WOODCOCK-JOHNSON® III: REPORTS, RECOMMENDATIONS, AND STRATEGIES

NANCY MATHER and LYNNE E. JAFFE

John Wiley & Sons, Inc.

"Tests do not think for themselves, nor do they directly communicate with patients. Like a stethoscope, a blood pressure gauge, or an MRI scan, a psychological test is a dumb tool, and the worth of the tool cannot be separated from the sophistication of the clinician who draws inferences from it and then communicates with patients and professionals."

—Meyer et al., 2001, p. 153

Acknowledgments

Many people have supported us in the development of this book. First, our families: Lynne's husband, Brian, was invariably encouraging and patient, and maintained a sense of humor, even when we lost ours. Lynne's son, David, became much more independent as he allowed his mother to spend countless hours "in time out," writing. Although he was only four years old when we completed the last book, his sentiment was the same: "Send it to Africa." Nancy's children, Ben and Dan, provided a certain amount of distraction, and a generous amount of love. Our parents, Bernie and Edith, and Chuck and Mildred, have provided their constant love throughout our lives. They taught us years ago that education, respect, tolerance, and nurturing are the central ingredients for a child's success at school and at home.

We would like to thank Jane Todorski, who has been our copyeditor on both editions of this book. We appreciate her expertise, eye for detail, endless patience and flexibility, and humor. ("Wait, Jane . . . we just have one more thing to add. Is it too late?") Edith Jaffe provided valuable help with reading galleys and making final edits. Lynne's colleagues at ASDB generously shared their prodigious expertise, and Earlene Dykes and Alan Myklebust were understanding and flexible about the time needed to complete this project. Patricia Foreman helped us format the text and graphics. Barbara Wendling, Rosalind Hill, and Judith Kroese developed score forms. Julie Reichman, Carol Anne Evans, and Rachel Friedman-Narr generously provided consultation and critique on the recommendations related to sensory impairment. John Willis and Ron Dumont were gracious and vigilant in making numerous corrections to the Score Equivalents table, helping to make the explanation of the RPI understandable, and infusing the process with levity. Dick Woodcock provided critical information and discussion. Tracey Belmont, from John Wiley & Sons, was supportive and patient during her management of this project ("For sure, Tracey, you'll have it by next month"). Susan Dodson and Paul McCurdy at Graphic Composition, Inc., were gracious about last-minute faxes and coordination of endless details.

Several colleagues graciously provided us with reports and bore with our adaptations and revisions of them. Unfortunately, our first draft of Section II: Reports was considerably longer than anticipated, forcing us to go through a grueling process of deleting some reports and shortening others. We are grateful to *all* of the evaluators for their willingness to share their work. Adaptations of reports provided by the following evaluators are included in Section II. Katia Alfaro and Beatriz Quintos; Lizabeth-Ann Brown; Lisa Coyner; Jeannette Devlin; Eric Jeffers; Michael Gerner; Jennifer Gilman; Noel Gregg and Chris Coleman; Melissa King; Judith Kroese; Janice Laz-Romo; Sheryl Maher; Eva Prince; Barbara Read; Ginny Reiss; Rhia Roberts; Janice Sammons; Caroline Tisot, Patricia Feuerstein, and Catherine Fiorello; and Patricia Tomlan. Fredrick Schrank provided a case to illustrate the WJ III Report Writer.

We are indebted to our mentors: Dr. Richard Woodcock for teaching us so much about assessment, and Dr. Samuel Kirk for training us in the importance of clinical judgment and the necessity of linking assessments with appropriate instructional recommendations. Finally, we are grateful to each other. We made it through another book, still the best of friends.

Table of Contents

INTRODUCTION   **1**

SECTION I: WJ III DESCRIPTIVE AND INTERPRETIVE INFORMATION   **3**

Introduction   3
Sample Score Forms   3
    Woodcock-Johnson III COG: Clusters/Tests Score Form   4
    Woodcock-Johnson III ACH: Clusters/Tests Score Form   5
    Woodcock-Johnson III COG: Cluster Descriptions and Scores   6
    Woodcock-Johnson III ACH: Cluster Descriptions and Scores   7
    Bell Curve Cluster/Test Comparison Chart   8
    Developmental Band Profile Worksheet— WJ III COG   9
    Instructional Zone Profile Worksheet— WJ III ACH   11
Average Grade Placement for Age   15
Score Equivalents and Classification Labels   16
WJ III COG Construct and Content Coverage   19
WJ III ACH Construct and Content Coverage   20
Example Items for the WJ III COG and WJ III ACH   21
Explanation of WJ III Scores, Interpretive Levels, and Discrepancies   25
    Level 1: Qualitative   25
       Task Analysis and Comparisons of Selected Tests   25
    Level 2: Level of Development   26
       W Scores   26
       Age Equivalents   26
       Grade Equivalents   26

    Level 3: Degree of Proficiency   26
       Relative Proficiency Index   27
       Cognitive-Academic Language Proficiency   28
       Age/Grade Profiles   28
    Level 4: Comparison with Peers   28
       Percentile Ranks   28
       Standard Scores   29
       Z Scores   29
       Standard Error of Measurement   29
    Discrepancy Terminology   29
Sample Statements for Reporting Scores and Score Discrepancies   30
    Score Levels Reported in Combination   30
    Level of Development   30
    Proficiency   30
    Peer Comparison   31
    Discrepancies   33
Test Comparisons and Error Pattern Analysis   35
    Tips for Interpretation   35
    Task Analysis and Comparisons of Selected Tests from the WJ III COG and WJ III ACH   36

SECTION II: REPORTS   **47**

Introduction   47
Test Names and Abbreviations   52
Diagnostic Reports   53

SECTION III: RECOMMENDATIONS   **267**

Introduction   267
CHC Factors: Descriptors, Possible Performance Implications, and Recommendations   268

Memory   272

Fluid Reasoning   276

Visual–Spatial Thinking/Visual Detail   277

Visual Processing Speed   281

Nonverbal Learning Disabilities (NLD)   282

Oral Language   284

Phonological Awareness   292

Basic Reading Skills   299

Reading Comprehension   315

Handwriting/Visual–Motor   326

Basic Writing Skills   335

Written Expression   342

Mathematics   353

Knowledge/Content Areas/Study Strategies   373

Homework/Time Management/Organization   377

Testing/Test-Taking   382

Attentional Disorders   386

Behavior Management and Intervention   397

Social Skills/Self-Esteem   403

Sensory Impairments   408

Transition   420

SECTION IV: STRATEGIES   425

Introduction   425

Addition Fact Memorization: Organizational
    Structures   425

Anticipation Guide   426

Addition Fact Chart   428

Behavior Rating Chart   429

Behavioral Contracts   430

Behavioral Interventions for the Whole Class   431

Carbo Method   433

Classroom Behavioral Interventions: Issues in
    Design   433

Classroom Rules: Guidelines   434

Cloze Procedure   435

Cohesive Devices: Types   436

Collaborative Strategic Reading   437

Content Area Instruction: Components of Effective
    Lessons   438

Context Clues   439

Directed Reading–Thinking Activity   440

Directed Vocabulary Thinking Activity   441

Elkonin Procedure: Adapted   441

Error Monitoring Strategy   443

Fernald Method for Reading   444

Fernald Method for Spelling Instruction   446

Fernald Method for Reading and Spelling: Modified   446

Flow List—Sight Words   447

Flow List—Sight Word/Spelling Flow List   448

Flow List—Spelling   449

Glass-Analysis for Decoding Only   449

Glass-Analysis for Spelling   450

Instant Words (300)   451

Great Leaps Reading   453

Kerrigan's Integrated Method of Teaching
    Composition   453

KWLS Strategy   454

Language Experience for Sight Words: Modified   455

Look-Sign-Fingerspell-Write   455

Look-Spell-See-Write   458

Math Computation Forms   459

Math Facts—Instructional Sequence   461

Math Problem-Solving Strategy   461

Memory: General Principles for Improvement   462

Multiplication Fact Chart   463

Mystery Motivator   464

Neurological Impress Method   464

Organization for Effective Instruction   465

Organization of Materials and Assignments   466

Phonics Check-Off Chart   467

Phonogram Activities   469

PIRATES Test-Taking Strategy   470

Positive Reinforcers   472

Precision Requests   473

Precision Teaching   473

Precision Teaching Graph   475

PreReading Plan   476

Presenting Technique   476

Principles of Effective Teaching for Students with
    Learning Difficulties   477

RAVE-O   478

Reciprocal Teaching   478

Repeated Readings   479

Repeated Readings Graph   480

ReQuest Procedure   481

ReQuest Procedure—Modified   481

Response-Cost   482

Self-Management Strategy for Improving Adolescent
    Behavior   482

Semantic Feature Analysis: Concepts   484

Semantic Feature Analysis: Vocabulary   485

Semantic Maps: Advance Organizers   486

Semantic Maps: Evaluating/Activating Prior
    Knowledge   486

Sight Word Association Procedure   487

Six Syllable Structures in English   488

Software Selection Tips   489

Speed Drills for Reading Fluency and Basic Skills   490

Spelling: General Teaching Principles   491

Spelling Rules: 43 Consistent Generalizations about the
    English Language   492

SQ3R: Survey, Question, Read, Recite, Review   494

STORE the Story   494

Study Guides   497

"Sure I Will" Program: Increasing Compliance   499

Talk-to-Yourself Chart   499

Taped Books   500

Telling Time Strategy   500

Token Economy Systems   501

Touch Math   503

Transitions Between Activities   504

Wilson Reading System   504

Wilson Reading System for Students with Visual
    Impairments: Adaptation   505

Word Bank Activities   506

Writing as a Process   507

Writing Process with Mapping for Individual
    Tutoring   508

TESTS CITED WITHIN THE BOOK   **510**

REFERENCES   **513**

List of Figures

Figure I.1   Describing and Reporting Scores   34

Figure II.1   Writing Sample of a Boy, Age 9-7, with Severe Dysgraphia   112

Figure II.2   Jonas's Drawing   113

Figure II.3   Math Classroom Work Sample of a Girl, Age 11-5, with a Visual–Motor Weakness and a Procedural Math Disorder   154

Figure II.4   Math Work Sample of a Girl, Age 11-5, with a Visual–Motor Weakness and a Procedural Math Disorder, Done on Grid Paper. One Problem Done Orally and Dictated to Evaluator.   154

Figure III.1   Illustration of a Pegword Mnemonic: Why Earthquakes Happen   275

Figure III.2a   Graphic Organizer for Expository Text Structure: Contrast   291

Figure III.2b   Graphic Organizer for Expository Text Structure: Description   291

Figure III.2c   Graphic Organizer for Expository Text Structure: Cause–Effect   291

Figure III.3   Illustration of the Use of Pictures to Explain Compound Words   296

Figure III.4   Sample Guide for Summarizing a Passage with a Cause–Effect Structure   324

Figure III.5a   Graphic Organizer for Expository Text Structure: Chronology   326

Figure III.5b   Graphic Organizer for Expository Text Structure: Main Ideas and Details   326

Figure III.5c   Graphic Organizer for Expository Text Structure: Description   326

Figure III.6   Picture of a Bed to Aid in Recalling the Correct Orientation of b and d   331

Figure III.7   Clock Face Overlaid with a Number 2 as a Cue to Number Orientation   331

Figure III.8   An Example of a Page Format for Writing a Simple Composition   332

Figure III.9a   Graphic Organizer for Expository Text Structure: Contrast   348

Figure III.9b   Graphic Organizer for Expository Text Structure: Compare–Contrast   349

Figure III.10   Format for Multiplication Algorithm   359

Figure III.11   Illustrations for Story of Place Value Houses   363

Figure III.12   Math Decision Map   367

Figure III.13   Mnemonic for the Steps of the Division Process   367

Figure III.14   Classroom Seating Arrangements for Facilitating Teacher Circulation   389

Figure IV.1   Math Fact Chart to Aid in Memorizing Addition Facts   426

Figure IV.2   Example Anticipation Guide Chart   427

Figure IV.3   Picture of a Sun for the Elkonin Procedure: Adapted   442

Figure IV.4   Illustration of Ways to Box Different Spelling Patterns in the Elkonin Procedure: Adapted   442

Figure IV.5   Example of Sight Word/Spelling Flow List with One Student's Responses Recorded   449

Figure IV.6   Examples of Notebook Dividers for Color-Correlation with Assignment Sheets   466

Figure IV.7   Example of an Assignment Sheet to Help Students Remember Their Homework   466

Figure IV.8   Student Cue Card for PIRATES Test-Taking Strategy   471

Figure IV.9   Example Relationship Chart for Semantic Feature Analysis: Concepts   484

Figure IV.10   Example Study Guide Utilizing Three
Levels of Comprehension   497

Figure IV.11   Example Study Guide Representing
Organizational Patterns   498

Figure IV.12   Model of Talk-to-Yourself Chart   499

Figure IV.13   Touch Math: Illustration of the
Touchpoints on Numbers 0–9   503

Figure IV.14   Touch Math: Example of Visual Cues for
Addition with Regrouping   503

Figure IV.15   Velcro Board for Wilson Reading System
as Used with Students with Visual
Impairments   505

Introduction

This reference book is intended to serve as a resource for evaluators using the Woodcock-Johnson III (WJ III) Cognitive (COG) and/or Achievement (ACH) tests in educational or clinical settings (Woodcock, McGrew, & Mather, 2001a, b, c). Its central purpose is to assist practitioners in preparing and writing psychological and educational reports using the WJ III, for individuals enrolled in a school setting from preschool through the postsecondary level. The book is divided into four sections.

The first section, WJ III Descriptive and Interpretive Information, presents material related to use and interpretation of the WJ III. The clusters and tests are described and sample test items are presented. An overview of the WJ III scores and interpretive information is provided, and a few sample forms are presented that may be used to summarize test data. In addition to the examiner's manuals, additional information on interpreting the WJ III can be found in two sources: Essentials of WJ III™ Cognitive Abilities Assessment (Schrank, Flanagan, Woodcock, & Mascolo, 2001) and Essentials of WJ III™ Tests of Achievement Assessment (Mather, Wendling, & Woodcock, 2001).

The second section, Reports, presents diagnostic reports that illustrate applications of the WJ III in both educational and clinical settings. These diagnostic reports depict a variety of learning problems in individuals from preschool to the postsecondary level. Information obtained from other diagnostic instruments is integrated into several of the sample reports to aid practitioners in interpreting the WJ III when used in combination with other assessment instruments as well as when used as the sole measure. Many different styles and formats of reports are presented.

The third section, Recommendations, provides a wide variety of educational recommendations. Recommendations are provided for oral language, and the achievement areas of reading, written language, mathematics, and knowledge/content. Additional recommendations are provided for areas such as memory, attention, behavior management, social skills/self-esteem, and for students with sensory impairments.

The last section, Strategies, contains summaries, arranged alphabetically, of methods and techniques that were included in the recommendations or the diagnostic reports. These summaries may be attached to a report so that general or special education teachers, educational therapists, or parents may implement the recommended procedures.

WJ III Descriptive and Interpretive Information

INTRODUCTION

The following score forms may be used to display and summarize an individual's test scores. The forms are followed by a chart that matches grade placement with chronological age. This chart is useful for determining the typical age for a given grade and whether disparities exist between grade placement and age. When differences exist (such as in the case of a retention), it is sometimes helpful to compare the individual's performance to both grade-peers and age-peers. Next, several tables are provided that describe the WJ III tests and the task requirements. These are followed by example test items for the WJ III COG and WJ III ACH. Because they are not actual items from the test, these sample items may be shared with a parent or teacher who is interested in knowing more about the nature or types of questions on the specific tests. The descriptive information includes an explanation of all the scores on the WJ III, with sample statements for reporting scores and describing the results from the discrepancy procedures. The last part of the section provides ideas for meaningful test comparisons, as well as tips for interpretation. These comparisons and tips can help an evaluator develop a diagnostic hypothesis to explain a particular pattern of test scores.

SAMPLE SCORE FORMS

The following score forms are intended to aid the evaluator in organizing the student's assessment results on the WJ III COG and WJ III ACH. The forms give the evaluator the choice of score level to use (i.e., qualitative, level of development, degree of proficiency, comparison with peers) and the level of specificity with which to analyze the results (test to factor/cluster). These forms are helpful for analysis of assessment results and as a visual framework for presenting this information to others.

Woodcock-Johnson III Tests of Cognitive Abilities: Clusters/Tests Score Form

Name: _____   Scores based on: Grade ____ Age ____ norms

Date of Birth: _____   Type of Score: SS___   %ile___   RPI___   Grade___   Age___

	Category/Factor	Scores		Standard Battery	Scores		Extended Battery	Scores	
Intellectual Ability	General Intellectual Ability			Verbal Comprehension			General Information		
				Visual-Auditory Learning			Retrieval Fluency		
				Spatial Relations			Picture Recognition		
				Sound Blending			Auditory Attention		
				Concept Formation			Analysis-Synthesis		
				Visual Matching			Decision Speed		
				Numbers Reversed			Memory for Words		
	Brief Intellectual Ability			Verbal Comprehension					
				Concept Formation					
				Visual Matching					
Cognitive Performance	Verbal Ability			Verbal Comprehension			General Information		
	Thinking Ability			Visual-Auditory Learning			Retrieval Fluency		
				Spatial Relations			Picture Recognition		
				Sound Blending			Auditory Attention		
				Concept Formation			Analysis-Synthesis		
	Cognitive Efficiency			Visual Matching			Decision Speed		
				Numbers Reversed			Memory for Words		
CHC Factors	Comprehension-Knowledge			Verbal Comprehension			General Information		
	Long-Term Retrieval			Visual-Auditory Learning			Retrieval Fluency		
	Visual-Spatial Thinking			Spatial Relations			Picture Recognition		
	Auditory Processing			Sound Blending			Auditory Attention		
	Fluid Reasoning			Concept Formation			Analysis-Synthesis		
	Processing Speed			Visual Matching			Decision Speed		
	Short-Term Memory			Numbers Reversed			Memory for Words		
Clinical Clusters	Phonemic Awareness			Sound Blending			[Sound Awareness]		
				Incomplete Words					
	Working Memory			Numbers Reversed					
				Auditory Working Memory					
	Broad Attention			Numbers Reversed			Auditory Attention		
				Auditory Working Memory			Pair Cancellation		
	Cognitive Fluency						Retrieval Fluency		
							Decision Speed		
							Rapid Picture Naming		
	Executive Processes			Concept Formation			Planning		
							Pair Cancellation		
	Delayed Recall						Visual-Auditory Learning–Delayed		
							_z_ score or PR		
							Story Recall–Delayed (ACH)		
							_z_ score or PR		
	Knowledge						General Information		
							Academic Knowledge (ACH)		

Mather, N., & Jaffe, L. (2002). *Woodcock-Johnson III: Reports, Recommendations, and Strategies.* New York: John Wiley & Sons.

Woodcock-Johnson III Tests of Achievement: Clusters/Tests Score Form

Name: _____   Scores based on: Grade _____ Age _____ norms

Date of Birth: _____   Type of Score: SS___ %ile___ RPI___ Grade___ Age___

Areas	Clusters	Scores		Standard Battery	Scores		Extended Battery	Scores	
Oral Language	Oral Language			Story Recall			Picture Vocabulary		
				Understanding Directions			Oral Comprehension		
	Listening Comprehension			Understanding Directions			Oral Comprehension		
	Oral Expression			Story Recall			Picture Vocabulary		
Reading	Broad Reading			Letter-Word Identification					
				Reading Fluency					
				Passage Comprehension					
	Basic Reading Skills			Letter-Word Identification			Word Attack		
	Reading Comprehension			Passage Comprehension			Reading Vocabulary		
Math	Broad Math			Calculation					
				Math Fluency					
				Applied Problems					
	Math Calculation Skills			Calculation					
				Math Fluency					
	Math Reasoning			Applied Problems			Quantitative Concepts		
Written Language	Broad Written Language			Spelling					
				Writing Fluency					
				Writing Samples					
	Basic Writing Skills			Spelling			Editing		
							[Punctuation & Capitalization]		
	Written Expression			Writing Fluency					
				Writing Samples					
Other Clusters	Academic Knowledge						Academic Knowledge		
	Phoneme/Grapheme Knowledge						Word Attack		
							Spelling of Sounds		
	Academic Skills			Letter-Word Identification					
				Spelling					
				Calculation					
	Academic Fluency			Reading Fluency					
				Writing Fluency					
				Math Fluency					
	Academic Applications			Passage Comprehension					
				Writing Samples					
				Applied Problems					
	Total Achievement			Letter-Word Identification					
				Reading Fluency					
				Passage Comprehension					
				Spelling					
				Writing Fluency					
				Writing Samples					
				Calculation					
				Math Fluency					
				Applied Problems					
	Supplemental Tests/Scores						Story Recall–Delayed *z* score or PR		
							Sound Awareness		
							Handwriting		

Mather, N., & Jaffe, L. (2002). *Woodcock-Johnson III: Reports, Recommendations, and Strategies.* New York: John Wiley & Sons.

Woodcock-Johnson III Tests of Cognitive Abilities: Cluster Descriptions and Scores

Name: _____

Grade:_____   Age:_____   Scores based on: Grade ____ Age ____ Norms

Factor/Cluster	Description	SS/PR	RPI	Level of Proficiency
Comprehension-Knowledge	General information and stores of acquired knowledge			
Long-Term Retrieval	Ability to store information efficiently and retrieve it later through associations			
Visual–Spatial Thinking	Ability to perceive, analyze, synthesize, and think with visual patterns, including the ability to store and recall visual representations			
Auditory Processing	Ability to analyze, synthesize, and discriminate auditory stimuli. Also related to phonological awareness			
Fluid Reasoning	Ability to reason, form concepts, and solve problems that often involve unfamiliar information or procedures			
Processing Speed	Speed and efficiency in performing automatic or simple cognitive tasks, visual scanning efficiency			
Short-Term Memory	Ability to hold orally presented information in immediate awareness and use it within a few seconds (memory span and working memory)			
Cognitive Fluency	Ease and speed by which an individual performs simple to complex cognitive tasks			
Executive Processes	Three aspects of executive functioning: strategic planning, proactive interference control, and the ability to shift mental set repeatedly			
Phonemic Awareness	Ability to analyze, synthesize, and manipulate speech sounds			
Working Memory	Ability to hold information in immediate awareness while performing a mental operation on the information			
Comments:				

Mather, N., & Jaffe, L. (2002). *Woodcock-Johnson III: Reports, Recommendations, and Strategies*. New York: John Wiley & Sons.

Woodcock-Johnson III Tests of Achievement: Cluster Descriptions and Scores

Name: _____

Grade:_____ Age:_____ Scores based on: Grade _____ Age _____ Norms

Cluster	Description	SS/PR	GE/RPI	Level of Proficiency
Broad Reading	Reading decoding, reading speed, and using syntactic and semantic cueing systems when reading for meaning			
Basic Reading	Sight vocabulary, phonics, and structural analysis skills			
Broad Math	Math achievement including problem solving, number facility, automaticity with facts, and reasoning			
Math Calculation Skills	Computational skills and automaticity with math facts			
Math Reasoning	Problem solving, concepts, and math vocabulary			
Broad Written Language	Spelling, writing rate, and written expression			
Written Expression	Quality of written sentences and fluency of production			
Academic Knowledge	Knowledge of science, social studies, and humanities			
Academic Skills	Basic academic skills			
Academic Fluency	Ease and speed by which an individual performs simple to more complex academic tasks			
Oral Language	Linguistic competency, listening ability, oral comprehension			
Comments:				

Mather, N., & Jaffe, L. (2002). *Woodcock-Johnson III: Reports, Recommendations, and Strategies.* New York: John Wiley & Sons.

Bell Curve Cluster/Test Comparison Chart

Name: _____   Date: _____

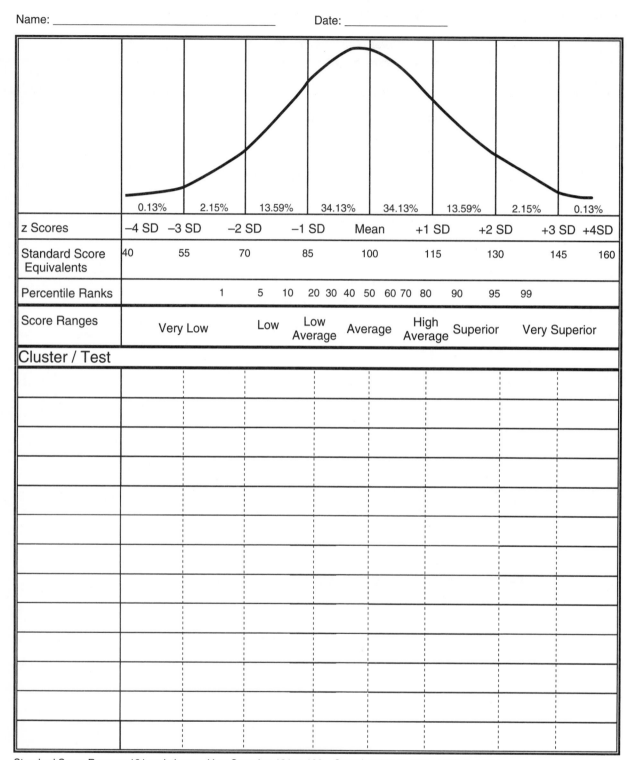

	0.13%	2.15%	13.59%	34.13%	34.13%	13.59%	2.15%	0.13%
z Scores	−4 SD −3 SD	−2 SD	−1 SD	Mean	+1 SD	+2 SD	+3 SD +4SD	
Standard Score Equivalents	40 55	70	85	100	115	130	145	160
Percentile Ranks		1	5 10	20 30 40 50	60 70 80	90	95 99	
Score Ranges	Very Low		Low	Low Average Average	High Average Superior		Very Superior	
Cluster / Test								

Standard Score Ranges: 131 and above = Very Superior; 121 to 130 = Superior; 111 to 120 = High Average;
90 to 110 = Average; 80 to 89 = Low Average; 70 to 79 = Low; 69 and below = Very Low.

Mather, N., & Jaffe, L. (2002). *Woodcock-Johnson III: Reports, Recommendations, and Strategies.* New York: John Wiley & Sons.

Developmental Band Profile Worksheet—WJ III Tests of Cognitive Abilities

Cognitive Factor/Clusters Cognitive Tests	Developmentally Difficult (weakness) RPI 75/90 & below	Developmentally Appropriate	Developmentally Easy (strength) RPI 96/90 & above
Comprehension-Knowledge (*Gc*)			
Verbal Comprehension			
General Information			
(Academic Knowledge—ACH)			
Long-Term Retrieval (*Glr*)			
Visual-Auditory Learning			
Retrieval Fluency			
Visual-Spatial Thinking (*Gv*)			
Spatial Relations			
Picture Recognition			
Auditory Processing (*Ga*)			
Sound Blending			
Auditory Attention			
Fluid Reasoning (*Gf*)			
Concept Formation			
Analysis-Synthesis			
Processing Speed (*Gs*)			
Visual Matching (1 or 2)			
Decision Speed			
Short-Term Memory (*Gsm*)			
Numbers Reversed			
Memory for Words			
Clinical Clusters	Developmentally Difficult (weakness)	Developmentally Appropriate	Developmentally Easy (strength)
Phonemic Awareness			
Sound Blending			
Incomplete Words			
(Sound Awareness—ACH)			
Working Memory			
Numbers Reversed			
Auditory Working Memory			
Broad Attention			
Numbers Reversed			
Auditory Attention			
Pair Cancellation			
Auditory Working Memory			
Cognitive Fluency			
Retrieval Fluency			
Decision Speed			
Rapid Picture Naming			
Executive Processes			
Concept Formation			
Planning			
Pair Cancellation			

Mather, N., & Jaffe, L. (2002). *Woodcock-Johnson III: Reports, Recommendations, and Strategies.* New York: John Wiley & Sons.

Developmental Band Profile Worksheet—WJ III Tests of Cognitive Abilities (*continued*)

Cognitive Performance Model	Developmentally Difficult (weakness)	Developmentally Appropriate	Developmentally Easy (strength)
Verbal Ability (Std)			
Verbal Comprehension			
Verbal Ability (Ext)			
Verbal Comprehension			
General Information			
Thinking Abilities (Std)			
Visual-Auditory Learning (*Glr*)			
Spatial Relations (*Gv*)			
Sound Blending (*Ga*)			
Concept Formation (*Gf*)			
Thinking Abilities (Ext)			
Visual-Auditory Learning (*Glr*)			
Retrieval Fluency (*Glr*)			
Spatial Relations (*Gv*)			
Picture Recognition (*Gv*)			
Sound Blending (*Ga*)			
Auditory Attention (*Ga*)			
Concept Formation (*Gf*)			
Analysis-Synthesis (*Gf*)			
Cognitive Efficiency (Std)			
Visual Matching (*Gs*)			
Numbers Reversed (*Gsm*)			
Cognitive Efficiency (Ext)			
Visual Matching (*Gs*)			
Decision Speed (*Gs*)			
Numbers Reversed (*Gsm*)			
Memory for Words (*Gsm*)			

Worksheet Instructions:
Use the Developmental Level Bands from the Student's Compuscore® (*Age/Grade Profile Selection in the "Reports" Menu*).
Place check marks in the appropriate column that shows whether a cluster/test is difficult, developmentally appropriate, or easy. The proficiency level (e.g., limited) can also be represented within each column.

Adapted from EDCS Inc., Barbara Read, Woodstock, VT. Unpublished.

Mather, N., & Jaffe, L. (2002). *Woodcock-Johnson III: Reports, Recommendations, and Strategies.* New York: John Wiley & Sons.

Instructional Zone Profile Worksheet—WJ III Tests of Achievement

Achievement Clusters / Achievement Tests	Developmentally Difficult (weakness) RPI 76/90 & below	Developmentally Appropriate	Developmentally Easy (strength) RPI 96/90 & above
Broad Reading			
Letter-Word Identification			
Reading Fluency			
Passage Comprehension			
Basic Reading			
Letter-Word Identification			
Word Attack			
Reading Comprehension			
Passage Comprehension			
Reading Vocabulary			
Oral Language (Std)			
Story Recall			
Understanding Direction			
Oral Language (Ext)			
Story Recall			
Understanding Directions			
Picture Vocabulary			
Oral Comprehension			
Oral Expression			
Story Recall			
Picture Vocabulary			
(Academic Knowledge)			
(General Information—COG)			
Listening Comprehension			
Understanding Directions			
Oral Comprehension			
Broad Written Language			
Spelling			
Writing Fluency			
Writing Samples			
Written Expression			
Writing Fluency			
Writing Samples			
Basic Writing Skills			
Spelling			
Editing			
(Punctuation & Capitalization)			
(Spelling of Sounds)			

Mather, N., & Jaffe, L. (2002). *Woodcock-Johnson III: Reports, Recommendations, and Strategies.* New York: John Wiley & Sons.

Instructional Zone Profile Worksheet—WJ III Tests of Achievement (*continued*)

Clusters/Tests	Instructionally Difficult (weakness)	Instructionally Appropriate (average)	Instructionally Easy (strength)
Phoneme/Grapheme			
Word Attack			
Spelling of Sounds			
(Sound Awareness)			
Broad Math			
Math Calculation			
Math Fluency			
Applied Problems			
Basic Math Skills			
Math Calculation			
Math Fluency			
Math Reasoning			
Applied Problems			
Quantitative Concepts			
Cross Academic Clusters	Instructionally Difficult (weakness)	Instructionally Appropriate (average)	Instructionally Easy (strength)
Academic Fluency			
Reading Fluency			
Writing Fluency			
Math Fluency			
Academic Skills			
Letter-Word Identification			
Spelling			
Math Calculation			
Academic Applications			
Passage Comprehension			
Applied Problems			
Writing Samples			

Worksheet Instructions:
Use the Instructional Range Bands from the Student's Compuscore® (*Age/Grade Profile Selection in the "Reports" Menu*).
Place check marks in the appropriate column that shows whether a cluster/test is difficult, developmentally appropriate, or easy. The proficiency level (e.g., limited) can also be represented within each column.

Adapted from EDCS Inc., Barbara Read, Woodstock, VT. Unpublished.

Mather, N., & Jaffe, L. (2002). *Woodcock-Johnson III: Reports, Recommendations, and Strategies.* New York: John Wiley & Sons.

Results of the WJ III Cognitive Factors and Clusters by Standard Score Range

		CHC Factors	Cognitive Performance and Clinical Clusters
Very Superior	131>		
Superior	121–130		
High Average	111–120		
Average	90–110		
Low Average	80–89		
Low	70–79		
Very Low	55–69		
↓	<55		

Developed by B. J. Wendling, Dallas, TX. Unpublished.

Mather, N., & Jaffe, L. (2002). *Woodcock-Johnson III: Reports, Recommendations, and Strategies.* New York: John Wiley & Sons.

Results of the WJ III Achievement Clusters by Standard Score Range

		Broad Clusters	Basic Skills and Application Clusters
Very Superior	131>		
Superior	121–130		
High Average	111–120		
Average	90–110		
Low Average	80–89		
Low	70–79		
Very Low	55–69		
⬇	<55		

Developed by B. J. Wendling, Dallas, TX. Unpublished.

Mather, N., & Jaffe, L. (2002). *Woodcock-Johnson III: Reports, Recommendations, and Strategies.* New York: John Wiley & Sons.

Table I.1. Average Grade Placement for Age

Yrs.-Mos.	Average Grade Placement	Yrs.-Mos.	Average Grade Placement	Yrs.-Mos.	Average Grade Placement
5-1	0.0	9-6	4.2	14.0	8.5
5-2	0.1	9-7	4.3	14.1	8.6
5-3	0.2	9-8	4.3	14.2	8.7
5-4	0.3	9-9	4.4	14.3	8.8
5-5	0.3	9-10	4.4	14.4	8.9
		9-11	4.5	14.5	9.0
5-6	0.3	10-0	4.6	14.6	9.1
5-7	0.4	10-1	4.7	14.7	9.1
5-8	0.4	10-2	4.8	14.8	9.2
5-9	0.5	10-3	4.9	14.9	9.3
5-10	0.5	10-4	5.0	14.10	9.3
5-11	0.6	10-5	5.1	14.11	9.4
6-0	0.7	10-6	5.2	15-0	9.5
6-1	0.9	10-7	5.3	15-1	9.6
6-2	1.0	10-8	5.3	15-2	9.7
6-3	1.1	10-9	5.4	15-3	9.8
6-4	1.2	10-10	5.4	15-4	9.9
6-5	1.3	10-11	5.5	15-5	10.0
6-6	1.3	11-0	5.5	15-6	10.1
6-7	1.4	11-1	5.6	15-7	10.2
6-8	1.4	11-2	5.7	15-8	10.2
6-9	1.4	11-3	5.8	15-9	10.3
6-10	1.5	11-4	5.9	15-10	10.4
6-11	1.5	11-5	6.0	15-11	10.4
7-0	1.6	11-6	6.1	16-0	10.5
7-1	1.8	11-7	6.2	16-1	10.6
7-2	1.9	11-8	6.2	16-2	10.7
7-3	2.0	11-9	6.3	16-3	10.8
7-4	2.1	11-10	6.3	16-4	11.0
7-5	2.2	11-11	6.4	16-5	11.1
7-6	2.2	12-0	6.5	16-6	11.2
7-7	2.3	12-1	6.7	16-7	11.2
7-8	2.3	12-2	6.8	16-8	11.3
7-9	2.4	12-3	6.9	16-9	11.4
7-10	2.4	12-4	6.9	16-10	11.5
7-11	2.5	12-5	7.0	16-11	11.6
8-0	2.6	12-6	7.1	17-0	11.8
8-1	2.8	12-7	7.2	17-1	11.9
8-2	2.9	12-8	7.2	17-2	12.0
8-3	3.0	12-9	7.3	17-3	12.1
8-4	3.1	12-10	7.3	17-4	12.2
8-5	3.1	12-11	7.4	17-5	12.3
8-6	3.2	13-0	7.5	17-6	12.4
8-7	3.3	13-1	7.7	17-7	12.5
8-8	3.3	13-2	7.8	17-8	12.6
8-9	3.4	13-3	7.9	17-9	12.7
8-10	3.4	13-4	8.0	17-10	12.8
8-11	3.5	13-5	8.1	17-11	12.9
9-0	3.6	13-6	8.2		
9-1	3.7	13-7	8.2		
9-2	3.8	13-8	8.2		
9-3	3.9	13-9	8.3		
9-4	4.0	13-10	8.3		
9-5	4.1	13-11	8.4		

Table I.2.   Score Equivalents and Classification Labels

Score	Mean	SD	Score	Mean	SD
Standard scores (SS)	100	15	Scaled score (ScS)	10	3
Percentile rank (PR)	50	NA	Stanine (Stan.)*	5	1.96
z score (z)	0.00	1.00	GRE-like scores (GRE)	500	100
T score (T)	50	10	*Shading indicates Stanine range		

WJ III Classif.**	SS	PR	z	T	ScS	Stan.	Wechsler Classif. **
	160	99.9	+4.00	90			
	159	99.9	+3.93				
	158	99.9	+3.87				
	157	99.9	+3.80	88			
	156	99.9	+3.73				
	155	99.9	+3.67				
	154	99.9	+3.60	86			
	153	99.9	+3.53				
	152	99.9	+3.47				
	151	99.9	+3.40	84			
	150	99.9	+3.33				
	149	99.9	+3.27				
	148	99.9	+3.20	82			
	147	99.9	+3.13				
Very Superior	146	99.9	+3.07				Very Superior
	145	99.9	+3.00	80	19		
	144	99.8	+2.93				
	143	99.8	+2.87				
	142	99.7	+2.80	78		9	
	141	99.7	+2.73				
	140	99.6	+2.67		18		
	139	99.5	+2.60	76			
	138	99	+2.53				
	137	99	+2.47				
	136	99	+2.40	74			
	135	99	+2.33		17		
	134	99	+2.27				
	133	99	+2.20	72			
	132	98	+2.13				
	131	98	+2.07				
	130	98	+2.00	70	16		
	129	97	+1.93				
	128	97	+1.87				
	127	96	+1.80	68			
Superior	126	96	+1.73				Superior
	125	95	+1.67		15		
	124	95	+1.60	66			
	123	94	+1.53			8	
	122	93	+1.47				
	121	92	+1.40	64			

Table I.2.   (*continued*)

WJ III Classif.**	SS	PR	z	T	ScS	Stan.	Wechsler Classif. **
High Average	120	91	+1.33		14		High Average
	119	90	+1.27				
	118	88	+1.20	62			
	117	87	+1.13				
	116	86	+1.07				
	115	84	+1.00	60	13	**7**	
	114	82	+0.93				
	113	81	+0.87				
	112	79	+0.80	58			
	111	77	+0.73				
Average	110	75	+0.67		12		Average
	109	73	+0.60	56			
	108	70	+0.53			**6**	
	107	68	+0.47				
	106	66	+0.40	54			
	105	63	+0.33		11		
	104	61	+0.27				
	103	58	+0.20	52			
	102	55	+0.13				
	101	53	+0.07				
	100	50	0.00	50	10	**5**	
	99	47	−0.07				
	98	45	−0.13				
	97	42	−0.20	48			
	96	39	−0.27				
	95	37	−0.33		9		
	94	34	−0.40	46			
	93	32	−0.47			**4**	
	92	30	−0.53				
	91	27	−0.60	44			
	90	25	−0.67		8		
Low Average	89	23	−0.73				Low Average
	88	21	−0.80	42			
	87	19	−0.87				
	86	18	−0.93				
	85	16	−1.00	40	7	**3**	
	84	14	−1.07				
	83	13	−1.13				
	82	12	−1.20	38			
	81	10	−1.27				
	80	09	−1.33		6		
Low	79	08	−1.40	36			Borderline
	78	07	−1.47			**2**	
	77	06	−1.53				
	76	05	−1.60	34			
	75	05	−1.67		5		
	74	04	−1.73				
	73	04	−1.80	32			
	72	03	−1.87				
	71	03	−1.93				
	70	02	−2.00	30	4		

(*continued*)

Table I.2.   (*continued*)

WJ III Classif.**	SS	PR	z	T	ScS	Stan.	Wechsler Classif. **
Very Low	69	02	−2.07				
	68	02	−2.13				
	67	01	−2.20	28			
	66	01	−2.27				
	65	01	−2.33		3		
	64	01	−2.40	26			
	63	01	−2.47				
	62	01	−2.53				
	61	0.5	−2.60	24		1	
	60	0.4	−2.67		2		
	59	0.3	−2.73				
	58	0.3	−2.80	22			
	57	0.2	−2.87				Intellectually Deficient (WISC-III)
	56	0.2	−2.93				
	55	0.1	−3.00	20	1		
	54	0.1	−3.07				Extremely Low (WAIS-III)
	53	0.1	−3.13				
	52	0.1	−3.20	18			
	51	0.1	−3.27				
	50	0.1	−3.33				
	49	0.1	−3.40	16			
	48	0.1	−3.47				
	47	0.1	−3.53				
	46	0.1	−3.60	14			
	45	0.1	−3.67				
	44	0.1	−3.73				
	43	0.1	−3.80	12			
	42	0.1	−3.87				
	41	0.1	−3.93				
	40	0.1	−4.00	10			

*The performance classification labels provided here are used by the WJ III, WISC III, and WAIS III. Other tests may use different classification labels.

Note: The WJ III separately computes Standard Scores and Percentile Ranks, so that the scores on the Compuscore may not be in precisely the same relationship as in Table I.16.

Adapted from

Dumont, R. P., & Willis, J. O. (2001). Score conversion tables for commonly used tests. Retrieved January 29, 2002 from Dumont and Willis on the Web: http://alpha.fdu.edu/psychology/

Willis, J. O., & Dumont, R. P. (1998). Guide to identification of learning disabilities (1998 New York State ed.) (pp. 240–241). Acton, MA: Copley.

Mather, N., & Jaffe, L. (2002). *Woodcock-Johnson III: Reports, Recommendations, and Strategies.* New York: John Wiley & Sons.

Table I.3. WJ III COG Construct and Content Coverage

Test	Primary Broad CHC Factor / *Narrow CHC Ability*	Stimuli	Test Requirement	Response
Test 1: Verbal Comprehension	Comprehension-Knowledge (*Gc*) / *Lexical knowledge / Language development*	Visual (pictures); Auditory (words)	Naming objects; knowledge of antonyms and synonyms; completing verbal analogies	Oral (word)
Test 2: Visual-Auditory Learning	Long-Term Retrieval (*Glr*) / *Associative memory*	Visual (rebuses)— Auditory (words) in the learning condition; Visual (rebuses) in the recognition condition	Learning and recalling pictographic representations of words	Oral (sentences)
Test 3: Spatial Relations	Visual-Spatial Thinking (*Gv*) / *Visualization / Spatial relations*	Visual (drawings)	Identifying the subset of pieces needed to form a complete shape	Oral (letters) or motoric (pointing)
Test 4: Sound Blending	Auditory Processing (*Ga*) / *Phonetic coding: Synthesis*	Auditory (phonemes)	Synthesizing language sounds (phonemes)	Oral (word)
Test 5: Concept Formation	Fluid Reasoning (*Gf*) / *Induction*	Visual (drawings)	Identifying, categorizing, and determining rules	Oral (words)
Test 6: Visual Matching	Processing Speed (*Gs*) / *Perceptual speed / Visual scanning*	Visual (numbers)	Rapidly locating and circling identical numbers from a defined set of numbers	Motoric (circling)
Test 7: Numbers Reversed	Short-Term Memory (*Gsm*) / *Working memory*	Auditory (numbers)	Holding a span of numbers in immediate awareness while reversing the sequence	Oral (numbers)
Test 8: Incomplete Words	Auditory Processing (*Ga*) / *Phonetic coding: Analysis*	Auditory (words)	Identifying words with missing phonemes	Oral (word)
Test 9: Auditory Working Memory	Short-Term Memory (*Gsm*) / *Working memory*	Auditory (words, numbers)	Holding a mixed set of numbers and words in immediate awareness while reordering into two sequences	Oral (words, numbers)
Test 10: Visual-Auditory Learning—Delayed	Long-Term Retrieval (*Glr*) / *Associative memory*	Visual (rebuses) in the recognition condition; Visual-auditory in the relearning condition	Recalling and relearning pictographic representations of words from 30 minutes to 8 days after initial presentation	Oral (sentences)
Test 11: General Information	Comprehension-Knowledge (*Gc*) / *General (verbal) information*	Auditory (questions)	Identifying where objects are found and what people typically do with an object	Oral (sentences)
Test 12: Retrieval Fluency	Long-Term Retrieval (*Glr*) / *Ideational fluency*	Auditory (directions only)	Naming as many examples as possible from a given category	Oral (words)
Test 13: Picture Recognition	Visual-Spatial Thinking (*Gv*) / *Visual memory*	Visual (pictures)	Identifying a subset of previously presented pictures within a field of distracting pictures	Oral (words) or Motoric (pointing)
Test 14: Auditory Attention	Auditory Processing (*Ga*) / *Speech-sound discrimination / Resistance to competing auditory stimulus*	Auditory (words) Visual (pictures)	Identifying orally presented words amid increasingly intense background noise	Motor (pointing)
Test 15: Analysis-Synthesis	Fluid Reasoning (*Gf*) / *General sequential (deductive) reasoning*	Visual (drawings)	Analyzing puzzles (using a given code) to determine missing components	Oral (words)
Test 16: Decision Speed	Processing Speed (*Gs*) / *Semantic processing speed*	Visual (pictures)	Identifying and circling the two most conceptually similar pictures in a row	Motoric (circling)
Test 17: Memory for Words	Short-Term Memory (*Gsm*) / *Memory span*	Auditory (words)	Repeating a list of unrelated words in correct sequence	Oral (words)
Test 18: Rapid Picture Naming	Processing Speed (*Gs*) / *Naming facility*	Visual (pictures)	Recognizing objects, then retrieving and articulating their names rapidly	Oral (words)
Test 19: Planning	Visual-Spatial Thinking (*Gv*) & Fluid Reasoning (*Gf*) / *Spatial scanning / General sequential reasoning*	Visual (drawings)	Tracing a pattern without removing the pencil from the paper or retracing any lines	Motoric (tracing)
Test 20: Pair Cancellation	Processing Speed (*Gs*) / *Attention and concentration / Visual scanning*	Visual (pictures)	Identifying and circling instances of a repeated pattern rapidly	Motoric (circling)

Table I.4. WJ III ACH Construct and Content Coverage

Test	Curricular Area *Narrow CHC Ability*	Stimuli	Test Requirement	Response
Test 1: Letter-Word Identification	Reading (*Grw*) *Reading decoding*	Visual (text)	Identifying printed letters and words	Oral (letter name, word)
Test 2: Reading Fluency	Reading (*Grw*) *Reading speed*	Visual (text)	Reading printed statements rapidly and responding true or false (Yes or No)	Motoric (circling)
Test 3: Story Recall	Oral Expression (*Gc*) *Language development* *Listening ability* *Meaningful memory*	Auditory	Listening to and recalling details of stories	Oral (sentence)
Test 4: Understanding Directions	Listening Comprehension (*Gc*) *Listening ability* *Language development*	Auditory	Listening to a sequence of instructions and then following the directions	Motoric (pointing)
Test 5: Calculation	Mathematics (*Gq*) *Math achievement* *Number fluency*	Visual (numeric)	Performing various mathematical calculations; retrieving math facts	Motoric (writing)
Test 6: Math Fluency	Mathematics (*Gq*) *Math achievement*	Visual (numeric)	Adding, subtracting, and multiplying rapidly	Motoric (writing)
Test 7: Spelling	Spelling (*Grw*) *Spelling ability*	Auditory (words)	Spelling orally presented words	Motoric (writing)
Test 8: Writing Fluency	Writing (*Grw*) *Writing speed*	Visual (words with picture)	Formulating and writing simple sentences rapidly	Motoric (writing)
Test 9: Passage Comprehension	Reading (*Grw*) *Reading comprehension* *Verbal (printed) language comprehension*	Visual (text)	Completing a sentence by giving the missing key word that makes sense in the context.	Oral (word)
Test 10: Applied Problems	Mathematics (*Gq*) *Quantitative reasoning* *Math achievement* *Math knowledge*	Auditory (questions); Visual (numeric, text, pictures)	Performing math calculations in response to orally presented problems	Oral
Test 11: Writing Samples	Writing (*Grw*) *Writing ability*	Auditory; Visual (text, pictures)	Writing meaningful sentences for a given purpose	Motoric (writing)
Test 12: Story Recall—Delayed	Long-Term Retrieval (*Glr*) *Meaningful memory*	Auditory (sentence)	Recalling previously presented story elements	Oral (passage)
Test 13: Word Attack	Reading (*Grw*) *Reading decoding* *Phonetic coding: analysis & synthesis*	Visual (word)	Reading phonically regular non-words	Oral (word)
Test 14: Picture Vocabulary	Oral Expression (*Gc*) *Language development* *Lexical knowledge*	Visual (picture)	Naming pictures	Oral (word)
Test 15: Oral Comprehension	Listening Comprehension (*Gc*) *Listening ability*	Auditory	Completing an oral sentence by giving the missing key word that makes sense in the context	Oral (word)
Test 16: Editing	Writing Skills (*Grw*) *Language development* *English usage*	Visual (text)	Identifying and correcting errors in written passages	Oral
Test 17: Reading Vocabulary	Reading (*Grw/Gc*) *Verbal (printed) language Comprehension* *Lexical knowledge*	Visual (word)	Reading words and supplying synonyms and antonyms; reading and completing verbal analogies	Oral (word)
Test 18: Quantitative Concepts	Mathematics (*Gq*) *Math knowledge* *Quantitative reasoning*	Auditory (question); Visual (numeric, text pictures)	Identifying math terms and formulae; identifying number patterns	Oral (word)
Test 19: Academic Knowledge	*General information (Gc)* *Science information* *Cultural information* *Geography achievement*	Auditory (question); Visual (text; picture)	Responding to questions about science, social studies, and humanities	Motoric (pointing), Oral (word, sentences)
Test 20: Spelling of Sounds	Spelling (*Grw/Ga*) *Spelling ability* *Phonetic coding: Analysis & synthesis*	Auditory (letter, word)	Spelling letter combinations that are regular patterns in written English	Motoric (writing)
Test 21: Sound Awareness	Reading (*Ga*) *Phonetic coding*	Auditory (letter, word)	Providing rhyming words; deleting, substituting, and reversing parts of words to make new words	Oral (word)
Test 22: Punctuation & Capitalization	Writing (*Grw*) *English usage*	Auditory (question) Visual (letters, words)	Applying punctuation and capitalization rules	Motoric (writing)

Table I.5. Example Items for the WJ III Tests of Cognitive Abilities: Standard Battery

Test 1: Verbal Comprehension
The test includes four orally presented tasks: Naming pictured objects, providing synonyms and antonyms, and completing analogies.

What are...
Tell me another word for "chase."
Tell me the opposite of "sit."
Pencil is to lead, as pen is to . . .

Test 2: Visual Auditory Learning
The task simulates a learning-to-read process. Symbols are first taught orally and then read in phrases and sentences.

What does this say?

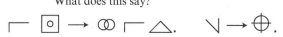

(This man is by the house.)   (He is happy)

Test 3: Spatial Relations
The task involves identifying from a series of shapes the pieces needed to form the whole shape.

Test 4: Sound Blending (taped)
The task is to synthesize a series of orally presented sounds (syllables and/or phonemes) to form a whole word.

/b/a/s/k/e/t/ would be "basket."

Test 5: Concept Formation
The task involves identifying and stating what is different about drawings that are inside a box from those that are outside the box.

Correct response: little and two
(The drawings inside the box are little and have two of each.)

Test 6: Visual Matching (timed)
The task is to match two identical numbers in a row. Numbers range from 1 to 3 digits.

Test 7: Numbers Reversed (taped)
Contains orally presented series of from 2 to 7 digits to be repeated in reverse order.

Item: 7-2-3-5
Correct: 5-3-2-7

Test 8: Incomplete Words (taped)
The task is to identify an orally presented word that is missing phonemes.

tur-le is "turtle"
com-u-ter is "computer" or "commuter"

Test 9: Auditory Working Memory (taped)
The task involves retaining two types of information (words and numbers) presented orally in a mixed order and then reordering that information and repeating first the words and then the numbers.

Item: boy – 1 – 4 – soap – 6
Correct: boy – soap – 1 – 4 – 6

Test 10: Visual-Auditory Learning—Delayed
The task is recalling, with corrective feedback, the visual-auditory associations from Test 2: Visual-Auditory Learning. The test may be presented after a delay of 20 minutes to 8 days.

Mather, N., & Jaffe, L. (2002). *Woodcock-Johnson III: Reports, Recommendations, and Strategies.* New York: John Wiley & Sons.

Table I.6. Example Items for the WJ III Tests of Cognitive Abilities: Extended Battery

Test 11: General Information

There are two tasks: Identifying where specified objects would usually be found and telling what people would usually do with a specified object.

What do people usually do with a ladder?
Where would you usually find eyeglasses?

Test 12: Retrieval Fluency (timed)

The task is to name as many items in a given category as possible in 1 minute. Three categories are presented.

Name different things that you can wear. Name them as fast as you can. Begin.

Test 13: Picture Recognition

The task is to identify a subset of previously presented pictures within a larger set of pictures.

Which two did you see?

Test 14: Auditory Attention (taped)

The task is to differentiate among similar sounding words with increasing levels of background noise. A word is pronounced and the subject points to the picture that represents the word (example: dog, log, fog).

Test 15: Analysis-Synthesis

The task is to analyze the components of an incomplete logic puzzle and to name the missing components by using a colored key at the top of the page.

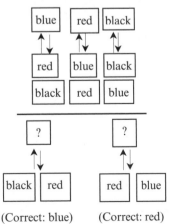

Test 16: Decision Speed (timed)

The task is to scan a row of seven pictures and then circle the two drawings that are the most closely associated.

Test 17: Memory for Words (taped)

The task is to repeat a list of unrelated words in the correct sequence.

Repeat what I say: ruler, book, what

Test 18: Rapid Picture Naming (timed)

The task is to name pictures of common objects presented in rows as rapidly as possible.

Test 19: Planning

The task requires tracing a form, covering as many segments of a visual pattern as possible without retracing or lifting the pencil.

Test 20: Pair Cancellation (timed)

The task is to scan rows of three pictures (hot air balloon, tree, balloon) that are randomly repeated, and circle each instance of the target pair (hot air balloon, tree).

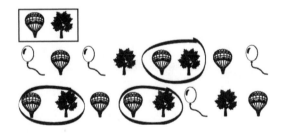

Mather, N., & Jaffe, L. (2002). *Woodcock-Johnson III: Reports, Recommendations, and Strategies.* New York: John Wiley & Sons.

Table I.7. Example Items for the WJ III Tests of Achievement: Standard Battery

Test 1: Letter-Word Identification
The task requires identifying and pronouncing isolated letters and words.

g   r   cat   palm

Test 2: Reading Fluency (timed)
The task requires rapidly reading and comprehending simple sentences.

The sky is green.	YES (NO)
You can sit on a chair.	(YES) NO
A bird has four wings.	YES (NO)

Test 3: Story Recall (taped)
The task requires listening to passages of gradually increasing length and complexity and then recalling the story elements.

Martha went to the store to buy groceries. When she got there, she discovered that she had forgotten her shopping list. She bought milk, eggs, and flour. When she got home she discovered that she had remembered to buy everything except the butter.

Test 4: Understanding Directions
The task requires pointing to objects in a picture after listening to instructions that increase in linguistic complexity.

Point to the man on the bike. Go.

Before you point to the third car, point to the tree closest to a corner. Go.

Test 5: Calculation
The task includes mathematical computations from simple addition facts to complex equations.

$2 + 4 =$ $3x + 3y = 15$

Test 6: Math Fluency (timed)
The task requires rapid recall or calculation of simple, single-digit addition, subtraction, and multiplication facts.

8	7	6
−3	+7	·9

Test 7: Spelling
The task requires the written spelling of words presented orally.

Spell the word "horn." She played the horn in the band. Horn.

Test 8: Writing Fluency (timed)
The task requires quickly formulating and writing simple sentences using three given words and a picture prompt.

books
likes
read

_____
_____
_____

Test 9: Passage Comprehension
The task requires reading a short passage silently and then supplying a key missing word.

The boy _____ off his bike. (Correct: fell, jumped)

The book is one of a series of over eighty volumes. Each volume is designed to provide convenient _____ to a wide range of carefully selected articles.
(Correct: access)

Test 10: Applied Problems
The task involves analyzing and solving practical mathematical problems.

Bill had $7.00. He bought a ball for $3.95 and a comb for $1.20. How much money did he have left?

Test 11: Writing Samples
The task requires writing sentences in response to a variety of demands. The sentences are evaluated based on the quality of expression.

Write a sentence to describe the picture.

Test 12: Story Recall–Delayed
The task requires the student to recall, after a 30 minute to 8-day delay, the story elements presented in the Story Recall test.

Yesterday you heard some short stories. I am going to read a few words from the story and I want you to tell me what you remember about the rest of the story. "Martha went to the store…"

Mather, N., & Jaffe, L. (2002). *Woodcock-Johnson III: Reports, Recommendations, and Strategies.* New York: John Wiley & Sons.

Table I.8. Example Items for the WJ III Tests of Achievement: Extended Battery

Test 13: Word Attack
The task requires pronouncing nonwords that conform to English spelling rules.

flib   bungic

Test 14: Picture Vocabulary
The task requires naming pictured objects ranging from common to specialized.

What is this person holding?
(Correct: gavel)

Test 15: Oral Comprehension (taped)
The task requires listening to short passages and then supplying the missing final word.

Without a doubt, his novels are more complex than the novels of many other contemporary _____.
(Correct: writers, novelists)

Test 16: Editing
The task requires identifying and correcting errors in spelling, punctuation, capitalization, or word usage in short typed passages.

Bobby's face was so sunburned, it looked like he had fell into a bucket of red paint.
(Correct: fallen)

Test 17: Reading Vocabulary
The test involves reading words for three different tasks: providing synonyms, providing antonyms, and completing analogies.

What is another word for curious?
Tell me the opposite of civilized.
Finish what I say: Student is to boxer as study is to . . .

Test 18: Quantitative Concepts
The task requires applying mathematical concepts and analyzing numerical relationships.
Point to the largest duck.
What number belongs in this series: 1 2 6 __ 120
(Correct: 24)

Test 19: Academic Knowledge
The task involves answering questions about curricular knowledge in various areas of the biological and physical sciences, history, geography, government, economics, art, music, and literature.

On a musical scale, how many notes are in an octave?

Test 20: Spelling of Sounds
The task requires the written spelling of nonwords according to English spelling rules.

barches   smuff

Test 21: Sound Awareness
The task includes four measures of phonological awareness (rhyming, deletion, substitution, and reversal).

Tell me a word that rhymes with goat. (rhyming)
(Correct: boat, wrote, any real word that rhymes)

Say the word "cat" without the /k/ sound. (deletion)
(Correct: at)

Change the /s/ in sack to /b/ . (substitution)
(Correct: back)

Say the sounds in the word "tire" backward. (reversal)
(Correct: right)

Test 22: Punctuation and Capitalization
The task requires using correct punctuation and capitalization in writing orally dictated words and phrases.

Write the month "September." (Scored for capitalization.)

Write the city and state "Chicago, Illinois." (Scored for comma.)

Mather, N., & Jaffe, L. (2002). *Woodcock-Johnson III: Reports, Recommendations, and Strategies.* New York: John Wiley & Sons.

EXPLANATION OF WJ III SCORES, INTERPRETIVE LEVELS, AND DISCREPANCIES

Level 1: Qualitative

Qualitative information is obtained through observation of behavior during testing, analysis of task demands, and error analysis of responses to test items. Qualitative information, though not a *score,* is a pivotal component for understanding and interpreting all scores obtained by the student. Oftentimes a description of how a student obtained a particular score is as important as the information provided by the score itself. Qualitative information is one of the critical components of proper individualized assessment and is

an integral part of the reporting and interpretation of test results (see Table 9).

Task Analysis and Comparisons of Selected Tests

The basis for qualitative analysis of a test is generally twofold: task analysis and error pattern analysis. In task analysis, the evaluator analyzes the cognitive and academic demands of the task, including the subskills the student needs to perform the task proficiently. The similarities and differences between the task demands, compared with the student's demonstrated proficiency (or lack thereof) on each task, suggest the type of task demands that are either easy or difficult for the student. In error pattern analysis, the evaluator examines the errors the student made and the

Table I.9. Hierarchy of WJ III COG Test Information

Level	Type of Information	Basis	Information and Scores	Uses
1	Qualitative (Criterion-Referenced)	Observations during testing and analysis of responses	Description of subject's reaction to the test situation Performance on finely defined skills at the item content level	Appreciation of the subject's behavior underlying obtained test score Prediction of the subject's behavior and responses in instructional situations Specific skill instructional recommendations
2	Level of Development (Norm-Referenced)	Sum of item scores Age or grade level in the norming sample at which the median score is the same as the subject's score	Raw score *Rasch Ability score (Example: Test or cluster W score) Age Equivalent (AE) Grade Equivalent (GE)	Reporting a subject's level of development Basis for describing the implications of developmental strengths and weaknesses Basis for initial recommendations regarding instructional level and materials Placement decisions based on a criterion of significantly advanced or delayed development
3	Proficiency (Criterion-Referenced)	Subject's distance on a • Rasch scale from an age or grade reference point • Equal interval units; preferred metric for statistical analyses	Quality of performance on reference tasks Rasch Difference score (Example: Test or cluster W DIFF) Relative Proficiency Index (RPI) Cognitive Academic Language Proficiency (CALP) Level Instructional / Developmental Zone	Proficiency on tasks of average difficulty for peers Developmental level at which typical tasks will be perceived as easy, mildly challenging, or very difficult by the subject Placement decisions based on a criterion of significantly good or poor proficiency
4	Relative Standing in a Group (Norm Referenced)	Relative position (A transformation of a difference score, such as dividing by the standard deviation of the reference group)	Standard Scores Percentile Ranks z scores	Communication of a subject's competitive position among peers Placement decisions based on a criterion of significantly high or low standing

strategy he or she used in doing the task (possibly in lieu of exercising the necessary skills) to discern the subskill(s) that have not been mastered.

Task analysis is frequently used to obtain information about a student's skills and abilities *other* than the ability that is the intended target of the test or cluster. A test is designed to measure a certain ability, but at times one recognizes through more detailed analysis that the intended ability was not measured. As an example, the Working Memory cluster is intended to measure the ability to hold information in immediate awareness while performing a mental operation on it. Low scores on Auditory Working Memory and Numbers Reversed might, quite reasonably, lead the evaluator to diagnose difficulties in working memory. Task analysis, however, shows that both tests require the student to visualize numbers. Suppose that error analysis of Auditory Working Memory showed errors only on repetition of numbers but not on objects—a question should arise as to whether the problem is in memory or in the student's ability to visualize/work with numbers. That question can then be answered by checking the student's performance on other tests that require memory but no numbers, such as Memory for Words and Visual-Auditory Learning. Visual Matching and Calculation would provide additional information regarding facility with numbers. Task analysis and error pattern analysis, then, help evaluators to obtain valuable information that may, or may not, require further investigation.

Level 2: Level of Development

Level 2 information is derived directly from the raw score. This information indicates the level of development and is usually transformed to metrics that compare raw scores to age- or grade-level groups. Raw scores are then entered into the WJ III Compuscore and Profiles Program (Schrank & Woodcock, 2001) or the Report Writer for the WJ III (Schrank & Woodcock, 2002).

W *Scores*
W scores are intermediate scores for test interpretation. These scores do not appear on the computer printout unless the examiner chooses that option in Program Options. The *W*-scale is a special transformation of the Rasch ability scale and provides a common scale of equal-interval measurement that represents both a person's ability and the task difficulty. The *W*-scale for each test is centered on a value of 500, which has been set to approximate the average

performance at age 10 years, 0 months. The *W* score for any cluster is the average *W* score for the tests included in the cluster. The *W* score is also used to plot the Age/Grade Profile, which illustrates Development Zones on the WJ III COG and Instructional Zones on the WJ III ACH (see Level 3: Degree of Mastery). The *W*-scale is particularly useful for the measurement of growth and can be considered a growth scale.

Age Equivalents (AE)
An age equivalent (AE), or age score, reflects the student's performance in terms of the age group in the norming sample in which the median raw score is the same as the student's raw score. If half the subjects of age 8-5 in the norming sample obtained a raw score of 20 or greater, and half the subjects of age 8-5 obtained a raw score of 20 or less, then the raw score of 20 is assigned the age equivalent of 8-5 (8 years, 5 months). All students, regardless of age, who obtain a raw score of 20 will have an 8-5 age equivalent assigned as their level of development. Age equivalents are expressed in years and months with a dash (-) as the delimiter. The age scale starts at 2-0 on some tests and 4-0 on the other tests, and extends to the age of peak median performance in the norming sample for each test.

Grade Equivalents (GE)
A grade equivalent (GE), or grade score, reflects the student's performance in terms of the grade level in the norming sample at which the median raw score is the same as the student's raw score. For example, if half the subjects in grade 3.6 in the norming sample obtained a raw score of 20 or greater, and half the subjects in grade 3.6 in the norming sample obtained a raw score of 20 or less, then the raw score of 20 is assigned the grade equivalent of 3.6 (third grade, sixth month). All students, regardless of age, who obtain a raw score of 20 will have a 3.6 grade equivalent assigned as their level of development. Grade equivalents are expressed in grade and month with a decimal point (.) as the delimiter. The grade scale ranges from <K.0 (below beginning kindergarten) to >18.0 (above beginning second year graduate school).

Level 3: Degree of Proficiency

Level 3 information indicates the quality of a student's performance on criterion tasks of known difficulty levels when compared to an age or grade reference group.

Relative Proficiency Index (RPI)

The Relative Proficiency Index (RPI) predicts a student's level of proficiency on tasks that typical age- or grade-peers (the reference group) would perform with 90% proficiency. For example, an RPI of 55/90 on the calculation test would indicate that, on similar math tasks, the student would demonstrate 55% proficiency, whereas average age- or grade-peers would demonstrate 90% proficiency. Interpretation guidelines, paralleling informal reading inventory criteria, are Independent Level (easy; 96/90 and above), Instructional Level (76/90 to 95/90); and Frustration Level (difficult; 75/90 and below).

RPIs are based on the W scale. The W scale is a special transformation of the Rasch ability scale (Rasch, 1960; Wright & Stone, 1979) and uses the same set of numbers for expressing both item difficulty and an individual's ability. As a consequence, the scale provides a mathematical basis for predicting performance based on the difference between a person's ability and difficulty of the task. WJ III users do not need to use W scores directly, although W scores can be provided by the Compuscore and Profiles Program, if desired.

For any skill or ability assessed, the RPI can document a performance deficit that may not be apparent in peer-comparison scores (e.g., standard scores, percentile ranks). When there appears to be a contradiction between interpretations of the standard score and the RPI, the evaluator must remember that these two kinds of scores are communicating different information and are not interchangeable. A common misconception is that peer-comparison scores indicate ability or achievement levels. In fact, peer-comparison scores do not provide direct information regarding a student's mastery of the skill or ability being assessed. Rather, they represent a rank ordering, indicating the position in which a student's score falls within the distribution of scores obtained by age- or grade-peers in the norming sample. Woodcock (1999) illustrates this difference as follows:

Persons with visual or hearing problems are usually classified as handicapped or in need of special services because they have significant deficits in the quality of their visual or aural performance, not because they fall below some point on a norm-referenced criterion scale. On the other hand, mental retardation has been based primarily on a norm-referenced criterion such as having an IQ that falls in the lower 3% of the general population (below 70). (Woodcock, 1999)

Occasionally, an evaluator may note an *apparent* contradiction between a standard score and the RPI. For example, on the Letter-Word Identification test, Tommy, a second-grade boy, obtained a standard score of 92 (average, albeit at the lower end), a percentile rank of 30, and an RPI of 62/90 (limited). These scores suggest that, even though many other second-graders (30%) demonstrated equally limited or more limited sight vocabularies, Tommy's skills were nonetheless deficient compared to the average proficiency of second-graders. He requires additional attention to sight-word acquisition. This *apparent* discrepancy is more likely to be observed during a period of rapid growth in a skill or ability. Consequently, it is important to consider proficiency scores as well as peer-comparison to determine a student's need for services.

Sample descriptive statements reflect a Fluid Reasoning *W* difference of –10 for a male student.

Proficiency: "His fluid reasoning ability is limited to average. . . ."
Functionality: "His fluid reasoning ability is mildly impaired to within normal limits. . . ."
Developmental: "His fluid reasoning ability is mildly delayed to age-appropriate. . . ."
Implications: "He will probably find age-level tasks requiring him to identify categories and relationships among categories, make inferences, recognize and form concepts, and draw conclusions difficult."

Table I.10. Criterion-Referenced Interpretation of RPI Scores

W Diff Values	Reported RPIs	Proficiency	Functionality	Development	Implications
+31 and above	100/90	Very Advanced	Very Advanced	Very Advanced	Extremely Easy
+14 to +30	98/90 to 100/90	Advanced	Advanced	Advanced	Very Easy
+7 to +13	95/90 to 98/90	Average to Advanced	Within Normal Limits to Advanced	Age-appropriate to Advanced	Easy
–6 to +6	82/90 to 95/90	Average	Within Normal Limits	Age-appropriate	Manageable
–13 to –7	67/90 to 82/90	Limited to Average	Mildly Impaired to Within Normal Limits	Mildly Delayed to Age-appropriate	Difficult
–30 to –14	24/90 to 67/90	Limited	Mildly Impaired	Mildly Delayed	Very Difficult
–50 to –31	3/90 to 24/90	Very Limited	Moderately Impaired	Moderately Delayed	Extremely Difficult
–51 and below	0/90 to 3/90	Negligible	Severely Impaired	Severely Delayed	Impossible

Table I.11. Instructional Interpretation of RPI Levels

RPI	Instructional Level
96/90 and above	Independent
76/90 to 95/90	Instructional
75/90 and below	Frustration

Cognitive-Academic Language Proficiency (CALP)

A CALP score is provided for all of the tests that measure English language proficiency, if this option is selected in the software. As with the RPI, the CALP level is based upon the *W* score differences. CALP levels describe how the student will perform on English language tasks when compared with others of the same age or grade. As illustrated in Table 12, the scores range from a CALP Level of 5 (Advanced), where the student will find the language demands in instructional situations to be very easy, to a CALP Level of 1 (Negligible), where the student will find the language demands in instructional situations impossible to manage.

Age/Grade Profiles

The Instructional Zone in the WJ III ACH and the Developmental Zone in the WJ III COG are special applications of the RPI. These bands extend from –10 *W* score units (easy) to +10 *W* score units (difficult). These bands display the range between an RPI of 96/90 (easy) to an RPI of 75/90 (difficult). The student will find tasks that are below the lower point of the band to be quite easy, and those above the higher point of the band to be quite difficult. The length of these bands on the Age/Grade Profile indirectly reflects the rate of growth of the measured trait in the population. In a period of development when growth is rapid, the Developmental or Instructional Zone bands will be quite narrow; in a period of development when little growth occurs, the

bands will be quite wide. For example, a narrow band for a second grade student on the Letter-Word Identification test indicates that growth in sight word acquisition is rapid at that grade level, whereas a wide band for a student in high school indicates that sight word acquisition takes place slowly during that developmental period.

The Age/Grade Profile displays the practical implications of the test or cluster scores (in contrast to the statistical implications displayed by the SS/PR Profiles). The Developmental and Instructional Zones suggest the level that which tasks will be easy for a person and the level at which tasks will be difficult, and may be used to describe the student's present level of functioning.

Level 4: Comparison with Peers

Level 4 information indicates relative standing in the group when compared to age- or grade-peers.

Percentile Ranks (PR)

A percentile rank describes a student's relative standing in a comparison group on a scale of 1 to 99 (see Table 13). The student's percentile rank indicates the percentage of students from the comparison group who had scores the same as or lower than the student's score. A student's percentile rank of 68 indicates that 68% of the comparison group had scores the same as or lower than the student's score. Extended percentile ranks provide scores down to a percentile rank of one-tenth (0.1) and up to a percentile rank of ninety-nine and nine-tenths (99.9). A student's percentile rank of 0.1 indicates that only 1 in 1,000 students in a reference group would score as low or lower. A student's percentile rank of 99.9 indicates that 999 in 1,000 students in a reference group would score the same or lower.

Table I.12. CALP Levels, Implications, and Comparisons to RPI Levels

CALP Level		English Language Demands at Age or Grade Level	RPI
5	Advanced	Very Easy	98/90 to 100/90
4–5 (4.5)	Fluent to Advanced	Easy	96/90 to 97/90
4	Fluent	Manageable	82/90 to 95/90
3–4 (3.5)	Limited to Fluent	Difficult	68/90 to 81/90
3	Limited	Very Difficult	34/90 to 67/90
2–3 (2.5)	Very Limited to Limited	Very Difficult to Extremely Difficult	19/90 to 33/90
2	Very Limited	Extremely Difficult	5/90 to 18/90
1–2 (1.5)	Negligible to Very Limited	Extremely Difficult to Impossible	3/90 to 4/90
1	Negligible	Impossible	0/90 to 2/90

Table I.13. Classification of Standard Score and Percentile Rank Ranges

Standard Score Range	Percentile Rank Range	WJ III Classification
131 and above	98 to 99.9	Very Superior
121 to 130	92 to 97	Superior
111 to 120	76 to 91	High Average
90 to 110	25 to 75	Average
80 to 89	9 to 24	Low Average
70 to 79	3 to 8	Low
69 and below	0.1 to 2	Very Low

Standard Scores (SS)

A standard score describes a student's performance relative to the average performance of the comparison group. It is based on an average score being assigned a value of 100, with a standard deviation, an indication of the variability of scores in the population, assigned a value of 15. The range of standard scores is 0 to over 200.

Z Scores

A *z* is a standard score that has a mean of 0 and a standard deviation of 1. A (+) sign means that the score is above the mean (e.g., +2.0 means two standard deviations above the mean) and a (–) sign means that the score is below the mean (e.g., –2.0 means two standard deviations below the mean).

Standard Error of Measurement (SEM)

The standard error of measurement is an estimate of the amount of error attached to an individual's standard score, or how much to expect a person's obtained score to vary from his or her true score if the person were administered the same test repeatedly. The WJ III provides the unique SEM associated with each possible score, rather than average SEMs based on entire samples, a feature made possible by the use of Rasch scaling.

Discrepancy Terminology

Actual SS: The student's obtained standard score on a cognitive or achievement cluster.

Predicted SS: The meaning of the predicted score varies depending upon the type of discrepancy comparison. For the ability/achievement discrepancies, the predicted score may be based on four options: (a) GIA-Std (Tests 1–7); (b) GIA-Ext (Tests 1–7, 11–17); (c) Predicted Achievement; or (d) Oral Language. The GIA score is based on a weighted combination of tests that provides the best overall estimate of general intelligence (g). The highest g-weights are for tests of Gc and Gf. In contrast, the Predicted Achievement score is based on the differential weightings of WJ III COG Tests 1–7 that best predict achievement in specific curriculum areas. The fundamental difference between the GIA g-weights and the PA prediction weights is the criterion upon which the weights are derived. The GIA weights use an internal validity criterion: which weights provide for the best g-estimate within the cognitive battery. In contrast, the PA weights use an external validity criterion: which weights provide for the best prediction of a criterion (achievement) outside the cognitive battery.

These PA test weights vary differentially according to the relative importance of different cognitive abilities at different age or grade levels and achievement. For example, in predicting reading in a first-grade student, the Sound Blending and Visual Matching tests are weighted more, whereas for a high school student the Verbal Comprehension test is weighted more heavily. for the oral language procedure, the Oral Language-Ext cluster score in the WJ III ACH is used.

These predicted scores obtained from the GIA, PA, and Oral Language ability measures are not the same as the obtained scores. The predicted scores represent the best estimate of a person's expected achievement after the effects of regression to the mean are accounted for (a statistical phenomenon that occurs when one variable is used to predict another and the two variables are imperfectly correlated). The obtained score is what the person actually obtains. After regression to the mean is accounted for in the prediction, the predicted score represents the best estimate of what we would expect the person to achieve based upon the developmental level (age or grade) and the particular achievement domain.

For the intra-ability discrepancies (intra-cognitive, intra-achievement, and intra-individual), the predicted score is based on the average of the person's other scores, as well as the correlations among the measures. For example, on the intra-achievement discrepancy using the WJ III ACH Standard Battery, Broad Reading would be compared to the average of the student's performance in the other three areas: Broad Mathematics, Broad Written Language, and Oral Language.

Standard Score Difference (SS DIFF): The SS DIFF score represents the Predicted SS subtracted from the Actual SS.

Discrepancy Percentile Rank (PR): For the ability/achievement discrepancies, this score represents the percent of the WJ III norm sample that had an SS DIFF of this magnitude.

For the intra-ability discrepancies, this score represents the percent of the WJ III norm sample of the same age or grade, and with the same predicted score as the student's, that obtained an ability score the same as, or lower, than the student's.

Discrepancy Standard Deviation (SD): The Discrepancy SD score reports the SS DIFF divided by the standard error of estimate (SEE), the appropriate standard deviation statistic for this application. This statistic is derived from the distributions of SS DIFF found in the WJ III norm sample. For the ability/achievement discrepancies, the score represents the number of standard deviations the SS DIFF is from the Predicted SS. For the intra-ability discrepancies, this score represents the number of standard deviations the SS DIFF is from the average of his or her other abilities.

SAMPLE STATEMENTS FOR REPORTING SCORES AND SCORE DISCREPANCIES

These statements provide examples of ways to describe various test scores in reports. Words in brackets will vary, depending on the cognitive or achievement test or ability being discussed.

Score Levels Reported in Combination

Lara demonstrated Low Average to Average performance on [the WJ III Spelling test], with a grade equivalent of early grade 3, and an RPI of 62/90.

Kara's [Broad Written Language] score bridged the Low to Low Average ranges (SS 77–83) with a grade equivalent of early grade 3 and an RPI of 75/90. When average grade-peers have 90% success, Kara will have 75% success on similar tasks.

Tara's CALP Level of 5, as well as her RPI of 99/90, suggest that she will find the language demands in instructional situations to be very easy.

Level of Development (Grade Equivalent, Age Equivalent)

Dick's scores indicate that his level of functioning on [paired associate learning and retrieval tasks] is typical compared to grade-mates.

Maria's obtained grade score on the [Broad Reading cluster] was approximately beginning third grade (GE = 3.1).

The number of items Marcos answered correctly is comparable to the average student in early grade 7.

Test results indicate that Diane's performance is comparable to that of average 8-year-olds.

On [phonemic awareness tasks], Felicia scored similarly to students in mid-grade 2.

Sally is a fourth-grader who currently performs at the first-grade level in [math computation].

Margaret scored at mid-second grade level on [the Broad Reading cluster].

Lucas's instructional level for [word identification] was mid-grade 3.

Proficiency

Relative Proficiency Index

Mark's level of proficiency on [the Broad Mathematics cluster] was in the Limited range (RPI: 66/90).

Sam's RPI of 21/90 on the [Phoneme/Grapheme cluster] indicates that on similar tasks, in which the average fourth-grade student would demonstrate 90% proficiency, Sam would demonstrate 21% proficiency. Sam's knowledge of [phoneme-grapheme correspondence and spelling patterns] is very limited.

Jason's RPI on the [Verbal Comprehension test] was 75/90, suggesting that when average age-peers have 90% success on similar [expressive vocabulary and reasoning tasks], Jason will have 75% success. This score places his proficiency at the lower end of the instructional range.

Although Nicholas's obtained standard score on [the Mathematics Reasoning cluster] is within the Average range for seventh-grade students overall, his RPI (45/90) indicates that he will have more difficulty than most of his grade-peers in [math problem solving].

Manuel is predicted to demonstrate 2% mastery on [short-term memory tasks] that average age-peers would perform with 90% mastery (RPI: 2/90), indicating that his functioning in this area is severely impaired.

Renee's RPI of 98/90 on [Visual-Spatial Thinking] signifies advanced proficiency. When average age-peers demonstrate 90% accuracy on similar tasks, Renee's expected accuracy would be approximately 98%.

Even though Sheila's standard scores on both [Broad Reading and Broad Mathematics] are in the Low range compared to other fifth-graders, her proficiency in [reading] (RPI 9/90) is markedly lower than her proficiency in [mathematics] (RPI 32/90).

Ben's performance on [Retrieval Fluency (RPI 90/90) and Rapid Picture Naming (RPI 88/90)] indicate that he has no difficulty with [rapid retrieval of familiar words from long-term memory].

David's RPI of 45/90 on [Short-Term Memory] represents a mild delay in the skills necessary for similar classroom tasks, such as [repeating a set of instructions to himself]. His expected success in doing so would be 45% compared with his classmates' 90%.

On a similar classroom task [reading one or two sentences and filling in the missing word], Bryn's proficiency would be within normal limits (RPI 82/90).

Although Luz scored considerably higher in [Quantitative Concepts] than in [Calculation and Fluency], her RPIs of 70/90 and 40/90 indicate that she will experience frustration in dealing with grade-level [math concepts and number relationships].

Geraldo's RPI of 84/90 indicates that his [academic knowledge] is comparable to that of his grade-peers.

Developmental and Instructional Zones

The Developmental Zone on the WJ III COG indicates that Martha will find tasks involving verbal comprehension to be easy at mid-grade 4 and frustrating at beginning grade 6.

The WJ III Age/Grade Profile indicates that appropriate instructional materials for teaching Jesse [word attack skills] would be early grade 2, and for [sight vocabulary and reading comprehension], early grade 3.

Stan's instructional zone indicates that he will find [reading] tasks to be easy at the beginning second-grade level and very difficult at the beginning third-grade level.

Ted's instructional zone on the WJ III Age/Grade Profile indicates that instructional materials in [basic writing skills] at beginning fourth-grade level will be very easy for Ted, while materials at mid-fifth grade level will be very difficult.

Appropriate instructional materials for June in basic mathematics and skills would range from beginning fifth-grade level [easy] to late fifth grade [instructional]. Materials at the early sixth-grade level would be frustrating for her.

Jared's performance on [Academic Applications] matches the median score of college sophomores on the tests of this cluster, suggesting that Jared would find instructional materials at the college sophomore level appropriately challenging.

Cognitive-Academic Language Proficiency

Kai met the criteria for fluency in all tests of oral language skills (CALP 4 to 4.5). He should find the English language demands of instruction at the twelfth-grade level manageable to easy.

Ingrid's CALP level of 2 on [the Verbal Ability cluster] indicates that she is very limited in [expressive vocabulary knowledge] and is likely to find the language demands of instruction related to English vocabulary at fourth-grade level extremely difficult.

Ruoli's performance on the WJ III Oral Language cluster (CALP level 1) suggests negligible functioning in [comprehension and expression of] English. Managing academic instruction in English, appropriate for 10-year-old native speakers, will be impossible for him.

Peer Comparison

Standard Score Ranges

Based on his standard score confidence bands, Jacob demonstrated performance commensurate with his age-peers on [the Oral Language–Extended cluster].

On the WJ III Total Achievement cluster, Bill's overall performance was in the Average range.

According to grade norms, Sara's level of achievement on the [Broad Reading cluster] falls in the Average range.

Juan's achievement in [basic writing] skills is Low Average for his grade.

Test results indicate that all of Jesse's [reading] abilities fall in the Low Average range when compared to grade-peers.

Oscar demonstrated Average ability to store [linguistic information] in memory and retrieve it later.

Kata's Average to High Average score on [Analysis-Synthesis] reflects her ability to [use deductive, linear logic for solving novel problems].

Fran's performance varied on the tests comprising the [Executive Processes] cluster. Her standard scores on the [Planning and Pair Cancellation] tests indicate a High Average level of ability when compared with her typical grade peers, whereas her performance was in the Low Average range on the [Concept Formation] test.

George's performance on the [Knowledge] cluster fell in the Low Average to Average range.

Max's [writing fluency, formulating and writing simple sentences quickly] bridges the High Average to Superior ranges (SS ± 1 SEM = 115–123).

TJ demonstrated a relative weakness in [word retrieval], scoring in the Low Average range on the [Rapid Picture Naming] test.

Nancy's overall [math] abilities, as represented by the [Broad Math] cluster score, are in the Low range with no significant discrepancies among the component tests of [Calculation, Math Fluency, and Applied Problems].

When Mr. Garibaldi was compared with the graduate school sample, his Comprehension-Knowledge factor score remained competitive (SS 114).

When compared with adults her age, Ms. Lancaster performed well within the Average range in each of the clinically relevant test clusters. In contrast, her scores decreased to the Low range when compared with the graduate school sample.

Lynne's Low to Low Average performance on [Applied Problems] reflects her apparent [confusion with math concepts].

Mariah demonstrated Superior [reasoning] skills, [using inductive and deductive logic to form concepts and solve problems using newly learned procedures (Fluid Reasoning: SS 127, PR 96)].

The WJ III SS/PR Profile indicates that Earl scored significantly higher on the [Broad Reading cluster] than he did on the [Broad Mathematics cluster].

Although in the Average range, Mariah's [visual-spatial] abilities appear to be significantly less well developed than her [reasoning/problem solving]. The separation of the confidence bands was [three] times the width of the SEM, whereas one is considered significant.

Rhia's standard score of 125 ± 5 indicates that her performance on the WJ III Broad Written Language cluster is in the Superior range.

Mary obtained a Broad Reading standard score of 98 ± 6. This score is within the Average range.

Martha scored in the Superior range on the Broad Reading cluster (SS ± 1 SEM: 119–131).

Tom's score on the Spelling test (SS ± 1 SEM: 98–110) was significantly higher than his score on the Writing Samples test (SS ± 1 SEM: 75–86).

Although Mark scored in the Low Average range on the Broad Mathematics cluster, his performance on the Calculation test (High Average) was significantly higher than his performance on the Applied Problems test (Very Low).

The statistically significant score discrepancy between the tests comprising the [Auditory Processing cluster (Sound Blending SS 125–132 vs. Auditory Attention SS 112–117)] are not considered to be educationally significant and do not warrant concern.

Percentile Ranks

Kay's percentile rank of 99.5 on the [Basic Math Skills cluster] indicates that only 5 out of 1,000 individuals of her age would have a score as high as or higher than hers.

On the [Broad Mathematics cluster], Sara scored at the 25th percentile, within the lower limits of the Average range.

Test results from the WJ III [Broad Mathematics cluster] indicated that Susan's overall [math] achievement is in the Low Average range (20th percentile).

Lawrence's frustration with classroom [writing] tasks is understandable given his obtained percentile rank of 3 on [Writing Samples]. Among students of his age, only 3 of 100 scored as low as or lower than he did on this test.

Glenda obtained a [Broad Reading cluster] percentile rank of 8 (SS = 78).

On the [reading] tests, a significant difference existed between Ruth's Low Average to Average performance on [Letter-Word Identification (PR ± 21–39)] and her Very Low to Low performance on [Passage Comprehension (PR ± 1–5)].

Bill's group standing in [problem-solving] ability (PR: 2) is significantly lower than his [calculation] skill (PR: 89).

Monica's [reading] skills (PR 98) are significantly higher than her mathematics skills (PR 10).

Angelica's [Auditory Working Memory] score was in the Low range, as low or lower than 94% of her grade-peers (PR 6).

Z Scores

The following z score statements are offered for use with reporting results of Visual-Auditory Learning—Delayed and

Story Recall—Delayed. These particular z scores represent the difference (if any) between a person's delayed recall score and the delayed recall scores of others of his or her grade or age who had obtained the same score on the first administration of the tests.

Theo's ability to recall key details in stories that had been read to him was equal to or better than 75% of his grade-peers (Story Recall, PR 75). His ability to retain this information and recall it later was significantly better (z score = +1.57) than those whose initial performance was similar to his.

Jesus performed in the Low Average range on a task requiring him to learn to associate words with a series of symbols. When asked to recall the words for the symbols a day later, he remembered about as many as would be predicted given his initial low performance (z score = +0.3).

Gerald's ability to recall key details of narrative information and associations between symbols and spoken words was in the Average range. Compared with grade-peers whose initial scores were the same as his, after several hours, his retention of word-symbol associations was similar; his recall of narrative details, however, significantly exceeded that of his grade-peers (+1.75 standard deviations).

Discrepancies

Intra-Ability Discrepancies

Jeanne does not demonstrate a significant discrepancy among the [four achievement] clusters.

When Bill's [Comprehension-Knowledge] cluster score is compared to his Average performance on the other six CHC factors, only 6 out of 100 students (PR: 6) would obtain a score as low as or lower than his.

When Sally's actual achievement score is compared to her predicted score, based upon the average of the other three achievement clusters, a significant discrepancy exists. Sally's Discrepancy Percentile Rank indicates that only 5% of the students of the same age and with the same predicted score would obtain a score as low as or lower than hers.

On the Intra-Individual Discrepancies, only 1 in 1,000 grade-peers (PR: 99.9) with Lila's same predicted [Broad Reading] score (the average of her other cluster scores) would obtain an actual [Broad Reading] score the same as or higher than hers.

In [Broad Written Language], only 3% of students whose predicted scores were the same as Alex's would obtain a standard score of 87 or lower.

Of Philip's grade-peers whose predicted standard scores were identical to his, only 2 out of 100 students would obtain a score as high as or higher than his actual standard score of 115 in [Broad Reading] (Discrepancy Percentile Rank = 98).

When D.J.'s [Broad Math] cluster standard score of 73 is compared to his average on the other three achievement clusters, only 1 out of 100 grade-peers with the same predicted score would have obtained a score as low as or lower than he did (Discrepancy PR = 0.1; SD Diff = –3.26).

Margaret evidences significant intra-individual strengths in [Auditory Processing and Phonemic Awareness] and weaknesses in [Processing Speed, Broad Reading, and Broad Math]. The likelihood of her age-peers with the same predicted score obtaining scores as high as or higher than hers is [1% for Auditory Processing and 3% for Phonemic Awareness]. In her areas of weakness, the probability of obtaining scores as low as or lower than hers, given the predicted scores, are [4% for Processing Speed and 3% for Broad Reading and Broad Math].

Michael's only significant Intra-Individual Discrepancy was in [Fluid Reasoning], indicating a severe deficit in [abstract, logical reasoning], compared to his other abilities. A discrepancy of this magnitude is found in only 1% of students of his age.

Ability/Achievement Discrepancies

No significant discrepancy exists between Shirin's General Intellectual Ability—Extended score and her present academic performance.

When Charlene's General Intellectual Ability—Extended (GIA-Ext) score is compared to her achievement, significant discrepancies exist between the GIA-Ext and [Basic Reading Skills]. Only 2 out of 100 individuals with a predicted standard score of 105 would obtain a score of 75 or lower.

When Jeff's predicted achievement standard score of 81 is compared to his actual achievement standard score of 55, only 1 out of 100 students (Discrepancy Percentile Rank = 1) would obtain a score the same or lower.

Current test results indicate that Spence has a significant discrepancy between his oral language abilities and his [reading] skills. When his Oral Language—Extended cluster (SS = 104) is compared to his [Basic Reading Skills] (SS = 65), and [Reading Comprehension] clusters (SS = 74), only 1 and 2 out of 100 individuals, respectively, would score the same or lower.

Based on her General Intellectual Ability—Standard and Oral Language scores, Gina's [Broad Reading, Broad Math, and Math Calculation] scores are significantly below expectations.

The WJ III provides predicted achievement scores for each academic area based on different weightings of seven cognitive abilities according to the student's age. Gerald scored significantly lower than predicted in [Broad Reading (Standard Error of Estimate [SEE] = –2.55), Basic Reading Skills (SEE = –1.61), and Broad Written Language (SEE = –1.60)].

When compared to his overall intellectual ability, Patrick's achievement was significantly lower than predicted in [all areas of written language].

Jerome's difficulties learning to [pronounce words and spell] are unpredicted given his advanced oral language abilities and superior phonemic awareness skills.

[Broad Reading, Math Calculation, and Academic Knowledge] were significantly lower than predicted, suggesting that Robert's cognitive abilities are more advanced than his present levels of academic performance.

Integrating Statements

When presenting combinations of score statements and describing the scores themselves, think of the steps of the process as forming an inverse pyramid. The organization proceeds from broad-based scores (e.g., Total Achievement and clusters) to narrow-based scores (e.g., test scores). Discuss individual test scores when significant differences exist among the scores. Although the different scores provide different information, it is not necessary to report all types of scores in the body of a report. In discussing scores, begin with peer comparison scores (e.g., standard scores or percentile ranks), then RPIs, Instructional Zones, and age or grade equivalents, and finally information obtained from error analysis and observation. Figure 1 illustrates the progression for describing and reporting scores. The following paragraph provides an example:

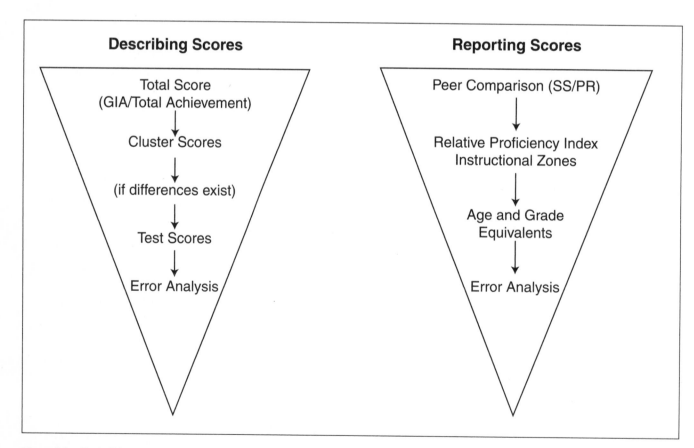

Figure I.1   Describing and Reporting Scores

Reading

On the WJ III ACH Broad Reading cluster, Kasey obtained a standard score of 66 ($\pm$1 SEM = 64–69). When Kasey's actual standard score in Broad Reading is compared to his predicted score (based on the average of the other three areas of achievement), only 1 out of 1,000 people would have obtained a score the same or lower. His Relative Proficiency Index of 5/90 indicates that when average grade-mates are having 90% success, Kasey will have approximately 5% success, performance well below the Frustration level. His grade scores on the Instructional Zone indicate that an easy level of reading for Kasey is mid–first grade, whereas a frustration level is beginning second grade. Although all reading scores were in the Low to Low Average range, Kasey's score on the Reading Fluency test, which requires rapid reading of simple sentences, was significantly lower than his scores on the Letter-Word Identification and Passage Comprehension tests. In general, many of Kasey's reading errors involved medial vowel sounds, such as pronouncing *must* as "mist." Even when accurate, his word recognition was slow. Kasey appeared to lack confidence in his reading ability, and he remarked during testing that reading has been difficult for him since first grade.

TEST COMPARISONS AND ERROR PATTERN ANALYSIS

This section offers suggestions for qualitative interpretation of the information available from the WJ III. Extensive and valuable information can be obtained from comparing a student's performance on various cognitive and achievement tests, based on similarities and differences in task demands, and from exploration of error patterns in item responses. Frequently, task analysis and error pattern analysis offer insights not obtainable from test scores alone regarding factors contributing to the student's difficulties and areas in need of further investigation.

The following test comparisons are not intended to be a complete or comprehensive listing of all of the possible task comparisons among the WJ III Tests of Cognitive Abilities and Tests of Achievement. They are illustrations of the qualitative information an evaluator can obtain from analysis at the individual test level. Both the table and the section that follow exemplify comparisons and possible performance implications when a difference of significance or probable significance exists between individual test scores within a cluster or between clusters—and sometimes, when they are all low. The section that follows, Tips for Interpretation, organized into cognitive and academic abilities as-

sessed by the WJ III, provides additional suggestions for error pattern analysis.

When making test comparisons, consider scores that represent proficiency (RPI) as well as standing among peers (standard scores). For each student, the evaluator is cautioned to interpret the implications of the suggested test comparisons in the context of other test and cluster scores from the WJ III as well as performance on additional tests, behavioral observations, classroom performance, parent and teacher reports, and student self-perceptions.

Table 14, Task Analysis and Comparisons of Selected Tests from the WJ III, has five columns. *Test Names* simply lists the tests involved in the comparison. *Similarities* lists the task demands or required subskills that the tests share. *Differences,* divided into two columns, lists the task demands and required subskills that are not shared and, thus, are the basis for the comparison. *Possible Implications* lists the implications of the test comparisons. The italic print describes the possible relationship between/among the test scores. The test(s) listed on the left side of the > symbol has (have) the higher score(s); the test(s) to the right has (have) the lower score(s). The sentence below, in regular print, describes one or more possible reasons, related to the student's cognitive or academic abilities, for this pattern of performance. Each sentence begins with three dots as a reminder that the phrase "If [A > B], *consider . . .*" is implied.

Tips for Interpretation

If significant discrepancies exist between or among the individual test scores within a factor or cluster, report performance on the narrow abilities and, using task analysis and other test results, attempt to explain the reason for the difference between the scores. Also, consider how this information may alter your interpretation or use of the factor/cluster score.

Example case: Alyssa's Cognitive Fluency cluster score falls in the Low Average range, with Decision Speed in the Average range and Retrieval Fluency and Rapid Picture Naming in the Very Low range.

Using these and other test results, the evaluator determines that Alyssa has a specific problem in word retrieval, a weakness limited to language tasks and, for the most part, expressive language tasks. Although weak word retrieval certainly can inhibit cognitive fluency, the evaluator must

Table I.14. Task Analysis and Comparisons of Selected Tests from the WJ III Tests of Cognitive Abilities and Tests of Achievement

Test Names	Similarities	Differences		Possible Implications *If* [the following test pattern], *consider* . . .
Picture Vocabulary Verbal Comprehension	Retrieval of single words from long-term storage	Retrieval of simple name (PV)	Retrieval of words based on associations and reasoning (VC)	*Picture Vocabulary > Verbal Comprehension or both low* . . . limited breadth and depth of vocabulary knowledge . . . difficulties with word retrieval
		Less linguistic complexity (PV)	More linguistic complexity (VC)	*Picture Vocabulary > Verbal Comprehension* . . . limited flexibility of word comprehension and usage
Retrieval Fluency Rapid Picture Naming Picture Vocabulary	Retrieval of single words from long-term storage	Retrieval of a specific word (RPN, PV)	Broader choice of acceptable responses (RF)	*Retrieval Fluency > Rapid Picture Naming & Picture Vocabulary* . . . difficulty with specificity of word retrieval (finding a specific word)
		Time constraint (RF, RPN)	No time constraint (PV)	
		Words are well-established in long-term storage (RF, RPN)	Words are less familiar or not known (PV)	*Retrieval Fluency & Picture Vocabulary > Rapid Picture Naming* . . . difficulty with automaticity of word retrieval (finding a specific word fast)
		Retrieval of words from a picture prompt (RPN, PV)	Retrieval of words without a picture prompt (RF)	*Picture Vocabulary & Rapid Picture Naming > Retrieval Fluency* . . . difficulty with self-generation of multiple responses . . . lack of strategy use in generating multiple responses (e.g., thinking of animals by habitat: pets, farm, ocean)
Sound Blending Sound Awareness Incomplete Words	Phonemic awareness	Trainable skills (SB, SA)	Less trainable skill (IW)	*Sound Blending & Sound Awareness > Incomplete Words* . . . weakness in auditory closure (*Consider possibility of prior training in phonemic awareness with lesser innate ability*)
		Directly related to basic reading skills (SB, SA)	Less well-established relation to reading skills (IW)	*Low Sound Blending and Sound Awareness* . . . undeveloped phonemic awareness skills
		Requires advanced skills (deletion, substitution, transposition, reversal) (SA)	Requires more basic skills (blending) (SB)	*Sound Blending > Sound Awareness* . . . difficulties with more advanced phonemic awareness skills (depends on age of student) (*Informally check ability to segment words into sounds; analyze errors on SA for level of breakdown*)
Sound Blending Sound Awareness Auditory Attention	Require speech sound discrimination	Perception of individual speech sounds and sequence (intentional) (SB, SA)	Detection of speech sounds (automatic) (AA)	*Sound Blending, Sound Awareness > Auditory Attention or all low* . . . poor hearing acuity and/or speech discrimination
		Stimuli presented in quiet conditions (SB, SA)	Stimuli presented in adverse auditory condition (AA)	
Concept Formation Analysis-Synthesis	Problem solving with new procedures Logical reasoning Learning task with corrective feedback Increase in complexity	Analysis of multiple attributes of a problem to *infer the rule* governing its organization (inductive logic) (CF)	Use of *given rules* (i.e., a code) to solve a problem (deductive logic) (AS)	*Analysis-Synthesis > Concept Formation* . . . limited ability to hold in awareness and work with multiple attributes of a problem simultaneously . . . limited flexibility in problem solving . . . limited apperception of similarities and differences
		Ability to hold many pieces of information in mind at once (simultaneous processing) (CF)	Ability to move step by step through a mental process (sequential processing) (AS)	*Concept Formation > Analysis-Synthesis* . . . difficulty with application of rules or procedures
		Rule changes with each problem (CF)	Rules and method of solution (use of code) stay constant (AS)	

Table I.14. (*continued*)

Test Names	Similarities	Differences		Possible Implications *If* [the following test pattern], *consider* . . .
Concept Formation Applied Problems	Ability to hold and work with multiple elements of a problem Ability to apply inductive reasoning, including categorization of critical elements	Minimal need for knowledge of numeric concepts and procedures (CF)	Strong need for knowledge of numeric concepts and procedures (AP)	*Concept Formation & Applied Problems low* . . . weakness in basic reasoning and conceptual foundation for math, contributing to inability to see the logical relationships among the elements *Concept Formation > Applied Problems* . . . limited math knowledge, but good reasoning (*Check amount and type of prior instruction*)
Analysis-Synthesis Calculation	Application of rules and procedures Deductive reasoning	Minimal need for knowledge of numeric concepts and procedures (AS)	Strong need for knowledge of numeric concepts and procedures (C)	*Analysis-Synthesis & Calculation low* . . . weakness in procedural knowledge and difficulty with application of rules *Analysis-Synthesis > Calculation* . . . weakness in procedural knowledge and skills despite ability to follow a procedure and use deductive reasoning (*Check amount and type of prior instruction*)
Visual Matching Decision Speed Pair Cancellation	Rapid visual scanning Rapid visual processing Response mode	Picture stimuli (DS, PC)	Number/symbol stimuli (VM)	*Visual Matching, Decision Speed, & Pair Cancellation all low* . . . difficulty with visual scanning (*Consider ocular-motor functioning*) . . . slow processing speed *Decision Speed & Pair Cancellation > Visual Matching* . . . poor symbol discrimination . . . lack of familiarity with numbers
Visual Matching Numbers Reversed Auditory Working Memory Calculation Math Fluency	Inclusion of numbers in test content	Numbers held in memory (NR, AWM)	Numbers constant on page (VM, C, MF)	*Visual Matching, Calculation, Math Fluency > Numbers Reversed, Auditory Working Memory* . . . weakness in working memory . . . difficulty with mental visualization of numbers (*Analyze items on AWM to see if errors were solely, or mostly, on repetition of numbers, rather than things.*) *Visual Matching, Numbers Reversed, Auditory Working Memory > Calculation, Math Fluency* . . . limited knowledge and/or ability to apply math concepts and procedures
		Numbers used for non-mathematical purpose (NR, AWM, VM)	Requires math knowledge (C, MF)	
Memory for Words Numbers Reversed Auditory Working Memory	Short-term memory of unrelated stimuli (i.e., single words, numbers)	Number stimuli (NR, AWM)	Word stimuli (MW, AWM)	*All low* . . . weakness in short-term memory *Memory for Words > Numbers Reversed (& Auditory Working Memory—problem solely with number repetition)* . . . difficulty visualizing numbers *Memory for Words > Numbers Reversed > Auditory Working Memory* . . . difficulty in working memory corresponding to task complexity
		Higher demands on working memory (NR, AWM)	Lower demands on working memory (MW)	
Understanding Directions Story Recall Oral Comprehension	Comprehension of meaningful sentences	Critical elements share a meaningful linguistic context (SR, OC)	Critical elements are minimally related by meaning (UD)	*Oral Comprehension & Story Recall > Understanding Directions* . . . difficulty holding critical elements in memory outside of a cohesive meaningful context . . . difficulty comprehending and/or holding in memory complex syntax and multiple linguistic concepts (e.g., spatial, temporal, conditional) *Understanding Directions & Oral Comprehension > Story Recall* . . . weakness in organization of story elements in memory
		Comprehension and memory of syntax supported by meaning (SR, OC)	Comprehension and short-term memory of syntax not supported by meaning (UD)	
		Mode of response: verbal: single word (OC) verbal: phrases, sentences (SR)	Mode of response: pointing, nonverbal (UD)	

(*continued*)

Table I.14. (*continued*)

Test Names	Similarities	Differences		Possible Implications *If* [the following test pattern], *consider . . .*
Oral Comprehension Story Recall Passage Comprehension	Comprehension of connected discourse	Oral stimuli (listening) (OC, SR)	Written stimuli (reading) (PC)	*Oral Comprehension & Story Recall > Passage Comprehension* . . . difficulty with reading decoding *All low* . . . limited comprehension of oral language
Word Attack Letter-Word Identification Reading Fluency Passage Comprehension	Require skills in word attack and sight word acquisition	Reading decoding (WA, LWI, RF, PC)	Reading comprehension (RF, PC)	*Word Attack & Letter-Word Identification > Passage Comprehension* . . . poor reading comprehension (*RF might be strong or weak*) *Word Attack > Letter-Word Identification, Retrieval Fluency, Passage Comprehension* . . . poor sight word acquisition impairs fluency and comprehension. *Letter-Word Identification > Word Attack* . . . limited word attack skills creates dependence on whole word reading (*may limit future sight word acquisition*) *All low* . . . limited decoding (word attack and sight words) as a major factor in weak fluency and comprehension
Calculation Math Fluency Applied Problems	Require accurate retrieval of math facts Require understanding of basic math concepts	Knowledge of algorithms (C) Knowledge of simple facts (MF) Math reasoning (AP)		*Applied Problems > Calculation & Math Fluency* . . . weakness in procedural knowledge but good reasoning (*Look for inefficient and compensatory strategies*) *Math Fluency & Calculation > Applied Problems* . . . weakness in math reasoning *Calculation > Math Fluency, Applied Problems, Quantitative Concepts* . . . substitution of inefficient strategies for procedural knowledge and facts produces average or better score. (*Consider limited understanding of foundational concepts in math, procedural knowledge, and acquired math knowledge.*) *All low* . . . weakness in foundational concepts in math, procedural knowledge, and acquired math knowledge

determine the meaning of the broad score—if it continues to describe general cognitive fluency or if a distinction should be made between fluency in verbal versus nonverbal processes.

Analyze the task demands of the tests administered to the student relative to the quality of her performance. Look for any similarities between/among the task demands and subskills required by the tests on which the student per-

formed well, in addition to similarities between/among the tests on which she performed poorly. Similarly, compare the differences between the task demands and subskills required on the tests on which she did well with those of the tests on which she did poorly. Examine also the types of errors made on test items, whether a pattern of errors exists, and strategies the student used as substitutes for the correct ones. Based on these comparisons, attempt to determine the narrow abilities that appear strong throughout testing and those that appear weak. [For examples, see the section entitled Explanation of WJ III Scores, Interpretive Levels, and Discrepancies, Level 1: Qualitative: Task Analysis and Comparisons of Selected Tests.]

When making determinations about cognitive and/or academic strengths and weaknesses, check both the standardized scores and the Relative Performance Indexes. Both provide valuable, and different, information. For making recommendations about the instructional level of the materials, refer to the Instructional Zone band on the WJ III ACH. This band provides an estimate of an easy level to a difficult level. The grade equivalent is in the center of the Zone. Note any behavioral changes in response to tests with different formats, subject areas, or response requirements. For example, compare the student's attitude, persistence, and level of cooperation on timed versus untimed measures, oral versus written measures, cognitive versus academic tests, and in various skill areas (e.g., reading vs. math). A pattern of behavior change may provide clues as to task demands that are easy and those that are difficult.

Memory

Compare performance on associative memory tests that require both visual and auditory associations (e.g., Visual-Auditory Learning) to those that require only auditory memory (e.g., Memory for Words).

Compare performance on working memory tests (e.g., Numbers Reversed and Auditory Working Memory) to performance on tests that measure memory span (e.g., Memory for Words). If performance on memory span tests is higher, consider that the student may have more difficulty with divided attention than with rote sequential memory.

If performance is low on tests of meaningful memory (e.g., Story Recall, Understanding Directions), consider the possible effect of the student's level of acquired knowledge and language development on performance. Low performance may be more a reflection of lack of experience and exposure or limited language abilities than of poor memory.

Compare performance on tasks that involve retrieval of old learning (e.g., Picture Vocabulary, General Information) to those that involve storage and retrieval of new learning (e.g., Visual-Auditory Learning). High performance on old learning in contrast to low performance on new learning suggests difficulty with comprehending and/or storing new information.

Compare performance on measures of delayed recall to measures of immediate recall (e.g., Visual-Auditory Learning, Story Recall). Check scores to see if material is retained efficiently over time in comparison to scores of other students who performed similarly on the initial presentation. Also, compare the student's responses on initial and delayed recall regarding the number of elements retained and if the same or different elements were named.

Compare performance on short-term memory tests (e.g., Memory for Words, Numbers Reversed) to performance on tests that require meaningful memory (e.g., Story Recall, Understanding Directions). Check to see if memory improves when information is more contextual. The elements in Story Recall are presented with more context than those in Understanding Directions.

Cognitive/Academic Fluency/Processing Speed

If Reading Fluency, Math Fluency, and Writing Fluency are all low, compare the Academic Fluency cluster score to the Processing Speed and Cognitive Fluency cluster scores to determine whether the student has a generalized slow speed of processing or is only slow when tasks involve printed material.

Compare performance on tasks involving rapid visual scanning (e.g., Visual Matching, Pair Cancellation) to that on those tasks involving rapid word retrieval (e.g., Rapid Picture Naming). If all are low, consider that slow naming was secondary to slow scanning of the pictures. If visual scanning is fast and picture naming is slow, the problem is more likely in naming speed or word retrieval.

If all tests requiring rapid visual scanning of symbols and pictures are low (e.g., Visual Matching, Pair Cancellation, Reading Fluency), consider the possibility of visual or ocular-motor problems. Other behaviors that may indicate ocular-motor problems include losing the place, skipping lines, and using a finger or pencil to aid in tracking along a line.

Note on Visual Matching whether the student matches one or more transposed numbers (e.g., 16 and 61), or skips lines. These behaviors suggest inefficiency with scanning and may be related to problems with efficient processing of print.

Attention Deficit Hyperactivity Disorder (ADHD)/Behavior

Do not assume that strong performance on the tests of the Executive Processes cluster or Broad Attention cluster is a contraindication of ADHD. Although the student may have the cognitive abilities to discern rules, shift mindset, plan a task, ignore visual distracters and, in general, effectively manage the task demands of the tests in the clusters during the test session, she may not be able to apply them consistently in practical situations. ADHD does not assume that these abilities are deficient—only that the affected person is not able to regulate their use volitionally and consistently.

Note difficulties with attention span, impulsive responses, lack of persistence, high activity level, and other behaviors indicative of ADHD that might affect test performance. Low scores on tests in which the student displays these behaviors may be more indicative of lack of considered thought than of a weakness in the skills being assessed.

Note the tests during which a student's ADHD-like behaviors increase. These may be the tests requiring skills that are most difficult for the student.

Review observations from the Test Session Observations Checklist on the front page of the Test Record. Target behaviors of concern to explore in more depth.

Note whether any behaviors or attitude adversely affected the student's performance (e.g., low frustration tolerance, poor attention, lack of persistence, impulsive responses, resentment towards testing) and note the possible effect in test results (e.g., "The student's low frustration tolerance appeared to affect his effort in the test situation. If he did not know an answer immediately, he refused to try to think it through and would not respond to encouragement. Consequently, his current scores may be an underestimation of his true abilities").

Record any comments the student makes indicating affective responses to tasks (e.g., "I hate math"), comments regarding school in general or any aspect of school (e.g., "The teacher always picks on me"), and comments about himself as a learner (e.g., "I never remember that," "I'm always the last one finished").

Oral Language

Although the tests of the WJ III are not sufficient to diagnose a primary language disorder, judicious comparisons of test results can provide strong indications as to generalized and specific language problems that would necessitate a referral to a Speech-Language Pathologist.

Compare the student's performance on Verbal Comprehension to Reading Vocabulary. If Verbal Comprehension and Reading Vocabulary are both low, consider that the student's limited oral vocabulary also limits his reading vocabulary. If the student's score on the oral test is high and the reading test low, consider that weak decoding skills prevent the student from demonstrating his word knowledge. In either case, check Picture Vocabulary, Letter-Word Identification, and Word Attack for additional diagnostic information.

Compare the student's responses on Story Recall, Writing Samples, and Writing Fluency as informal measures of sentence formulation. Behaviors on Story Recall that might indicate difficulties in this area include responses that indicate knowledge of the content but are poorly organized and unclear. Indicative behaviors on Writing Samples include omissions of keywords and sentence structure that is particularly simple (on the higher items) or has sufficiently awkward syntax to obscure the meaning of the sentence.

Compare the student's performance on tests of oral vocabulary (e.g., Verbal Comprehension, Picture Vocabulary) to tests of oral comprehension of connected discourse (e.g., Oral Comprehension, Story Recall, Understanding Directions). If vocabulary is significantly better than discourse comprehension, consider a weakness in comprehension of syntax and/or linguistic concepts. Serious weaknesses in short-term memory might also contribute to difficulties with comprehension.

Consider that limited oral vocabulary and background knowledge can be caused by limited reading experiences, especially from middle school on. If the student has poor basic reading skills, she is not reading, or comprehending, sufficient text from which to learn new words and information at the same rate as her age- or grade-peers.

Consider that the student may have a primary language disorder if all oral language tests are low (Verbal Comprehension, Picture Vocabulary, Sound Blending, Retrieval Fluency, Story Recall, Oral Comprehension, Understanding Directions), but tests that involve minimal oral language (e.g., simple instructions along with pictures) are higher (e.g., Spatial Relations, Visual Matching, Numbers Reversed, Picture Recognition, Decision Speed). Poor short-term memory for linguistic information (e.g., Memory for Words) is also likely to be low. Acquisition of academic knowledge, reading comprehension, and written expression are based on primary language ability and so are also likely to be low.

Compare the student's performance on Picture Vocabulary, Retrieval Fluency, and Rapid Picture Naming—all relatively simple tasks that require the student to retrieve known words from long-term storage. If the student performs well on Picture Vocabulary but poorly on Rapid Picture Naming, consider a problem with word retrieval. Although both require retrieval of a specific word, only Rapid Picture Naming has a time constraint, increasing the need for automaticity of response. Although low Retrieval Fluency may reinforce the possibility of a word retrieval problem, average performance would not exclude it. Because Retrieval Fluency allows a broader range of acceptable responses, it may not be as sensitive as Rapid Picture Naming. Difficulty with both Rapid Picture Naming and Retrieval Fluency also could be related to speed of processing.

Phonological Awareness to Print

Keep in mind that the progression of phonological awareness is developmental. Generally, the progression is as follows:

- preschool: segmenting sentences into words;
- preschool to kindergarten: rhyming;
- kindergarten: segmenting words into syllables and deleting syllables;
- grade 1: blending, segmenting, deleting, and adding phonemes;
- grades 1–2: manipulation (e.g., substitution, transposition) of phonemes.

Many children are not able to perform the types of phoneme manipulation tasks measured in the WJ III Sound Awareness test until the end of second grade.

If Auditory Attention, Incomplete Words, Sound Blending, Sound Awareness, and Spelling of Sounds are all significantly weak, note whether or not the student had difficulty on the training items of Auditory Attention as well as during the noise condition. If so, and if she has not had a recent hearing test, request a screening for hearing acuity and speech discrimination to rule out a hearing loss. If these abilities are intact, consider a central auditory processing disorder. Look for other indications of misperceptions of speech or problems interpreting speech in compromised acoustic environments.

If a student has low performance on Sound Blending, determine if she can segment words into phonemes. Ask her to count the number of sounds that she hears in various words. Include words she can spell but in which the number of letters does not match the number of sounds (e.g., fox [4], cow [2]). If she also has difficulty on this type of task, recommend instruction in blending (synthesizing sounds) and segmenting (analyzing sounds).

If Incomplete Words is significantly lower than Sound Blending, consider the nature of the instructional program. Whereas reading instruction may help to develop the student's ability to blend sounds, it is less likely to develop the auditory closure ability measured by Incomplete Words.

Although Sound Awareness gives only a total score, analyze performance on the four subtests. Determine if the student's performance differs on rhyming tasks versus sound manipulation tasks to get a sense of the level at which the student's phonological abilities are breaking down.

Some individuals have trouble learning to rhyme but can learn to blend and segment sounds. If a student has difficulty with rhyming, as well as with the other tasks on Sound Awareness, check performance on the Sound Blending test to see if he may have developed some of the intermediate phonological awareness skills.

Phonological awareness abilities can be developed through carefully planned instruction. In interpreting assessment results, consider how the current or past method of instruction may have affected scores measuring this ability rather than assuming that the student developed these abilities through incidental learning.

Before deciding that a student has a weakness in orthographic processing (i.e., recall of spelling patterns), make sure that phonological awareness skills are developed. Phonological awareness provides the foundation on which orthographic coding skills can be built.

Students who speak English as a second language may misperceive some English phonemes and obtain low scores on measures of phonological awareness. These low scores may be more a reflection of their limited familiarity with English language phonemes, rather than poor phonological awareness.

The most critical phonemic awareness abilities for decoding and encoding are blending and segmentation. When writing recommendations, place greater emphasis on teaching these abilities than on teaching rhyming.

Compare performance on phonological awareness tests to performance on phoneme/grapheme knowledge tests (Word Attack, Spelling of Sounds). If phonological awareness is significantly higher than phoneme/grapheme knowledge, recommend instruction in letter/sound relationships (phonics). If performance is low on both, recommend activities to build phonological awareness, as well as procedures to build phoneme/grapheme knowledge.

If analysis of Sound Awareness indicates good rhyming ability but a weakness in manipulating phonemes within words, and Sound Blending is low, the student may benefit from a word family approach to reading instruction while learning the more complex phonological awareness skills that will enable her to make better use of phonics.

Before recommending phonological awareness training for older students with reading disabilities, make sure that their problems are not related to the orthographic features of words (recalling letter patterns) rather than to the phonological features. If the student sequences sounds correctly on the Spelling of Sounds and Spelling tests (even though the word may be misspelled), instruction in phonological awareness is probably unnecessary. The following performance patterns may indicate that instruction should instead be directed to mastery of common English spelling patterns:

- spellings on Spelling of Sounds, Spelling, and Writing Samples that are phonically accurate (correct sound/symbol correspondence) but violate spelling rules and include letter combinations that are unlikely in written English (*kw* instead of *qu*);
- attempts to sound out words phonetically that would normally be recognized as sight words (e.g., *was*);
- scores on Sound Blending and Sound Awareness are average or better but Letter-Word Identification, Word Attack, Reading Fluency and Spelling are weak. Word Attack may be higher if the student has acquired phoneme/grapheme correspondences.

Basic Reading and Writing Skills

Record errors on both the Letter-Word Identification and Word Attack tests for later error analysis. Attempt to discern patterns of performance, such as if the student is able to identify initial and final sounds, but struggles with medial vowel sounds.

If Letter-Word Identification is higher than Word Attack, the student may be depending on sight word recognition rather than phonics skills. Determine whether or not the student has a weakness in phonological processing that may be contributing to poor phonics skills.

Compare Reading Fluency to Letter-Word Identification and Word Attack. If all are low, consider that poor basic reading skills are preventing the development of fluency.

If the student demonstrates weaknesses on basic reading skills, check her performance on the tests of phonological awareness to determine if weak phonological awareness is contributing to weak basic reading skills. If the results are inconclusive, consider administering a standardized test of phonological awareness skills that also includes tests of rapid automatized naming.

Compare performance on Spelling and Spelling of Sounds. Check to see whether or not the student has mastered spellings of high frequency words.

Compare performance on Spelling of Sounds to Word Attack. Check to see that the student can use grapheme/phoneme correspondences for both spelling and pronouncing nonwords.

Review errors on the Editing and the Punctuation and Capitalization tests. Make a list of the rules that the student knows and does not know.

On Editing, make a note of whether or not the student is able to detect the error, even if he cannot correct it.

Reading Comprehension

Review the errors items on the Reading Fluency test. By analyzing other tests, determine whether errors indicate weak word reading skills or poor literal reading comprehension.

Consider performance on Letter-Word Identification and Word Attack to determine whether or not poor decoding skill is affecting reading comprehension. If decoding skill is adequate but reading comprehension scores are low, check to see if limited knowledge and weak oral language abilities are contributing factors.

Notice if the student attempts to maintain meaning on items on the Passage Comprehension test.

Analyze errors on Passage Comprehension to see if the student's answers are syntactically correct. If many error items are not syntactically correct, consider the possibility of a problem in comprehension of oral syntax.

Record any oral reading errors on the Reading Vocabulary test. Attempt to determine if a low score is more a reflection of weak word identification skills or limited vocabulary.

Consider performance on Academic Knowledge, General Information, and the oral vocabulary tests. Limited background knowledge or vocabulary may be the reason for poor reading comprehension.

Compare performance on Passage Comprehension to Oral Comprehension and Reading Vocabulary to Verbal Comprehension to see if a difference exists between comprehension of written versus oral text. In general, high correlations exist between these measures unless the student is having trouble with basic reading skills. In secondary and postsecondary students, reading comprehension may be higher than listening comprehension because in written text, language is visible and the memory demands decrease.

Compare results on the Reading Fluency and Passage Comprehension tests to tasks that involve processing of higher-level discourse.

Written Expression
Compare performance on Writing Samples to measures and observations of oral language abilities. Attempt to determine if the quality of written expression is similar to oral expression. Compare performance on Writing Samples and Writing Fluency to determine if a difference exists between writing speed and ideation.

Compare the syntactic complexity of the sentences produced on Writing Samples and Writing Fluency. Determine if the student is able to write both short, simple sentences, as well as longer, more complex, sentences with more content.

Analyze spelling on Writing Samples and compare to performance on Spelling and Spelling of Sounds. See if spelling performance deteriorates when the student has to focus on and integrate many aspects of writing.

Analyze the student's use of punctuation and capitalization on Writing Samples. Compare to Editing to see if the student knows the rules and can correct errors when she does not have to write but cannot formulate a sentence, retrieve spellings, execute the mechanical act of writing, and attend simultaneously to punctuation, capitalization, and usage.

Compare performance on Writing Fluency to performance on Reading Fluency and Math Fluency to determine if the student has a similar rate on all timed measures.

Handwriting
Use the Handwriting Elements Checklist to evaluate and record the specific factors affecting legibility: slant, spacing, size, horizontal alignment, letter formation, and line quality. List the elements that need improvement.

Compare the student's performance on Writing Fluency, a timed test, to performance on Writing Samples and Spelling. Writing Fluency is most indicative of a student's fastest handwriting, whereas Writing Samples and Spelling represent handwriting under typical writing conditions. If the student writes legibly on the Writing Samples and

Spelling tests, conclude that handwriting is adequate under typical conditions.

For older students (middle school and up), writing rate has more of an effect on writing skill than does poor quality of handwriting. If a student has a compromised writing rate, specific accommodations are often necessary.

Check to see whether or not a student struggling with handwriting has developed keyboarding skill. If not, recommend instruction in word processing.

If the student evidences significantly poor quality of manuscript (print) handwriting, observe her as she writes. Note if the strokes she uses to make her letters are made in the correct sequence and if the direction of the strokes is correct (generally left to right, top to bottom). Multiple errors of this type impede the development of writing fluency and automaticity.

Note the student's pencil grip as she writes. An awkward or particularly odd grip could indicate weakness in the fine muscles of the hand.

Note the student's posture as she writes. An extreme tilt of the head to one side or the other may indicate inefficient visual functioning such as the suppression of one eye. After the test, ask the student about her ability to see the paper and the reason for turning her head.

Note how the student uses her non-writing hand (e.g., steadies her paper, supports her chin).

Mathematics
General
If the student has particular difficulty with visual–motor coordination and spatial organization of numbers on the page, as she works through a computation problem, the increasing visual confusion may lead to errors. When testing is completed, distinguish between math difficulty and visual confusion resulting from poorly lined up and sloppy numbers. Ask the student to dictate the solution to a problem similar to one that she got wrong while you write for her.

If the student is slow on tests of Processing Speed (especially Visual Matching) and Math Fluency, and makes many errors on Calculation, and Applied Problems, consider that slow processing may have impeded the development of automaticity of math facts and procedures, thus leaving little cognitive attention available for more complex application of those skills.

If the student has difficulty with all math tests as well as Numbers Reversed and Visual Matching, analyze Auditory Working Memory to see if she had difficulty with only the numbers but not the "things." If so, consider that she may have specific difficulty visualizing and working with number symbols.

Math Fluency

Analyze the student's errors on Math Fluency. Many incorrect responses may indicate a weakness in understanding the operations, inattention to the operation signs, and/or poor fact knowledge; correct but few answers may indicate lack of automaticity.

Compare performance on Math Fluency to Calculation to see if low performance in basic skills is a result of delayed automaticity with math facts and/or limited procedural knowledge.

Compare results on Math Fluency to tests of Reading and Writing Fluency to determine whether or not performances on all timed academic tests are similar.

Calculation

Errors are often rule-governed. The student misunderstands the rule, misapplies the rule, or has made up a rule for herself. Analyze errors on Calculation and on Applied Problems to attempt to determine why she made errors on specific items. If needed, ask her to solve a similar problem and explain her procedure as she does so.

> Example case: The student attempts to solve 7×13 (in a vertical format) and comes up with an answer of 22. Verbalizing her procedure, she said, "7 times 3 is 21." She then points to the 1 in the 13 and says, "Add the one and that's 22." Her process indicates that she did not understand the problem as 7 groups of 13.
>
> Consider that the student may obtain an average or better score on Calculation without having the grade-expected skills. If the student has used a variety of inefficient processes (e.g., counting on fingers, repeated addition instead of multiplication) to compensate for lack of procedural (e.g., use of algorithms) or conceptual (e.g., place value) knowledge and math information (e.g., units of measurement equivalencies), report the difference between her score and her proficiency as well as her areas of difficulty.

Applied Problems

Attempt to determine reasons for a low score on Applied Problems (e.g., poor basic skills, difficulty sequencing multiple steps, word problem structure, language processing difficulties, or poor mathematical reasoning).

Analyze the student's errors on Applied Problems to see if she understands the logical structure of a problem but does not know how to use the appropriate procedure.

> Example case: The student is given the problem: "12 people each have 25 cents to spend. How much money do they have altogether?" She writes a column of twelve 25s with an addition sign and then tries to add them. She understands the logic of the problem and can reason out how to solve it but either does not know that multiplication is the more efficient operation to use or does not know the procedure.

If the student has difficulty with Applied Problems but Calculation appears adequate, check her performance on Concept Formation to see whether or not she has difficulty working with multiple elements of a problem simultaneously and abstracting the superordinate features.

Quantitative Concepts

Analyze the errors on Quantitative Concepts to see if the student does not understand math terminology and concepts or if she is not able to discern the relationships among numbers.

If the student is having difficulty with discerning number patterns, see if the level at which she breaks down gives you any information about her flexibility with number relationships.

> Example case: The student can respond correctly as long as the increment between numbers is static (e.g., 6–9–12 . . .) but has difficulty when the increment changes within a pattern (e.g., 6–9–13–18 . . .).

Specific Math Disorders

Consider that the student who has good language, fluid reasoning, and working memory, ascertains the logical structure of word problems, differentiates relevant from extraneous information, and selects the appropriate operations, but becomes confused while working through the computation, may have a procedural math disorder. A procedural disorder is characterized by ". . . relatively frequent use of developmentally immature procedures, frequent errors in the execution of procedures, potential developmental delay in the understanding of the concepts underlying procedural use, and difficulties sequencing the multiple steps in complex procedures" (Geary, 2000, p. 6).

If the student has limited ability to retrieve math facts, the math facts she does retrieve are frequently wrong, her error responses are associated with the numbers in the problem, and the solution times for correct retrieval are not systematic, consider the possibility of a mathematical disorder in semantic memory. This disorder appears to occur with phonologically-based reading disorders (Geary, 2000).

If the student has difficulty with spatial representation of numerical information (e.g., misalignment of numbers, number reversals), misinterpretation of numerical information related to position (e.g., place value errors), and, possibly, has difficulties in other areas of math that depend on spatial abilities (e.g., geometry), consider a visuospatial mathematical disorder (Geary, 2000).

SECTION II

Reports

INTRODUCTION

This section provides a variety of sample diagnostic reports that illustrate how the Woodcock-Johnson III may be used and explained in assessments. The purposes of these diagnostic reports are to help the reader (a) increase understanding of the use and interpretation of WJ III results, both alone and in combination with other assessment instruments; (b) tailor the written report to the purpose of the evaluation; and (c) use the assessment results to generate recommendations for appropriate supports, adjustments, and interventions. Although the WJ III can provide helpful information for vocational planning, the focus of this section is on students enrolled in a school setting from preschool to postsecondary.

In building a new skill or polishing a frequently used one, a model is often helpful. Rather than "starting from scratch," one may adopt what fits and adapt what does not. The diagnostic reports are based on real people evaluated by the authors, their colleagues, and graduate interns. For the sake of confidentiality, all names and identifying information have been changed. The diagnostic reports were chosen to illustrate a wide variety of reasons for referral, student ages and backgrounds, educational situations, and diagnoses. Although many different diagnoses are represented here, the types of cases are far from exhaustive.

Occasionally, it is appropriate to report a person's race or ethnicity in a diagnostic report, especially when cultural factors might affect the interpretation of the results. Many school districts indicate a student's race or ethnicity by an ethnic code placed with the identifying information. In the following reports, race or ethnic background has been noted only when this information might have some bearing on the interpretation of the test results.

Most of the diagnostic information for these reports was derived from WJ III assessments, student work samples, and interviews with parents and/or teachers. In instances in which the evaluator wanted more information, supplementary testing was conducted using other assessment instruments. Where contributing factors outside the expertise of the evaluator were suspected, such as a severe language impairment, Attention Deficit Hyperactivity Disorder, or clinical depression, a recommendation was made for further evaluation by an appropriate professional. In some cases, this evaluation was incorporated into the initial assessment process. Although this arrangement is often not possible in a school setting, it is preferable to have all pertinent information before writing the final report so that all findings may be integrated. Comprehensive diagnosis of conditions affecting a person's ability to function efficiently in the appropriate setting, such as the school or workplace, makes it possible to write more useful recommendations for enhancing performance. A list of examinees, with their ages, their diagnoses, and tests used, is presented, to facilitate locating types of cases in which the reader may have specific interest.

Types of Evaluations

Evaluations may be requested for a variety of reasons, leading to different types of assessments and recommendations. Likewise, the setting in which the evaluation takes place, such as a school, hospital, private clinic, postsecondary setting, or vocational training center, may dictate the scope and type of testing done. For a child or adult without a previous diagnosis, a full battery of tests may be administered with language, occupational therapy, medical, and psychological evaluations as indicated. Where continued eligibility for special education services is the primary issue, administration of selected cognitive and academic clusters of the WJ III, supplemented by informal testing and work samples, may be sufficient. Where evaluation or documentation of progress in academic skills is needed, the evaluator might decide to administer only the WJ III Tests of Achievement: Standard Battery.

Depth of Information

The purpose and setting of an evaluation might also influence the levels of information sought through testing and interpretation, as well as the amount of detail included in the report. A lengthy report with detailed information does not necessarily signal the complexity of the case, although a person with many difficulties and/or an atypical background may certainly warrant more extensive evaluation and a more complex report. In a private setting, more time may be allotted to each case and more in-depth information presented in the report. In a school setting, practicality may dictate less time for testing, error analysis, and writing reports. An advantage of the school setting, however, is the ongoing opportunity for diagnostic teaching and observation.

The setting in which a person is evaluated, as well as the purpose for evaluation, might also influence the level of diagnosis or the manner in which it is worded. In a clinical or private setting, the principal evaluator may diagnose a specific learning disability or some other disability. In the school setting, the evaluator would be more likely to report that the child met certain criteria for a disability and make a referral to the multidisciplinary team for the final decisions.

Types of Scores

Depending upon the purpose of the evaluation and specific information offered within the report, the evaluator might report different types of scores. For example, information concerning the most appropriate level of instructional materials to be used for a variety of tasks would be reported by Instructional Zones, representing the range of easy to difficult tasks and materials for each skill area. The grade equivalent (GE) score expresses an approximate instructional level. In using the Instructional Zone as a guideline, use caution in equating the grade equivalent score with the level of instructional materials. Although the grade equivalent score shows a person's developmental standing within the normative sample, it may not directly match the level of

performance among peers in a specific educational environment. Considering the variability of schools and individual classes across the nation, a third-grade child could receive a grade equivalent score 1 year below his or her actual grade level, but be at the same level of instruction as the average third-grader in the specific school. Moreover, different materials intended for a certain grade level may vary considerably from each other in the initial level of student skill and knowledge assumed. The Relative Proficiency Index (RPI) is useful for describing how successful a person will be on similar tasks.

If the evaluation is mainly for purposes of diagnosing a disability and determining eligibility for special education services, common practice is to use standard scores or percentile ranks, as these scores express a person's relative standing in a group of age- or grade-peers. Some of the diagnostic reports in this section include both standard scores and percentile ranks. Although both types of scores provide the same information, percentile ranks are easier for many people to interpret, whereas standard scores are necessary for inter–test comparisons and eligibility decisions. CALP scores represent Cognitive-Academic Language Proficiency. They are particularly useful with subjects who are English language learners (ELL) to indicate the proficiency with which they can understand the language used in an educational setting. Some of the cases presented here include ELL subjects and CALP scores. Some schools or institutions may require Stanine scores, Normal Curve Equivalents, or *T* scores, all of which are available from the WJ III.

Some of the sample reports have scores embedded in the narrative. Other reports in this section include a notation stating, "All test scores are attached to the end of this report." Scores from the WJ III Compuscore and Profiles Program (Schrank & Woodcock, 2001) are included for several reports. Students and evaluators who are new to the WJ III may want to study the obtained scores and draw conclusions before reading the report.

Recommendations

Reports might also differ in scope and specificity of recommendations. In some reports, whether private or school-based, recommendations may be written to cover all areas: cognitive, academic, and behavioral. Other reports might include recommendations only for areas seen as critical for immediate intervention. Reports may refer to general interventions, others include suggestions for specific techniques and materials, or defer to recommendations made by the educational team when the evaluation results are discussed.

Discrepancy Interpretation

The reader may note that some of the children in the reports who were diagnosed as having learning disabilities do not show a significant ability/achievement discrepancy. The lack of an ability/achievement discrepancy does not necessarily indicate the absence of a learning disability. This discrepancy may not be found, as the person's performance on tests of cognitive abilities particularly related to the academic areas in question may be low. It is precisely this poor performance on some cognitive abilities, relative to others, that suggests the presence of a learning disability. In this case, it would be more appropriate to look for an intra-individual discrepancy.

Sources and Uses of Information

The information in these diagnostic reports was based on many types of data gathered from a variety of sources. Information regarding the home environment; physical, emotional, social, and cognitive development; sensory faculties; functioning in the educational setting; previous educational opportunities; results of previous evaluations; and the person's description of the problem provide a basis for interpreting and judging the validity of the new test data. Additionally, full use of information from formal and informal tests includes consideration of scores, behavior during testing, and analysis of error patterns. In some cases, as with some school reports, this information is collected by different people and integrated at the multidisciplinary conference.

Ultimately, the quality and validity of evaluation results for any specific individual depend on the skill of the evaluator in (a) selecting and administering the tests; (b) evaluating the validity of individual test scores in light of possible interfering factors (e.g., fatigue, inattention, reluctance to test, cultural differences, sensory impairments); (c) interpreting and integrating test results; (d) analyzing error patterns; (e) discerning the person's strategies and compensations; and (f) deriving appropriate recommendations.

Outline

An outline is often helpful in structuring reports, although the nature of each assessment will ultimately determine the information to be included. The following outline may be used as a starting point.

1. Identifying Information—Provide the following in the heading of the report:
   a) student's name and date of birth
   b) student's age and grade
   c) testing and report (optional) date(s)
   d) evaluator's name
   e) school, parents' names, teachers' name (optional)
   f) ethnicity (optional)
2. Reason for Referral
   a) identify the person who referred the student
   b) discuss the reason for the referral
   c) explain the specific concerns of the referral source and the purpose of the evaluation
3. Background Information
   a) include relevant family history (include familial history of learning/behavioral problems)
   b) describe current family and living situation
   c) discuss any pertinent health/developmental history
   d) review any relevant educational history (e.g., special services, retentions)
   e) describe current behaviors and behavioral history in school and at home (if the reason for referral includes behavioral concerns)
4. Classroom Observations (for elementary and secondary school, may be required by local educational agency)
   a) state number of students, teachers, and instructional aides in classroom
   b) describe class activity and general class demeanor
   c) describe the task on which the student was working
   d) discuss student's attention and effort, task success, general behavior
5. Previous Evaluations and Results
   a) report findings of past medical, psychological, and educational evaluations
   b) note results from recent vision and hearing screenings
6. Tests Administered
   a) list the names of tests administered
   b) describe any informal assessments
   c) list people interviewed (e.g., teachers, parents)
7. Assessment Procedures Used
   a) state adherence or exceptions to legal criteria and best testing practices
   b) describe cautions or limitations regarding findings
   c) state types of norms used (e.g., age, grade)

d) explain scores reported (e.g., standard scores, Relative Proficiency Index, grade equivalents) (optional)

8. Behavioral Observations (see Test Observations Checklist on front of the Test Record)
   a) discuss reactions to assessment
   b) report general response style (impulsive to reflective)
   c) describe activity level
   d) discuss general attitude
   e) note verbal communication skills
   f) note response to success, failure, and feedback

9. Intellectual/Cognitive Abilities and/or Achievement
   a) report scores in text, list within the body of this section, or attach at end
   b) interpret and integrate data
   c) consider findings from a variety of sources (e.g., classroom work samples, diagnostic teaching)
   d) separate paragraphs for each cognitive and academic area, such as reading, mathematics
   e) analyze responses and errors and provide specific examples to document clinical interpretation

10. Summary and Conclusions
    a) briefly summarize test results
    b) state implication of results (conclusions)
    c) do not include new information
    d) include statement of diagnosis or refer to multidisciplinary team for consideration of next step

11. Recommendations
    a) note any further testing or observations needed
    b) develop a list of appropriate accommodations
    c) provide and explain realistic and practical interventions based on the student's strengths and weaknesses
    d) involve student, parents, and teachers

Guidelines for Writing Educational Assessment Reports

Name: _____ School: _____
Date of Birth: _____ Date of Testing: _____
Age: ___ Examiner: _____
Grade: ___

Reason for Referral
- State the reason for referral and, where appropriate, the name and role of the referring person.
- Remember that the reason for referral is your reason for testing. Your assessment results should help clarify the concerns on which the referral is based.
- Be concise. This section can usually be written in one short paragraph.

Background Information
- Summarize information from school records, medical records, interviews, and reports.
- Include information from a variety of sources, including interviews, previous educational history, the results from prior evaluations and reports, and relevant interventions.
- Include relevant information about medical and developmental history and behavioral and social development. If possible, before testing, make sure that the student has had a recent vision and hearing screening. This gives the evaluator the opportunity to provide accommodations or modifications, if necessary, and prevents invalid results due to unrecognized sensory conditions that may influence the student's performance.
- Discuss relevant information about the school setting, the family, and the student's current living arrangements.

Assessment Procedures Used
- Include all formal and informal assessments administered. State the full name of the assessment device used including the form or edition, followed by the initials or shortened name in parentheses. The test can then be referred to by its initials throughout the remainder of the report. If you administer only selected subtests, state subtest names followed by the full test name. The WJ III is a battery of tests, rather than subtests. For the sake of brevity, the tests may be designated, in this section, by their numbers (e.g., Woodcock-Johnson III Tests of Cognitive Abilities: Tests 1–14).
- State the purpose for administering the test used. For example: "Selected tests from the Woodcock-Johnson III (WJ III) were administered to Jane to assess her skills in reading."
- State adherence to or exceptions to best assessment practices (e.g., ethnicity and race considered in test selection; educational disadvantage or other exclusionary factors were not primary factors in test results; tests were administered in the student's primary language).
- State adherence to or exceptions to standardized administration (e.g., accommodations, modifications).
- Describe any cautions or limitations regarding findings (e.g., normative sample was not based primarily on students with similar characteristics, such as sensory impairment; student's performance may have been negatively affected by impulsivity and attentional difficulties).
- State the type of norms used (e.g., age, grade).
- Explain how the scores reported are interpreted (e.g.,

Relative Proficiency Index indicates the student's proficiency in similar tasks when grade- or age-peers would achieve 90% success).

Behaviors During Testing
- Confine comments here to general observations concerning the student's reaction to the testing situation as well as his or her involvement and motivation throughout the test.
- Cite specific examples if possible, such as "he rocked back and forth in his chair frequently during the assessment procedure," or "she looked out the window and avoided eye contact with the examiner."
- Do not label the behavior (e.g., "John was hyperactive during testing").
- Save comments relevant to specific tests or tasks for the "Results" section.

Summary of Scores
- This is your quantitative data. List all relevant scores.
- Report the scores in ranges when possible and state the level of confidence (e.g., 68% confidence interval).
- Present the information in an organized manner; a table format is recommended.
- You may attach scores at the end of your report.

Results and Interpretation
In this section, discuss test results, as well as qualitative information. For each area of performance to be discussed:

- Make a general statement about the student's performance followed by more specific comments.
- Include results from error analysis, particularly if they are related to the reason for referral or suggest remediation procedures.
- Organize the discussion as follows: total test scores; composites, cluster, or factors; tests and subtests; and qualitative information (comments, information from error analysis).
- When test scores within a cluster differ significantly, discuss the reason for the difference.

Recommendations
Make recommendations specific to the referral question and/or to the findings, if different from the referral question.

Further Testing
- Recommend further testing to yield more specific information, if necessary.
- Recommend further testing for problems that have become evident as a result of the evaluation but were not included in the referral concern (e.g., a student referred for reading problems performs poorly on oral language tests).

Instruction
- List suggestions for teaching approaches and materials.
- Base your suggestions on information gathered in this assessment procedure as well as knowledge from additional sources.

General Suggestions
- Use the third person (i.e., "the examiner" or "the evaluator").
- Use formal language but avoid jargon. Attempt to use terminology that will be familiar to the reader.
- Capitalize names of tests, subtests, and clusters.
- In most instances, if working with a multidisciplinary team within a school system, do not state whether a student does or does not have a specific educational classification (e.g., learning disabilities, mental retardation) unless this has been determined previously by a multidisciplinary team. Instead, make a recommendation that the team will consider eligibility for special services.

TEST NAMES AND ABBREVIATIONS

Woodcock-Johnson III Tests of Cognitive Abilities   WJ III® COG
Woodcock-Johnson III Tests of Achievement   WJ III® ACH

Supplemental Tests

Achenbach Child Behavior Checklist   CBCL
Analytic Reading Inventory, Sixth Edition   ARI
Beck Anxiety Inventory   BAI®
Beck Depression Inventory—II   BDI®-II
Beery-Buktenica Developmental Test of Visual-Motor Integration (4th ed.)   VMI
Behavior Assessment System for Children: Adolescent Form   BASC
Boehm Tests of Basic Concepts—3   Boehm-3
Brigance Diagnostic Inventory of Basic Skills   BRIGANCE®
Children's Auditory Verbal Learning Test—2   CAVLT-2
Children's Memory Scale   CMS
Clinical Evaluation of Language Fundamentals—3   CELF®-3
Colorado Perceptual Speed Trial III   CPST III
Comprehensive Test of Phonological Processing   CTOPP
Conners' Teacher Rating Scale—Revised   CTRS—R
Conners' Parent Rating Scale—Revised   CPRS—R
Controlled Oral Word Association Test   COWAT
Expressive Vocabulary Test   EVT
Goldman-Fristoe Test of Articulation   GFTA
Illinois Test of Psycholinguistic Abilities—3   ITPA-3
Key Math Diagnostic Arithmetic Tests—Revised   Key Math-R
The Listening Test
Nelson-Denny Reading Test   Nelson-Denny
Oral and Written Language Scales   OWLS
Peabody Picture Vocabulary Test—III   PPVT-III, PPVT-IIIA
Phonological Awareness Test   PAT
Qualitative Reading Inventory—III   QRI-III
Rey Complex Figure Test and Recognition Trial   RCFT
Speech Sounds Perception Test   SSPT
Stanford-Binet Intelligence Scale, Fourth Edition   SB-4
Test of Language Competence—Expanded Edition, Level 1   TLC-Expanded
Test of Mathematical Abilities—2   TOMA-2
Test of Word Finding—2   TWF-2
Test of Written Language, Third Edition   TOWL-3
Vineland Adaptive Behavior Scales: Interview Edition   Vineland
Wechsler Adult Intelligence Scale—Third Edition   WAIS®-III
Wechsler Intelligence Scale For Children—III   WISC®-III
Wechsler Memory Scale—Third Edition   WMS®-III
Wide Range Achievement Test—3   WRAT3
Woodcock-Muñoz Language Survey: English Form   WMLS-English
Woodcock-Muñoz Language Survey: Spanish Form   WMLS-Spanish
The Word–R Test   Word-R

DIAGNOSTIC REPORTS

Name	Age	Diagnosis/Concerns	Tests Used	
Jack Langdon	4-5	Disorders of oral language and speech articulation delay development of reading readiness skills.	WJ III COG WJ III ACH	VMI
Rebecca Williams	4-7	Developmental delays impede acquisition of preschool skills	WJ III COG WJ III ACH	PPVT-IIIA
Bart Huxley	5-6	Phonological dyslexia, dysgraphia and attentional problems impede reading and writing development.	WJ III COG CBCL	VMI CTOPP
Christina Begay	6-9	Low cognitive abilities complicated by limited access to language (hearing impairment), poor attention, and limited school attendance interfere with development of language and academic skills.	WJ III COG WJ III ACH	
Juliette Reid	7-3	Oral language disorder and ADHD contribute to disabilities in reading, math and written expression.	WJ III COG WJ III ACH BOEHM-3 CAVLT-2 PPVT-III	RCFT WISC-III VMI CELF-3
Nathan Thalgott	7-5	Possible nonverbal learning disabilities	WJ III COG WJ III ACH	
Victor Rodriguez	7-7	Weakness in working memory and long-term retrieval. To be combined with academic and speech-language findings re: concern about reading and writing difficulties.	WJ III COG VMI	
Gregory Blackhawk	7-10	Visual impairment, problems in auditory short-term memory, visual memory for symbols, and attention contribute to severe delay in basic reading, writing, and math skills.	WJ III COG WJ III ACH PAT CPRS-R CTRS-R	Diagnostic teaching and informal assessment
Casey Hanson	8-1	Medical condition and medication side effects affect response speed and limit academic progress.	WJ III COG	
Josephine Baxter	9-6	Difficulties with word retrieval, emotional lability and organization.	WJ III COG CBCL CTOPP PPVT-III WRAT3	EVT Word-R TWF-2 TLC-Expanded
Jonas Pierce	9-7	Dysgraphia severely impedes production of written symbols.	WJ III COG WJ III ACH	WISC-III
Renee Sandoval	9-7	Oral language disorder in English language learner contributes to difficulties in academic achievement.	WJ III COG WJ III ACH PPVT-III ARI	Woodcock-Muñoz Language Survey: English & Spanish
Charlie Wilbrahan	10-2	Oral language disorder and problems with abstract reasoning limit development of academic and interpersonal skills.	WJ III COG WJ III ACH	
Rose Schmidt	10-3	Weaknesses in processing speed, rapid automatized naming, memory for numbers, and inductive reasoning impede development of basic reading, writing, and math skills.	WJ III COG WJ III ACH ITPA-3	CTOPP QRI-3 Writing sample
Maria Whitehurst	11-0	WJ III Report Writer Sample Difficulties in math and writing skills	WJ III COG WJ III ACH	
Joy Wiley-Evans	11-5	Procedural math disability	WJ III COG WJ III ACH	VMI
Michael Jansen	11-8	Mild hearing impairment, mild developmental delay, emotional disorder, specific deficits in word retrieval and phonological coding of words, and attentional problems contribute to severe delays in all academic areas, language acquisition, and interpersonal skills.	WJ III COG WJ III ACH Vineland Listening Test	VMI CTOPP Word–R QRI-3
Frankie Espinosa	10-10	Oral language disorder interferes with acquisition of all academic skills.	WJ III COG WJ III ACH	ITPA-3
Tony Haliday	12-7	Fluctuating hearing, variable memory for auditory information, and difficulties with processing speed, transfer of new learning to long-term storage, and deductive reasoning interfere with development of reading fluency, reading comprehension, written language, and math skills.	WJ III COG WJ III ACH Key Math-R TOWL-3	ITPA-3 VMI ARI

(continued)

DIAGNOSTIC REPORTS (*continued*)

Name	Age	Diagnosis/Concerns	Tests Used	
Boyd Moore	13-5	Weaknesses in associative memory and inductive reasoning with average oral language and academic achievement	WJ III COG WJ III ACH	CMS OWLS
Jen Charbonneau	13-11	Gifted	WJ III COG	
Josh Cloud	13-11	Question regarding retention for low academic performance Recommendation: further testing, not retention	WJ III ACH	
Paul Matthews	14-4	Attention Deficit Hyperactivity Disorder	WJ III COG WJ III ACH	SB-4
Steven Parker	15-8	Weaknesses in processing speed, inductive reasoning, memory, vocabulary, phonemic awareness, orthography, and possibly auditory processing contribute to severe deficiencies in academic achievement and knowledge; complicated by intermittent school attendance and cultural influences.	WJ III COG WJ III ACH	Nelson-Denny
Helen Chapman	15-9	Difficulties in spatial/sequential thinking and perceptual speed impede acquisition of math skills.	WJ III COG WJ III ACH	TOMA-2
Anjeline Gregg	16-2	Orthographic dyslexia	WJ III COG WJ III ACH	Science text book
Donald Ramona	17-8	Weak short-term memory and attention indicate learning disabilities in basic reading and math skills.	WJ III ACH	
Ophelia Jones	20	Orthographic dyslexia	WJ III COG WAIS-III WMS-III SSPT COWAT	CPST OWLS BAI BDI-II
Gavin Carver	25	Phonological dyslexia	WJ III COG WJ III ACH	WAIS-III
Stacy Alexander	29	Oral language disorder negatively affects reading comprehension, written expression, and math problem solving	WJ III COG WJ III ACH	
Marcus Gibbons	49	Relative weakness in memory, identifying essential elements in new information, and ADHD contribute to difficulties in written expression. Comparison of age and grade scores.	WJ III COG WJ III ACH	

Diagnostic Evaluation Report

Name:	Jack Langdon	Parents:	Edward Langdon and Mary Ann Martin
Date of Birth:	January 14, 1997	School:	Waterton Preschool
Date of Evaluation:	June 12, 2001	Referred by:	Elizabeth Gregg, Early Education Teacher
Age at Evaluation:	4 years, 5 months		

REASONS FOR REFERRAL

Jack's preschool teacher, Elizabeth Gregg, referred him for an evaluation of his language and pre-literacy skills. Jack has previously been diagnosed with a moderate to severe expressive language disorder, and information is being sought regarding his ability to develop reading and writing skills. Specific recommendations are being requested that will help Jack acquire a foundation for literacy learning.

BACKGROUND INFORMATION

Jack is the product of a full-term pregnancy and uncomplicated birth. His birth weight was 7 pounds, 10 ounces. Developmental milestones other than language were acquired within normal limits. Ms. Martin, Jack's mother, reported that Jack produced no speech sounds at the age of 2. Melissa Price, SLP-CCC, who has worked with Jack since he was 2, reported that he did not acquire speech sounds in the normal developmental pattern.

Jack's medical history is unremarkable. He did not experience an atypical amount of ear infections, but did have chronic fluid in both ears. Jack's father reported that he had chronic ear infections as a child that affected his acquisition of reading and spelling skills. Jack's brother was recently diagnosed with developmental dyslexia.

Jack's mother described him as active but with good ability to focus. He fights frequently with his older brother, but gets along well with his peers. Ms. Martin stated that Jack shares well and loves visiting friends. Jack's interests include nature (he loves to catch and observe frogs and snakes), art (drawing, cutting, and gluing), building with Legos, and pretend play.

Jack spent 1½ years at the South Mountain Children's Developmental Center for day care and attended Gateway Preschool for 1 year, 2 days a week for 2 hours each day. According to Ms. Price, Jack's language and articulation are improving, and he is now able to name basic colors and count to 5. She judged his speech to be approximately 80% intelligible to someone familiar with the context.

Jack's preschool teacher, Elizabeth Gregg, described him as an imaginative and playful boy who loves nature and enjoys telling stories about the spiders and other creatures he has caught, building with Legos, playing with cars, and drawing. Ms. Gregg reported that Jack learned to write his name easily. She described Jack's language as immature and noted that he tends to repeat whole words when trying to express himself, especially when he has a lot to say. She expressed concerns about Jack's ability to memorize new information but noted that with much repetition, he has learned simple songs and poems. Ms. Gregg is concerned that Jack's linguistic and memory difficulties will affect his reading and writing development.

ASSESSMENT SUMMARY

Jack's cognitive, fine motor, and language abilities were assessed using selected tests from the Woodcock-Johnson III Tests of Cognitive Abilities (WJ III COG) and Tests of Achievement (WJ III ACH), the Beery-Buktenica Developmental Test of Visual-Motor Integration—4th Edition (VMI), and interviews with the teacher and mother. Scores from the WJ III are attached.

Assessment Results

The results of this evaluation indicate that Jack has strong nonverbal abilities. He demonstrated excellent logical problem solving using geometric shapes and fine-motor skills for drawing, within the highest 1% and 5% of his age group, respectively. On tests related to visual abilities, such as thinking with patterns and designs and speed of visual processing, Jack's performance was solidly average for his age level. Similarly, he obtained a score in the Average range in understanding oral directions. These results suggest that Jack has at least age-appropriate abilities on tasks that have minimal expressive language demands.

Consistent with his previous diagnosis, Jack's expressive language difficulties are apparent in poor development of phonological processing (i.e., recognition that spoken language can be broken down into smaller units, such as words), syntax, grammar, and efficient retrieval of words, which are likely caused by a combination of problems with phonology and semantics. Jack did not understand the concepts of synonym or antonym, nor did he grasp the idea from trial items, placing his performance within the lowest 5% of his age-peers in expressive vocabulary and word associations. Jack also evidenced weaknesses in rapidly retrieving the names for familiar pictured objects (e.g., "car," "dog") and names of things to fit in given categories (e.g., "things people wear"). In contrast, his ability to listen to, hold in memory, and carry out oral directions is better than approximately 59% of his peers, solidly average.

Additionally, Jack has difficulty with phonological skills. He was unable to discriminate rhyming words from non-rhyming words (the easiest level of rhyming), nor was he able to complete or produce rhymes. These skills are typically acquired during the preschool years. In initial reading tasks, Jack was able to name two letters, but did not know any sounds of letters. Ms. Gregg commented that he can recognize only those letters in his first name.

Given Jack's family history and obvious delays in phonological processing, production of speech sounds, and expressive vocabulary, he is at significant risk for developing reading and spelling difficulties.

RECOMMENDATIONS

Speech and Language Services

1. Jack would benefit from attendance at a full-time preschool that runs 9 months per year, with summer services available.
2. This summer, Jack would benefit from speech services twice a week for 45–60 minutes, and in the fall, three times a week. Emphasis should continue on speech production, increased length of utterance, pre-literacy phonological skills (e.g., rhyming and syllable segmentation), and categorizing words into semantic classes for improving retrieval. Ms. Price should spend 45–60 minutes each week consulting with Jack's preschool teacher so that phonological awareness and pre-literacy skills Jack learns in therapy can be incorporated into classroom activities.

Language and Literacy Instruction

1. Provide phonological awareness activities as an integral part of Jack's preschool experience, using a developmental sequence of skills such as rhyme recognition (e.g., "Does *Sam* rhyme with *Pam*?"), rhyme completion (e.g., "One, two, buckle my . . ."), rhyme production (e.g., "Tell me a word that rhymes with *cat*"), and syllable segmentation (e.g., "*oc-to-pus*"). Recommended resources for Jack's teacher include *Phonemic Awareness in Young Children: A Classroom Curriculum,* by M. Adams, B. Foorman, I. Lundberg, and T. Beeler, Brookes Publishing Co., 1998; and *Ladders to Literacy: A Kindergarten Activity Book,* by R. O'Connor, A. Notari-Syverson, and P. Vadasy, Brookes Publishing Co., 1998.
2. Help Jack learn additional letter names. The book *Alphabet Art: A to Z Animal Art,* by Judy Press, published by Williamson Publishing Co., Charlotte, VT, is an excellent resource for children ages 2–6. Simple art activities are provided for each letter, such as "Octavio, the Octopus." Facts are provided about the octopus, as well, and can entice a child who may be more motivated by the informational aspect.
3. Repetition and multisensory experiences (visual, auditory, tactile, and kinesthetic) will be necessary for Jack to learn and retain verbal concepts and labels. For example, when teaching letters, have Jack trace large letters in a variety of substances, such as sand, mud, or shaving cream, and elicit the letter name, keyword, and sound (e.g., "S"—*snake*—/s/).
4. Because of Jack's interest in nature, use books about bugs and animals to stimulate interest and language development.
5. Help Jack categorize and classify information to help improve knowledge and vocabulary.

Mathematics

1. Using a model, help Jack make numbers out of clay to help him become familiar with their shapes. Subsequently, use them in activities.
2. Once he has gained some familiarity with the shapes, help Jack make sandpaper numbers for tracing. Teach number recognition and counting by tracing numbers.
3. Use songs, games, and hands-on activities to teach the days of the week, names of shapes, and other pre-math skills.

In the Home

1. Continue reading to Jack. Encourage him to listen to books on tape, and read favorite picture books to him so that he can memorize them and "read along."
2. Play rhyming games and games that require counting, matching, and memory (e.g., Grandmother's Trunk, Concentration).
3. Provide Jack with opportunities to reinforce skills using computer software. To reinforce alphabet and number knowledge, consider *Bailey's Book House* and *Minnie's Math House,* both published by Edmark (800-320-8377).

Compuscore Version 1.1b: Score Report: WJ III

Norms based on age 4–5   Date of Testing: 06/12/2001

CLUSTER	AE	EASY	to DIFF	RPI	PR	SS (68% BAND)
VERBAL ABILITY (Ext)	3-4	2-10	4-0	60/90	11	81 (77–86)
THINKING ABILITY	4-10	4-0	5-11	94/90	69	107 (103–112)
COMP-KNOWLEDGE (*Gc*)	3-4	2-10	4-0	60/90	11	81 (77–86)
L-T RETRIEVAL (*Glr*)	3-5	<3-0	4-6	77/90	18	86 (79–93)
VIS-SPATIAL THINK (*Gv*)	4-4	3-7	5-6	89/90	49	99 (96–103)
BASIC READING SKILLS	3-2	<3-0	4-0	62/90	20	87 (79–96)
Verbal Comprehension	3-4	2-9	3-11	59/90	5	76 (68–84)
Visual-Auditory Learning	3-10	3-2	4-8	81/90	34	94 (86–101)
Spatial Relations	4-9	3-11	5-11	93/90	60	104 (98–110)
Sound Blending	3-5	3-0	4-0	62/90	23	89 (84–93)
Concept Formation	7-7	6-8	8-10	100/90	99	133 (129–138)
Visual Matching	4-6	4-2	4-10	92/90	53	101 (99–103)
General Information	3-5	2-11	4-0	60/90	17	86 (80–91)
Retrieval Fluency 7	2-7	<2-0	4-2	72/90	9	79 (73–85)
Picture Recognition	3-11	3-1	5-1	84/90	40	96 (92–100)
Rapid Picture Naming	2-4	2-1	2-8	2/90	2	68 (66–70)
Form A of the following achievement tests was administered:						
Letter-Word Identification	3-0	2-5	3-7	32/90	11	81 (73–90)
Understanding Directions	4-8	3-11	5-5	93/90	59	103 (99–108)
Spelling	3-7	3-3	3-10	30/90	17	86 (80–91)
Word Attack	<3-8	<3-0	<5-0			
Sound Awareness	<4-3	<4-0	<4-8			

Adapted from Melissa M. King, M.Ed.

Early Development Evaluation

Name: Rebecca Williams
Birthdate: 2/10/97
Chronological Age: 4–7
Grade: Preschool

Parent: Margaret Williams
Agency: Dept. of Economic Security
Test dates: 9/6/01, 9/10/01

REASON FOR REFERRAL

Rebecca was referred for an evaluation by her social worker at the Department of Economic Security (DES), Amelia Forrester. Ms. Forrester reported that Rebecca's preschool teacher felt she was immature and slow in developing pre-academic skills. Ms. Forrester requested a brief assessment to help determine pre-academic educational goals for Rebecca.

BACKGROUND INFORMATION

Rebecca is a Caucasian child, the sixth of eight siblings. Her mother, Margaret Williams, a single parent, works full-time at night and attends school in the daytime to complete her GED. Mrs. Williams is not in contact with any of the children's fathers. She reported that all of her children attend day care and that she has little time to spend with them. An elderly neighbor spends evenings at her house to prepare dinner and then get the children in bed. The caretaker reports that Rebecca spends most afternoons and evenings "glued to the TV."

Mrs. Williams stated that during her pregnancy with Rebecca, she developed gestational diabetes. Rebecca was delivered by Caesarian section and subsequently had respiratory distress. Mrs. Williams recalled that Rebecca attained all of her developmental milestones on the late side of normal. She described her as a quiet, cooperative child.

Records indicated that Mrs. Williams has been in several abusive relationships in the past 5 years. The police were called to the home by neighbors four times within 1 year. Three years prior, all of the children were placed in foster care for a 6-month period. After Mrs. Williams completed a counseling and drug rehabilitation program, the children were returned to the home with the stipulation of monthly monitoring by a social worker from DES. Results of Rebecca's vision and hearing tests, arranged by DES, were normal.

TESTS ADMINISTERED

Woodcock-Johnson III Tests of Cognitive Abilities
    (WJ III COG): Tests 1–7

Woodcock-Johnson III Tests of Achievement (WJ III
    ACH): Tests 1, 3–4, 7, 10
Peabody Picture Vocabulary Test—IIIA (PPVT-IIIA)

BEHAVIORAL OBSERVATIONS

Rebecca is a small child with a hesitant smile. She was cooperative and pleasant throughout the 1½-hour testing session. In general, her attention to tasks diminished as items increased in difficulty. She occasionally initiated conversation during a test by asking a question, but was easily redirected to the task.

TEST RESULTS

Rebecca was administered a set of tests from the WJ III COG and the WJ III ACH, Form A, which were scored according to age norms. Standard scores are reported as 68% confidence bands. A 68% confidence band is expressed as ±1 standard error of measurement (SS ±1 SEM).

Cognitive Abilities

Test results (see Tables 1 and 2) indicated that Rebecca's overall intellectual ability falls in the Low to Low Average range. Her general thinking ability, composed of those skills necessary for new learning and performance on difficult or novel tasks, is in the Low range. Her abilities to learn associations between symbols and words, to blend syllables and sounds into words, to process visual symbols rapidly, and to identify categories of similarities and differences are generally in the Low Average range. Rebecca was not able to hold two digits in memory while reversing their order (e.g., changing 2-5 to 5-2). In considering these findings, one must factor in Rebecca's limited educational and environmental opportunities. The obtained scores may be primarily a reflection of limited experiences and opportunities.

Table 1. WJ III COG Scores

CLUSTER/Tests	AE	EASY to DIFF		RPI	PR	SS (SS ±1 SEM)
GIA	3-6	3-0	4-1	54/90	8	79 (76–83)
THINKING ABILITY	3-4	<3-0	4-0	57/90	7	78 (73–83)
Visual-Auditory Learning	3-3	<3-0	4-0	59/90	14	84 (75–92)
Spatial Relations	3-1	2-9	3-7	36/90	4	73 (67–80)
Sound Blending	3-5	3-0	4-0	56/90	20	87 (83–92)
Concept Formation	3-10	2-11	4-8	76/90	26	90 (79–101)
Visual Matching	4-0	3-8	4-3	49/90	23	89 (87–91)
Numbers Reversed	<5-0	<4-11	<5-1			

Table 2. WJ III Oral Language Scores

CLUSTER/Tests	AE	EASY to DIFF		RPI	PR	SS (SS ±1 SEM)
Verbal Comprehension	3-0	2-6	3-7	39/90	1	66 (58–73)
ORAL LANGUAGE (WJ III ACH)	3-4	2-6	4-5	72/90	19	87 (83–91)
Story Recall	2-9	<2-0	5-0	78/90	19	87 (79–95)
Understanding Directions	3-7	2-11	4-3	64/90	19	87 (82–92)

Oral Language

Rebecca's oral language skills are Low Average when compared to the range of scores obtained by others at her age level. She was able to recall several details in orally presented stories and to follow directions that contained one to two commands (e.g., "Point to the house and then the tree"). Her performance on the PPVT-IIIA (SS ±1 SEM: 76–90, AE: 3–7) a test of receptive vocabulary, was consistent with the oral language results of the WJ III ACH. In contrast, her expressive vocabulary and ability to grasp and articulate the relationships among word meanings (e.g., antonyms, synonyms, analogies) were in the Very Low range when compared to others at her age level. Occasionally, Rebecca seemed to have some familiarity with the name for the picture presented, but lacked the specific label. For example, she identified scissors as "cutters." Rebecca's RPI scores suggest that while comprehension of connected, contextual language may be difficult for her, tasks with more constrained and specific language demands will be very difficult.

Academic Achievement

As shown in Table 3, Rebecca's standard score on the WJ III Letter-Word Identification test was in the Average range. Her RPI of 86/90 indicates average proficiency when compared to her age-peers on identifying letters. In contrast, Rebecca scored in the Low range on the Spelling test. Her RPI of 6/90 indicates that her prewriting skills are moderately delayed. Rebecca was able to write the first letter of her name.

Rebecca was also asked to copy some geometric forms. Although her pencil grip was correct, she seemed to have difficulty planning how to move the pencil to form letters and shapes. She was successful with the circle and the right-slanting oblique line but was unable to make the lines intersect on the square and the cross.

Rebecca scored in the Low Average range on Applied Problems. Her RPI of 29/90 indicated that her mastery of number concepts is moderately to mildly delayed. She demonstrated knowledge of one-to-one correspondence in choosing sets of objects to match numbers up to 7. On in-

Table 3. WJ III ACH Scores

CLUSTER/Tests	AE	EASY to DIFF		RPI	PR	SS (SS ±1 SEM)
Letter-Word Identification	4-5	3-11	4-10	86/90	45	98 (93–103)
Spelling	3-2	2-11	3-6	6/90	6	76 (70–82)
Applied Problems	3-6	3-1	3-10	29/90	11	81 (77–86)

formal tasks, she was able to rote-count to 11, but could only count objects up to 8. She was able to point to all common body parts as they were named, with the exception of "chest" and "ankle." She identified all primary colors correctly, but did not know any secondary colors.

SUMMARY AND IMPLICATIONS

Formal and informal test results indicate that Rebecca is mildly delayed in the development of cognitive, linguistic, and pre-academic skills, with relative weaknesses in expressive vocabulary and flexibility of vocabulary usage, short-term memory, part/whole relationships, and fine motor skills.

Rebecca's experiences and educational opportunities must be considered when reviewing the results of the evaluation. Weaknesses in her abilities may primarily reflect limited exposure and opportunity, rather than limited talents and abilities.

RECOMMENDATIONS

General

1. If she meets the criteria, enroll Rebecca in her school district's specialized developmental preschool program in which the emphasis is on developing concepts and language through experiential learning.
2. If Rebecca does not meet the criteria for the district program, secure agreement from her current preschool teacher to focus on development of concepts, receptive and expressive vocabulary, and language reasoning skills. Ask that she write behavioral objectives based on the following recommendations and cooperate with the monitoring of Rebecca's progress by the social worker.
3. Expose Rebecca to as wide a variety of experiences as possible with an adult who can explain what is happening, name objects and actions, and answer questions. Encourage verbal responses from Rebecca.
4. At school or at home, limit Rebecca's television viewing to shows that focus on early literacy, such as "Sesame Street" or "Reading Between the Lions" on PBS.
5. Provide activities at home that she can do independently, such as jigsaw puzzles, coloring in coloring books, free-hand art, simple mazes and dot-to-dot pictures, and sorting household objects. Encourage out-

side activities with her siblings, such as playing catch or hopscotch.

Oral Language Development

1. Provide consultation from a speech–language pathologist to Mrs. Williams and Rebecca's preschool teacher for specific ways to enhance vocabulary and language development.
2. Play games that focus on the sounds of words. These include rhyming games and songs, thinking of words that start with a particular sound, and counting the "beats" (syllables) of words.
3. Play games that focus on the meaning of words. These include thinking of words that go together, making collages of pictures that go together and discussing them, and thinking of opposites. Ask Rebecca to describe what she has created so that she expands her vocabulary accordingly.
4. Increase Rebecca's exposure to literature. Read to her and discuss the stories with her. Explain words that may not be familiar to Rebecca as they come up in stories and provide practice using them. Occasionally, stop during the action of a story and ask what she thinks will happen next and why. Read further and then discuss whether or not she was right.
5. Teach/reinforce positional (e.g., first/last), and directional (e.g., right/left) concepts.

Phonological Development and Reading

1. Provide Rebecca with many activities to promote phonological awareness and early literacy skills.
   a) While reading to Rebecca, help her to recognize the relationship between the print on the page and the oral story you are telling.
   b) Help Rebecca to develop the concepts of words and sentences, oral and printed, and book-handling skills (e.g., holding the book upright, turning pages, looking at the left page before the right).
   c) Provide ample exposure to both lower- and upper-case letters using games and puzzles. Later, use games and puzzles to match lower- and uppercase letters.
   d) Use a simple electronic game so that Rebecca can key in a letter and hear the letter name or choose a key, guess the name, and check herself.

2. When Rebecca is thoroughly familiar with many of the consonants and vowels, explain to her how letters are put together to make up words; then relate these to the words and sentences in stories. Reinforce the concept that letters and words are the building blocks of writing.

Number Concepts

1. Teach number concepts using the following progression:
   a) Teach the concept of sets (classification) using familiar physical objects that may be sorted in a variety of ways (e.g., size, color, shape, use). Later, introduce manipulatives such as pictures on flannel boards, Attribute Logic Blocks, Cuisenaire Rods, and Snap Cubes.
   b) Use pictures to represent physical objects in sets.
   c) Name sets by the major identifying attribute (e.g., "big").
   d) Reinforce one-to-one correspondence. Help Rebecca learn to match each element of a set with a counting number to determine the cardinal number of the set (i.e., answers the question, "How many?"). At this point, teach quantitative vocabulary and concepts (e.g., more, less, same). Move from using physical objects to match sets (concrete level), to using pictures (semi-concrete), to using tallies (semi-abstract), to identifying cardinal numbers (abstract).
   e) Teach Rebecca that a number can be compared with any other number (e.g., "bigger than," "the same as").
   f) Do not expect Rebecca to write numerals. Provide her with numeral tiles or cards and plastic numbers to use for matching activities. Provide ample exposure to the image of the numbers for later writing.
2. For specific activities, refer to *Today's Mathematics: Part 1, Concepts and Classroom Methods,* Tenth Edition, and *Today's Mathematics, Part 2, Activities and Instructional Ideas,* both by James Heddens and William Speer (John Wiley & Sons, 2000). Other excellent math recommendations may be found at the website for the National Council of Teachers of Mathematics (http://www.nctm.org/corners/teachers/index.htm).

Fine-Motor Skills

1. Provide Rebecca with lots of practice using crayons, markers, and pencils in activities that will give her the opportunity to plan and execute movements using the small muscles of her hand. If necessary, directly teach Rebecca how to visualize where the point of her pencil, marker, scissors, or other tool should be at the end of each stroke or cut.
2. Use activities such as tracing, using templates, and coloring within simple, bold-line drawings before moving on to copying forms and drawing pictures.
3. Provide ample positive reinforcement for effort rather than just for quality of her product.

Diagnostic Evaluation Report

Name:	Bart Huxley		Parents:	Earl and Dottie Huxley
Date of Birth:	August 6, 1995		School:	Montessori Academy
Age at Evaluation:	5 years, 6 months		Date of Evaluation:	February 16, 2001
Grade:	P1 (equivalent to kindergarten)			

REASONS FOR REFERRAL

Mr. and Mrs. Huxley requested a comprehensive evaluation of their son Bart to determine whether or not he is displaying early signs of dyslexia. The Huxleys and Bart's teacher feel he is not developing at the pace of other children his age in regard to learning the alphabet, writing, and fine-motor skills.

BACKGROUND INFORMATION

Mrs. Huxley, Bart's mother, reported that he is the product of a full-term pregnancy and uncomplicated delivery. Developmental milestones were achieved within normal limits. Bart experienced bouts of otitis media from the age of 15 months to 4½ years. He had a mild case of chicken pox at the age of 3; otherwise, his medical history has been unremarkable. Vision and hearing exams last August revealed normal results.

   In regard to family history, dyslexia is common on the paternal side of the family, including Bart's father, grandfather, and great aunt. A maternal uncle is said to have attention problems. Bart lives at home with both parents and a younger brother, age 3. The Huxleys describe Bart as a happy child with a pleasant disposition. He gets along well with other children. Mrs. Huxley reported that Bart demonstrates poor handwriting. At school, he has had difficulty sitting still although this has become less problematic in the last year.

   Nadelle Lee, Bart's teacher at the Montessori school, and Gwen Schmidt, his tutor, completed the Child Behavior Checklist and participated in interviews. Bart is enjoying his first year in school, in the 3- to 6-year-old class. He is positive and enthusiastic, and he strives to please. Ms. Lee uses a variety of methods and materials, including Primary Phonics, hands-on materials for mathematical learning, and D'Nealian for handwriting. Ms. Schmidt, who tutors Bart in letter names, sounds, and formation, uses both Montessori and Orton-Gillingham materials. Both Ms. Lee and Ms. Schmidt reported that Bart seems unable to acquire and retain basic language-based information, particularly letter names and sounds, and rhyming skills, but does better with numbers and quantities. Ms. Schmidt added that Bart's recall of letter sounds improves if he traces the letter and uses a keyword as a prompt for the sound. Bart is also reported to have difficulty producing certain shapes without a model but is comfortable working with the 4-year-olds on writing tasks. Bart has difficulty remaining focused during circle time and in large-group activities (10 students). In one-to-one tutoring, although he is attentive throughout the 30-minute session, he generally tires after 20–25 minutes. Bart's behavior and social skills are fine. He seems particularly to enjoy hands-on visual–spatial tasks, such as building with blocks and assembling puzzles.

TESTS ADMINISTERED

Achenbach Child Behavior Checklist (CBCL)
Woodcock-Johnson III Tests of Cognitive Abilities
   (WJ III COG): Tests 1–9
Beery-Buktenica Developmental Test of Visual-Motor Integration (4th ed.) (VMI)
Comprehensive Test of Phonological Processing (CTOPP)
Informal assessment of alphabetic knowledge
Interview

BEHAVIORAL OBSERVATIONS

Overall Bart worked diligently and demonstrated adequate attention in this one-on-one environment. Several breaks were taken to ensure that he was putting forth his best effort. On many of the tests, he was unable to learn the task from the sample items. The current test results are deemed valid indicators of his present levels of functioning and readiness at this time.

ATTENTION AND BEHAVIOR

Bart's mother completed the Achenbach Child Behavior Checklist (CBCL). Across eight behavioral categories, Bart's ratings were in the average range in comparison to other boys his age.

COGNITIVE ABILITY

The Woodcock-Johnson III Tests of Cognitive Abilities was administered to obtain an understanding of Bart's strengths and weaknesses. Bart's scores were calculated using age norms. When no significant difference was found among the tests of a cluster, only the cluster standard score (SS) is discussed. The percentile rank (PR) indicates the percentage of students of Bart's age who obtained the same score or a lower score than Bart. Relative Proficiency Indexes (RPI) allow statements to be generated about a subject's predicted quality of performance on tasks similar to the ones tested. For example, an RPI of 71/90 is interpreted to mean that when others at the student's age show 90% success on a certain task, the student is predicted to show only 71% success.

Bart's performance on individual cognitive performance clusters (representing broad categories of cognitive abilities) is presented in Table 1.

Bart's performance indicated that, currently, he is functioning within the Low Average range of general intellectual abilities (GIA). Bart's scores on the Verbal Ability (standard) and Thinking Ability (standard) clusters were consistent with his GIA. The Verbal Ability cluster represents his knowledge of individual word meanings and understanding of the relationships among word meanings; the Thinking Ability cluster represents a sampling of the different thinking processes. Among the four tests of this cluster, Bart performed in the Low Average range on learning and retrieving associations between unfamiliar visual symbols and known words (Visual-Auditory Learning). Bart experienced considerable difficulty retrieving the words for the picture symbols, especially those representing function words such as prepositions and pronouns, even though some were quite illustrative of their associated verbal label. Bart scored in the Low to Low Average range in a test of categorical reasoning based on principles of inductive logic (Concept Formation). He experienced difficulty determining the rule governing each set of patterns. His performance was in the Average range when identifying the two or three pieces of a design that, when assembled, would form the complete shape (Spatial Relations), as well as on a test that requires blending orally presented phonemes and syllables into words (Sound Blending).

Cognitive Efficiency represents the capacity of the cognitive system to process information automatically. On Visual Matching, a test of rapid scanning and visual discrimination to find matching numbers, Bart completed only four items in 2 minutes and rubbed his eyes several times. His circling of the numbers appeared labored and negatively affected his score (SS 73, Low). No score was obtained for Numbers Reversed because Bart was not able to repeat two digits in reverse sequence. In contrast, Bart scored in the Average range on a task in which he had to remember items given in random order and give them back in categories (Auditory Working Memory). Bart needed three practice trials before he could perform this task successfully. Phonemic Awareness, analyzing and synthesizing speech sounds, was in the Average range.

In summary, Bart demonstrated a unique blend of cognitive strengths and weaknesses, which when combined, yielded General Intellectual Ability in the Low Average range. Strengths for Bart included his ability to manipulate visual–spatial information mentally, especially when linguistic reasoning was not required. He also displayed some good phonological awareness skills that can be capitalized upon to facilitate his reading and spelling development. Weaknesses included his knowledge of word meanings and relationships, his ability to learn visual/auditory associations, and his ability to perceive categories based on similarities and differences. His speed in processing visual symbols was unusually low. These weaknesses would be expected to impact the ease with which he learns sound/symbol correspondences, printed words, and visual representations of letters and numbers.

Visual–Motor Integration

To investigate further Bart's motor skills, he was administered the VMI. After the first of three subtests, copying

Table 1. WJ III Cognitive Performance Cluster Scores

WJ III COG CLUSTER	SS	PR	RPI
General Intellectual Ability (GIA)—Standard	81	10	57/90
Verbal Ability	86	18	75/90
Thinking Ability	88	22	78/90
Cognitive Efficiency	73	3	12/90
Phonemic Awareness	94	34	83/90
Working Memory	86	18	57/90

forms of increasing complexity, presented one at a time, he began to display considerable fatigue; consequently, to avoid possibly invalid results, the Visual Discrimination and Motor Coordination subtests were not administered. Bart did, however, exert effort on the copying task; he was able to copy a vertical line, horizontal line, and a circle with sufficient accuracy but not any figures with diagonal or intersecting lines. Bart obtained a standard score of 52, below the 1st percentile for his age.

Oral Language

Phonology

Bart's phonological skills were investigated further through administration of the CTOPP. Weaknesses in phonological awareness, phonological memory, and low naming speed, are often associated with reading difficulties. On the CTOPP, Bart obtained the score profile shown in Table 2.

On the Phonological Awareness composite, Bart performed within the Average range on blending two sounds to make a familiar word (e.g., "What word is this? /n/–/o/") or deleting syllables from two-syllable words (e.g., *napkin* without *-kin*). Using blocks to represent the syllables was clearly helpful for him. On items requiring the deletion of individual sounds (e.g., *cup* without the /k/), he was successful with one initial sound but no final sounds. Bart's Sound Matching score, in the Low Average range, indicates that he is having some difficulty isolating the initial sounds of words (e.g., *mouse* and *moon* both start with /m/). He was unable to discriminate and match final sounds. Developmentally, isolation of initial phonemes in words occurs be-

fore the end of kindergarten and is an important prerequisite to learning phonics.

Bart experienced difficulty on Phonological Memory tasks. He could recall a series of no more than three digits and repeated accurately only two-syllable nonsense words. Most likely, underdeveloped phonological memory is a major contributing factor to Bart's difficulty in learning sound/symbol correspondence.

Of the three areas assessed on the CTOPP, Bart had most difficulty with Rapid Naming. He made no errors but was slow in retrieving the words for the pictures. (Pretesting ensured that Bart knew the names of the colors and objects presented.) Slow retrieval affects the ability to automatically associate letters with sounds for decoding and whole words with their oral equivalents for sight word acquisition and, ultimately, reading fluency.

In summary, Bart is showing age-appropriate syllable deletion and sound-blending skills, both important for developing successful reading and spelling skills. Bart has weaknesses on phonemic manipulation tasks at the individual sound level, understanding that words are composed of sounds and that those sounds can be moved around. Particular difficulties were noted in isolation of initial and final sounds; sound matching; and phonological memory, especially for digits. His lowest area was in rapid naming.

ACADEMIC ABILITIES

Bart's knowledge of the alphabet was assessed informally. Bart named nine printed letters: *r, z, m, v, e, x, s, c,* and *w.* He recalled the keyword he had been taught more easily than the actual letter name. For example, when shown the letter *w,* Bart said, "Begins with wagon." Bart could give the sound for /t/ but not the letter name. He provided sounds for eight letters: /b/, /r/, /m/, /h/, /v/, /c/, /s/, and /o/ (short sound). When providing the sound for /h/, Bart added the /schwa/ sound, making the /h/ sound like "huh." The examiner tried to model "clipping" the sounds but Bart was not successful at doing so. Twice Bart confused the letter *t* for *x.*

Bart wrote his first name and the first two letters of his last name. On dictation, he produced only the letters *m, c, e, o, s,* and *r.* He commented that he knows *c* because his brother's name is Carter. Bart was able to count to 14.

Overall, Bart's knowledge of the alphabet, including the names and sounds of letters, is below average for children in his school. Bart himself volunteered, "I can't read." He does have a beginning base of knowledge, however, and his recall appears to be enhanced by meaning (e.g., recalling a key-

Table 2. CTOPP Score Profile

CTOPP COMPOSITE/Subtest	Scaled Score	Standard Score	Percentile Rank
PHONOLOGICAL AWARENESS		91	27
Elision	9		37
Blending Words	10		50
Sound Matching	7		16
PHONOLOGICAL MEMORY		82	12
Memory for Digits	6		9
Nonword Repetition	8		25
RAPID NAMING		70	2
Rapid Color Naming	6		9
Rapid Object Naming	4		2

Scaled Score ($M = 10$, $SD = 3$); Standard Score ($M = 100$, $SD = 15$)

word rather than a letter name). His letter formation resembled that of a younger child. Counting skills were also below expectancy for his age and experience.

SUMMARY

Bart's parents referred him for an evaluation based on concerns regarding his difficulties learning letters and numbers. Reports from teachers and results of this evaluation indicate that Bart is functioning intellectually in the Low Average range. He possesses a well-developed understanding of spatial relationships and has acquired some good phonological skills. Areas of difficulty that may be negatively affecting his ability to learn basic reading, writing, and arithmetic skills involve higher level reasoning, learning and retrieving symbol/word associations, reasoning with word meanings, short-term memory, phonological awareness at the level of individual sounds, and visual–fine motor skills. Although his Low Average Verbal Ability and Thinking Ability cluster scores are consistent with his GIA, the combination of his significantly underdeveloped visual–fine motor coordination, slow visual processing of symbols, and slow rate of rapid naming suggest that problems are not primarily due to a generally slow rate of learning. These areas of specific weakness suggest that Bart has developmental dyslexia and dysgraphia (i.e., a disturbance in visual–motor integration that affects a child's ability to write or copy letters, words, and numbers). Bart's attentional difficulties in class may be secondary to his difficulties with so many of the classroom activities or may represent a concomitant primary disorder of attention that may require later evaluation.

RECOMMENDATIONS FOR INSTRUCTION

Reading

1. Bart needs to improve his foundation skills before formally learning "how to read." More work needs to be done to help Bart learn letter names and sounds. A recommended resource for teaching the alphabet is the *Alphabet Learning Center Activities Kit* by Nancy Fetzer and Sandra Reif (Center for Applied Research in Education, www.Phedu.com). The Fernald method (summary attached) will be helpful to reinforce letter names, sounds, and formation.
2. Bart will need *daily* multisensory instruction in written language. As soon as this can begin, Bart will start to ex-

perience literacy success. Due to his weakness in phonological memory, instruction will need to be redundant, with many opportunities for practice in different settings (e.g., classroom, home, remedial setting). The following resource is recommended for Bart's parents: *Starting Out Right: A Guide to Promoting Children's Reading Success* (National Academy Press, Washington, D.C., 1999). This guide offers activities to promote rhyming and other aspects of phonological awareness and provides lists of children's books and software for enhancing literacy development.
3. Create a Resource Notebook for Bart in which each page is devoted to a letter. Have him cut out and paste in pictures that begin with the target sound with emphasis on the keyword. Teach him that like animals, letters have names and make a sound. Make sure he knows the names and sounds, and the difference between them. He will rely, for some time at least, on a keyword to recall the letter name/sound association.
4. Begin daily literacy lessons with phonological awareness exercises (about 10–15 minutes) that expand Bart's ability to analyze the sounds within words. LinguiSystems (www.linguisystems.com, 800-776-4332) offers a wide variety of instructional materials to address these needs.

Visual–Motor Development

1. Refer Bart for an occupational therapy evaluation. The therapist can observe Bart's posture, pencil grip, hand skills, chair and desk size, and paper position and make recommendations for developing more efficient motor skills and physical stability.
2. Provide Bart with many opportunities to use fine-motor skills in activities consistent with his current ability level. Such activities may include simple paper folding; cutting out large, simple shapes with bold borders; and copying large, simple shapes on the chalkboard. Use a variety of fun and interesting mediums, such as finger-paints, watercolors, pudding (to lick off his finger after making a shape), and glitter-on-glue designs. Also provide many activities in which the goal is simply free-form designs.
3. D'Nealian is a good method of handwriting instruction, although *Handwriting Without Tears* may be more therapeutic for Bart (www.hwtears.com, 301-983-8409). Use tracing and drawing activities on a vertical plane before moving to a horizontal plane. Use materials that provide friction, such as chalk on a chalkboard or markers on paper.

Mathematics

Continue Montessori methods for teaching math using concrete manipulatives. Progress carefully in a sequence of real objects, manipulatives, pictorial representations, and, finally, the most abstract level, numerical notation. Use a number line to help Bart develop the idea of what number comes before or after another number.

ACCOMMODATIONS

1. Limit the time spent on drill and practice. Be gentle, encouraging, and yet persistent with Bart when it comes to reading and fine-motor tasks and take cues from him in terms of when enough is enough. Use of extrinsic rewards, such as 5 minutes of a simple computer game or stickers, is encouraged to help him maintain motivation to practice difficult tasks.

2. While learning letters, use magnetic letters or letter tiles instead of having Bart write letters he cannot yet form easily. Keep an alphabet strip on his desk for reference and reinforcement.

3. Provide Bart with opportunities to reinforce skills using computer software. One example of an appropriate program would be *School Zone Alphabet Express* (Scholastic, www.scholastic.com/bookclubs).

If Bart does not make sufficient progress and continues to need considerable assistance, refer him for a comprehensive evaluation in first grade to determine eligibility for special education services. If Bart's attentional difficulties continue and appear to be significantly interfering with his learning, request an evaluation specifically addressing this concern.

Adapted from Melissa M. King, M.Ed.

Educational Evaluation

Name:	Christina Begay	Parents:	Lee and Ronald Begay
Chronological Age:	6 Years, 9 Months	Ethnicity:	Native American
Report Date:	March 14, 2001	Primary Language:	English
Educational Program:	Whitesell State Schools for the Deaf and the Blind—Elementary		

REASON FOR REFERRAL

Christina was referred for an evaluation of her cognitive and academic functioning levels by her educational program team at the Whitesell State Schools for the Deaf and the Blind (WSDB) and by her local education agency, Jefferson Unified School District, to assist in decisions regarding educational program options. Christina's teacher notes that her level of academic functioning appears to be within the preschool skills level and that her educational performance is inconsistent.

BACKGROUND INFORMATION

Christina is the daughter of Lee and Ronald Begay. She resides at home with her parents and her five siblings, ranging from 1 year to 8 years of age. English is the primary language of the home. Christina was born at 32 weeks after an induced labor following her mother's 1-month hospitalization due to low fluid in the amniotic sac. Mother reports that the umbilical cord was wrapped around Christina's neck at birth; she was born blue and was placed on a respirator for 2 weeks for administration of oxygen. Christina's weight and height are below the 5th percentile for her age. She is healthy overall, though she has historically presented with balance and coordination problems.

Christina's hearing problem was suspected and diagnosed shortly after her birth. Her family received outreach services from Whitesell School for the Deaf and the Blind (WSDB), and Christina was fitted with binaural hearing aids at 3 years of age. Yearly audiological testing indicates that Christina experiences a mild-to-moderate sensorineural hearing loss bilaterally. She wears two behind-the-ear hearing aids in all educational settings and is encouraged to use these aids in all home activities. As the Begays have not yet completed the enrollment process with Children's Rehabilitation Services to provide Christina with her own hearing aids without cost, she is wearing aids on loan from the school. From preschool to the present,

Christina has a history of losing or misplacing her hearing aids, resulting in extended periods of time without amplification. Christina passed all vision screening measures administered in school.

Christina attended the Preschool for Hearing Impaired Children from 1997 to 1999. She was enrolled in her local education agency, Summerton School District, for a brief period of time in the fall of 1999. She demonstrated poor behavioral control and limited participation in this setting. She was then referred for placement consideration to WSDB to address the educational issues connected to her hearing loss. Her WSDB teachers describe Christina as an active, fun-loving girl whose level of maturity is below her chronological age. She is dependent on boundaries set by staff to maintain age-appropriate behavior in educational settings. She often attempts to avoid educational or therapeutic tasks in which she is disinterested. Christina is absent from school frequently.

During the past 2 years of enrollment at WSDB, educational staff report noted progress in the areas of motor development and communication skills. She receives consultative support from Occupational Therapy through classroom activities for fine-motor needs and direct service from Physical Therapy for gross-motor development relating to balance and coordination. Her communicative competency has improved in the areas of speech articulation (though several sound substitutions are consistently noted), maturity of communicative intent when using her aural/oral skills, and expansion of her signing skills to a three-word sign string for communication with staff who are deaf.

ASSESSMENT STRATEGY

Christina was observed in two settings: her elementary classroom while working on a small group activity with her teacher and one other student and on the playground during the elementary school recess.

Subsequently, Christina worked in the one-to-one test

setting with this evaluator over a 2-week period. These sessions lasted for 60 to 75 minutes as she participated in various tests selected from the Woodcock Johnson III Tests of Cognitive Abilities (WJ III COG, Tests 1–9, 13–14, 17–18) and the WJ III Tests of Achievement (WJ III ACH, Tests 3–5, 7, 9–10). All standardized testing was conducted in English, with Christina using digital hearing aids that were configured by the school's audiologist to match her hearing loss. To allow for optimum auditory input and best reduction of sound-field noise, a cabling system was attached to her hearing aids for use with the audio-taped test material. Sign language was rarely used with Christina as she is not a fluent signer and relies on her hearing and speech for communication purposes. Christina's speech is judged to be 100% intelligible with some substitutions or distortions noted in her word productions.

Test results are presented with Christina's cultural and sensory background taken into consideration. Her test performance is not judged to be impacted by severe educational disadvantage though her excessive absences are acknowledged and suspected to have affected her school achievement.

BEHAVIORAL OBSERVATIONS

Testing

Christina was friendly and enthusiastic in all testing activities. She willingly accompanied the evaluator to the testing room and was helpful in setting up and putting away testing materials. Several accommodations to standardized testing were required when working with Christina in this setting due to her limited attention span and impulsive response style. These accommodations included using a behavior management program based on tangible rewards for performance, reducing the amount of visually presented items on a page by covering preceding or subsequent test items, changing Christina's position between sitting and standing based on her waning focus or excessive fidgeting, and taking frequent breaks in the testing sessions.

Classroom

In the classroom, Christina was working on a letter identification activity with her teacher and one other student who is profoundly deaf. Her teacher primarily used conceptually based, sign-supported speech when communicating with both students, but frequently dropped the signing when working solely with Christina. Her responses and participation were similar regardless of whether the teacher used sign-supported speech or speech alone. Her responses were often incorrect or tangential to the instructional request. As Christina turned to interact with her classmate within the task, she employed only speech. When reminded that she needed to use sign language with this student, Christina turned off her voice and pantomimed a few gestures in an attempt to make her message clear.

On the playground, Christina interacted predominantly with children with visual impairments. She walked up to their play area on the swings and chatted with both students and staff. She asked them to push her on the swings, talked to another student about her winter coat, and asked about the dark sunglasses that the student was wearing. During the 15-minute playground observation, Christina did not join her age-mates with hearing impairments in their play activities or in their interactions.

ASSESSMENT FINDINGS

The findings of this formal assessment are offered as good indicators of Christina's cognitive and academic abilities in comparison to her age-peers without a hearing impairment. These findings should be used in conjunction with other educational measures and observations in determining Christina's true levels of performance to assist in the development of educational programming to meet her specific needs. The interpretations of these findings and her present level of performance should also be viewed in light of her neonatal problems, her hearing impairment (with sporadic use of hearing aids), and intermittent school attendance.

According to standardized measures obtained from the WJ III COG, Christina's verbal ability (acquired knowledge and language comprehension) is in the Very Low range when compared to others at her age level. Her overall performance, representing general intellectual ability (based on her language development, short-term memory, associative memory, auditory processing, and visual problem solving), indicates that Christina is performing at the 1st percentile ranking among her age-peers. Her thinking ability (intentional cognitive processing) is in the Low range, better than only 4% of her age-peers. Also, Christina's cognitive efficiency (automatic cognitive processing) is assessed to be in the Very Low range, better than only 2 out of 1,000 age-peers.

When compared to others at her age level, Christina's

performance is Low Average in visual-spatial thinking; however, this cognitive ability is noted to be an area of relative strength as her performance placed her at the 11th percentile rank for her age. Christina's oral language skills are in the Low range when compared to the range of scores obtained by age-peers with normal hearing. Her skills in auditory processing and short-term memory are in the Very Low range; her performance was at or below the 1st percentile.

The WJ III ACH presented to Christina produced results indicating that she is performing most academic tasks at or below skill levels usually achieved by or during the kindergarten year. She was able to write only a few upper-case letters of the alphabet and demonstrated no sight word recognition other than her own name. Results of phonemic awareness tests indicate that she is unaware of the sound components in words, is unable to blend sounds to make words, and has no knowledge of sound/symbol relationships. This finding is not surprising as Christina's current educational program has attempted to maximize her language development, and phonological awareness training has not been a part of her instructional plan. Christina could recall only a single element from the oral presentation of a brief story. A second presentation of the story, using sign-supported speech, produced similar results. Christina demonstrated the understanding of one-to-one correspondence of numbers and quantities to 10 but was unable to work with the concepts of adding to or taking away quantities from a set of manipulatives.

Christina's high level of distractibility and tendency to respond impulsively compounded her difficulty with cognitive, language, and academic tasks. Christina had brief moments of focused attention, which the evaluator attempted to extend through prompting, prodding, and rewards. Despite limited opportunities for distraction, an optimized sound system, and a tangible reward system, Christina's ability to focus, attend, and reflect on the tasks before responding was below expected developmental levels.

SUMMARY

Christina's overall cognitive abilities, whether examining her verbal abilities, visual reasoning abilities, or a compilation of both, are assessed to be significantly below those of her peers without a hearing impairment. These performance levels should be viewed with caution as Christina's cognitive and academic development have been compro-

mised by a variety of circumstances. Her hearing impairment, though within mild-to-moderate levels, is assumed to have had a negative impact on her global communication and educational development. Christina has not been consistently aided with auditory equipment since the confirmation of her hearing impairment. Even when aided, the clarity of the auditory signal may be compromised due to the sensorineural nature of her hearing impairment. Christina's language development opportunities have been compromised by inconsistent and less-than-optimum auditory input during formative developmental years. Also, it is likely that excessive absences from school may have contributed to her delays in both cognitive and academic skills. Finally, Christina's birth history suggests a traumatic beginning; the impact of her respiratory distress during her first days of life is unknown.

Christina's cognitive profile does not indicate that her visual channel is significantly stronger for reception and processing of information than her auditory channel. Rather, both modalities are in the Very Low range at this point. Christina's hearing impairment is significant in nature and should be accommodated in educational settings. She requires a learning environment that promotes reduced distractions for optimum performance as Christina is auditorially and visually distractible and expresses discomfort with increased levels of background noise during listening tasks.

RECOMMENDATIONS

In light of assessment findings, observations, and staffings with Christina's educational team, the following recommendations are made to address the referral question:

1. Christina's levels of academic skill are progressing but at a very slow rate in comparison to her age-peers. The educational and communication staff currently working with Christina are gathering data regarding which communication modality may best enhance Christina's rate of learning. Her educational team is encouraged to consider that information along with the possible benefits of a formal approach to phonemic awareness. This approach to reading may promote Christina's access to the world of print at a rate greater than that which she is currently demonstrating.
2. Christina is very dependent on her residual hearing and demonstrates obvious benefit from her aids. Christina should be involved in developing a behavioral system

that would encourage responsible care of such equipment.

3. Christina should wear her hearing aids in all educational settings. Use of a personal amplification system that highlights the teacher's voice and reduces the natural background noise within a classroom should be explored.

4. Assessed cognitive levels and performance observations indicate that Christina requires modifications to the general elementary-level curriculum. Most likely, she will learn at a slower pace than her age-peers, will require much review and repetition, and will benefit from activities that promote the application of curriculum skills to her real-life activities.

5. Christina's visual distractibility requires accommoda-tions by reducing the amount of information presented on a page or in an instructional activity. Christina is likely to have a better opportunity for success when the student-to-teacher ratio is low. This may be accomplished in a reduced class size or by focusing Christina's instruction in a small group within the scope of a regular class size.

6. The integrated support services of occupational and physical therapy currently provided to Christina have produced positive growth in the areas of fine- and gross-motor skills. Therapy staff indicate that these developmental areas continue to require refinement and that services should continue.

Adapted from Eva M. Prince, Ed.S., School Psychologist

WOODCOCK-JOHNSON III TESTS OF COGNITIVE ABILITIES AND TESTS OF ACHIEVEMENT

CLUSTER/Test	AE	EASY	to DIFF	RPI	PR	SS(68% BAND)
GIA	4-5	3-10	5-1	24/90	1	67 (64–70)
VERBAL ABILITY	4-1	3-5	4-10	26/90	1	63 (56–70)
THINKING ABILITY	4-8	3-11	5-8	56/90	4	74 (70–78)
COG EFFICIENCY	4-10	4-9	5-0	1/90	0.2	56 (50–61)
VIS-SPATIAL THINK (Gv)	4-11	3-11	6-4	72/90	11	81 (76–86)
AUDITORY PROCESS (Ga)	3-9	3-2	4-7	35/90	1	67 (63–72)
SHORT-TERM MEM (Gsm)	4-9	4-8	4-11	2/90	0.3	59 (53–65)
PHONEMIC AWARE	3-11	3-3	4-9	43/90	3	71 (65–76)
WORKING MEMORY	<4-10	<4-8	<4-11			
ORAL LANGUAGE	4-2	3-2	5-3	47/90	3	71 (65–77)

CLUSTER/Test	AE	EASY	to DIFF	RPI	PR	SS(68% BAND)
Verbal Comprehension	4-1	3-5	4-10	26/90	1	63 (56–70)
Visual-Auditory Learning	5-0	4-1	6-3	69/90	8	79 (75–83)
Spatial Relations	5-7	4-6	7-4	81/90	29	92 (88–96)
Sound Blending	3-5	3-0	4-0	17/90	3	71 (65–76)
Concept Formation	5-4	4-7	6-1	59/90	16	85 (79–91)
Visual Matching	4-9	4-5	5-0	2/90	2	68 (65–70)
Numbers Reversed	<5-0	<4-11	<5-1			
Incomplete Words	4-9	3-9	6-6	74/90	23	89 (84–94)
Auditory Work Memory	<3-6	<3-6	<3-8			
Picture Recognition	4-2	3-3	5-6	60/90	12	82 (76–88)
Auditory Attention	4-3	3-5	5-6	58/90	7	78 (74–83)
Memory for Words	4-0	3-6	4-7	13/90	5	75 (71–80)
Rapid Picture Naming	4-6	4-0	5-0	16/90	10	80 (79–82)

Form A of the following achievement tests was administered:

CLUSTER/Test	AE	EASY	to DIFF	RPI	PR	SS(68% BAND)
Story Recall	4-1	2-3	6-10	75/90	8	79 (63–95)
Understanding Directions	4-2	3-6	4-11	20/90	2	70 (66–74)
Calculation	<5-5	<5-2	<5-8			
Spelling	4-6	4-2	4-10	1/90	1	64 (59–69)
Passage Comprehension	5-6	5-3	5-10	5/90	5	75 (70–81)
Applied Problems	4-8	4-3	5-1	7/90	4	73 (69–77)

DISCREPANCIES	STANDARD SCORES			DISCREPANCY		Significant
	Actual	Predicted	Difference	PR	SD	±1.50 SD (SEE)
VERBAL ABILITY	63	76	–13	13	–1.12	No
THINKING ABILITY	74	68	+6	68	+0.48	No
COG EFFICIENCY	56	83	–27	2	–1.98	Yes

Neuropsychological Evaluation

Name:	Juliette Reid		Parents:	Michael and Nancy Reid
Birthdate:	11/23/93		Dates of Evaluation:	2/14/01, 2/19/01, 2/26/01
Age:	7 years, 3 months		School:	Goode Elementary
Grade:	1			

REASON FOR REFERRAL

Juliette Reid was seen for a neuropsychological evaluation at the request of her parents, Michael and Nancy Reid, who were concerned about her lack of progress in school. Mrs. Reid stated that "Juliette cannot read, does not know her numbers, and takes lots of time to recall the letters." They requested the evaluation to help determine the cause of her learning difficulties and to determine strategies for teaching her.

BACKGROUND INFORMATION

Family Background

Juliette was adopted as an infant and currently lives with her parents; an older, non-biologically related, adopted brother, Zadon (9 years); and a sister, Tania (3 years), who is the natural child of the Reids. The father is a district sales manager, and the mother manages the household. Both parents completed college. Mrs. Reid describes Juliette as a "very fun-loving child who causes no real problems. She loves to talk and play make-believe. She also loves to play with Barbies and dolls." She gets along well with her siblings and loves to play with children of all ages. Discipline is provided by both parents with the use of a "sticker chart" for reinforcement.

Developmental History

As Juliette is an adopted child, scant information is available on her biological mother's pregnancy and her birth history. She weighed 7 lbs., 5 oz. at birth and reportedly received an Apgar score of 8. Developmental milestones were reported to be within the normal range. She experienced some allergies when the family moved approximately 5 years ago, but these have reportedly subsided. She has had two ear infections in the past; her hearing was normal bilaterally when tested in September 2001. She wears eyeglasses for farsightedness. Other medical history is unre-

markable. She is a patient of Dr. Susan Keebler, whom she sees for yearly examinations. She was seen for a psychiatric evaluation by Dr. Kevin Ash on 10/31/00. He diagnosed Attention Deficit/Hyperactivity Disorder (ADHD), Predominantly Inattentive type, for which he prescribed Ritalin. Since mid-November 2000, she has taken 5 mg. in the morning and at noon. Her mother reports that there has been a dramatic improvement in her ability to attend since she began medication.

Educational History and Previous Testing

Juliette attended preschool for 3 mornings per week beginning at the age of 4 years. She was enrolled for kindergarten and the first half of first grade at the Parker Academy and received special education help for ½ hour per day through the local school district. In February of 2001, she began attending her home public school, Goode Elementary. She continues to receive special education assistance for 1 hour per day.

Problems with Juliette's learning were noted by the parents during her late preschool years when she had difficulty learning color names and also persisted in substituting object pronouns (e.g., "me," "her") for subject pronouns (e.g., "I," "she") in her oral language. Her preschool teacher, Jennifer Sammons, noted that she had difficulty with "left/right orientation" of letters and could not recognize letters or numbers, although she was able to count by rote. Further, she commented that Juliette had "good auditory discrimination," as well as "good story comprehension and retelling ability."

A preschool screening, completed by Pamela Becker, Early Intervention Specialist, on 6/7/99, revealed that Juliette was performing within the Low Average range in the cognitive and motor domains with performance significantly below average in language, specifically in expressive language.

In January of Juliette's kindergarten year, her teacher noted that she was experiencing significant difficulties with attention and with learning in reading and math. She was able to identify many letters ("Point to *m*") and give the sounds for some, but was unable to name letters when they were shown to her. She was, however, able to identify several words beginning with particular letter sounds and could give the sounds of several of the letters. She was also experiencing significant problems in maintaining her attention to tasks. Because of these difficulties, Juliette was referred for comprehensive psychoeducational, speech/language, and occupational therapy evaluations through her school. These evaluations took place over a 2-month period ending in late March 2000.

A psychological evaluation completed by Marjorie Rhein, school psychologist, revealed intellectual functioning within the Low Average to Average range (WISC-III Full Scale IQ: 84; Verbal IQ: 83; Performance IQ: 89). She noted strengths in vocabulary and social judgment with weaknesses in short-term memory, abstract reasoning, and arithmetic reasoning. She also noted problems with distractibility and focusing of attention. Results of selected tests from the Woodcock-Johnson Psychoeducational Battery—Revised, administered by Carmen Freeman, diagnostician, indicated Average abilities in visual processing of pictures, Low Average abilities in visual processing speed and auditory processing. Similar to the results of the WISC-III, she displayed a weakness in short-term memory. All academic skills were in the Low range. Juliette also evidenced problems with color naming and with visual–motor coordination. Results of a language assessment administered by Dorothy Moreno, SLP-CCC, resulted in language scores ranging from Low Average/Average to significantly below average. In contrast to findings on the WISC III, vocabulary was a weakness. In a language sample of 75 utterances, the only error noted was in pronoun usage (her/she). An occupational therapy evaluation by Helen Kongsgaard, OTR, found that Juliette's gross motor, motor planning, bilateral coordination, and—contrary to Ms. Freeman's findings—fine manipulative skills were adequate. Thus, this comprehensive evaluation resulted in consistent findings of weak short-term memory but inconsistencies regarding vocabulary and visual–motor integration. Following these evaluations, Juliette was provided educational services for students with learning disabilities, with goals to improve her reading, writing, and math readiness.

Prior to Juliette's psychiatric evaluation in October 2000 (noted previously), her first-grade teacher at Goode Elementary wrote classroom observations about her progress. She described Juliette's continued difficulties with attention, memory (particularly delayed recall), reading, spelling, and math. She also noted that Juliette did fairly well with some assistance on phonics worksheets. When spelling, she was often able to discriminate the beginning

and ending sounds of words but was unable to recall the associated letters. The teacher further noted that Juliette frequently confused verb tenses and pronouns.

OBSERVATIONS AND IMPRESSIONS

Juliette navigated the rather extensive formal testing sessions with ease. She was well-mannered and conversed easily about many topics, often introducing new ones in the middle of formal tests. Although she easily focused on a task initially, she had substantial difficulty maintaining her attention. She immediately responded appropriately to redirection. Many times, though, her attention to a task was good (particularly on timed tasks), and she seemed determined to do a good job. She did not seem frustrated when tasks became difficult. At times, she realistically stated that she was unable to do a task or item. Juliette was on medication for ADHD on all three examination dates. The results of this evaluation are considered to be valid estimates of her current levels of functioning in the areas assessed.

TESTS ADMINISTERED

Beery-Buktenica Developmental Test of Visual-Motor Integration (4th ed.) (VMI)
Boehm Tests of Basic Concepts—3 (Boehm-3)
Children's Auditory Verbal Learning Test—2 (CAVLT-2)
Clinical Evaluation of Language Fundamentals—3 (CELF-3)
Peabody Picture Vocabulary Test—III (PPVT-III)
Rey Complex Figure Test and Recognition Trial (RCFT)
Wechsler Intelligence Scale for Children—Third Edition (WISC-III)
Woodcock-Johnson III Tests of Cognitive Abilities (WJ III COG)
Woodcock-Johnson III Tests of Achievement (WJ III ACH)
Review of history and informal observations

TEST RESULTS AND INTERPRETATION

Intellectual Functioning

Juliette's performance on tests of overall intellectual functioning (see Table 1) was within the Low Average range. On

Table 1. Tests of Overall Intellectual Functioning

	COMPOSITE	SS	PR
WJ III COG	GIA	84	14
WISC-III	FS IQ	80	9
	VS IQ	74	4
	PS IQ	90	25

SS = Standard Score (M = 100, SD = 15);
PR = Percentile Rank

the WISC-III, Juliette's verbal abilities were significantly low, as well as being significantly lower than her non-verbal abilities. The 16-point discrepancy occurs in approximately 22% of the population and is beyond the .05 level of significance for a 7-year-old child.

On the WJ III COG, substantial differences among cluster scores reflected fairly wide variations in cognitive abilities, from the Low range to the higher end of the Average range. Considered together, Juliette's performances on tests of intellectual functioning and on cognitive abilities that are predictive of specific academic skills suggest that her academic achievement should be within the Low Average range.

Attention, Organization, and Processing Speed

Juliette's obtained scores within the Average range on speed of visual processing (see Table 2). These scores reflect adequate ability to maintain her attention to complete tasks in a timed situation. Time pressure appeared to motivate her to increase her effort. Her attention during untimed tasks was problematic in that she frequently interjected comments unrelated to the task at hand. She was not distracted by environmental visual or auditory stimuli during this evaluation.

Juliette also performed in the Average range on tasks assessing her ability to focus her attention (Auditory Attention) and in the Low Average range in dividing attention within a memory task. (Auditory Working Memory). Her ability to shift her mental set was within the Low Average range (Concept Formation). Thus, her attentional abilities appear to be improved in this one-to-one situation, in relatively brief tasks, and when she is on medication, in comparison to the previously reported difficulties when not on medication.

Juliette's ability to plan and organize was assessed on two different tasks. Although she performed within the High Average range on a task assessing her ability to trace a pattern with a pencil without removing the pencil from the paper or retracing any lines (Planning), she performed quite poorly on a task requiring her to copy a complex geometric figure (RCFT). She drew the figure in parts, duplicated some, and did not integrate the parts, rendering the figure unscorable. One of the obvious differences between these two tasks was the tracing of the figures (already integrated) on the one test (Planning) and the requirement of completely reproducing the figure on the other test (RCFT). As Juliette's visual–motor abilities on reproduction of simple geometric designs were adequate (VMI), the differences in task demands and results among the three tests suggest that her problems on the RCFT were more related to a combination of poor planning, the complexity of the visual–motor integration required, and the low structure of the task. These difficulties are consistent with her diagnosis of ADHD in that individuals with this disorder often display problems with planning and organization, particularly on unstructured tasks.

Memory and Retrieval

Previously reported short-term memory difficulties were also apparent during this testing (see Table 3). Juliette's scores in this area were generally within the Low to Low Average range. However, on two tasks requiring her to follow directions and remember story information, her performance improved. Thus, meaning seems to facilitate performance.

On a list-learning task, Juliette was able to perform within the Average range and was able to maintain that level after the interference of having to repeat a different list. She also, however, included words that were not on the original list. On another task requiring her to learn words associated with rebus-like symbols, she performed in the Low range. She also showed substantial problems with maintaining her level of learning after a delay.

Juliette's ability to retrieve information from long-term memory was significantly impaired. Her difficulties with

Table 2. Tests of Attention, Organization, and Functioning

	CLUSTER/ COMPOSITE/Test	SS	PR
WJ III COG	PROCESSING SPEED	93	32
	Pair Cancellation	101	52
	Auditory Attention	110	75
	Auditory Working Memory	88	21
	Concept Formation	89	23
	Planning	114	83
WISC-III	PROCESSING SPEED INDEX	106	66
CAVLT-2	Intrusions		16
RCFT		unscorable	unscorable
VMI		85	16

Table 3.   Tests of Memory and Retrieval

		CLUSTER/COMPOSITE/Test	SS*	PR	ScS*
Short-Term Memory	WISC-III	Digit Span		9	6
	WJ III COG	Numbers Reversed	82	11	
	CELF-3	Recalling Sentences		5	5
		Concepts and Directions		2	4
	WJ III COG	Understanding Directions	89	22	
		Story Recall	94	33	
	CAVLT-2	Immediate Memory Span	99	47	
		Interference Trial	96	39	
		Immediate Recall	96	39	
Long-Term Retrieval Retrieval Fluency	WJ III COG	Visual-Auditory Learning	70	2	
		Story Recall–Delayed	no score	no score	
	CAVLT-2	Delayed Recall	78	7	
		Recognition Accuracy	85	16	
	WJ III COG	LONG-TERM RETRIEVAL	63	1	
		Retrieval Fluency	70	1	
		Rapid Picture Naming	67	1	

*SS: M = 100, SD = 15.   *ScS: M = 10, SD = 3.

accurate and timely retrieval of information were also apparent in her oral expression, where finding specific words appeared to be difficult for her (see the following section). Problems in these areas have interfered greatly in her learning and are substantiated by descriptions from her parents and former teachers regarding her inability to recall information learned in the past (e.g., color names, letters, numbers). Although it may be problematic, at times, to discern if her observed behavior is related to difficulties storing information in long-term memory or retrieval of information from long-term memory, it is likely that both areas are weak and will continue to affect learning.

Visual-Spatial Functioning
Juliette's abilities in the area of visual–spatial functioning appear to be within the Average range with no obvious

weaknesses. (See Table 4.) No assessment of orthographic functioning (her ability to process letters and letter patterns) was completed due to the low level of her reading and spelling knowledge. However, it is strongly suspected that observations of "reversals" noted by her previous teachers are related to problems with retrieval of exact information rather than to initial visual processing. The similarities in form and sound between the letters b and d (/b/ and /d/ are both voiced stop sounds) cause her confusion when required to retrieve the letter/sound associations..

Juliette's ability to combine visual–spatial processing with a motor response was within the Low Average range when copying simple geometric figures but significantly impaired when attempting to copy a complex geometric figure. Her ability to *trace* simple and more complex geometric figures was in the High Average range. Thus, her visual–spatial construction appears adequate when structure is provided and on relatively simple tasks but breaks down significantly on more unstructured, visually complex tasks.

Table 4.   Tests of Visual–Spatial Functioning

	CLUSTER/ COMPOSITE/Test	SS	PR	ScS
WJ III COG	VISUAL-SPATIAL THINKING	102	56	
	Spatial Relations	111	77	
	Picture Recognition	95	36	
WISC-III	Picture Completion		37	9
	Block Design		37	9
	Object Assembly		25	8
	Coding		75	12
	Symbol Search		50	10

Table 5.   Tests of Visual–Spatial Construction

	CLUSTER/Test	SS	PR	ScS
WJ III COG	Planning	114	83	
VMI		85	16	
RCFT		unscorable	unscorable	

Oral Language

Juliette's abilities in the area of oral language range from significantly below average to average. (See Table 6.) Her auditory processing of speech sounds appears to be within the Low Average to Average range. Furthermore, her ability to discriminate speech sounds under distorted conditions was in the Average range. Thus, phonemic awareness skills, often a contributing factor to problems in learning to read, do not appear to be a weakness. With regard to phonological production, she was heard to occasionally produce sound substitutions in her conversational speech (e.g., /f/ for voiceless "/th/"). The sound substitution errors were inconsistent and, therefore, are not of concern at this time.

With regard to semantics, or understanding meaning, Juliette performed within the Low Average to Average range. On tasks where she had to show her understanding of meaning through oral expression, her performance ranged from Low Average to Average, with some indications that she had more difficulty on tasks requiring specific words and on tasks requiring convergent thinking.

In the area of syntax, or her understanding and use of the form of language, Juliette performed within the Low Average to Average range receptively, but in the Low range expressively. Her conversational language contained noticeable syntactical errors; her utterances often contained grammatical errors with occasional difficulties in conjoining sentences. She had occasional difficulty with subject/verb agreement (e.g., "My friends who has a dog . . .") and verb tense (e.g., "I ride with the girl again" for "I rode . . ."), but had frequent difficulty with the use of irregular verb forms (e.g., "sitted"/"sat," "comed"/"came," "ranned"/"ran") and noun forms (e.g., "mans"/"men"). Some utterances were also incomplete (e.g., "Why has two of them?"). Many of these errors (particularly the application of the regular past tense form in place of irregular verb forms) seem to be related to her difficulties with retrieval of information (noted earlier) which has contributed to difficulties with accurate word retrieval. Word-finding problems may also be part of her difficulty on tasks requiring specific vocabulary and convergent thinking. These problems in word finding are undoubtedly also interfering with her learning in school and with her school performance. It is difficult for her to show what she knows on tasks requiring her to recall specific information (e.g., class discussions of learned information).

Academic Achievement

Reading

Juliette is essentially a beginning reader. Formal assessment findings were in the Very Low and Low ranges, significantly

Table 6.   Tests of Oral Language

		CLUSTER/COMPOSITE/Test	SS	PR	ScS
Phonemic Awareness Auditory Processing	WJ III COG	AUDITORY PROCESSING	98	45	
		PHONEMIC AWARENESS III	87	20	
		Sound Blending	92	30	
		Incomplete Words	95	38	
		Sound Awareness	86	17	
		Auditory Attention	110	75	
Semantics: Receptive	Boehm-3			17	
	CELF-3	Word Classes		37	9
	PPVT-3		84	14	
Semantics: Expressive	WISC-III	Information		9	6
		Comprehension		37	9
		Similarities		2	4
		Vocabulary		5	5
	WJ III COG	General Information	86	17	
		Picture Vocabulary	91	27	
		Oral Comprehension	87	19	
		Verbal Comprehension	77	6	
Syntax	CELF-3	RECEPTIVE LANGUAGE	86	18	
		Sentence Structure		50	10
		EXPRESSIVE LANGUAGE	69	2	
		Word Structure		9	6
		Formulated Sentences		9	6

Table 7.   Tests of Academic Achievement

	CLUSTER/Test	SS	PR
WJ III COG	BROAD READING	60	4
	Letter-Word Identification	72	3
	Word Attack	79	8
	Passage Comprehension	59	0.3
	Spelling	81	11
	Spelling of Sounds	90	26
	Calculation	82	11
	Math Fluency	84	14
	Applied Problems	75	5

below her overall level of intellectual functioning and her levels of predicted achievement. (See Table 7.)

On an informal task assessing her ability to give letter names and sounds in response to printed letters, Juliette was able to give the correct names or sounds 33% of the time, and these correct responses were frequently in response to hints/guidance from the examiner. Occasionally, she recited the entire alphabet in order to retrieve the name of a letter. Although she was able to recite most of the alphabet correctly, she said "n n" for "m n" and "x n o z" for "x y z."

Written Language

Consistent with her performance in reading, Juliette's development in writing has been slow. On formal testing she performed within the Low Average range on tests of spelling, reflecting her ability to write some letters corresponding to letter names or sounds and to write letters corresponding to the beginning and/or ending sounds of words/nonsense words (reflecting her relatively good phonemic awareness). She was unable to write enough to complete either the Writing Fluency or Writing Samples tests on the WJ III ACH. She wrote her first name correctly; in response to being asked to write the alphabet, she wrote, "ACBOgfxyihnokq." Thus, formal test results do not really reflect her limited progress in this area.

Math

On formal math testing, Juliette performed within the Low Average range on tests of computation (while performing in the Low range on a test assessing her ability to apply math concepts). Informally, she was able to recite numbers correctly from 1 to 23. It is likely that the problems related to recall of number symbols and number names noted by her previous teachers are related to her difficulty with retrieval of information from long-term memory and continue to affect her math learning. It is possible that her ability to apply

math concepts is strongly influenced by the fact that her attention in math is often directed toward recalling specific information (symbols, names, facts), rather than to thinking through solutions to problems. Although her math achievement scores are not significantly below predicted achievement, they are much lower than would be expected of a child her age.

SUMMARY AND CONCLUSIONS

Juliette Reid was seen for a neuropsychological evaluation to assess her cognitive strengths and weaknesses and current levels of functioning. Her overall intellectual functioning and her predicted achievement levels are within the Low Average range. Her auditory and visual processing abilities are within the Low Average to Average range. She displays significant weaknesses in short-term memory and the ability to retrieve information from long-term memory. Her retrieval problems significantly interfere with her oral expression and with her academic learning in the areas of reading, writing, and math. Her oral language abilities regarding semantics are generally in the Low Average range but she displays significant problems in expressive syntax. Consistent with her previous diagnosis of ADHD, for which she is receiving medication, she has difficulty with planning and organization, particularly on complex and divergent tasks.

Diagnosis

Reading Disorder
Mathematical Disorder
Disorder of Written Expression
Expressive Language Disorder
Attention-Deficit/Hyperactivity Disorder, Predominantly
   Inattentive type

RECOMMENDATIONS

Programmatic Recommendations

1. Because of the significant discrepancy between current reading levels and her level of intellectual functioning and predicted achievement levels, Juliette should continue to be served in the special education learning disabilities program. Additionally, although her current scores in math and written language are not significantly discrepant from cognitive functioning, these are obvious

problematic areas for her, and she would also benefit from intensive help in these areas.

2. Juliette's scores on formal testing during this evaluation strongly suggest that she should qualify for speech/language services. Therefore, it is recommended that the IEP team and the Speech/Language Pathologist at Goode Elementary review these results to determine if further evaluation and/or consideration for placement are appropriate at this time.

3. The nature and significance of Juliette's problems also strongly suggest that she will profit more from small group and individual pull-out or self-contained services rather than inclusion or consultative services, because she will need intensive, specific therapy.

4. Reportedly, there has been some consideration given to retaining Juliette for the next school year. Although it is understandable that local school professionals are concerned about her ability to function in a second-grade classroom, it is strongly recommended that she not be retained. She will have significant difficulties in either a first- or second-grade classroom that will not be alleviated unless her programming is responsive to her specific needs. Retention will not have any favorable impact on development and may, in fact, give a false sense of progress in relation to her classmates while masking her language and learning problems.

5. Juliette will need at least one after-school activity that she enjoys to help preserve her good self-image. Try to provide immediate reinforcement and feedback for small accomplishments.

Instructional Recommendations

Some of the following recommendations are adapted from those developed by the Atlanta Speech School, Atlanta, Georgia.

Oral Language, Word Finding, and Retrieval

1. Juliette's significant problems with retrieval of information have affected her ability to retrieve words. Strengthening Juliette's vocabulary knowledge and the relationships between words and word classes should significantly improve her ability to retrieve specific words. Overlearning of specific words will help her to retrieve specific word forms such as irregular verbs. A program that is particularly helpful in this area is the *Language Processing Kit* (LinguiSystems, 800-776-4332, www.linguisystems.com).

2. Because of Juliette's problems with retrieval of information, it will be helpful for her parents and teachers to provide her with cues to aid her recall. She may frequently describe a concept or word but be unable to "pull" the exact word. A summary of techniques for prompting word retrieval is attached to this report.

3. Teach Juliette strategies for self-prompting word retrieval. A helpful program is the *Word Finding Intervention Program* (PRO-ED, 800-897-3202, www.proedinc.com).

4. Because of Juliette's memory difficulties, give directions in small units and use advance organizers.
   a) Instead of saying, "Take out your math book, turn to page 75, and copy the problems in columns 1 and 3. Use lined paper," give the instructions in smaller chunks, allowing Juliette to complete each before giving the next one. As she is more successful, gradually increase the number of steps she is required to remember at one time.
   b) Give her advance organizers before giving her directions so that she knows what to expect. For example, say, "I want you to do 10 math problems in your math book now. I will want you to copy the problems first on a clean sheet of lined paper," prior to beginning the specific directions. It may also be helpful to tell her in advance the number of steps in the directions.

5. Teach Juliette some simple cognitive strategies for facilitating both storage and retrieval of information. A summary of strategies is attached.

6. When Juliette makes an error in grammar or syntax, model the correct usage and occasionally ask Juliette to repeat it.

7. Help Juliette identify what listeners need to know when beginning to relate an experience or summarize a story. Discuss the need to let the listener know the general situation and the people involved. Give examples of summaries beginning with nonspecific terms such as "he" versus specific terms such as "a little boy who was lost." Help her identify problems in your summaries before requiring her to improve her own.

8. Because of Juliette's retrieval problems, she will have more difficulty with a presentation style that has fast-paced oral questions or drills and one that requires recitations and explanations. She will perform best when instruction is presented in multiple ways, assessment is varied in format, pace of presentation is slower, and a multiple-choice format is provided when needed (e.g., "Was the boy sad or mad?").

Reading and Written Language

1. Juliette's difficulties with memory and retrieval are causing significant delays in her development of reading, spelling, and written expression. Therefore, she will need intensive, specialized instruction to "jump start" her skills in these areas. Drill and practice to promote "overlearning" will be important to her development. Organize the sound/letter system to facilitate Juliette's learning and retrieval of letter sounds. An organizational system that would be helpful is the "natural" system inherent in the way speech sounds are produced by the mouth. A program that uses this approach is the *Lindamood Phoneme Sequencing Program* (LiPS) (PRO-ED, 800-897-3202, www.proedinc.com).

   If LiPS is not used, select a highly systematic, explicit, and multisensory program for teaching basic reading skills and provide ample practice reading in decodable text for reinforcement and generalization of skills learned.

2. As Juliette begins to develop her decoding and spelling skills, it will be important also to develop her fluency in reading. Use a research-validated commercial program such as *Great Leaps Reading* (Diarmuid, 877-475-3277, www.greatleaps.com), a repeated reading procedure, and/or speed drills to train rapid recognition of words and word parts.

Mathematics

1. Give Juliette an organizational system that will help her understand basic arithmetic concepts. For example, keep a number line available for her to refer to until she has learned all number symbols. To help her learn numbers, point to the number in the number line and then ask her to recall the correct number name. Encourage her to rely less and less on the cueing system as she becomes more proficient in recalling number names. As Juliette becomes more proficient at using the number line, show her how to use it in solving written math problems. Ensure that when she is solving simple addition and subtraction problems she understands the processes.

2. Provide counting activities using the technique, "count it–move it" (e.g., moving a token to the side as she counts it, jumping from number tile to number tile placed on the floor) so that her movement will reinforce her understanding of one-to-one correspondence.

3. Have her use concrete manipulatives or motor activities to solve math addition and subtraction problems before introducing pictures or math symbols in problems. Keep the number line visible so that she can refer to it (both as an aid to retrieval of the number names and as an aid to adding and subtracting). Permit her to use her fingers to aid in adding and subtracting until she no longer needs to do it.

4. When Juliette has mastered her facts, provide drill with timed math and flash cards so that she can increase her speed in retrieving math facts.

ADHD

Although Juliette's ADHD appears to be well-managed with the help of the medication, some suggestions for further benefiting Juliette's development of attention strategies, organizational skills, and self-esteem are provided in an addendum.

Adapted from Judith M. Kroese, Ph.D., CCC-SLP

Wechsler Intelligence Scale for Children—Third Edition (WISC-III)

Subtest	Scaled Score	Subtest	Scaled Score
Information	6	Picture Completion	9
Similarities	4	Coding	12
Arithmetic	3	Picture Arrangement	4
Vocabulary	5	Block Design	9
Comprehension	9	Object Assembly	8
Digit Span	6	Symbol Search	10

Composites	SS	PR	
Verbal	74	4	
Performance	90	25	
Full Scale	80	9	
Verbal Comprehension	79	8	
Perceptual Organization	86	18	
Freedom from Distractibility	69	2	
Processing Speed	106	66	

Subject's Name: ___Juliette Reid_____ Scores Based on Grade ____ Age 7-3 Norms

Date of Birth: _____11-23-93_____ Type of Score: SS X   PR__ RPI__ Grade__ Age__

Woodcock-Johnson III Factors/Clusters and Tests of Cognitive Abilities—Score Profile

	Category/Factor	Score	Standard Battery	Score	Extended Battery	Score
Intellectual Ability	General Intellectual Ability	84	Verbal Comprehension	77	General Information	86
			Visual-Auditory Learning	70	Retrieval Fluency	70
			Spatial Relations	111	Picture Recognition	95
			Sound Blending	92	Auditory Attention	110
			Concept Formation	89	Analysis-Synthesis	105
			Visual Matching	93	Decision Speed	94
			Numbers Reversed	82	Memory for Words	NA
	Brief Intellectual Ability		Verbal Comprehension			
			Concept Formation			
			Visual Matching			
Cognitive Performance	Verbal Ability	82	Verbal Comprehension	77	General Information	86
	Thinking Ability	92	Visual-Auditory Learning	70	Retrieval Fluency	70
			Spatial Relations	111	Picture Recognition	95
			Sound Blending	92	Auditory Attention	110
			Concept Formation	89	Analysis-Synthesis	105
	Cognitive Efficiency	85	Visual Matching	93	Decision Speed	94
			Numbers Reversed	82	Memory for Words	
CHC Factors	Comprehension-Knowledge	82	Verbal Comprehension	77	General Information	86
	Long-Term Retrieval	63	Visual-Auditory Learning	70	Retrieval Fluency	70
	Visual-Spatial Thinking	102	Spatial Relations	111	Picture Recognition	95
	Auditory Processing	98	Sound Blending	92	Auditory Attention	110
	Fluid Reasoning	97	Concept Formation	89	Analysis-Synthesis	105
	Processing Speed	93	Visual Matching	93	Decision Speed	94
	Short-Term Memory		Numbers Reversed	82	Memory for Words	NA
Clinical Clusters	Phonemic Awareness	87	Sound Blending	92	[Sound Awareness]	86
			Incomplete Words	95		
	Working Memory	82	Numbers Reversed	82		
			Auditory Working Memory	88		
	Broad Attention	89	Numbers Reversed	82	Auditory Attention	110
			Auditory Working Memory	88	Pair Cancellation	101
	Cognitive Fluency	67			Retrieval Fluency	70
					Decision Speed	94
					Rapid Picture Naming	67
	Executive Processes	96	Concept Formation	89	Planning	114
					Pair Cancellation	101
	Delayed Recall				Visual-Auditory Learning–Delayed	(z/PR)
					Story Recall–Delayed (ACH)	(z/PR)
	Knowledge	NA			General Information	86
					Academic Knowledge (ACH)	NA

NA = Not administered.

NS = No score obtained.

Subject's Name: _____Juliette Reid_____   Scores Based on Grade __ Age <u>7-3</u> Norms
Date of Birth: _____11-23-93_____   Type of Score: SS <u>X</u>   PR__ RPI__ Grade__ Age__

Woodcock-Johnson III Clusters and Tests of Achievement—Score Profile

Areas	Clusters	Score	Standard Battery	Score	Extended Battery	Score
Reading	Broad Reading	60	Letter-Word Identification	72		
			Reading Fluency	NS		
			Passage Comprehension	59		
	Basic Reading Skills	74	Letter-Word Identification	72	Word Attack	79
	Reading Comprehension		Passage Comprehension	59	Reading Vocabulary	NA
Oral Language	Oral Language	84	Story Recall	94	Picture Vocabulary	91
			Understanding Directions	89	Oral Comprehension	87
	Listening Comprehension	84	Understanding Directions	89	Oral Comprehension	87
	Oral Expression	90	Story Recall	94	Picture Vocabulary	91
Math	Broad Math	78	Calculation	82		
			Math Fluency	84		
			Applied Problems	75		
	Math Calculation Skills	82	Calculation	82		
			Math Fluency	84		
	Math Reasoning		Applied Problems	75	Quantitative Concepts	
Written Language	Broad Written Language	NA	Spelling	81		
			Writing Fluency	NS		
			Writing Samples	NA		
	Basic Writing Skills	NA	Spelling	81	Editing	
	Written Expression	NA	Writing Fluency	NS		
			Writing Samples	NA		
Other Clusters	Academic Knowledge	NA			Academic Knowledge	NA
	Phoneme/Grapheme Knowledge	83			Word Attack	79
					Spelling of Sounds	90
	Academic Skills	73	Letter-Word Identification	72		
			Spelling	81		
			Calculation	82		
	Academic Fluency	69	Reading Fluency	NS		
			Writing Fluency	NS		
			Math Fluency	84		
	Academic Applications	NA	Passage Comprehension	59		
			Writing Samples	NA		
			Applied Problems	75		
	Total Achievement		Letter-Word Identification	72		
			Reading Fluency	NS		
			Passage Comprehension	59		
			Spelling	81		
			Writing Fluency	NS		
			Writing Samples	NA		
			Calculation	82		
			Math Fluency	84		
			Applied Problems	75		
	Supplemental Tests/Scores				Story Recall—Delayed	NS
					Sound Awareness	86
					Punctuation & Capitalization	NA
					Handwriting	NA

NA = Not administered.

NS = No score obtained.

Educational Evaluation Report

Name: Nathan Thalgott
Age: 7-5
Grade: 2.2

Dates of Evaluation: 11/1, 11/14, 11/15/01
School: Hobson Elementary School
Referred by: Ms. Jana Carnes

REASON FOR REFERRAL

Nathan's teachers and parents requested this educational evaluation to help increase their understanding of Nathan's strengths and weaknesses and to help generate instructional recommendations to assist him within the school setting. Ms. Carnes, the special education teacher at Hobson Elementary School, made the formal referral for an educational evaluation.

BACKGROUND INFORMATION

The following information was obtained from a review of the Evaluation Referral Form completed by Nathan's teacher, his school records, and interviews with school staff working with Nathan. Nathan resides with his parents and younger twin sisters in Rivertown, CT. His family situation is stable and supportive. Nathan's family history reveals other members who have experienced attentional and/or learning difficulties.

Although Nathan is not described as having primary health or medical difficulties, school referral information indicates that he has frequent sinus problems and some food sensitivities/allergies. Nathan's fine- and gross-motor skills and problems with interpersonal relationships are described as areas of concern. Since kindergarten, Nathan has received occupational therapy support.

In addition to concerns regarding motor and social development, a number of other issues prompted this referral. Nathan's teacher described the following problems: Nathan becomes overstimulated easily and is perceived to have an inconsistent span of attention and concentration; he shows difficulties with transitions between activities and following directions in the classroom. He demonstrates unusual and repetitive behaviors, does not readily pick up on social cues, has limited affect, seems in his own world and uninvolved in classroom activities, shows problems in developing and maintaining peer relationships, and draws his letters in an upward manner.

Ms. Carnes reports that Nathan engages in a repetitive behavior of putting his index fingers into his nose and then touching his eyes. Nathan's parents and teachers are concerned about this behavior for obvious health and hygiene reasons. Nathan is currently being treated for conjunctivitis. This behavior persists despite a number of strategies and informal interventions tried by Nathan's parents and teacher.

EVALUATION PLAN

Woodcock-Johnson III Tests of Cognitive Abilities
    (WJ III COG): Tests 1–9, 11–17, 19–20
Woodcock-Johnson III Tests of Achievement
    (WJ III ACH), Form A: Tests 1–11, 15, 17–18
Informal assessments and diagnostic teaching activities

OBSERVATIONS DURING TESTING

Testing was conducted over three sessions at Hobson Elementary School. Nathan came cooperatively to all sessions. He presented himself as a generally affable child with a somewhat detached manner. His affect tended to be relatively flat and reserved. His interpersonal style and conversational tone lacked a level of modulation typical for a child his age. He did not show much expression or animation— even when discussing topics of apparent interest. A few moments into the first testing session, Nathan placed his fingers in his nose and then touched his eyes. To reduce this behavior during testing, a behavioral strategy was implemented whereby, at the evaluator's whispered prompt, "Hands," Nathan was to fold his hands in his lap and would then receive a positive comment. After several practices, Nathan was able to respond successfully. Twice, Nathan started to raise his fingers to his face, caught himself, and folded his hands into his lap without a prompt. During informal conversation and discussions, Nathan was able to demonstrate a generally age-appropriate level of background knowledge. He stated that he liked school and that his favorite time is "free time," during which he enjoys playing with the building materials. Nathan says that he sometimes finds math to be hard but that he likes writing his own stories. Nathan seemed to have difficulty responding to open-ended questions, relating information in a somewhat

BORDERS.
BOOKS MUSIC MOVIES CAFE

Borders Books #0267
1390 W. University Avenue
St. Paul, MN 55104
Phone: 651.641.0026
Fax: 651.641.0142

Packing List

512766638 - 000

Bill To

DAVID SCHROT
757 SEXTANT AVE. W.

ROSEVILLE MN 55113

Ship To

David Schrot
757 Sextant Ave. W.
Roseville MN 55113
United States Of America

Order# 25537253	**Order Date** 09/10/05	**Ship Date** 9/12/05	**Shipped Via** USPS DELIVERY CONFIRM

Title	Author	Title Number	Qty
WOODCOCK JOHNSON (R) 3 REPORTS RECOMMEND	MATHER, NANCY	0471419990	1

Thank you for shopping at Borders!

Have questions about this order?
Please contact Customer Service at 1-888-81BOOKS.

Borders Online Reserve

At BordersStores.com, you can search for and reserve items from the comfort of home and pick them up later at the Borders store
of your choice.

Returns

Returns will be accepted at any Borders store. Please bring your original receipt along with this packing list.

For your reference, the Borders store return policy is as follows:

Merchandise presented for return, including sale or marked-down items, must be accompanied by the original Borders store receipt.
Returns must be completed within 30 days of purchase. The purchase price will be refunded in the medium of purchase (cash,
credit card or gift card). Items purchased by check may be returned for cash after 10 business days.

Merchandise unaccompanied by the original Borders store receipt, or presented for return beyond 30 days from date of purchase,
must be carried by Borders at the time of the return. The lowest price offered for the item during the 12 month period prior
to the return will be refunded via a gift card.

Opened videos, discs, and cassettes may only be exchanged for replacement copies of the original item. Periodicals, newspapers,
out-of-print, collectible and pre-owned items may not be returned. Returned merchandise must be in saleable condition.

For Easy Shipping orders, we will refund shipping and gift wrap fees if the return is a result of our error.

MOE7246007

disjointed or disorganized manner. When questions were more structured, Nathan formulated a response more easily.

Nathan consistently used his right hand for all pencil/paper tasks. He grasped the pencil close to the tip with an awkward grip. Throughout testing, Nathan was generally accepting of feedback and strategies, but did not find it easy to generalize a strategy from one task to another. His attention and concentration were somewhat inconsistent for his grade, but manageable in a one-to-one setting. Nathan's attention diminished when tasks became more abstract or re-quired sustained listening. The current results are considered valid and reasonable estimates of Nathan's abilities and skills at this time.

RESULTS OF COGNITIVE TESTING

The WJ III Tests of Cognitive Abilities is a comprehensive battery of individually administered tests measuring different intellectual/cognitive abilities. Nathan obtained scores on the WJ III COG as shown in Table 1.

Table 1. WJ III COG Scores

Cluster/Test	Age	Easy to Diff		RPI	PR	SS (±1 SEM)
GIA (Ext)	**7-2**	**6-2**	**8-6**	**88/90**	**42**	**97 (94–99)**
Comp-Knowledge	**9-0**	**7-8**	**10-9**	**97/90**	**83**	**114 (110–119)**
Verbal Comprehension	9-3	7-10	11-0	97/90	85	115 (110–121)
General Information	8-10	7-5	10-6	97/90	79	112 (106–118)
Long-Term Retrieval	**7-10**	**5-6**	**15-3**	**91/90**	**63**	**105 (99–110)**
Visual-Auditory Learning	8-1	6-3	12-6	93/90	65	106 (101–111)
Retrieval Fluency	7-4	4-1	22	90/90	48	99 (94–105)
Visual-Spatial Thinking	**5-0**	**4-0**	**6-7**	**66/90**	**6**	**76 (72–81)**
Spatial Relations	5-9	4-7	7-8	77/90	22	89 (84–93)
Picture Recognition	4-3	3-4	5-7	54/90	7	78 (73–83)
Auditory Processing	**9-9**	**7-1**	**15-9**	**96/90**	**84**	**115 (109–121)**
Sound Blending	11-11	8-9	18-1	98/90	92	121 (114–128)
Auditory Attention	7-7	5-7	12-0	91/90	53	101 (95–107)
Fluid Reasoning	**5-6**	**4-9**	**6-2**	**31/90**	**5**	**76 (71–81)**
Concept Formation	5-9	4-11	6-6	50/90	12	82 (77–87)
Analysis-Synthesis	5-3	4-5	5-10	17/90	2	70 (61–79)
Processing Speed	**7-0**	**6-6**	**7-8**	**82/90**	**36**	**95 (92–97)**
Visual Matching	6-11	6-6	7-5	74/90	33	93 (90–96)
Decision Speed	7-3	6-5	8-2	88/90	45	98 (94–102)
Short-Term Memory	**8-0**	**6-11**	**9-7**	**94/90**	**63**	**105 (98–111)**
Numbers Reversed	6-6	6-1	7-3	70/90	32	93 (88–97)
Memory for Words	11-4	9-2	15-4	99/90	86	116 (108–124)
Phonemic Awareness	**13-8**	**8-10**	**>28**	**98/90**	**97**	**127 (121–133)**
Sound Blending	11-11	8-9	18-1	98/90	92	121 (114–128)
Incomplete Words	19	9-2	>33	98/90	96	127 (119–135)
Working Memory	**6-5**	**5-10**	**7-3**	**72/90**	**27**	**91 (87–95)**
Numbers Reversed	6-6	6-1	7-3	70/90	32	93 (88–97)
Auditory Work Memory	6-3	5-3	7-5	75/90	26	90 (85–96)
Executive Processes	**6-3**	**5-3**	**7-6**	**77/90**	**20**	**87 (84–91)**
Concept Formation	5-9	4-11	6-6	50/90	12	82 (77–87)
Pair Cancellation	6-9	5-11	7-9	81/90	34	94 (92–96)
Planning	7-2	4-0	>28	90/90	47	99 (84–114)

	Standard Scores			Discrepancy		Significant
Intra-Cognitive Discrepancies	Actual	Predicted	Difference	PR	SD	SS (±1.5 SEE)
Comp-Knowledge	114	96	+18	93	+1.46	No
Long-Term Retrieval	105	97	+8	73	+0.60	No
Visual-Spatial Thinking	76	101	−25	4	−1.72	Yes
Auditory Processing	115	97	+18	93	+1.45	No
Fluid Reasoning	76	102	−26	1	−2.19	Yes
Processing Speed	95	99	−4	38	−0.31	No
Short-Term Memory	105	98	+7	71	+0.56	No
Phonemic Awareness	127	97	+30	98	+2.13	Yes
Working Memory	91	97	−6	29	−0.54	No

Discussion of Cognitive Testing

Although Nathan's overall cognitive/intellectual ability score suggests average functioning, his cognitive profile is characterized by variation among his abilities, from Low Average to Superior. As the differences among Nathan's abilities are both statistically and developmentally significant, any "full-scale" or global composite score, such as the GIA, should be interpreted with caution.

Nathan demonstrates a number of cognitive strengths and assets. He is quite proficient in phonological awareness skills and in his ability to focus his auditory attention selectively.

Nathan also possesses good vocabulary knowledge and experiential information but demonstrates these best in response to structured questions. He becomes somewhat less effective when he is required to work with verbal information at a more abstract level.

Nathan demonstrates average abilities to retrieve newly learned associations between visual and verbal information (e.g., familiar words for unfamiliar visual symbols). The ability to store and recall information undoubtedly assists Nathan in acquiring and then conveying his knowledge and information, and is critical to learning basic academic skills.

Nathan demonstrates good capability with short-term memory, particularly in immediate awareness and memory span. He has greater difficulty with tasks that require him mentally to manipulate and reorganize information while holding it in memory.

Nathan shows considerable difficulties with tasks involving visual–spatial thinking. On the Spatial Relations test Nathan was able to determine which "parts" made up a "whole" as long as the shapes of the pieces were obviously different from each other and required no mental rotation. As the problems increased in complexity, Nathan appeared perplexed, became distracted, and needed encouragement to continue. After only a few more complex items, Nathan stated that they were too hard, and appeared to guess on the remaining items. Similar difficulties were noted with a picture recognition–memory test. As the amount of visual information increased, Nathan's attention and effectiveness decreased.

Although scoring technically in the Average range, Nathan has begun to show some frustration and inefficient performance on perceptual accuracy and speed. Nathan's RPI score of 74/90 on the Visual Matching test suggests that even under the optimal conditions of the test setting (i.e., 3-minute task, no environmental distractions), Nathan is still working at frustration level. He did not have difficulty on a timed test requiring matching of pictures based on conceptual similarity (e.g., *rose,* car, shovel, *tulip,* fork).

Nathan's most significant area of cognitive weakness appears to be in his ability to work with abstract relationships and novel problem solving. Nathan demonstrated difficulties on both measures of fluid reasoning, measures of the ability to determine essential from nonessential elements, group information based on superordinate attributes, or by using and extending given rules. Administration procedures of both tests involve explicit instruction, correction and clarification when necessary, and positive feedback for correct responses. Despite this highly structured format, Nathan found the tasks to be very confusing. These types of abilities are necessary for higher-order reasoning.

The pattern of strengths and weaknesses that Nathan demonstrates within this cognitive profile, as well as his behaviors, are consistent with a syndrome referred to as "nonverbal learning disabilities," although this term is somewhat misleading. In fact, a number of elements of receptive language processing and organized expressive language can be affected profoundly by the types of cognitive difficulties associated with this type of learning disability. The term "nonverbal" essentially attempts to set up a distinction between this type of profile and a pattern of linguistic difficulties often associated with phonological dyslexia.

Nathan's current profile is just that—a profile of test results situated in the presence of other concerns. Nathan also shows motoric difficulties, behavioral compulsions, and poor social skills. Additional school anecdotal records indicate that Nathan is easily overstimulated and finds it difficult to move readily from one activity to another. These additional characteristics may ultimately serve as diagnostic support confirming a profile of nonverbal learning disabilities. This type of profile and the accompanying behavioral characteristics can also be present in a variety of other low-incidence neurological disorders, or they can be part of broader patterns encompassing other neurological–physiological or psychological issues. Therefore the Evaluation and Planning Team should consider this current profile for Nathan as a *preliminary indication* of the need for further neurological or neuropsychological evaluation before an accurate differential diagnosis can be determined.

Discrepancies

Nathan's WJ III cognitive profile indicates significant weaknesses in Visual-Spatial Thinking (discrepancy =

–1.72) and Fluid Reasoning (–2.19) in relation to his other cognitive abilities. He has considerable strengths (albeit not quite achieving statistical significance) in Comprehension-Knowledge (discrepancy = +1.46) and Auditory Processing (+1.45), and a significant strength in Phonemic Awareness (+2.13).

Additionally, Nathan's intracognitive discrepancy profile should be considered from a pragmatic perspective. The differences among Nathan's abilities undoubtedly create confusion and frustration for Nathan's teachers, parents, and indeed for Nathan himself. Nathan "knows" much information and is often quite competent in presenting what he knows when the questions are specific. He is much less proficient if the task requires him to manipulate, categorize, or work inferentially with what he knows. It is sometimes hard to appreciate the fact that youngsters who appear "bright" and capable and have a good fund of knowledge may still require assistance in "discovering" patterns and conceptual relationships among the things that they "know" or in generalizing connections from one situation or type of information to another.

RESULTS OF ACHIEVEMENT TESTING

The WJ III Tests of Achievement comprise a comprehensive battery of individually administered tests measuring oral language, reading, mathematics, written language, and general knowledge. Nathan's scored levels of performance in each skill area are shown in Table 2.

Discussion of Achievement Testing

Nathan's academic profile indicates that he has been developing at a more or less average rate relative to his grade-peers. However, certain responses reflect the difficulties that were observed within his cognitive profile. (Note: Examples are *not* actual test items.)

The impact of Nathan's cognitive weaknesses apparently affects elements of his language comprehension, especially when he is required to interpret spatial information framed in increasingly complex syntax. The Understanding Directions test required Nathan to point to various objects in a

Table 2. WJ III ACH Scores

Cluster/Test	Grade	Easy to Diff.		RPI	PR	SS (± SEM)
Oral Language	**1.0**	**<K.0**	**3.0**	**85/90**	**33**	**94 (90–97)**
Story Recall	5.5	1.0	>18.0	95/90	85	115 (108–123)
Understanding Directions	K.1	<K.0	1.1	62/90	17	86 (82–89)
Listening Comprehension	**1.7**	**K.7**	**3.0**	**89/90**	**48**	**99 (95–103)**
Understanding Directions	K.1	<K.0	1.1	62/90	17	86 (82–89)
Oral Comprehension	3.5	2.3	5.1	98/90	81	113 (108–119)
Broad Reading	**2.6**	**2.3**	**3.1**	**98/90**	**75**	**110 (108–112)**
Letter-Word Identification	2.8	2.5	3.2	99/90	78	112 (109–114)
Reading Fluency	2.6	2.1	3.1	97/90	67	106 (104–109)
Passage Comprehension	2.4	2.0	3.0	95/90	64	105 (101–109)
Reading Comprehension	**2.3**	**1.8**	**3.0**	**94/90**	**64**	**105 (102–108)**
Passage Comprehension	2.4	2.0	3.0	95/90	64	105 (101–109)
Reading Vocabulary	2.1	1.7	2.9	94/90	60	104 (101–107)
Broad Mathematics	**2.2**	**1.6**	**3.0**	**93/90**	**61**	**104 (100–109)**
Calculation	2.6	2.1	3.3	97/90	77	111 (104–118)
Math Fluency	2.4	K.6	4.5	92/90	62	104 (101–108)
Applied Problems	1.8	1.3	2.4	85/90	43	97 (93–101)
Math Calculation Skills	**2.6**	**1.8**	**3.6**	**95/90**	**76**	**110 (105–116)**
Calculation	2.6	2.1	3.3	97/90	77	111 (104–118)
Math Fluency	2.4	K.6	4.5	92/90	62	104 (101–108)
Math Reasoning	**1.7**	**1.2**	**2.2**	**81/90**	**35**	**94 (91–98)**
Applied Problems	1.8	1.3	2.4	85/90	43	97 (93–101)
Quantitative Concepts	1.5	1.0	2.1	75/90	29	92 (87–96)
Broad Written Language	**2.0**	**1.5**	**2.8**	**92/90**	**56**	**102 (98–106)**
Spelling	2.2	1.8	2.8	96/90	67	107 (102–111)
Writing Fluency	2.3	1.6	3.1	90/90	51	100 (94–107)
Writing Samples	1.6	1.2	2.3	85/90	38	95 (90–100)
Written Expression	**1.9**	**1.4**	**2.8**	**88/90**	**42**	**97 (92–102)**
Writing Fluency	2.3	1.6	3.1	90/90	51	100 (94–107)
Writing Samples	1.6	1.2	2.3	85/90	38	95 (90–100)

picture after listening to a sequence of recorded instructions. Initially, the instructions were relatively simple (e.g., "Point to the star," "Point to the dog and then point to the flower"); however, they steadily increased in the number of steps in the sequence (i.e., items to be remembered), complexity of syntax (e.g., "Point to the car and then *either* point to the chair *or* the couch"), and inclusion of linguistic concepts (e.g., spatial—in front of, under; temporal—before, while; conditional—if, unless). When the instructions began to denote subtler, more sophisticated relationships, Nathan's efficiency was lost.

Nathan's difficulties with this task, in light of his cognitive profile, have profound implications for numerous academic tasks—beginning at the basic level of following directions in his classroom. Teachers or other individuals in a school setting often present children with strings of instructions that have implicit changes in tense, sequence, or condition, or use vocabulary that presumes an understanding of temporal or spatial concepts.

In noticeable contrast to these difficulties, Nathan performed in the High Average range on two other oral language tests, Story Recall and Oral Comprehension. He displayed good ability to use his associative recall and memory for contextual language to retell the important elements of stories and to demonstrate his understanding of short discourse. Despite his excellent performance, however, Nathan's errors on the latter test suggested problems in understanding certain syntactic patterns.

Nathan has acquired an average level of academic skill in reading and written language. His recitation of the alphabet was slow but accurate. His handwriting showed inconsistent spacing between letters and between words. At his grade level, the curriculum demands in these areas remain relatively concrete. Nathan is likely to require assistance with higher-level comprehension tasks in reading and for organization of expository writing, once the curriculum demands begin to present him with the need to *apply* his skills, especially in those areas where understanding of relationships among events and elements of information are critical, such as science and social studies, and fiction with multiple plots and sophisticated character development.

Nathan's performance in basic math skills was strong. His ability to rote skip-count and knowledge of simple calendar concepts (days of the week, days in a month) were age appropriate. His performance in math reasoning, especially in Quantitative Concepts, however, reflects his weakness in abstract reasoning and visual–spatial thinking. Math is an area that is inherently more abstract even at the initial stages of learning, and Nathan's performance on Quantita-

tive Concepts has started to indicate conceptual problems. Nathan had difficulties with ordinal numbers (e.g., "Show me the fourth in line"), with some basic mathematical vocabulary and symbols, and in the logic governing number sequences and patterns.

Right now Nathan is able to do simple single-digit addition and subtraction, and showed an understanding of a basic multiplication by skip-counting by 5s. These skills are fairly concrete and are generally able to be learned by rote memorization; however, the abstract concepts that lay the foundation for learning higher-level calculation skills such as place value and regrouping for addition and subtraction are more problematic and have a strong spatial component.

Nathan's cognitive profile suggests that he is *significantly at risk* for academic difficulties in the coming years in all academic tasks that require reasoning with abstract concepts, organization, sequencing, conceptualization, and extended written production. Nathan's parents and teachers need to consider and anticipate the tasks that are likely to present Nathan with difficulties, and should not wait until he has failed or fallen significantly behind his classmates before providing supportive educational services and making appropriate modifications and accommodations.

ABILITY/ACHIEVEMENT DISCREPANCY

Presently, Nathan's actual academic skill levels are generally within his own predicted levels. (See Table 3.) However, caution is needed when interpreting these results. A lack of discrepancy does not rule out a *clinical* diagnosis of learning disabilities or another clinically definable condition.

SUMMARY AND RECOMMENDATIONS

Nathan's current evaluation suggests that he is a youngster with *at least* average overall cognitive/intellectual ability. His cognitive profile indicates a significant amount of variation among his abilities. His primary difficulties are with visual–spatial thinking and higher-order abstract reasoning. Related difficulties are also noted on tasks that require rapid visual processing of symbols and mental reorganization of information in working memory. In contrast, Nathan has a good fund of general information and vocabulary knowledge, strong auditory and phonological awareness skills, and good associative learning and recall.

Nathan's pattern of cognitive strengths and weaknesses

Table 3. Ability/Achievement Discrepancies*

Discrepancies	Standard Scores			Discrepancy		
	Actual	Predicted	Difference	PR	SD	Significant
Broad Reading	110	98	+12	85	+1.04	No
Reading Comprehension	105	98	+7	75	+0.66	No
Broad Math	104	98	+6	71	+0.56	No
Math Calc Skills	110	98	+12	83	+0.96	No
Math Reasoning	94	98	−4	37	−0.33	No
Broad Written Lang	102	98	+4	63	+0.34	No
Written Expression	97	98	−1	48	−0.06	No
Oral Language	94	98	−4	34	−0.41	No
Listening Comprehension	99	98	+1	55	+0.12	No

*These discrepancies are based on GIA (Ext) with ACH Broad, Basic, and Applied clusters.

is reflected in his current academic functioning. His cognitive strengths have helped him to acquire initial skills in all academic areas. Nevertheless, he is beginning to show difficulties with language tasks that involve comprehension of complex syntax and general sequencing of information. He is also starting to show signs of confusion with elements of mathematics. Since Nathan's cognitive weaknesses relate to tasks that are only beginning to increase in importance within the curriculum, it is not surprising that his achievement test scores are within the Average range. In fact, children who demonstrate cognitive weaknesses such as Nathan's often do not manifest academic difficulties until the fourth grade, when the curriculum demands shift to the application and generalization of learned skills. As was noted earlier, the *lack* of a numerical discrepancy at this time should not be interpreted as ruling out learning disabilities or some other clinical disorder. These Average levels of performance will not necessarily hold constant—particularly given Nathan's difficulties with higher-order thinking skills.

By report, Nathan also has difficulty with fine- and gross-motor tasks, as well as social perception and integration. He displays repetitive, nonfunctional behaviors that are resistant to intervention. This combination of factors along with Nathan's cognitive, language, and academic profile may indicate an emerging pattern of nonverbal learning disabilities. This diagnosis, however, requires that other possible disorders have been ruled out. Nonverbal learning disabilities are thought to exist at the mild end of a broader spectrum that includes other types of low-incidence neurological syndromes. Therefore, a consultation and evaluation by a pediatric neurologist or neuropsychologist who has specific expertise in the neurological bases of learning disabilities is warranted and recommended.

With regard to school instruction, several recommendations are presented:

General Considerations

1. The Evaluation and Planning Team should seek out additional information to assist in establishing a differential diagnosis prior to eligibility discussions. The profile that Nathan demonstrates is one that will have clinical and educational implications (e.g., whether he meets the criteria for special education eligibility or is determined to be best served by modifications and accommodations at this time). A comprehensive view of Nathan's cognitive and behavioral abilities and difficulties, including his pattern of performance during this evaluation, is strongly suggestive of a syndrome termed "nonverbal learning disabilities" (NLD). An excellent resource to assist the parents and school staff in understanding Nathan's current profile of NLD and the possible developmental progression, and in developing instructional techniques, is *The Source for Nonverbal Learning Disorders,* from LinguiSystems, (800) 776-4332, www.linguisystems.com.

2. Monitor Nathan frequently during any independent work to ensure that he does not repeatedly "practice" doing something incorrectly. Independent work needs to be at the level that presumes Nathan knows the concepts he is practicing. Do not expect him to learn concepts or skills initially from such materials.

3. Keep in mind that tasks involving abstract information will be more challenging to Nathan, and that he will need reinforcement and additional support on these types of tasks.

4. The more complex a task is, the greater will be the likeli-

hood that Nathan will require some assistance in organizing himself and the task. Simplify complex/multiple-step assignments by breaking them into shorter and more manageable "chunks" to be completed over multiple sessions. At the beginning of a new session, review with Nathan the previous work that was accomplished and remind him of the end goal of the activity.

5. Because of his problems with visual–spatial organization, provide Nathan with visually clear and logical materials that contain a limited amount of information, ample workspace, and plenty of blank space separating units of visual information (e.g., different tasks). Help him to structure his blank work space (e.g., partitioning his paper into large boxes—one for each math problem). (Samples of structured forms for math computation are attached.)

6. Help Nathan learn strategies to help him through sequential and spatial tasks (e.g., mathematics activities including word problems or novel writing assignments). Teach him how to tell which strategy to use for different tasks.

7. Whenever possible encourage Nathan to verbalize ideas and concepts. Model how to organize these into a logical, sequential order using visual outlines before teaching him how to do so. Any graphic organizers used should be linear and move logically from element to element (e.g., from the top down, or from left to right). Spidery, brainstorming types of webs are confusing for students with visual–spatial difficulties.

Do not view Nathan's repetitive or peculiar behaviors as deliberately disobeying previous instructions (e.g., continuing to put his fingers in his nose then his eyes, despite a previous discussion of the dangers of doing so). As many of these behaviors are not consciously mediated, discussions with Nathan regarding them are not likely to effect changes. Instead, a repetitive or interfering behavior may be more effectively ameliorated by use of a cueing system. Choose a specific word or gesture and teach him a specific behavior to perform in response to it—a behavior that requires the cessation of the behavior targeted for extinction (e.g., The word "hands" prompted him to fold his hands in his lap, keeping them away from his eyes). Focus on the positive response to the cue, rather than reminding him *not* to do something. Practice several times in private before using this system around others. If a nonverbal cue is chosen, provide Nathan explicit verbal instruction in recognizing and interpreting it, as this is an area of weakness for him. This system is designed to afford Nathan positive behavioral opportunities where he practices and learns how to inter-

rupt, divert, and ultimately control some of his tendencies for interfering or repetitive behaviors.

Mathematics

1. Nathan's accuracy in computation should not be compromised because of spatial or organizational difficulties. As math operations and problems incorporate more steps and spatial components (e.g., long division—the order of steps, working left to right, writing the results of each step in the proper place in relation to the other digits), provide materials and strategies to help Nathan with spatial organization (e.g., lining up rows/columns of numbers is easier on graph paper or on lined paper turned "landscape" style so that the lines are vertical).

2. Nathan needs a systematic organizational process for approaching word problems. Below is a sample of one that Nathan may find helpful. He will need to have it as a written reference until the sequence is internalized and automatic for him.

   a) See the situation—Have Nathan read the problem and orally describe the setting or situation.

   b) Determine the question—Have Nathan ascertain the problem to be solved. What is the question?

   c) Gather data—Have Nathan read the problem again (orally or silently) and list the data required to solve the problem. Later, when introducing extraneous information, have him draw a line down the center of the paper and list irrelevant information on the other side.

   d) Analyze relationships—Help Nathan analyze the relationships among the data (e.g., What did we start with? What number is related to it? What happened next?).

   e) Decide the operation—Nathan must decide which computational process should be used to solve the problem. Alert him to keywords (e.g., *total, difference*) that suggest basic operations. Have Nathan state the problem as a complete mathematical sentence.

   f) Estimate answers—Have Nathan practice estimating a reasonable answer. If he understands the reasoning behind the problem, he should be able to do this.

   g) Practice and generalize—After Nathan has worked through one type of problem correctly, provide him with similar problems with different numbers.

3. When teaching new math procedures and operations, activate Nathan's prior knowledge of similar concepts and make sure he develops an understanding of the new

key concepts. Use concrete, manipulative materials, and reinforce the concepts by talking through them.

Oral and Written Language

1. All individuals working with Nathan need to understand that higher-order tasks involving visual–spatial thinking, complex language, and abstract reasoning will be difficult for him.
2. As the syntax of reading material becomes more complex, watch Nathan for indications that he is having difficulty with comprehension. He is likely to need direct instruction in interpreting complex syntax and the types of words that signal the relationship between clauses and between sentences (e.g., words indicating that there is more information to come, such as "then" and "again"; words that indicate a change of direction in the flow of ideas, such as "although" and "but").
3. Nathan may tend to respond slowly to questions that are vague or open-ended, especially during discussions. Whenever possible, word questions so that the answer called for is specific rather than one that requires him to reformulate concepts. Provide Nathan with the time and assistance he may need to formulate his responses.
4. Continue to help Nathan develop handwriting using a formal and developmentally structured writing program. *Daily practice* in 15- to 20-minute increments with modeled writing assignments should prove effective. The goal is for Nathan to reach a level where his handwriting is both fluent and legible.
5. Before assigning reading material, use a strategy to promote or activate Nathan's prior knowledge of the topic. Include techniques that incorporate new vocabulary, key ideas, events, and characters. These activities will help Nathan associate the information from his reading with prior experiences and known information.

Adapted from Barbara G. Read, M.Ed.

Psychological Report

Name:	Victor Rodriguez	Home Language:	Spanish (determined by parent report)
Date of Birth:	5/27/1994		
Parents:	Tony and Maria Rodriguez	Ethnicity:	Hispanic
Date of Testing:	3/15/2002	Chronological Age:	7-7
Primary Language:	English/Spanish (determined by Language Assessment Scales [LAS])	Grade:	Second
		School:	Irwin Elementary

REASON FOR REFERRAL

Victor was referred for evaluation by the Student Study Team at Irwin Elementary because he is having difficulty developing reading and language arts skills. He was enrolled in bilingual instruction in kindergarten and first grade. Last year he was in an English immersion classroom. He currently participates in English Language Development (ELD) daily. Victor has made good progress with oral English skills. His current LAS indicates he is fluent in English. Victor was retained last year and is repeating second grade because he failed to meet bottom-line grade-level standards.

EVALUATION PROCEDURES

The following procedures were components of the evaluation:

Woodcock-Johnson III Tests of Cognitive Abilities
(WJ III COG): Tests 1–7, 9–10, 12, 14, 18
Beery-Buktenica Developmental Test of Visual-Motor Integration (4th ed.) (VMI)
Developmental history
Vision and hearing screening
Review of school records and previous assessment records
Classroom observation

DEVELOPMENTAL HISTORY

According to the developmental history form completed by his mother, Victor's prenatal, neonatal, and birth history was without complication and is unremarkable. Victor attained the motor and language milestones within normal limits. Nothing is noted in the developmental assessment that would adversely impact Victor's educational performance.

MEDICAL HISTORY

Victor's general health is good. On 9/2001, vision and hearing screenings yielded results within normal limits. His health history is void of any conditions that might affect academic performance.

HOME AND COMMUNITY

Victor presently resides with his biological parents. He is the youngest of three children. Spanish is the primary language of the home; however, Victor speaks English with his older brother and sister, who are ages 13 and 15. His mother describes Victor's activity level as typical of children his age. She also indicated Victor tends to have friends of the same age and gets along well with peers.

EDUCATIONAL HISTORY

Victor attended a preschool program and then the local home school. He has an excellent attendance history. He was retained in the second grade, but has never received special education services. The second-grade teacher reports that Victor's math skills are close to grade level. He demonstrates good fine-motor skills and always works hard despite limited progress.

PRIOR EVALUATIONS

Stanford 9 Achievement Test Series (4/01)

Composite/Test	PR
Total Reading	5
Word Study Skills	7
Vocabulary	4
Reading Comprehension	10
Total Math	30
Problem Solving	32
Procedures	32
Language	10
Spelling	7

ATTEMPTS TO EDUCATE IN THE GENERAL EDUCATION CLASSROOM

Interventions previously attempted in an effort to maintain Victor in the general education program include modified or shortened assignments, individualized classroom help, one-on-one with the teacher, tasks broken into smaller steps, and additional time.

For 2 consecutive years, Victor has attended a special reading program, after school interventions, and summer school. His teacher works with him in a small reading group at the first-grade level and provides additional help on all reading and language arts assignments. She reports Victor continues to struggle in reading, has not developed a sight word vocabulary, and cannot remember high-frequency words from one day to the next. He cannot remember long vowel sounds, blends, or digraphs. When reading and writing, he frequently confuses "b" and "d." On a recent phonemic awareness assessment (11/01), Victor had difficulty blending sounds and rhyming.

CLASSROOM OBSERVATIONS

Lorena De La Cruz, Ed.S., school psychologist, observed Victor in his general education classroom on 1/9/2002 during a class reading assessment. He acted in a manner typical for children of his age. His attention span appeared to be good; he showed good effort; and he worked on tasks to completion. He was seated at a table by himself. The task was to read a set of short sentences and select the correct word from a list of four words to correctly complete each sentence.

Victor attempted to read each sentence out loud. He sounded out each word, letter by letter, then attempted to read it as a whole word. He appeared to have difficulty blending the sounds, read all vowels as short, and confused "b" and "d." He did attempt to use context cues to help him figure out the words, but frequently, when he reread a sentence, he read it differently than he had initially.

Victor attempted to follow teacher directions when reading but did not always apply them correctly. For example, the teacher instructed the students that if they could not pronounce the names of people in the sentences, they should just call them by their first letter and continue reading the sentence. Victor pointed to all capital letters (including the first word in each sentence) and read them as if they were names. The class then turned to another section of the test that had the same instructions printed in large, bold letters at the top of the page. Victor spent a consider-

able amount of time trying to read the directions and, consequently, spent little time on the task.

TEST SESSION OBSERVATIONS

Victor's performance during formal testing appeared to represent his best effort. Overall, the results of the present testing and evaluation procedures appear to be valid for the purpose of addressing the reason for referral.

Victor's conversational proficiency was typical for his age level. He was cooperative and attentive throughout the examination; he responded promptly, but carefully, to test questions, generally persisting with difficult tasks. Victor used both Spanish and English to respond to the verbal items. His activity level seemed typical for his age.

INTELLECTUAL AND PROCESSING ASSESSMENTS

Woodcock-Johnson III Tests of Cognitive Abilities

Victor was administered a set of tests from the WJ III Tests of Cognitive Abilities. (See Table 1.) Comparisons among Victor's cognitive ability scores help determine the presence and significance of any strengths and weaknesses among his abilities. Test results indicate that Victor's overall intellectual ability is in the Low Average range when compared to others of his age level. His thinking ability (intentional cognitive processing) appears to be in the Average range. His expressive vocabulary and verbal reasoning, at the level of individual words, auditory processing (analysis and manipulation of speech sounds), and cognitive efficiency (automatic cognitive processing), fall into the Low Average range. Victor had particular difficulty on tasks of working memory (holding information in immediate awareness while working with it), as well as with long-term retrieval of learned associations (word/symbol). His scores fell into the Low to Low Average range and Low range, respectively.

Results of the VMI indicated that Victor's visual–motor skills are as good as or better than 91% of his age peers.

SUMMARY AND RECOMMENDATIONS

Based on the information obtained during the course of this evaluation, educational, environmental, economic disadvantage, or cultural or ethnic differences are not considered to be the primary factors influencing Victor's educational

Table 1. Scores: Woodcock-Johnson III Tests of Cognitive Abilities*

CLUSTER/Test	AE	EASY	to DIFF	RPI	PR	SS (68% Band)	CALP
GIA	7-3	6-5	8-5	72/90	18	87 (84–89)	
VERBAL ABILITY	6-11	5-10	8-2	68/90	16	85 (80–91)	3-4
THINKING ABILITY	8-0	6-5	10-8	87/90	37	95 (92–98)	
COG EFFICIENCY	6-11	6-5	7-6	37/90	11	81 (77–85)	
L-T RETRIEVAL (Glr)	5-8	4-2	8-1	72/90	1	67 (62–71)	
AUD PROCESS (Ga)	8-0	6-0	11-6	88/90	41	97 (92–102)	
WORKING MEMORY	6-3	5-9	7-1	42/90	9	80 (75–85)	
Verbal Comprehension	6-11	5-10	8-2	68/90	16	85 (80–91)	
Visual-Auditory Learning	5-9	4-8	7-5	63/90	4	75 (71–78)	
Spatial Relations	10-0	6-10	>25	93/90	64	105 (100–110)	
Sound Blending	7-4	5-9	9-8	83/90	34	94 (88–100)	
Concept Formation	9-6	8-0	12-4	94/90	63	105 (101–109)	
Visual Matching	7-7	7-1	8-1	51/90	19	87 (84–90)	
Numbers Reversed	6-1	5-9	6-7	24/90	10	81 (75–87)	
Auditory Work Memory	6-8	5-7	7-10	62/90	17	85 (80–91)	
Retrieval Fluency	5-3	3-2		80/90	4	73 (66–80)	
Auditory Attention	9-1	6-5	>20	91/90	57	103 (96–109)	
Rapid Picture Naming	4-2	3-9	4-8	1/90	1	65 (64–67)	
Vis-Aud Learn-Del.						(z score) +39	

*Norms based on age 8-7.

difficulties. Victor is a bilingual student who entered school with limited oral English skills and is currently classified as fluent in oral English. He has made good progress in math but has considerable difficulty in reading and writing. Results of this evaluation indicate that weaknesses in working memory and long-term retrieval are likely to be interfering with his ability to acquire basic reading and writing skills.

These results will be combined with the educational and speech and language evaluations to determine how best to meet Victor's educational needs. Victor appears to require a consistent, systematic approach to reading and writing instruction to enable him to develop basic skills.

Adapted from Janice Laz-Romo, Ed.S., School Psychologist.

Psychoeducational Evaluation

Student: Gregory Blackhawk
Birthdate: December 10, 1993
Chron. Age: 7-10

Parents: Betty and Anthony Blackhawk
Test Dates: October 11–13, 2001
Grade: 2

REASON FOR REFERRAL

Gregory was referred for evaluation by Tania Martin, Certified Teacher of the Visually Impaired, due to his poor attention in class and extreme difficulty learning basic reading, spelling, and math skills. Ms. Martin and Gregory's teachers wondered if a learning disability and/or Attention-Deficit/Hyperactivity Disorder (ADHD) could be contributing to his academic difficulties.

BACKGROUND INFORMATION

A comprehensive summary of Gregory's history regarding health and visual functioning was provided by Dr. Gary Olsen, School Psychologist, in his evaluation dated 9-10-00. His report and Ms. Martin's functional vision report provide additional information.

Gregory Blackhawk is a 7-year-old, second-grade boy who is diagnosed with ocular albinism, the result of which is impaired acuity and moderate horizontal nystagmus. Results of a functional vision evaluation completed by Ms. Martin last year indicated near acuity approximating 20/160 and distance acuity of 20/100. He has astigmatism, mild myopia in the right eye, and a left eye muscle imbalance. Gregory has binocular vision at a distance of up to 2 feet; at greater distances, he uses only his right eye. Gregory also has the pigmentation of albinism, with pale skin, light blond hair, and light blue eyes.

Gregory lives with his parents, two brothers, and a sister on the Navajo reservation. The younger brother also has ocular albinism. Mrs. Blackhawk works as an instructional aide at the reservation preschool, and Mr. Blackhawk works in maintenance at the tribal casino. The Blackhawks currently live with Mrs. Blackhawk's sister and her husband, and their three children, in Mrs. Blackhawk's mother's home.

Gregory's parents describe him as well-behaved. He does not have any regular chores, as Mr. Blackhawk wants his children to be free to play without a lot of responsibilities. Given occasional tasks, Gregory does them without reminding. Gregory prefers to be outside and very active all of the time, playing with friends, but in the house he can settle down to play with cars, color, or watch television. Mr. Blackhawk noted that Gregory is even-tempered, but when he does get angry, it is usually a "sudden eruption." At his mother's direction, Gregory does his homework each day when he gets home from school. She sits with him to ensure that he does it with reasonable quality. Frequently, Gregory tells his mother he doesn't have homework, but she usually finds the assignments in his backpack. Familial history is positive, on both sides of the family, for learning and attentional problems.

All of Gregory's previous and current teachers provided remarkably similar information regarding his behavioral and learning patterns. Since kindergarten Gregory has demonstrated significant difficulty with sustained attention. He is easily distracted, even on academic tasks that are well within his capability. The teachers acknowledged that they may not recognize the extent to which Gregory is off-task because he is quiet and does not draw attention to himself. When he's not working, Gregory plays with a pencil or looks at the lights. Gregory's attention is better in academic tasks that are interactive, physically active, or hands-on. He has a tendency to rush through tasks and overlook his errors. Ms. Martin sees the same behaviors when she works with him one-on-one and in the classroom but does not think that they are related to his visual impairment. She noted that it is not uncommon for children with low vision to look at lights.

The teachers also reported that Gregory does not retain learned skills, even day to day. He forgets letter names and sounds, how to form letters, and how to read and spell simple words. He does not recognize simple words that he has been exposed to hundreds of times (e.g., *and, you*). He has difficulty with rote counting, naming numbers, and with most other arithmetic skills. In contrast, if he is paying attention, he understands spoken language (e.g., stories, expository information) quite well, can remember events in sequence, and appears to have vocabulary on par with most other children his age. He understands and uses humor well and gets along well with his peers. In the classroom, Gregory informs teachers when he cannot see or needs to change his seat.

CLASSROOM OBSERVATIONS

The desks in Gregory's classroom, except for his, are arranged in pods of three and four. Gregory is seated by himself in the front, far left side of the room, directly in front of the white board but away from other students. Mrs. Thompson stated that she rarely uses the white board except for Daily Written Language, which the students copy from the board, and as a screen for the overhead projector. Mrs. Thompson's desk is in the rear, far right side of the room. Although a CCTV is on a desk placed at a right angle to his, Gregory rarely uses it or his hand-held magnifiers. Printed text and assignments are generally enlarged for him and printed on cream-colored paper. For reading, he has a white guide card. The classroom is lighted by overhead fluorescent lights recessed into the ceiling. Mrs. Thompson has requested that one set of lights be covered to reduce the glare for Gregory, but this has not yet been done.

The school has adopted the "Success for All" program, a highly systematic program addressing all components of language arts. Gregory is in a group of 12 students with Ms. Mewes for direct reading instruction for 1½ hours a day. During this observation, the children sat on the floor, and Ms. Mewes led a series of short activities. The activities included naming the type of business pictured in a photograph, giving the sounds for letters, practicing letter formation in the air with large arm movements, segmenting words into sounds, blending sounds into words, reading sight words, spelling words orally, and reviewing story elements on a worksheet. The print on Gregory's worksheet was not enlarged although the teacher said it usually is. He did not appear to have any overt difficulty with it although it is unlikely that he read more than a few words of the print. Between some of the activities, to refocus attention, the students sang short songs. Based on 10-second interval data taken during this 30-minute period, Gregory appeared to be on task 96% of the time. After one reminder, he usually raised his hand before speaking. During the next hour, the class sat around a circular table to read their story books. Gregory's book was enlarged. Gregory tried to follow along while students took turns reading aloud but quickly lost his place. His guide card is only about ⅔ the length of the line. He did not steady the book or the guide card with his left hand, so that while tracking along the line with his right hand, they both moved. When it was Gregory's turn to read, Ms. Mewes had to help him find the right page. Then, rather than reading, he made up a sentence based on the picture above the text and the few sight words he knew. When the class split up into pairs to read to each other, Gre-

gory and two other boys stayed with Ms. Mewes. As the other boys took their turns reading, Gregory often looked away from the book. When he did look at the book, he pointed to words on the wrong line. When it was his turn, he again "read" a sentence based on the picture rather than on the words.

The group reassembled to practice written spelling. The teacher pronounced phonetically regular three- and four-sound words, sound by sound, and the students wrote the letter for each sound. Gregory could not keep up and omitted many letters.

BEHAVIORAL OBSERVATIONS DURING TESTING

Gregory was tested over 3 days in one 1-hour session, three 1½-hour sessions, and one 2½-hour session. Only diagnostic teaching and informal testing were done during the 2½-hour session. All sessions included games, often integrated into the task, and breaks for choosing rewards for attention and effort.

Gregory and the examiner established rapport quickly and easily. Gregory was an easy conversationalist and was happy to answer questions about himself. Asked about his family, he casually stated, "My little brother is white like me and he wears glasses like me. My other brother is dark." Gregory came willingly with the evaluator for every session, maintained a good attitude, and attempted to cooperate. When tasks became even minimally challenging, he was unable to sustain attention unless a game was incorporated. It is the evaluator's impression that Gregory's ability to consider test items was seriously and pervasively impaired by his limited attention. For some entire tests and sections of others, the examiner had to refocus Gregory's attention before every item. He looked around the room, pointing at and commenting on things, and made casual comments regarding an association triggered by a test item. During the 5-second intervals allowed for studying the pictures on a memory test, he repeatedly commented, "This guy looks like my dad," "I found a bug, looked like this, once." Scores on the tests of Long-Term Retrieval are not available as his visual impairment prevented administration of one and his poor attention invalidated the other.

On some tests, Gregory seemed to forget instructions that he initially understood. Only occasionally did he appear discouraged; however, during a vocabulary test he exclaimed, "Everybody knows more than me." When items became challenging, Gregory responded too quickly to have given them adequate thought; moreover, he interrupted his own thought process so frequently that it would not have been possible for him to develop a strategy to meet the task demands. Consequently, interpretation of these test results needs to be considered in light of Gregory's visual impairments and limited attention.

TEST ACCOMMODATIONS FOR VISUAL IMPAIRMENT

Gregory was tested in a conference room with little outside noise. The overhead lights did not reflect on the materials, and Gregory was asked to rearrange test materials before each task, both to reduce glare and to accommodate his nystagmus as much as possible. All printed test materials (letters, numbers) had been reprinted in a sans serif font, size 4m, on cream-colored paper. For diagnostic teaching and informal testing, materials made on the spot were hand-printed in D'Nealian style, at least 8m in size, on cream-colored paper. All tests that required vision were interspersed with one or more tests that did not. When asked if his eyes were tired, Gregory always responded that they were not.

TESTS ADMINISTERED

Woodcock-Johnson III Tests of Cognitive Abilities (WJ III COG): Tests #1, 4–5, 7–9, 11–15, 17–18
Woodcock-Johnson III Tests of Achievement:
    (WJ III ACH): Tests #1, 3–5, 7, 9–10, 13–15, 19
Phonological Awareness Test (PAT)
Diagnostic teaching and informal assessments
Conners' Parent and Teacher Rating Scales—Revised
Teacher and parent interviews

Gregory's ethnicity, culture, and visual impairment were considered in choosing the assessment instruments for this evaluation. The test instruments used were considered to be the best available. Accommodations and modifications were made to minimize the effects of his visual impairment. The consequent effect on the validity of the norms is considered in the interpretation of test results. Interpretation also considered Gregory's cultural upbringing and possible effects on performance. The following were considered and ruled out as contributing factors to the referral concerns: educational disadvantage, environmental deprivation, economic factors, primary language of the home, motor prob-

lems, communication problems. The results of this evaluation are considered valid within the constraints of the cautions, regarding Gregory's visual impairment and Navajo culture, discussed throughout the test and in the Summary and Conclusions section.

TEST RESULTS

The tests of the WJ III were scored according to grade norms. When no difference was found between the two component tests of a cognitive factor or achievement cluster, only the factor/cluster score is discussed. Standard scores (SS) are reported as 68% confidence bands (Mean = 100; SD = 15). The verbal classification (range) is based on the SEM and indicates Gregory's standing in comparison to the scores obtained by subjects in the first month of second grade in the norm sample: Very Low (SS 69 or below), Low (SS 70–79), Low Average (SS 80–89), Average (SS 90–110), High Average (SS 111–120), Superior (SS 121–130), Very Superior (SS 131 and above). Percentile ranks (PR) describe the percentage of grade-peers in the norm sample who obtained a score the same as or lower than his. The Relative Proficiency Index (RPI) indicates the level of proficiency with which Gregory could handle classroom tasks similar to those on the test when his grade-peers would achieve 90% proficiency. The grade equivalent (GE) or age equivalent (AE) is based on Gregory's raw score (the number of items correct on a test). It indicates the grade or age level in the norming sample at which the median raw score was the same as Gregory's raw score. Unless noted, all of the factors, clusters, and tests discussed next are from the WJ III COG or WJ III ACH.

Cognitive Abilities

Consistent with previous psychoeducational assessments, test results indicate that Gregory's abstract reasoning ability is on par with grade-peers (SS 98–104, PR 51). Given instruction and corrective feedback, Gregory was able to learn new procedures to solve increasingly complex logic problems, based on visual patterns. The RPIs indicated that Gregory is relatively more adept in deductive reasoning (using given rules to work through a problem in a step-by-step fashion) than in the inductive reasoning process (looking at multiple elements of a problem and figuring out the rule governing its organization).

Gregory's High Average performance on the Picture Recognition test (SS 107–122, RPI 97/90) showed advanced ability to note visual details in pictures and hold them in memory for later use.

Gregory's Low to Low Average scores on the factors of Short-term Memory (SS 77–88, RPI 43/90) and Working Memory (SS 74–85, RPI 37/90) indicate that, *with his current level of attention,* he has difficulty remembering spoken words and numbers when they are not related by a meaningful context. When he has to hold "meaningless" information in mind while trying to do some mental operation on it, he loses pieces and gives up. This apparent weakness is in sharp contrast with his strong ability to recall the information presented in a more meaningful verbal context.

Oral Language

Test results indicate that Gregory has at least average ability to understand and reason with linguistic information conveying meaningful content. The Oral Language cluster (SS 91–98, RPI 85/90) is composed of tests of vocabulary, story memory, listening comprehension, and following oral directions. His scores in the Low Average and lower end of the Average range on tests of vocabulary and word associations (Picture Vocabulary, Verbal Comprehension) appeared to be affected by cultural differences and possibly by limited visual experience. (For example, he was unable to answer a question referring to the grass around a house. The reservation is on desert land, and houses do not have lawns.) In contrast, he easily demonstrated his comprehension of short passages and brief stories presented on audiotape. His retelling of the stories was organized and included the key elements. As well, *if he is paying attention,* Gregory can understand instructions incorporating a variety of linguistic concepts and complex syntax, hold them in memory, and then follow the directions. The stimuli for this test were colored pictures, which he viewed on a CCTV (closed circuit television: a television monitor that enlarges whatever is placed on the viewing screen to the dimensions chosen by the viewer). He clearly thought that this was a game, and his attention was excellent.

Phonological Awareness
Phonological awareness skills are critical to developing basic reading and spelling skills. Gregory's performance on tests of the WJ III and the PAT indicate that he has developed phonological awareness skills (i.e., the ability to perceive and manipulate word parts) as well as or better than other students of his age and grade (WJ III Phonemic Awareness, SS 97–109, RPI 91/90; Auditory Processing, SS 102–112, RPI 94/90). He demonstrates strengths in accurately identifying speech sounds in the presence of noise; rhyming; blending syllables and sounds (up to four) into whole words; dividing words into syllables and sounds (up to three); identifying initial sounds in words and, to a lesser extent, final sounds; and—using manipulatives—identifying the position of a sound that has been changed in a word. He is not yet able to identify medial sounds in words, or to drop syllables or sounds from words to make new words.

Academic Achievement

Since kindergarten, Gregory's instruction in language arts has been in a program that is highly structured and explicit in teaching phonological awareness, basic reading and spelling skills, and D'Nealian handwriting. After explicit instruction and ample practice, skills are continuously reviewed in isolation, as well as integrated into students' daily use.

Reading
Test results indicate that Gregory is seriously delayed in his knowledge of letter sounds (PAT: AE <5-9), his ability to sound out phonetically regular nonsense words (WJ III Word Attack: SS 82, PR 11, RPI 25/90; PAT: SS 67, PR 3, AE 5-11), and his ability to read sight words (WJ III Letter-Word Identification: SS 63, PR 1, RPI 0/90). Despite a highly structured, systematic, and well-balanced reading program, his estimated instructional level in basic reading skills is late kindergarten.

In informal testing, Gregory differentiated between letters and numbers and named each group (numbers, "ABCs"). He confused letter shapes and could not name all of the letters consistently. He sang the alphabet to try and remember the name for *v* but failed. At one point, he looked at a *g* and said to himself, "What is that? *b? p?* It's a lowercase *c.*" Gregory was able to sound out words with up to three sounds if he recognized all of the letters in the word and easily recalled their sounds. Sometimes he pronounced each sound but then omitted the first one when blending them. Of the 14 words on the class sight word list, Gregory read only four or five, and these inconsistently. At times he said them almost immediately and at other times acted as if he had never seen the word before. As noted previously, he recognized very few words as sight words, tried to sound out words he undoubtedly had seen hundreds of times (e.g., *and, on*), and simply could not attempt others (e.g., *said*).

Gregory was unable to read any of the sentences on the Passage Comprehension test. Although his obtained score was at the 5th percentile, it was based on three correct guesses at the words accompanying a choice of pictures.

Writing
On the Spelling test, Gregory was not able to write any of the dictated letters correctly. Compared to grade-peers, Gregory would have scored better than only 1 in 1,000. His instructional level was mid-kindergarten (SS 55, RPI 0/90). Although Gregory can write 17 letters of the alphabet, he does not have each firmly associated with its name. When printing, Gregory forms each letter in reasonably proper D'Nealian style but often writes the individual strokes incorrectly (e.g., bottom to top) and out of sequence. As with reading, Gregory spells by sounding out a word and writing a letter for each sound. He cannot spell words that do not look like they sound. Although Gregory has a great advantage in being able to perceive up to four individual sounds in a word, he presently does not know or consistently recall which letter goes with the sound, and depends on the clue contained in the letter names. For example, he spelled "water" as *yodr*. He isolated the initial sound, /w/, associated it with the name of *Y,* and spelled the rest of the word sound by sound.

In diagnostic teaching, Gregory studied two words, *look* and *camp* (which he had just misspelled as *cip* on a class spelling drill) through a modified Fernald technique. This method includes saying the word, saying it sound by sound while tracing each letter, and writing repeatedly without a model. Gregory was able to read and spell *camp* the next morning and then again in the afternoon. He spelled "look" as *cook*. As his D'Nealian style *l* looks similar to an elongated *c,* while studying, he said the /l/ sound as he traced what he perceived to be a *c* and learned the word that way. Nevertheless, used cautiously, a multimodality instructional technique such as Fernald appears to be useful for Gregory in teaching sight words and reinforcing reading and writing instruction.

Mathematics
On the Calculation test, Gregory scored in the Very Low range (SS 67–77, PR 3, RPI 15/90). He counted on his fingers for simple addition fact problems with sums up to 5, counting up from one each time, using an inefficient system of touching the fingers of one hand to the fingers of the other and to his face. He did not recognize subtraction problems, treating them as addition. His score on automatic knowledge of math facts was higher than only 1% of his grade-peers. He completed only the addition problems, and counted on his fingers to arrive at the solutions.

On the Applied Problems test (practical application of math skills), Gregory's score bordered the Low to Low Average range (SS 74–84, PR 8, RPI 23/90). With picture clues, Gregory was able to add and subtract but could not imagine what was not pictured (e.g., "Here are 3 pencils. If we put in 2 more, how many will there be?"). On informal testing, using real objects, Gregory showed more facility with this skill. When given 2 cookies and asked how many more he would need to ask for to have 4, he immediately said, "May I have 2 cookies?" He counted by rote from 1 to 20 but became confused when asked to continue. Gregory named a sampling of printed numbers under 20 correctly, but was unable to name any higher numbers correctly. He was able to tell time to the hour on an analog clock. He did not know the value of any coins.

General Knowledge
Gregory performed relatively better on the Academic Knowledge test (Science, Social Studies, Humanities) than on General Information (SS 75–87, RPI 54/90), a difference that appeared to be affected by culture and limited visual experience. The information needed for Academic Knowledge is more likely to be taught in school, where Gregory will be exposed to it. Conversely, General Information calls for knowledge acquired through daily experience with objects in one's environment, some of which are not prevalent in Gregory's environment. For example, there are few, if any, stop signs on the reservation, but many in the school hallways reminding students not to run. Accordingly, a reasonable answer to, "Where would you find a stop sign?" is "In the hallway." Although other children might notice stop signs when riding around town in a car, Gregory would not be able to see one clearly unless he were right next to it and it were pointed out to him.

Attention

The Conners' Rating Scales—Revised (table of scores attached) did not include children with severe visual impairments or a significant number of Navajo children in the sample and, as such, may not accurately represent behavior of Navajo children with severe visual impairments.

Gregory's parents describe him as attentive at home except during homework time. Their elevated rating on the

Cognitive Problem/Inattention subscale reflects academic problems and reports of inattention at school. The profile of the three teachers' ratings and their item responses indicated academic and attentional problems, although on the whole their responses to specific items did not reflect the level of concern they stated in their interviews. Overall, the ratings indicated a level of clinical significance for Attention-Deficit/Hyperactivity Disorder, Predominantly Inattentive Type.

SUMMARY AND CONCLUSIONS

According to the results of this evaluation, Gregory has at least average intelligence, reasoning ability, oral language comprehension and expression, memory for linguistic information presented in a meaningful context, and, despite his visual impairment, the ability to recognize and recall pictorial details. Additionally, Gregory clearly acquires and retains information from school and from life experiences as long as he has a knowledge base to which he can relate it.

Gregory evidences weaknesses in memory span and working memory, specifically for discrete, unrelated pieces of information. Moreover, an inherent weakness in memory is likely to be exacerbated by the inability to sustain attention long enough to process information sufficiently to transfer it into long-term storage. Consequently, Gregory will benefit from having a strong understanding of the concepts underlying any data that he is expected to memorize.

Despite his cognitive strengths and a language arts program that is explicit and highly systematic in teaching phonological awareness, phonics, sight words, spelling, and writing skills, Gregory is severely delayed in all of these skills, as well as in the most basic of math skills.

Gregory's memory weaknesses appear to contribute substantially to his difficulty in establishing stable associations among letter forms, letter names, letter sounds, and in learning sequences or sets of inherently unrelated words (e.g., the alphabet, counting). Memory problems are evident also in his phonological abilities, for example, his omission of a sound when attempting to blend three sounds into a word.

Additionally, Gregory's error patterns, attempted compensations, and positive response to a multisensory technique with a tracing component are compelling indicators of severe difficulty in recognizing, storing, and/or retrieving visual symbols and symbol patterns. Unlike a picture, whose meaning is transparent (at least at second-grade level), the meaning of a letter or number is arbitrary (not in-

herent in the symbol itself) and abstract (not represented by real-world objects), and thus depends heavily on memory.

Although Gregory's visual impairment clearly is not the primary cause of this pattern of learning difficulties, his nystagmus and poor acuity unquestionably compound his difficulty in learning these skills. Moreover, given his inability to sustain attention to activities that are not inherently engaging to him, it is likely that he often misses out on the instruction and reinforcement of skills that he so desperately needs.

SUMMARY

Gregory Blackhawk is a 7-year-old Navajo boy with ocular albinism, causing nystagmus and reduced acuity. Both the visual impairment and limited attention make the validity of test scores questionable. One can assume from test results in the Average range that Gregory has intellectual ability, including reasoning and oral language skills, *at least* on par with second-grade children. Weaknesses in auditory short-term memory, specifically for unrelated pieces of information, and in visual recognition and memory for symbols appear to be interfering with his development of basic reading, writing, and arithmetic skills, thus constituting specific learning disabilities. The effects of the learning disabilities are compounded by Gregory's behaviors, consistent with Attention-Deficit/Hyperactivity Disorder–Inattentive type, and by his visual impairment. Notwithstanding, with Gregory's intellectual and language capability, given early and appropriate intervention, he should be successful in developing basic academic skills and in applying them to higher-order tasks.

RECOMMENDATIONS

General

1. The classroom teacher, visual impairment specialist, and learning disabilities specialist should meet to decide what role each will take in providing Gregory the multiple services he needs, how to reinforce what the others are teaching, and how to communicate problems as they arise. Set up meetings at regular intervals to review his progress.
2. The learning disabilities specialist, psychologist, or counselor should, as simply as possible, explain the findings of this report to Gregory, ensuring that he under-

stands why he is having difficulty and emphasizing that he is smart and capable.

3. Provide all specialized instruction in a pull-out model of service. Gregory is already too aware of his differences from other children, and remedial instruction in the classroom would be embarrassing.

4. For any computer to which Gregory has access, secure and install a screen magnifier program to magnify print and graphics to any chosen size and a screen reader program to read all printed and graphic information on the computer. Request assistance from Ms. Martin in selecting programs appropriate to Gregory's needs and skill levels. Provide Gregory direct instruction in the use of these programs.

5. To reduce Gregory's feelings about being different, seat him in a pod with other children with his CCTV at right angles to his desk as it is now. Make a desk available to him near the front of the room to which he can move when the overhead projector is being used.

6. Despite Gregory's significant visual impairment, he demonstrates a strength in his ability to note critical details in pictures and remember them later. Thus, the use of pictures will be an important instructional device in helping him to learn new concepts and remember rote information.

7. Whenever possible, use a game format for learning (e.g., reviewing for a test by playing Jeopardy with the target information). Gregory will find it easier to attend to the information and hold it in mind long enough to process it more effectively.

General Principles of Instruction for Students with Learning Disabilities

1. Provide work in all basic skills at Gregory's instructional level. As much as Gregory wants to do the same work as everyone else, having him work at tasks at his frustration level will not benefit him, will add to his frustration, and will take already limited time away from appropriate instruction and practice.

2. In teaching new skills to Gregory, do not progress to the next skill until the current one is learned to mastery. Then, as you teach the next skill, continuously review the previous one and incorporate it into daily work.

3. Before assigning any task, analyze it to make sure that Gregory can do the component skills. For example, to write a word from dictation, he must segment the word into sounds, recall what letter makes each sound, re-

call how the letter looks, and know how to print the letter.

Visual Impairment

1. Ask Ms. Martin to provide an inservice for all staff working with Gregory to explain how he sees his world, how his visual impairments affect his learning, and the importance of providing the accommodations she has recommended.

2. Modify the light over Gregory's desk to minimize glare. Consider doing this also in the reading classroom.

3. Rather than use a line guide, teach Gregory to use his left hand to steady his book and to track along the line he is reading with his right forefinger.

Attention-Deficit/Hyperactivity Disorder

1. Share this report with Gregory's pediatrician or with a physician with expertise in Attention-Deficit/Hyperactivity Disorder to rule in or rule out ADHD and to consider problems that might present as such but require other treatment.

2. *If* the physician diagnoses ADHD, and the Blackhawks decide on a trial of medication, the school staff working with Gregory should establish a system for monitoring his response and providing feedback to his parents and the physician. For example, the teachers could complete a simple behavior rating chart after each activity period throughout the day and, at the end of each week, send copies to the parents and, with their permission, the physician. This rating chart will allow the physician to see if the medication is effective, adjust the dosage amounts and times, and monitor possible side effects. A sample behavioral chart is attached to this report.

3. Before giving instructions, ensure that you have Gregory's attention. In cooperation with Gregory, make up and use a private signal, such as a touch on the shoulder, as a reminder to return to task.

4. Seat Gregory around students who pay attention. With Gregory's permission, arrange for another student to give Gregory an unobtrusive signal when his attention wanders.

5. Reduce class and homework assignments to the extent that Gregory will not have to spend more time on them than other students.

Content Area Instruction

Because Gregory is immersed in the Navajo culture and lives on the reservation (as do most of his classmates), a critical aspect of introducing all new content area instruction will be to evaluate prior knowledge and spend whatever time is needed to fill in missing concepts and experience.

Basic Reading and Writing Skills

1. Use the current language arts program as a guide or "skeleton," but start from the beginning with Gregory. Teach letter recognition, names, sounds, and formation. At every step, supplement the recommended techniques with additional techniques and strategies to promote and reinforce his learning of each skill. For example, Gregory is not able to remember all of the SFA letter/keyword associations; he would be more likely to do so if the picture of the keyword incorporated the associated letter. For the letter/sound associations that are still problematic, change the keyword to one that can incorporate the letter in its picture (e.g., a cup with a *C* for a handle; an octopus made out of an *O*). Color the letter form so that it stands out from the picture.

2. Teach sight words and phonograms using a multisensory method such as modified Fernald. Provide frequent practice in reading and written spelling.

3. Once Gregory has learned the sound of a letter or phonogram, provide for overlearning by having him read it and spell it in nonsense words as well as real words, multiple times a day, on a schedule that allows for gradual fade-out.

4. When teaching sight words, directly teach Gregory to recognize common letter patterns within the word (e.g., *ight* in sight, *oo* in look). Reinforce automatic recognition of the letter pattern by giving practice finding it in other words and discriminating it from similar patterns. A progressive sequence might be (a) recognition: on a worksheet of words containing the grapheme *oo*, Gregory uses his pencil to track across each line, circling all the *oo*'s he finds; (b) discrimination: on a worksheet of *oo* words interspersed with words containing other vowel teams, Gregory circles only the *oo* grapheme; (c) speed drills: use speed drills to reinforce the grapheme/phoneme correspondence. (A description of Speed Drills for Reading Fluency is attached.)

5. To enhance interest and attention, provide drill and practice in letter/sound relationships and letter patterns on computer programs.

6. Supplement the SFA storybooks with additional decodable text, such as the Steck-Vaughn Phonics Readers.

7. Provide Gregory the DWL sentences printed on paper so that he can make the corrections directly on the paper rather than having to copy the sentences before editing them. Use simple sentences with words Gregory can read.

8. Observe Gregory forming each letter and reteach those formed incorrectly (sequence and direction of strokes). Monitor his practice until you are sure he will independently continue to write it correctly. Provide continued practice, in isolation and incorporated into other tasks, until he has established the pattern in memory (i.e., can write it correctly without thinking).

Mathematics

1. Ensure that Gregory knows that the number sequence begins with zero. Show him how the 0 to 9 number pattern repeats as the numbers progress (e.g., numbers in the units place change with each number but repeat; numbers in the tens place change every 10 numbers). Use color-coding to highlight the repeating patterns.

2. Tie instruction in counting to instruction in reading numbers.

3. Teach all math skills with manipulatives to ensure that Gregory understands the concept, then directly associate what you are doing with the manipulatives to the numbers. In doing this, teach Gregory to count on rather than always starting from one.

    • •   • → • • • $2 + 1 = 3$

4. Play games using manipulatives such as Unifix Cubes, Snap Cubes, or Base Ten Blocks to teach place value. Teach Gregory the meaning of printed numbers above 9 using a place value mat (columns on large paper with headings for ones and tens). Associate the manipulatives in each column with printed numbers.

SCORES

Conners' Parent and Teacher Rating Scales—Revised (CRS-R) (long version)

Scales	Ratings				Common Behaviors of Children with this Problem
	Martin	Mewes	Davis	Parents	
Oppositional	45	58	45	50	Breaks rules; problems with authority, easily annoyed
Cognitive Problems/Inattention	72	73	75	65	Inattentive; organizational problems, difficulty completing tasks; concentration problems
Hyperactivity	43	46	48	61	Difficulty sitting still; restless and impulsive
Anxious-Shy	61	55	61	51	Has worries and fears; emotional, sensitive to criticism, shy and withdrawn
Perfectionism	44	50	44	49	High goals; fastidious and obsessive
Social Problems	45	53	45	50	Few friends; low self-esteem and self-confidence; feels socially detached from peers
Psychosomatic	n/a	n/a	n/a	48	Reports unusual amount of aches and pains
Conners' ADHD Index	52	59	61	54	"At risk" for ADHD
Conners' Global Index: Restless-Impulsive	51	59	61	59	Restless, impulsive, and inattentive
Conners' Global Index: Emotional Lability	44	48	48	46	Prone to more emotional responses/behaviors (crying, anger, etc.) than is typical
Conners' Global Index: Total	48	56	58	55	Hyperactive; broad range of behavior problems
DSM-IV: Inattentive	59	65	65	60	Behavior consistent with DSM-IV diagnostic criteria for Inattentive type ADHD
DSM-IV: Hyperactive-Impulsive	42	46	46	63	Behavior consistent with DSM-IV diagnostic criteria for Hyperactive-Impulsive type ADHD
DSM-IV: Total	50	56	55	62	Behavior consistent with the DSM-IV diagnostic criteria for Combined type ADHD

Mean = 50, SD = 10. Elevated scores indicate a higher than average occurrence of problem behaviors. *T* scores of 65 and above are usually taken to indicate a clinically significant problem. Scores of 61 to 64 are interpreted as a possibly significant problem requiring monitoring.

Psychological Report

Name:	Casey Hanson		Ethnicity:	Caucasian
Date of Birth:	11/30/1993		Gender:	Female
Chronological Age:	8-1		Parent:	Esther Hanson
Grade:	Third		Language:	English
Home School:	Benson Elementary		Evaluation Date:	1/10/02

REASON FOR REFERRAL

Casey's mother requested a full evaluation to determine whether she qualifies for special education services.

EVALUATION PROCEDURES

The following procedures were components of the evaluation:

Developmental history
Medical history
Vision and hearing screening
Classroom observation
Woodcock-Johnson III Tests of Cognitive Abilities
    (WJ III COG): Tests 1–7, 11–14, 16

BACKGROUND INFORMATION

Ms. Hanson described Casey's prenatal history as unremarkable. Her birth history, however, was complicated due to the diagnosis of a heart murmur and tachycardia. Casey was placed on medication for the tachycardia at 2 weeks of age. Although Casey attained the major developmental milestones at a typical rate, monitoring of her condition has required numerous doctor visits and frequent school absences. Medical concerns were the only factors noted in the developmental history that would adversely impact Casey's educational performance.

Medical History

Casey's general health is fair. She had heart surgery at age 3. She is currently prescribed Atenolol 25 mg daily for supraventricular tachycardia. A cardiologist with expertise in this condition follows her closely. Her apparent fatigue and slow response time may be due to the tachycardia and/or the medication, which lists fatigue as a possible side effect.

On 8/2001 Casey's vision was screened, and on 9/2001 her hearing was screened. Both vision and hearing screenings yielded results within normal limits.

Home and Community

Casey presently resides with her mother, stepfather, stepbrother, and two younger stepsisters. She has a 12-year-old sister who lives with their biological father, both of whom she sees on a regular basis. Her mother reports that Casey is slow at times at home and sometimes has difficulty concentrating on homework. Ms. Hanson suspects that Casey's medication may be responsible for her limited attention. She also reports that Casey's biological father was in special education.

Educational History

Casey attended a preschool program and then entered Benson Elementary School. Because of health problems, she has a history of frequent excused absences and tardiness. She has never received special education services. In second grade her classroom teacher described Casey's performance at a Student Study Meeting on 3/13/2001. She reported that Casey was functioning below grade level in all academics, worked very slowly, had poor spelling skills, often appeared withdrawn, had few learning strengths, had trouble working independently, and had difficulty following directions and expressing herself orally.

Interventions previously attempted in an effort to maintain Casey in the general education program include individualized classroom help, communications between parent and school, one-on-one work with the teacher, additional time, peer tutors, preferential seating, and tasks broken into smaller steps. Casey has also participated in the Reach for Reading program and after-school interventions. A positive work chart has been used for the purposes of enhancing effort and motivation.

CLASSROOM OBSERVATIONS

Lorena De La Cruz, Ed.S., school psychologist, observed Casey in her general education class on 1/8/2002. Casey appeared to work slowly during the observation. Although her concentration was good, she was not able to complete the task within the allotted time frame.

Her ability to relate to others was fair. Her maturity appeared typical for her age. She was cooperative and compliant and followed rules without prompts. Her approach to tasks was affected by her slow response style. When new material was presented, Casey did not participate in class discussions. When the teacher called on her, Casey needed extra clues before she could give a verbal response indicating that she understood the material.

TEST SESSION OBSERVATIONS

Casey's conversational proficiency seemed limited for her age level. Although she was cooperative, she seemed lethargic throughout the examination. She seemed attentive to the tasks but at times appeared tense or worried. Casey's response time was very slow, and she was hesitant in answering test questions. She needed items repeated because of the time lag. She generally persisted with difficult tasks. Casey's performance during formal testing did not appear to be affected adversely by failure or frustration. She did not require any adaptations or modifications to the standardized procedures. She did not require an excessive amount of reinforcement and praise. Overall, the results of the present testing and evaluation procedures appear to be valid for the purpose of addressing the reason for referral.

TEST RESULTS

Casey was administered a set of tests from the WJ III COG. When compared to others of her age level, she is Average in overall intellectual ability, verbal ability (acquired knowledge and language comprehension), thinking ability (intentional cognitive processing), and cognitive efficiency (automatic cognitive processing). Similarly, Casey's performance is Average in visual–spatial thinking, auditory processing, and processing speed, and Low Average in long-term retrieval. Although no significant discrepancies were found among Casey's cognitive abilities, her cognitive performance may be negatively influenced by her cognitive fluency (limited), specifically response speed and word retrieval.

SUMMARY AND CONCLUSIONS

Casey is a student who has a history of academic difficulty in her school. She is diagnosed with a heart condition for which she takes medication. She is subject to fatigue, which may be affecting her school performance. Based on the information obtained during the course of this evaluation, no educational, environmental, economic disadvantage, or cultural or ethnic differences are considered to be the primary factors influencing Casey's educational difficulties. Casey does appear to demonstrate an educational disability—specifically, Other Health Impaired. Formal cognitive assessment indicates average cognitive functioning with weaknesses in response speed and word retrieval. Casey's slow cognitive response time and possible mental fatigue may be due to her medical condition/medication or to word-retrieval difficulties. If the IEP team determines that her academic performance is being significantly affected, Casey would qualify for special education under the category of Other Health Impairment.

RECOMMENDATIONS

1. Mrs. Hanson should discuss Casey's fatigue, slow cognitive pace, and difficulties with sustained attention with the doctor who prescribes her medication, to rule out or confirm the medication as a major contributing factor to these behaviors. This information should be communicated to the school team as soon as possible.
2. Refer Casey to the speech-language pathologist and the educational diagnostician to assess further her difficulties in word retrieval, oral language, and academic performance.
3. If Casey is going to continue to be absent from school frequently, provide her mother with schoolwork that Casey can complete at home.

After evaluations are completed by the speech-language pathologist and the educational diagnostician, the multidisciplinary team should meet to develop specific recommendations to address her academic needs. Recommendations should address adaptations to assignments and plans for increasing Casey's ability to work independently and to follow directions. Casey may need to have school assignments shortened and the criteria adjusted so that she can meet academic objectives. She may benefit from learning mnemonic strategies to assist with tasks involving memorization.

Adapted from Janice Laz-Romo, Ed.S.

Diagnostic Evaluation Report

Name:	Josephine Baxter	Parents:	Charles and Nadine Baxter
Date of Birth:	September 2, 1992	School:	Park Cove Elementary
Age at Evaluation:	9 years, 6 months	Grade:	Fourth
Dates of Evaluation:	January 18 and 19, 2002		

REASONS FOR REFERRAL

Mr. and Mrs. Baxter requested a comprehensive evaluation with emphasis on Josephine's speech and language development. Josephine suffered a closed head injury at the age of 7; since that accident Mrs. Baxter, who is a speech-language pathologist, has observed word-finding difficulties, emotional lability, and problems in organization.

BACKGROUND INFORMATION

According to the parent questionnaire completed by Mrs. Baxter, Josephine is the product of a full-term pregnancy. Vacuum extraction was used to facilitate Josephine's birth, and the umbilical cord was wrapped around Josephine's neck and shoulder. No complications resulted. Josephine's developmental milestones were acquired during normal time frames. At the age of 2 she spoke in complete sentences.

Josephine has been healthy throughout her early developmental years. At the end of second grade, however, she was hit by a car while skating. Although she did not lose consciousness, Josephine cannot remember the accident. CAT scan results indicated "no significant abnormality," and Josephine was sent home. Josephine's hearing and vision are normal, and there is no family history of learning disabilities. Josephine lives at home with both parents and two younger siblings, ages 6 and 3.

Mrs. Baxter described Josephine as somewhat shy, well-behaved, sweet, and fun loving. Immediately following the accident, Josephine had many nightmares, but these have diminished. Josephine is said to get along with younger children fairly well but avoids socializing with age-peers.

Josephine began school at the age of 3, and her school attendance has been regular. Overall Josephine is said to be doing well in school. Mrs. Baxter has observed that since the accident Josephine is at times hesitant in her speech and demonstrates word-finding problems in conversation. Examples include saying "dress" for nightgown, "brownie" for cupcake, "clock" for watch, "geyser" for visor, "table" for counter, and "fountain" for faucet. Mrs. Baxter reported that Josephine says "um, um . . ." frequently in the middle of sentences during conversation. Shortly after the accident Josephine reportedly forgot how to use a phone book, which was something she had done regularly prior to her head injury. Mrs. Baxter also shared that during the first few weeks after the accident Josephine's speech was somewhat garbled. Although the third-grade teacher expressed concerns about reading comprehension, her fourth-grade teacher reported that Josephine does not experience any difficulties in her classroom. The Baxters did note that Josephine's speech and word-finding problems have continued to improve since the accident.

PREVIOUS TESTING

When Josephine was age 4 years, 9 months (June 1996), Mrs. Baxter administered the Peabody Picture Vocabulary Test—Revised, a measure of receptive vocabulary. Josephine's score was in the upper end of the Average range for her age group. Her standard score (SS) was 110. Kindergarten records indicate that Josephine's receptive and expressive language and gross-motor skills were considered "moderately above age level"; her auditory and visual memory were "considerably above age level." Her visual discrimination and fine-motor skills were at "expected age level." At the end of second grade, before her accident, Josephine was administered the Vermont Developmental Reading Assessment and achieved the standards for Reading Accuracy and Reading Comprehension "with honors."

Subsequent to the accident, in December 1999, Dr. Kathryn Heilman, Ph.D., a neuropsychologist, evaluated Josephine at the Monroe Child Development Clinic. She administered the Wechsler Intelligence Scale for Children—Third Edition (WISC-III) and reported a Full Scale IQ of 129, 97th percentile (Superior). Dr. Heilman summarized that neurocognitively, no significant impairments were evident. She did state, however, that while formal testing of word finding did not reveal problems, some problems in word retrieval were evident during the evaluation and these tended to occur on tasks that required expanded discourse or more elaborated responses. Dr. Heilman observed a mild latency in Josephine's response to oral questions. While speaking in informal conversation or in answers to direct questions, Josephine would often stop mid-sentence as she attempted to retrieve a particular word from memory. Dr. Heilman wrote that, "I would agree with Mrs. Baxter's observations that Josephine does have mild problems retrieving specific words from memory; however, I suspect that this may be a mild, residual effect and given the subtle nature of the problem, I would anticipate that this difficulty will likely resolve in the upcoming months."

TESTS ADMINISTERED

Achenbach Child Behavior Checklist (CBCL)
Woodcock-Johnson III Tests of Cognitive Abilities
    (WJ III COG): Tests 1–8, 11–18
Comprehensive Test of Phonological Processing (CTOPP)
Peabody Picture Vocabulary Test—Third Edition
    (PPVT-III), Form A
Expressive Vocabulary Test (EVT)
The Word Test—Revised
Test of Word Finding—2
Test of Language Competence—Expanded Edition,
    Level 1 (TLC-Expanded)
Wide Range Achievement Test—3 (WRAT3)
Parent interview

BEHAVIORAL OBSERVATIONS

Josephine was seen on two separate occasions. Each time she was pleasant and cooperative. She seemed to enjoy challenging tasks and demonstrated excellent attention and concentration. On several occasions, when trying to explain concepts, she expressed frustration in not being able to find the word she intended to use.

Possible word-finding errors were noticed twice in casual conversation. Josephine commented that after testing, her parents were going to "let me go to the Baby [instead of Baby Gap store] to pick out something." Later, Josephine said that while she was testing, she was missing her school's "Stanford 9 practice assembly." The examiner questioned "assembly" and Josephine corrected herself saying, "I mean assessment." The present results are deemed valid indicators of her functioning at this time.

ATTENTION AND BEHAVIOR

The Child Behavior Checklists were completed by Josephine's mother and fourth-grade teacher, Nicole Lynn Hussey. Mrs. Baxter's responses resulted in elevated (abnormal) scores on only one of the eight behavioral categories. Behaviors characterized as Social Problems were in the Clinically Significant range (acts young, clings, teased, not liked, clumsy, prefers younger children). Overall, Josephine's *T* scores for Internalizing Behaviors and Externalizing Behaviors were in the Average range.

Ms. Hussey's rating scale was not significant in any behavioral domain. She described Josephine as hard working and friendly. What concerned her most is that Josephine sometimes talks with classmates during independent work time.

DIAGNOSTIC EVALUATION RESULTS

Cognitive Ability

The Woodcock-Johnson III Tests of Cognitive Abilities (WJ III COG) were given to Josephine to obtain an impression of her intellectual functioning. Results revealed General Intellectual Ability (GIA) Extended in the High Average to Superior range (SS 120). Her scores on the clusters of the WJ III COG (representing broad categories of cognitive abilities) are shown in Table 1.

Josephine performed predominantly in the High Average range of intellectual functioning. This included her expressive vocabulary, her ability to grasp the relationships among word meanings, and the breadth and depth of her acquired knowledge (Verbal Ability/Comprehension-

Table 1.   Scores on the WJ III COG

CLUSTER	SS	PR	RPI	AE
GIA (Ext)	120	91	97/90	12-0
Verbal Ability (Ext)/Comp-Knowl.	113	80	97/90	11-5
Thinking Ability (Ext)	117	88	95/90	13-2
Cognitive Efficiency (Ext)	116	85	97/90	11-3
Long-Term Retrieval	106	65	92/90	10-8
Visual-Spatial Thinking	100	49	90/90	9-5
Auditory Processing	119	90	97/90	16-0
Processing Speed	109	73	96/90	10-4
Short-Term Memory	115	84	98/90	13-8
Phonemic Awareness	118	89	97/90	15-7
Cognitive Fluency	81	10	62/90	7-4

Knowledge), her general thinking processes (Thinking Ability), and her cognitive capacity to process information automatically (Cognitive Efficiency). Josephine obtained scores in the High Average range in Auditory Processing, Short-Term Memory, and Phonemic Awareness. These measure one's ability to analyze, synthesize, and discriminate speech sounds, and to apprehend and hold verbal information in immediate awareness and then use it within a few seconds.

Josephine demonstrated a variety of cognitive abilities in the Average range. These included Long-Term Retrieval, the ability to store information and fluently retrieve it later in the process of thinking. On one of the Long-Term Retrieval tests, Retrieval Fluency, Josephine did not appear to use an organizing strategy for naming items but appeared to name them at random. Other abilities on which she demonstrated Average facility were Processing Speed, or the ability to perform simple or well-practiced cognitive tasks rapidly, particularly when under pressure to maintain focused attention, and Visual Spatial Thinking, the ability to perceive, analyze, and synthesize visual patterns.

On each of four cognitive clusters, the tests comprising the cluster indicated significantly different narrow abilities, so that use of the cluster score alone would be misleading. On the tests of the Cognitive Fluency cluster, intended to measure the ease and speed by which an individual performs cognitive tasks, Josephine was able to quickly discern conceptual similarities among pictures, and rapidly name words to fit a given category. In contrast, her performance on the Rapid Picture Naming test, speed of direct recall of simple vocabulary, was in the Low range. When naming pictures, Josephine frequently said "um" before responding. She tracked each row with her finger and called the fish a "salmon," then self-corrected. (She laughed and said "salmon" was on her spelling list that week.)

Within the Fluid Reasoning cluster, Josephine performed in the Superior range on Concept Formation, a test of inductive reasoning requiring the subject to ascertain the critical attribute that differentiates one set of drawings from another. In comparison, she scored in the Average range on Analysis-Synthesis, a test of deductive reasoning, requiring the application of rules to novel problems. The stimuli for these tests are visual patterns, and corrective feedback is provided.

The statistically significant discrepancies within Comprehension-Knowledge and Auditory Processing are not considered to be educationally significant and do not warrant concern.

In summary, Josephine is a child with high average intellectual abilities overall. Her performance on the WJ III COG tests suggests a child with good verbal comprehension, memory and reasoning abilities, and stores of acquired knowledge. A significant weakness was observed on the test of Rapid Picture Naming.

Oral Language

Phonology and Rapid Naming

The Comprehensive Test of Phonological Processing (CTOPP) was administered to assess phonological awareness, phonological memory, and rapid naming. Phonological awareness is a critical foundation for reading and spelling. On the CTOPP, Josephine obtained the score profile shown in Table 2.

Josephine's overall performance on the CTOPP indicates that she is aware of the individual sounds in words, can manipulate them, and can hold them in short-term memory for immediate repetition.

Josephine had more difficulty on rapid naming tasks. On color, object, and letter naming, her performance was in the lower end of the Average range.

Though Josephine's performance on the CTOPP Rapid Naming and Alternate Rapid Naming tests was within the Average range, her performance was significantly weaker (by more than one standard deviation) than her performance on the Phonological Awareness and Phonological Memory composites.

Table 2. Scores on the CTOPP

CTOPP COMPOSITE/Subtest	SS	ScS	PR
PHONOLOGICAL AWARENESS	115		84
Elision		14	91
Blending Words		11	63
PHONOLOGICAL MEMORY	121		92
Memory for Digits		15	95
Nonword Repetition		12	75
RAPID NAMING	97		42
Rapid Digit Naming		11	63
Rapid Letter Naming		8	25
ALTERNATE RAPID NAMING	91		27
Rapid Color Naming		8	25
Rapid Object Naming		9	37

Table 3. Vocabulary and Word Finding Scores

TEST/Subtest	SS	PR	AE
PEABODY PICTURE VOCABULARY TEST—III	108	70	10-4
EXPRESSIVE VOCABULARY TEST	102	55	9-6
THE WORD TEST-REVISED			
Associations	107	64	9-9
Synonyms	111	74	10-0
Semantic Absurdities	109	67	9-11
Antonyms	111	73	10-8
Definitions	99	39	8-6
Multiple Definitions	104	54	9-2
TOTAL TEST	108	66	9-8

Vocabulary and Word Finding

To examine single word comprehension and usage, word associations, and semantics, the Peabody Picture Vocabulary Test—Third Edition (PPVT-III), the Expressive Vocabulary Test (EVT), and The Word Test—Revised were given. Scores are shown in Table 3.

All scores on these tests and subtests of word knowledge were in the mid- to upper end of the Average range. Josephine did, however, appear to struggle with word retrieval when required to provide precise definitions for stimulus words (The Word Test, Definitions). She made comments such as "I can't think of a name," "I know it but I just can't explain it," and "It's on the tip of my tongue but I can't get it out!"

The Test of Word Finding—2 (TWF-2) specifically assesses word-finding skills in single word naming. The TWF-2 formal analysis revealed weak word-finding skills. In contrast to her 97% word comprehension score, Josephine earned a word-finding quotient of 73 (PR 3), almost two standard deviations below the mean. The TWF-2 informal analyses indicated that, when cued with the first syllable of the target word, Josephine was able to retrieve 71% of the missed words and was able to imitate all two- and three-syllable target words on which she had made errors. An analysis of her noun target word substitutions indicated that the majority were semantic (e.g., "flower" for rose) with a smaller number of phonemic substitutions (e.g., "oculars" for binoculars).

The TWF-2 formal and informal test findings indicate that Josephine had difficulty retrieving target words that she knew and could articulate. Her high incidence of semantic substitutions coupled with her responsiveness to phonemic cueing suggests that many of her semantic word substitutions may have stemmed from difficulties accessing

Table 4. Test of Language Competence—Expanded Edition Scores

TLC-Expanded COMPOSITE / Subtests	SS	ScS	PR
INTERPRETING INTENTS	118		
Ambiguous Sentences		10	50
Listening Comprehension: Making Inferences		14	91
EXPRESSING INTENTS	110		
Oral Expression: Recreating Sentences		10	50
Figurative Language		12	75

the phonological form of the target words. Further, her phonemic approximations of target words (phonemic substitutions) also indicate difficulty accessing the complete phonology of the target words.

Connected Language

To assess Josephine's comprehension and usage of connected language in terms of syntax, semantics, and pragmatics, the Test of Language Competence—Expanded Edition (TLC-Expanded) was administered. (See Table 4.) Josephine demonstrated High Average ability to understand spoken language and Average ability to express herself using age-appropriate grammar and syntax.

ACADEMIC SKILLS

Academic achievement was assessed in basic reading, spelling, and computation skills on the Wide Range Achievement Test—3 (WRAT3). Josephine obtained the scores shown in Table 5.

Josephine displayed High Average single word reading decoding, spelling, and paper pencil computation skills. Her achievement scores were consistent with her high average aptitude for academic success.

Analysis of the WRAT3 Arithmetic subtest indicated that Josephine can perform addition and subtraction of multiple-digit numbers with renaming, and simple multiplication and division. She has yet to learn how to manipu-

Table 5. Wide Range Achievement Test—3 Scores

WRAT3: Subtests	SS	PR
Reading	114	83
Spelling	117	87
Arithmetic	120	91

late fractions or compute long division problems. Most likely, these math skills have not yet been taught.

SUMMARY AND CONCLUSIONS

Mr. and Mrs. Baxter requested a comprehensive evaluation primarily to assess Josephine's speech and language development with particular concern regarding word-retrieval difficulties. Results of this evaluation indicate that Josephine is a child with High Average intellectual abilities overall. She scored in the Average to High Average range in all areas of cognitive abilities with the exception of rapid naming. Her single word vocabulary skills were Average to High Average, as was her comprehension and expression of longer discourse. Her well-developed phonemic awareness skills provide a strong foundation for her High Average reading decoding, sight word, and spelling achievement. Her computation skills are also strong.

Present results suggest that Josephine has word-retrieval difficulties. A weakness in rapid naming was evident on both the WJ III COG and the CTOPP. On the TWF-2, Josephine clearly demonstrated specific word-retrieval deficits, largely related to phonemic retrieval. Test behaviors, informal conversation, anecdotal records, previous testing by Dr. Kathryn Heilman, and observations by Mrs. Baxter provide support for these findings.

By history, Josephine's word-retrieval difficulties appear to be the result of the closed head injury she suffered at the age of 7. A pediatric neurologist would be helpful in determining whether or not Josephine's constellation of cognitive and linguistic strengths and weaknesses is typical of a closed head injury such as the one she experienced. Time and the ever-increasing academic demands of school will reveal what impact such retrieval difficulties will have on Josephine's academic and social development.

RECOMMENDATIONS

1. The Baxters should share the results of this evaluation with Josephine's pediatrician and request a referral to a pediatric neurologist.
2. Though Josephine's reading skills are strong, monitor her rate of reading to ensure that fluency develops commensurate with decoding and comprehension. Periodic timings of oral reading can be used to ensure progress.
3. Provide a copy of this report to the school Child Study Team and request the services of a speech-language pathologist to work with Josephine on strategies for facilitating word retrieval.
4. The following are some of the strategies often used to facilitate word retrieval:
   a) Provide activities to reinforce the association of recently learned words with known words within a strong conceptual framework. Examples include games (e.g., board games, computer software, games you might play in the car) that require Josephine to categorize information such as vegetables, fruit, things you drink, and things you wear.
   b) Teach Josephine to visualize the object or the spelling of the word to prompt recall of the verbal label.
   c) Teach Josephine to visualize a different context for the word and mentally describe it with a sentence. Example: For "blocks," she might think, "Children build with _____."

Adapted from Melissa M. King, M.Ed.

Educational Evaluation

Name: Jonas Pierce   Parents: Roger and Jeanette Pierce
Date of Birth: 07/07/1991   Grade: 4.6
Age: 9 years, 7 months   School: Walnut Cove Elementary
Sex: Male   Dates of Testing: 02/12 and 2/16/2001

REASON FOR REFERRAL

Jonas was referred for his 3-year review of special education services. For the past 3 years, he has been receiving occupational therapy and learning disability services in a resource setting. In addition, his parents have expressed concern about his overall motor development and poor handwriting.

BACKGROUND INFORMATION

Jonas is the adopted son of Roger and Jeanette Pierce. He lives with his parents and an older brother, Jeremy, who is also adopted. The Pierces adopted Jonas at birth. His biological mother was 14 years old and smoked during the pregnancy. Although little is known about prenatal care, concerns have also been raised about possible drug and/or alcohol use during pregnancy.

Jonas attended preschool for 2 years and then entered Walnut Cove Elementary for kindergarten. Based on parental and teacher concerns regarding motor development, Jonas was referred for an occupational therapy evaluation in first grade. Results from the Peabody Developmental Motor Scale indicated delays of up to 17 months in fine-motor development and up to 26 months in gross-motor development. He demonstrated weakness in his flexor muscles, particularly abdominals and hip flexors, toe-walking, and weaknesses in visual–motor planning. Jonas was unable to hop on one foot without losing his balance. On the Gardner Test of Visual-Perceptual Skills (non-motor), Jonas obtained Average scores on measures of visual discrimination and visual–spatial relations, and a Below Average score in visual memory. Recommendations were made for occupational therapy with the goals of improving fine- and gross-motor skills, visual–perceptual motor planning, and muscle weaknesses. In addition, Jonas began to receive resource support for reading, writing, and math.

The Pierces report that although Jonas has tried to participate in team sports (both soccer and baseball), the experiences were not positive. During baseball games, Jonas would often sit down in the outfield. On the soccer field, Jonas tried to stay away from the ball. His mother reported that on several occasions when she picked Jonas up from practice, he would be crying. Presently, Jonas is enrolled in a karate program that he attends once a week. He reports that his favorite activities are playing with his Game Boy, watching television, and eating candy.

Delays are still noted in gross-motor development. At the age of 9, Jonas is unable to ride a bike or tie his shoes with ease. He walks with an awkward gait and often trips. Because of continued toe walking, Jonas is currently wearing casts on both legs to stretch his heel cords and position his feet flat on the ground. When the casts are removed, Jonas is scheduled for physical therapy to help strengthen his legs. Recent results from a brain magnetic resonance imaging (MRI) indicated subtle cortical dysplasia involving the cerebellar hemispheres (the area of the brain involving motor development and balance). These findings are supported by clinical observations.

Jonas is currently in the fourth grade. For the past 3 years, he has received special education services in a resource setting under the category of Specific Learning Disability. He has also received ½ hour weekly of Occupational Therapy services. He currently uses an Alpha Smart in his classroom to assist with lengthy writing assignments. Jonas's parents note that he is creative and has a good vocabulary and sense of humor. When asked to write what he likes to do on the weekends, Jonas wrote: "Watch TV, play Nintendo, and fall down the stairs."

ASSESSMENTS

Jonas was administered the Wechsler Intelligence Scale for Children—III and a set of tests from the Woodcock-Johnson III Tests of Cognitive Ability (WJ III COG) (Tests 1–7 and 11–17) and the Woodcock-Johnson III Tests of Achievement (WJ III ACH), Standard Battery (Tests 1–11). In addition, Jonas was observed in the classroom and a writing sample was collected. Testing was conducted over four sessions.

CLASSROOM OBSERVATION

Jonas was observed in his classroom on March 23 at 1:00. The class was preparing to move to a room next door where they were about to have a fourth-grade "United Classrooms" meeting. Four classes, including Jonas's, were together in one room in order to discuss the updated behavior plan. Jonas was sitting in the back of the room. He looked at the floor and his shoes, glancing up only occasionally. He appeared to be listening. Fifteen minutes into the discussion, Jonas began digging into the tread of his shoe with a pencil. He then removed his shoe and continued to run the tip of his pencil through the shoe treads, until a nearby student, then a teacher aide, prompted him to put his shoe back on and listen.

BEHAVIORAL OBSERVATIONS DURING TESTING

For the WISC-III administration, Jonas was tested through two sessions. During the first session, Jonas complained of being tired, yawned, and kept his head down on the desk. He said that he did not get much sleep, then became teary eyed and asked if he could please finish tomorrow. He completed two subtests before he was dismissed to go back to class. Jonas returned for testing the next morning and was once again mildly to moderately resistant. He complained that the examiner, while trying to get him engaged in the testing, was "annoying" him. When reminded that he agreed to come back to finish the test after being allowed to stop the day before, he became more cooperative. Nonetheless, he did not seem to have much stamina and struggled to maintain an adequate energy level. During hands-on subtests, he showed persistence and enthusiasm.

For the WJ III testing, Jonas was fairly cooperative in both testing sessions. He was informed that he could earn coupons for "free time" by complying with requests and trying his hardest. He appeared at ease, comfortable, and attentive. In the first session, testing was conducted at the end of the school day, and toward the end of the session Jonas appeared tired. He yawned and asked when the testing would be finished. He responded promptly, but carefully, to test questions and generally persisted with difficult tasks.

INTELLECTUAL/COGNITIVE TESTING

Results from the WISC-III are presented in Table 1.

Jonas's Full Scale IQ score of 93 fell within the Average range at the 32nd percentile. This IQ score provides an estimate of general intelligence and scholastic aptitude. The

Table 1.   WISC-III Scores

Subtests (Mean = 10, SD = 3, Average Range = 7 to 13)			
Verbal	Scaled Score	Performance	Scaled Score
Information	08	Picture Completion	07
Similarities	11	Coding	03
Arithmetic	09	Picture Arrangement	08
Vocabulary	13	Block Design	10
Comprehension	10	Object Assembly	11
Digit Span	(14)		

( ) indicates scores not included in the computation of IQ scores.

IQ Score (Mean = 100, SD = 15) (Average Range = 85 to 115)			
	Standard Score	Range	Percentile
Verbal Score	101	95–107	53
Performance Score	86	79–95	18
Full Scale Score	93	88–99	32
Index Scores			
Verbal Comprehension	103	96–110	58
Perceptual Organization	94	86–103	34
Freedom from Distractibility	109	98–117	73

Full Scale is composed of the Verbal and Performance scales. He obtained a Verbal IQ of 101, which is in the Average range at the 53rd percentile. The Verbal Scale provides an indication of Jonas's verbal abilities, including language comprehension and expression, recall of information, and the ability to reason with words. He obtained a Performance Scale score of 86, which falls within the Low Average range at the 18th percentile. The Performance Scale score reflects Jonas's abilities to employ visual images in problem solving and to use perceptual organization skills. The 15-point difference between scores is statistically significant and indicates a strength in verbal abilities, and a relative weakness in visual and visual–motor abilities.

Jonas obtained the following Index Scores. His score of 103 in Verbal Comprehension is Average and shows adequate ability in areas related to providing oral definitions of words and abstract verbal reasoning. A score of 94 in Perceptual Organization is also Average, indicating adequate abilities related to nonverbal problem solving. His score of 109 on Freedom from Distractibility indicates that Jonas shows average ability to concentrate and perform mental operations, with especially good immediate recall of a series of orally presented numbers. Although Jonas did not complete the additional test needed for the Processing Speed Index, it is clear that he struggles with speed of processing, particularly when it comes to paper-and-pencil ef-

Table 2. Woodcock-Johnson III Tests of Cognitive Abilities

CLUSTER/Test	AE	EASY to DIFF		RPI	PR	SS(68% BAND)
GIA (Ext)	9-7	8-0	11-11	90/90	51	100 (98–103)
VERBAL ABILITY (Ext)	9-5	7-11	11-3	89/90	47	99 (95–103)
THINKING ABILITY (Ext)	10-4	7-7	17-5	92/90	62	105 (101–108)
COG EFFICIENCY (Ext)	9-4	8-3	10-8	88/90	45	98 (95–101)
COMP-KNOWLEDGE (Gc)	9-5	7-11	11-3	89/90	47	99 (95–103)
L-T RETRIEVAL (Glr)	7-10	5-6	15-3	85/90	20	87 (82–92)
VIS-SPATIAL THINK (Gv)	8-10	6-3	15-11	88/90	42	97 (93–101)
AUDITORY PROCESS (Ga)	>25	11-7	>25	98/90	96	126 (120–132)
FLUID REASONING (Gf)	9-6	7-11	12-5	90/90	49	100 (96–103)
PROCESS SPEED (Gs)	8-7	7-10	9-4	70/90	23	89 (86–92)
SHORT-TERM MEM (Gsm)	11-6	9-4	14-7	96/90	69	108 (102–113)
Verbal Comprehension	9-10	8-4	11-9	91/90	55	102 (97–107)
Visual-Auditory Learning	8-9	6-7	16-8	87/90	39	96 (91–101)
Spatial Relations	7-7	5-8	12-1	83/90	30	92 (88–96)
Sound Blending	>26	>26	>26	100/90	99	136 (129–142)
Concept Formation	11-7	9-1	15-7	95/90	67	107 (103–111)
Visual Matching	8-8	8-1	9-3	63/90	24	89 (86–93)
Numbers Reversed	7-6	6-8	8-8	63/90	25	90 (85–95)
General Information	9-0	7-7	10-9	86/90	40	96 (90–102)
Retrieval Fluency	6-3	3-7	14-4	82/90	6	77 (70–84)
Picture Recognition	10-7	7-1	>25	92/90	57	103 (98–108)
Auditory Attention	8-6	6-2	17-3	87/90	39	96 (90–102)
Analysis-Synthesis	8-1	7-1	10-0	78/90	31	93 (88–97)
Decision Speed	8-5	7-5	9-7	75/90	28	91 (87–95)
Memory for Words	>23	20	>23	100/90	94	123 (116–130)

ficiency. His score on the Coding subtest shows slow processing of visual information with a motoric response during a timed paper-and-pencil task.

On the WJ III COG, Jonas's overall intellectual ability also fell in the Average range. (See Table 2.) Relative strengths and weaknesses were noted among the factor scores. When compared to age-peers, his performance is Superior in Auditory Processing, the ability to analyze and manipulate language sounds. He had Average performance in four areas: Comprehension-Knowledge, a measure of acquired knowledge and vocabulary; Visual-Spatial Thinking, the ability to think with designs and patterns; Fluid Reasoning, the ability to solve novel problems; and Short-Term Memory, the ability to hold information in immediate awareness and then repeat it within a few seconds. He scored in the Low Average range in Long-Term Retrieval, the ability to store and retrieve associations, and Processing Speed, the ability to scan symbolic information rapidly. Jonas appears to have relative strengths in language-related activities and relative weaknesses on tasks involving quick motor responses and the visual processing of symbols.

A significant difference existed between the two tests of the Short-Term Memory factor. Jonas's performance was higher on Memory for Words, a measure of memory span, than it was on Numbers Reversed, a measure of working memory that involves both memory span and visualization.

Jonas appears to have a strength in short-term memory for sequential information, but has more difficulty on tasks involving reordering of information. The difference between words and numbers as the stimuli may also contribute to the difficulty or ease of the task.

A significant difference also existed between the two tests in the Auditory Processing cluster. Jonas's performance was higher on Sound Blending (Very Superior), the ability to listen to sounds and then blend them together to form a whole word, than it was on Auditory Attention (Average), the ability to discriminate sounds in increasing levels of background noise. This high score on Sound Blending may be attributed to early reading intervention that focused upon phonemic awareness activities involving the oral manipulation of speech sounds.

A possible difference existed between the two tests in the Long-Term Retrieval cluster. Jonas's performance on Visual-Auditory Learning, a task requiring learning and retrieving symbol/word associations, was higher than his performance on Retrieval Fluency, a timed task measuring speed of word retrieval. Jonas's low score on Retrieval Fluency may be more a reflection of fatigue than of ability. He did not seem to put forth his best effort. Several times during the timed test, he stopped saying words and yawned. Other quantitative and qualitative information suggest that Jonas retrieves words easily when speaking.

Table 3. Intra-Cognitive Discrepancies

Intra-Cognitive DISCREPANCIES	STANDARD SCORES			DISCREPANCY		Significant at
	Actual	Predicted	Difference	PR	SD	+ or − 1.50 SD (SEE)
COMP-KNOWLEDGE (Gc)	99	101	−2	44	−0.16	No
L-T RETRIEVAL (Glr)	87	103	−16	11	−1.21	No
VIS-SPATIAL THINK (Gv)	97	101	−4	39	−0.28	No
AUDITORY PROCESS (Ga)	126	97	+29	98	+2.16	Yes
FLUID REASONING (Gf)	100	101	−1	45	−0.11	No
PROCESS SPEED (Gs)	89	102	−13	18	−0.90	No
SHORT-TERM MEM (Gsm)	108	100	+8	74	+0.63	No

Difficulties with motor skills were noted on tests involving the marking of symbols or pictures. When Jonas was forming circles on timed tests, he started the circle at the bottom and then proceeded to the right. He held the pencil with an awkward grip with his thumb sticking straight out. His circles were of irregular size and shape, and on several circles the line went in and out forming sharp angles. Jonas's relatively slow performance on measures of processing speed may be more related to motor speed than to symbolic processing speed.

Intra-Cognitive Discrepancies

When his performance among abilities is compared, Jonas shows a significant strength in Auditory Processing. Only 2 out of 100 students would obtain a score as high or higher. (See Table 3.)

ACADEMIC TESTING

Jonas's Total Achievement score was in the Average range, as was his performance in Broad Reading, Broad Math, and Oral Language. When viewed across the academic subjects of reading, writing, and math, Jonas's performance was lowest on measures of Academic Fluency that involve rate and automaticity. Jonas's performance was Low Average in math calculation skills and written language. Performance in these areas is described briefly below and in Table 4.

Written Language

Jonas obtained scores in the Low Average range on all aspects of writing. Several responses on both the Writing Samples and Writing Fluency tests were scored as "0" because they were illegible. His writing style is characterized by a mix of upper- and lowercase letters that appear to be based upon ease of formation. Analyses of handwriting indicated poor spacing between letters and between words, letter formation errors, oversized letters, and numerous spelling errors. Many of his letters were produced incorrectly. For example, he formed the letter "y" by writing the letter "v" and then adding a line at the bottom. He formed the letter "a" by making a loop. The line that should go down the side extends out from the top, so that his "a's" appear more like "o's." The letter "l" is written as a capital "L" and is often oriented sideways so that it appears to be the letter "v." He reversed many letters, particularly the letter "c." The frequent reversals of this letter are most likely the result of the way Jonas forms circles (from the bottom up to the right) rather than misperception of letter orientation.

The same types of difficulties are apparent in his classroom writing. Figure II.1 presents a writing sample from Jonas. As noted on the writing tests of the WJ III, Jonas has extreme difficulty with letter formation. He consistently reverses the let-

Figure II.1 Writing Sample of a Boy, Age 9-7, with Severe Dysgraphia

Translation: Mom and Dad my room toys are going crazy candy. Send me my game boy and games.

Figure II.2   Jonas's Drawing

ter "c," and forms several letters incorrectly. He has difficulty with spacing and size and mixes upper- and lowercase letters.

Despite his severe difficulties with handwriting, Jonas enjoys drawing and is able to produce detailed designs and pictures, such as the one shown in Figure II.2.

Math Calculation Skills

Jonas's lowest score was on Math Fluency, a test requiring the rapid computation of simple addition, subtraction, and multiplication facts. This low performance may be partially attributed to his difficulty writing numbers. On both the Calculation and Math Fluency tests, he inconsistently reversed the number "7," and consistently reversed the numbers "6" and "9." The way Jonas forms a "6," it appears to be the number "2." Although Jonas was able to add and subtract simple problems, he missed several because he did not pay attention to the sign. He did not regroup on a two-digit subtraction problem.

SUMMARY

Jonas is a fourth-grade student with a history of delays in the development of both fine- and gross-motor skills. Presently, his greatest area of difficulty is written language,

Table 4. Woodcock-Johnson III Tests of Achievement

CLUSTER/Test	AE	EASY to DIFF		RPI	PR	SS (68% BAND)
ORAL LANGUAGE	9-11	7-6	16-0	91/90	55	102 (97–107)
TOTAL ACHIEVEMENT	8-8	8-0	9-8	77/90	27	91 (89–92)
BROAD READING	9-2	8-6	10-1	84/90	42	97 (95–99)
BROAD MATH	9-1	8-2	10-3	84/90	39	96 (93–98)
BROAD WRITTEN LANG	7-11	7-4	8-8	56/90	10	81 (78–84)
MATH CALC SKILLS	8-8	7-8	9-11	79/90	27	91 (87–94)
WRITTEN EXPRESSION	8-0	7-1	9-3	70/90	14	84 (79–89)
ACADEMIC SKILLS	9-1	8-6	10-1	83/90	41	97 (95–99)
ACADEMIC FLUENCY	8-0	7-2	8-10	58/90	13	83 (81–85)
ACADEMIC APPS	9-0	8-0	10-4	84/90	40	96 (94–99)
Form A of the following achievement tests was administered:						
Letter-Word Identification	11-8	10-5	13-0	99/90	79	112 (109–115)
Reading Fluency	7-10	7-5	8-4	26/90	13	83 (81–85)
Story Recall	9-8	5-9	>21	90/90	51	101 (92–109)
Understanding Directions	10-0	8-2	14-0	92/90	56	102 (97–107)
Calculation	9-0	8-3	9-11	82/90	37	95 (90–100)
Math Fluency	7-9	5-10	9-9	77/90	7	78 (75–81)
Spelling	7-10	7-6	8-3	26/90	11	82 (78–85)
Writing Fluency	8-4	7-5	9-4	70/90	21	88 (82–93)
Passage Comprehension	9-0	8-1	10-6	84/90	42	97 (94–100)
Applied Problems	9-9	8-11	10-8	92/90	54	101 (96–106)
Writing Samples	7-7	6-9	9-1	71/90	15	84 (78–90)

| *Intra-Achievement* DISCREPANCIES | STANDARD SCORES | | | DISCREPANCY | | Significant at |
	Actual	Predicted	Difference	PR	SD	+ or – 1.50 SD (SEE)
BROAD READING	97	93	+4	64	+0.37	No
BROAD MATH	96	95	+1	53	+0.08	No
BROAD WRITTEN LANG	81	98	–17	4	–1.77	Yes
ORAL LANGUAGE	102	94	+8	73	+0.63	No

primarily in the production of written symbols. His difficulty in transcription results in slow, labored performance on all tasks involving writing (e.g., spelling, math facts). Jonas has particular strengths in his ability to blend language sounds, an important ability for reading and spelling. It is likely that apparent relative weaknesses in abilities related to the speed of processing and producing symbols are solely due to the requirement of a motor response. With the exception of written language, Jonas is performing close to grade level in all subjects. His problems with written language appear to be related primarily to difficulties in motor production, rather than to problems in ideation or expression.

Based upon severe difficulties in fine-motor skills, Jonas will continue to benefit from occupational therapy and writing instruction. Care should be taken to ensure that Jonas's teachers understand that his difficulties with writing are not based upon weaknesses in language or conceptual abilities, but rather upon poor motor skills. These assessment results will be reviewed with the multidisciplinary team to consider continued eligibility for services and instructional programming.

RECOMMENDATIONS AND ACCOMMODATIONS

1. Continue use of the *Alpha Smart* in the classroom.
2. Continue systematic instruction in keyboarding so that Jonas will become proficient in keyboarding and can complete written assignments in a timely manner.
3. When providing feedback on written language, place the emphasis on the ideas presented, rather than on the appearance of the writing. Praise Jonas's attempts to write, regardless of appearance.
4. Minimize copying activities by providing the information on worksheets or handouts. Provide short answer activity sheets that will review skills and knowledge without requiring lengthy written answers.
5. Provide additional time or shortened assignments on any tasks involving writing.
6. Permit Jonas to take content area exams orally.
7. Consult with the Occupational Therapist for recommendations regarding further activities for the classroom to improve gross- and fine-motor skills.
8. Use multisensory procedures (tracing and saying) to help teach proper letter and number formation and reduce frequent letter and number reversals. Begin with the letters "c" and "o" and the numbers "6," "7," and "9."
9. Provide instruction in basic math skills, including regrouping, multiplication, and division.
10. Encourage Jonas to put forth his best effort. When needed, set up a behavior management plan where Jonas can earn rewards for on-task behavior and completion of work.

Evaluated by Janice Sammons, M.A., Jennifer Gilman, M.A., Eric Jeffers, Ed.S.

Wheeling Instructional Center Educational Evaluation

Name: Renee Sandoval
Date of Birth: 08/07/1992
Age: 9-7

School: Johnson Elementary School
Grade: 3.6
Dates of Evaluation: 3/20/2002, 3/22/2002

REASON FOR REFERRAL

Renee's mother, Delia Sandoval, referred Renee for a private evaluation. Mrs. Sandoval was concerned about her daughter's difficulty expressing herself in both English and Spanish, as well as her limited educational progress. She wanted to gain a better understanding of her daughter's strengths and weaknesses and her present levels of language proficiency in both English and Spanish, and receive some ideas for educational planning.

BACKGROUND INFORMATION

Presently, Renee lives with both her parents and an older sister, Carmen. Spanish is the primary language of the home. Her father is a computer technician and her mother directs the preschool program at a parochial school. Both her father and sister have a history of learning difficulties. Her father dropped out of school in the eighth grade and then, at 18 years of age, entered a trade school. In fourth grade, Carmen was diagnosed as having both a learning disability and a specific language impairment. Carmen is currently receiving special education and speech and language services in her middle school.

Renee is currently a third-grade student at Johnson Elementary School. She attends a general ESL classroom and special education classes for 7 hours per week with an emphasis on reading and writing instruction. According to written records and a parent interview, developmental milestones, except for language, were achieved within normal limits. Mrs. Sandoval reported that Renee did not begin speaking until she was 2½ years old and responded with single words until the age of 3.

Renee was retained in kindergarten due to limited academic progress. From kindergarten to second grade she has attended bilingual classrooms and participated in an early reading intervention program referred to as the Reading Assistance Program (RAP). Her second-grade teacher, Margaret Sanders, reported that Renee seemed to have difficulty retaining information presented in the classroom. She also noted that Renee had trouble working independently and would attempt to avoid working when tasks were difficult. She referred Renee for an evaluation because of limited academic progress in all areas, including her progress in the RAP Program.

PRIOR ASSESSMENT

In April of 2001, Renee was given the Woodcock Johnson Psycho-Educational Battery—Revised Tests of Cognitive Ability (WJ-R COG) and Tests of Achievement (WJ-R ACH) and the Batería—R Woodcock-Muñoz (Spanish) Tests of Cognitive Abilities and Tests of Achievement. Results from the WJ-R COG reflected High Average Visual Processing abilities, but severely deficient performance on the factors of Short-Term Memory, Auditory Processing, and Comprehension-Knowledge.

Scores from the WJ-R ACH placed her in the Very Low range in Reading, Written Language, and Knowledge. She scored in the Low Average range on both the Math Skills and Math Reasoning clusters. Achievement results from the Batería—R Woodcock-Muñoz administered in Spanish were similar.

Two speech-language pathologists also evaluated Renee. One evaluation was conducted in English and the other in Spanish. The tests administered were the Clinical Evaluation of Language Fundamentals—Third Edition, Spanish Edition; Test de Vocabulario en Imagenes Peabody; and Peabody Picture Vocabulary Test—III. The Spanish speech-language evaluation report, completed in April 2001, indicated Average receptive and Low Average expressive language skills. According to the therapist, Renee appeared at a linguistic crossroads where she was trying to speak more English, but losing her Spanish skills. The therapist further noted that Renee's conversations were interrupted frequently with false starts, reformulations, and pauses, which seemed indicative of word-finding problems. Assessment of English speech and language abilities indicated that Renee had below average abilities in English as compared to monolingual English speakers. Her English language scores were all in the Low to Low Average range. Based upon her Average performance in receptive language, her language development in Spanish was described as more advanced than her development in English.

At this first staffing, Renee was determined to be eligible for special education services under the category of Specific Learning Disabilities. The multidisciplinary team determined that Renee did not meet the school district criteria for language impairment.

CURRENT EVALUATION

The following formal and informal assessments were conducted with Renee. The racial and ethnic background of the student was considered and the selected assessments were deemed appropriate.

Tests Administered

Woodcock-Muñoz Language Survey: English Form
Woodcock-Muñoz Language Survey: Spanish Form
Woodcock-Johnson III Tests of Achievement (WJ III ACH) Standard and Extended
Woodcock-Johnson III Tests of Cognitive Abilities (WJ III COG) Standard and Extended
Analytic Reading Inventory, Sixth Edition (ARI)
Peabody Picture Vocabulary Test—Third Edition (PPVT-III)
Reading and writing interview
Miscue analysis in the reading of a book and oral retellings

Due to her retention in kindergarten, both grade and age norms were used to score Renee's performance on the tests of the WJ III. The age norms appear most appropriate for examining cognitive development since most of the abilities assessed are not directly taught in school. Conversely, the opportunity she has had to learn academic skills is similar to her grade-peers. As the use of two sets of norms is confusing and disallows use of the discrepancy scores, grade norms are used throughout this report. Where the difference between her scores on grade and age norms were considered educationally significant, both are reported. The reader should be aware, however, that since Renee is a year older than most of her grade-peers, the scores reported here are, in general, slightly higher than the age norms produced. In addition, when interpreting Renee's performance on tests presented in English, consider that Renee is an En-

glish language learner whose first language is Spanish. Therefore, some of her scores may be underestimates of her language-related abilities.

Behavioral Observations

Renee appeared to try her best on most of the tests that were administered. When she was able to accomplish the tasks, she remained attentive and cooperative. On several occasions, when tasks became too difficult, she would ask to go to the bathroom or to get a drink of water. She sometimes responded to questions using both English and Spanish. During testing, Renee revealed a lack of confidence in regard to her academic abilities, particularly her reading and writing skills. For example, when asked to read a word, she stated, "I don't know the word. Yo no se leer" (I don't know how to read).

Assessment Results

Oral Language
Oral language abilities were measured with the Woodcock-Muñoz Language Survey (English and Spanish), selected tests from the WJ III, and the PPVT-III (English). Results from the Woodcock-Muñoz Language Survey revealed that tasks involving oral language in English would be "extremely difficult" for her (CALP 2), whereas tasks in Spanish would be "very difficult to extremely difficult" (CALP 2–3). Renee will find written tasks in English "impossible" (CALP 1) and in Spanish, "extremely difficult to impossible" (CALP 1–2). Consistent with the results of the Woodcock-Muñoz Language Survey, Renee evidenced severe difficulty in all of the oral language tests of the WJ III COG and ACH and on the PPVT-III. Her standard scores ranged from the Very Low range to the Low range (SS 50 to 80) on tests assessing her breadth and depth of vocabulary knowledge, facility in linguistic reasoning using analogies, comprehension of varying amounts of short discourse, ability to recall and retell story details, ability to follow a series of instructions using a variety of linguistic concepts (e.g., spatial, temporal, exceptionality), and acquisition of general knowledge usually learned through language and experience. Renee's CALP levels on these tests ranged from 2 to 3, again indicating that with her current language proficiency in English, she will find the language demands for instruction at third-grade level "very difficult" to "extremely difficult."

Cognitive Processing

Renee was administered tests measuring a wide range of cognitive abilities. As the WJ III Tests of Cognitive Abilities were administered in English, Renee's second language, and wide variation existed among her scores, a General Intellectual Ability score is not reported here.

Visual-Spatial Skills

Renee's strongest cognitive ability appears to be her facility with spatial orientation, analyzing and synthesizing visual patterns, and holding images in memory for subsequent recognition. Her scores indicate that her performance was typical of her grade-peers.

Memory and Retrieval

Renee's performance on three of the cognitive clusters suggests memory weaknesses. Her ability to hold information in immediate awareness (memory span), as well as to work with that information while doing so (working memory), is in the Low range compared to grade-peers. Her RPIs suggest that while other third-graders would experience 90% success on similar tasks, Renee would experience 37% success on tasks requiring memory span and 25% on tasks requiring working memory.

Regarding Long-Term Retrieval, Renee's scores fell into the Very Low range on both of the component tests. Her actual proficiency in recalling known information from long-term memory stores (Retrieval Fluency, RPI 75/90) appears to be significantly better than her proficiency in learning new information, storing it in memory, and retrieving it even over a few minutes (Visual-Auditory Learning, RPI 47/90).

Severe difficulties with long-term retrieval were noted on a test requiring Renee to name pictures of common objects rapidly (Rapid Picture Naming, SS 52, RPI 0/90). She knew the names, but she retrieved them slowly. Although both are administered with time constraints, differences exist between the formats of Rapid Picture Naming and Retrieval Fluency. Rapid Picture Naming requires a person to come up with a specific word (as does Visual-Auditory Learning), whereas Retrieval Fluency allows considerably more flexibility in coming up with a variety of words within a category. These results suggest that Renee may have a specific problem in word finding. Further difficulties with word retrieval were noted during informal assessments. Although Renee demonstrated knowledge of most of the letter names and sounds, she sometimes had to rely on a strategy to help her remember a letter name (e.g., to recall the name for "W," she had to say the whole alphabet to herself; to recall a day of the week, she had to recite the days in order).

Auditory Processing and Phonemic Awareness

The broad areas of auditory processing and phonemic awareness, necessary for acquiring reading decoding skills, include the abilities to discriminate, analyze, and synthesize speech sounds. Renee had no difficulty discriminating among similar speech sounds in words (Auditory Attention SS 102; RPI 91/90) even in the presence of background noise. Her performance in recognizing a spoken word with some of the sounds missing (Incomplete Words) and in changing the sounds in words to form different words (Sound Awareness) placed her in the Low Average range among third-graders. In contrast, her performance in blending a series of speech sounds together to form a word (Sound Blending) was in the Low range. Because these abilities are developing rapidly during this developmental period, it is possible that a child's standard score could be within the Average range—or in this case, the Low Average range—for her grade-peers even though she was not proficient in handling the demands of the task. Based on her RPIs, Renee's proficiency in manipulating the individual sounds of language is limited and tasks requiring these skills will prove frustrating for her.

Processing Speed

Processing speed refers to the speed and efficiency of carrying out simple or frequently repeated cognitive tasks, especially when under time constraints. Her performance on these timed tests was significantly higher when identifying the two most conceptually similar pictures in a row (e.g., "shoe," "boot") (Decision Speed, SS 92, RPI 78/90) than when identifying the two matching numbers in a row (Visual Matching, SS 73, RPI 18/90). Her score on Pair Cancellation, another speeded, simple task, was Low Average with an RPI at the frustration level (SS 86, RPI 63/90). Although her mastery of tasks similar to Decision Speed is (just) within the Average limits for third-grade level, it is limited when compared with age-peers. Notwithstanding the differences in her scores, Renee does appear to need more time than her grade- and age-peers to complete tasks.

Fluid Reasoning

Fluid reasoning involves abstract, logical reasoning. Renee's score on a test of deductive thinking, using a given code to solve increasingly difficult puzzles composed of colored squares, bridged the Low Average to Average range

(Analysis-Synthesis SS 91, RPI 79/90). She had more difficulty on a test requiring her to consider the attributes of two sets of drawings and come up with the rules governing their separation (Concept Formation SS 77, RPI 24/90). This test appears to depend more on linguistic reasoning than does Analysis-Synthesis, as well as requiring the simultaneous consideration of multiple elements or attributes.

Intra-Cognitive Discrepancies

When Renee's scores on each cognitive cluster were compared with the average of her other cognitive cluster scores, only Long-Term Retrieval is significantly lower than expected, due mainly to her low score on Visual-Auditory Learning.

Academic Achievement

When compared to others at her grade level, Renee's knowledge, academic skills, fluency with academic tasks, and ability to apply academic skills are all within the Very Low range, with no significant discrepancies among them. Renee's performance is Low Average in math calculation skills; Low in math reasoning; and Very Low in basic reading skills, reading comprehension, basic writing skills, and written expression. Her knowledge of phoneme/grapheme relationships is also Low.

Reading

The following information is based on Renee's results on the WJ III Broad Reading cluster, the ARI, the reading interview, and informal activities. Based on the Broad Reading cluster (SS 48, PR < 0.1, RPI 0/90), Renee's reading abilities, compared with her grade-peers,' are in the Very Low range. Only 1 in 1,000 third-graders would obtain a score as low as or lower than hers. Instructional materials at late kindergarten level should be appropriate for her. When attempting to decode unfamiliar words, she tried to sound out each letter but did not recognize consonant digraphs and blends (e.g., /sh/, /gl/). She recalled letter names and sounds when presented in isolation, except for /q/ and /y/ and the soft sound of /c/. She knew only the short sounds of the vowels.

On the ARI, an informal reading inventory, she made several miscues (word errors) that interfered with meaning and did not self-correct when her miscues did not result in a real word. When reading, all of her cognitive energy is focused on decoding, leaving little attention or memory available to focus on meaning. She had great difficulty retelling the events of the passages she read. Her summarization of a story that had been read to her was, "He did not want to

help her mom, and the mom said if they wanted to help and they said no." Although Renee's lack of proficiency in oral language undoubtedly will impair reading comprehension at some point, currently her decoding skills are too low to measure this.

Renee is self-conscious about her reading difficulties. On several occasions, she stated that she is not a reader and can only read "baby-books." Nevertheless, in the clinic, she showed interest and enthusiasm when reading meaningful books.

Written Language

Renee's abilities in written language were assessed based on the WJ III and analyses of classroom writing samples. Writing skills assessed by the WJ III included spelling, writing fluency, writing a variety of complete sentences, and editing sentences with errors in them. Her performance on Broad Written Language (SS 59) was within the lowest 3 in 1,000 of her grade-peers. Her RPI suggests proficiency in writing skills at 13% compared with typical third-graders' 90%. Appropriate instructional materials would be approximately beginning first-grade level.

Observation and error analysis of these tasks suggest the following:

- Renee writes the words just as they sound to her; she is as yet unaware of English spelling patterns that might differ from one-to-one letter/sound correspondence, such as the irregular components of words.
- Renee's difficulty discriminating between the short vowel sound for /e/ and /i/ may be due to the pronunciation of their names in Spanish.
- Letter orientation errors (e.g., *p, d, b*) were also evident in her written work.
- Renee erases frequently when writing and often asks for help to spell words. The fact that she is worried about sounding out every word coupled with her difficulty retrieving information makes her writing very slow and effortful. Her willingness to write in her interactive journal improved when she understood that she did not have to spell the words correctly.
- Renee tends to start her sentences with the same phrases. Her sentence structure is very simple and reveals her lack of language proficiency and limited background knowledge.

Mathematics

Mathematics was Renee's strongest academic area. The WJ III Broad Mathematics cluster measures calculation skills, fluency in recalling math facts, and application of these skills to practical situations. Her Broad Mathematics cluster score was in the lower end of the Low Average range (SS 82) with an RPI of 54/90. Her math calculation skills (RPI 73/90) are stronger than her math reasoning skills (RPI 16/90). The Age/Grade Instructional Zone indicates that Renee could benefit from instruction in computation skills at about mid-second grade level but would need instruction in application of math skills at about mid-first grade level.

Renee demonstrated understanding of the concepts of addition and subtraction and added and subtracted one-and-two-digit numbers without regrouping. While performing math computations, she counted aloud in English. She did not know any multiplication facts and did not understand the concept of multiplication. She enjoyed the math activities and commented that math was the only thing that she knew how to do.

Academic Knowledge
Similar to her general knowledge (General Information SS 69), Renee's store of information in the areas of humanities, social sciences, and physical sciences is in the Very Low range, similar to that of a beginning kindergarten student.

Intra-Achievement Discrepancies
No discrepancies were found among Renee's performance on the achievement clusters.

Ability/Achievement Discrepancies

Oral Language Discrepancies
Even though her English language abilities are low, Renee's oral language abilities are considerably more advanced than are her present levels of reading and writing performance. When Oral Language is used to predict her academic achievement, the following discrepancies are significant: Broad Reading, Basic Reading Skills, Reading Comprehension, Broad Written Language, and Basic Writing Skills.

Intellectual Ability/Achievement Discrepancies
Even if one considers the GIA to be an underestimation of Renee's cognitive abilities, predictions of academic achievement made using this score indicate that Renee should be making far more academic progress than she shows on this evaluation. Most of her scores on the Achievement cluster (including Oral Language) are significantly lower than her predicted scores. These include the clusters noted above and Oral Language, Oral Expression, and Academic Knowledge.

SUMMARY

Renee is currently a third-grade student, retained in kindergarten, at Johnson Elementary School. Her primary language is Spanish. She is making limited progress in all areas of academic achievement although math facts and calculation are relative strengths. Results from previous and current testing and informal observations suggest that Renee has cognitive strengths in visual–spatial processing and memory, speech discrimination, and deductive, linear reasoning. Renee evidences significant weaknesses, compared to grade-peers, in phonemic manipulation, memory span, working memory, long-term retrieval, transfer of new information into long-term memory stores, processing speed, inductive logical reasoning, and acquired knowledge. It is difficult to ascertain whether these cognitive weaknesses are the foundation for her slow language development or are mutually impairing. The current evaluation, with findings of oral language weaknesses in both Spanish and English, indicates the existence of a primary language disorder which, along with the other cognitive weaknesses, severely impacts Renee's ability to develop academic concepts and skills. She presently requires intensive and specialized remedial education in oral language as well as in academics.

RECOMMENDATIONS

The following recommendations are provided to help Renee with classroom performance and academic development. Additional recommendations for language development and therapy can be found in the speech-language evaluations in Renee's cumulative folder.

Further Evaluation

1. Refer Renee to a bilingual speech-language pathologist for an in-depth evaluation of receptive and expressive language abilities, including word retrieval.
2. Due to her slow scanning and processing of visual symbols, refer Renee to a developmental optometrist specifically to rule out or confirm ocular-motor problems as well as other vision conditions that might interfere with visual processing.
3. Administer an adaptive behavior scale to Renee's parents and teacher to obtain more information about her general level of functioning and, hopefully, to rule out a generalized developmental delay.

General Recommendations

1. Although Spanish is Renee's first language, presently she demonstrates limited proficiency in both English and Spanish. When assigning all academic tasks, adjust the language demands to her current developmental levels. Establish reasonable, reduced expectations for all assignments.
2. To increase her self-confidence and decrease her dependence on others, encourage Renee to evaluate her own performance on tasks. For example, have her chart her progress on a specific type of skill such as speed of math facts or letter/sound correspondences learned.
3. To reduce avoidance behaviors, provide Renee with several passes per day for visits to the drinking fountain and bathroom.
4. Because Renee will have difficulty understanding lengthy instructions and complex sentences, when giving instructions to her, provide clear, simple explanations. Clarify vocabulary. When needed, provide clarifications of English instructions in Spanish.
5. Provide a variety of multisensory interventions that involve a lot of purposeful repetition to help Renee memorize material (e.g., visual cues, tracing, listening, saying, singing).
6. Before assigning a reading, writing, or content area task, provide activities to promote related language development. Spend time on activities that promote oral discussions, build vocabulary, and increase background knowledge.
7. When providing instruction, to be followed by assignments, explain and model the task and provide guided practice. When Renee is able to complete the task successfully, provide independent practice.
8. Read Renee simple stories. Speak slowly, repeat phrases, as necessary, and use picture cues to illustrate the meaning.

Reading

1. Teach phonics through a highly structured, synthetic program that will help Renee form a strong association between letters and their corresponding sounds. Teach letter/sound relationships directly and systematically. Teach her how to blend sounds to form words. Combine phonics instruction with a reading program that uses decodable text (i.e., reading materials that incorporate only the phonics skills taught so far so that the student practices what she has been taught but is not confronted with letter/word patterns that have not yet been introduced). This will allow Renee to learn to apply her newly acquired skills successfully and develop automaticity.
2. Have Renee work with a more competent reader with whom she could do guided reading and partner-reading, follow along with taped books, and listen to oral reading.
3. Encourage extension activities that promote oral discussions about the books read.
4. Supplement phonics instruction and the use of decodable text with patterned language books to help Renee make the connections between oral language and printed words, and to become more familiar with common English spelling and sentence patterns. Use highly predictable reading materials that contain rhyming words and repeated syntactic patterns.
5. As they come up in her reading program, help Renee master common English spelling patterns (e.g., -ing, -ed, -tch, -ck) and understand the rules that govern them. Provide for overlearning of spelling patterns.

Writing

1. Use a whole-word approach to teaching spelling only for the high-frequency sight words that come up in the systematic reading program; otherwise, focus Renee's spelling practice on the phonics patterns she is learning. For whole-word spelling, use a multisensory method such as the Modified Fernald Technique to incorporate visual, oral, and kinesthetic-tactile components.
2. Use a Spelling Flow List, or other type of chart, so that Renee can monitor her growth and progress. Select a few words from her reading sight words and provide daily, then distributed, reinforcement and testing. After mastery has been established, test on a monthly basis.
3. Integrate writing activities with the use of a patterned language text. After reading a book at an independent level, use an extension activity in which Renee creates her own book. Have her follow the book's pattern, but choose her own objects and characters.
4. As with reading, prewriting activities to increase vocabulary and background knowledge are essential.
5. As writing skill develops, use sentence-combining activities to improve Renee's ability to write sentences with more complex structures. Present Renee with a set of simple sentences to combine into one longer sentence.

Mathematics

1. When providing instruction in math, adjust the level of instruction to match Renee's current level of language proficiency.
2. For the math facts, Renee profits from purposeful repeti-

tion within different activities, such as singing songs, saying them as well as writing them, and including them in games.

3. Provide manipulatives and practical activities to promote math reasoning. To help Renee and her classmates understand word problems, set up practical situations, such as a simulated store, and have the students make up specific situations requiring math calculations (e.g., figuring out the cost of two objects, making change) and

put them into words, while someone else writes the problem down. Later, use the same written problems for problem-solving practice and substitute other objects, numbers, and situations.

4. Because of her limited level of reading skill, provide Renee with assistance in reading the math textbook.

Adapted from Katia Alfaro, M.A. and Beatriz Quintos, M.A.

COMPUSCORE VERSION 1.1b: SCORE REPORT

Name: Sandoval, Renee   School: Johnson Elementary School

TABLE OF SCORES: *Woodcock-Johnson III Tests of Cognitive Abilities* and *Tests of Achievement (Form A)* **Norms based on grade 3.6**

CLUSTER/Test	GE	EASY	to DIFF	RPI	PR	SS(68% BAND)	z
GIA (Ext)	K.7	K.0	1.7	43/90	2	68 (66–70)	−2.13
VERBAL ABILITY (Ext)	K.2	<K.0	1.0	17/90	1	64 (60–68)	−2.40
THINKING ABILITY (Ext)	1.4	K.3	3.2	72/90	10	81 (79–83)	−1.26
COG EFFICIENCY (Ext)	1.6	1.0	2.4	42/90	5	76 (72–80)	−1.61
COMP-KNOWLEDGE (*Gc*)	K.2	<K.0	1.0	17/90	1	64 (60–68)	−2.40
L-T RETRIEVAL (*Glr*)	K.3	<K.0	1.9	62/90	0.1	54 (50–59)	−3.03
VIS-SPATIAL THINK (*Gv*)	2.6	K.5	7.3	87/90	36	94 (90–99)	−0.37
AUDITORY PROCESS (*Ga*)	1.3	K.3	4.4	78/90	17	85 (80–91)	−0.97
FLUID REASONING (*Gf*)	1.5	K.9	2.4	53/90	10	81 (78–85)	−1.26
PROCESS SPEED (*Gs*)	2.0	1.4	2.7	47/90	8	79 (76–82)	−1.39
SHORT-TERM MEM (*Gsm*)	1.1	K.4	2.0	37/90	8	79 (74–85)	−1.40
PHONEMIC AWARE III	1.1	K.3	2.5	65/90	7	78 (74–82)	−1.49
WORKING MEMORY	K.8	K.1	1.6	25/90	3	73 (68–78)	−1.83
BROAD ATTENTION	1.4	K.5	2.4	54/90	5	76 (72–80)	−1.61
COGNITIVE FLUENCY	<K.0	<K.0	K.8	20/90	0.4	60 (57–62)	−2.68
EXEC PROCESSES	1.6	K.6	2.9	65/90	9	80 (77–83)	−1.32
KNOWLEDGE	K.1	<K.0	K.8	14/90	1	62 (58–66)	−2.51
ORAL LANGUAGE (Ext)	<K.0	<K.0	K.9	31/90	0.4	60 (55–64)	−2.69
ORAL EXPRESSION	<K.0	<K.0	K.6	36/90	1	64 (58–71)	−2.37
LISTENING COMP	K.2	<K.0	1.2	27/90	1	65 (61–69)	−2.34
TOTAL ACHIEVEMENT	1.2	K.9	1.6	6/90	0.4	60 (58–62)	−2.67
BROAD READING	K.9	<K.8	1.2	0/90	<0.1	48 (45–52)	−3.46
BROAD MATH	2.1	1.5	2.8	54/90	11	82 (79–85)	−1.23
BROAD WRITTEN LANG	1.1	K.7	1.5	13/90	0.3	59 (55–64)	−2.71
BASIC READING SKILLS	1.4	1.2	1.6	1/90	0.3	59 (55–63)	−2.75
READING COMP	K.9	<K.7	1.2	2/90	<0.1	53 (49–57)	−3.11
MATH CALC SKILLS	2.5	1.7	3.5	73/90	18	86 (82–91)	−0.91
MATH REASONING	1.4	1.0	2.0	16/90	4	74 (70–77)	−1.76
BASIC WRITING SKILLS	<1.2	<1.2	1.2	2/90	0.2	56 (50–62)	−2.93
WRITTEN EXPRESSION	1.4	K.9	2.0	36/90	1	67 (60–74)	−2.21
ACADEMIC SKILLS	1.4	1.2	1.7	3/90	0.1	55 (52–58)	−2.99
ACADEMIC FLUENCY	K.9	<K.8	1.5	12/90	0.3	59 (53–65)	−2.73
ACADEMIC APPS	1.1	K.8	1.5	8/90	0.5	61 (58–65)	−2.57
ACADEMIC KNOWLEDGE	K.1	<K.0	K.6	10/90	0.5	61 (56–66)	−2.59
PHON/GRAPH KNOW	1.6	1.3	1.9	27/90	7	77 (73–82)	−1.50

(*continued*)

TABLE OF SCORES: *(continued)*

CLUSTER/Test	GE	EASY to DIFF		RPI	PR	SS(68% BAND)	z
Verbal Comprehension	K.1	<K.0	K.9	15/90	0.4	60 (55–66)	−2.64
Visual-Auditory Learning	K.3	<K.0	1.4	47/90	1	65 (61–69)	−2.33
Spatial Relations	3.7	1.0	9.7	90/90	51	101 (96–105)	0.04
Sound Blending	K.4	<K.0	1.5	55/90	7	77 (71–84)	−1.51
Concept Formation	K.9	K.3	1.6	24/90	6	77 (73–81)	−1.56
Visual Matching	1.7	1.2	2.2	18/90	4	73 (70–77)	−1.77
Numbers Reversed	1.0	K.5	1.6	20/90	7	78 (71–84)	−1.49
Incomplete Words	K.3	<K.0	3.4	74/90	16	85 (79–91)	−0.98
Auditory Working Memory	K.5	<K.0	1.5	31/90	6	76 (71–81)	−1.58
General Information	K.2	<K.0	1.1	19/90	2	69 (64–74)	−2.06
Retrieval Fluency	K.3	<K.0	3.7	75/90	1	63 (55–71)	−2.45
Picture Recognition	1.8	K.2	5.1	81/90	28	91 (87–96)	−0.57
Auditory Attention	4.6	1.1	12.9	91/90	56	102 (96–109)	0.16
Analysis-Synthesis	2.4	1.5	4.1	79/90	28	91 (86–97)	−0.57
Decision Speed	2.7	1.8	3.8	78/90	31	92 (88–97)	−0.51
Memory for Words	1.3	K.3	2.6	59/90	21	88 (82–94)	−0.80
Rapid Picture Naming	<K.0	<K.0	<K.0	0/90	<0.1	52 (50–54)	−3.20
Planning	10.1	K.0	>18.0	92/90	87	117 (97–137)	1.14
Pair Cancellation	2.0	1.1	3.0	63/90	17	86 (83–88)	−0.96
Letter-Word Identification	1.4	1.2	1.6	0/90	0.4	60 (57–63)	−2.69
Reading Fluency	<K.8	<K.8	<1.0	—	—	—	—
Story Recall	<K.0	<K.0	K.4	50/90	<0.1	50 (30–70)	−3.33
Understanding Directions	K.9	<K.0	2.2	56/90	9	80 (75–84)	−1.36
Calculation	2.6	2.1	3.3	66/90	23	89 (84–94)	−0.74
Math Fluency	2.0	K.2	4.0	79/90	11	81 (78–85)	−1.24
Spelling	K.7	K.5	1.0	1/90	0.2	56 (51–62)	−2.90
Writing Fluency	1.2	<K.0	1.9	21/90	3	71 (62–79)	−1.96
Passage Comprehension	K.7	K.5	K.9	0/90	<0.1	49 (44–54)	−3.39
Applied Problems	1.6	1.1	2.1	18/90	8	79 (76–83)	−1.37
Writing Samples	1.5	1.1	2.1	54/90	1	67 (58–76)	−2.22
Story Recall—Delayed	—	—	—	—	—	—	2.76
Word Attack	1.4	1.2	1.6	4/90	4	73 (68–79)	−1.79
Picture Vocabulary	<K.0	<K.0	K.7	24/90	4	74 (70–79)	−1.71
Oral Comprehension	<K.0	<K.0	K.4	10/90	1	66 (61–71)	−2.26
Editing	<1.2	<1.2	<1.6	—	—	—	—
Reading Vocabulary	1.2	K.8	1.5	9/90	2	69 (64–74)	−2.07
Quantitative Concepts	1.2	K.8	1.8	15/90	3	71 (66–76)	−1.94
Academic Knowledge	K.1	<K.0	K.6	10/90	0.5	61 (56–66)	−2.59
Spelling of Sounds	2.1	1.5	4.1	79/90	28	91 (87–96)	−0.59
Sound Awareness	1.9	1.2	2.9	64/90	16	85 (82–89)	−0.98
Punctuation & Capitalization	1.2	K.8	1.7	16/90	1	65 (56–74)	−2.34

	STANDARD SCORES			DISCREPANCY			
INTRA-COGNITIVE DISCREPANCIES	Actual	Predicted	Difference	PR	SD	Significant at + or − 1.50 SD (SEE)
COMP-KNOWLEDGE (*Gc*)	64	80	−16	8	−1.40	No
L-T RETRIEVAL (*Glr*)	54	80	−26	2	−2.08	Yes
VIS-SPATIAL THINK (*Gv*)	94	84	+10	78	+0.76	No
AUDITORY PROCESS (*Ga*)	85	83	+2	59	+0.22	No
FLUID REASONING (*Gf*)	81	78	+3	61	+0.28	No
PROCESS SPEED (*Gs*)	79	85	−6	33	−0.45	No
SHORT-TERM MEM (*Gsm*)	79	83	−4	39	−0.28	No
PHONEMIC AWARE	76	82	−6	32	−0.46	No
WORKING MEMORY	73	82	−9	22	−0.76	No

TABLE OF SCORES: *(continued)*

INTRA-ACHIEVEMENT DISCREPANCIES	STANDARD SCORES			DISCREPANCY		
	Actual	Predicted	Difference	PR	SD	Significant at + or – 1.50 SD (SEE)
BASIC READING SKILLS	59	61	–2	38	–0.30	No
READING COMP	53	66	–13	9	–1.34	No
MATH CALC SKILLS	86	73	+13	85	+1.05	No
MATH REASONING	74	65	+9	79	+0.82	No
BASIC WRITING SKILLS	56	67	–11	16	–0.99	No
WRITTEN EXPRESSION	67	70	–3	39	–0.28	No
ORAL EXPRESSION	64	73	–9	23	–0.73	No
LISTENING COMP	65	70	–5	35	–0.39	No
ACADEMIC KNOWLEDGE	61	70	–9	21	–0.80	No

INTELLECTUAL ABILITY/ ACHIEVEMENT DISCREPANCIES	STANDARD SCORES			DISCREPANCY		
	Actual	Predicted	Difference	PR	SD	Significant at + or – 1.50 SD (SEE)
BROAD READING	48	78	–30	0.4	–2.67	Yes
BASIC READING SKILLS	59	83	–24	2	–2.09	Yes
READING COMP	53	79	–26	1	–2.40	Yes
BROAD MATH	82	83	–1	44	–0.15	No
MATH CALC SKILLS	86	86	0	50	0.00	No
MATH REASONING	74	81	–7	24	–0.71	No
BROAD WRITTEN LANG	59	83	–24	2	–2.13	Yes
BASIC WRITING SKILLS	56	81	–25	1	–2.19	Yes
WRITTEN EXPRESSION	67	82	–15	10	–1.27	No
ORAL LANGUAGE (Ext)	60	80	–20	5	–1.67	Yes
ORAL EXPRESSION	64	83	–19	5	–1.61	Yes
LISTENING COMP	65	81	–16	10	–1.26	No
ACADEMIC KNOWLEDGE	61	80	–19	4	–1.73	Yes

These discrepancies based on GIA (Ext) with ACH Broad, Basic, and Applied clusters.

ORAL LANGUAGE/ACHIEVEMENT DISCREPANCIES	STANDARD SCORES			DISCREPANCY		
	Actual	Predicted	Difference	PR	SD	Significant at + or – 1.50 SD (SEE)
BROAD READING	48	82	–34	0.3	–2.78	Yes
BASIC READING SKILLS	59	80	–21	3	–1.85	Yes
READING COMP	53	81	–28	2	–2.14	Yes
BROAD MATH	82	82	0	49	–0.02	No
MATH CALC SKILLS	86	87	–1	48	–0.04	No
MATH REASONING	74	78	–4	37	–0.33	No
BROAD WRITTEN LANG	59	80	–21	6	–1.52	Yes
BASIC WRITING SKILLS	56	84	–28	2	–2.03	Yes
WRITTEN EXPRESSION	67	86	–19	7	–1.46	No
ACADEMIC KNOWLEDGE	61	76	–15	9	–1.35	No

These discrepancies based on Oral Language (Ext) with ACH Broad, Basic, and Applied clusters.

Rangely Public Schools Evaluation Report

Name: Charlie Wilbrahan   School: Peter Douglas School
Date of Birth: 01/08/92   Teacher: Ms. Minskoff
Age: 10-2   Grade: 4.5
                                             Dates of Testing: 2/14/02, 2/26/02

REASON FOR REFERRAL

Charlie was referred to complete his 3-year reevaluation to determine his continuing eligibility for special education services.

BACKGROUND

Charlie had an anoxic episode at 3 weeks of age and was revived only when his mother administered CPR. He was hospitalized and diagnosed with infantile apnea. He was sent home on a monitor and, until he was approximately 7 months old, continued to have frequent, repeated episodes where he stopped breathing. Subsequent neurological assessment indicated abnormal activity in the left cerebral hemisphere. He was late to develop language, began to speak discernable words at age 3, and was nearly 5 when he began to speak in two- or three-word, somewhat unintelligible, utterances. At the age of 4, he was diagnosed as having oral dyspraxia. Charlie attended a language-based preschool and then entered kindergarten. Since kindergarten, he has been in an "inclusion" classroom where there is a teacher, a special educator, and an assistant. He has received additional services for speech and language, as well as pull-out instruction for reading, writing, and math with the special educator. In contrast to his language deficits, he functions well in classroom tasks that tap nonverbal problem-solving skills.

TESTS ADMINISTERED

The WJ III COG and the WJ III ACH are comprehensive batteries of individually administered tests measuring a variety of intellectual/cognitive abilities, scholastic aptitudes, and achievement in academic areas. Because these two batteries are co-normed, direct comparisons can be made among Charlie's overall intellectual ability, his oral language, and his achievement scores. These comparisons help determine the presence and significance of any strengths and weaknesses among his abilities. Charlie was administered Tests 1–20 from the *WJ III Tests of Cognitive Abilities* (WJ III COG) (administered on 02/14/02) and Tests 1–8, 10–11, 13–15, and 18–19 from the *WJ III Tests of Achievement* (WJ III ACH) (administered on 02/26/02).

Standard scores (SS) between 90 and 110 and percentile ranks (PR) between 25 and 75 fall in the Average range. The Relative Proficiency Index (RPI) predicts a student's proficiency on tasks similar to those tested. An RPI of 80/90 means that a student would be expected to demonstrate 80% proficiency with similar tasks that average individuals in the comparison group (age or grade) would perform with 90% proficiency. The tests of the WJ III were scored according to age norms.

TEST SESSION OBSERVATIONS

Charlie was at ease and attentive during the evaluation. He often reminded himself to "work my hardest and try my best" and was willing to persist with difficult tasks. His activity level was typical for his age. He sometimes responded too quickly to test questions. Inaccurate responses and difficulty understanding the directions of certain tests appeared related to difficulties understanding language.

Although Charlie's conversational proficiency was limited for his age level, he engaged in simple conversation. His sentence structure has improved over the past year and he incorporates details into his conversation. He was unable to respond to questioning that involved higher-order thinking or required his own interpretations and feelings.

Overall testing behavior appeared more similar to peers than in the past. Charlie was able to engage in tasks effectively and complete tests accurately. Prior evaluation observations and test scores indicate that he was unable to process directions and/or expectations on many tests and, consequently, no baselines were established for future comparison. On the current evaluation, while he could not respond correctly to many items on some tests, he was able to process directions and begin each test.

RESULTS OF COGNITIVE TESTING

Charlie's performance on the WJ III COG resulted in the scores shown in Table 1.

Memory (Long-Term Retrieval, Short-Term Memory, Working Memory)

Long-Term Retrieval is the ability to store information and retrieve it later through association. Charlie was able to complete the Visual-Auditory Learning test, which measures the ability to associate new visual symbols with known (oral) words and then "read" sentences made up of the symbols. He was able to manage the demands of the test and effectively respond even as the symbols became more abstract and were introduced in increasingly complex sentences. Charlie experienced greater difficulty with the Retrieval Fluency test, which measures fluency of retrieval of information from stored knowledge. He was able to name very few examples from a given category under the pressure of limited time.

Short-term memory, an aspect of cognitive efficiency, is closely identified with memory span, a limited capacity system where information is typically retained for only a few seconds. Once an individual uses the information to perform a task, it is either stored or lost. Charlie's ability to apprehend information and use it within a short time frame is significantly impaired as demonstrated by his Low performance in repeating sequences of unrelated words and, in reverse order, sequences of digits. Charlie's RPI indicates that his proficiency in similar memory tasks would be 4% compared with typical age-peers' 90%.

Processing (Auditory, Visual-Spatial, Processing Speed)

Processing speed is the ability to perform simple cognitive tasks quickly, particularly when under pressure to maintain focused attention. Processing speed tasks are typically easy enough that most individuals would get all the items correct if the test were not timed. Within the Processing Speed cluster, Charlie demonstrated Average ability to generate simple concepts quickly—in this case, matching pictures based on their conceptual similarities (e.g., "bush" and "tree"). Charlie demonstrated Low Average ability in discriminating between visual symbols. His performance was significantly lower

Table 1. WJ III COG Scores

Cluster Score	Description	SS	RPI	Demands of Related Tasks
Comprehension-Knowledge	Ability to communicate one's knowledge and the ability to reason using previously learned experiences and procedures.	67	22/90	Extremely Difficult
Long-Term Retrieval	Ability to store information efficiently and retrieve it later through associations	67	73/90	Difficult
Visual Spatial Thinking	Ability to perceive, analyze, synthesize, and think with visual patterns, including the ability to store and recall visual representations	101	91/90	Manageable
Auditory Processing	Ability to analyze, synthesize, and discriminate auditory stimuli. Also related to phonological awareness	84	75/90	Difficult
Fluid Reasoning	Ability to reason, form concepts, and solve problems that often involve unfamiliar information or procedures	54	6/90	Extremely Difficult
Processing Speed	Speed and efficiency in performing automatic or very simple cognitive tasks	96	84/90	Manageable
Short-Term Memory	Ability to hold orally presented information in immediate awareness and then use it within a few seconds. Includes memory span and working memory	62	4/90	Extremely Difficult to Impossible
Cognitive Fluency	Measures the ease and speed by which an individual performs simple cognitive tasks	77	54/90	Very Difficult
Executive Processes	Includes three aspects of executive functioning: strategic planning, proactive interference control, and the ability to shift repeatedly one's mental set	67	79/90	Difficult
Phonemic Awareness	Ability to analyze, synthesize, and manipulate speech sounds	73	63/90	Very Difficult to Difficult
Working Memory	Ability to hold information in immediate awareness while performing a mental operation on the information	56	1/90	Impossible

(Very Low) in rapidly retrieving common words from long-term memory storage.

Test results indicate that compared to age-peers, Charlie's ability to discriminate speech sounds in the presence of noise is Average and his ability to blend individual syllables and sounds to make a whole word is Low Average. Despite an overall Low Average score in the Auditory Processing factor, Charlie's RPI indicates that classroom tasks requiring these abilities will be difficult for him.

Charlie scored in the Average range on the tests indicating the ability to perceive, analyze, synthesize, and think with visual patterns, including the ability to store and recall visual representations, such as pictures. He demonstrated ability commensurate with his age-peers in mentally manipulating pieces of abstract designs to match a whole design and differentiating pictures he had been shown previously from similar pictures that had not been presented.

Acquired Knowledge and Reasoning

Charlie scored in the Very Low range in the factors of Comprehension-Knowledge and Fluid Reasoning. The Comprehension-Knowledge cluster represents the breadth and depth of one's knowledge, including the ability to communicate one's knowledge based on previously learned experiences or procedures. Charlie's store of language-based knowledge accumulated from general life experiences and education is very limited (RPI 22/90). He also struggled with tasks that measure the ability to reason, form concepts and solve problems using unfamiliar information or novel procedures. Inductive and deductive reasoning skills continue to be an area of significant weakness for Charlie (RPI 6/90).

RESULTS OF ACHIEVEMENT TESTING

The WJ III ACH measures oral language and the academic areas of reading, mathematics, written language, and academic knowledge. The Relative Proficiency Indexes for the achievement section of this report are based on Charlie's age (10-2). (See Table 2.)

Oral Language

The Oral Language cluster provides a broad sample of linguistic competency, listening ability, and comprehension.

Table 2. WJ III ACH Scores

Cluster	Description	Grade Equiv.	RPI	Demands of related tasks at grade level
Broad Reading	Measures reading achievement including reading decoding, reading speed, and the ability to comprehend connected discourse while reading	2.9	20/90	Extremely Difficult
Basic Reading	Measures sight vocabulary, phonics, and structural analysis	2.5	16/90	Extremely Difficult
Broad Math	Measures math achievement including problem solving, number facility, automaticity and reasoning	3.0	60/90	Very Difficult
Math Calculation	Measures computational skills and automaticity of math facts	4.1	85/90	Manageable
Math Reasoning	Measures problem solving, analysis, reasoning, and vocabulary	1.7	9/90	Extremely Difficult
Broad Written Language	Measures written language achievement and includes measures of spelling, writing fluency, and written expression	1.5	13/90	Extremely Difficult
Written Expression	Measures the quality of written sentences and fluency of production	2.4	57/90	Very Difficult
Academic Knowledge	Measures learned knowledge in science, social studies, and humanities	1.5	30/90	Very Difficult to Extremely Difficult
Academic Skills	Measures basic academic skills	2.3	9/90	Extremely Difficult
Academic Fluency	Measures the ease and speed by which an individual performs simple academic tasks	3.0	56/90	Very Difficult
Oral Language	Measures linguistic competency, listening ability, and oral comprehension	K.0	19/90	Extremely Difficult

Charlie's performance in this domain was well below expectations. Related tasks at grade level will be extremely difficult. The scope of these tests, however, does not incorporate areas of language in which Charlie has made his most impressive gains. These include connected, spontaneous language and the clarity, content and structure of language necessary for conversation and communication.

Academic Achievement

Charlie has made gains in his overall academic development. Although his proficiency in word identification skills and reading fluency is still very limited, he has made significant improvement. Tasks that require comprehension, vocabulary, and reasoning continue to be exceedingly difficult for him. These test findings indicate that Charlie is approaching age-level proficiency in math computational skills and has met proficiency criteria in fluency in addition, subtraction, and multiplication facts. In contrast, application of math skills, including problem solving, number facility, and reasoning, continue to be very limited. Written language achievement, including spelling, speed of production, and quality of expression continue to improve; however, they still remain areas of significant weakness.

SUMMARY AND RECOMMENDATIONS

Charlie demonstrates consistent growth in all cognitive and academic domains. When compared to others at his age level, Charlie's performance is Average in Visual-Spatial Thinking and Processing Speed; Low Average in Auditory Processing; and Very Low in Comprehension-Knowledge, Short-Term Memory, Long-Term Retrieval, and Fluid Reasoning. His executive processing skills, including strategic planning, ignoring distracters, and flexibility in shifting his mental set, remain significantly underdeveloped.

Charlie's Oral Language skills are Very Low when compared to the range of scores obtained by others at his age level. In contrast, his performance approached age/grade expectancy levels when tasks were simplistic in language demands and supported with visual materials. No significant discrepancies were found between his oral language ability and his achievement in reading, mathematics, written language, or knowledge. Nevertheless, Charlie has made solid academic growth in all areas of the curriculum. Math calculation and reading fluency continue to represent the most impressive areas of improvement while improvement in reading comprehension and written language will be dependent on development of reading decoding and encoding skills, sight word acquisition, and receptive and expressive language abilities.

When compared to others at his age level, Charlie's academic skills are within the Low range. His fluency with academic tasks is Low Average and his level of knowledge is Low. Charlie's performance is Average in math calculation skills; Low Average in basic reading skills; Low in math reasoning and written expression; and Very Low in written language.

Based on his performance and responses to various accommodations/modifications (e.g., simplification and repetition of information, questions, and directions; use of visual aids), Charlie is able to demonstrate understanding and use of oral and written language effectively, albeit within limits. He continues to exhibit significant linguistic and reasoning difficulties that impact his ability to express himself and understand problems that involve reasoning. Although team members will make the final decision, results from this evaluation suggest the need for continued speech-language and special educational services.

The team supports the continued use of Reading Milestones and Saxon Math, supported by visual aids and manipulatives. Both programs provide Charlie with controlled text presented within a systematic, repetitive framework. Use of visual aids continues to be an integral part of his program. The team continues to assess and evaluate various visual techniques and approaches in an effort to help Charlie reach his full potential. Additional recommendations will be determined at the team meeting.

Adapted from Lizabeth-Ann Brown.

Psychoeducational Evaluation

Student: Rose Schmidt
Birth Date: 11/19/81
Chron. Age: 10-3
Grade: 4.4

Parents: Drs. Jessamine and Lyle Schmidt
Test Dates: February 18–19, 2002
Report Date: March 4, 2002

REASON FOR REFERRAL

Rose was referred for evaluation by Martha Brownell, Educational Therapist, due to ongoing difficulty in learning basic reading, spelling, and math skills despite strong language skills.

BACKGROUND INFORMATION

Rose is a 10-year-old girl who, along with her 6-year-old brother, attends Hilltop Gardens, a private school. Rose was born in Austria, the result of a normal pregnancy and delivery. Her mother, a British cardiologist, reported that her developmental milestones were all within normal limits. Rose's father, Dr. Lyle Schmidt, who is Austrian and also a cardiologist, was the head of a prestigious teaching hospital in Austria. Both Drs. Schmidt travel broadly, doing surgical demonstrations and lecturing in other countries. Rose's maternal grandparents, who share their house, provide childcare while the Schmidts are away. Dr. Jessamine Schmidt's father, a retired physician, and her brother's son have been diagnosed with dyslexia.

In Austria, Rose attended kindergarten intermittently. Just before her 7th birthday, the family moved to Albuquerque. She started first grade at Hilltop Gardens as a monolingual German speaker. Currently, since Rose's grandparents do not speak German and her father's English is somewhat limited, the family speaks English about 70% of the time. The children speak only German when the family returns to their home in Austria for 3 months each summer and, sometimes, for a month in winter.

In first grade, Rose was seriously delayed in academic readiness skills, both because of her limited English language skills and, possibly, because she had not acquired the skills American children learn in kindergarten. Her mother reported that Rose did not know the English words for many of the phonological awareness activities and later did not recognize sight words she had been told repeatedly. She had great difficulty learning the concept of addition. In second grade, she was still unable to grasp the concept that a

nickel equaled five pennies. Her mother also noted that in Austria, the piano teacher said that Rose forgot what she had learned from one week to the next. In contrast, she is a logical thinker and easily comprehends and remembers "real-world" information, in which she has a specific interest, such as facts about animals.

PREVIOUS EVALUATIONS

At the beginning of grade 2, Joanna Hanson, M.Ed., director of Hanson Academy, a private school for students with learning disabilities, evaluated and diagnosed Rose as dyslexic with deficits in visual discrimination and memory and strengths in auditory sequential memory and processing of sounds. Ms. Hanson noted that Rose was slow to complete tasks and appeared to lack automatic recall of letter forms. She suggested that Rose may be slow in processing information. The possible contributions of English as a second language and lack of kindergarten experience were not addressed.

Throughout her third grade year, during the school day, Rose received private instruction from Martha Brownell, Educational Therapist, in basic reading and spelling skills using the Lindamood Phoneme Sequencing Program for Reading, Spelling, and Speech (LiPS). The program emphasizes the development of phonemic awareness skills. Ms. Brownell used the Seeing Stars program for training visualization of sight words and had started fluency training. In May, posttesting on the Woodcock Reading Mastery Test—Revised and the Analytical Reading Inventory indicated that Rose was performing at the grade 6 level in decoding nonsense words, grade 3 in word identification and passage comprehension, and grade 4 in oral reading of words in context. Standard scores were not reported. Ms. Brownell reported that Rose still needed instruction in sight words, decoding of multisyllable words, and fluency. She also noted Rose's apparently slow processing, especially for sight words. Specialized instruction was discontinued at that point at the recommendation of the director of Hilltop Gardens school. She felt that Rose had made enough progress that she could remain in the classroom throughout the day with extra help from the classroom teacher. Hilltop Gardens does not offer special education.

Rose does not feel socially accepted at school and reports that she has only one real friend, who is in another class. Due to the general education teacher's absence throughout the first semester, her class had multiple substitute teachers and occasionally was combined with another class. Rose's mother stated that Rose cries almost nightly due to her social isolation and academic frustration. Within the last 2 months, Rose's violin teacher has begun to tutor her daily in school subjects and accompany her to school to provide supplementary help in the classroom.

Rose wears her glasses at all times. Dr. David Goldman, a behavioral optometrist, recently examined her vision and gave her a slightly weaker prescription than her previous glasses. He found no ocular-motor problems. Rose has no remarkable developmental or medical characteristics.

BEHAVIORAL OBSERVATIONS

Rose appeared as a poised and attractive girl. Her conversational proficiency and activity level seemed typical for her grade level. She was exceptionally cooperative throughout the examination and generally appeared at ease, comfortable, and attentive to the tasks. She responded promptly, but carefully, to test questions, generally persisting with difficult tasks. Initially, she asked questions such as "Will you tell me what to do?" and "Can I ask questions if I don't understand?" She relaxed as she came to understand the general procedures of the assessment process.

TESTS ADMINISTERED

Woodcock-Johnson III Tests of Cognitive Ability
    (WJ III COG): #1–18, 20
Woodcock-Johnson III Tests of Achievement
    (WJ III ACH): #1–15, 17–21
Comprehensive Test of Phonological Processing
    (CTOPP): Subtests 1–7, 9–11
Illinois Test of Psycholinguistic Abilities—Third Edition
    (ITPA-3): Subtests 4, 9–12
Qualitative Reading Inventory—3 (QRI-3)
Spontaneous writing sample
Interviews with Drs. Jessamine and Lyle Schmidt and
    Martha Brownell

TEST RESULTS

The WJ III Tests of Cognitive Abilities and Tests of Achievement were scored according to grade norms. Because these two batteries are co-normed, direct comparisons can be made among Rose's cognitive and achievement scores. These comparisons help determine the presence and significance of any strengths and weaknesses among her abilities. Rose's abilities measured by the components of the WJ III are described as standard score (SS) ranges created by 68% confidence bands (SS ± 1 SEM). (See Table 1.) When the individual tests comprising a cognitive factor or achievement cluster have overlapping confidence bands, only the factor or cluster score is presented.

The percentile rank (PR) indicates where Rose's score would fall within the scores of 100 students of the same school grade and month. For example, a PR of 75 would indicate that her score was as high as or higher than 75 out of 100 grade-peers in the norm sample. The grade equivalent (GE) indicates that Rose's raw score on a test is the same as the median raw score of students in that month and year of school. The Relative Proficiency Index (RPI) is a qualitative measure indicating Rose's expected level of proficiency on similar tasks if her grade-peers score 90%. Cognitive-Academic Language Proficiency (CALP) represents the language proficiency necessary for learning academic skills and concepts. The ITPA-3 and the CTOPP were scored according to age levels and provide scaled scores ($M = 10$, $SD = 3$), standard scores ($M = 100$, $SD = 15$), and percentile ranks. The QRI-3 is an informal reading inventory and provides approximate grade equivalents based on the level of difficulty of the passages. A complete set of test scores is appended to this report.

Cognitive Abilities

Based on the tests of the WJ III COG, Rose's General Intellectual Ability—Extended score, indicating general cognitive abilities, is in the Average range (SS 96, SS ± 1 SEM 94–98), as are most of her cognitive abilities. Rose demonstrated abilities commensurate with her grade-peers in the cognitive areas described below.

Table 1.   WJ III Standard Score Ranges

SS	69 & below	70–79	80–89	90–110	111–120	121–130	131+
Range	Very Low	Low	Low Average	Average	High Average	Superior	Very Superior

Table 2.   WJ III COG Oral Language Scores

WJ III CLUSTER/Test	RPI	PR	SS (± 1 SEM)	CALP
ORAL LANGUAGE (Ext)	91/90	55	102 (98–106)	4
COMP-KNOWLEDGE	91/90	53	101 (96–106)	4

Oral Language

Because Rose began her education in the United States as a monolingual German speaker, her current level of fluency in English should be considered. Rose met criteria for fluency and demonstrated performance commensurate with her grade-peers in the tests of oral language (see Table 2), consisting of vocabulary knowledge, the ability to follow multiple-step directions (including spatial, temporal, conditional, exception, and numeric terms), identification of the relationship between verbal concepts (analogies), comprehension of spoken information, and retelling narrative information. Rose demonstrated no difficulty rapidly retrieving familiar words from long-term memory. Nevertheless, one must keep in mind that during her primary grades, when many basic concepts were taught, Rose was just learning the language. Rose stated that she is now more comfortable speaking English than German and considers it her primary language.

Memory and Retrieval

Rose demonstrated Average ability to store linguistic information in memory and retrieve it later. (See Table 3.) The

Table 3.   WJ III Memory and Retrieval Scores

WJ III CLUSTER/Test	RPI	PR	SS (± 1 SEM)	z
SHORT-TERM MEMORY	89/90	47	99 (93–105)	
Numbers Reversed	74/90	32	93 (88–98)	
Memory for Words	96/90	64	105 (98–113)	
WORKING MEMORY	84/90	38	95 (91–99)	
Numbers Reversed	74/90	32	93 (88–98)	
Auditory Working Memory	90/90	50	100 (95–105)	
LONG-TERM RETRIEVAL	90/90	49	100 (95–105)	
Visual-Auditory Learning	87/90	38	95 (90–100)	
Retrieval Fluency	92/90	76	111 (105–116)	
DELAYED RECALL				–0.25
KNOWLEDGE	90/90	51	100 (96–105)	

TEST/Subtest	PR	Scaled Score*
ITPA-3 Syntactic Sentences	63	11
CTOPP Memory for Digits	9	6

*M = 10, SD = 3.

skills assessed were memory span (the number of elements one can hold in memory simultaneously) and working memory (the ability to hold information in immediate awareness while performing a mental operation on it).

Rose demonstrated Average abilities in long-term retrieval and delayed recall. These tasks required Rose to learn new information (e.g., short stories and associations between symbols and spoken words), use it over a period of a few minutes, and retrieve it from memory up to 2 days later.

In contrast to her strong memory for linguistic information, Rose appeared to have relative difficulty holding in numbers in memory and working with them. Her difficulty increased with the number of digits in the series. On the Auditory Working Memory test, Rose was unable to repeat more than one digit correctly, although she did not evidence difficulty repeating the names of objects. On Numbers Reversed, she could repeat only three digits in reverse order and, on the CTOPP Memory for Digits subtest, was inconsistent in repeating four and five digits in the order given. The pattern described here suggests a relative weakness with memory for numbers.

Visual-Spatial Thinking

Results of the WJ III Visual-Spatial Thinking cluster (see Table 4) indicate that Rose can think with visual patterns, such as recalling pictures after a brief interval, perceiving part/whole relationships, and mentally manipulating pieces of a pattern to match a complete design. Her recognition-memory for pictorial detail is a significant strength.

Reasoning

Rose's performance on the tests of the Fluid Reasoning cluster (see Table 5) indicates that she is significantly more

Table 4.   WJ III Visual-Spatial Thinking Scores

WJ III CLUSTER/Test	RPI	PR	SS (± 1 SEM)
VIS-SPATIAL THINK	93/90	66	106 (101–111)
Spatial Relations	85/90	35	94 (90–98)
Picture Recognition	97/90	85	116 (109–122)

Table 5.   WJ III Reasoning Scores

WJ III CLUSTER/Test	RPI	PR	SS (± 1 SEM)
FLUID REASONING	84/90	38	95 (92–99)
Concept Formation	49/90	16	85 (81–88)
Analysis-Synthesis	97/90	77	111 (105–117)

competent in using deductive than inductive logic for solving novel, mainly nonverbal, problems using newly learned procedures. Her Average to High Average score on Analysis-Synthesis reflects her ability to use given rules, or a code, to work through problems in a step-by-step fashion. Concept Formation requires that one consider multiple elements within two sets of drawings and ascertain the rule for the separation of groups. The rules become increasing complex and change with each problem. Thus, this test requires not only the ability to figure out the rules that govern a particular pattern but flexibility in shifting one's mindset from one problem to the next. Rose appeared to have difficulty grasping and working with multiple attributes of the visual stimuli simultaneously. Both types of reasoning skills are important for math concepts.

Phonological Processing

Rose demonstrated competency in phonological processing. (See Table 6.) She demonstrated Superior skill in sound blending, sound segmenting, and sound discrimination. In contrast, her score on the CTOPP Elision (sound deletion) subtest was Low to Low Average and on WJ III Sound Awareness, Average to High Average. The variation among her phonological processing scores may simply mean that her instruction in phonemic awareness skills was highly successful but that sound deletion was not trained. Moreover, any difficulties Rose may have with phonological and phonemic awareness skills must be considered in light of her change in primary language at age 7. These tasks assume familiarity with the sound patterns of words in English and, although Rose is now a fluent English speaker, one cannot assume that she has developed this level of automaticity. Ms. Brownell indicated that initially these skills did not come easily to Rose.

Processing Speed

Cognitive efficiency is the facility with which the cognitive system can process information automatically, without conscious thought, thus freeing it up for more complex thinking and reasoning tasks. Speed of processing is a critical correlate, reflecting the ability to automatize simple or frequently practiced tasks. An example is driving a car. When learning, one is consciously aware and deliberate in each move—but eventually, as the procedure becomes automatic, one can drive a familiar route and arrive at a destination with no memory of having done so. Rose had difficulty on both tests of processing speed (see Table 7): scanning rows of numbers to find the two that matched, and scanning rows of pictures to find the two that were most similar conceptually. Despite her accuracy on all items she attempted, her test results indicated that her speed in simple tasks was as low as or lower than 96% of her grade-peers.

Rapid Automatized Naming

Rose demonstrated a weakness in rapid automatized naming (RAN), scoring in the Low Average range on both composites of the CTOPP. (See Table 8.) RAN tasks require the subject to name a series of visually presented digits, letters, colors, or pictured objects as fast as possible. They differ from the retrieval fluency tasks discussed above in that a limited number of items appear repeatedly. Due to a trial run before each task, the name of each item has already been activated in memory before the test starts. Research in a variety of languages, including German, indicates that RAN is related to the development of basic reading and spelling skills. Distinct from phonological skills, it appears to predict a person's facility with orthographic processing,

Table 6. WJ III Phonological Processing Scores

WJ III CLUSTER/Test	RPI	PR	SS (± 1 SEM)
AUDITORY PROCESSING	98/90	96	126 (121–132)
PHONEMIC AWARE III	97/90	90	120 (114–125)

CTOPP Subtest	PR	Scaled Score*
Blending Words	84	13
Blending Nonwords	63	11
Segmenting Words	63	11
Elision	5	5
PHONOLOGICAL MEMORY	12	82
Memory for Digits	9	6
Nonword Repetition	25	8

*M = 10, SD = 3.

Table 7. WJ III Processing Speed Scores

WJ III CLUSTER/Test	RPI	PR	SS (± 1 SEM)
PROCESSING SPEED	33/90	4	74 (71–78)
Visual Matching	22/90	6	77 (74–81)
Decision Speed	47/90	10	81 (77–85)

Table 8. CTOPP Composite Scores

CTOPP COMPOSITE	PR	SS
RAPID NAMING	12	82
ALTERNATE RAPID NAMING	16	85

the ability to perceive, store, and recall familiar letter combinations (words and word parts) as immediately recognizable visual patterns.

Academic Achievement

Reading

Rose demonstrates considerable difficulty with reading grade-level text although she clearly uses the phonemic awareness and phonics skills she learned in the LiPS program. Rose's WJ III Broad Reading score was in the Low range, placing her within the lowest 6% of her grade-peers (PR 6). Her RPI of 17/90 predicts that on similar classroom tasks, Rose would have 17% accuracy compared with her classmates' 90%.

Basic Reading and Spelling Skills

Because basic reading and spelling skills are so highly related, they are discussed together here. (See Table 9 for Reading and Spelling scores.) As noted previously, the development of these skills may be affected by performance in phonological awareness and orthographic processing. Typically, good readers have a strong foundation in phonology and learn easily to perceive and manipulate the sounds of spoken words. As they learn to associate the sounds with letters (phonics), they begin to "sound out" new words. After sounding out the same word repeatedly, it becomes a sight word; the reader recognizes the visual pattern as a whole, instantaneously recalling the word name. One aspect of orthographic processing is this ability to recognize letter combinations and whole words as visual patterns. As a reader increases her store of sight words, reading becomes more fluent and only new words need to be sounded out. At the same time, good readers learn to recognize common word parts (e.g., *re, tion, port*) and use these larger chunks, rather than individual letters, to pronounce new words. Thus, phonological skills form the foundation for phonics, and orthographic skills facilitate sight word development and fluency.

Rose continues to have serious weaknesses in word identification. Her instructional level for reading words out of context is mid-second grade and in context, third grade, indicating that she applies her language skills when reading in context to help her figure out unfamiliar words. On tasks requiring her to read words in lists, Rose would be expected to experience 7% accuracy compared with her grade-peers' 90%. Rose demonstrated Low Average to Average performance on the WJ III Spelling test, with a grade equivalent of early grade 3, and an RPI of 62/90.

Rose performed significantly better when reading and spelling phonetically regular nonsense and real words (i.e., words that are spelled as they sound, such as *flidret* and *grab*) than words with an irregular element (e.g., *said, laugh*). Reading and spelling phonetically irregular words requires one to have stored, and be able to retrieve, a visual image of the word. This pattern suggests that Rose depends to a large extent on phonology and phonics skills to read and spell but has not developed grade-expected orthographic knowledge. Rose requires further instruction in phonics skills, in immediate recognition of common letter patterns, in reading/spelling rules, and in syllabication and structural analysis.

Reading Fluency

Reading fluency is the ability to read rapidly and smoothly, without hesitation or errors, and with comprehension. Rose scored in the Low Average range (see Table 10). Her dysfluency was obvious in her reading of the passages of the QRI-3. Her average reading speed was 45 words per minute, partially due to sounding out words that should be sight words by now, self-correcting errors, and repeating

Table 9.   Reading and Spelling Scores

WJ III CLUSTER/Test	GE	RPI	PR	SS (± 1 SEM)
Letter-Word Identification	2.5	7/90	7	78 (75–81)
Word Attack	3.3	80/90	40	96 (94–98)
Spelling	3.1	62/90	24	89 (86–93)

ITPA-3 Subtest	GE	AE	PR	Scaled Score*
Sound Decoding	5.4	10-6	50	10
Sound Spelling	>8.0	>12-11	84	13
Sight Decoding	3.7	8-9	25	8
Sight Spelling	3.4	8-6	25	8

*M = 10, SD = 3.

QRI-3	Passage Level
Word Identification in Lists	2
Word Identification in Context	3

Table 10.   Reading Fluency Scores

WJ III CLUSTER/Test	GE	RPI	PR	SS (± 1 SEM)
Reading Fluency	2.5	20/90	13	83 (81–85)
QRI-3 Reading Rate	45 wpm			

Table 11.   Reading Comprehension Scores

WJ III CLUSTER/Test	GE	RPI	PR	SS (± 1 SEM)
READING COMP	2.6	62/90	17	86 (83–89)
Passage Comprehension	2.1	30/90	8	79 (75–83)
Reading Vocabulary	3.9	86/90	43	97 (94–101)

QRI-3	Passage Level
Passage Comprehension	3

words and phrases. Even when not having any apparent difficulty with the particular words, she read slowly.

Reading Comprehension

Rose's Average score on Reading Vocabulary indicates that if she can read a word, she is likely to know its meaning. (See Table 11.) The majority of her errors were in decoding the words incorrectly. On a similar classroom task, reading one or two sentences and filling in the missing word, Rose's expected proficiency would be 30% compared with her classmates' 90%. Although her performance on the WJ III placed her instructional level for comprehension of short passages at early grade 2, Rose was able to retell and answer questions adequately about both the second and third grade passages of the QRI-3. Given Rose's comprehension of spoken language and reading vocabulary, poor reading comprehension is most likely a reflection of weak decoding skills (e.g., word attack, word identification, structural analysis) and fluency, and should improve as her basic reading skills improve.

Written Language

Rose's Broad Written Language score and each of the component test scores bridged the Low Average to Average ranges with a grade equivalent of early grade 3 and an RPI of 75/90. (See Table 12.) Broad Written Language includes measures of spelling words (discussed above), formulating and writing sentences, and writing fluency.

Written Expression

The Writing Samples test measures skill in formulating and writing sentences or phrases in response to a variety of de-

Table 12.   Written Language Scores

WJ III CLUSTER/Test	GE	RPI	PR	SS (± 1 SEM)
BROAD WRITTEN LANG	3.2	75/90	23	89 (86–92)
WRITTEN EXPRESSION	3.3	80/90	26	90 (86–95)

mands. Her answers were generally acceptable but lacked elaboration and detail. In a spontaneous writing sample, Rose's organization of ideas was good but her use of punctuation was minimal and she had many run-on sentences. In contractions, she wrote the apostrophe on the baseline, like a comma. Her RPI of 86/90 indicates that Rose would find classroom writing assignments manageable if they were evaluated with respect to the quality of the ideas rather than spelling, grammar, or punctuation.

Writing Fluency

Compared to grade-peers, Rose's writing fluency, formulating and writing simple sentences quickly, is Limited to Average (RPI 72/90). Rose worked slowly, completing only eleven items in 7 minutes, and she could not formulate a sentence for three items.

Math

Rose's overall math abilities, as represented by the Broad Math cluster score (see Table 13), are in the Low range with no significant discrepancies among the component tests of Calculation, Math Fluency, and Applied Problems. The number of items she answered correctly is comparable to a student in early grade 2. Her RPI indicates that her overall proficiency on similar math tasks is limited (RPI 39/90) compared to her grade-peers.

Calculation

Rose did not attend to process signs consistently and miscounted the pictures in one problem, without noticing that her answer was unlikely. She has not memorized all addition, subtraction, and multiplication facts, so she uses her fingers and touchpoints (not always correctly). Rose demonstrated competence in adding two-digit numbers with renaming, unless 0 was used as a place-holder, and subtraction of two-digit from two-digit numbers without

Table 13.   Math Scores

WJ III CLUSTER/Test	GE	RPI	PR	SS (± 1 SEM)
BROAD MATH	2.2	39/90	6	77 (73–80)
MATH CALC SKILLS	2.2	47/90	4	74 (69–78)
Calculation	2.4	30/90	6	77 (72–83)
Math Fluency	1.6	66/90	3	71 (68–74)
MATH REASONING	2.8	49/90	16	85 (82–88)
Applied Problems	2.3	24/90	11	82 (78–86)
Quantitative Concepts	3.4	74/90	29	92 (87–96)

renaming. She did not know the algorithm for doing a two-digit by one-digit multiplication problem and her strategy indicated that she might not understand the concept. For example, given 7×13 (in a vertical format), she said, "7 times 3 is 21, add the one and that's 22." She did not understand the problem as 7 groups of 13 or multiple addition.

Application and Quantitative Concepts

Rose's RPI of 49/90 in Math Reasoning reflects her apparent confusion with math concepts. It indicates that she will experience extreme difficulty in dealing with grade-expected concepts and application of skills. Throughout all math tasks, Rose did not seem to have a clear understanding of number concepts and relationships. She appears to have learned the information by rote. Regarding money, although she was able to state the value of a nickel and a dime in terms of pennies, and that 4 quarters equal a dollar, she could not see that 2 nickels were the equivalent of a dime. She did not know the value of a quarter and was unsure about a dollar. When she was informed that a dollar is equivalent to 100 pennies, she stated that a person could not carry that many and that she could fill the 5-gallon water jug at home with them. Similarly, Rose had difficulty with time and calendar information such as the order of days in the week, months in the year, and seasons; the number of minutes in an hour, hours in a day, and months in the year. Although she had just named 11 of the months, when asked how many there are, she guessed 4 or 5. Rose used her fingers to count by 2s and was unable to do so correctly after 10. She could not discern the patterns in number sequences (e.g., 6 8 _ 12) if the interval between numbers was more than one.

Rose demonstrated confusion in sorting out and organizing the information given in word problems. Despite good effort, she was unable to translate any word problems into computation and tended to say "I don't know" rather than try. She did not use paper and pencil unless the evaluator suggested it. On one problem, she made a good attempt at drawing the problem but used the wrong numbers.

General Knowledge

Rose's ability to learn and recall linguistic information facilitates her acquisition of general world knowledge. She appears to have caught up with her grade-peers in knowledge of information likely to be learned both through life activities, such as the uses for different objects, and in school, such as information related to science and humani-

ties. Fourth grade is a turning point for most students, however, when they are expected to begin to learn new information and vocabulary independently through reading.

WJ III DISCREPANCIES

On the WJ III, intra-individual discrepancies are computed to show the likelihood of a person obtaining a particular score, given the average of their other cognitive and achievement cluster scores. Large discrepancies indicate significant strengths and weaknesses. Rose evidences significant intra-cognitive strengths in Auditory Processing and Phonemic Awareness, undoubtedly due to her training in LiPS. She demonstrates significant weaknesses in Processing Speed.

Additionally, based on her General Intellectual Ability and Oral Language scores, Rose's Broad Reading, Broad Math, and Math Calculation scores are significantly below expectations. Reading Comprehension did not appear as a significant weakness because, within the cluster, Rose's Reading Vocabulary score reduced the effect of the low Passage Comprehension score. Similarly, Rose's score on Quantitative Concepts balanced out the low Applied Problems score so that Math Reasoning does not show as a significant weakness.

SUMMARY AND CONCLUSIONS

Rose is a 10-year-old girl from a highly educated family who started school in first grade, in English, as a monolingual German speaker. There is a maternal family history of dyslexia. According to the current test results, Rose has at least average general intellectual ability, comprehension and expression of oral language in English, and memory for linguistic information. Findings of at least average memory abilities included working memory and long-term retrieval. Her phonemic awareness skills, previously trained with the Lindamood program, are strong. She appears to reason well using deductive, linear logic for problem solving.

Current test results indicate a severe deficit in processing speed, a cognitive ability that provides a critical foundation for learning and automatizing procedures and facts. This finding does not mean that Rose simply needs more time to learn new information and procedures but that different techniques may be necessary in some areas of learning. Certainly, to develop automaticity, she will require extensive practice and application of skills as they are learned. Relative weaknesses in memory for numbers and inductive reasoning would exacerbate the difficulty of learning and recalling information related to math, including basic number concepts, facts, and problem solving.

Rose also demonstrates weak rapid automatized naming (RAN), an ability that has been related to the acquisition of sight words and retrieval of spelling patterns. Current research indicates that RAN difficulties interfere with learning to read and spell words that are not phonetically regular, and with reading fluency.

Additionally, Rose started school at a severe disadvantage—having to learn English while being expected to learn basic pre-academic and academic concepts and skills in English, and without the prerequisites taught in American kindergartens.

The effects of these cognitive difficulties are evident in Rose's serious weaknesses in basic reading, writing, and math skills. Rose's knowledge of general world information and school-related information, in sharp contrast, is well within the Average range for her grade-peers. This is most likely due to her general intelligence, language abilities, and memory. From fourth grade on, however, reading becomes a major resource for acquiring knowledge and new vocabulary. Children with reading difficulties often develop delays in knowledge and vocabulary, specifically due to lack of exposure to printed information. Consequently, the provision of specialized instruction at this point is critical.

The results of this evaluation indicate that Rose has learning disabilities that impede her development of basic reading, writing, and math skills. The specific cognitive weaknesses that appear to be contributing to her difficulties are processing speed and, to a lesser extent, memory for numbers and inductive reasoning. Difficulty with rapid automatized naming indicates further cognitive inefficiency. Rose requires specialized instruction from a teacher with expertise in teaching children with learning disabilities.

EDUCATIONAL RECOMMENDATIONS

Parents

1. Rose's areas of academic difficulties are varied and will require significant time in specialized instruction to allow her to catch up and keep pace with her peers. She is also involved in many extracurricular activities. When scheduling her time, make sure that she has ample time to relax and to play and that there are days when she is not expected to do academic work.

2. Provide Rose with educational therapy with a learning disabilities specialist or a reading specialist with expertise in working with children with learning disabilities. Educational therapy is a continuous process of diagnostic teaching and requires a high level of specialized training. Alternatively, consider enrolling Rose in a school that provides specialized instruction for children with learning disabilities and in which teachers are familiar with providing accommodations for students with learning challenges.

3. Rose is at risk for developing learned helplessness, a condition in which a child is not able to function competently in the school setting because she has come to believe that she cannot learn on her own. Support intended to foster independence can sometimes create dependency instead. Now that the general education teacher has returned, replace Rose's in-class tutor with appropriate accommodations that will allow her to function effectively in class without highlighting her learning problems.

4. Until Rose's reading ability approximates her oral language comprehension, provide her with taped versions of her classroom textbooks and assigned trade books. In the content areas, the priority is that she learn the information, which she is unlikely to be able to do if she is struggling through the reading. Because Rose has been identified as having learning disabilities that interfere with reading, you may obtain taped books from Recording for the Blind & Dyslexic (RFB&D). Information on how to do so is attached. It is best to find out what books Rose will need to be reading as much ahead of time as possible so as to have time to obtain the tapes from RFB&D. Taped novels can be obtained from the public library.

5. To aid with word pronunciation, provide Rose with a talking pen. One example is the Reading Pen II, a small portable scanner that scans any word from printed text, displays the word in large print, reads the word aloud from a built-in speaker or earphones, and defines words. Available from Wizcom Technologies, 257 Great Road, Acton, MA 01720, (888) 777-0552, www.wizcomtech.com.

6. To aid with spelling, buy Rose a pocket-sized computerized spell-checker, such as the Franklin Spelling Ace. Because she can spell words as they sound, she will be able to approximate the pronunciation of most words well enough for the spell-checker to come up with the correct spelling. Available at electronics and office supply stores.

7. Provide Rose with high interest/low vocabulary books so

that she can practice reading enjoyable books independently. Scholastic, Inc. (www.scholastic.com) and High Noon, a subsidiary of Academic Therapy Publishing Company (www.AcademicTherapy.com), have many such books. Also, check with the children's librarian at the public library.

Teacher and/or Educational Therapist

General

The classroom teacher and the educational therapist should try to coordinate their programs so that they are mutually supportive. For example, base Rose's school spelling lists on the spelling patterns the educational therapist is teaching. As much as possible, try to incorporate the specialized teaching being provided outside the classroom into class assignments. It would be helpful for the educational therapist and the teacher to meet at regular intervals to share progress notes and coordinate instruction.

Sight Word Recognition and Fluency

Currently, Rose has mastered the phonics skills needed for reading and spelling but she is not able to apply these skills or recognize words easily and automatically. The following strategies can be used to increase sight word recognition and build speed:

1. As Rose does not easily perceive and remember the letter patterns in words, teach spelling rules explicitly and provide extensive activities in which Rose retrieves spelling patterns from memory and identifies examples of them in various types of text. In all reading and spelling instruction, make sure to focus specifically on letter patterns. Incorporate activities to draw her attention to these such as color coding, circling, or searching for specific letter patterns in text.
2. To build speed and accuracy in pronouncing sight words and phonetically irregular words, use Speed Drills for Reading Fluency and Basic Skills. A summary of this technique is attached.

Math

Further Evaluation

Evaluate Rose's understanding of the concepts underlying addition and subtraction in a variety of situations and with a variety of materials. Make sure she understands that numbers represent the quantity of any type of entity within a set, that addition is the combining of sets, and that 0 also represents a set that has nothing in it. Before Rose will be able to

make sense of the value of money and equivalencies in money (e.g., the number of nickels in a quarter and the reason) and measurement (e.g., time: seconds, minutes, hours, days, weeks, months, years), she must understand sets and how they can be combined.

Math Instruction: Concepts

1. Teach all new math concepts and processes through direct instruction, not a discovery method. Rose will benefit most from instruction that is explicit, structured, and step-by-step.
2. Teach all new concepts and extensions of known concepts using concrete materials first. Make sure Rose has a chance to experiment with the materials, and experiences and understands the different aspects of the math concepts she will be expected to use. For example, when teaching simple fractions, use a variety of materials (e.g., tiles, pizza, Cuisenaire rods) to represent the whole and the fraction. Make sure she understands the meaning of the related terminology (e.g., numerator, denominator) by having her talk about what she is doing with the materials. Provide plenty of practice in manipulating the materials to solve problems. Then present similar types of problems using pictures and requiring her to draw pictures to represent the problems posed. When she has mastered this step, associate these materials with numbers. The last step is to use numbers alone to represent fractional concepts. [Adapted from Principles and Standards for School Mathematics (PSSM), National Council of Teachers of Mathematics, 2000.] The following websites are excellent for checking out PSSM and instructional ideas and examples: www.nctm.org and www.illuminations.nctm.org.
3. Develop inductive reasoning by providing practice in classification and flexibility of classification. For example, take a set of objects and divide them into groups based on a particular attribute (tools and cooking utensils). Have Rose explain on what basis you separated them (What are the differences between groups and what are the similarities within groups?). Then, reassemble the objects into one group and ask Rose to group them on some other basis (e.g., metal and wood) and discuss the attribute on which she made the distinction (in this case, what they are made of). Take turns classifying objects in different ways. When she appears to have a solid understanding of this concept, continue the tasks using two attributes to differentiate between groups (e.g., height and function). Progress to more complex relationships (e.g., color or function). Gradually move to more abstract materials such as Attribute Logic Blocks,

Tangrams, and Cuisenaire Rods, and eventually number and letter patterns.

4. Concentrate on teaching Rose the supporting concepts and algorithms of addition and subtraction. She is not ready for multiplication until she has mastered these operations.

5. Using manipulatives, teach Rose the concept of place value. In doing so, teach her to understand and work with numbers in expanded notation. When she has a solid understanding of place value, introduce 0 (the null set) as a placeholder.

Math Facts and Algorithms

1. Reteach addition and subtraction facts incorporating strategies to help Rose make sense of them and organize them in her mind. A specific sequence for teaching addition and multiplication facts is appended to this report. Teach subtraction facts as a reformulation of addition facts. Continue fact practice even when she seems to know them automatically.

2. For computation problems, give Rose a pocket-sized addition fact chart. Teach her how to use it for subtraction also. Encourage her to use it any time she wants for the answers to math facts but tell her to guess the answer before looking. That way, she gets immediate reinforcement if she is right and immediate correction if she is wrong. Eventually, visualizing the location of the answer may help in remembering it. When a fact has become truly automatic, Rose should black it out. This will continuously strengthen her recall of the fact as well as allow her to see how few facts are left to learn.

3. Before Rose works a page of computation problems, have her highlight the process signs.

4. When Rose has to memorize rote information, such as units of measurement, help her to create visual or auditory associations as memory aids. For example, 12 inches in a foot could be drawn as a footprint of a bare foot with 12 inchworms end to end crawling across it.

Math Application

1. Create situations based on daily activities and using common objects to illustrate addition and subtraction concepts. Guide Rose to verbalize the situation incorporating the language of math. Move from this to writing the problem.

2. As a next step, provide Rose with extensive guided practice in reading addition and subtraction word problems, setting them up with manipulatives and then as computation problems, and solving them. Use problems that incorporate many types of objects, first tangible objects (e.g., eggs, nickels) and then generalize to intangibles (e.g., miles, minutes). Try to use situations that would be familiar to her as well as practical.

Classroom Accommodations

1. Make it comfortable for Rose to ask for clarification or repetition of instructions, or for clarification of any information related to an assignment.

2. Due to Rose's difficulty with basic reading, spelling, and arithmetic skills, reduce the amount of work in each area assigned for in-class assignments and homework so that Rose can complete her assignment in approximately the same amount of time other students are expected to spend. When figuring the grade, the reduced amount assigned is considered as 100%. Examples are: solving the odd-numbered math problems instead of all the items, studying 10 spelling words instead of 20, and writing a paragraph instead of a whole page.

3. Do not require Rose to do assignments that do not have obvious academic application, such as doing word searches or making cards. Her general work pace and the extra academic help she will be receiving will continuously take up more of her time than other students spend in doing schoolwork.

4. Give Rose extended time for tests and in-class assignments that cannot be shortened.

5. Do not ask Rose to read aloud in class unless she volunteers to do so. When possible, prior to asking Rose to read aloud, privately assign a passage to her so that she can get help with the words and practice the passage several times before she has to read it.

WJ III Score Discrepancies

DISCREPANCIES	STANDARD SCORES			DISCREPANCY		Significant at ± 1.50 SD (SEE)
	Actual	Predicted	Difference	PR	SD	
Intra-Cognitive						
COMP-KNOWLEDGE (*Gc*)	101	100	+1	53	+0.07	No
L-T RETRIEVAL (*Glr*)	100	100	0	48	−0.05	No
VIS-SPATIAL THINK (*Gv*)	106	100	+6	69	+0.48	No
AUDITORY PROCESS (*Ga*)	126	97	+29	99	+2.22	Yes
FLUID REASONING (*Gf*)	95	101	−6	31	−0.49	No
PROCESS SPEED (*Gs*)	74	103	−29	2	−2.08	Yes
SHORT-TERM MEM (*Gsm*)	99	100	−1	45	−0.11	No
PHONEMIC AWARE	119	97	+22	96	+1.75	Yes
WORKING MEMORY	95	100	−5	34	−0.41	No

DISCREPANCIES	STANDARD SCORES			DISCREPANCY		Significant at ± 1.50 SD (SEE)
	Actual	Predicted	Difference	PR	SD	
Intra-Achievement						
BROAD READING	76	90	−14	11	−1.21	No
BROAD MATH	77	91	−14	10	−1.27	No
BROAD WRITTEN LANG	89	85	+4	63	+0.34	No
ORAL LANGUAGE	98	87	+11	80	+0.83	No

DISCREPANCIES	STANDARD SCORES			DISCREPANCY		Significant at ± 1.50 SD (SEE)
	Actual	Predicted	Difference	PR	SD	
*Predicted Achievement/Achievement Discrepancies**						
BROAD READING	76	92	−16	7	−1.51	Yes
BASIC READING SKILLS	85	95	−10	19	−0.88	No
READING COMP	86	95	−9	20	−0.86	No
BROAD MATH	77	88	−11	14	−1.10	No
MATH CALC SKILLS	74	88	−14	11	−1.23	No
MATH REASONING	85	90	−5	31	−0.50	No
BROAD WRITTEN LANG	89	92	−3	41	−0.22	No
WRITTEN EXPRESSION	90	92	−2	44	−0.15	No
ORAL LANGUAGE (Ext)	102	98	+4	63	+0.34	No
ORAL EXPRESSION	100	100	0	48	−0.05	No
LISTENING COMP	104	96	+8	73	+0.61	No
ACADEMIC KNOWLEDGE	95	97	−2	42	−0.19	No

*These discrepancies based on predicted achievement scores with ACH Broad, Basic, and Applied clusters.

DISCREPANCIES	STANDARD SCORES			DISCREPANCY		Significant at ± 1.50 SD (SEE)
	Actual	Predicted	Difference	PR	SD	
*Intellectual Ability/Achievement Discrepancies**						
BROAD READING	76	97	−21	3	−1.94	Yes
BASIC READING SKILLS	85	98	−13	13	−1.12	No
READING COMP	86	97	−11	14	−1.08	No
BROAD MATH	77	98	−21	2	−1.97	Yes
MATH CALC SKILLS	74	98	−24	3	−1.95	Yes
MATH REASONING	85	98	−13	11	−1.22	No
BROAD WRITTEN LANG	89	98	−9	21	−0.79	No
WRITTEN EXPRESSION	90	98	−8	26	−0.63	No
ORAL LANGUAGE (Ext)	102	98	+4	64	+0.37	No
ORAL EXPRESSION	100	98	+2	56	+0.15	No
LISTENING COMP	104	98	+6	67	+0.45	No
ACADEMIC KNOWLEDGE	95	98	−3	41	−0.23	No

*These discrepancies based on GIA (Ext) with ACH Broad, Basic, and Applied clusters.

DISCREPANCIES	STANDARD SCORES			DISCREPANCY		
	Actual	Predicted	Difference	PR	SD	Significant at + or – 1.50 SD (SEE)
*Oral Language/Achievement Discrepancies**						
BROAD READING	76	101	–25	3	–1.94	Yes
BASIC READING SKILLS	85	101	–16	10	–1.28	No
READING COMP	86	101	–15	13	–1.11	No
BROAD MATH	77	101	–24	3	–1.83	Yes
MATH CALC SKILLS	74	101	–27	3	–1.85	Yes
MATH REASONING	85	101	–16	10	–1.30	No
BROAD WRITTEN LANG	89	101	–12	19	–0.87	No
WRITTEN EXPRESSION	90	101	–11	22	–0.77	No
ACADEMIC KNOWLEDGE	95	101	–6	29	–0.55	No

*These discrepancies based on Oral Language (Ext) with ACH Broad, Basic, and Applied clusters.

Comprehensive Test of Phonological Processing

Subtest*	Age Equivalent	Grade Equivalent	Percentile Rank	Standard Score
Elision	7-0	2.0	5	5
Blending Words	>14.9	>9.7	84	13
Memory for Digits	5-6	K.4	9	6
Rapid Digit Naming	8-0	3.0	16	7
Nonword Repetition	6-6	1.4	25	8
Rapid Letter Naming	8-0	3.0	16	7
Rapid Color Naming	8-9	3.7	25	8
Rapid Object Naming	7-9	2.7	16	7
Blending Nonwords	13-6	8.4	63	11
Segmenting Words	>14-9	>9.7	63	11
COMPOSITES**				
Phonological Memory			12	82
Rapid Naming			12	82
Alternate Rapid Naming			16	85

*Mean = 10, SD = 3.
**Mean = 100, SD = 15.

Illinois Test of Psycholinguistic Abilities—Third Edition

Subtest*	Age Equivalent	Grade Equivalent	Percentile Rank	Standard Score
Sight Decoding	8-9	3.7	25	8
Sound Decoding	10-6	5.4	50	10
Sight Spelling	8-6	3.4	25	8
Sound Spelling	>12-11	>8.0	84	13
Syntactic Sentences	11-0	6.0	63	11

*Mean = 10, SD = 3.

Sample Report from F. A. Schrank & R. W. Woodcock (2002). *Report Writer for the WJ III.* Itasca, IL: Riverside.

Cognitive and Educational Evaluation

Name:	Whitehurst, Maria	School:	Glenview Intermediate
Date of Birth:	11/10/1990	Teacher:	Mr. Costa
Age:	11 years, 0 months	Grade:	6.2
Sex:	Female	Examiner:	Chris Smith
Dates of Testing:	10/25/2001; 11/07/2001		

REASON FOR REFERRAL

John Whitehurst, Maria's father, referred her for an evaluation of a suspected learning disability. Additionally, Maria appears to be far behind her classmates in math despite several years of special attention in this area. This evaluation is intended to address the following questions: What cognitive and/or academic strengths and weaknesses exist? Is there evidence for an ability/achievement discrepancy? What are Maria's cognitive and academic developmental levels?

FATHER'S REPORT

Mr. Whitehurst provided the following information. Maria lives with her mother and father, along with two other children, aged 17 and 14. There have been no significant changes in Maria's family life recently.

According to her father, Maria is usually in good health and is physically fit. Mr. Whitehurst reported that Maria's vision is normal, and that her vision was tested recently by an optometrist (March 2001). Mr. Whitehurst reported that Maria's hearing is normal, but Maria has not had a recent hearing test. At night, Maria typically sleeps for 7 or 8 hours, but she doesn't seem to be able to sleep soundly.

During pregnancy, Maria's mother had no significant health problems. Maria's delivery was normal. Immediately after birth, Maria was healthy.

Maria's father remembers Maria as a determined infant and toddler but a shy and fearful one. Her early motor skills, such as sitting up, crawling, and learning to walk, developed normally. Her early language development, such as first words, asking simple questions, and talking in sentences, seemed to be typical.

Maria did not attend preschool. She seemed to learn things later, or with more difficulty, than other children did. She seemed to have more difficulty developing social skills than most other children. According to her father, Maria's behavior was somewhat difficult to manage during her preschool years.

Maria received special educational services beginning at age 10 (currently she is on a modified grade 6 program). Mr. Whitehurst believes that Maria has learning problems (especially in math) and has been concerned about this for at least 5 years.

At the time of this assessment, Mr. Whitehurst described Maria as independent, happy, and caring. (The following descriptions are based on Mr. Whitehurst's observations of Maria over the previous year.) Maria is usually happy; her mood varies normally. She often has difficulty awaiting her turn and often interrupts or intrudes on others. Mr. Whitehurst said that Maria generally likes school but it seems like she doesn't try to succeed at schoolwork.

Mr. Whitehurst reported that Maria always, or almost always, remembers to do her assigned chores. Some other things that Mr. Whitehurst reported may be significant. Maria frequently fails to give close attention to details or makes careless mistakes. She often does not follow through on instructions and fails to finish her homework. She usually attempts, but gives up easily, when confronted with difficult tasks.

Mr. Whitehurst reported that Maria demonstrates anxious behavior at home, which he rated as slightly serious (hair pulling and nail biting).

TEACHER'S REPORT

Sam Costa, Maria's teacher, described Maria as distractible, unmotivated, and insecure. (The following information, provided by Mr. Costa, represents his observations of Maria over the previous month.) At times, Maria seems unhappy. He said that Maria needs more one-to-one attention but completes about as much schoolwork as other girls in her grade.

Mr. Costa reported a characteristic that likely facilitates Maria's classroom performance: Maria generally persists with difficult tasks.

In contrast, some reported behaviors may be inhibiting performance. Maria frequently fails to give close attention to details or makes careless mistakes. She seems to have difficulty sustaining attention in tasks or play activities. She often does not seem to listen when spoken to directly. Maria's oral responses to questions are very slow and hesitant. She often forgets what she is supposed to do. She is easily distracted.

When seated, Maria is often lethargic. Her social interaction skills are typical for girls in her grade. Maria's listening ability is of most concern to Mr. Costa; he believes this seriously impairs Maria's classroom performance.

Mr. Costa reported that Maria demonstrates very serious inattentive behaviors in the classroom (sometimes sits lethargically; she seems sleep deprived). However, these behaviors are not disruptive. Other problem behaviors include uncooperative behavior; anxiousness; and withdrawal. She demonstrates aggressive behaviors, but these were rated as neither serious nor disruptive.

Mr. Costa rated Maria's level of oral expression as average. Her levels of listening comprehension, basic reading skill, reading comprehension, mathematics calculation, basic writing skill, and written expression were rated as limited. Her level of mathematics reasoning was rated as very limited.

Maria is being instructed at the grade 4 level in basic writing skills and written expression. Her level of instruction in basic reading skills, reading comprehension, math calculation, and math reasoning is at the grade 3 level. Classroom oral expression demands are at the grade 4 level; listening comprehension demands are at the grade 3 level.

CLASSROOM OBSERVATIONS

Maria was observed in the classroom on 06/02/2001. Chris Smith was the observer. A teacher-directed large classroom activity was observed. Maria takes medication to help her manage her behavior; however, she was not on medication during this observation.

When compared to another female student who was identified as typical, Maria was observed as having more off-task behaviors. During the 15-minute observation, the comparison student was off-task 4 times; Maria was off-task 8 times. Inattentive behaviors (looking around the classroom) were observed; these behaviors were not serious or disruptive to others. Withdrawn behaviors (daydreaming; playing with neighbor's hair) were observed; these behaviors were not serious but slightly disruptive to others. Other inappropriate behaviors (talking with neighbor) were observed; these behaviors were slightly serious and slightly dis-

ruptive to others. The primary problem behavior observed was talking to others when she should have been working.

According to Maria's teacher, her behavior during this observation was typical for her.

Maria was also observed in the classroom later on 06/02/2001. As before, Chris Smith was the observer. Individual activity (seatwork) was observed. As earlier, Maria was not on her behavior-management medication during this observation.

When compared to another female student who was identified as typical, Maria was observed as having more off-task behaviors. During the 15-minute observation, the comparison student was off-task 3 times; Maria was off-task 7 times. Inattentive behaviors (looking around the classroom), overactive behaviors (out of seat), and withdrawn behaviors (daydreaming; playing with pen) were observed; these behaviors were not serious or disruptive to others. Other inappropriate behaviors (talking) were observed; these behaviors were not serious but slightly disruptive to others. The primary problem behavior observed was withdrawal.

According to Maria's teacher, her behavior during this observation was also typical for her.

TESTS ADMINISTERED

WJ III Tests of Cognitive Abilities (administered on 10/25/2001)
WJ III Tests of Achievement (administered on 11/07/2001)

These tests provide measures of Maria's overall intellectual ability, specific cognitive abilities, academic achievement, and oral language abilities. Relative strengths and weaknesses among her cognitive and academic abilities are described in this report. A description of each ability is provided. Maria's performance in each broad category is compared to grade peers using a standard score range. Her level of task accuracy is described by a comparison to the average individual at a specified grade. Maria's proficiency is described categorically, ranging from very limited to average; her test performance can be generalized to similar, nontest, grade-level tasks. Clinical interpretation (with qualitative observations) of cognitive and academic task performance is provided.

INTELLECTUAL ABILITY

Maria's general intellectual ability, as measured by the WJ III GIA (Ext) score, is in the low average range of others her grade. There is a 68% probability that her true GIA score would be included in the range of scores from 87 to 91.

COGNITIVE ABILITIES

Phonemic Awareness includes the knowledge and skills related to analyzing and synthesizing speech sounds. Maria's awareness of phonemes is comparable to that of the average individual in grade 9.3. When compared to others in her grade, her standard score is within the average to high average range (percentile rank range of 56 to 82; standard score range of 102 to 114) for her grade. Her awareness of phonemes is average; Maria will probably find grade-level tasks requiring the ability to apply phonemic information in immediate awareness manageable.

Processing Speed measures Maria's ability to perform simple and automatic cognitive tasks rapidly, particularly when under pressure to maintain focused attention. Maria's processing speed is comparable to that of the average individual in grade 7.2. Her standard score is within the average range (percentile rank range of 56 to 76; standard score range of 102 to 110) for her grade. Her processing speed is average; it is likely that Maria will find grade-level tasks requiring cognitive speediness manageable.

Visual-Spatial Thinking is an index of Maria's ability to perceive, analyze, synthesize, and think with visual patterns, including her ability to store and recall visual representations. Maria's visual processing ability is comparable to that of the average individual in grade 4.8. Her standard score is within the average range (percentile rank range of 29 to 51; standard score range of 92 to 100) for her grade. Her visual processing ability is average; this suggests that Maria will find grade-level tasks requiring visual memory or mental manipulation of visual images manageable.

Auditory Processing measures Maria's ability to analyze, synthesize, and discriminate auditory stimuli, including her ability to process and discriminate speech sounds presented under distorted conditions. Maria's auditory processing ability is comparable to that of the average individual in grade 4.2. Her standard score is within the average range (percentile rank range of 25 to 49; standard score range of 90 to 100) for her grade. Her auditory processing ability is average; it is predicted that Maria will find grade-level tasks requiring synthesizing and discriminating speech sounds manageable.

Comprehension-Knowledge is a measure of the breadth and depth of Maria's language-based knowledge. It includes the ability to verbally communicate her knowledge and comprehension. Maria's knowledge and comprehension is comparable to that of the average individual in grade 4.5. Her standard score is within the low average to average range (percentile rank range of 20 to 36; standard score range of 87 to 94) for her grade. Her knowledge and comprehension are limited to average; Maria will likely find grade-level verbal communication, knowledge, and comprehension tasks difficult.

Fluid Reasoning is the ability to reason, form concepts, and solve problems using unfamiliar information or novel procedures. Maria's fluid reasoning ability is comparable to that of the average individual in grade 3.2. Her standard score is within the low average to average range (percentile rank range of 14 to 26; standard score range of 84 to 90) for her grade. Her fluid reasoning ability is limited; Maria will probably find grade-level tasks requiring identifying categories and relations, drawing and generalizing inferences, recognizing and forming concepts, and drawing conclusions very difficult.

Long-Term Retrieval is the ability to store and retrieve information. Maria's long-term retrieval is comparable to that of the average individual in grade 3.0. Her standard score is within the low average to average range (percentile rank range of 10 to 25; standard score range of 81 to 90) for her grade. Her long-term retrieval is average; it is likely that Maria will find grade-level tasks requiring strategies to store, and fluency to retrieve, information manageable. Overall, Maria's ability to recall information and relearn associations that were previously learned is within normal limits.

Short-Term Memory is the ability to hold information in immediate awareness and use it within a few seconds. Although Maria's overall short-term memory standard score is within the low average range, her performance varied on two different types of tasks measuring immediate memory capacity. Maria's performance is average on auditory memory span tasks. Her performance is very limited on tasks requiring her to attend to information held in immediate awareness while working with or changing it.

Among her cognitive abilities, Maria has a relative weakness in Working Memory. Working Memory measures Maria's ability to hold information in immediate awareness while performing a mental operation on the information. Her working memory capacity is comparable to that of the average individual in grade 1.7. Her standard score is within the very low to low range (percentile rank range of 1 to 5; standard score range of 66 to 75) for her grade. Maria's working memory capacity is very limited; this suggests that she will find grade-level tasks requiring complex processing of information in immediate memory extremely difficult.

Clinical Interpretation of Cognitive Fluency and Executive Processing

Maria's speed in performing simple to complex cognitive tasks is average. Specifically, her performance on tasks measuring speed of forming simple concepts was advanced; she made decisions quickly. Her performance on tasks measuring fluency of retrieval from stored knowledge was average. On tasks measuring speed of direct recall of simple vocabulary, Maria's performance was limited.

Maria's overall ability to plan, monitor, and arrive at solutions to problems is limited to average. For example, on tasks measuring her ability to plan and implement solutions to problems, her performance was average. She appeared to have difficulty shifting concepts; her performance on tasks measuring adaptive learning and flexibility in thinking was limited. Maria's ability to maintain focus on a task amid visual distractors was limited; her task vigilance was low. During testing, her ability to focus her attention on relevant stimuli for information processing purposes was limited.

ACHIEVEMENT

When compared to others in her grade, Maria's academic achievement is average in Academic Knowledge (science knowledge, social studies knowledge, and cultural knowledge).

Listening Comprehension includes listening ability and verbal comprehension. Maria's listening and oral comprehension abilities are comparable to those of the average individual in grade 4.8. Her standard score is within the average range (percentile rank range of 27 to 46; standard score range of 91 to 98) for her grade. Her listening and oral comprehension abilities are average; it is predicted that Maria will find grade-level tasks requiring listening skills and oral comprehension manageable.

Oral Expression measures Maria's linguistic competency in spoken English. Maria's overall ability to express herself orally is comparable to that of the average individual in grade 4.0. Her standard score is within the low average to average range (percentile rank range of 19 to 37; standard score range of 87 to 95) for her grade. Her overall ability to express herself orally is average; Maria will likely find grade-level tasks requiring listening skills and English-language oral vocabulary development manageable.

Basic Reading Skills includes sight vocabulary, phonics, and structural analysis skills. Maria's basic reading skills are comparable to those of the average individual in grade 3.2. Her standard score is within the low average range (percentile rank range of 12 to 17; standard score range of 82 to 86) for her grade. Her basic reading skills are limited; tasks measuring reading skills above the grade 3.9 level will be quite difficult for her.

Reading Comprehension measures Maria's reading vocabulary and her ability to comprehend connected discourse while reading. Maria's reading comprehension is comparable to that of the average individual in grade 3.2. Her standard score is within the low to low average range (percentile rank range of 8 to 16; standard score range of 79 to 85) for her grade. Her reading comprehension is limited; reading comprehension tasks above the grade 4.5 level will be quite difficult for her.

Written Expression measures Maria's fluency of production and quality of expression in writing. Maria's overall ability to express herself in writing is comparable to that of the average individual in grade 3.1. Her standard score is within the low to low average range (percentile rank range of 4 to 12; standard score range of 74 to 82) for her grade. Her overall ability to express herself in writing is limited; writing fluency tasks above the grade 4.6 level will be quite difficult for her.

Basic Writing Skills includes spelling skills and knowledge of English language usage. Maria's basic writing skills are comparable to those of the average individual in grade 2.7. Her standard score is within the low range (percentile rank range of 3 to 7; standard score range of 72 to 78) for her grade. Her basic writing skills are very limited; tasks measuring effective expression in written language above the grade 3.5 level will be quite difficult for her.

Mathematics Reasoning includes mathematical knowledge and reasoning. Maria's mathematics reasoning ability is comparable to that of the average individual in grade 2.4. Her standard score is within the very low to low range (percentile rank range of 1 to 3; standard score range of 66 to 72) for her grade. Her mathematics reasoning ability is very limited; math reasoning tasks above the grade 3.1 level will be quite difficult for her.

Among her achievement and oral language abilities, Maria has a relative weakness in Math Calculation Skills. Math Calculation Skills measures Maria's computational skills and automaticity with basic math facts. Her mathematics calculation skills are comparable to those of the average individual in grade 2.5. Her standard score is within the very low range (percentile rank range of <1 to 2; standard score range of 60 to 68) for her grade. Maria's mathematics calculation skills are limited; math calculation tasks above the grade 3.5 level will be quite difficult for her.

Clinical Interpretation of Academic Processing

Academic Skills
Maria's sight reading ability is very limited and nonautomatic. As the test items became more difficult, she required increased time and greater attention to phoneme-grapheme relationships to determine the correct response. Maria's math calculation was nonautomatic and very limited. She gave incorrect responses on math calculation items involving addition, subtraction, and advanced addition. Maria's spelling is very limited; words dictated to her were spelled in a slow, laborious manner (nonautomatically).

The fluency with which Maria performs academic tasks is limited. In particular, her fluency with mathematics problems is limited to average; she solved problems slowly and made several errors. Maria had trouble formulating or writing sentences quickly; her writing fluency is limited. Maria's fluency with reading tasks is very limited; although she read sentences at a rate typical for her peers, she also made several errors.

Academic Applications
On a passage comprehension task, Maria struggled with use of syntactic and semantic cues; her performance was limited. Maria's writing ability is limited; the sentences she wrote were inadequate when compared to what would be expected for her grade. Maria's quantitative reasoning is negligible; she appeared to have limited understanding of grade-appropriate math application tasks. She gave incorrect responses on math reasoning items involving addition, money, and time.

Maria's knowledge of phoneme-grapheme relationships is limited. Specifically, her ability to pronounce nonwords is limited and nonautomatic (she sounded out nonwords slowly and then attempted to blend the sounds). Maria's ability to spell nonwords is limited. Her ability to sequence sounds and knowledge of common English spelling patterns are limited.

Informal Writing Evaluation
Additional information about Maria's writing abilities was obtained from an evaluation of an expository writing assignment.

Maria's handwriting was rated as poor to adequate. Her abilities to form letters correctly and to stay on the line were adequate; her abilities to use consistent spacing and to form letters automatically were poor. Maria's spelling of reg-
ular words was adequate, but her spelling of exception words was poor. Maria's punctuation and capitalization skills were very poor to adequate. Specifically, her ability to use capital letters correctly was adequate; her abilities to end sentences with correct punctuation and to indent paragraphs were poor; her ability to use internal punctuation correctly was very poor. Maria's use of vocabulary (including age-appropriate, varied, and precise vocabulary) was adequate. Maria's syntax and usage ranged from poor to adequate. Her abilities to use correct word endings, to use pronouns correctly, and to write sentences with varied lengths and structures were adequate. Her abilities to maintain verb tense and to write complete sentences were poor.

Maria's expository text structure was rated as very poor to adequate. Her abilities to highlight important ideas, to sequence ideas logically, and to include major details were adequate. Her ability to use appropriate words to link ideas together was poor; her ability to combine sentences into cohesive paragraphs was very poor.

Overall, Maria demonstrated adequate ability to maintain focus and intent; she demonstrated poor ability to maintain appropriate voice and discourse genre. Maria maintained a positive attitude and appeared confident when writing.

TEST SESSION OBSERVATIONS

Maria's conversational proficiency seemed typical for her grade level. She was cooperative throughout the examination; her activity level seemed typical for her grade. She appeared at ease, comfortable, and attentive to the tasks during the examination. She responded promptly, but carefully, to test questions, but she gave up easily after attempting difficult tasks.

SUMMARY

Maria was referred for an evaluation of a suspected learning disability.

Maria's overall intellectual ability, as measured by the WJ III GIA (Ext), is in the low average range.

When compared to others at her grade level, Maria's performance is average in comprehension-knowledge, visual-spatial thinking, auditory processing, processing speed, and phonemic awareness; low average in long-term retrieval, fluid reasoning, and short-term memory; and low in working memory. Under delayed conditions, her ability to recall and relearn previously learned information is within normal limits. When her cognitive abilities are compared, she demonstrated a significant relative weakness in working memory.

Maria's English oral language skills (oral expression and listening comprehension) are average when compared to others at her grade level. Her level of knowledge is average. Her fluency with academic tasks is low average. Maria's academic skills and her ability to apply those skills are both within the low range.

When compared to others at her grade level, Maria's performance is low average in broad reading, basic reading skills, and reading comprehension; low in basic writing skills and written expression; and very low in math calculation skills and math reasoning. Her knowledge of phoneme-grapheme relationships is low average. When her achievement areas are compared, she demonstrated a significant relative weakness in math calculation skills.

To help determine if any ability/achievement discrepancies exist, comparisons were made among Maria's cognitive, oral language, and achievement scores. When compared to her overall intellectual ability, her achievement is significantly lower than predicted in the areas of mathematics, math calculation skills, math reasoning, written language, and basic writing skills. Based on a mix of the cognitive tasks associated with performance in the particular academic area and most relevant to the specific achievement domain, Maria's achievement is also significantly lower than predicted in the areas of mathematics, math calculation skills, and math reasoning. Also, her mathematics, math calculation skills, math reasoning, written language, and basic writing skills are significantly lower than would be predicted by her English oral language ability.

Anxious behaviors at home were reported by Maria's father. Uncooperative behaviors were reported by her teacher. During classroom observations, inappropriate (nonaggressive) behavior was observed.

Based on her measured ability levels, it appears that Maria is being instructed at a level that is too difficult for her in reading, written language, and mathematics.

Chris Smith, Ed.S.
School Psychologist

TABLE OF SCORES: Woodcock-Johnson III Tests of Cognitive Abilities and Tests of Achievement
Report Writer for the WJ III, Version 1.0
Norms based on grade 6.2

CLUSTER/Test	Raw	GE	EASY	to DIFF	RPI	PR	SS(68% BAND)	AE
GIA (Ext)	—	4.1	2.3	6.8	79/90	23	89 (87–91)	9-6
VERBAL ABILITY (*Ext*)	—	4.5	3.1	6.3	76/90	27	91 (87–94)	9-10
THINKING ABILITY (*Ext*)	—	3.6	1.5	8.4	82/90	24	90 (87–92)	9-1
COG EFFICIENCY (*Ext*)	—	4.9	3.6	6.5	79/90	28	91 (87–96)	10-3
COMP-KNOWLEDGE (*Gc*)	—	4.5	3.1	6.3	76/90	27	91 (87–94)	9-10
L-T RETRIEVAL (*Glr*)	—	3.0	K.9	13.5	84/90	16	85 (81–90)	8-8
VIS-SPATIAL THINK (*Gv*)	—	4.8	1.6	13.0	87/90	39	96 (92–100)	10-0
AUDITORY PROCESS (*Ga*)	—	4.2	1.2	10.6	86/90	36	95 (90–100)	9-9
FLUID REASONING (*Gf*)	—	3.2	2.0	5.0	65/90	20	87 (84–90)	8-6
PROCESS SPEED (*Gs*)	—	7.2	5.8	9.1	95/90	66	106 (102–110)	12-5
SHORT-TERM MEM (*Gsm*)	—	2.4	1.5	3.6	42/90	10	81 (75–87)	7-6
PHONEMIC AWARE	—	9.3	3.6	14.3	94/90	71	108 (102–114)	14-5
PHONEMIC AWARE III	—	5.8	2.5	12.5	89/90	47	99 (95–103)	11-5
WORKING MEMORY	—	1.7	K.9	2.6	21/90	2	71 (66–75)	6-10
BROAD ATTENTION	—	2.2	1.2	3.6	45/90	2	70 (66–74)	7-7
COGNITIVE FLUENCY	—	5.2	3.3	7.4	84/90	35	94 (91–97)	10-4
EXEC PROCESSES	—	3.5	2.0	5.9	73/90	15	84 (82–87)	8-11
KNOWLEDGE	—	5.3	3.8	7.1	84/90	37	95 (92–99)	10-6
ORAL LANGUAGE (Ext)	—	4.4	2.5	7.8	82/90	29	92 (89–95)	10-0
ORAL EXPRESSION	—	4.0	1.7	7.3	81/90	27	91 (87–95)	9-8
LISTENING COMP	—	4.8	3.0	8.3	84/90	36	95 (91–98)	10-3
TOTAL ACHIEVEMENT	—	2.9	2.3	3.7	25/90	4	74 (73–76)	8-3

(*continued*)

TABLE OF SCORES (*continued*)

CLUSTER/Test	Raw	GE	EASY	to DIFF	RPI	PR	SS(68% BAND)	AE
BROAD READING	—	3.5	2.9	4.2	28/90	10	81 (79–83)	8-9
BROAD MATH	—	2.2	1.6	3.0	13/90	1	63 (59–66)	7-7
BROAD WRITTEN LANG	—	2.9	2.1	4.0	39/90	4	74 (71–78)	8-2
BASIC READING SKILLS	—	3.2	2.7	3.9	26/90	14	84 (82–86)	8-6
READING COMP	—	3.2	2.4	4.5	55/90	11	82 (79–85)	8-7
MATH CALC SKILLS	—	2.5	1.8	3.5	30/90	1	64 (60–68)	7-11
MATH REASONING	—	2.4	1.9	3.1	9/90	2	69 (66–72)	7-10
BASIC WRITING SKILLS	—	2.7	2.2	3.5	20/90	5	75 (72–78)	8-0
WRITTEN EXPRESSION	—	3.1	2.1	4.6	55/90	7	78 (74–82)	8-7
ACADEMIC SKILLS	—	2.9	2.5	3.5	13/90	3	71 (68–73)	8-3
ACADEMIC FLUENCY	—	3.6	2.8	4.7	44/90	11	81 (79–83)	9-0
ACADEMIC APPS	—	2.3	1.8	3.1	24/90	3	71 (68–74)	7-9
ACADEMIC KNOWLEDGE	—	4.7	3.3	6.3	76/90	29	92 (88–96)	9-10
PHON/GRAPH KNOW	—	2.5	1.9	3.9	49/90	14	84 (81–86)	8-0
Verbal Comprehension	—	3.2	2.1	4.6	54/90	13	83 (79–87)	8-7
Visual-Auditory Learning	19-E	2.5	1.1	9.1	80/90	18	86 (81–91)	8-3
Spatial Relations	61-D	3.7	1.0	9.7	84/90	34	94 (90–98)	8-9
Sound Blending	20	6.8	2.7	11.9	91/90	54	101 (96–107)	11-11
Concept Formation	20-E	3.1	2.1	4.6	60/90	22	89 (85–92)	8-6
Visual Matching	42-2	5.8	4.9	7.0	86/90	44	98 (93–102)	11-1
Numbers Reversed	6	1.0	K.5	1.6	5/90	2	68 (61–74)	6-1
Incomplete Words	26	13.1	5.0	>18.0	96/90	82	114 (107–121)	27
Auditory Work Memory	13	2.9	1.7	4.4	54/90	14	84 (79–88)	8-6
General Information	—	6.0	4.3	8.2	89/90	48	99 (94–104)	11-5
Retrieval Fluency	55	4.2	K.4	>18.0	88/90	29	92 (86–98)	9-10
Picture Recognition	48-D	6.1	2.2	>18.0	90/90	49	100 (95–105)	11-6
Auditory Attention	32	1.7	K.4	7.6	78/90	20	88 (82–93)	7-7
Analysis-Synthesis	20-D	3.2	2.0	5.5	70/90	21	88 (83–93)	8-6
Decision Speed	36	10.3	7.5	>18.0	98/90	86	116 (111–122)	15-2
Memory for Words	17	6.2	4.0	9.3	90/90	50	100 (93–107)	11-4
Rapid Picture Naming	87	2.4	1.5	3.5	27/90	12	83 (81–85)	7-7
Planning	—	2.7	<K.0	>18.0	88/90	28	91 (82–101)	8-3
Pair Cancellation	51	4.0	2.8	5.4	65/90	20	87 (85–89)	9-5

Form A of the following achievement tests was administered:

CLUSTER/Test	Raw	GE	EASY	to DIFF	RPI	PR	SS(68% BAND)	AE
Letter-Word Identification	46	3.5	3.1	4.1	20/90	13	83 (80–86)	8-10
Reading Fluency	34	3.6	3.0	4.2	18/90	14	84 (82–86)	9-0
Story Recall	—	3.3	K.2	13.5	85/90	23	89 (81–96)	8-9
Understanding Directions	—	4.2	2.3	8.3	82/90	32	93 (88–98)	9-7
Calculation	10	2.4	1.9	3.0	8/90	1	64 (58–70)	7-9
Math Fluency	42	3.2	1.3	5.4	67/90	7	77 (75–80)	8-7
Spelling	25	2.6	2.1	3.3	15/90	5	76 (72–80)	8-0
Writing Fluency	13	3.9	3.0	4.9	50/90	15	85 (81–89)	9-4
Passage Comprehension	26	3.1	2.4	4.3	53/90	13	83 (79–88)	8-5
Applied Problems	24	1.8	1.3	2.4	2/90	1	67 (63–71)	7-2
Writing Samples	6-C	1.9	1.4	3.4	59/90	1	63 (53–73)	7-7
Word Attack	13	2.5	2.1	3.5	34/90	17	86 (83–88)	8-1
Picture Vocabulary	24	4.3	2.6	6.2	75/90	30	92 (88–97)	9-11
Oral Comprehension	20	5.2	3.5	8.3	85/90	41	97 (92–101)	10-9
Editing	7	2.9	2.3	3.6	27/90	7	78 (74–83)	8-2
Reading Vocabulary	—	3.2	2.3	4.8	56/90	16	85 (82–88)	8-9
Quantitative Concepts	—	3.3	2.5	4.2	33/90	8	79 (74–83)	8-7
Academic Knowledge	—	4.7	3.3	6.3	76/90	29	92 (88–96)	9-10
Spelling of Sounds	21	2.3	1.5	4.6	65/90	14	84 (79–88)	7-10
Sound Awareness	34	3.0	2.0	5.3	71/90	21	88 (83–92)	8-8
Punctuation & Capitals	11	2.1	1.5	2.8	16/90	1	63 (55–71)	7-6

TABLE OF SCORES (*continued*)

| DISCREPANCIES | STANDARD SCORES | | | DISCREPANCY | | Significant at |
	Actual	Predicted	Difference	PR	SD	± 1.50 SD (SEE)
Intra-Cognitive						
COMP-KNOWLEDGE (*Gc*)	91	92	−1	46	−0.09	No
L-T RETRIEVAL (*Glr*)	85	93	−8	29	−0.56	No
VIS-SPATIAL THINK (*Gv*)	96	95	1	54	+0.09	No
AUDITORY PROCESS (*Ga*)	95	94	1	53	+0.08	No
FLUID REASONING (*Gf*)	87	93	−6	31	−0.49	No
PROCESS SPEED (*Gs*)	106	93	13	84	+0.99	No
SHORT-TERM MEM (*Gsm*)	81	95	−14	13	−1.11	No
PHONEMIC AWARE	108	93	15	88	+1.19	No
WORKING MEMORY	71	95	−24	3	−1.88	Yes

| DISCREPANCIES | STANDARD SCORES | | | DISCREPANCY | | Significant at |
	Actual	Predicted	Difference	PR	SD	± 1.50 SD (SEE)
Intra-Achievement						
BASIC READING SKILLS	84	79	5	72	+0.59	No
READING COMP	82	81	1	55	+0.13	No
MATH CALC SKILLS	64	88	−24	3	−1.84	Yes
MATH REASONING	69	83	−14	10	−1.31	No
BASIC WRITING SKILLS	75	82	−7	26	−0.64	No
WRITTEN EXPRESSION	78	84	−6	31	−0.51	No
ORAL EXPRESSION	91	84	7	72	+0.59	No
LISTENING COMP	95	82	13	85	+1.02	No
ACADEMIC KNOWLEDGE	92	81	11	86	+1.08	No

| DISCREPANCIES | STANDARD SCORES | | | DISCREPANCY | | Significant at |
	Actual	Predicted	Difference	PR	SD	± 1.50 SD (SEE)
*Intellectual Ability/Achievement Discrepancies**						
BROAD READING	81	92	−11	13	−1.11	No
BASIC READING SKILLS	84	94	−10	18	−0.90	No
READING COMP	82	93	−11	14	−1.07	No
BROAD MATH	63	94	−31	0.1	−2.98	Yes
MATH CALC SKILLS	64	95	−31	1	−2.36	Yes
MATH REASONING	69	93	−24	1	−2.36	Yes
BROAD WRITTEN LANG	74	94	−20	4	−1.76	Yes
BASIC WRITING SKILLS	75	93	−18	5	−1.60	Yes
WRITTEN EXPRESSION	78	93	−15	9	−1.33	No
ORAL LANGUAGE (*Ext*)	92	93	−1	47	−0.06	No
ORAL EXPRESSION	91	94	−3	41	−0.24	No
LISTENING COMP	95	93	2	55	+0.12	No
ACADEMIC KNOWLEDGE	92	93	−1	46	−0.09	No

*These discrepancies compare GIA (Ext) with Broad, Basic, and Applied ACH clusters.

(*continued*)

TABLE OF SCORES (*continued*)

DISCREPANCIES	STANDARD SCORES			DISCREPANCY		Significant at
	Actual	Predicted	Difference	PR	SD	± 1.50 SD (SEE)
*Oral Language/Achievement Discrepancies**						
BROAD READING	81	96	–15	12	–1.16	No
BASIC READING SKILLS	84	96	–12	19	–0.87	No
READING COMP	82	95	–13	15	–1.03	No
BROAD MATH	63	96	–33	0.5	–2.57	Yes
MATH CALC SKILLS	64	97	–33	1	–2.27	Yes
MATH REASONING	69	95	–26	2	–2.16	Yes
BROAD WRITTEN LANG	74	96	–22	5	–1.67	Yes
BASIC WRITING SKILLS	75	96	–21	6	–1.56	Yes
WRITTEN EXPRESSION	78	97	–19	8	–1.38	No
ACADEMIC KNOWLEDGE	92	95	–3	39	–0.29	No

*These discrepancies compare Oral Language (Ext) with Broad, Basic, and Applied ACH clusters.

DISCREPANCIES	STANDARD SCORES			DISCREPANCY		Significant at
	Actual	Predicted	Difference	PR	SD	± 1.50 SD (SEE)
*Predicted Achievement/Achievement Discrepancies**						
BROAD READING	81	87	–6	27	–0.63	No
BASIC READING SKILLS	84	87	–3	39	–0.27	No
READING COMP	82	86	–4	32	–0.47	No
BROAD MATH	63	86	–23	1	–2.31	Yes
MATH CALC SKILLS	64	90	–26	1	–2.36	Yes
MATH REASONING	69	84	–15	7	–1.51	Yes
BROAD WRITTEN LANG	74	89	–15	9	–1.35	No
BASIC WRITING SKILLS	75	87	–12	15	–1.05	No
WRITTEN EXPRESSION	78	91	–13	13	–1.11	No
ORAL LANGUAGE (Ext)	92	91	1	53	+0.08	No
ORAL EXPRESSION	91	93	–2	43	–0.18	No
LISTENING COMP	95	91	4	63	+0.34	No
ACADEMIC KNOWLEDGE	92	86	6	73	+0.60	No

*These discrepancies compare predicted achievement scores with Broad, Basic, and Applied ACH clusters.

DISCREPANCIES	DISCREPANCY		Significant at ± 1.50 SD (SEE)	Interpretation
	PR	SD (or *z*)		
*Measures of delayed recall**				
DELAYED RECALL	13	–1.14	No	Within normal limits
Vis-Aud Lrng-Delayed	16	–1.01	No	Within normal limits
Story Recall-Delayed	20	–0.83	No	Within normal limits

*These discrepancies based on predicted difference between initial and delayed scores.

EDUCATIONAL ASSESSMENT

Name:	Joy Wiley Evans		Parents:	Tanya Wiley, Benjamin Evans
Birthdate:	9-22-89		Grade:	5.4
Chronological Age:	11-4		Dates of Testing:	1/14 and 1/24/01
School:	St. Elizabeth's School		Report Date:	2-12-01

REASON FOR REFERRAL

Joy was referred for a private evaluation by her parents due to difficulty in learning and retaining math skills despite long-term math tutoring. They would like to know why she is having so much difficulty and how she will be able to learn math more successfully.

BACKGROUND INFORMATION

Joy is the 11-year-old child of Tanya Wiley and Benjamin Evans. Ms. Wiley and Mr. Evans are both professionals with graduate degrees. Joy has two older brothers, Randy, 19, and Sam, 15, who has been identified as having learning disabilities affecting reading and writing. The language of the home is English.

Since kindergarten, Joy has attended St. Elizabeth's School, a private school known for its accelerated pace. Due to her September birthday, her parents decided to have her repeat kindergarten.

Joy is currently in the fifth grade at St. Elizabeth's. Her fifth-grade teacher, Ms. Jessica Stein, reports that Joy rarely completes her math work and is constantly asking questions about how to solve certain problems that have already been reviewed in class. She does quite well in all other subjects.

Since second grade, Joy has experienced escalating anxiety concerning math, which increasingly interferes with her ability to apply skills she appears to know. Sara Phelan, a certified Special Education Teacher with expertise in teaching math, has tutored Joy once to twice a week for the past $2\frac{1}{2}$ years. For the past two summers, Joy has participated in a small math tutoring group run by Ms. Phelan to maintain and develop her math skills. According to Ms. Phelan, Joy has always had difficulty recalling facts accurately, had trouble learning to sequence count, and frequently copies down problems incorrectly. During summer instruction, she had trouble with rote tasks but was faster than the other girls in reasoning tasks. Although Ms. Phelan and Ms. Wiley have been working with her on long di-

vision with one-digit, then two-digit divisors since the beginning of this school year, she still makes errors and seems to get lost in the steps. Ms. Phelan commented that Joy leaves out a step, they work on it until she knows it, and in the next session she omits a different step. Recently, Ms. Phelan found that if Joy dictated the solution of a long division problem and Ms. Phelan did the writing, she did not make mistakes.

Since last December, Joy's anxiety has developed into school phobia. Frequently, she gets up in the morning but crawls back into bed, refusing to go to school and begging her mother for home schooling. She has uncontrollable crying jags and bouts of despair, feeling overwhelmed and unable to cope with the demands of school. At the current time, Margaret White, Ph.D., Psychologist, is providing therapy for school phobia.

Ms. Wiley describes Joy as somewhat impulsive but rarely a behavior problem. Except in the area of math, she is a good student. Ms. Stein has noticed Joy's increasing frustration with math activities, reporting that sometimes she stops attending to the task and sits doing nothing, as though she has "shut down." Other teachers do not see this behavior.

PREVIOUS EVALUATIONS

This is Joy's second evaluation to find the reason for her longstanding difficulties with math. In June 1999, this examiner evaluated her and found that although she had difficulty learning math facts and used some immature procedures in algorithms, her score on the WJ-R Broad Mathematics cluster was in the Superior range, with no significant difference between Calculation and Applied Problems. At that time, severe math anxiety appeared to be a major contributor to her difficulty with math along with possible difficulties in attention. In April 2000, Joy took the Stanford 9 Tests of Achievement. On the seven subtests other than math, Joy's percentile rank (PR) scores ranged from 83 to 99, with most above 90. Her Computation score was PR 33 and Mathematics, which included a wider range of math concepts and skills, was PR 63.

In 1999, Joy's score on the Broad Cognitive Abilities cluster (Standard) of the Woodcock-Johnson Psycho-Educational Battery (WJ-R) bridged the Superior to Very Superior range. The current General Intellectual Ability cluster score (WJ III GIA—Std) is somewhat lower, bridging the High Average to Superior range. A comparison between the two scores requires caution as the composition of this broad score has changed. Only one of the seven tests that comprise the WJ-R BCA is included in the WJ III GIA. Consequently, it is not Joy's intelligence that has changed, but the fact that different facets of performance have been evaluated. The decrease in her general cognitive ability score should be understood as an artifact of the change in tests.

OBSERVATIONS

Joy is familiar with this evaluator; consequently, comfortable rapport was already established. Joy's conversational proficiency is advanced for her grade level. She was exceptionally cooperative throughout the examination and gave careful thought to the test items. She was generally persistent with difficult tasks but realistic when she knew they were beyond her ability. She did not evidence anxiety even on difficult tasks but occasionally stated, "I know I learned this but I can't remember how to do it."

ASSESSMENT MEASURES

Joy was administered the Woodcock-Johnson III, Tests of Cognitive Ability (WJ III COG) 1–7, 9, 13, 15, 16, 19–20; Tests of Achievement (WJ III ACH) 2–3, 5–6, 9, 10, 12, 18; and the Beery-Buktenica Developmental Test of Visual-Motor Integration—Fourth Edition (VMI). Joy also participated in a 2-hour session of diagnostic teaching with the evaluator. Ms. Wiley and Ms. Phelan provided observations of Joy's strengths and specific problems in learning math concepts and skills and in solving math problems.

TEST RESULTS

Cognitive Abilities

Based on the Standard Battery of the WJ III COG, Joy's General Intellectual Ability (GIA) bridges the High Average and Superior ranges. Joy demonstrated Superior rea-

soning skills, using inductive and deductive logic to form concepts and solve problems using newly learned procedures (Fluid Reasoning). These included an algebraic-type task and discerning complex rules for differentiating between sets of designs. Typically, the abilities measured by Fluid Reasoning are strongly related to math achievement. Joy's performance on tests of working memory was in the High Average range and Average in tests of visual–spatial thinking using nonsymbolic designs and pictures. Albeit in the Average range, Joy's visual–spatial abilities appear to be significantly less well developed than her reasoning/problem solving. The separation of the confidence bands was four times the width of the standard error of measurement, whereas one is considered significant. Joy demonstrated significantly discrepant abilities (1.5 SD) within the Processing Speed cluster. She scored in the Superior range on a test requiring rapid decisions regarding conceptual associations between pictures but Average in rapid scanning and matching of numbers.

According to the results of the VMI, Joy's visual–fine motor integration, the ability to plan and execute the movement of the hand to create a visual representation, is weak, as low as, or lower than 12% of her age-peers. On the figure of two intersecting hexagons, she drew the left figure and went on to the next design, not noticing that she had not drawn the second hexagon.

Oral Language and Academic Achievement

For the purposes of comparison, Joy was administered selected tests in which she was not expected to have difficulty. The tests represented language comprehension and recall, reading comprehension, and reading fluency. Joy's ability to recall key details in stories that had been read to her was equal to or better than 75% of her grade-peers. Her ability to retain this information and recall it later was significantly better than those whose initial performance was similar to hers, indicating that her ability to store and retrieve meaningful linguistic information is excellent. Joy's ability to read and comprehend short passages was commensurate with her story recall (PR 73) and her ability to read quickly with comprehension was equal to or above 85% of her grade-peers. Joy's grade equivalent scores on the three tests were mid- to late-11th, 7th, and 8th grades, respectively.

Mathematics
Joy's overall performance on the Broad Mathematics cluster of the WJ III ACH, compared to her grade-peers, was

Average (GE 5.0) with no significant discrepancies among the three component tests: Calculation (computation), Math Fluency (timed math facts), and Applied Problems (application of math knowledge to practical situations), or between these and Quantitative Concepts (pattern recognition, basic concepts).

Although Joy's results are average when compared to grade-peers in the norm sample, her math performance, as reported by her teacher and parents, is below the mathematical standards and expectations at St. Elizabeth's. In addition, to interpret her "average" performance, one must consider that Joy has received over 2 years of private educational therapy in mathematics in addition to nightly help from her mother. Over time, based on her GIA and language-based academic skills, one would expect Joy's math performance to increase at least commensurately with grade-peers. In contrast, her standard scores on Calculation and Applied Problems have dropped dramatically since her last evaluation.

The following sections list math skills through fifth grade in which Joy demonstrated knowledge of the process and those in which she did not.

Math Strengths
1. Use of algorithms for adding and subtracting multiple-digit numbers with renaming, for multiplying a two-digit by a two-digit number with renaming, and for dividing a five-digit dividend by a two-digit divisor (if working with a scribe);
2. Analysis of the information in word problems and translation into the necessary computation for one-step multiplication and division problems and two-step addition and subtraction problems. Joy's strong reasoning allowed her to analyze a considerably more complex word problem but she could not see the most obvious and efficient way to translate it into computation. Her solution would have worked but was far too complex and she could not carry it through to completion;
3. Elimination of extraneous information;
4. Identification of missing information that is necessary to the solution;
5. Knowledge of the value of all the coins and the ability to count change;
6. Ability to analyze the pattern in a series of numbers if the interval between each number was static (e.g., 6 8 _ 12).

Math Weaknesses
1. Attention to operation signs;
2. Retrieval of math facts;

3. Use of fractions at any level of operation;
4. Use of decimal numbers in multiplication or division;
5. Counting elapsed time, using hours and minutes (although she did this correctly in the previous evaluation);
6. Declarative (factual) knowledge regarding units of measure (e.g., number of inches in a foot, weeks in a year, minutes in an hour) although she recalled learning this information. Ability to analyze the pattern in a series of numbers if the interval between numbers changed (e.g., 4 5 _ 10).

Error Patterns
Joy was inconsistent in her performance of all skills tested no matter how simple the problem or how well she seemed to understand the process. She worked a variety of problems correctly and made errors on essentially identical ones. The unpredictability of her errors indicates the instability of her skills and her application of them. Nevertheless, analysis of her error patterns indicates the following:

1. Joy appears unable to visualize numerical relationships. Consistently, she went through all of the substeps of a process that others do in one mental step. Moreover, she had to see it on paper to keep track of what she was doing, increasing the complexity of the task. For example, when trying to estimate the number of times 6 goes into 123, she could not visualize "6 into 12." She finally wrote down $6\overline{)123}$, then covered the 3 with her finger.
2. Although she understands the concept of place value, Joy could not keep track of the value of each digit in a two-digit divisor.
3. Joy did not monitor her work. Many times, within the steps of an algorithm, she made errors that led her into clearly impossible situations (e.g., 32 − 287).

Visual–Motor Skills
Consistent with her performance on the VMI, when doing a numerical task, Joy's numbers are large, poorly formed, poorly spaced, and hard to distinguish from each other. Her placement of problems on a work page is spatially disorganized. Although, with effort, Joy can write reasonably neatly, she said, "When I try, I can't remember what I'm doing." Figure II.3, a sample of a classroom assignment, illustrates the impact of this difficulty.

During diagnostic teaching, Joy gave up in confusion half-way through a long division problem. The evaluator offered to act as scribe and recopied the problem. Joy gave the evaluator explicit instructions of what numbers to write and where to write them, solving the problem without errors. Joy explained, "When I have to write it, I forget what I was going to do. When you write it, it's easier to remember what to do." Joy found special paper and a colored marker helpful. The 3/8" grid on the paper helped her to keep her numbers lined up, and dividing the paper into quadrangles provided for plenty of space around each problem. Writing the problem in colored fine-tip marker and working it in pencil helped her to differentiate the numbers in the problem from her work. Figure II.4 is a sample of work done on grid paper during diagnostic teaching and the division problem done with the evaluator as scribe.

SUMMARY AND DISCUSSION

Results of this evaluation indicate that Joy's overall intellectual ability bridges the High Average to Superior range. Her abstract reasoning is in the Superior range; working memory in the High Average to Superior range; and visual–spatial thinking in the higher end of the Average range. Oral language comprehension, reading comprehension, and reading fluency were in the Average to High Average range; math skills were in the lower area of the Average range. Her Relative Proficiency Indexes were in general agreement with her standard scores, indicating that her reading proficiency is advanced and that her math proficiency is average compared with grade-peers.

Despite her Average math scores, clinical analysis and diagnostic teaching provide strong evidence that Joy experiences multiple problems related to math functioning. She has great difficulty retrieving math facts from memory and remembering rote information such as measurement equivalents (declarative knowledge); she has not automatized the sequence of steps in algorithms (procedural knowledge) or the conceptual basis for the steps (e.g., division as repeated subtraction); and she has difficulty visualizing numerical relationships.

Joy's facility with language and excellent logical analysis skills generally enable her to find the underlying structure of word problems, sort out necessary from extraneous information, and ascertain the operations needed to solve them. But, because she has not internalized math procedures and declarative knowledge, once she is involved in the computation process, her need to focus on the mechanics forces her into a lock-step linear sequence. Additionally, her inability to visualize numerical relationships vastly increases the number of steps involved and in turn, the burden on memory. With cognitive effort and attention focused on procedures that should be automatic, the legibility and spatial organization of her writing deteriorate, obscuring her written work and further complicating the process. Working in this manner requires a great deal of cognitive energy and attention, and overloads working memory. Thus, despite excellent abstract reasoning and problem-solving abilities, Joy is not able to use metacognitive strategies to monitor the plausibility of her work ("Does this make sense?") and enhance her efficiency.

CONCLUSIONS

The research literature describes three subtypes of mathematics disabilities. One of these, a procedural disorder, is characterized by "relatively frequent use of developmentally immature procedures, frequent errors in the execution of procedures, potential developmental delay in the understanding of the concepts underlying procedural use, and difficulties sequencing the multiple steps in complex procedures" (Geary, 2000, p. 6).

Joy's dramatic drop in test scores and limited progress in math in the past $1\frac{1}{2}$ years, despite classroom instruction, professional tutoring, and nightly help from her mother, contrasted with consistently good performance in her other academic skills suggest a specific math disability. Test results and observation of her reasoning strengths, error patterns, compensatory strategies, and response to diagnostic teaching are consistent with the procedural subtype. The difficulty this disorder presents is exacerbated by her weak visual–motor skills. Additionally, Joy's tendency to "shut down" when frustrated with math further taxes her already overloaded effort to maintain cognitive focus. The combination of math anxiety, weakness in visual–motor coordination and the resultant visual–spatial confusion, and difficulty sustaining attention in this circumstance, presents a serious impediment to learning. Additionally, Joy is unable to demonstrate and receive credit for those math skills she *has* learned. In light of these findings, her anxiety is an understandable response to her frustration, an ongoing sense of failure, and the stark contrast between her math weakness and her relatively easy success in other areas.

Joy requires educational programming as a person with specific learning disabilities, especially in math facts, declarative information, and procedures as well as in visual–motor integration.

RECOMMENDATIONS

General

1. Accommodations and remedial procedures for Joy should focus on relieving the burden on working memory, automating lower-level skills, and alleviating the visual confusion caused by her handwriting, enhancing orderliness on the worksheet.
2. Because of her excellent reasoning and problem-solving skills, do not hold Joy back from learning more advanced mathematics concepts and skills.
3. Frequent communication between Joy's math teacher and math tutor would be particularly helpful. As much as possible, Ms. Phelan should teach new concepts and procedures *before* they are presented in the classroom. The tutor will need a copy of the class math book to prepare lessons.

Instructional Approaches

1. Teach all new math concepts and processes through direct instruction and *guided* discovery. Structure discovery activities so that Joy is sure to make the connection. Then help her describe the new concepts and numerical relationships she has discovered. In doing so, she will clarify them for herself.
2. Rather than drill Joy on math facts at this point, find out what strategies she is using and help her become more efficient in those that are reasonable. As much as possible, teach her strategies for coming up with the answers. Use addition facts to teach subtraction and multiplication to teach division. Continue fact practice even when she seems to know them automatically. Use computer programs to motivate drill and practice but do not let them replace regular monitoring of fact knowledge through flash cards.
3. When Joy has to memorize rote information, such as units of measurement, help her to create visual or auditory associations to help her remember them. For example, a yard can be drawn as 3 bare footprints heel-to-toe across a fenced yard, with 12 inchworms crawling the length of each foot.
4. Use mnemonics to help Joy remember rules such as the order in which to do steps of an algorithm or the steps in an operation.
5. Immediately after Joy has demonstrated what appears to be true understanding of a process or concept, ask her to teach it to someone else.

Accommodations

1. Reduce Joy's homework and classroom assignments so that she can complete her work in the same amount of time as do other students. Start by cutting her work by 50% but in such a way that she experiences each type of problem (e.g., all the odd numbers).
2. Teach Joy to use a calculator and allow her to use it for word problems. Use of the calculator for the basic arithmetic will allow you to challenge her reasoning with more advanced word problems.
3. For computation problems, give Joy pocket-sized charts with addition and multiplication facts. Teach her how to use the addition chart for subtraction and the multiplication chart for division. Encourage her to use them any time she wants for the answers to math facts but tell her to guess the answer before looking. That way, she gets immediate reinforcement if she is right and immediate correction if she is wrong. Eventually, visualizing the location of the answer may help in remembering it. When a fact has become truly automatic, Joy should black it out. This will continuously strengthen her recall of the fact as well as allow her to see how few facts are left to learn.
4. Before Joy works a page of computation problems, have her highlight the process signs. Have her assign a specific color to each sign and give her a highlighter in each color.
5. Do not have Joy do timed tests, written or oral. She will make errors in written tests and her anxiety will be increased in oral tests. Provide her as much time as she needs to complete a test. If extra time cannot be made available, reduce the number of problems she is expected to do.
6. Keep a supply of Joy's special graph paper (squares 3/8" with bold lines dividing the paper into quadrangles) in the classroom. This paper will help her line up her numbers correctly and keep her work on different problems separated from each other. Remind Joy to leave plenty of space around any problem she is working.
7. Do not have Joy copy problems from books or the board as she is likely either to copy incorrectly or have difficulty reading her own handwriting. Instead, write the problems in colored marker on her special grid worksheets, one digit to a square. Have Joy work the problems in pencil to provide for good contrast between the problem and her work.

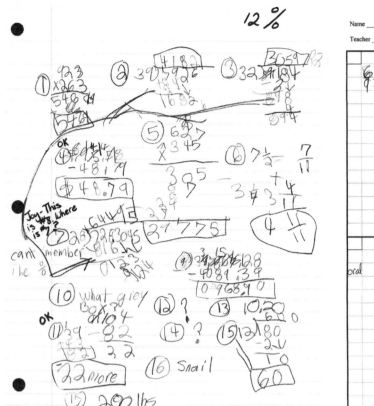

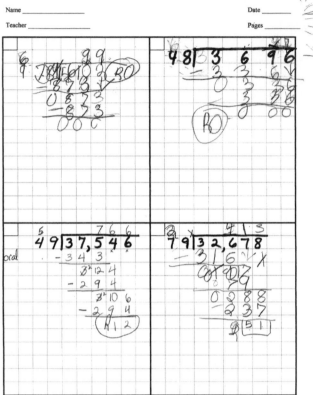

Figure II.3 Math Classroom Work Sample of a Girl, Age 11-5, with a Visual–Motor Weakness and a Procedural Math Disorder

Figure II.4 Math Work Sample of a Girl, Age 11-5, with a Visual–Motor Weakness and a Procedural Math Disorder, Done on Grid Paper. One Problem Done Orally and Dictated to Evaluator.

WOODCOCK-JOHNSON III TESTS OF COGNITIVE ABILITIES

Name: Joy Wiley-Evans

Scores based on: Grade <u>X</u>   Age __ Norms

Date of Birth: 8-22-89

Chronological Age: 11-5

	CLUSTER/ FACTOR	SS	SS ±1 SEM	RPI	Standard Battery	SS	SS ±1 SEM	RPI	Extended Battery	SS	SS ±1 SEM	RPI
Intellectual Ability	General Intellectual Ability	118	115–121	97/90	Verbal Comp.	119	113–124	98/90				
					Vis.-Aud. Learning	91	86–96	84/90				
					Spatial Relations	108	102–113	94/90	Picture Recog.	104	98–110	93/90
					Sound Blending	107	101–113	95/90				
					Concept Formation	122	117–128	99/90	Anal.-Synth.	124	118–131	99/90
					Visual Matching	101	96–106	91/90	Decision Spd.	124	119–130	99/90
					Numbers Reversed	118	112–123	99/90				
CHC Factors	Visual-Spatial Thinking	107	102–112	93/90	Spatial Relations	108	102–113	94/90	Picture Recog.	104	98–110	93/90
	Fluid Reasoning	127	122–131	99/90	Concept Formation	122	117–128	99/90	Anal.-Synth.	124	118–131	99/90
	Processing Spd.	113	109–117	97/90	Visual Matching	101	96–106	91/90	Decision Spd.	124	119–130	99/90
Clinical Clusters	Working Memory	119	114–123	98/90	Numbers Reversed	118	112–123	99/90				
					Aud. Work Memory	113	108–117	97/90				
	Executive Processes	119	115–123	97/90	Concept Formation	122	117–128	99/90	Planning	109	98–119	91/90
									Pair Cancel.	108	106–111	96/90
	Delayed Recall								Story Recall– Delayed (ACH)		(z-score) +1.47	

WOODCOCK-JOHNSON III TESTS OF ACHIEVEMENT

	CLUSTERS	SS	SS ±1 SEM	RPI	Standard Battery	SS	SS ±1 SEM	RPI	Extended Battery	SS	SS ±1 SEM	RPI
					Story Recall	110	100–119	93/90				
Math	Broad Math	97	94–99	86/90	Calculation	96	92–101	85/90				
					Math Fluency	91	88–93	84/90				
					Applied Problems	100	97–103	90/90				
	Math Calculation	94	90–98	84/90	Calculation	96	92–101	85/90				
					Math Fluency	91	88–93	84/90				
	Math Reason.	99	96–102	89/90	Applied Problems	100	97–103	90/90	Quant Concepts	98	94–102	87/90
					Reading Fluency	116	113–118	100/90				
					Passage Comp.	109	103–116	96/90				

Psychoeducational Evaluation

Name:	Michael Jansen	Parents:	Julia and Eric Jansen
Birth Date:	4/14/89	Student's Primary Language:	English
Chronological Age:	11 years, 8 months	Parents' Primary Language:	English
Ethnicity:	Caucasian	Dates Tested:	10/26/00, 11/09/00, 11/10/00, 11/21/00,
Educational Disadvantage:	None		12/06/00, 12/08/00, 12/18/00, 01/10/01,
Language of the Home:	Oral and signed English		01/12/01
Evaluator:		Report Date:	3/15/01

REASON FOR REFERRAL

Michael was referred for evaluation by his parents to see if learning disabilities, in addition to his psychiatric diagnoses, could be identified as a contributing factor in his difficulty learning and retaining academic skills. His mother stated that after years of trying to keep Michael's emotional and behavioral difficulties a secret, she now felt that he would be better served if the educational staff understand clearly the severity of his psychological problems. Additionally, she wanted a thorough evaluation that would provide a comprehensive explanation of the reasons for his learning difficulties and lack of academic progress. Furthermore, the Jansens and the educational team have requested that this evaluation provide information to aid in determining effective instructional techniques, as well as the best educational program and placement for Michael.

BACKGROUND INFORMATION

Family History

Michael is an attractive 11-year-old boy, big for his age, who is a sixth-grade student in a self-contained classroom for students with hearing impairments at Thomas Mann Middle School in Willamette. Michael lives with his mother, Julia Jansen, an airlines ticket agent; his father, Eric Jansen, an electrician; his sister, Lila, age 16, who is deaf, and his brother Matthew, age 9, who is visually impaired and medically fragile. Another brother, age 19, also deaf, lives independently.

Michael and Matthew were both adopted. According to Mrs. Jansen, Michael was abandoned by his biological mother at 4 months and was found malnourished and dehydrated at a crack house in the inner city. The hospital where he was stabilized before being placed in foster care did not test for drugs in his system. Nothing is known about

his biological mother or his genetic history. He lived in two foster homes before being adopted by the Jansen's at age 20 months.

Oral English and sign-supported English are used about equally in the home, depending on who is present at the time. Michael states that he is equally comfortable with oral English and sign-supported oral English.

Medical History

Michael has been diagnosed with Goldenhar Syndrome, a genetic syndrome that can cause unilateral structural abnormalities and facial skin tags and is often associated with learning and behavior problems. Michael's only noticeable feature is the small size of his left ear.

Michael has always had normal hearing acuity and speech discrimination in his right ear. Malformation of the left ear caused a severe conductive hearing loss below 1000 Hz rising to a mild to moderate loss above 1000 Hz. Additionally, hearing in the left ear fluctuated due to chronic infections that were resistant to medical treatment due to the narrowness of the ear canal. Michael wears a hearing aid in the left ear. Last summer, otologic surgery was successful in resolving the infection, creating a normal-sized ear canal and an eardrum, and in unfusing the bones in the middle ear. A unintended result of the surgery, however, is a profound hearing loss above 1000 Hz, through the range of speech sounds. An audiological evaluation done in November 2000 found normal middle ear function bilaterally. Speech discrimination at conversational levels was excellent in the right ear. In the left ear, word recognition was poor (32%) and sentence recognition was fair (80%) at 70 dB with auditory clues only. Just prior to this evaluation, Michael's digitally programmable hearing aid was reconfigured for optimal gain and clarity in a variety of sound environments.

In March 2001, Michael saw Dr. David Feinman for a

behavioral optometric exam. Dr. Feinman found normal ocular motility, binocular coordination, depth perception, color discrimination, and eye health. Dr. Feinman also noted some difficulty in visual perceptual processes. He prescribed new lenses for mild nearsightedness and astigmatism. Michael is to wear his glasses at all times except for physical exercise. Michael is physically healthy.

Developmental History

Michael was delayed in meeting all developmental milestones. He sat at 9½ months, walked at 14 months, and was toilet trained at 5 years. Mrs. Jansen reported that Michael never crawled and rarely walked. He ran until he hit the wall, fell, got up and did it again. He did not seem to know how to slow down. Michael started to talk at 3 years; through age 5 he had acute difficulty with word retrieval and sentence formulation, resulting in severe frustration. The Jansens taught him to sign. Although his sign was rudimentary, it allowed him to communicate sufficiently so that his parents could ask questions and in doing so, give him the words he needed to express his needs.

Mental Health History

The Jansens have worked with a variety of counselors and psychologists and currently are working with a psychiatrist, Dr. Andrea Fox. Michael receives school-based case management services from Margaret Darcy, MSW, CMSW, who coordinates school and community agency services for Michael.

Since Michael's early childhood, he has demonstrated a variety of abnormal behaviors with sufficient consistency to have acquired a host of psychiatric diagnoses including Fetal Alcohol Effect (FAE), Bipolar Disorder (BP), Attention Deficit Hyperactivity Disorder (ADHD), Depression NOS, Intermittent Explosive Disorder, Obsessive Compulsive Disorder (OCD), Reactive Attachment Disorder (RAD), Sensory Integration Disorder, and Disruptive Behavior Disorder. Michael currently takes Risperdal, 1 mg in the morning and at bedtime, for anxiety, paranoia, and ADHD symptoms, and Doxipin, 100 mg at bedtime to alleviate anxiety, improve sleep, and prevent sleepwalking. The current medications are clearly helpful but not optimal in effect; however, previous medications, Depakote, Neurontin, Tegretol, and Lithium, caused intolerable behavioral side effects.

With small class sizes, careful structure, individualized attention, and the extra services that have been provided at Thomas Mann, Michael usually manages to maintain acceptable behavior and cope with everyday situations until the school day is over. By the time he arrives home, however, he is no longer able to maintain that control. The behaviors he demonstrates outside of the school setting are more illustrative of his subjective reality. (See results of the Vineland, below.) The incidents described are not isolated incidents but longstanding patterns of behavior that are made more difficult for the people around him by the unpredictability of the events.

Limited examples of Michael's maladaptive behaviors are provided to give teachers, counselors, and other professionals working with Michael a clearer understanding of the difficulty he has functioning in a reasonably normal manner throughout the day, as well as insight into his mental–emotional health. For a variety of reasons, this has not been fully addressed in previous evaluations and, at this point, these issues are seen as equal to or more important than his academic learning needs, especially when considering future educational programming.

Activity and strong proprioceptive resistance are critical in helping Michael cope with emotional buildup. At school, Michael is helped to maintain control throughout the day by the knowledge that the last period of the day will be spent in hard physical activity, using movement equipment in the occupational therapy room or wrestling with Steven Angelo, Physical Therapist. Last year, his teacher, Bryn Sokall, incorporated movement and activities of muscle resistance into classroom time with a trampoline and a set of weights. She found that Michael could not be touched without his previous permission and that when he was upset, she could usually calm him down in a private discussion outside the classroom. At home, Michael is outside and active almost all of the time, running or riding his bike or scooter. He often wears wrist and leg weights and a tight stretchy vest to enhance proprioception. He has a large cloth bag he likes to crawl into and close to help him pull himself together when he is upset.

Educational History and Previous Testing

Michael began receiving preschool education services at age 4, then was enrolled in a special education kindergarten in Bowman Smith Primary School. Psychological evaluations done at ages 6-0 and 7-4 indicated Full Scale IQ scores of 69 and 78, respectively, with variability in strengths and weaknesses, and significantly delayed adaptive behavior skills. On the 1997–98 IEP, his special education teacher stated that he was making good progress in Reading Mastery (a highly systematized basic reading program), and had developed beginning decoding skills on primer level. In September of 1998, at age 9-3, Michael transferred into the self-contained classroom at Thomas Mann for students who are deaf or hard of hearing. The new IEP specified that reintegration would be considered ". . . when Michael can communicate directly with hearing peers and adults, taking into consideration his emotional development."

He was placed in Bryn Sokall's class for the 1998–99 and 1999–2000 school years. An evaluation done in February 1999 revealed significant problems in math achievement, language processing, visual perceptual skills, visual–motor skills, and all behavior scales of the Devereux Scales of Mental Disorders (DSMD). Although Michael has demonstrated significant behavioral difficulties at home, for the past 2½ years, he has been able to maintain his behavior and emotional responses within acceptable limits at school. This may be attributed to a variety of factors: support and perceptiveness regarding his needs from his teacher, a consistent and structured educational program, counseling, and medication. Detailed reports of these evaluations are available in Michael's educational file.

Michael has received speech-language services since his enrollment at Thomas Mann. During the third quarter of the 1999–2000 school year, Michael was involved in a pilot project of small-group instruction in phonological awareness and phonics skills for 45 minutes, 4 days a week, with speech instruction integrated twice a week and individual speech sessions once a week. The direct instruction program was discontinued after the planned 8 weeks and, subsequently, Ms. Sokall tried to infuse phonics instruction throughout the day.

Michael's current teacher, Phillip Anderson, usually uses Total Communication, speaking while using conceptually accurate sign in English word order. Sometimes, however, he drops his voice so he can sign in ASL. Michael stated that he wants a teacher who voices all the time with or without sign. He also said that he wants to move to a class that "does things," such as cooking and other experiential learning, and he wants a music class.

Mrs. Jansen described some of the difficulties that Michael has when reading orally from one of the classroom storybooks, simple picture-texts with three to four lines of large print per page. Michael recognizes most words in the book as sight words and can sound out simple, short-vowel, one-syllable words. He may read a word correctly in one sentence, then draw a blank when he sees it in the next sentence. His strategy, which is usually successful, is to mark his place with his finger, find and reread the previous sentence in which he read the word correctly, and then go back to where he left off. He often loses his place while reading, usually in the middle of the line, and is unable to find it without help. Pages with only two or three lines of large print are easiest for him to read. If he can decode all of the words easily, and if the information is very simple, he understands what he is reading, but cannot sequence the events. He cannot scan a passage he has read to find the answer to a question composed of the same words.

Michael has difficulty coping with homework even with parent help. He becomes frustrated quickly when mildly challenged by the task (e.g., finding specific words within a simple story), and will scream at his mother, "I hate you. I can't do this," and sometimes rips up the paper. Mr. Anderson no longer assigns homework to Michael and this has eased the situation at home. Michael also rips up notes from his teacher to his mother, fearing that they say "something bad" about him, even if Mr. Anderson has read it to Michael already. Communication now takes place through e-mail to alleviate Michael's anxiety.

CLASSROOM OBSERVATION AND TEACHER INTERVIEW

Michael was observed twice in his classroom by Dr. Rosen and multiple times by Dr. Janice Borgstrom who has worked in the class twice weekly throughout the school year. During one observation, the students worked on a worksheet, using their reading books. Mr. Anderson had previously explained and modeled the tasks and queried individual students regarding their understanding of each one. Michael worked independently and with good concentration but did not do the task, an exercise in use of context clues, correctly. Michael made up his own sentences for given words rather than copying the sentences in the book in which they were used. The reading books were approximately first-grade reading level and appeared to be an appropriate instructional level for Michael. During another observation, Dr. Borgstrom conducted a class lesson regarding the categorization of different types of nouns. Michael listened to Dr. Borgstrom, watched appropriately when other students had their turns, and responded correctly when it was his turn.

According to Mr. Anderson, Michael demonstrated few behavioral or attentional problems throughout the first semester. On one occasion, he left the classroom when he was upset, having decided to call his mother. During the current semester, however, Michael has had more difficulty. He has, at times, refused to have his work corrected, refused to work, refused to look at Mr. Anderson, pulled his jacket over his head making a small opening from which to look out, whistled, made noises despite other students' requests to stop, and fallen asleep in class. His handwriting has deteriorated. Mrs. Jansen commented that at home Michael makes noises, whistles, and rocks to calm himself. Mr. Anderson commented that some days, when he needs to correct Michael, Michael clearly resents the assistance. Michael will work with Mr. Anderson outside the classroom but this is only an option when another adult is in the class. In an attempt to teach Michael to advocate for himself, Mr. Anderson and Michael have decided that when Michael is upset, he can ask for permission to go and sit by himself in the middle school office until he feels that he can return to class.

TESTS ADMINISTERED

Woodcock-Johnson III Tests of Cognitive Abilities
(WJ III COG): Tests 1–13, 15–20
Woodcock-Johnson III Tests of Achievement
(WJ III ACH): Tests 1–11, 13–15, 18–19, 21
Vineland Adaptive Behavior Scales: Interview Edition
The Listening Test (administered by Dr. Janice
Borgstrom)
The Word—R Test: A Test of Expressive Vocabulary and
Semantics (Word-R) (administered by Dr. Janice
Borgstrom)
Comprehensive Test of Phonological Processing (CTOPP)
Beery-Buktenica Developmental Test of Visual-Motor Integration (4th ed.) (VMI)
Qualitative Reading Inventory—3 (QRI-3)
Classroom observation
Interviews with previous and current classroom teachers
Interview with Julia Jansen

BEHAVIORAL OBSERVATIONS DURING TESTING

Michael's behavior during testing varied greatly according to the day, the type of test, the reinforcement system, and the evaluator. When working with Dr. Borgstrom, Michael evidenced rapid fatigue and deterioration of attention and effort after 15 to 20 minutes. He requested repetition on many

items, which was given for the purpose of gaining further qualitative information although it altered the standardization process. With advance warning of this difficulty, this evaluator set up a reinforcement system for attention, cooperation, and effort, with frequent opportunities to earn, and choose, a reward. This intervention took up very little time and was quite effective in helping Michael sustain attention and enthusiasm. During the first two sessions, if Michael became tired, discouraged, or frustrated, he had the option of going outside to ride his scooter (which his mother had brought in for this purpose) for a few minutes. He used this option during the first two testing sessions but did not request it after that. Michael was generally able to work well for an hour to 1½ hours with a break. After reviewing the differences in scores on tests given under different circumstances, the decision was made to readminister certain items from The Word-R Test and The Listening Test using the behavioral reinforcement system. Michael responded correctly in this situation to many items he had previously missed. Clearly, his attention and emotional state have a considerable impact on his ability to perform.

Michael conversed easily in the test setting although the topics were limited to recent events in his life. He was usually cooperative and persisted in tasks that were difficult for him. Michael readily accepted the explanation that each test would start out fairly easy and become quite hard. Subsequently, when Michael began to become frustrated, a reminder of this reestablished a level of emotional comfort. Twice, testing was discontinued because Michael did not want to continue. Michael's activity level was appropriate throughout testing. Overall, Michael appeared self-confident through most of the tests.

The following modifications were made to the standardized testing procedures for the WJ III Tests of Cognitive Abilities: voice presentation was used on Incomplete Words, possibly inflating the score, and on the latter part of Oral Comprehension because Michael interrupted the test to say, "That voice is really beginning to annoy me," and refused to continue to listen to it.

The results of this evaluation are considered a valid representation of Michael's cognitive and academic abilities given optimal circumstances and good motivation.

EVALUATION RESULTS

Michael's ethnic and racial background were considered and determined to have no effect on test selection or interpretation, nor were they found to be a primary factor in his

Table 1.   WJ III Score Ranges

SS	Below 70	70–79	80–89	90–110	111–120	121–130	Above 130
Range	Very Low	Low	Low Average	Average	High Average	Superior	Very Superior

educational placement. No significant educational disadvantages were noted other than those commonly associated with a hearing impairment. All assessments were conducted using oral English or sign-supported English. Michael wore his hearing aid, which was checked and found to be in working order before each session.

The WJ III Tests of Cognitive Abilities and Tests of Achievement were scored according to age norms. Because these two batteries are co-normed, direct comparisons can be made between Michael's cognitive and achievement scores. Michael's abilities as measured by the tests and clusters of the WJ III are described as percentile ranks (PR), indicating where Michael's score would fall within the scores of 100 students of the same age and month, and standard score (SS) ranges created by 68% confidence bands (SS ± 1 SEM). When the scores of the component tests within a cognitive factor are similar, only the factor score, representing a broader ability, is reported, as this is the more reliable score. (See Table 1.)

The Relative Proficiency Index (RPI) is also used to describe the quality of Michael's test performance. For example, an RPI of 75/90 indicates that Michael would demonstrate 75% proficiency on a task when typical grade-peers demonstrated 90%. An RPI of 75/90 or below indicates that similar classroom tasks would be at the student's frustration level (difficult to impossible); an RPI of 96/90 or above, at his independent level (easy to extremely easy); and between 76/90 to 95/90, within his instructional range. The CTOPP also was scored according to age norms. The QRI-3 is an informal reading inventory and provides only approximate grade equivalents based on the level of difficulty of the word lists and passages. The scores of the Word-R and the Listening Test are not valid, due to the repeated administration of the tests, multiple repetition of items within the tests, and unstandardized probes on test items. These tests were used to obtain qualitative information.

Adaptive Behavior

According to the results of the Vineland Adaptive Behavior Scales, when compared with age-peers without a hearing impairment, Michael's skills in each of the domains of Communication, Daily Living, and Socialization are sig-

nificantly low, in the range of Mild to Moderate Deficit, giving him an Adaptive Behavior Composite score in the Moderate Deficit range. During the Vineland interview, Michael's mother provided the information that follows.

Domains

Communication

According to Mrs. Jansen, Michael still has difficulty with the verbal specificity and organization necessary for a discussion more involved than light conversation. Although he uses complex sentences in his speech, he has difficulty processing complex syntax and abstract meaning. He needs instructions given one step at a time, in concrete terms, because he appears to forget or process only pieces of multiple-step instructions. Although usually asked to repeat instructions aloud, Michael still may not carry them out and is puzzled when he's reminded. As yet, Michael is unable to provide his complete home address.

Daily Living Skills

Michael takes care of his toileting needs independently but must be reminded about certain grooming needs such as brushing his teeth or washing his hair when he takes a shower. He dresses himself and chooses his own clothes. He is not affected by weather conditions and thus, does not dress accordingly unless specifically told what to wear (e.g., jacket, long pants). Subsequently, he continues to dress that way until given some other type of instruction. Michael has no awareness of taking personal responsibility for his health and is not always aware of when he himself is sick.

Mrs. Jansen reported that Michael's table manners are "terrible;" he often eats with his hands (although he knows how to use utensils) and talks with his mouth full. When younger, Michael received eating therapy because he habitually stuffed his mouth so full of food that, unable to chew, he choked. He can now judge the amount so that he stops just short of being unable to chew. Despite many interventions, the Jansens have been unable to change his eating habits; consequently, his parents rarely take Michael to restaurants, other than fast food chains. His siblings will not eat with him in public.

Other than a few specific items he is allowed to heat in the microwave, Michael is not permitted to prepare food unsupervised. He does certain chores independently, such as setting the table and taking care of his dog. Other than these, he never completes what he has been told to do (e.g., put his clothes away), even if it is something he loves to do and it is broken down into steps for him.

Community

Although when asked, Michael will say that it is unsafe to go somewhere with a stranger, his judgment is not sufficiently reliable for him to go places, such as into a store, by himself; consequently, he is rarely in a situation in which he could independently demonstrate safety awareness (e.g., walk/don't walk lights). Michael answers the phone correctly but if the person for whom the call is intended is unavailable, he gets scared and hangs up. He knows to call 911 in an emergency but his judgment of what constitutes an emergency may be distorted. On one occasion, Michael called 911 because his respite sitter was making him watch TV, which he hates, and he was convinced that his parents were never coming back. Michael repeated the words, "Something is wrong here" until the police arrived and contacted Michael's parents.

Michael can tell time to the hour and half-hour and understands that clock time is related to the schedule of routine events in his day. He does not really understand the value of money. He earns money for doing chores but tends to lose it unless he gives it to his mother to hold. Michael knows how to order for himself in fast food restaurants but is afraid to approach the counter if other patrons are there.

Socialization

Michael is content playing at home, outside, by himself. Sometimes Mrs. Jansen sees him through the window having conversations with himself in sign, moving to take the part of each speaker. These are not the body shifts required by ASL syntax to indicate a change of speakers, but complete changes of position.

Michael has only one friend whom he sees out of school, a boy 2 years younger who enjoys being very active and playing pretend games with Michael, like "army." At school, Michael tends to separate himself from his peer-group, even if playing the same game at the same time.

Michael has a limited understanding of rules for games. Last year, on a soccer team, he could not understand why he could not just run and kick the ball whenever he wanted. Football and track had too many rules, too many participants, and too much going on. Recently, he has done well on the middle school wrestling team. The rules of card or board games tend to be too complex for him. Even when rules are simplified for him in family games, he tends to lose interest after about 10 minutes.

Because Michael is limited in judgment and forethought, opportunities to demonstrate personal responsibility are infrequent. His mother did state, however, that he is responsible about returning things borrowed, such as from the library.

Maladaptive Behaviors

Compared with other 11-year-olds in the Vineland norm sample, Michael's Maladaptive Behavior Domain score is significantly elevated. His maladaptive behaviors are of significant concern whether he is rated on his medications or off his medications, and whether he is compared to the general norm sample or to children with emotional disturbances who live in residential facilities.

Michael has severe difficulty identifying and coping with emotions. He tends to identify all emotions, even positive ones, as anger. He runs away when he thinks someone is angry with him and destroys things when he is angry. In the school setting, he has made significant progress in this area. Outside of the school environment, Michael's anger and resultant actions are often completely out of proportion to the precipitating event. For example, angry at being told to come into the house, he went into his bedroom, ripped down blinds, kicked holes in the doors, and broke his brother's toys. In these instances, Michael cannot be physically restrained, as this makes him panic and fight harder. When he calms down, he does not understand the reason for his behavior or that it was wrong; nor does he feel sorry for what he has done. When Michael is in a situation in which he does not understand what is happening, he withdraws into a "mental cocoon." His mother perceives him as exhibiting excessive unhappiness almost all of the time, regardless of his medication.

Generally, in school and at home, Michael does not appear to generalize rules from one situation to another. He does not appear to have developed a sense of moral values. His ability to follow school rules may be more of a factor of learning the routine in each situation. Michael is unaware if he has done something wrong or has hurt someone's feelings. He appears to lack empathy and does not feel remorse. Michael has a history of hurting and killing small animals and doing things that cause them to die or be hurt. Over the past 2 years, however, Michael has not hurt any people or animals except for hitting family members in anger. After careful consideration, his parents gave him a puppy. He is closely supervised with it, and has been caring for it well.

Michael incorporates things he hears into his own reality. For example, he heard something on TV about a child being hit with a belt and the next day told his teacher, "Did you know my dad hit me with a belt?" Once Michael thinks of an event in this way, he believes it really happened. Mrs. Jansen stated that Child Protective Services finally stopped coming out to investigate but would just call to check on Michael's latest story.

Sometimes Michael does things that could be viewed as

malicious, except that he does not appear to be fully aware of his actions or to consider the consequences, removing the element of deliberateness. As one example, last month, Michael took the brakes off his father's new $300 bicycle to use on his own. Once engaged, he continued to dismantle the bike, cutting through the spokes and cables and disassembling the parts. His mother happened upon him and called to him repeatedly as she walked towards him. She was not able to get his attention until she touched him. He startled, as though coming out of a trance, and appeared surprised as he realized what he had done. About a week ago, as he passed another boy in the hall, he signed, "I'm going to kill your girlfriend." Michael had not been interacting with the boy and was not angry at him. Later, he came to the evaluator's office where his mother was being interviewed, explained his threat, and stated: "It just showed up in my mind. I don't know why." Mrs. Jansen stated that when Michael is angry, he frequently threatens to kill her, and sometimes his brother, but has never before threatened to kill someone else.

Michael lives with delusions and extreme anxiety. For example, on a car trip last January, an 18-wheeler passed their car and the driver, seeing a young boy in the back seat, waved. Michael became hysterical. Screaming that the truck driver was going to kill them, he threw himself down on the floor and kicked at the windows, trying to escape from the moving car. He can become literally paralyzed with fear in situations that are out of his everyday experience or in situations that are quite familiar. On a recent family vacation, he was unable to move from a spot in the hotel room, certain that he was going to be kidnapped. Although he loves to swim, he repeatedly refuses to swim in his backyard pool for fear of being attacked by sharks. His current medication allows him to accept that there are no sharks in the pool and to remember that his mother has proven this in the past. Occasionally, still, he cannot get past this fear and is unable to get into the water.

Michael has compulsive behaviors and peculiar mannerisms. He stashes food under his bed—even food that clearly will not keep, such as ice cream. No matter how many times Mrs. Jansen makes Michael help her clean it up, he feels that he must have the food there and replaces it. As a toddler, he hid his bottles in his father's boots. Michael also has a habit of hiding under his bed and making animal and other, unrecognizable, noises. When asked what he is doing, he says he's just talking and wants to be left alone. In some activities, such as lining up his toy cars, Michael cannot be interrupted, no matter what the reason, until he is finished.

Michael has self-injurious behaviors such as picking at his skin until he bleeds and, a few months ago, he repeatedly hit his head against the outside wall of their house for over an hour, continuing while it bled. He was finally lured away from the wall with ice cream sandwiches. Mrs. Jansen suspects this behavior was a side effect of Neurontin.

In summary, Michael frequently behaves in ways that indicate a lack of forethought or inhibitory control. Moreover, he does not realize the societal view of his actions at the time and his mother is doubtful as to whether he really understands the wrongness or inappropriateness of his actions. Based on his mother's description of his behavioral history and that included in a community agency report several years ago, his perspective of reality is clearly distorted. He has bouts of acute depression and has stated suicidal ideations but, to date, has never formulated a plan.

Intelligence/Cognitive Abilities

According to the results of the WJ III COG, Michael's general cognitive/intellectual ability is in the Very Low range (General Intellectual Ability-Extended [GIA]: SS 62–66), slightly lower than findings of previous assessments. This score places him within the lowest 1% of age-peers. Although he had considerable variation (3.5 SD) among the scores comprising this cluster, with spikes of abilities in the Average range, his lowest scores were in the areas weighted most heavily.

Reasoning

Abstract thinking and logical reasoning appear to be Michael's most impaired abilities. Despite repeated training and corrective feedback, Michael simply could not understand what was required on the inductive and deductive reasoning tasks of the Fluid Reasoning cluster. (See Table 2.) His score was lower than 1 out of 1000 of his age-peers. As information is processed, abstract thinking and logical reasoning allow one to go beyond what he already knows, perceive or create the connections between new and known information, and develop new concepts. The thinking/rea-

Table 2.   Fluid Reasoning Scores

WJ III FACTOR/Test	SS	68% BAND	PR	RPI	AE
FLUID REASONING	51	46–56	<0.1	4/90	5-7

Table 3.   Short-Term and Working Memory Scores

WJ III FACTOR/ CLUSTER/Test	SS	68% Band	PR	RPI	AE
SHORT-TERM MEMORY	77	73–81	6	26/90	6-10
Numbers Reversed	102	96–108	55	92/90	12-2
Memory for Words	59	54–64	0.3	1/90	4-3
WORKING MEMORY	86	81–90	17	62/90	8-8
Numbers Reversed	102	96–108	55	92/90	12-2
Auditory Working Memory	71	66–76	3	18/90	6-8

CTOPP COMPOSITE/Test					
PHONOLOGICAL MEMORY	55		<1		

soning process is the foundation for forethought, judgment, inference, and rule generalization.

Short-Term Memory and Working Memory

Short-term memory (memory span, the amount of information that can be held in conscious awareness at one time) and working memory (the ability to perform a mental operation on this information) are critical facilitators for thinking as they allow information taken in by the senses or retrieved from long-term stores to be held in mind for processing.

Test results (see Table 3) indicate that Michael has severe problems with short-term memory and working memory. He did, however, create and demonstrate effective use of a memory strategy, using a combination of anchoring (assigning a digit to a finger) and signed numbers to repeat a string of digits in reverse order. Weak memory obviously contributed to Michael's Low performance on many areas of the evaluation—most notably on the oral language tests.

Long-Term Storage and Retrieval

The significant discrepancy between Michael's scores on the two tests comprising the Long-Term Retrieval factor (see Table 4) suggest that his ability to retrieve information from long-term memory depends on the type of task involved. Michael scored in the Very Low to Low range when required to learn and retrieve new associations between rebus-like symbols and familiar words (e.g., to, cat, yellow). In contrast, when given a specific category (e.g., foods) and asked to come up with examples from his own store of knowledge, his score and his proficiency were Average for

Table 4.   Long-Term Retrieval Scores

WJ III FACTOR/Test	SS	68% Band	PR	RPI	AE
LONG-TERM RETRIEVAL	74	70–78	4	77/90	7-4
Retrieval Fluency	99	93–105	46	90/90	11-3
Visual-Auditory Learning	72	68–75	3	57/90	6-5

age-peers. Additionally, he used a strategy of organizing words into subcategories (e.g., drinks, dinners, sweets). The difference in his performance between the two tests suggests that he may have had difficulty with the added requirement of learning new information (as opposed to retrieving known information). A number of factors may have contributed to this difficulty: having to grasp the abstract relationship between symbols and words, working at a proscribed pace, and the restriction in word choice (only one correct response).

Lexical Access/Word Retrieval

In addition to his strong performance on Retrieval Fluency, Michael performed as rapidly and accurately as his age-peers when naming printed letters and digits (Rapid Naming). (See Table 5.) Michael appears to have a strength in rapidly retrieving words from long-term memory when the association between prompt (visual or oral) and word to be recalled is overlearned and automatic (e.g., letter naming) or when his response does not have to be specific (e.g., category naming).

Michael had considerably more difficulty retrieving words for pictured objects and colors rapidly. He scored in the Low range (CTOPP Alternate Rapid Naming). Despite his Low Average WJ III Rapid Picture Naming score, his RPI of 27/90 indicated that similar grade-level tasks would be very difficult to extremely difficult for him. Michael signed the names for the objects and colors as he said them. When he was finished, the evaluator had him repeat one of the tests without signing to see if this might reduce his response time. Instead, his subsequent responses were slower and less fluent.

Table 5.   Lexical Access/Word Retrieval Scores

CTOPP COMPOSITE/Test	SS	68% BAND	PR	RPI	AE
RAPID NAMING (digits, letters)	91		27		
ALTERNATE RAPID NAMING (colors, objects)	73		3		
WJ III Rapid Picture Naming	84	82–86	14	27/90	8-0

Language Development and Acquired Knowledge

Michael's difficulties in abstract, logical reasoning and memory were apparent in his performance on oral language tasks and in his spontaneous conversation. Facility in primary language (oral or sign) is inseparable from stores of acquired knowledge. Acquired knowledge, to a large extent, is the mediator by which new information is processed and a catalyst for thinking and new learning. Likewise, the expansion of acquired knowledge both produces and enhances language development. As Michael considers himself a beginning signer and is far more proficient in oral English, only his oral English skills were formally assessed. Nevertheless, Michael often signs while he speaks, even to hearing people. This may be a habit developed by being in a signing environment throughout the day.

Acquired Knowledge

According to the results of the WJ III (see Table 6), Michael's knowledge of the world around him, both based on daily experiences and school presentation, is in the Very Low range, within the lowest 1% of his age-peers. The difficulty that Michael demonstrates with oral language skills provides both a basis for and a reflection of his limited knowledge.

Language Comprehension

Word Level

A variety of measures indicates that Michael's understanding of and flexibility with word meanings is limited. Although his Picture Vocabulary score was in the Average

Table 6.   Language Development and Acquired Knowledge Scores

WJ III FACTOR/ CLUSTER/Test	SS	68% BAND	PR	RPI	AE
KNOWLEDGE	67	63–70	1	16/90	6-7
COMPREHENSION- KNOWLEDGE	72	68–75	3	30/90	7-2
ORAL LANGUAGE (Ext)	70	66–73	2	52/90	7-7
Understanding Directions	73	69–77	4	34/90	6-10
Oral Comprehension	69	64–74	2	14/90	6-7
Story Recall	88	82–94	20	84/90	8-7
Picture Vocabulary	92	87–97	30	76/90	9-11

QRI-3 Listening Comprehension (informal)	Lowest passage administered— Grade level 3: Frustration level
The Listening Test	Scores invalid due to nonstandardized administration but most were significantly low. Results of qualitative analysis reported.
The Word R Test	

range, his RPI indicates that he would perceive a similar task at grade level as difficult. In all of the language comprehension tests, Michael had difficulty grasping the critical elements in word meanings. This, in turn, limited his ability to apprehend relationships among words such as are necessary for higher language skills (e.g., classification, generalization, analogy, ambiguity, and absurdity). For example, he could not find the absurdity inherent in a "married bachelor" because he did not know the meaning of "bachelor." Asked which one didn't fit, "pizza, candy, sugar, honey," he responded, "All of them are food."

Connected Discourse

Michael's performance on the WJ III indicated that his comprehension of connected discourse of one to two sentences in length is within the lowest 1% of his age-peers (Oral Comprehension). Holding the brief spoken passages in memory appeared to be a particular problem, as he requested repetition of many passages (not given), and could not consistently follow two-step directions.

Michael was more proficient in retelling (WJ III Story Recall, Low Average) and answering questions (The Listening Test) about brief, simple stories (three to four sentences), but when presented with a seven-sentence story with slightly more complex syntax, he remarked, "This gets harder 'cause of long sentences'" and remembered almost none of it. Michael had considerable difficulty understanding and retelling the longer (250–350 words), orally presented stories of the QRI-3 intended for grades 3 and 4.

Analysis of Language Comprehension

Analysis of Michael's responses on the combination of language tests administered yielded the following information. For adequate comprehension of linguistic information, Michael must have solid prior knowledge and, preferably, experience of the concepts involved and the vocabulary (as he will not infer the meaning from context). On the lower-level passages of Story Recall, The Listening Test, and the QRI-3 (which he read), Michael was able to: identify relevant details, state the main idea, make inferences about events, and predict what might happen next. These passages all had content within the realm of his experience, used familiar vocabulary, and had relatively uncomplicated syntax.

Michael does not understand long sentences, those with very complex sentence structure, and those in which the clausal relationships (if/then, except, otherwise) change a surface interpretation of the meaning (e.g., "In the cocoon, caterpillars will change into butterflies, *except* in particularly hot and dry weather conditions or *if* there are no plants for them to eat *when* they emerge"). Michael appears unable to comprehend instructions and information incorporating complex temporal concepts (e.g., statements in which the order of events is different from the order of mention, such as "Before you ride your bike, you need to do your homework"). Also, he tends to interpret information concretely; consequently, he does not grasp implied relationships among events. For example, he listened to a story about Amelia Earhart's attempt to fly around the world and the disappearance of her plane over the Pacific Ocean. Asked why he thought her plane was never found, he stated, "Because she disappeared. She's gone." Asked what Earhart was attempting to do when her plane disappeared, he responded, "Trying to get back—or get out," rather than "fly around the world."

Michael's concrete understanding of language and his difficulties identifying critical elements, noting similarities and differences, making inferences, and considering alternate ways to solve problems contribute to and are influenced by his difficulties with reasoning and memory.

Language Expression

Michael's word-retrieval difficulties, as well as the more generalized memory deficits, severely hamper his ability to express his thoughts. Difficulty with word retrieval and an inability to recognize and focus on the critical elements within his intended message are major contributing factors to his acute weakness in formulating sentences and organizing longer discourse. The following is his response to: "What is a bear?"

A bear is a animal and it—You want me to describe it? It has big—about this size of a foot (shows with his hands) and the back [of the] foot has to be about here and the front [of the] foot, um, I say is about this big. And then the balls [claws]. It has brown—some are black—furry and the face sometimes has like tan . . . tan . . . than on the . . . on the like the face sometimes it's all brown. It has brown hair all that stuff and the tail . . . it has the tail, it has eyes, nose. And sometimes the nose is brown, or black. And that's all I know.

In retelling a brief story, the content of which was well within his comprehension, he sequenced most of the key events but confused specific details.

First, they asked their mom—their dad I mean—their father, if they can go to the movies. He said, "I'm sorry girls but if you find something the game, I'll call you. And soon, Mary and Sue went in their movies [room].

Michael has more difficulty in spontaneous, extended discourse than in retelling a story. In addition to disorganization of his main points, he mispronounces words (see Auditory/Phonological Processing) and uses incorrect syntax (e.g., "in case the bus brokes down"), verb tense (e.g., "One time, I went with Bryn to Mexico. We want to go to Mexico and I go to Mexico."), and referents (e.g., "Then the car stopped and fix—and helped fix the bus").

Use of Sign-Supported Oral English

Because Michael seems to use sign to help himself with different types of tasks, and chooses to sign while speaking, extension testing was conducted to see if the addition of sign improves his language comprehension. After a standardized administration of the Story Recall test, the evaluator read the passages to Michael. Simultaneously, a certified interpreter (with whom Michael is quite familiar) interpreted in conceptually accurate sign in English word order (Michael's preference over American Sign Language). Although Michael's performance did improve on two passages with the addition of sign, it is unclear if the sign actually helped his comprehension, helped him to focus his attention (thus aiding comprehension), or if repetition of the story was the major factor. The last two passages were clearly too difficult for him and the sign did not help.

Michael does use sign as an effective medium for recalling the spelling of words and for retrieving words in speech—sometimes as a prompt for oral retrieval and occasionally as a substitute.

Auditory/Phonological Processing

Phoneme Detection and Initial Processing

Michael's performance on the WJ III Auditory Attention test (see Table 7) is consistent with the results of the audiological speech discrimination tests. These results indicate that Michael's detection and initial processing of speech sounds within words are accurate, even in noise that almost masked the words. Moreover, he had no difficulty recognizing words that were presented with sounds omitted (Incomplete Words).

Phonological Processing and Memory

In contrast, Michael's phonological memory, immediate memory for the sounds in words, is exceedingly weak. His scores on the CTOPP Phonological Memory composite and the WJ III Memory for Words test (Table 7) placed his performance below the lowest 1% of his age-peers.

Table 7.   Auditory/Phonological Processing Scores

WJ III FACTOR/ CLUSTER/Test	SS	68% BAND	PR	RPI	AE
AUDITORY PROCESSING	97	91–103	42	88/90	10-9
Auditory Attention	111	103–119	76	94/90	>20
Sound Blending	89	82–96	23	77/90	8-9
PHONEMIC AWARENESS	92	86–98	31	85/90	9-8
Incomplete Words	101	93–108	52	90/90	11-10
Sound Blending	89	82–96	23	77/90	8-9
Memory for Words	59	54–64	0.3	1/90	4-3

CTOPP COMPOSITE/Test	SS	ScS*	PR	GE	AE
PHONOLOGICAL AWARENESS	64		<1		
Elision		3	1	1.2	6-3
Blending Words		5	5	1.4	6-6
PHONOLOGICAL MEMORY	55		<1		
Memory for Digits		1	<1	<K.0	<5-0
Nonword Repetition		4	2	<K.0	<5-0
Segmenting Words		8	25		<7-0

*Scaled scores have a mean of 10 and a standard deviation of 3

Michael mispronounces many words in spontaneous speech (e.g., "*hamugurber*"/hamburger, "*glode*"/globe, "*priers*"/pliers, "*fluzzy*"/blurry). Dr. Borgstrom noted that his error patterns are not consistent with his past or present hearing impairment, nor are they errors that children with hearing impairments typically make, such as confusing phonemes that sound different but look the same on the mouth (e.g., /p//b/, /g//k/) or phonemes that are out of their range of detectable sounds. Michael also mispronounces less familiar words within a few minutes of hearing them (e.g., "*evrelina-anair*"/Amelia Earhart, "*persissa*"/Pacific). Despite specific training in sound blending, Michael still has great difficulty, and comes up with unlikely responses in simple sound blending tasks (e.g., "ball" for "*b-ŏ-n*," "dad" for "*m-ă-d*").

These error patterns indicate that while Michael detects and initially processes the sounds in words accurately, he codes them in short-term memory incorrectly (with the wrong sounds). When he retrieves the word for speech, he retrieves it as it has been miscoded in long-term memory, and pronounces it incorrectly, thus reinforcing his mispronunciation.

Michael also struggled with the more complex phonological tasks of sound segmentation and sound deletion. Although he scored in the Average range on the Segmenting Words subtest (CTOPP), he did so by visualizing the spelling of the target word and saying the sound for each letter (e.g., "*h-ŏ-t*" for "hot," "*ĕ-g-g*" for "egg"). Still, he made some phonological errors even on words he can spell (e.g., "*p-ō-k*" for "pig").

Table 8.   Processing Speed Scores

WJ III FACTOR/Test	SS	68% BAND	PR	RPI	AE
PROCESSING SPEED	81	78–84	10	45/90	9-4
Visual Matching	73	69–77	4	16/90	8-10
Decision Speed	93	89–97	32	79/90	10-4

Processing Speed

Processing speed is the ability to do simple cognitive tasks quickly, allowing procedures that have been done repeatedly to become automatic, and freeing higher-level thinking for more complex or difficult tasks. Michael had particular difficulty rapidly scanning rows of numbers under timed conditions. (See Table 8.) His score was significantly higher, in the Average range, on a task of scanning rows of pictures to find the two that were most alike conceptually (e.g., *boot* and *shoe*). Although his RPI was relatively low (79/90) on the latter task, Michael does appear to process pictures more rapidly and easily than symbols.

Visual–Spatial and Visual–Motor Skills

Visual–Spatial Skills
Results of the WJ III COG indicate that Michael's visual–spatial abilities are varied. (See Table 9.) He exhibited strengths, with scores solidly in the Average range, in the ability to form and store mental images of pictures for later recognition and to plan a route through a spatial field by choosing which lines to follow. Age-level tasks in perceiving part/whole and spatial relationships in abstract figures, however, would be difficult (RPI 73/90). As noted above, Michael appears to have difficulty processing symbols rapidly. A visual skills assessment conducted by Grace Laskey, O. T., 2 years ago also indicated great variability among visual perceptual skills.

Michael's perception of the stimuli on one of the reasoning tests was notable. One of two geometric shapes has a line drawing of a box around it simply to distinguish it as separate from the other. Asked to state what was different

Table 9.   Visual–Spatial and Visual–Motor Skills Scores

WJ III FACTOR/Test	SS	68% BAND	PR	RPI	AE
VISUAL-SPATIAL THINKING	88	84–92	21	80/90	8-3
Spatial Relations	85	81–89	15	73/90	7-2
Picture Recognition	96	91–101	39	86/90	9-10
Planning	95	85–105	37	89/90	9-6

about the drawing inside the box from the drawing outside the box (e.g., shape, color), Michael kept describing the drawing, the "square" around it, and the white space between them as components of the target figure. He was unable to focus just on the figure and ignore the rest as background.

Visual–Motor Skills

Michael is right-handed. He demonstrated significant difficulty in visual–motor coordination on the VMI, in the lowest 1% of his age-peers. He obtained the same score on the same test 2 years ago. This difficulty is reflected in his limited handwriting control despite his good tripod pencil grip (WJ III Handwriting: SS 66, PR 1, AE 5-0).

Executive Processing and Strategic Thinking

Despite his low performance on so many cognitive tests, Michael created strategies to enhance his performance in a variety of tasks. Although some of them were inefficient, they did appear to improve his performance, even if just (possibly) to focus his attention. His strategies were:

- to remember a string of digits, he used a mixture of fingerspelling and mentally "anchoring" them on his fingers;
- to remember elements of a story read to him, he asked if he could take notes. The notes were scribbled, mostly illegible words, marks, and numbers, scattered randomly on a 3 × 3 piece of paper. (He was offered other paper but said the one he had was fine.)

Table 10.   Academic Achievement Scores

WJ III CLUSTER/Test	SS	68% BAND	PR	RPI	GE*	AE*
BROAD READING	63	61–65	1	1/90	2.0	7-4
BROAD WRITTEN LANGUAGE	72	69–76	3	33/90	2.7	8-0
BROAD MATH	66	64–69	1	13/90	2.2	7-7
ACADEMIC KNOWLEDGE	65	61–70	1	10/90	1.2	6-5

*Age/Grade Equivalent: The age/grade at which the median score matched Michael's raw score.

QRI-3 Passage Level	Words in Lists	Oral Reading in Context	Oral Reading Rate	Reading Comprehension
Primer	Independent	Instructional	59 wpm	Independent
Grade 1	Instructional	Frustration	52 wpm	Instructional
Grade 2	Frustration	Frustration	48 wpm	Questionable

- to segment the sounds in a word, he visualized the spelling and said the sound of each letter;
- to name things within a given category, he organized his responses into subcategories;
- to recall the names of pictured objects, he signed them; and
- to remember the spelling of words, he fingerspelled portions of them.

Academic Achievement

All of Michael's academic skills are severely delayed with no significant discrepancies within or between any of the achievement clusters. His Total Achievement cluster score was within the lowest 2 in 1000 age-peers. Notwithstanding, analysis of his performance on the academic tests demonstrates that he has learned, retained, and does attempt to use certain skills, suggesting paths for instruction.

Reading

Michael was more successful reading words in lists than in context. When reading in context, he performed well at the primer level in passages of up to about 100 words. Michael made an excellent attempt at reading with expression. He was deliberate in his use of his limited phonics skills and tried to sound out many words. He has developed a small sight vocabulary. After Michael read the QRI-3 level 2 passage, the evaluator had him look again at the mispronounced words. Michael corrected 25 of 36 words without help, indicating that he has some decoding skills, but they are not yet automatic.

Despite his many processing deficits, Michael has abilities that can be developed toward functional literacy. His comprehension indicates that if he learns to decode and increase his sight vocabulary, he may be able to comprehend print material considerably closer to the level of his oral comprehension.

Writing

Michael's development in phonological and phonics skills is evident in his spelling as he clearly attempts to use a phonetic approximation (e.g., *rein*/rain, *senkn*/second, *becse*/because). In his spelling of other words, his difficulty with phonological and phonics skills is more evident (e.g., *trak*/talks, *wokrest*/rewards). Usually, however, his difficulty recalling the visual letter patterns is evident.

At this point, the greatest impediments to Michael's writing ability are his limited spelling abilities and fine-motor control. He can write simple and even some complex sentences but the need to try and recall and form the letters of a word or to sound it out continually interrupts his thought processes. These difficulties make it hard for him to focus on expressing his ideas in writing.

Math

Michael appears to lack a solid understanding of basic number concepts, the concepts underlying addition and subtraction, and place value. Asked to do simple math problems using pictures, Michael used his finger to cover those he was supposed to subtract as well as to count imaginary objects he was supposed to add. He used his fingers for most addition and subtraction facts, misperceived or ignored operation signs, and subtracted the least number from the higher number regardless of their position in the problem. He identified a quarter and a dime by name but not their values. He was unable to translate any word problems into computation correctly.

Michael correctly used a calendar to find specific days and dates, counted by 2s to 10, read a thermometer, named some basic arithmetic symbols (+, =) and abbreviations, and counted nickels and pennies. He enjoyed figuring out number patterns and was successful as long as the interval change represented sequence counting (e.g., 2 4 6 _). Again, he used a strategy (e.g., "2 skips to 4, 4 skips to 6").

DISCREPANCIES

Intra-Individual Discrepancies

To find if significant strengths and weaknesses exist among the cognitive and academic abilities within an individual, each cluster score is compared to the average of all the others. Despite the finding that Michael's overall intellectual ability is in the lowest 1% of his age-peers, he experiences an additional intra-individual weakness in Fluid Reasoning, indicating a severe problem in abstract, logical reasoning, compared to his other abilities. A discrepancy of this magnitude is found in only 1% of children of his age.

Intellectual Ability/Achievement Discrepancies

Using the GIA-Ext to predict levels of academic achievement allows one to see if a student is learning as expected based on his or her intellectual ability. Based on Michael's GIA-Ext standard score of 64, Basic Reading Skills, Broad Math, and Math Calculation were significantly lower than predicted, suggesting that Michael's cognitive abilities are more advanced than his present levels of academic performance in those areas. In this case, other possible contributory factors must be considered, such as mental and emotional availability for learning, instructional approaches, and educational program.

SUMMARY AND DISCUSSION

Michael Jansen is an 11-year-old sixth-grade student at Thomas Mann Middle School. He is an adopted child, carefully supervised, in a loving, intact, two-parent household in which both oral English and signed English are used. Michael has a unilateral hearing loss, wears glasses, is physically healthy, and has good ocular-motor skills.

Michael also has a history of significant psychiatric problems. His behavior at school is considerably more controlled than the behavior he displays outside of the school environment.

Adaptive Behavior

According to Mrs. Jansen's ratings of Michael on the Vineland, he has a moderate deficit in overall adaptive behavior with a generally flat profile in communication, daily living, and socialization skills. His maladaptive behaviors, as summarized above, are significant and of great concern. Michael does not seem to have an internal structure of moral or rule-governed behavior. He does not think in terms of consequences and appears to lack awareness of his destructive behaviors even while he is engaged in them. He lacks empathy, has irrational compulsive behaviors and extreme anxiety, incorporates fictional events into his reality, experiences overwhelming fear of unlikely-to-impossible situations, and, at times, engages in self-injurious behaviors. His medications are helpful but not optimal. Strong proprioceptive resistance and movement help him maintain emotional and behavioral control.

Intellectual/Cognitive Abilities

Michael's performance on the cognitive measures of the current evaluation indicates that his general intellectual functioning is Very Low, within the range of mild mental retardation. Michael processes information slowly and evidences severe deficits in memory and retrieval skills, acquired knowledge, and oral language. All of these abilities were measured in the Low and Very Low ranges. Additionally, he demonstrates a significant deficit in abstract, logical reasoning.

Michael demonstrates significant problems with word retrieval, contributing to his difficulty in formulating sentences and his inability to read a word in one sentence that he has just read in the previous sentence, as Mrs. Jansen observed. Michael codes the phonology of spoken words incorrectly, causing mispronunciations and exacerbating his word-retrieval problems. Michael appears to have difficulty with some aspects of visual perception, specifically figure/ground relationships. His visual–motor coordination is severely limited; handwriting is very difficult for him.

Michael has some important cognitive strengths. Once he has learned information or a procedure to an automatic level, he retrieves it quickly. Michael appears to have intact detection and initial processing of speech sounds, providing an inroad to teach the phonology necessary for accurate pronunciation of words for reading and spelling. Also, Michael has a relative strength in processing, storing, and retaining pictorial information. In oral or written language, Michael can comprehend stories, sequence the events, and make predictions, as long as the elements of the language are within his functioning level and experience. This allows a base for development of language/reading comprehension skills. Because Michael creates strategies to help him with difficult tasks, using strategies to teach him new skills and procedures should prove effective.

Michael feels that he needs a teacher who uses oral English all of the time, with or without sign. He identifies oral English as his primary language. Test results indicate that he is accurate in this assessment, although he appears to benefit from his own use of sign in some instances.

Academic Achievement

Michael was uniformly low in reading, writing, math, and academic knowledge. His present performance levels in reading and math were significantly lower than predicted based on his intellectual abilities. This suggests that he should be able to improve those skills if other factors critical for learning are available to support this progress. These may include his emotional and attentional availability for learning, consideration of different instructional approaches and/or service delivery, and adjusted educational expectations.

In reading and spelling, Michael does show a reliance on and some basic facility with phonics skills. He demonstrated that at least through first-grade reading level, he understands what he reads. Thus, every attempt should be made to bring his decoding and word identification skills at least up to the level of his oral language comprehension. Likewise, Michael's writing skills should be developed for practical purposes in daily life, such as writing phone messages and shopping lists. Michael lacks basic number concepts and is delayed in learning math facts. Use of technology, such as a calculator, and a strong focus on understanding basic concepts tied to a few areas of daily living skills will be important.

Discussion

In accordance with Michael's consistently low scores in cognitive abilities, academic achievement, and adaptive behavior skills, he meets the special education eligibility criteria as a child with Mild Mental Retardation. Additionally, Michael meets the eligibility criteria as a child with Emotional Disability under the following provisions: inappropriate types of behavior or feelings under normal circumstances; general pervasive mood of unhappiness or depression; and a tendency to develop physical symptoms or fears associated with personal or school problems. He has exhibited these characteristics to a marked degree throughout his childhood to this point; his emotional disabilities adversely affect his performance in the educational environment.

On the surface, Michael does not present as a child with cognitive skills as impaired as his performance on this evaluation would indicate and he does not have the affect that is often seen with this level of developmental delay. Additionally, within the current school setting, with small, structured classes, the level of accommodations created for Michael, and the consistent attention to his need for certain kinds of physical stimulation to maintain emotional control, he is functioning appropriately. He does not present with the level of psychological/emotional deviancy that is so apparent outside of this setting. His appearance of higher level functioning and "normalcy," advantageous in many situations, is likely to mislead others into unrealistic expectations for Michael in many life arenas, such as academic achievement, problem-solving, self-sufficiency, social interactions, and emotional coping. A comprehensive educational team, including Michael's parents, counselor, and case manager, need to convene to discuss realistic goals for Michael and a program, with clear delineation of roles, for accomplishing them. At the IEP meeting, the educational team will make decisions regarding educational placement.

RECOMMENDATIONS

General

1. Michael would benefit from an educational program focused on functional academics. He needs intensive, specialized instruction in basic academic skills geared toward practical daily living needs and training in nonacademic daily living skills, social interactions and expectations, getting around in the community, and accessing community resources.
2. Michael clearly benefits from his daily physical therapy activities to help him maintain emotional and behavioral control throughout the school day. Continue this program on a daily basis, preferably at the end of the day, as anticipation of this emotional/physical release appears to help Michael maintain control.
3. Michael appears to use sign as an effective medium for recalling the spelling of words and for retrieving words in speech—sometimes as a prompt for oral retrieval and occasionally as a substitute. He would benefit from continued development of sign skills and fingerspelling for these purposes.
4. Provide Michael with continued communication therapy to address the following issues: strategies for word retrieval in speech and reading, continued emphasis on word pronunciation, comprehension of narrative information at gradually increasing language levels, and organization of concepts for expository information.

For the Teacher

1. In most areas of instruction, Michael will need extra time, more repetition, and, frequently, alternate techniques to learn concepts, information, and procedures that others integrate with reasonable ease.

2. Ensure that Michael learns any skill and procedure to a fully automatic level if he is expected to retain, use, and build on it. Automaticity exceeds mastery in level of integration. Once skills and associations are automatic, he is able to retrieve them quickly.
3. When introducing new concepts, information, and procedures
   a) Activate and evaluate prior knowledge of the topic. If necessary, preteach key vocabulary and foundational concepts before beginning the instructional unit.
   b) Use pictures and nonsymbolic visual information along with any other input—oral, sign-supported speech, or print.
4. Use learning strategies where appropriate to strengthen his ability to hold information in short-term memory while working with it and to help him retrieve the steps of procedures.
5. For reading and spelling instruction, use an intensive, explicit, and highly systematic phonics approach to decoding and spelling with a simultaneous, integrated emphasis on recognition of common letter patterns, such as the Wilson Reading System or RAVE-O. Despite problems with phonological coding and visual perception, Michael does use phonics both to sound out words and as a clue to whole-word identification. This is a viable learning method for him. Within this instruction, pay particular attention to Michael's pronunciation.
6. Go back to basics in math instruction, incorporating manipulatives to teach basic number concepts, the concepts underlying addition and subtraction, and place value. Incorporate objects in his world. Help Michael make a gradual transition from manipulatives, to pictures, to tallies/tokens, to numbers.
7. Request consultation from an occupational therapist with expertise in handwriting skills for ways to make handwriting easier for Michael and practice techniques to help automatize the motor act of letter formation.
8. To compensate for Michael's inaccurate phonological coding of spoken words, work with the communication specialist to provide direct instruction in the pronunciation of new vocabulary and known but mispronounced words. Show him the word in print, pointing out the parts of the word and their spelling and model saying the parts. Have Michael pronounce the word himself several times, with guidance to ensure accuracy, to establish accurate coding in working memory. As with any other skill, provide for frequent practice

pronouncing the word, with feedback as to his accuracy, until correct pronunciation is automatic. Make sure that Michael knows the meaning, and preferably multiple meanings, of any word he is learning to pronounce. This procedure will also help Michael's retention and retrieval of sight words.

9. To help Michael differentiate the print from the background, reading materials should be in large print, approximately 16 point, depending on the font, with ample white space between the lines of print. Fewer lines on a page will be easier for him to perceive.

10. Modify the spatial format of worksheets and forms for clarity. Use worksheets that contain only the needed visual information. Rather than boxing information or using lines to separate areas, use plenty of space, even if it means using more than one paper. Provide graph paper or specialized forms (see attached sample) to help organize the digits in math computation.

For the Parents

1. A neuropsychological evaluation and a pediatric neurological evaluation may provide valuable insights into a more comprehensive view of Michael's psychological, emotional, and cognitive problems, identify specific areas of neurological damage, rule out seizure activity that may be presenting as dissociation, and suggest treatment and remedial options that have not yet been considered.

2. To help with Michael's behavior outside of school, Mr. and Mrs. Jansen might want to consider seeking consultation from a psychologist or social worker with expertise in behavioral management of children. Additionally, they might want to contact MIKID (Mentally Ill Kids in Distress), an education and support organization for families of children with serious behavior and emotional problems.

SCORES

Vineland Adaptive Behavior Scales: Interview Edition   **Informant: Julia Jansen, mother**

Domains	PR	SS*	SS ±1 SEM	Adaptive Level
COMMUNICATION	0.1	53	46–60	Mild-Mod. Deficit
Receptive				Low
Expressive				Low
Written				Low
DAILY LIVING SKILLS	<0.1	50	44–56	Mild-Mod. Deficit
Personal				Low
Domestic				Low
Community				Low
SOCIALIZATION	0.2	56	50–62	Mild-Mod. Deficit
Interpersonal Relations				Low
Play & Leisure Time				Low
Coping Skills				Low
ADAPTIVE BEHAVIOR COMPOSITE	<0.1	49	45–53	Moderate Deficit
MALADAPTIVE BEHAVIOR				Significant, rated on or off meds

SS: *Mean = 100, SD = 15.

Comprehensive Test of Phonological Processing

COMPOSITE/Subtest	AE	GE	PR	ScS	SS
CORE TESTS					
PHONOLOGICAL AWARENESS			<1		64
Elision	6-3	1.2	1	3	
Blending Words	6-6	1.4	5	5	
PHONOLOGICAL MEMORY			<1		55
Memory for Digits	<5-0	<K.0	<1	1	
Nonword Repetition	<5-0	<K.0	2	4	
RAPID NAMING			27		91
Rapid Digit Naming	10-0	5.0	25	8	
Rapid Letter Naming	10-6	5.4	37	9	
SUPPLEMENTAL TESTS					
ALTERNATE RAPID NAMING			3		73
Rapid Color Naming	6-6	1.4	5	5	
Rapid Object Naming	8-3	3.2	9	6	
Blending Nonwords (not administered)					
Segmenting Words	<7-0	<2.0	25	8	

SS: Mean = 100, SD = 15; ScS: Mean = 10, SD = 3.

Qualitative Reading Inventory—3

Level	Words in Lists	Oral Reading in Passages	Passage Comprehension	Oral Reading Rate	Listening Comprehension
Primer	Independent	Instructional	Independent	59 wpm	N/A
1	Instructional	Frustration	Instructional	52 wpm	N/A
2	Frustration	Frustration	Frustration	48 wpm	N/A
3	—	—	—	—	Frustration
4	—	—	—	—	Frustration

Beery-Buktenica Test of Visual–Motor Integration—Fourth Edition: SS 66, PR, 1

The Listening Test
Scores Invalid: Nonstandardized Administration

	Age Equivalent		Percentile Rank		Standard Score	
Subtest	1st admin.	2nd admin.	1st admin.	2nd admin.	1st admin.	2nd admin.
Main Idea	7-3	8-10	6	19	88	112
Details	8-1	>11-2	16	75	86	112
Concepts	6-4	8-2	1	12	<55	80
Reasoning	8-7	no change	18	no change	86	no change
Story Comprehension	10-3	8-10	43	26	101	93
TOTAL TEST	7-8	9-1	4	18	69	89

The Word-R Test
Scores Invalid: Nonstandardized Administration

	Age Equiv.		Percentile Rank		Standard Score	
Subtest	1st admin.	2nd admin.	1st admin.	2nd admin.	1st admin.	2nd admin.
Associations	6-10	—	BN*	10	BN	78
Synonyms	6-11	—	BN	1	BN	55
Semantic Absurdities	7-0	—	1	8	<55	76
Antonyms	6-7	—	BN	16	BN	85
Definitions	7-11	—	5	12	77	82
Multiple Definitions	7-8	—	3	7	67	75
TOTAL TEST	7-4	—	BN	13	BN	64

*BN indicates that the obtained score was below the norms.

Psychoeducational Evaluation

Name: Frankie Espinosa
Date of Birth: 04/05/1990
Age: 11 years, 10 months
Grade: 6.5

Sex: Male
Parents: Flora and Martin Espinosa
Report Date: 2/20/02
Dates of Testing: 1/31/02, 2/05/02

REASON FOR TESTING

Mrs. Espinosa, Frankie's mother, requested an evaluation update because she was concerned about Frankie's slow academic progress despite special education services for the past 2 years. She wants to know if Frankie's current placement provides him with appropriate support for academic success.

BACKGROUND INFORMATION

Frankie lives at home with his father, mother, two sisters, and maternal grandmother. His mother reported that Frankie met all the developmental milestones within the normal limits. Frankie is bilingual; he speaks English to his father, sisters, and all his friends, and Spanish to his mother and grandmother. Frankie reports that he finds reading and writing, especially spelling, difficult in both English and Spanish. Math is "a little difficult." Frankie enjoys drawing and says he wants to be an artist when he is finished with school.

PREVIOUS TESTING

Two years ago, Frankie was given a language proficiency test and it was determined that although he was more proficient in English than in Spanish, his abilities in both languages were somewhat delayed. At the same time, he was given selected tests from the Spanish version of the WJ-R Tests of Cognitive Ability and Tests of Achievement (Bateria-R). His scores on The Oral Language and Auditory Processing tests were in the Low/Low Average range as were his scores in Broad Reading and Broad Written Language. In Broad Mathematics he scored in the Low Average/Average range. Frankie was considered eligible for services as a student with a learning disability in "auditory processing" and has been receiving resource assistance for one period daily since that time.

TESTING OBSERVATIONS

Frankie was cooperative and attentive during each of the three testing sessions. His attention to tasks with minimal linguistic demands was high and he was careful in considering his responses. Frankie appeared confident and self-assured when attempting tasks with reduced language demands but appeared tense, anxious, and hesitant to respond on tasks with high linguistic demands. Frankie generally persisted with difficult tasks but would often make self-derogatory comments, such as: "I'll try, but I can't do it!" and "This stuff is too hard for me."

TESTS ADMINISTERED

Frankie was administered a set of tests from the WJ III Tests of Cognitive Abilities (WJ III COG) and from the WJ III Tests of Achievement (WJ III ACH). The WJ III COG measures overall intellectual functioning and specific cognitive abilities. The WJ III ACH measures various aspects of oral language and scholastic achievement. Because the WJ III COG and WJ III ACH were co-normed, direct comparisons can be made among Frankie's cognitive and achievement scores. These comparisons can help determine the presence and significance of any strengths and weaknesses among his abilities. In addition to the WJ III, Frankie was administered the Illinois Test of Psycholinguistic Abilities—Third Edition (ITPA-3).

This report describes Frankie's performance as an individual in the fifth month of sixth grade. Interpretation is referenced to his grade placement and includes degree of proficiency (RPI) and peer comparison scores (standard scores and percentile ranks). Standard scores (SS) are reported in ranges (SS ±1 Standard Error of Measurement [SEM]), the 68% confidence interval. (See Table 1.)

The percentile rank (PR) indicates where Frankie's score would fall within the scores of 100 students of the same school grade and month. For example, a PR of 75 would indicate that 75 out of 100 grade-peers in the norm sample

Table 1. WJ III Score Range

SS	Below 70	70–79	80–89	90–110	111–120	121–130	Above 130
Range	Very Low	Low	Low Average	Average	High Average	Superior	Very Superior

scored the same as or lower than he did. In addition, Frankie's Cognitive-Academic Language Proficiency (CALP) levels are reported. CALP scores indicate a person's language proficiency regarding the ability to learn new academic skills and concepts in the language of instruction, in this case, English. A score of 4 indicates that the student will be able to handle the language demands easily; a score of 1 indicates that the language demands will be impossible. Cluster discrepancy scores are found within the report and individual test scores are attached at the end.

TEST RESULTS

Cognitive Functioning

General Intellectual Ability-Extended (GIA-Ext) is a broad measure of cognitive functioning based on a weighted composite of 14 tests measuring a variety of cognitive abilities. Across the cognitive and language abilities, however, Frankie's abilities appear polarized into the Very Low to Low ranges and the High Average to Superior ranges. (See Table 2.) Thus, reporting one global score to represent his overall intellectual ability would be misleading.

Based on the results of the WJ III Tests of Cognitive Abilities, Frankie has strengths, represented by scores in the High Average to Superior ranges, in visual–spatial

thinking, processing speed, working memory, broad attention, and executive processes. More specifically, Frankie demonstrates well-developed abilities in:

* perceiving, analyzing, and synthesizing visual patterns as well as holding visual images in memory (Visual-Spatial Thinking, SS 114–126, PR 91);
* speed and efficiency in performing simple or frequently repeated cognitive tasks and procedures (Processing Speed, SS 119–127, PR 94);
* holding information in immediate awareness while simultaneously working with or manipulating that information (Working Memory, SS 108–116, PR 78);
* general attentiveness to and focus on stimuli for information processing (Broad Attention, SS 112–120, PR 86); and
* self-monitoring of his activities within a task to produce the best outcome (Executive Processes, SS 106–112, PR 72).

Frankie demonstrated strengths as well in abstract reasoning and short-term memory, although within each area, his performance on one test was in the Average range and the other in the High Average range. Frankie's performance on the Fluid Reasoning tests indicated that he is relatively stronger in deductive reasoning, or using rules to move step-by-step through the solution of a problem (Analysis-Synthesis, SS 111–124, PR 88), than he is in inductive reasoning, or considering multiple elements of a problem at the same time, and ascertaining the critical attributes (similarities and differences) that govern the solution (Concept Formation, SS 96–102, PR 48).

Regarding short-term memory, Frankie appears to be

Table 2. Cognitive Functioning Scores

CHC Factor	Easy to Difficult		RPI	PR	SS (±1 SEM)
Comprehension-Knowledge (*Gc*)	<K.0	1.6	6/90	0.3	58 (55–62)
Long-Term Retrieval (*Glr*)	K.4	9.0	79/90	5	75 (71–80)
Visual-Spatial Thinking (*Gv*)	7.4	>18.0	97/90	91	120 (114–126)
Fluid Reasoning (*Gf*)	5.7	13.7	95/90	71	108 (104–112)
Processing Speed (*Gs*)	9.1	>18.0	99/90	94	123 (119–127)
Short-Term Memory (*Gsm*)	6.2	12.9	96/90	70	108 (102–114)
Clinical Cluster	Easy to Difficult		RPI	PR	SS (±1 SEM)
Working Memory	7.0	13.0	97/90	78	112 (108–116)
Broad Attention	6.4	13.0	96/90	86	116 (112–120)
Cognitive Fluency	1.7	4.7	54/90	7	77 (75–80)
Executive Processes	5.0	4.0	94/90	72	109 (106–112)
Knowledge	K.4	2.1	10/90	1	63 (60–66)

relatively better able to hold a series of digits in mind, and even reorder them, than to simply repeat, in the order given, a series of words (Numbers Reversed, SS 109–119, PR 83; Memory for Words, SS 93–106, PR 48).

The stimuli for many of the tests described above are pictures or designs, and Frankie enjoyed these. At one point, he commented, "This is really fun."

Intra-Cognitive Discrepancies

Strengths and weaknesses in cognitive functioning are identified by comparing a person's standard score for each cognitive ability cluster (obtained score) with the average of his other six cluster scores (predicted score). A difference of 1.5 SEM is considered significant.

Frankie's score comparisons indicated significant strengths in Visual-Spatial Thinking and Processing Speed, with scores in the High Average/Superior range. (See Table 3.) Tests comprising these clusters have limited linguistic demands. Fluid Reasoning, Short-Term Memory, and Working Memory are also strengths, with scores in the Average/High Average range. The discrepancies are educationally, if not statistically, significant. The linguistic demands involved in the tests of these clusters are greater than for the two clusters on which Frankie attained his highest scores, suggesting that limited language proficiency is affecting performance.

The indication of problems specifically in language continued into Frankie's lowest cluster scores. In Compre-hension-Knowledge, Phonemic Awareness, Long-Term Retrieval, and Auditory Processing, all with moderate to high linguistic demands, Frankie's obtained scores were significantly lower than his predicted scores.

Oral Language and Long-Term Retrieval

In sharp contrast to his self-assuredness in working on the tests measuring his cognitive strengths, Frankie demonstrated considerable difficulty and frustration on the tests most strongly based in oral language and auditory processing. Frankie's CALP level on the Oral Language cluster was 2.5, indicating that his language abilities in English for these types of tasks are "very limited to limited" and that he will find the demands of instruction in English at his grade level "very difficult to extremely difficult." (See Table 4.)

Although Frankie did well on tests of immediate memory, his ability to retrieve linguistic information, specifically words, from long-term memory was somewhat more complicated. Analysis of his standard scores and Relative Performance Indexes, and the task demands of each test, suggests that Frankie has weaknesses in rote learning of seemingly arbitrary associations (no inherent or obvious relationship) and/or in the rapid transfer of these associations to long-term memory. Once information is in his long-term memory, he does appear to have difficulty in retrieving specific words (where only one is right), and language context clues do not seem to help him (Visual-Auditory Learning, SS 73–82, PR 7, RPI 70/90; Retrieval Fluency,

Table 3.   Intra-Cognitive Discrepancies

Intra-Cognitive Discrepancies	Standard Scores			Discrepancy		Significant at ±1.50 SEE
	Actual	Predicted	Difference	PR	SD	
Comprehension-Knowledge (*Gc*)	58	102	–44	<0.1	–3.65	Yes
Long-Term Retrieval (*Glr*)	75	99	–24	3	–1.83	Yes
Visual-Spatial Thinking (*Gv*)	120	95	+25	97	+1.83	Yes
Auditory Processing (*Ga*)	76	99	–23	4	–1.80	Yes
Fluid Reasoning (*Gf*)	108	94	+14	90	+1.31	No
Processing Speed (*Gs*)	123	94	+29	98	+2.14	Yes
Short-Term Memory (*Gsm*)	108	95	+13	84	+0.99	No
Phonemic Awareness	58	99	–41	<0.1	–3.30	Yes
Working Memory	112	95	+17	90	+1.30	No

Table 4.   Oral Language and Long-Term Retrieval Scores

Cluster	GE	Easy to Difficult		RPI	PR	SS (±1 SEM)	CALP
Oral Language (Ext)	K.8	<K.0	2.2	27/90	0.5	61 (58–65)	2-3
Oral Expression	K.7	<K.0	2.6	40/90	2	70 (66–74)	3
Listening Comprehension	K.8	<K.0	1.9	17/90	1	63 (59–67)	2

SS 77–90, PR 14, RPI 85/90; Rapid Picture Naming, SS 54–57, PR 0.1, RPI 0/90).

On other tests strongly related to oral language, Frankie completely lost the confidence he had on the less verbal tests and clearly struggled with the task demands. His scores were all in the Very Low range, compared to the scores of other sixth-graders. Frankie's standard scores and RPIs indicate that his abilities are very limited in the following areas:

- general culture-related knowledge, usually learned through language or experience, regarding what a variety of common objects are used for and where they might be found;
- breadth and depth of vocabulary knowledge and word associations (including antonyms and synonyms);
- ability to grasp and express the relationships among word meanings (i.e., analogies);
- comprehension of connected discourse from one sentence in length to brief stories;
- ability to recognize the key elements in a story and include them in retelling the story;
- ability to understand, hold in memory, and follow verbal instructions;
- comprehension of a variety of linguistic concepts used in context, such as spatial terms (e.g., *over, near*), temporal terms (e.g., *before, first*), terms of exceptionality (e.g., *except, but not*), conditional (e.g., *if, unless*), and numeric (e.g., *three, group*).

Because Frankie has spoken English throughout his life and performance is low in both languages, his difficulties appear to be due to general linguistic weaknesses, rather than issues surrounding learning a second language.

Phonemic Awareness and Auditory Processing

A different aspect of oral language with which Frankie had significant difficulty was phonemic awareness, the ability to perceive, manipulate, and alter the individual sounds in words. These skills are not necessary for oral communication but are critical for the development of basic reading and spelling skills. They include, but are not limited to, blending together separate sounds into a word (e.g., /k/ /ă/ /t/ is "cat"), saying the individual sounds in a word (e.g., the sounds in "cat" are "/k/ /ă/ /t/"), omitting sounds from words (e.g., "flat" without /l/ is "fat"). All of Frankie's phonemic awareness scores were in the Very Low range (Phonemic Awareness, SS 57–64, PR 0.4, RPI 30/90; Sound Blending, SS 57–68, PR 1, RPI 18/90).

In contrast, Frankie exhibits good speech–sound discrimination and the ability to filter out and ignore background noise even as it increasingly obscures the sounds (Auditory Attention, SS 95–108, PR 54, RPI 91/90). (See Table 5.)

Academic Achievement

Basic Reading and Spelling Skills

Academic Achievement scores are shown in Table 6. Frankie's Age/Grade Instructional Zone indicates that his knowledge of letter/sound associations (i.e., phonics) is similar to that of a child in mid-first grade. On similar tasks, Frankie would experience 13% success compared to his grade-peers' 90% (Phoneme-Grapheme Knowledge, SS 67–73, PR 2). When spelling real or nonsense words, he wrote the first letter for the first sound and moved on to the next, keeping track of where he was in the word by seeing the letters on paper. To a large extent, Frankie used the same strategy for spelling real words (Spelling, SS 54–63, PR 0.3, RPI 1/90). His errors included omission of letters for sounds, especially those that are hard to notice, such as the /s/ in a final /st/ blend, and putting in letters that suggest that he was paying attention to his mouth movements to compensate for his difficulty perceiving the individual sounds (e.g., "*ous*" for "was," "*uran*" for "rain").

Frankie scored in the Very Low range on all of the reading measures, indicating extreme limitations in word attack skills, sight word acquisition, fluency, and comprehension. No strengths were apparent. Most of the words he read correctly were read as whole words after some hesitation. If he did not know a word as a whole, he did not have a strategy for sounding it out. It was interesting to note, therefore, that when trying to read phonically regular nonsense

Table 5.   Phonemic Awareness and Auditory Processing Scores

Factor/Cluster	GE	Easy to Difficult		RPI	PR	SS (±1 SEM)
Auditory Processing (Ga)	K.9	K.1	3.1	60/90	5	76 (71–81)
Phonemic Awareness III	K.5	<K.0	1.5	30/90	0.4	60 (57–64)

Table 6.   Academic Achievement Scores

Cluster	GE	Easy to Difficult		RPI	PR	SS (±1 SEM)	CALP
Broad Reading	2.2	1.9	2.5	1/90	0.4	61 (59–63)	1
Broad Math	3.9	3.0	5.0	52/90	9	80 (77–83)	—
Broad Written Language	2.0	1.5	2.8	14/90	0.5	61 (58–65)	2
Basic Reading Skills	2.0	1.8	2.3	1/90	1	67 (64–69)	—
Reading Comprehension	2.0	1.7	2.6	14/90	1	64 (61–67)	2
Math Calculation Skills	4.9	3.6	6.7	77/90	22	88 (85–92)	—
Math Reasoning	3.9	3.1	4.8	41/90	13	83 (79–86)	—
Basic Writing Skills	2.0	1.6	2.5	5/90	1	63 (60–67)	—
Written Expression	2.6	1.8	3.9	39/90	3	71 (67–76)	3
Academic Skills	2.6	2.2	3.0	5/90	1	62 (60–65)	—
Academic Fluency	2.5	1.8	3.4	13/90	2	69 (67–71)	—
Academic Applications	2.3	1.8	3.1	23/90	3	71 (68–74)	—
Academic Knowledge	1.5	K.7	2.6	14/90	2	69 (65–74)	2
Phoneme/Grapheme Knowledge	1.7	1.4	2.1	13/90	2	70 (67–73)	—

words, he read some as real words with similar spelling patterns (e.g., *foy* as "toy"). Frankie's RPIs and CALP levels indicate that his proficiency in basic reading skills is negligible and that reading tasks at his grade level will be impossible. Given Frankie's language difficulties and the high correlation between oral language and reading, these results are expected.

Written Language

The WJ III ACH tests of written language measure skills in spelling, writing fluency (speed of writing short, simple sentences), editing (correcting errors in written sentences), and written expression (formulating and writing sentences according to a variety of task demands). Once again, Frankie's scores on all of the clusters fell into the Very Low range with none of the individual tests emerging as a particular strength. It is likely that his score on Writing Samples would have been higher than his obtained standard score of 63 but some of his spelling was not decipherable and he occasionally omitted a word that was key to the coherence of the sentence, lowering his score. His CALP level of 2 on the Broad Written Language cluster indicates that the language demands of grade-level writing instruction will be "extremely difficult." These results also are consistent with Frankie's weakness in oral language abilities. During the Writing Samples test, Frankie muttered under his breath, "I hate writing. It's bull——." Then he glanced up, said, "Sorry," and went back to writing.

Math

Math is clearly Frankie's strongest area of academic performance. He relaxed visibly when he was handed a page of

math fact problems, saying in relief, "I can do this." Within the WJ III math tests, Frankie was strongest on Quantitative Concepts (demonstrating comprehension of math concepts, terminology, and number patterns). His score and RPI were solidly in the Average range. His performance on Calculation was in the lower end of the Average range. His RPI of 78/90 suggests that he is proficient enough to benefit from grade-level instruction but will find it more challenging than his typical classmates. He had difficulty with long division and with basic operations using fractions. As Frankie used a combination of his fingers, hatch marks, and Touch Math for working the computation problems, it was not surprising that his Math Fluency score was in the Low Average range and, in terms of proficiency, between the frustration and instructional level. His math facts are not automatic although he was pretty accurate in using his compensations. Frankie's most difficult math challenge was the Applied Problems test, with his score in the Low range and his RPI at 10/90. This test is much more language-laden than the other math tests. Although all of the problems were read aloud to him, the reasoning that is required is, to a large extent, linguistic in nature.

Academic Knowledge

From fourth grade on, most of the content area information students learn in school is acquired through reading or some form of oral language (e.g., lecture, discussion, oral reports). With Frankie's very limited oral language skills, and even more limited reading skills, his opportunity for acquiring school-based knowledge has been severely limited as well. His academic knowledge, such as social studies, physical sciences, and humanities, is also in the Very Low range. His RPI of 14/90 indicates the level of impoverishment of his school-acquired knowledge.

Discrepancies

Intra-Achievement Discrepancies
Although math is a relative strength for Frankie, when his obtained WJ III ACH cluster scores are compared to his predicted scores, no specific area shows a significant strength or deficiency. (See Table 7.)

Ability/Achievement Discrepancies

General Intellectual Ability/Achievement
Due to his wide range of scores, Frankie's General Intellectual Ability score (GIA-Ext) is low. Even using this low score as a predictor, his functioning in oral language and academic skills is significantly lower than was predicted.

(See Table 8.) Significant discrepancies between ability and achievement were found in five of the seven areas under which an individual can qualify as having a learning disability under the Individuals with Disabilities Education Act: basic reading, reading comprehension, written expression, listening comprehension, and oral expression. The role that language plays in the measurement of intellectual functioning and achievement is critical. It is inextricable from both cognitive development and academic achievement. Consequently, the significant ability/achievement discrepancies are described as a specific language impairment.

Oral Language Ability/Achievement
The Oral Language Ability/Achievement discrepancies indicate that apart from Broad Reading, none of Frankie's attained scores were discrepant from his predicted score based on his oral language ability. (See Table 9.) It appears, therefore, that his low language abilities are consistent with

Table 7.   Intra-Achievement Discrepancies

Intra-Achievement Discrepancies	Standard Scores			Discrepancy		Significant at
	Actual	Predicted	Difference	PR	SD	±1.50 SEE
Basic Reading Skills	67	69	−2	41	−0.24	No
Reading Comprehension	64	71	−7	23	−0.74	No
Math Calculation Skills	88	77	+11	80	+0.86	No
Math Reasoning	83	70	+13	89	+1.20	No
Basic Writing Skills	63	72	−9	19	−0.86	No
Written Expression	71	75	−4	39	−0.29	No
Oral Expression	70	77	−7	27	−0.60	No
Listening Comprehension	63	75	−12	16	−1.01	No
Academic Knowledge	69	73	−4	37	−0.33	No

Table 8.   Ability/Achievement Discrepancies

Intellectual Ability/ Achievement Discrepancies	Standard Scores			Discrepancy		Significant at
	Actual	Predicted	Diff	PR	SD	±1.50 SEE
Broad Reading	61	93	−32	<0.1	−3.30	Yes
Basic Reading Skills	67	95	−28	1	−2.44	Yes
Reading Comprehension	64	94	−30	0.1	−3.02	Yes
Broad Math	80	95	−15	9	−1.37	No
Math Calculation Skills	88	96	−8	29	−0.56	No
Math Reasoning	83	94	−11	13	−1.12	No
Broad Written Language	61	95	−34	0.1	−3.03	Yes
Basic Writing Skills	63	94	−31	0.3	−2.73	Yes
Written Expression	71	94	−23	2	−2.01	Yes
Oral Language (Ext)	61	94	−33	0.1	−3.08	Yes
Oral Expression	70	94	−24	1	−2.20	Yes
Listening Comprehension	63	94	−31	0.4	−2.66	Yes
Academic Knowledge	69	94	−25	1	−2.41	Yes

These discrepancies based on GIA (Ext) with ACH Broad, Basic, and Applied clusters.

Table 9.   Oral Language Ability/Achievement Discrepancies

Oral Language/ Achievement Discrepancies	Standard Scores			Discrepancy		Significant at ±1.50 SEE
	Actual	Predicted	Difference	PR	SD	
Broad Reading	61	81	−20	5	−1.61	Yes
Basic Reading Skills	67	81	−14	15	−1.05	No
Reading Comp	64	78	−14	14	−1.10	No
Broad Math	80	81	−1	48	−0.05	No
Math Calc Skills	88	86	+2	56	+0.14	No
Math Reasoning	83	77	+6	67	+0.45	No
Broad Written Lang	61	80	−19	7	−1.46	No
Basic Writing Skills	63	82	−19	8	−1.40	No
Written Expression	71	84	−13	17	−0.94	No
Academic Knowledge	69	75	−6	29	−0.55	No

These discrepancies based on Oral Language (Ext) with ACH Broad, Basic, and Applied clusters.

academic performance and are the primary reason for his academic difficulties.

Illinois Test of Psycholinguistic Abilities, Third Edition

The Illinois Test of Psycholinguistic Abilities, Third Edition (ITPA-3) was administered to further investigate Frankie's language deficiencies and their probable basis for his academic deficits. The ITPA-3 produces three Global Composites of General Language, Spoken Language, and Written Language. Individuals with specific reading and writing disabilities will tend to score higher on the Spoken Language than on the Written Language composite. Individuals with primary language difficulties, however, will tend to score low on both composites.

Frankie's score on all three Global Composites fell into the Very Low range (with SS of 62, 65, and 62, consecutively). Frankie's scores on all eight Specific Composites (Semantics, Grammar, Phonology, Comprehension, Word Identification, Spelling, Sight-Symbol Processing, and Sound-Symbol Processing) also fell into the Very Low/Low ranges. Results from both the WJ III and the ITPA-3 suggest that Frankie's current educational difficulties are primarily the result of an oral language impairment.

SUMMARY

Frankie's GIA-Ext score, in the Low Average/Average range, is not an adequate representation of performance because of the marked strengths and weaknesses among his abilities. Scores of all tests with minimal language demands fall into the Average to Superior ranges. In contrast, Frankie's oral language skills are Very Low when compared

to the range of scores obtained by others at his grade level. When compared to others at his grade level, Frankie's knowledge, his academic skills, his fluency with academic tasks, and his ability to apply academic skills are all within the Very Low/Low range. No discrepancies were found among Frankie's achievement areas.

When compared to his overall intellectual ability, Frankie's achievement is significantly lower than predicted in oral language and in all areas of reading, written language, and academic knowledge. Using Oral Language as the predictor, however, only Broad Reading yields a significant discrepancy. This fact along with Frankie's attainment of scores in the Very Poor range on General Language, Spoken Language, and Written Language Composites of the ITPA-3 indicate that his difficulties are due to an oral language impairment that has affected development in both English and Spanish. A comprehensive speech-language evaluation is recommended to determine appropriate educational programming, as well as instructional goals.

RECOMMENDATIONS

1. Refer Frankie for a comprehensive speech-language evaluation. The goals of this evaluation would be to determine placement options, as well as objectives for language therapy.
2. Because of the documented relationship between poor phonological awareness and delayed literacy development, provide Frankie with an intensive program of intervention in English phonology. The goal should be to improve phonological awareness, as well as to increase knowledge of phoneme/grapheme relationships.
3. Provide Frankie with a systematic and explicit program of instruction in basic reading and spelling at the same

time as he is learning strategies to improve oral language comprehension. As his decoding and sight word knowledge improve to the point where he can read text that is somewhat substantive, guide him in applying his oral comprehension strategies to his reading.

4. Provide Frankie with a variety of classroom activities that will help increase oral language.

5. When possible, provide opportunities for Frankie to learn information in ways that do not involve language or are substantially supplemented with nonlinguistic information such as pictures, videos, and computer programs that are strong on graphics. Visuals will give him something on which to hang new language and concepts. Likewise, try to find ways for Frankie to demonstrate his knowledge that do not have strong language requirements.

Adapted from Rhia Roberts, Ph.D.

WJ III Tests of Cognitive Abilities: Individual Test Scores

Test Name	Raw	GE	Easy to Difficult		RPI	PR	SS (±1 SEM)
Verbal Comprehension	—	K.6	<K.0	1.5	5/90	0.3	58 (54–62)
Visual-Auditory Learning	25-E	1.8	K.6	4.7	70/90	7	78 (73–82)
Spatial Relations	74-D	16.8	7.0	>18.0	97/90	85	116 (110–122)
Sound Blending	9	<K.0	<K.0	K.5	18/90	1	63 (57–68)
Concept Formation	28-E	6.1	3.9	9.7	89/90	48	99 (96–102)
Visual Matching	51-2	10.4	8.5	12.9	99/90	90	119 (114–124)
Numbers Reversed	16	12.9	9.0	14.7	99/90	83	114 (109–119)
Incomplete Words	11	<K.0	<K.0	1.1	45/90	1	66 (59–73)
Auditory Working Memory	23	7.8	5.3	11.3	94/90	63	105 (100–110)
General Information	—	K.8	<K.0	1.7	6/90	1	63 (59–68)
Retrieval Fluency	48	3.0	K.1	>18.0	85/90	14	84 (77–90)
Picture Recognition	54-D	>18.0	7.9	>18.0	97/90	85	115 (109–122)
Auditory Attention	38	7.3	1.6	13.0	91/90	54	101 (95–108)
Analysis-Synthesis	28-E	13.4	8.5	>18.0	98/90	88	118 (111–124)
Decision Speed	39	>18.0	10.0	>18.0	99/90	94	123 (117–129)
Memory for Words	17	6.2	4.0	9.3	89/90	48	99 (93–106)
Rapid Picture Naming	54	<K.0	<K.0	<K.0	0/90	0.1	55 (54–57)
Planning	—	13.8	K.3	>18.0	92/90	77	111 (99–123)
Pair Cancellation	69	9.7	7.3	12.8	98/90	83	114 (112–117)

WJ III Tests of Achievement: Individual Test Scores

Test Name	Raw	GE	Easy to Difficult		RPI	PR	SS (±1 SEM)
Letter-Word Identification	35	2.3	2.1	2.6	0/90	1	63 (60–66)
Reading Fluency	13	1.9	1.5	2.3	0/90	1	66 (64–68)
Story Recall	—	K.7	<K.0	4.7	71/90	2	68 (57–78)
Understanding Directions	—	K.5	<K.0	1.5	21/90	0.5	62 (56–67)
Calculation	19	5.3	4.2	6.7	78/90	31	93 (88–97)
Math Fluency	55	4.2	2.2	6.6	76/90	15	84 (82–87)
Spelling	19	1.5	1.1	1.9	1/90	0.3	58 (54–63)
Writing Fluency	10	3.0	2.3	3.9	22/90	5	76 (72–80)
Passage Comprehension	20	2.1	1.8	2.6	14/90	2	68 (63–72)
Applied Problems	28	2.8	2.3	3.5	10/90	6	76 (72–80)
Writing Samples	13-B	2.0	1.5	3.7	60/90	1	63 (53–74)
Word Attack	6	1.7	1.5	2.0	3/90	3	71 (67–75)
Picture Vocabulary	17	K.7	<K.0	2.1	16/90	3	73 (68–77)
Oral Comprehension	11	1.2	K.2	2.2	14/90	3	71 (67–76)
Editing	6	2.6	2.1	3.3	17/90	4	74 (70–79)
Reading Vocabulary	—	1.9	1.5	2.5	15/90	2	70 (66–73)
Quantitative Concepts	—	5.6	4.4	7.2	82/90	37	95 (90–100)
Academic Knowledge	—	1.5	K.7	2.6	14/90	2	69 (65–74)
Spelling of Sounds	16	1.6	1.2	2.5	39/90	3	73 (68–77)
Sound Awareness	24	1.5	K.9	2.4	29/90	3	71 (67–75)
Punctuation & Capitals	14	3.2	2.4	4.4	47/90	7	78 (71–84)

Achievement test scores based on Form A.

Educational Assessment Report

Name:	Tony Haliday		Dates:	March 5–7, 10–13, 2001
Date of Birth:	8-3-88		Grade:	7.7
Age:	12-7		School:	Stanford Math-Science Magnet Middle School

REASON FOR REFERRAL

Tony was referred by his itinerant Teacher of the Hearing Impaired (HI), Pat Adler, to the University clinic for 3 weeks of diagnostic teaching and testing. She stated concerns regarding his ongoing difficulties in written language and mathematics, which are affecting his success in middle school. She requested more information as to the reasons for these difficulties as well as recommendations for remediation.

BACKGROUND INFORMATION

Tony lives with his younger brother, his father, and his mother. His parents have never married, but have lived together since his birth. Tony's father works as a painter. Tony's mother reported that she received special education services when she was in the public school system until she was in the fifth grade. She is currently going to school to become a hairdresser and noted that she has no difficulty with the practical aspects of her courses, but has trouble memorizing information for her tests.

Tony's mother reported a normal pregnancy and delivery, and no developmental delays were noted in his preschool years. On a routine visit to the doctor, Tony's pediatrician noted that he had an unusual head shape. Upon further testing by specialists, he was diagnosed with cranial sagittal synostosis (the premature closure of the sagittal sutures over the fontanel). Such fusion limits the ability of the skull to expand in a direction perpendicular to the suture, resulting in characteristic head shapes. Typically, a diagnosis of craniosynostosis comes before a child is 2 years old but Tony was not accurately diagnosed until he was 3. His neurologist recommended that he have surgery to correct this problem but also said that he had never performed this kind of surgery on a child over 2 years of age. Immediately prior to this diagnosis, Tony had a tonsillectomy and adenoidectomy. After consulting with his pediatrician, Tony's mother decided against the corrective surgery because of his older age and the other recent medical operations. Craniosynostosis along the sagittal ridge is seldom associated with any neurological deficits.

As a young child, Tony experienced reoccurring ear infections for which he twice had tubes inserted. In 1997, he failed the school's hearing screening and was referred for an evaluation by an audiologist. Initially, he was diagnosed with a mild conductive hearing loss in his left ear and with borderline-to-normal hearing in his right ear. Annual audiograms show that his hearing has continued to deteriorate. He currently has a fluctuating bilateral hearing loss, which ranges from normal hearing to mild hearing loss in the right ear and normal hearing to moderate hearing loss in the left ear. He does not use any kind of amplification to compensate for his hearing loss in the classroom. At one point he was introduced to, and instructed in, the use of an auditory trainer. He did not want to continue to use it in the middle school because he did not want to carry it to all seven of his classes. His mother also thought that this was too much responsibility for him. Currently, he has frequent complaints about sharp pains in his ear and headaches. He is scheduled to have a third set of tubes placed in his ears in April and has an appointment scheduled in May with his neurologist.

Tony attended Humphrey Elementary School. From first through fifth grades, he received resource services for learning disabilities in reading and math, and language instruction from the speech-language pathologist. In the latter half of fifth-grade, his special education classification was changed to Multiple Disability (MD) and he began receiving support from the itinerant teacher of the hearing impaired.

Presently, Tony attends Stanford Math-Science Magnet Middle School. The curriculum at Stanford emphasizes accelerated science and math courses. Tony follows a regular seventh-grade schedule, including PE, language arts, engineering, math, science, social studies, and reading. The language arts, math, and social studies classes are designated as special education classes. The science class is designated as an inclusion class.

Tony also receives specialized instruction from his social studies teacher who is certified in special education, from the itinerant teacher of the hearing impaired, and from a speech-language pathologist. He is having some difficulty adjusting to the format of middle school. He is receiving D's in mathematics and computer, F's in science, and B's and C's in other classes. His teachers state that he is frequently absent. When he is in school, he appears to try but frequently appears "lost," asks for help, and needs individual assistance.

OBSERVATIONS DURING ASSESSMENT

At the beginning of the first session of the evaluation, Tony expressed his concerns about the testing. He asked many questions such as: "Do I have to come here?" and "What would happen if I got in a fight and was on in-school suspension?" Once he understood that the purpose of the assessment was to find ways to help him in school, he was polite, friendly, and cooperative. He did, however, express his dislike of taking tests, anxiety regarding his abilities, and frustration with certain tasks. He remarked, "I'm not good at this" and "It's too hard." Often, at the end of specific tests he asked, "How do you expect me to know that?" Although it was explained many times that these tests include material for older students, he continued to make statements that reflected a poor academic self-concept.

While attending the 3-week clinic, Tony engaged in many tasks that were difficult for him. Daily, he was asked to read, write, work on math, or participate in an oral language activity. Despite his difficulty with these tasks, he always put forth effort. He expressed desire to improve his writing, stating that he plans to go to college and, therefore, needs to do better in school now. An amplification system (an auditory trainer) was used throughout the test and diagnostic teaching sessions. The batteries and settings were checked daily to ensure that it was in working order. Tony was reminded several times per session to tell the evaluator if he noticed any difficulty hearing her voice or the tapes.

TESTS ADMINISTERED

Woodcock Johnson III Tests of Cognitive Abilities (WJ III COG), Tests 1–20 and Tests of Achievement (WJ III ACH), Tests 1–22, Standard (Std) and Extended (Ext) batteries (Scores based on grade norms)
Analytical Reading Inventory (ARI)
Beery-Buktenica Developmental Test of Visual Motor Integration—Fourth Edition (VMI)
Illinois Test of Psycholinguistic Abilities—Third Edition (ITPA-3)
Key Math Diagnostic Arithmetic Tests—Revised
Test of Written Language—Third Edition (TOWL-3)

RESULTS OF PRIOR EVALUATION

Wechsler Intelligence Scale for Children—Third Edition (WISC-III)

Verbal	Scaled Score
Information	12
Similarities	9
Arithmetic	9
Vocabulary	10
Comprehension	12

Performance	Scaled Score
Picture Completion	11
Coding	7
Picture Arrangement	5
Block Design	8
Object Assembly	7

Intelligence Quotients	Standard Score
Verbal	102
Performance	84
Full Scale	93

In 1999, Tony was administered the WISC-III. His Verbal Scale IQ (Average) was over one standard deviation (SD) above his Performance Scale IQ (Low Average). He was reasonably accurate, but slow, in arranging pictures into a story sequence, in putting together the pieces of a puzzle with limited visual detail, and in writing symbols corresponding to a given code. The Coding subtest requires rapid back-and-forth visual scanning, good visual-motor coordination, and attention and memory for visual detail. Tony qualified for continued learning disability services but the nature of his learning disability was not discussed in the report.

RESULTS AND INTERPRETATION

Intellectual Functioning

In March, 2002, the Woodcock-Johnson III Tests of Cognitive Abilities (WJ III COG) Standard and Extended Batteries were administered to examine Tony's cognitive strengths and weaknesses. The WJ III COG measures broad abilities within the area of cognition. Each broad ability, represented by a factor or cluster score, is composed of narrower abilities, represented by the individual test scores. Where Tony's performance on the narrow abilities within a broad ability were similar, only the factor/cluster score is discussed, as that is the more reliable score. Where the scores of the component tests are significantly dissimilar, only individual scores are discussed, as they are not considered to represent the broader ability.

Tony's General Intellectual Ability score (GIA) was 81 (SS 80–83), in the Low to Low Average range. This score must be interpreted with caution, however, due to Tony's hearing impairment, which may have affected his performance on these tests, despite amplification, and which also has undoubtedly affected his acquisition of skills and knowledge throughout his life.

Memory

Tony's performance varied on the tests of short-term memory and working memory. Tony's best score was on Auditory Working Memory (SS 89–97, RPI 80/90), a test of divided attention as well as memory. Given an oral list of objects and digits in random order, he gave back the objects named, then the digits, in their original sequence. The Memory for Words test (repeating back a string of unconnected words) proved more difficult for him. Despite his standard score in the lower end of the Average range (SS 86–98), his RPI (70/90) indicated that in tasks requiring verbal rehearsal (mental repetition of spoken information to prevent erosion in memory), he would retain about 70% of the information compared to his average grade-peers' 90%. On Numbers Reversed, Tony's score was in the Low range (SS 71–82). His RPI of 20/90 indicates that tasks requiring him to hold a string of digits in memory while changing their order will be "extremely difficult" for him.

Despite variation in his test scores, in many circumstances, information that Tony is holding in memory is likely to erode before he has adequate opportunity to process the information for transfer to long-term memory or use it to perform tasks. This can affect almost all new learning of academic skills as well as more complex procedures such as following directions, problem solving, reading comprehension, and written expression.

Processing Speed

According to his RPI scores, Tony processes visual information slowly and/or has particular difficulty rapidly scanning rows of symbols and small pictures (Decision Speed, SS 84–93, Low Average to Average, RPI 67/90; Visual Matching, SS 40–47, Very Low, RPI 0/90; Pair Cancellation SS 83–87, Low Average, RPI 59/90). Tony had difficulty on all tests requiring rapid visual scanning, the severity of

which corresponded to the size and complexity of the symbols involved. The severity of Tony's difficulty in visual scanning/discrimination is too extreme to be accepted as a processing deficit prima facie. Tony should have an ophthalmologic or behavioral optometric examination to ensure that his eyes are functioning normally.

If, in fact, this is a problem of processing speed (the time required for the cognitive system to interpret the information received through the eyes), Tony's ability to perform tasks involving visual symbols (e.g., reading, writing, math) is severely compromised and he will find it exceedingly difficult to automatize the lower-level skills, such as coming up with the answers to simple math facts while working out a multiple-step word problem, forming letters and spelling words while formulating written sentences, and fluently recognizing sight words or decoding unfamiliar words to facilitate reading comprehension.

Visual-Spatial Thinking

Tony's performance on the Visual-Spatial Thinking factor (SS 98–108, Average, RPI 92/90) indicated a relative strength in manipulating visual images and working with patterns and puzzles.

Visual-Motor Skills

The results of the VMI suggest that Tony's perception of the increasingly complex forms appears to be reasonably accurate (SS 93, Average). The quality of his reproductions when copying the forms, however, indicates that the addition of a motor demand increases the difficulty of the task (SS 84, Low Average). The effect of this weakness in coordinating visual information with motor output is observed in Tony's poor handwriting and frustration at copying material from the board.

Auditory and Phonological Processing

Tony's scores on the two tests of the WJ III Auditory Processing factor were extremely discrepant. Tony's apparent limited ability to "attend" to speech sounds in the presence of distracting noise (Auditory Attention, SS 68–79, Low) may well reflect inaccurate detection of the sounds, secondary to his hearing loss, rather than a problem in processing or attention. Tony is likely to have difficulty understanding directions and information presented orally in class or in other situations, especially in the presence of background noise. In contrast, he seems to have Average ability in blending individual speech sounds into a familiar word (Sound Blending, SS 102–113, RPI 95/90) and in perceiving the gestalt of a word, even with sounds missing (Incomplete Words, SS 91–103, RPI 88/90). He had considerably more difficulty with the more complex skills of manipulating sounds within words, such as phoneme deletion, substitution, and reversal (Sound Awareness SS 79–87, RPI 61/90). It should be noted that Tony's relative strength in phonemic awareness may be a direct result of the services he has received from his resource specialists. Nevertheless, despite Tony's hearing impairment, phonological awareness appears to be a relative strength that contributes to his basic reading skills.

Long-Term Retrieval

Tony appears to have some difficulty in learning new associations between symbols (visual) and words (oral) and/or retrieving these associations from long-term memory over a few minutes (Visual-Auditory Learning, SS 77–86, RPI 75/90). He appears to have no difficulty, however, retrieving known words from his long-term memory stores to fit a given category (e.g., "Name all the things you can think of that people can ride") (Retrieval Fluency, SS 90–102, RPI 89/90). This task differs from other word-retrieval tasks in that it allows the subject flexibility in choosing among the words he knows rather than having to find a specific word. Thus, retrieving known information from long-term memory may be relatively easy but learning and retrieving new associations may be a struggle.

Logical Reasoning

The ease with which Tony can solve problems using novel stimuli and logical reasoning appears to depend on the type of task. His use of inductive reasoning to discern the rule governing the difference between two sets of drawings (Concept Formation, SS 93–99, RPI 83/90) was considerably better than his ability to use deductive reasoning to apply a code in a mini-math system of colored squares, similar to algebraic equations (Analysis-Synthesis, SS 77–87, RPI 53/90).

Oral Language

Tony's oral vocabulary appears to be Average for his grade (Picture Vocabulary, SS 95–104, RPI 89/90; Verbal Comprehension, SS 93–102, RPI 87/90). Tony's knowledge of grammar also appears to be in the Average range (ITPA-3 Grammar, SS 97). His understanding of connected discourse, however, appears somewhat compromised. Tony's performance in recalling the key events in short stories spanned the Low and Low Average ranges (Story Recall,

SS 72–91). (The reason for such a wide span is that the ability to retell stories, once developed, is fairly stable over time.) His comprehension of brief discourse (one to two sentences) was in the lower end of the Average range (Oral Comprehension, SS 91–100). Tony's RPIs on both tests (81/90 and 83/90, respectively) indicate that this type of task, at grade level, would be within his instructional range but just manageable.

The ARI was also used to assess Tony's comprehension of oral language. His listening comprehension level was fourth grade on the ARI compared to early fifth grade on the WJ III Oral Comprehension test. The latter test requires the subject to listen to one or two sentences and fill in the missing word, whereas the ARI requires the subject to retell a much longer passage and answer comprehension questions. Tony had difficulty giving accurate and sequenced details, explaining vocabulary terms, and making inferences.

Tony may have difficulty interpreting picture details. He had particular difficulty on the Understanding Directions test (SS 79–90, RPI 68/90), comprehending, holding in memory, and following a series of instructions to point to objects in detailed pictures. Over both batteries (COG and ACH), he had difficulty in seven of eight tests requiring the ability to process pictures relatively quickly. Although this test does not have a time limit, one must hold all of the instructions in short-term memory until he has performed the related action. Possible difficulty interpreting pictorial detail is not consistent with his Average score on Picture Recognition (SS 100–112, RPI 94/90), and the other tests require many other subskills beside interpretation of pictures.

Despite his language strengths, Tony evidenced specific difficulties in word retrieval. In contrast to his solid performance on the Retrieval Fluency test, Tony was very slow in accessing the specific names for common objects in response to picture prompts (Rapid Picture Naming, SS 66–70, RPI 2/90). Over the 3 weeks of clinic work, informal language probes and observations confirmed this difficulty. Tony often used sound effects and hand motions to replace words when speaking. For example, telling how he scored a goal in his soccer game, he moved his hand in a zigzag fashion. Also, rather than use a precise word for his intended meaning, he frequently used words that were semantically related. For example, he used the word "ground" when describing the tile floor in a building. Limited word retrieval may negatively affect oral and written expression; Tony may encounter that "It's on the tip of my tongue" experience so often as to interfere significantly with sentence formulation in speaking and writing.

In diagnostic teaching, Tony also demonstrated problems conceptualizing and/or expressing sequential order. He described events using a "shotgun approach" to the details and made errors in using terms such as "first, second, next, last" when describing the order of events.

Academic Achievement

Reading

The following information is based on Tony's scores on the WJ III ACH, ITPA-3, ARI, and data collected from various diagnostic teaching procedures. Tony demonstrated Average skill on the Basic Reading Skills cluster (SS 97–101, RPI 88/90, GE 6.3), reading sight words and decoding phonically regular nonsense words. On the ARI word lists, his sight word instructional level was seventh grade.

Despite Tony's strong decoding skills, his reading was slow and labored (Reading Fluency, SS 84–88, RPI 25/90, GE 4.1), possibly reflecting his speed of scanning and processing visual symbols. His lack of fluency undoubtedly interferes with his ability to focus his attention on the meaning inherent in the text.

Although Tony's standard score on the WJ III ACH Passage Comprehension test is in the Average range (SS 87–97), his RPI of 77/90 and his grade equivalent of 4.5 suggests that he will have difficulty comprehending textual material at his grade level. His instructional level on the considerably longer passages of the ARI was also fourth grade. His retellings and responses to comprehension questions indicated difficulties with using syntactic clues, sequencing events in stories, making inferences, and interpreting figurative language. For example, after reading a passage in which a character was described as "being as scared as a mouse in front of a python," he incorporated "the python" into his retelling. Tony's reading comprehension difficulties are clearly related to his difficulties with comprehension of oral language and are exacerbated by his dysfluent reading.

Written Language

The following information is based on formal test results and information from diagnostic teaching procedures. The writing tests of the WJ III include Writing Samples (SS 60–80, RPI 68/90, GE 2.3), writing one sentence per item in response to a variety of task demands; Spelling (SS 84–91, RPI 53/90, GE 4.1), writing words from dictation; and Writing Fluency (SS 79–87, RPI 43/90, GE 3.9), rapidly formulating and writing simple sentences, given the keywords and picture prompts. The TOWL-3 Spontaneous Writing subtest (SS 81) requires the subject to write a story in response to a picture prompt.

Analysis of Tony's story indicated that he does not recognize the difference between conversational language and the more formal style used in writing. He used few complete sentences and those were simple in structure and devoid of description. His pronouns generally lacked referents. His story was short, the plot inadequately defined and poorly resolved, the events poorly sequenced, and the ending abrupt. Tony made many spelling, capitalization, and punctuation errors. His handwriting is labored, with poor letter formation and inadequate space between words; at times, his writing is illegible. Tony demonstrated the same difficulties in basic writing skills, fluency, and expression in all of the writing tests administered and in informal tasks.

Math

Tony's overall math ability as measured by the WJ III Broad Math cluster (SS 70–76, RPI 32/90, GE 3.2) and Key-Math (SS 69) indicate that Tony is severely delayed in his development of arithmetic concepts and skills. Results of diagnostic teaching confirmed the validity of these scores. Tony's Low Average score on the Key-Math Basic Concepts composite (SS 88) is misleading. Tony read and wrote numbers incorrectly, did not understand place value, and was unable to round numbers. He did read fractions correctly when presented as numbers (e.g., $\frac{1}{2}$) and as a shaded part of an illustration. Otherwise, he was unable to work with any form of rational numbers. Tony was able to solve some problems using geometric figures, a skill that may be related to his strength in working with visual patterns (as opposed to pictures).

Results of the WJ III Calculation (SS 64–75, RPI 16/90, GE 2.9) and Math Fluency (SS 68–73, RPI 55/90, GE 2.6) tests and the Key-Math Operations composite (SS 55), suggest that Tony has learned very basic math algorithms but does not understand fundamental numerical concepts. For example, he did not know what to do with problems involving 0 (e.g., 8 – 8, 8 + 0). Tony has not memorized basic math facts and counting on his fingers proves slow, awkward, and inaccurate. He solved simple addition and subtraction problems without regrouping. He could not solve any multiplication problems but did demonstrate his understanding of multiplication as repeated addition. He did not attempt any division problems. He became extremely frustrated during the Mental Computation subtest, a working memory task requiring the subject to hold numerical information in short-term memory while performing basic computation. He solved only two problems and was confused when the problems involved more than one piece of information.

Tony's scores on the Key-Math Applications composite

(SS 72) and the WJ III Applied Problems (SS 80–88, RPI 31/90, GE 3.8) and Quantitative Concepts (SS 67–77, RPI 17/90, GE 2.8) tests correspond to his limited knowledge in the more basic concepts. Tony solved basic measurement problems that involved a ruler. He could not add coins or make change. He did not understand various measurement terms and could not interpret charts or graphs.

Tony's extreme weakness in math is of particular concern due to the math/science focus of his school and the accelerated courses in these areas.

SUMMARY OF ASSESSMENT FINDINGS

Intellectual/Cognitive Abilities

Tony is a seventh-grade student with a fluctuating bilateral conductive hearing loss, for which he uses no amplification. He is classified for special education purposes as Multiply Disabled and receives services from a special education teacher, a speech-language pathologist, and a teacher of the hearing impaired. A comparison of Tony's performance on the WISC-III, administered when he was age 9, and on similar tasks of the WJ III, albeit not directly comparable, indicate stability in some cognitive strengths and weaknesses and a steep decline in arithmetic and general information, suggesting that his knowledge in these areas has not increased commensurate with his peers'. His previous low scores in visual–spatial tests are puzzling, given his current performance. One possible explanation is that the WISC-III subtests also required time-limited processing of pictures.

Within the tests comprising the GIA cluster, Tony's scores ranged from a standard score of 44 to a standard score of 107. On the current evaluation, Tony demonstrated strong visual–spatial skills and memory for designs and pictures. Tony's ability to maintain auditory information in short-term memory appears extremely variable, possibly depending on the task, his hearing, the environment, and his level of attention and effort. Memory for numbers appears especially difficult. Tony appears to be able to retrieve from long-term memory information that he knows well; in contrast, he may have considerable difficulty transferring new learning to long-term storage. Tony's test performance evidences significantly slow speed of processing. Tony's ability to use inductive reasoning (i.e., making a generalization based on observed similarities and differences) appears stronger than his deductive reasoning (i.e., drawing a conclusion based on the use of available information in an "if/then" approach). The inductive reasoning task appears to require more linguistic reasoning than the deductive task, which is similar to a mathematical system.

The results of this evaluation reinforce Tony's classification as a student with a specific language impairment. Although he appears to have average vocabulary knowledge, ability to reason using individual words (e.g., analogies), and comprehension of discourse of a few sentences, he struggles to comprehend longer discourse and express his thoughts clearly when speaking or writing. Receptively, he has difficulty with organization of information, complex syntax, and figurative language; expressively, he has significant problems with word finding and sentence formulation, including complex syntax.

Results of Academic Assessment

Tony appears to have had some good training in reading decoding skills, which are within the Average range, and in the basic phonemic skills underlying them. Tony's limited comprehension of reading material, currently at a third-grade instructional level, is related to his deficits in comprehension of oral language and dysfluent reading.

Tony presents significant weaknesses in all basic writing skills (i.e., spelling, punctuation, capitalization, handwriting); in sentence-level skills (e.g., sentence structure, use of cohesive devices); and organization of ideas at the paragraph level. Written expression is largely based in expressive oral language abilities. Tony's overall writing skills are at the mid-third grade level.

Tony evidences the features of a specific math disorder in slow processing, poor memory for numbers, and limited deductive reasoning. He does not appear to understand fundamental number concepts (e.g., sets, place value, comparisons of amounts) although some of the cognitive skills required (e.g., discerning similarities and differences) appear to be available to him. Consequently, his math skills are fragmented and he is unable to apply them.

Tony's general world knowledge is limited and similar to that of the average student in late-third grade.

RECOMMENDATIONS

Further Evaluation

1. Tony requires a vision examination from an optometrist who specializes in behavioral optometry (i.e., how the eyes function in tandem and individually in the practical

tasks of daily life) or an ophthalmologist who has expertise in behavioral optometry.

2. Tony needs appropriate amplification throughout the school day. Contact an educational audiologist for an audiological examination (including ear health, acuity, speech thresholds, and speech discrimination) and information on the newer technology in programmable hearing aids. Since Tony's hearing loss fluctuates, set up a schedule of exams, preferably in school. Have the audiologist teach Tony how to program his hearing aids according to the results. Discuss this recommendation with the physician who will be performing the myringotomy (placement of tubes).

3. Contact Ms. Haliday, Tony's mother, to obtain the written results of the vision, audiological, and neurological exams.

General Accommodations

1. Seat Tony near the teacher to allow him to hear him or her more easily and away from competing noise.

2. Provide Tony with a copy of the teacher's notes, or designate a capable student with good handwriting to give him a copy of the notes (along with permission to copy the notes on the school copier).

3. Provide Tony with daily instruction and practice in keyboarding and using a word-processing program. As he becomes more proficient, provide him with a portable word processor to use in his classes.

4. Tony does not have the basic academic skills to benefit from the accelerated classes and strong focus on science and math in his school. Additionally, he requires the services of a learning disabilities specialist. Consider a transfer to a middle school that has a wider range of instructional levels and a certified learning disabilities specialist.

5. Whatever staff member is responsible for developing specific learning techniques and strategies for Tony should explain them to Tony's parents so they can facilitate use at home.

6. Arrange for the learning disabilities specialist, the speech-language pathologist, teacher of the hearing impaired, and specific class teachers to meet to develop ways to coordinate instruction. This will provide for reinforcement of skills as well as prevent fragmentation of instruction.

Oral Language

1. Teach Tony strategies to facilitate word retrieval, including learning to recognize when he is having difficulty retrieving a word so that he may use a retrieval strategy. Share the strategies with Tony's teachers so that they will be able to prompt him in class when he is stuck on a word.

2. Limit sentence length and complexity when speaking to Tony.

3. Teach Tony to recognize when he has not understood and to request repetition or rephrasing of instructions, questions, or statements when necessary.

4. When calling on Tony in class, provide him with as much time as he needs to organize his thoughts and formulate a response. Privately, alert him to this plan so that he does not feel pressured to come up with answers quickly. When possible, tell him in advance the question that he will be asked.

5. In high school, either waive the foreign language requirement or allow Tony to take American Sign Language (if available) to fulfill the requirement.

6. Teach Tony strategies for organizing the ideas, events, or details in narrative and expository information.

Content Area Classes

1. Make sure that the presentation of new information and concepts is organized.

2. Minimize the amount of required writing on tests by using multiple-choice questions, matching, fill-in-the-blank, or short answers. When necessary, allow Tony to take exams with one of the specialists so that he may have the questions read to him and he can dictate the answers.

3. On all tests and assignments, allow extended time.

4. Employ cueing strategies with Tony in the classroom. Teach him keywords that will alert him to important information, to the sequence of ideas, and to the organization of the information.

Reading

1. Help Tony increase his reading speed. Possible methods include repeated readings, speed drills, and commercial programs, such as Great Leaps Reading. (Summaries of these methods/programs are attached.)

2. Provide activities to help Tony process and comprehend what he reads, as he reads. Some suggested activities are Directed Reading Thinking Activity, Reciprocal Teaching, and the Request Procedure. (Summaries of these techniques are attached.)

3. Apply activities to improve oral language comprehension to reading comprehension. In this regard, the speech-language pathologist and learning disabilities

specialist could collaborate on adapting or developing specific strategies and then meet with Tony's content area teachers and his HI teacher, to determine ways to use these strategies in the classroom.

Writing

1. Initially, focus instruction on writing complete and well-structured sentences. The Sentence Writing Strategy (Schumaker & Sheldon, 1985) is an example of an effective strategy.
2. To reinforce sentence structures, read to Tony from a book in which the sentence structure is relatively basic (e.g., simple, compound, complex), but the content is interesting (e.g., Goosebumps). Guide Tony in listening to the flow of the sentences and then go back and read the sentences individually, discussing whether or not the sentence sounds complete. Read some sentence fragments to help him hear the difference.
3. Teach Tony simple frameworks around which he can organize different types of writing and, where possible, provide a visual format to help him understand. (Illustrations of graphic organizers and the type of writing they represent are attached.)
4. Teach Tony the rules for capitalization and punctuation use. Provide him with a cue card with abbreviations of the rules for quick reference.

5. When writing on a word processor, teach Tony how to use the spell checker. So that he can make sure that the spelling he has chosen matches the meaning he intended (e.g., *there, their, they're*), show him how to use the thesaurus on the word-processing program.

Math

1. Review basic number concepts such as ordering and conservation of matter; sets and place value; and the meaning of math terms (e.g., more, less) in conjunction with comparison of sets. An excellent source of a developmental sequence of math concepts and instructional activities is *Today's Mathematics* (10th edition): *Part 1, Concepts and Classroom Methods* and *Part 2, Activities and Instructional Ideas* (Heddens & Speer, 2000a, b).
2. When teaching new concepts and skills, or extending previously learned concepts and skills, use manipulatives, before using numbers.
3. Consider using Touch Math as a method of teaching computation skills so that Tony may continue to use the basic algorithms without errors.
4. While teaching practical application of math skills, allow Tony to use a calculator for the computation so that he can concentrate on the reasoning.

Adapted from Jennifer Gilman, M.A.

Woodcock-Johnson III: Tests of Cognitive Abilities: Factors/Clusters/Test Scores

Name: Tony Haliday

Scores based on: Grade: _7.7_ Age ___ Norms

Date of Birth _8-3-88_

Type of Score: SS _X_ Grade___ Age___

	Category/Factor	SS	68% Band	RPI	Standard Battery	SS	68% Band	RPI	Extended Battery	SS	68% Band	RPI
	GIA	81	80–83	66/90								
CHC Factors	Comprehension Knowledge	88	84–91	67/90	Verbal Comp.	97	93–102	87/90	General Information	80	76–85	40/90
	Long-Term Retrieval	83	79–88	83/90	Visual-Aud. Learning	81	77–86	75/90	Retrieval Fluency	96	90–102	89/90
	Visual-Spatial Thinking	103	98–108	92/90	Spatial Relations	98	94–103	89/90	Picture Recognition	106	100–112	94/90
	Auditory Processing	91	87–96	83/90	Sound Blending	107	102–113	95/90	Auditory Attention	74	68–79	54/90
	Fluid Reasoning	89	86–92	70/90	Concept Formation	96	93–99	83/90	Analysis-Synthesis	82	77–87	53/90
	Processing Speed	60	57–63	6/90	Visual Matching	44	40–47	0/90	Decision Speed	88	84–93	67/90
	Short-Term Memory	81	76–86	43/90	Numbers Reversed	76	71–82	20/90	Memory for Words	92	86–98	70/90
Clinical Clusters	Phonological Awareness III	95	91–98	86/90	Sound Blend	107	102–113	95/90	Sound Awareness	83	79–87	61/90
					Incomp. Words	97	91–103	88/90				
	Working Memory	82	78–86	49/90	Numbers Rev.	76	71–82	20/90				
					Aud. Working Memory	93	89–97	80/90				
	Cognitive Fluency	72	70–74	41/90					Retrieval Fluency	96	90–102	89/90
									Decision Speed	88	84–93	67/90
									Rapid Pict. Naming	68	66–70	2/90
	Executive Processes	90	87–92	80/90	Concept Form	96	93–99	83/90	Planning	100	88–112	90/90
									Pair Cancel	85	83–87	59/90
	Delayed Recall								Vis-Aud. Lrng-Del.	+0.56		
									Story Recall-Del.	+0.20		
	Knowledge	84	81–87	56/90					Gen'l Info	80	76–85	40/90
									Acad. Know.	91	86–95	72/90

Woodcock-Johnson III: Tests of Achievement

Name: Tony Haliday

Date of Birth 8–3–88

Scores based on: Grade: _X_ Age ___ Norms

Type of Score: SS_X_ %ile ___ RPI _X_ Grade___ Age___

	Clusters	SS	Band	RPI	Standard	SS	Band	RPI	Extended	SS	Band	RPI
Oral Language	Oral Language	91	88–95	81/90	Story Recall	81	72–91	81/90	Pict. Vocab.	99	95–104	89/90
					Underst. Direct.	84	79–90	68/90	Oral Comp.	96	91–100	83/90
	Listen. Comp.	90	86–94	76/90	Underst. Direct.	84	79–90	68/90	Oral Comp.	96	91–100	83/90
	Oral Expr.	95	91–100	86/90	Story Recall	81	72–91	81/90	Pict Vocab	99	95–104	89/90
Reading					Let-Wd. Ident.	97	95–100	84/90				
					Rdg. Fluency	86	84–88	25/90				
	Broad Rdg.	90	89–92	64/90	Passage Comp.	92	87–97	77/90				
	Basic Rdg.	99	97–101	88/90	Let-Wd. Ident.	97	95–100	84/90	Wd. Attack	100	96–105	91/90
	Rdg. Comp.	93	90–96	81/90	Passage Comp.	92	87–97	77/90	Rdg. Vocab.	96	92–99	84/90
Math					Calculation	70	64–75	16/90				
					Math Fluency	70	68–73	55/90				
	Broad Math.	73	70–76	32/90	App Problems	84	80–88	31/90				
					Calculation	70	64–75	16/90				
	Math Calc.	65	61–70	32/90	Math Fluency	70	68–73	55/90				
	Math Rsng.	77	74–80	24/90	App. Problems	84	80–88	31/90	Quant. Conc.	72	67–77	17/90
Written Language					Spelling	87	84–91	53/90				
					Writ. Fluency	83	79–87	43/90				
	Broad Written Language	81	78–84	55/90	Writ. Samples	70	60–80	68/90				
	Basic Writing	85	82–88	52/90	Spelling	87	84–91	53/90	Editing	85	81–90	51/90
					Writ. Fluency	83	79–87	43/90				
	Written Expr.	79	74–83	56/90	Writ. Samples	70	60–80	68/90				
Other Clusters	Acad. Know.	91	86–95	72/90					Acad. Knowl.	91	86–95	72/90
	Phn-Grph. Knowl.	91	89–94	73/90					Wd. Attack	100	96–105	91/90
									Spell Sound	74	70–79	43/90
	Academic Skills	84	82–87	51/90	Let-Wd. Ident.	97	95–100	84/90				
					Spelling	87	84–91	53/90				
					Calculation	70	64–75	16/90				
	Academic Fluency	81	79–83	40/90	Rdg. Fluency	86	84–88	25/90				
					Writ. Fluency	83	79–87	43/90				
					Math Fluency	70	68–73	55/90				
	Academic Applic	85	82–87	60/90	Passage Comp.	92	87–97	77/90				
					Writ. Samples	70	60–80	68/90				
					App. Problems	84	80–88	31/90				
Supplemental Tests									Story Rec. Del.	z = +0.2		
									Sound Awar.	83	79–87	61/90
									Punc. & Cap.	84	79–90	64/90

Psychoeducational Evaluation

Name:	Boyd Moore	Parents:	Mary and James Moore
Birth Date:	10/27/87	School:	Tuller Middle School
Chronological Age:	13-5	Dates of Evaluation:	3/27–29/01
Grade:	7.5	Evaluator:	

REASON FOR REFERRAL

Ms. Moore, Boyd's mother, referred him for an evaluation because Boyd performs poorly on science tests and on standardized tests. She also stated that she believes Boyd may have difficulties with expressive and possibly receptive language. Ms. Moore wishes to better understand Boyd's learning style and strengths and weaknesses, and seeks strategies to be employed by a tutor to help Boyd improve his scores on tests.

BACKGROUND INFORMATION

Boyd is a 13-year-old male who resides with his mother, Mary Moore, his father, James Moore, and his 11-year-old sister. Boyd attends Tuller Middle School and is in the seventh grade. Both of his parents are professionals.

Ms. Moore reported no problems or concerns during her pregnancy with Boyd. He was delivered via Caesarian section, due to lack of labor progress, with no complications. According to Ms. Moore, Boyd's developmental milestones were reached within normal limits.

During his early childhood, Boyd had fevers as high as 104 degrees and once experienced a seizure due to high fever. Boyd still experiences high fevers when ill. Boyd is allergic to sulfa drugs, and used to be allergic to bee stings though they do not appear to affect him now. Boyd has normal vision and hearing.

Boyd attended a day care center from 13 months until age 5, a cooperative private school from kindergarten to third grade, and a private school from third to sixth grade.

Ms. Moore reported that Boyd was later than his peers in learning to read. She stated that his first-grade teacher used a whole language approach, which did not work well for Boyd. He received tutoring at that time, employing a phonics approach, and was decoding words by the end of first grade. Boyd's parents report that he has made great strides in reading and experiences no difficulties now. Boyd has also received tutoring to improve his writing skills during fifth and sixth grade. His mother reported that his writing was immature, stilted, and disconnected. She added that the tutoring has helped improve his writing.

His parents reported that Boyd performed lower than his school grades would predict on standardized tests. They indicated that this has negatively impacted Boyd's school career. For example, they stated that based on his school performance, Boyd was invited to visit some of the upscale private schools in the area. However, he was rejected when they received his Stanford-9 test scores (Reading: Average to Above Average; Mathematics: Average to Low Average; Language: Average). They reported that this was very frustrating to Boyd because many of his friends were accepted to these schools. Boyd's father believes that Boyd experiences test anxiety, whereas his mother believes Boyd lacks test-taking strategies. Because Boyd is nearing high school, his parents are concerned about his performance on the high school entrance tests. They would like him to attend a competitive high school and fear that he may not be accepted if he does not improve his standardized test scores. His parents reported that Boyd has excellent social skills and has always performed well in school. They added that he has many friends, both in school and in the neighborhood.

Boyd was recently administered the Wechsler Intelligence Scale for Children, Third Edition (WISC-III) and received a Full Scale IQ of 107 (68th percentile). His Verbal IQ was 99 (47th percentile) and his Performance IQ was 115 (84th percentile). According to the report, Boyd seemed anxious and needed reassurance during testing. The examiner reported that his anxiety might have interfered with his performance.

Boyd's first trimester report card at Tuller Middle School indicates that he is doing well in school overall. He received an A in social studies, an A– in Spanish, a B in math, and a B– in both science and language arts. Test performance brought down his grades for science and math.

CLASSROOM OBSERVATIONS

Boyd was observed at school during homeroom, Spanish, and language arts. During homeroom, Boyd and his classmates read quietly as his homeroom teacher graded papers. The small classroom had a traditional arrangement, consisting of rows of desks facing a blackboard. There were 18 students in the classroom. The Spanish classroom was arranged with two rows of desks facing each other, leaving a center aisle. Boyd and his classmates were tested in Spanish class. The Spanish test consisted of a written component and an oral extra credit component. Boyd appeared calm during the test and finished in a timely fashion. He exhibited no anxious behavior during the test and appeared to have no difficulty with either the written or oral component. After he finished his test, he promptly began his homework assignment that consisted of translating Spanish text into English. Boyd concentrated on his work and was able to maintain focus in the midst of considerable noise generated by many of his classmates who were involved in casual conversations.

Like the homeroom, Boyd's language arts classroom was also arranged with desks facing a blackboard. The lesson consisted of the mechanics of writing, specifically, how to correctly punctuate dialogue. Boyd appeared attentive to the lesson. Each student was required to write and punctuate four sentences of dialogue on the board. Boyd's sentences were simple (e.g., "How are you?" said Dick); however, he did not punctuate the sentences correctly, consistently omitting question marks and periods. Boyd's teacher wrote on his report card that his writing contains garbled syntax and many mechanical errors.

INTERVIEW WITH TEACHERS

Boyd's Spanish teacher reported that he does well in her class and works very well independently. Boyd's science teacher stated that he demonstrated difficulty on tests requiring him to extract information to plug into mathematical formulae. Boyd's math teacher reported that Boyd has difficulty with the "problem of the week" exercises, which involve abstract reasoning skills. Boyd's language arts teacher expressed some concerns about his writing skills and his difficulty drawing inferences from readings.

TESTING OBSERVATIONS

Boyd was tested over three sessions. His appearance was neat and he presented as a friendly young man. Rapport was easily established and he appeared comfortable and confident regarding testing. Boyd did not seek reassurance or appear anxious or fidgety at any time during testing. At times, he appeared weary, but seemed able to maintain focus throughout the session. During the first and second sessions, two breaks were taken for him to walk around and to have a drink and snack. Because the third session was of a shorter duration, Boyd stated that he did not feel the need to take a break. The examiner did notice that he seemed to state that he did not know a response rather hastily at times but most of the time was thoughtful regarding his responses. It is notable that Boyd worked slowly during the mathematics portion of testing. Also, when presented with science questions taken directly from a school quiz, Boyd stated that he was confused regarding the mathematical procedure. Considering his level of cooperation and focus, these results appear to be indicative of his functioning at this time.

TEST RESULTS AND INTERPRETATION

Cognitive Assessment

Woodcock-Johnson Tests of Cognitive Abilities III (WJ III COG)
Children's Memory Scale (CMS) (selected subtests)
Woodcock-Johnson Tests of Achievement III (WJ III ACH) (selected tests)

General Intellectual Ability

Boyd's General Intellectual Ability (GIA) was found to be in the Average range as measured by the Woodcock-Johnson Tests of Cognitive Abilities III (WJ III COG). This finding is consistent with previous testing on the Wechsler Intelligence Scales for Children—III (WISC-III). The tests of the WJ III COG are combined in meaningful groups along with selected tests of the WJ III ACH and subtests of the CMS to better understand Boyd's strengths and needs. (See Table 1.)

Acquired Knowledge

Acquired knowledge, which is based on prior learning and experience, should be immediately available for recall and processing. Boyd's acquired knowledge was assessed in three areas: (a) crystallized ability, defined as language development and breadth and depth of knowledge of a cul-

Table 1.   WJ III COG and ACH, and CMS Scores

Domain	Factor	Skill Area	Test	Test/Subtest	Standard Score	Classification
Acquired Knowledge	Crystallized Ability		WJ III COG	Verbal Comp.	89	Low Average
			WJ III COG	General Information	80	
			WJ III ACH	Picture Vocabulary	98	Average
	Quantitative Knowledge		WJ III ACH	Quantitative Concepts	80	Low/Low Average
	Academic Knowledge			Science Social Studies Humanities	91	Low Average/Average
High-Level Processing and Reasoning	Fluid Reasoning	Deductive Reasoning	WJ III COG	Analysis-Synthesis	104	Average
		Inductive Reasoning		Concept Formation	78	Low
	Long-Term Storage and Retrieval	Word Finding and Retrieval	WJ III COG	Retrieval Fluency	101	Average
				Rapid Picture Naming	97	
		Meaningful Memory	WJ III ACH	Story Recall	93	Average
			CMS	Stories	85	Low Average
		Associative Memory and Learning	WJ III COG	Visual-Auditory Learning	84	Low Average
			CMS	Word Pairs	75	Low
				Word Lists	80	Low/Low Average
	Auditory Processing		WJ III COG	Sound Blending	111	High Average
				Incomplete Words	118	
				Auditory Attention	115	
	Visual Processing		WJ III COG	Spatial Relations	103	Average
				Picture Recognition	99	
Low-level Processing	Short Term Memory		WJ III COG	Numbers Reversed	106	Average
				Aud. Working Memory	110	
				Memory for Words	112	
	Processing Speed		WJ III COG	Visual Matching	98	Average
				Decision Speed	98	

ture; (b) quantitative knowledge, defined as general information about numerical concepts and mathematical quantities; and (c) academic knowledge, that which is acquired through formal academic study. Boyd performed in the Low Average range on tasks assessing crystallized ability. He had difficulty identifying common items, generating synonyms and antonyms for words, and completing word analogies. He scored similarly in quantitative knowledge, demonstrating difficulty in identifying the rules and patterns underlying number sequences, and in stating general factual knowledge regarding time and quantities.

Boyd performed in the lower portion of the Average range on tasks assessing academic knowledge. Boyd may have performed somewhat better on measures of academic knowledge than on crystallized knowledge because the former information is explicitly taught and drilled in school, whereas the latter requires the individual to assimilate in-

formation actively from the environment that is not explicitly taught. General information is gathered through active learning, that is, through a combination of information seeking, associative memory, and inductive reasoning. Boyd learns adequately when information is directly presented to him and drilled.

Information Processing

Above and beyond acquired knowledge, one must employ higher-level processing, or thinking abilities, to carry out novel learning or problem solving. This domain includes a variety of cognitive abilities that require processing information, rather than simply recalling it. The abilities within this domain are fluid reasoning, long-term retrieval, visual processing, and auditory processing. Because Boyd's functioning within this domain is varied, each of these areas needs to be considered separately.

Fluid Reasoning

New learning may involve novel reasoning and problem solving, known as fluid reasoning. Two different skills within this area were assessed, and Boyd showed varied abilities. Boyd performed in the Average range on a task assessing deductive reasoning ability but performed in the Low range on a task assessing inductive reasoning ability. This finding suggests that Boyd may reason effectively if presented with the rules and guidelines from which to draw his conclusions. He may, however, experience difficulty solving problems that require him to discover underlying generalizations and apply them, or when the rules for solving problems are not explicitly stated.

Long-Term Retrieval and Associative Memory

Learning new information requires the ability to store information in long-term memory and retrieve it fluently at a later time. Boyd's performance differed greatly depending on the skill area assessed by the tasks. He was found to function in the Average range on tasks requiring him to retrieve previously learned information, such as names for common items (e.g., ball, cup) and words in a semantic category (e.g., clothing). Boyd demonstrated Low Average ability on tasks requiring him to store and recall information in a meaningful context, such as stories. He was better at recalling general story themes and ideas than specific facts.

On tasks requiring Boyd to use associative memory, in which new material is learned and remembered by linking it to previously learned information, Boyd was found to function in the Low Average range. This finding suggests that Boyd is adequately able to retrieve information already stored in long-term memory, but has difficulty assimilating new information into his knowledge store. For example, Boyd demonstrated difficulty on a task requiring him to remember pairs of semantically unrelated words. This task requires the use of active strategies, such as verbal mediation and/or repetition, to create linkages between the words. Boyd's performance was similar on another task in which he was required to learn a list of words. Again, he should have used active strategies to form associations between the words to be able to recall them. Hence, Boyd does not appear to use active strategies to put information into context and make connections between new and known information.

Phonemic Awareness

Boyd performed in the Above Average range on tasks assessing auditory processing, the ability to analyze and synthesize auditory information at the level of individual sounds. Hence, Boyd possesses excellent phonetic awareness skills which are helpful when hearing new words, and for learning the sounds of a foreign language.

Visual Processing

Some tasks involve visual processing, which is the ability to analyze and synthesize visual–spatial information and manipulate visual shapes. Boyd performed in the Average range, thus demonstrating adequate ability to process, recall, and manipulate visual information. The ability to visualize adequately is helpful especially for conceptualizing information and solving mathematical problems.

Learning is also influenced by an individual's low-level processing, the ability to process information automatically in an efficient manner. Two distinct influences on automatic information processing, short-term memory and processing speed, are measured. If either of these areas is impaired, the ability to carry out tasks with little or no conscious thought and the efficiency of higher-level skills can be reduced. Short-term memory is the ability to hold information and use it within a few seconds, and includes auditory memory span (i.e., the number of elements one can hold in immediate awareness at one time) and working memory (i.e., the ability to perform operations on information held in memory). Processing speed is the ability to quickly execute a task while maintaining focused attention. Boyd was found to function in the Average range in both of these areas. Thus, his low-level processing skills are adequate to allow higher-level thinking to proceed without interference.

Academic Achievement

Oral and Written Language Scales (OWLS)
Woodcock-Johnson Tests of Achievement, Third Edition (WJ III ACH)

Boyd's achievement was assessed in oral language and the academic areas of reading, written language, and math. These areas were assessed using selected tests of the WJ III ACH, and of the OWLS. (See Table 2.) Boyd's achievement

Table 2. Academic Achievement Scores

Academic Area	Domain	Test	Test/Subtest	Standard Score	Percentile Rank	Range
Oral Language	Listening Comprehension	OWLS	Listening Comprehension	105	63	Average
		WJ III ACH	Understanding Directions	110	74	
	Oral Expression	OWLS	Oral Expression	109	73	Average
Reading	Basic Reading	WJ III ACH	Word Attack	95	38	Average
			Letter-Word Identification	97	43	
	Reading Comprehension		Passage Comprehension	95	38	Average
			Reading Fluency	101	52	
Writing Ability	Mechanics	WJ III ACH	Spelling	91	28	Average
			Punctuation and Capitals	91	28	
			Editing	95	38	
	Written Expression	OWLS	Written Expression	98	45	Average
		WJ III ACH	Writing Fluency	101	54	
Mathematics	Calculation	WJ III ACH	Calculation	92	29	Average
			Math Fluency	86	18	Low Average
	Mathematics Reasoning		Applied Problems	100	49	Average

was assessed in the skill areas of basic reading and reading comprehension. He demonstrated Average ability to decode and recognize words, indicating that these skills are adequate to support reading comprehension. Boyd's ability to comprehend written material was also within the Average range, as was his ability to quickly (fluently) read and understand simple sentences.

To assess Boyd's oral language skills, he was administered the OWLS, which yields scores in the areas of listening comprehension and oral expression. Boyd scored overall in the Average range. Thus, he demonstrated that he is adequately able to engage in basic interpersonal communication, and is adequately able to understand basic oral communication. It is notable, however, that his performance on measures of crystallized ability, which are also measures of verbal ability, suggests that Boyd's command of abstract, academic language is not as well developed.

To assess Boyd's written language skills, he was administered subtests of the OWLS and tests of the WJ III ACH. Boyd demonstrated Average achievement in both basic mechanics and the ability to communicate in written form. In addition, Boyd's ability to produce grammatically correct simple sentences fluently under a time limit was also Average. When writing an essay, however, Boyd's concepts and ideas were better developed than his spelling and punctuation skills.

Boyd's mathematical skills were assessed in three areas: math fluency, math calculation, and mathematical reasoning. Boyd had difficulty quickly solving simple addition, subtraction, and multiplication problems, scoring in the

Low Average range. Fluency in basic mathematical operations depends upon thorough learning that automates the process. When given unlimited time, however, Boyd performed in the Average range on math computation, although he often used less efficient means to solve the problems. For example, when solving two-digit multiplication problems, he added numbers as opposed to utilizing times tables. Boyd also performed in the Average range on untimed mathematical reasoning. He worked slowly and often used concrete methods as opposed to underlying rules and automated processes.

SUMMARY

Boyd is a 13-year 6-month-old male in the seventh grade at Tuller Middle School. His parents are seeking strategies to help improve his school performance and his standardized test scores. Boyd has experienced no significant developmental or educational concerns that would have impacted his learning. Both at school and in the testing sessions, Boyd has presented as a polite, respectful child who is pleasant, focused, and cooperative. His teachers speak well of him regarding behavior and academics. Some also expressed that he has difficulties in certain areas, such as finding relevant information in text to use in an application or to derive a rule, and in using correct syntax and mechanics when writing.

Boyd's cognitive abilities affect his learning and have implications for instruction. His low-level processing, including short-term memory and processing speed, is adequate to allow efficient learning. His stores of acquired knowledge appear not to reflect his educational experiences and opportunities, and may not be adequate to easily support new learning. Boyd's higher-level processing was more varied, with strong skills in auditory processing, and adequate skills in the areas of deductive reasoning, visual processing, and retrieval of overlearned information. However, his inductive reasoning, his ability to add new knowledge to long-term memory stores, and his abstract, academic language skills were all below average. These areas interact and impact academic success.

Boyd's performances on tasks assessing receptive and expressive language, reading, written language, and mathematics reasoning were all in the Average range. However, Boyd demonstrated difficulty with fluent application of math skills. He had difficulty quickly executing simple math operations (procedural knowledge), identifying rules underlying number sequences (inductive reasoning), and did not demonstrate adequate knowledge of quantitative concepts (quantitative knowledge). Boyd's difficulties regarding associative memory and inductive reasoning appear to underlie his academic difficulties. He performs lower than expected on tests requiring specific factual information.

Boyd's pattern of performance is consistent with what is typically seen in students having learning disabilities. Therefore, he would greatly benefit from strategies and accommodations to support his learning style. It is notable that Boyd's superior schooling history, parental support, and past tutoring have had a tremendous effect on his academic functioning in school, for his grades are all above average in a competitive academic environment. He is no doubt a hard-working, motivated, and tenacious student. In addition, Boyd possesses superior social skills, which are an asset for him in the classroom. Through the utilization of his many strengths, coupled with appropriate accommodations and adaptations, he is likely to be successful in a supportive academic environment.

RECOMMENDATIONS

Due to weaknesses in cognitive processing, including associative memory and learning, inductive reasoning, and verbal ability, coupled with weaknesses in basic writing skills and mathematical calculation, Boyd is experiencing difficulty in certain aspects of school. The results of this evaluation should be reviewed by the Tuller Middle School mul-

tidisciplinary team to determine whether Boyd meets the criteria for Learning Disability according to the Pennsylvania Special Education Regulations. In addition, the following accommodations and adaptations are warranted:

1. Allow extended time on classroom and standardized tests.
2. Boyd's acquisition of knowledge may be best represented on alternative assessments that allow him to elaborate and explain his answers.
3. Provide or aid him in creating written outlines to prepare for tests.
4. Provide visual aids to help him understand concepts and organize information.
5. Allow the use of a calculator.
6. Have Boyd review key points orally.
7. Due to Boyd's weakness in associative memory functioning and factual knowledge, he would benefit from the following strategies.
   a) Use of verbal mediation with a partner to help Boyd find connections and link information to that which was previously learned;
   b) Have Boyd teach the information to someone else. This will compel him to find metaphors, analogies, and connections in an attempt to convey an understanding of the subject matter to the learner;
   c) Use of mnemonic strategies and acronyms to link and remember information;
   d) Additional drill and repetition of basic information will be necessary at a more intense level than an average student will require. Use of computer programs to drill Boyd until he has mastered basic skills to an automatic level may be useful; and
   e) The level of factual knowledge assessed on standardized tests is also quite high, so review of test preparation materials, especially vocabulary and math procedures that are known to be assessed, will be essential.

Due to Boyd's difficulty using inductive reasoning, he would benefit from the following strategies:

1. Boyd should be encouraged to consider and search consciously and verbally for underlying principles and rules.
2. Boyd should be talked through the process while a teacher models the derivation and application of rules to a new problem.
3. Different types of tests (e.g., essay, multiple-choice, true/false) require different types of strategies. Teach Boyd the structure of different types of tests and test-

taking strategies so that he may be more efficient and successful in test situations. Do not assume that Boyd can derive these strategies from experience alone.

4. Due to Boyd's lack of procedural knowledge regarding simple mathematical calculations, he would benefit from drill on basic calculations to automate the processes. Internet resources such as ArithmAttack, Arithm, and Automaths are helpful in this capacity. Many activities and ideas for lessons are available on http://archives. math.utk.edu/topics/arithmetic.html, its parent site, http://archives.math.utk.edu (University of Tennessee), and http://forum.swarthmore.edu/library.

5. Drill and practice games, such as Math Blaster, may also be helpful.

6. Because Boyd works hard, wants to succeed, and is frustrated at not living up to expectations, his achievements should be acknowledged often by his family.

Developed by Caroline Tisot, M.Ed., Patricia Feuerstein, Ph.D., and Catherine A. Fiorello, Ph.D., Temple University.

Cognitive Evaluation

Name: Jen Charbonneau   School: Stillwater Creek Middle School
Date of Birth: 03/02/1988   Date of Testing: 05/06/2001
Chronological Age: 13-2

REASON FOR REFERRAL

The purpose of the present evaluation was to determine Jen's eligibility for a gifted and talented education program and, depending on the outcome, to consider ways to adapt and enrich the curriculum to challenge her.

BACKGROUND INFORMATION

Jen lives with her parents, Drs. Judith and Marcus Charbonneau, both of whom teach at the state university, and her younger sister. Currently, Jen is completing her seventh-grade year at Stillwater Creek Middle School. Jen stated that she does not find middle school very engaging and is bored by the lecture approach used by most of her teachers. Her mother noted that the curriculum is not sufficiently challenging for Jen, that she has not been assigned any significant projects or reports this year, and she has already mastered the eighth- and ninth-grade math curriculums via a computer-based tutoring program through Stanford University.

TESTS ADMINISTERED AND BEHAVIORAL OBSERVATIONS

Jen was administered the Woodcock-Johnson III Tests of Cognitive Abilities (WJ III COG) (Tests 1–20). Testing was conducted in one 2 ½-hour session with two short breaks.

Jen was cooperative throughout the testing session. She was at ease and attentive to the tasks although she tended to get a bit silly at times. She responded promptly and confidently to test questions. She easily engaged in difficult tasks but adopted a somewhat casual attitude on tasks that she felt were too easy. The results of this evaluation are considered to be a valid representation of her current functioning although some scores may slightly underestimate her actual ability.

OVERALL COGNITIVE ABILITY

On the WJ III General Intellectual Ability (Extended), a measure of overall cognitive performance, Jen scored in the

Very Superior range. This score places her overall intellectual standing among her age-peers within the top 3 in 1000. Cluster scores indicated that Jen has cognitive abilities in the Very Superior range in the extent of her acquired knowledge, vocabulary, verbal reasoning at the individual word level, and inductive and deductive abstract reasoning for problem-solving. Her performance indicated abilities in the Superior range in thinking with visual designs and patterns, analyzing and manipulating the sounds of language, and rapidly scanning and making decisions regarding symbolic information. Although Jen's standard scores indicated High Average ability in short-term memory, the capacity to hold information in memory for use within a few seconds, her Relative Proficiency Indexes (RPI) on all short-term memory tests (Memory for Words, Numbers Reversed, Auditory Working Memory) indicated that on similar tasks, she would demonstrate 99% proficiency compared to her average classmates' 90%. Her only score in the Average range was in the ability to store and retrieve associations. This last finding is not considered educationally significant, and may not even be an accurate representation of her abilities in this area, as Jen demonstrates advanced abilities in academic tasks requiring storage and retrieval of diverse types of associations.

Although some of the cluster scores were composed of individual test scores that were significantly discrepant from each other, the lowest of Jen's scores were in the upper end of the Average range and, as noted above, do not seem to reflect even relative difficulties in Jen's performance in academic endeavors.

INTRA-COGNITIVE DISCREPANCIES

Jen demonstrated a strength, significantly above her other cognitive abilities, in Comprehension-Knowledge, suggesting particular facility in vocabulary knowledge, reasoning with word meanings, and acquisition of information about the environment based on daily activities. Only 2 out of 100 age-peers with the same predicted score (the average of her scores on the other cognitive clusters) would obtain a score as high or higher. Although not included in the calculation of discrepancies, Jen's best performance was on Executive

Processes (SS 160), a combination of abilities composed of planning ahead, flexibility in shifting mindset in solving problems, and ignoring distractors. Only 1 in 1000 students would have scored as high as or higher than she did.

SUMMARY AND CONCLUSIONS

Jen's performance on the WJ III Tests of Cognitive Abilities indicate very advanced cognitive functioning in almost all areas assessed. Given these findings and her high academic grades, she meets the criteria for the Gifted and Talented Education Program (GTEP) in this district. Class placement and appropriate curriculum for Jen will be determined at the next meeting of the GTEP team.

RECOMMENDATIONS

The following recommendations are offered for the consideration of this team:

1. Use "Curriculum Compacting" to teach content areas at a quicker pace (especially in the areas of social studies and math).
2. As Jen is particularly advanced in math (per her completion of the Stanford course), consider the possibility of transporting her to the high school to take advanced algebra next year.
3. Enroll Jen in the enriched language arts class for eighth grade.
4. In content area classes, use a contract learning approach to allow Jen to engage actively in the decision-making process and to participate in designing her course of study. Rather than have her doing all of the regular class assignments, give her the option to design some in-depth projects requiring more advanced research skills than might be expected of her classmates.
5. Provide enrichment activities for Jen. For example, have Jen research information on the computer and (a) find URL's to complete a project, (b) determine the accuracy of the information the sites provide, or (c) create a school website.
6. Provide Jen with rich field trip opportunities to have a hands-on experience with past, present, and future trends in art, music, history, or environmental issues.
7. Guide Jen into opportunities for leadership positions (e.g., peer editing, involvement on the school newspaper, student council).
8. Next year, ensure that Jen makes application to and takes the qualifying test for University High School.

Adapted from Jeannette Devlin, M.A.

COMPUSCORE VERSION 1.1B: SCORE REPORT

Name: Charbonneau, Jen
Date of Birth: 03/02/1988
Date of Testing: 05/06/2001

Age: 13 years, 2 months
Grade: 7.8
Sex: Female

TABLE OF SCORES: Woodcock-Johnson III Tests of Cognitive Abilities
Norms based on age 13-2

CLUSTER/Test	RAW	AE	EASY to DIFF		RPI	PR	SS (68% BAND)
GIA (Ext)		>24	20	>24	99/90	99.7	142 (139–144)
VERBAL ABILITY (Ext)		>25	>25	>25	100/90	99.9	146 (142–151)
THINKING ABILITY (Ext)		>22	19	>22	98/90	99	137 (132–142)
COG EFFICIENCY (Ext)		>21	17-0	>21	99/90	95	125 (120–129)
COMP-KNOWLEDGE (Gc)		>25	>25	>25	100/90	99.9	146 (142–151)
L-T RETRIEVAL (Glr)		>22	8-8	>22	93/90	73	109 (104–114)
VIS-SPATIAL THINK (Gv)		>25	>25	>25	98/90	97	128 (120–135)
AUDITORY PROCESS (Ga)		>25	>25	>25	98/90	97	129 (122–135)
FLUID REASONING (Gf)		>21	>21	>21	99/90	99	133 (126–139)
PROCESS SPEED (Gs)		>21	17-2	>21	99/90	94	123 (118–127)
SHORT-TERM MEM (Gsm)		>22	16-9	>22	99/90	86	116 (111–121)
PHONEMIC AWARE		>28	20	>28	98/90	95	125 (119–131)
WORKING MEMORY		>22	16-6	>22	99/90	91	120 (116–124)
BROAD ATTENTION		>21	17-9	>21	99/90	99	134 (130–138)
COGNITIVE FLUENCY		16-8	12-11	>22	96/90	75	110 (107–113)
EXEC PROCESSES		>20	>20	>20	100/90	>99.9	160 (150–170)
Verbal Comprehension		>24	22	>24	100/90	99.7	141 (136–147)
Visual-Auditory Learning	7-E	>19	9-3	>19	93/90	63	105 (99–111)
Spatial Relations	79-D	>25	>25	>25	99/90	97	128 (119–137)
Sound Blending	30	>26	>26	>26	100/90	98	130 (123–136)
Concept Formation	39-E	>21	>21	>21	100/90	97	129 (120–138)
Visual Matching	56-2	>23	19	>23	100/90	93	122 (116–127)
Numbers Reversed	17	19	16-1	>22	99/90	84	115 (110–120)
Incomplete Words	24	16-1	8-3	>33	92/90	61	104 (97–111)
Auditory Work Memory	32	>22	17-8	>22	99/90	92	121 (116–126)
Vis-Aud Learn—Delayed							
General Information		>40	>40	>40	100/90	99.9	145 (138–151)
Retrieval Fluency	87	>30	7-7	>30	93/90	86	116 (111–122)
Picture Recognition	54-D	>25	13-3	>25	96/90	81	113 (106–120)
Auditory Attention	41	>20	9-2	>20	93/90	69	108 (99–116)
Analysis-Synthesis	31-E	>20	>20	>20	99/90	96	127 (120–
Decision Speed	40	>20	15-11	>20	99/90	88	118 (112–123)
Memory for Worbds	19	>23	20	>23	99/90	81	113 (106–120)
Rapid Picture Naming	20	13-10	11-11	16-7	93/90	54	102 (99–104)
Planning		>28	>28	>28	100/90	>99.9	244 (180–300)
Pair Cancellation	66	>19	>19	>19	100/90	99	137 (135–140)

TABLE OF SCORES (*continued*)

DISCREPANCIES	STANDARD SCORES			DISCREPANCY		Significant at ± 1.50 SD (SEE)
	Actual	Predicted	Difference	PR	SD	
Intra-Cognitive						
COMP-KNOWLEDGE (*Gc*)	146	120	+26	98	+2.16	Yes
L-T RETRIEVAL (*Glr*)	109	128	−19	6	−1.55	Yes
VIS-SPATIAL THINK (*Gv*)	128	117	+11	79	+0.79	No
AUDITORY PROCESS (*Ga*)	129	119	+10	76	+0.70	No
FLUID REASONING (*Gf*)	133	123	+10	80	+0.86	No
PROCESS SPEED (*Gs*)	123	119	+4	62	+0.31	No
SHORT-TERM MEM (*Gsm*)	116	122	−6	32	−0.48	No
PHONEMIC AWARE	125	119	+6	68	+0.47	No
WORKING MEMORY	120	123	−3	41	−0.24	No

WJ III Cognitive Factors/Clusters by Level

SS Classification	SS Range	CHC Factors	Cognitive Performance, Clinical Clusters, and CHC Factors	
Very Superior	>130	Gc	Executive Processes	(160)
			Verbal Ability/Comprehension Knowledge	(146)
			Thinking Ability	(137)
			Broad Attention	(134)
		Gf	Fluid Reasoning	(133)
Superior	121–130	Gv Ga Gs	Auditory Processing	(129)
			Visual-Spatial Thinking	(128)
			Phonemic Awareness	(125)
			Cognitive Efficiency	(125)
			Processing Speed	(123)
High Average	111–120	Gsm	Working Memory	(120)
			Short-Term Memory	(116)
Average	90–110	Glr	Cognitive Fluency	(110)
			Long-Term Retrieval	(109)

Developed by Barbara Wendling, Dallas, TX

Available from Dumont, R., & Willis, J. O. (2001). WJ III Computer Template [Computer software]. Plattsburgh, NY: Authors [http://alpha.fdu.edu/psychology/WJIII_Computer.htm].

Educational Evaluation

Name: Josh Cloud
Birth Date: 7/10/77
Chronological Age: 13-11
Grade: 7.9

Grandmother: Mrs. Rachel Cloud
School: Callaway Middle School
Test Date: 5/29/91

REASON FOR REFERRAL

Josh was referred to an academic tutoring center for an evaluation by his grandmother, Mrs. Rachel Cloud. Mrs. Cloud was concerned about Josh's poor school grades. Josh has just failed most of his seventh-grade classes and retention has been recommended. Mrs. Cloud wanted an estimate of how far behind Josh was in school, whether or not he should be referred for a comprehensive evaluation in his school, and an opinion regarding the advantages and disadvantages of repeating seventh grade.

BACKGROUND INFORMATION

Josh has lived with his maternal grandmother since birth. His biological mother disappeared shortly after his birth and has not had contact with Josh or her mother since. Parental rights were terminated when Josh was 2 years old and Mrs. Cloud became the legal guardian for Josh. In an interview, Mrs. Cloud reported that Josh did not begin speaking single words until the age of 4. He received speech-language therapy for 2 years. By the time he entered kindergarten, Mrs. Cloud felt his speech was comparable to his peers'. Near the end of kindergarten, Josh contracted Neisseria meningitis. Although he recovered over a 2-month period, the brain inflammation from this type of bacterial meningitis could contribute to learning problems, hearing loss, and/or changes in vision. Mrs. Cloud stated results from an audiological screening and vision exam indicated normal hearing and vision within 6 months after his illness as well as 3 months prior to this evaluation. Presently, Mrs. Cloud describes Josh as a quiet child who appears to be able to make himself understood when he wishes. She further noted that he does not appear to listen very well, particularly when she is telling him something that he does not want to do.

Josh attended Johnson Elementary school. He was retained in fifth grade because he was behind in all subjects. This past year, in Liberty Middle School, he failed most of his courses, thus prompting the recommendation for an-

other retention. Mrs. Cloud commented that Josh had given up on school this year and had not turned in any homework assignments. In turn, she felt that his teachers had given up on him. Mrs. Cloud fears that repeating seventh grade will not solve the problem and will only contribute further to Josh's low self-esteem and dislike of school.

TESTS ADMINISTERED

Josh was administered the Woodcock-Johnson III Tests of Achievement, Standard battery, Form A (WJ III ACH). Testing was conducted in two sessions, 1 hour and 2 hours, respectively. The WJ III ACH was scored according to grade norms. Although Josh has been retained, grade norms, rather than age norms, were selected because the referral question requires information regarding academic achievement relative to Josh's current school placement and the academic requirements he will face at the next grade level.

BEHAVIORAL OBSERVATIONS

In general, Josh was attentive and cooperative throughout the testing session. On occasion, he showed a puzzled expression, indicating that he did not understand the test questions. He needed to have several questions repeated several times before he was able to respond. When test items were repeated, he was able to respond appropriately. At times, he appeared to be distracted, and on three occasions, he asked questions that were unrelated to the task. When asked about what subjects he liked in school, he responded, "None."

ACHIEVEMENT TEST RESULTS

In general, test scores indicate that Josh is achieving considerably below grade level (Low Average range) in all academic areas tested with no significant differences among the achievement areas. Josh's academic deficiencies are of particular concern when his Relative Proficiency Indexes are considered. On tasks similar to those on the Reading, Written Language, Math, and Oral Language clusters, Josh's accuracy would range from 45% to 63% success compared to 90% accuracy for average students of his grade.

Reading

Broad Reading includes a measure of word identification, a measure of rate, and a measure of comprehension. His RPI of 50/90 suggests that when average grade-mates are experiencing 90% accuracy, Josh will experience 50% accuracy. In attempting to pronounce words, Josh had particular difficulty on medial vowel sounds, vowel combinations, and consonant blends. When Josh had to identify missing words in a short passage, he read the item, shrugged his shoulders, and guessed. Many of Josh's responses indicated that he did not understand the concepts or vocabulary involved.

Broad Written Language

Broad Written Language includes a measure of spelling, a measure of writing fluency, and a measure of written expression. Josh's RPI of 45/90 suggests that when average grade-mates have 90% success on writing tasks, Josh will only have 45% success and will be performing at the frustration level. When asked to write, Josh did not seem to sustain his best effort. For example, when asked to produce sentences, he commented that his hand was tired from writing and he then began to write short, incomplete sentences. When asked to write a short paragraph about something he wanted to do, he wrote: "Get on my ATC, get my dog a lot of dog food, and then move to Alaska so I wouldn't have to go to school."

Mathematics

Broad Mathematics includes a measure of computation, a measure of automaticity with math facts, and a measure of problem solving. As with other areas of achievement, Josh's RPI of 63/90 indicates that he will be frustrated when given grade-level mathematical tasks. Josh's limited mastery of mathematical operations and applications was also apparent in his responses. For example, when asked to solve a long division problem, such as $126 \div 42$, Josh pointed to the 2 in 42 and asked if he was supposed to divide 126 by the 2.

Oral Language

When compared to others at his grade level, Josh's Oral Language RPI was 60/90. He would have 60% success on oral language tasks when average grade-mates are having 90% success. His performance was better on tasks that depended more upon general knowledge and vocabulary than on those requiring listening and memory. When attempting to retell a short passage that he had just heard, he hit his head with his palm and said, "I'm supposed to tell that all *back* to you?" He then asked if he could listen to the story again.

RECOMMENDATIONS

Because Josh is significantly below grade level in all academic areas, retention is not an appropriate option, as it would not solve the problem. Instructional materials at a seventh-grade level would still be too difficult for Josh. Appropriate instructional materials for Josh in reading and math would be early fourth-grade level; in written language, mid-third grade level; and in oral language, mid-fourth grade level. Additionally, another retention would be damaging to his self-esteem. Instead, Mrs. Cloud should request help from district personnel to find an appropriate educational placement for Josh in a program that is designed to accommodate students at diverse performance levels and provides hands-on and visual activities as part of the curriculum. A critical aspect to any solution to this problem must answer the question, "What will school personnel do *differently* to alter the outcome?" In order to plan the most effective educational program, the following recommendations are made:

1. Request that a full evaluation be conducted either by school personnel or a private agency. This evaluation should include a thorough assessment of intellectual and cognitive abilities and receptive and expressive language abilities. In addition, the evaluation should attempt to determine whether his difficulties with listening and following directions might be related to poor memory or, possibly, auditory processing.
2. During a quiet time, ask Josh if he is aware of having difficulty hearing during any of his daily situations and if it is difficult for him to hear or make sense of what some-

one is saying when there is competing or background noise (e.g., other people talking, cafeteria noise). This will not negate the necessity of a more in-depth hearing evaluation but may give you valuable information to share with any evaluators.

3. Despite Josh's normal results on the audiological screening done 3 months ago, have his hearing thoroughly tested by an educational audiologist who regularly sees children who have had meningitis. Request that the evaluation include pure tone testing and speech discrimination testing in each ear and bilaterally. Request testing for a central auditory processing disorder.

4. A professional knowledgeable about Attention Deficit/Hyperactivity Disorder should obtain a complete developmental history and profile of current behaviors either to rule out ADHD as a contributing factor to Josh's learning difficulties or to make a further referral to a developmental pediatrician or psychologist.

5. After a full evaluation, request a conference to discuss any special education services for which Josh might be eligible, including what accommodations and compensations can be provided in the general education classroom for a student who is several years below grade level in academic functioning.

6. If Josh is not eligible for special education, Mrs. Cloud may wish to hire an educational therapist to tutor Josh.

7. At the beginning of each school year, Mrs. Cloud and Josh should meet with his teachers and share their concerns and plan strategies to help Josh increase classroom success.

8. These types of evaluations will take some time to set up and complete. In the meantime, try to improve what might be Josh's "selective" hearing with a behavioral strategy. Before you speak with him, call him by name and direct him to look at your face. Begin speaking only when he has done so. If he begins to do what you have told him within 30 seconds, or at the time you have both agreed on, fine. If not, assign him a second chore to be done immediately after the first one. You might write a list of minor chores (e.g., cleaning and refilling the cat's water, sweeping the kitchen), write each one on a slip of paper, and put them into a "job jar." Then, whenever Josh "forgets" or "did not hear" what he has just watched and listened to you say to him, have him choose a job from the "job jar," then do the first task you assigned and immediately after, the second. Explain this system clearly to Josh before initiating it so that he is well aware of why you are asking him to look at you and what the consequences of ignoring or forgetting are. Just having him look at your face before speaking to him may solve the problem.

Josh's instructional needs must be addressed immediately to ensure that he does not quit trying and that he progresses academically. With a highly structured teaching situation and with appropriate activities and materials modified to his performance levels, he should make progress, gain self-confidence, and renew his interest in learning. Josh's progress should be monitored closely by his grandmother and his teachers in the following school year.

Psychological Report

Name:	Paul Matthews		Ethnicity:	Hispanic
Birth Date:	8/22/87		School/Grade:	APA/9th
Age at Evaluation:	14 years, 4 months		Primary Home Language:	English
Evaluation Date:	December 22, 2001		Primary Student Language:	English

REASON FOR REFERRAL

Although he is an intellectually capable student, Paul currently is failing several classes at Westfield High School. His teachers referred him for an evaluation after a conference with his parents. They are concerned about his weak academic performance and lack of effort, and question whether there is a "processing deficit" of some kind. The parents asked specifically about an auditory processing problem.

BACKGROUND INFORMATION

Information Provided by the Parents

Paul currently resides with his father, Stan Matthews, and stepmother, Arlene Hoffman. Although Paul's parents are divorced, he maintains a close relationship with his mother, who lives two blocks away. The Developmental History/Home Study Questionnaire was completed by Paul's father. There are no known medical conditions and Paul's general health appears good.

Paul was adopted when he was 2 days old. Mr. Matthews reports that as an infant he was extremely active. He spent an extra year in preschool because of difficulties sitting still and participating in groups, and because he still appeared "too young to go to kindergarten." School history indicates that until this year, Paul has attended private schools that have a small student/teacher ratio, a somewhat individualized curriculum, and frequent home communication. According to his father, Paul was successful in elementary school and "held his own" in middle school, but at Westfield High, his grades have deteriorated considerably. Paul also is reported to have been going to outside counseling over the past couple of months. English is the language of Paul's home and it is his first and only language.

Performance in the General Curriculum

Paul began attending Westfield Middle School in seventh grade. His final eighth grade marks ranged from A's (Drama) to B's (Spanish I) and C's (English, Geography, Science, and Math). At the end of eighth grade, a teacher wrote that Paul should not be considered for continuation in the Honors Program in high school unless he made significant strides in maturity. Now in ninth grade, Paul is doing even less than he was previously and this has caused several course failures. The latest grade report showed a first semester GPA of 1.43. Despite poor grades, teachers report that he is a personable student who seems interested and participates in class discussions. On the other hand, Paul is somewhat distractible in the classroom and he needs to be redirected often; sometimes he does do the work, other times he does not begin to make an effort. Teachers uniformly observe that Paul seems capable but does not appear to get gratification from success in school—it just does not seem very important to him.

Previous Standardized Test Results

The Arizona State Achievement Test results in Spring 2000 showed that Paul's score of 512 and 500 in reading and writing, respectively, met the standards, while his score of 478 in mathematics approached the standard. On the eighth-grade Stanford—9, taken in April 2000, Paul earned a total reading score that exceeded 80% of adolescents at the eighth-grade level nationally, his total mathematics score surpassed 87%, and his total written language score exceeded 95%.

Vision and Hearing

Paul passed school vision and hearing screenings in October 2000.

Effects of Culture, Educational Disadvantage, and Limited English Proficiency

Paul is a Hispanic adolescent who is fully functional in oral and receptive English; in fact he has Superior verbal ability. He has regularly attended school and he has had adequate instruction in the basic academic areas. There is no evidence that educational disadvantage, environmental disadvantage, or cultural factors are influences that primarily account for his academic difficulties.

BEHAVIORAL OBSERVATIONS

Evaluation

During the evaluation, Paul put forth good effort and the results are viewed as being an accurate estimate of his current abilities. He was socially appropriate and respectful of the examiner and the testing process. Paul showed a good sense of humor and sophisticated verbal abilities to describe his feelings and interests about a variety of topics. He described a major problem for himself as putting things off and then not getting them done. Also, he reports that he does not know how to go about studying for tests, but he believes he has the ability to resolve these issues better than he has so far this year.

Classroom

Paul was observed in his American Literature class during a time when the teacher handed back essays and vocabulary tests. While this was happening and after the teacher began giving directions, Paul talked to a peer nearby and he did not get out his materials with his classmates. Paul looked at the teacher and listened momentarily. He called out an example after she gave one herself, but while she was getting a text for him to use he talked so loudly to a classmate that he could be heard across the room. There were several additional instances of students referring to portions of the assignment as the teacher responded to questions; however, Paul continued to talk with a classmate. The class ended with the teacher emphasizing the importance of completing their notebooks for collection the following week. Paul whistled and left the room. The boy he had been talking to asked the teacher if he could be moved to a different desk. Analysis of 30-second interval data over the 50-minute period showed that Paul was on task 60% of the time in comparison to a randomly selected comparison student who was on task 91%.

MEASURES USED

Stanford-Binet Intelligence Scale, Fourth Edition
Woodcock-Johnson III Tests of Cognitive Abilities
    (WJ III COG) Tests 4, 7, 9, 14, 20

Woodcock-Johnson III Tests of Achievement
    (WJ III ACH) Tests 1, 5–6, 8–11, 13, 17–18
Behavior Assessment System for Children (BASC):
    Adolescent form
        Parent Rating Scales: Respondents: Father,
            Stepmother
        Teacher Rating Scales: Respondents: Biology
            teacher, English teacher
Behavioral observations, record review, interview

INTERPRETATION

Evaluation Design and Test Considerations

Paul's cognitive profile, general adjustment, and academic skills was investigated as one source of information for educational planning in conjunction with teacher and parent observations, educational history, and present levels of academic performance. The Partial Composite IQ score of the Stanford-Binet Intelligence Scale was used for contrast with Paul's achievement to determine if a severe discrepancy exists between ability and achievement, required by this state to qualify a student for special educational services in the area of learning disabilities. The WJ III COG and WJ III ACH were used to provide a cognitive profile for investigation of the existence of a processing deficit and the possible influence on achievement. '

The Stanford-Binet was selected for administration because it clearly separates verbal and nonverbal intelligence, and it is a "power test" where speed of performance is not as important as other measures. The WJ III COG was chosen to investigate three specific cognitive domains that were of special interest in Paul's case. Information concerning his attention capacity (overall ability to process and attend to stimuli), working memory (ability to hold and manipulate stimuli in immediate memory), and auditory processing (phonemic awareness and sound sensitivity/integration under distracting conditions) was pertinent since attention problems were observed and his parents questioned auditory processing as a possible reason for them.

Test performance is reported as standard scores (SS), verbal classifications of standard score ranges (SS ± 1 SEM: Very Low, Low, Low Average, Average, High Average, Superior, Very Superior), and percentile ranks (PR). Achievement scores are also reported as grade equivalents (GE).

Intellectual/Cognitive Performance

Paul earned a Stanford-Binet Partial Composite IQ score of 122±4, which surpassed 92% of adolescents his age and falls within the Superior range. His ability to express his intelligence verbally and understand conceptual information communicated orally surpassed 97% of his age-peers on the Verbal Reasoning factor (131±5 standard score). Paul was equally proficient in precisely defining increasingly difficult words and using advanced language to explain the fundamental reasons accounting for common social practices. A superior learning channel for Paul is listening to information explained orally and then verbally demonstrating his understanding, assuming requisite interest and effort at the time of presentation. Not only did he fully comprehend the topic, he extended the ideas to reach new conclusions and insights.

Paul's nonverbal intelligence, the ability to use higher-order nonverbal reasoning to organize complex visual relationships, surpassed 71% of adolescents his age on the Visual/Nonverbal Reasoning factor (109±5 standard score). He was successful at recalling visual patterns and working with problems that involved flexible thinking to integrate shapes into a general pattern. Although Paul's nonverbal problem solving is not as proficient as his Superior to Very Superior oral/verbal reasoning, it is nevertheless above average.

Three cognitive domains were of special interest in Paul's case: his attentional capacity, working memory, and sound sensitivity and integration (e.g., phonemic awareness). Broad Attention requires aspects of short-term memory, sequencing, and the ability to attend to stimuli when interference exists. Working Memory is related to the effort and mental focus required to plan, hold, and manipulate stimuli in immediate memory so that it does not erode. Auditory Processing requires a person to be able to hear, integrate, and discern elementary sound units as well as discern auditory information in distracting conditions. The pattern of results for these three cognitive domains was that Paul consistently performed in the Superior to Very Superior range. His Broad Attention cluster on the Woodcock-Johnson III exceeded 95% of adolescents his age (SS 124); Working Memory surpassed 97% of adolescents his age (SS 127); and his Auditory Processing exceeded 98% of a national sample of students (SS 132). These results suggest that Paul is able to sustain attention on specific tasks for a short period of time. These scores should not be interpreted as negating the existence of an attention-related disorder, however, in that the ability to recognize when attention is needed and the appropriate target of attention, and the ability to self-initiate attention and to sustain it as long as necessary, are not measured by these tests.

Academic Performance

Achievement testing on the Woodcock-Johnson III shows Above Average to Superior range academic skills. Paul scored beyond 96% of adolescents his age (SS 127, GE >18.0) on the Basic Reading Skills cluster, which is composed of sight word recognition and word attack skills. He scored beyond 97% of age-peers on the Reading Comprehension cluster, which required him to supply a missing word in a complex passage as well as to provide synonyms and antonyms for printed words, and to complete verbal analogies. On the Mathematics Skills cluster, including automaticity of math facts and computation, Paul surpassed 76% of students his age (SS 111, GE 12.0). On the Math Reasoning cluster, including solving multiple-step word problems as well as recall of formulae, symbols, and specific processes, Paul surpassed 93% of his peers (SS 122, GE >18.0). On the Written Expression cluster, composed of tasks assessing speed of written sentence formulation and brief written content, Paul scored beyond 79% of adolescents his age (SS 112, GE 12.9).

BEHAVIOR RATING SCALES

Parent Rating Scales

On the BASC, Mr. Matthews rated the following behaviors as significant concerns: lying to get out of trouble, rapidly changing moods, needing too much supervision, and tendency to act without thinking. In contrast, his ratings indicated that Paul has lots of ideas, compliments others, and has no trouble being social or making new friends. Nevertheless, the extent of his behavior problems at home resulted in a Behavioral Symptoms Index (BSI, composed of the Hyperactivity, Aggression, Anxiety, Depression, Atypicality, and Attention Problems subscales) that surpassed 91% of his peers; only 9% of adolescents in the norm sample had parent ratings as high (negatively), related to attention and adjustment problems.

Ms. Hoffman's ratings differed to the extent that she did not observe any hyperactivity. Like Paul's father, she noted instances of lying and frequent trouble concentrating. While Paul is "sometimes" creative and "often" polite, his stepmother's ratings resulted in a BSI surpassing 89% of his peers. Both Paul's father and stepmother rated his Leadership skills as significantly low. They responded "never" or "sometimes" regarding the characteristics: good at getting people to work together, self-starter, usually chosen as a leader, energetic, and involved in organized social clubs or groups. For someone of Paul's superior cognitive and academic skills, his ratings in Leadership are highly atypical.

Teacher Rating Scales

To obtain a comprehensive measure of Paul's school behavior, his ninth-grade Science and English teachers completed the BASC Teacher Rating Scale. The Science teacher's ratings supported the evaluator's impression of an adolescent who is not depressed, overanxious, or demonstrating any significant learning problems. Conversely, he "often" is distractible, rushes through assigned work, is overactive, bothers other students, and demonstrates poor study skills. Paul's BSI score surpassed 88% of adolescents his age nationally. This score falls within the "at-risk" range (85% and above), suggesting behavioral problems in the classroom that require further investigation and monitoring.

Paul's English teacher also indicated that Paul shows no significant symptoms of depression or learning problems. In contrast, she rated Paul as "almost always" demonstrating behaviors that comprise the domains of attention problems, hyperactivity, and anxiety. These behaviors include bothering others who are working, frequently seeking attention, difficulty waiting his turn, maintaining he is not good at something, and often seeming nervous. Paul's BSI score surpassed 95% of adolescents his age nationally, which falls within the "clinically significant" range (95% and above), suggesting a severe behavioral problem in the classroom.

Ratings provided by Paul's father, stepmother, Science teacher, and English teacher indicate that he has behaviors consistent with the symptoms of Attention Deficit Hyperactivity Disorder (ADHD) and to an extent that they represent significant impediments to his functioning in those environments.

ABILITY/ACHIEVEMENT DISCREPANCY

None of Paul's achievement test standard scores were significantly below the predicted level. In fact, he shows a pat-

tern of High Average to Superior academic achievement, language development, and cognitive abilities although these qualities are not reflected in his school grades.

SUMMARY AND CONCLUSIONS

This evaluation indicates that among Paul's learning-related strengths is overall school-related intelligence that surpasses 92% of adolescents his age across the United States. Paul has well-developed higher-order intelligence, and his analytical reasoning suggests that he is capable of solving sophisticated problems and understanding very advanced topics. Paul far exceeds his peers in learning activities calling for verbal comprehension and conceptual reasoning. Moreover, Paul surpasses 96% of adolescents nationally in the development of his reading skills, and written expression and mathematics are High Average to Superior. This evaluation found no consistent pattern of cognitive weakness suggestive of a learning disability, information processing problem, or academic deficits.

Paul's major difficulty is not his knowledge, his conceptual understanding, or his ability to learn through conventional instructional approaches. Rather, the issues appear to be the consistency of both Paul's mental availability for learning and his application of knowledge and skills (e.g., maintaining attention in class, reflective work, completing assignments). The results of this evaluation indicate that Paul has many behaviors consistent with ADHD. Moreover, these behaviors are significantly more severe than in a national sample of adolescents his age, requiring him to put forth more energy than his peers to maintain his concentration, to plan and manage time, to persevere on learning-related tasks, and self-monitor his learning/work process. Paul meets the DSM-IV criteria for Attention Deficit Hyperactivity Disorder, combined type.

ELIGIBILITY QUESTIONS

Eligibility for special educational services, modifications, and/or accommodations requires the Multidisciplinary Team to consider three criteria:

1. Is there indication of a diagnosable disability?

Processing weaknesses and ADHD are relevant considerations for eligibility for specialized services under Specific Learning Disability and Other Health Impaired, respectively, under the Individuals with Disabilities Education Act (IDEA). Either may also qualify as a handicapping condition under Section 504 of the Rehabilitation Act of 1973 (Section 504). This evaluation suggests that Paul does not have cognitive processing deficits. His behaviors, however, symptomatic of ADHD, do appear to be significantly impacting his ability to participate fully in his education. Specifically, Paul appears limited in his attention in class, in his inhibition of inappropriate behaviors (e.g., disturbing other students by talking during a teacher-directed activity), and in his initiation of tasks in a timely manner both at home and at school.

2. Does a disability significantly impact educational performance?

Paul's school grades are considerably lower than his performance on standardized cognitive and academic measures. This discrepancy appears directly related to Paul's behaviors, consistent with ADHD, that significantly interfere with his completion of and the quality of his schoolwork. The underlying cognitive weaknesses related to ADHD reduce his cognitive vigilance and mental availability for learning. This, in turn, reduces the educational benefit he receives from school, contributes to lower grades, and decreases the likelihood that he will continue to put forth effort in school. The pattern of a downward spiral is already evident.

3. Does the student require a uniquely designed program of special instruction in order to make reasonable educational progress?

Current evaluation results, background information, and behavioral observations suggest that Paul also does not appear to need a special instructional program for academic progress. While he shows very serious underperformance, his academic abilities suggest that, if his attention is focused and he is monitoring his work processes, he obtains good benefit from the type of instruction offered at Westfield and in his previous schools. To minimize the impediments posed by his attentional and behavioral difficulties and to actualize his ability in school performance, however, he may require behavioral training and accommodations. The Multidisciplinary Team will make the final decision regarding Paul's eligibility for special education services and/or accommodations under the guidelines of IDEA and Section 504, and the necessity of either for Paul to make reasonable educational progress. (Paul was receiving ac-

commodations under a 504 Plan pending the results of this evaluation.)

RECOMMENDATIONS

Recommendations for the School

1. If possible, schedule a study hall at the end of the school day in which Paul can start his homework under the supervision of the study hall teacher. If a tutor is hired, consider allowing him or her to meet with Paul in school during that time.
2. Employ a behavioral intervention to help Paul develop control over his attention to task, his monitoring of work quality, and his recognition of the rights of others to work without interruption. A summary of the Self-Management Strategy for Improving Adolescent Behavior is attached.

Recommendations for the Parents

1. Make an appointment with Paul's physician or a physician with specific expertise in ADHD regarding this diagnosis and treatment options, including medical management. Previous to the appointment, send a copy of this report.
2. Seek regular, in-depth counseling for Paul for the purposes of: (a) facilitating an understanding of ADHD, the effect it has on him, and the responses he has developed over the years; (b) developing techniques for behavioral self-management; (c) assisting him in beginning to actualize his superior abilities; (d) supporting him in making more effective personal choices; (e) encouraging him in putting forth more effort. Periodic family participation in counseling would improve benefit for all of them.
3. Hire a tutor to work with Paul regularly and frequently (ideally three times a week). The tutor would communicate with Paul's teachers, help him prepare for tests, and teach him functional study habits, organizational skills, and time management.
4. Set aside a regular time for Paul to work on homework and, if possible, a place where he can work without distractions but where his parents can oversee his work processes.

SCORES

Stanford-Binet Intelligence Scale: Fourth Edition (M = 100, SD = 15)

FACTOR/Subtest	SS	PR	Standard Score Range
Vocabulary	130		
Comprehension	126		
VERBAL REASONING	131 ± 5	97	Superior to Very Superior
Pattern Analysis	108		
Bead Memory	108		
VISUAL/NONVERBAL REASONING	109 ± 5	71	Average to Above Average
ABILITY SCORE (IQ)	122 ± 8	92	Superior

Woodcock-Johnson III

CLUSTER/Test	SS	PR	Standard Score Range
Numbers Reversed	129	97	
Auditory Working Memory	117	87	
Auditory Attention	110	74	
Pair Cancellation	100	50	
WORKING MEMORY	127	97	Superior
BROAD ATTENTION	124	95	Superior (all tests)
Sound Blending	132	98	
Auditory Attention	110	74	
AUDITORY PROCESSING	132	98	Superior to Very Superior

Woodcock-Johnson III Tests of Achievement (Form A)

CLUSTER/Test	SS	PR	GE
Letter-Word Identification	127	96th	>18.0
Word Attack	120	91st	>18.0
BASIC READING SKILLS	127	96th	>18.0
Reading Vocabulary	128	97th	>18.0
Passage Comprehension	116	81st	>18.0
READING COMPREHENSION	127	97th	>18.0
Calculation	112	78th	12.9
Math Fluency (Speed)	105	62nd	10.2
MATH CALCULATION SKILLS	111	76th	12.0
Quantitative Concepts	129	97th	>18.0
Applied Problems	116	86th	>18.0
MATH REASONING	122	93rd	>18.0
Writing Samples	118	88th	17.7
Writing Fluency (Speed)	107	69th	11.4
WRITTEN EXPRESSION	112	79th	12.9

Behavior Assessment System for Children (BASC)

BASC Parent Rating Scale	Father		Step-mother	
COMPOSITE/Scale	*T* Score	Percentile	*T* Score	Percentile
Hyperactivity	63	90	52	62
Aggression	47	45	50	56
Conduct Problems	70	95	66	92
EXTERNALIZING PROBLEMS	62	88	57	80
Anxiety	48	47	50	59
Depression	68	94	55	75
Somatization	41	15	52	67
INTERNALIZING PROBLEMS	53	68	53	68
Social Skills	46	34	40	16
Leadership	37	11	37	11
ADAPTIVE SKILLS	41	19	37	12
Atypicality	63	90	72	96
Withdrawal	44	30	57	79
Attention Problems	73	98	76	99
BEHAVIORAL SYMPTOMS INDEX	64	91	63	89

BASC Teacher Rating Scale	Biology teacher		English teacher	
COMPOSITE/Scale	*T* Score	Percentile	*T* Score	Percentile
Hyperactivity	75	97	77	98
Aggression	64	91	63	89
Conduct Problems	63	91	44	25
EXTERNALIZING PROBLEMS	69	94	63	88
Anxiety	42	22	71	96
Depression	42	13	59	87
Somatization	49	63	49	63
INTERNALIZING PROBLEMS	43	30	61	87
Social Skills	42	1	47	41
Leadership	44	3	43	26
Study Skills	38	13	41	22
ADAPTIVE SKILLS	41	20	43	28
Attention Problems	71	97	77	99
Learning Problems	53	67	59	82
SCHOOL PROBLEMS	63	88	69	95
Atypicality	64	91	51	69
Withdrawal	44	31	40	11
BEHAVIORAL SYMPTOMS INDEX	62	88	71	95

Note. With the exception of Adaptive Skills, *T* scores of 60–69 indicate that the subject is "at-risk" regarding the corresponding behavioral category (e.g., Hyperactivity, Depression) and requires close monitoring. *T* scores of 70 and above indicate clinically significant (severe) problems needing immediate attention. On the Adaptive Skills subscale, scores below 40 designate "at risk" and scores of 30 and below designate "clinical significance." The Behavior Symptoms Index (BSI) is the best global indicator of an adolescent's behavioral functioning.

Educational Evaluation

Name: Steven Parker   School: Py Charter
Date of Birth: 07-29-86   Dates of Testing: 03-29-02, 03-30-02
Age: 15 Years, 8 Months   Grade: 9.7

REASON FOR REFERRAL

Steven was referred for testing by his teacher who is concerned about his low academic skills, especially in reading and writing, as well as his slow rate of progress. She was also concerned about the upcoming state standardized testing and wondered if Steven would benefit from additional time. Throughout his elementary school years, Steven's standardized test results have been low and have consistently indicated stronger math than reading skills. This is Steven's first referral for a formal educational evaluation.

HISTORY AND BACKGROUND INFORMATION

Steven is a 15-year-old Native American male who belongs to the Yaqui Tribe. His first language is English, although he understands bits of Spanish, and Yoeme, the indigenous language of the Yaquis. He lives on the Yaqui Reservation with his natural parents and two adopted female siblings. Steven reported that the two girls, ages 4 and 6 years, were adopted 2 years ago because "their mom was doing drugs on the 'res' and their dad was in prison." Steven's own prenatal, infancy, and childhood histories seem unremarkable, and his mother reported that he achieved developmental milestones at normal rates. Steven's father is a security guard for a local business and his mother is a secretary in the Human Resources Department for the Nation. Mr. Parker never completed high school. Mrs. Parker is a high school graduate and very much wants her son to be one too. Steven reported that he gets along well with them both, although he and his mother argue, usually about doing chores around the house. Steven said, "I try to help her sometimes, but mostly I'm too lazy and she has to keep reminding me." He described himself as being "kick-back," shy, and sensitive. He mentioned that he cries easily, although the last time he remembers crying was more than a year ago when some neighborhood dogs killed his kitten. Steven said that he is troubled by negative thoughts, mostly that he is "stupid." He tells himself, "I can't do it" and "I don't want to do it." Steven feels that these thoughts are harmful and would like to stop them. He said he used to worry about money but he "got rid of that." When asked whether he could apply that

same strategy to these other negative thoughts, Steven replied, "I could do it, but I can't put my heart on it yet."

Steven thinks that the quality of his life would improve if he could drop out of school. He currently attends a small ungraded high school classroom of 17 students, ages 14 to 21 years old, in a local charter school. The school offers a self-paced, prescriptive learning program that focuses on remediating deficiencies in basic reading, math and writing skills through individualized course work. Steven likes the school because it is close to his house and because the daily sessions are only 4 hours long. He generally dislikes the academic work, although he doesn't mind math and says he enjoys writing. He said that since he's been at this school, he has been trying to learn for the first time in his educational career. Steven has been working with a volunteer tutor 3 hours per week. Prior to the charter school, Steven attended an elementary and middle school near the Reservation. Of his tenure there, Steven said, "I was bad." Pressed for more information, Steven said he never paid attention, ditched frequently, wouldn't do his work, and didn't like the superior attitude of the teachers. He barely passed and thinks they probably should not have graduated him. He didn't go on to the local high school as many of his friends did. He said, "It would have been too hard anyway."

ASSESSMENT STRATEGY

Steven was administered selected tests from the Woodcock-Johnson III Tests of Cognitive Abilities (WJ III COG) (Tests 1–7 and 11–17) and Woodcock-Johnson III Tests of Achievement (WJ III ACH) (Tests 1–22). Testing was completed in two 2-hour sessions over 2 days. The tests were scored according to grade norms. A complete set of WJ III scores is appended to this report. Within the narrative, discussion of Steven's performance will focus on standard score ranges (SS) and Relative Proficiency Indexes (RPI). The standard score ranges are shown in Table 1.

Table 1. WJ III Score Ranges

SS	Below 70	70–79	80–89	90–110	111–120	121–130	Above 130
Range	Very Low	Low	Low Average	Average	High Average	Superior	Very Superior

Table 2.   Instructional Implications of RPIs

RPI	0/90 to 3/90	3/90 to 24/90	24/90 to 67/90	67/90 to 82/90	82/90 to 95/90	95/90 to 98/90
Instructional Implication	Impossible	Extremely Difficult	Very Difficult	Difficult	Manageable	Easy
Instructional Levels	Frustration 0/90 to 74/90				Instructional 75/90 to 96/90	Independent 97/90 to 100/90

The RPI is a qualitative measure indicating Steven's expected level of proficiency on tasks similar to those on the test, compared to the proficiency of average grade-peers. For example, an RPI of 25/90 indicates that when average grade-peers experience 90% proficiency on a task, the student will experience only 25% proficiency. The instructional implications represented by the RPIs are shown in Table 2.

For the purposes of this evaluation, the lowest three categories (Very Difficult, Extremely Difficult, Impossible) are collapsed, as any degree of task challenge from Very Difficult to Impossible will cause serious problems in learning. Standard scores and RPIs give different types of information and, as such, do not always correspond with each other. For example, a student's performance on a test may place him within the Average range compared to other students in his grade although he still may not have the proficiency to find the task manageable at grade level.

Further indications of appropriate instructional levels in academic achievement may be described as grade equivalents (GE). The GE is the grade level of whatever group in the norm sample has a median raw score that is the same as Steven's. So, if Steven's raw score on a test is 10, and the normative group having a median raw score of 10 on that test is in the second month of sixth grade, Steven's GE on that test would be 6.2.

Steven also was administered the Nelson Denny Reading Test and several passages from the Qualitative Reading Inventory—3 (QRI-3).

BEHAVIORAL OBSERVATIONS

Steven already had developed a good relationship with the test examiner, who is employed by the charter school he attends. He appeared to be fairly comfortable with the testing situation. He did mention that he was very nervous about it the night before. He showed good effort, although on a few questions he appeared to respond quickly and seemed satisfied to guess at some items rather than taking the time to work them out. When asked if he was putting forth his best effort, Steven replied in the affirmative. On tests that involved writing, Steven's response style was very slow and steady, something that is normal for him according to his teacher. He

sat very still, and when required to circle items or write sentences, he did so slowly, even when he was aware that the test was timed. Steven tended to slump over when writing, almost as if he were trying to hide his work. When questioned about his posture he said, "I always work this way."

COGNITIVE TESTING

Steven's General Intellectual Ability (GIA-Ext), as measured by the WJ III COG, is in the Low Average range; however, because his scores on the tests that comprise this measure are so widely scattered (SS 70 to 118), one score or score range does not represent his general intelligence. Rather, a profile of strengths and weaknesses within his cognitive and oral language abilities more accurately explains past academic difficulties, realistic expectations, and recommendations for future instruction.

Steven demonstrated a clear strength in visual–spatial thinking, scoring in the High Average range in the ability to think with and remember designs and patterns. His RPI indicated that similar tasks would be easy for him.

Steven scored well within the Average range and demonstrated proficiency in:

- Applying a given set of rules to solve problems (deductive reasoning) based on visual patterns (Analysis-Synthesis, RPI 80/90);
- Understanding and recalling spoken information presented in narrative form (Story Recall, RPI 90/90; Oral Comprehension, RPI 80/90);
- Learning, storing, and retrieving from memory associations between familiar words and unfamiliar symbols within a language context (Visual-Auditory Learning, RPI 90/90);
- Holding in immediate awareness a variety of unrelated elements, while reorganizing them into categories (Auditory Working Memory, RPI 90/90);
- Discriminating between speech sounds in similar-sounding words against a background of noise (Auditory Attention, RPI 86/90);
- Blending individual sounds together to make a word (Sound Blending, RPI 87/90).

Steven demonstrated a variety of abilities within the Low Average range and into the lower end of the Average range. The RPIs indicated that similar classroom tasks would be at his frustration level:

- Short-term memory: the ability to hold information in immediate awareness and repeat it to prevent its erosion in memory. Steven had considerably more difficulty re-ordering numbers while holding them in mind (Numbers Reversed, RPI 56/90) than mentally rehearsing strings of words in the order given (Memory for Words, RPI 73/90);
- Expressive vocabulary: knowledge of the names of objects (Picture Vocabulary, RPI 68/90);
- Inductive reasoning: the ability to look at and analyze the elements of a problem and figure out the rules by which it was constructed (Concept Formation, RPI 32/90);
- Holding in mind multiple-step instructions for a task, incorporating complex syntax and linguistic concepts (e.g., temporal, spatial, exception) (Understanding Directions, RPI 70/90);
- Rapidly naming pictures of common objects (Rapid Picture Naming, RPI 57/90);

Based on the above RPIs and his performance within the Low Average standard score range, Steven will have particular difficulty with mentally reordering numbers, inductive reasoning, and *rapidly* retrieving *specific* words from memory. In contrast, although Retrieval Fluency bridged the Low and Low Average ranges, Steven appears to be proficient (RPI 84/90) in retrieving words from memory within a familiar category (e.g., clothing, food), possibly because this affords him a choice among a wider range of responses rather than having to retrieve a specific word.

Steven's standard scores place the following cognitive abilities in the Very Low and Low ranges when compared with other ninth-graders. His RPIs indicate that he will find tasks similar to those tested very difficult to impossible.

- Knowledge about one's environment typically acquired through daily experiences and verbal interactions (e.g., where different things are found and their uses) and academic knowledge typically acquired in school (e.g., science, social studies) (Knowledge cluster, RPI 28/90);
- Expressive vocabulary and reasoning with word meanings (e.g., synonyms, antonyms, completing analogies) (Verbal Comprehension, RPI 33/90);

- Manipulating sounds within words to come up with other words (Sound Awareness, RPI 47/90);
- Rapidly processing symbols and pictures to recognize visual and conceptual similarities (Processing Speed, RPI 17/90). Although Steven was aware that these tests were timed, he seemed unhurried in drawing the circles to indicate his choices, contributing to his low scores;
- Auditory closure, or figuring out what word was said when heard with sounds left out, such as might happen when trying to listen to someone speak in a noisy room (Incomplete Words, RPI 36/90).

ACADEMIC TESTING

Reading

Results of the WJ III ACH Basic Reading Skills cluster indicate that Steven's word identification and word attack skills are in the Low range, based on standard scores. His RPI indicated that his proficiency in basic reading skills similar to those tested would be 21% in comparison to average grade-peers' 90%. His instructional level is beginning fourth grade. Results of the Nelson Denny Reading Test and the Qualitative Reading Inventory (QRI) were similar.

Error analysis on all reading tests yielded qualitative information. When Steven read words in lists, some of his productions were meaningless but had some auditory resemblance to the target word. Clearly, the majority of the words were not within his sight vocabulary. His knowledge of phonics was limited, especially regarding vowels and vowel combinations. Steven's strategy on unfamiliar words was to say the initial consonant sound(s), and then guess, ignoring the rest of the letters in the word. When reading in passages, Steven had frequent hesitations and repetitions, inserted and substituted words that altered the meaning of the passage, and read with little expression.

Results of the WJ III Reading Comprehension cluster (comprehension of brief passages and reading vocabulary) also placed Steven's abilities in reading comprehension in the Low range. Comprehension of grade-level reading material far exceeds his frustration level (RPI 43/90). His instructional level in reading comprehension is also beginning fourth grade.

Steven reads exceedingly slowly and dysfluently on all tests. On a timed reading task, whereas his average grade-peers would have 90% proficiency, Steven would have 6%

(WJ III Reading Fluency). Results from the Nelson Denny were similarly poor (4th percentile).

Reading is clearly a slow and laborious process for Steven. Although he demonstrated proficiency in oral sound blending, he does not have the phonics knowledge that would allow him to retrieve the correct sounds from memory and to retrieve known correspondences instantaneously. Additionally, sound blending appears to be the limit of his ability to manipulate sounds in his mind, which is not sufficient for fluent, automatic decoding and development of new sight words. On the Nelson Denny, Steven's reading comprehension improved from the 6th percentile to the 40th percentile when he was given extra time. Considering Steven's oral language abilities, it is apparent that the major impediment to his comprehension of reading matter is a combination of weak word attack skills, limited sight vocabulary, and poor reading fluency.

Written Language

Steven's performance on the Basic Writing Skills cluster of the WJ III ACH bridged the Low to Low Average ranges. Editing and Punctuation & Capitalization were in the Low Average range, Spelling was in the Low range, and Spelling of Sounds (not included in the cluster) was below the Very Low range. Regardless of the variations in standard score ranges, Steven's RPIs indicated that he would find similar tasks at the ninth-grade level very difficult to extremely difficult, negating the learning benefit of such tasks.

Error analysis of Steven's spelling (Spelling, Spelling of Sounds) indicated, again, that he has difficulty analyzing oral words into their component sounds. This finding is consistent with his weakness in segmenting and manipulating sounds in words. He displayed a tendency to change or omit sounds in the final syllable of multisyllable words (e.g., *advence* for "adventure," *beautifly* for "beautiful," *cristly* for "crystal"). Furthermore, he frequently does not know what letter or letter combinations to use to represent the sounds (Phoneme-Grapheme Knowledge, RPI 21/90). He appears to know how to spell certain word endings (e.g., *ly*) but does not have them well linked to their oral equivalent (e.g., "əl" rather than "lē"). Steven's handwriting was clear and legible.

Steven's performance on the Written Expression cluster was in the Low range. The Writing Fluency RPI indicates that Steven is extremely slow in writing simple sentences (e.g., *My cup is full*). In this test, the keywords for each item are printed next to the response line, which should make sentence formulation and spelling easier. As this is a timed test, Steven's generally slow response style may have negatively affected his performance.

The Writing Samples test does not have a time limit. It requires one-sentence written responses to a variety of task demands. Steven did not always write complete sentences. As well, he used a restricted vocabulary because, given the choice, he tended to use only words he knew how to spell.

As part of a history unit, Steven was asked to write a brief paper about the topic of prejudice. He chose to write about a personal experience in which he felt he had been the object of prejudice as a Native American. His writing sample and a translation are presented below. Steven wrote his first draft using a word processor.

I consider my slef as T. O. when I was in 5 or 6 grade my teacher mis . . . iwent to the story and got somting to drenk. Wll when I got to school iwent strait tomy classroom because I was running light. i sat my drenk on the table where I sat some kid rickey spild it. My teacher got mad and stared to call me names Like you stupid Yaqui then she was also telling don't you know anting. She is agenc Yaqui people because she was colling me Yaqui when she was colling namesi was not paing no atticion to what she was saining. She went to for abowt the Yaqui people I finoley got mad and tould heair to come dowen and quit hating.

Translation: I consider myself as T. O. [Tohono O'odham]. When I was in fifth or sixth grade, my teacher Miss _____. I went to the store and got something to drink. Well, when I got to school, I went straight to my classroom because I was running late. I sat my drink on the table where I sat. Some kid, Ricky, spilled it. My teacher got mad and started to call me names like, "You stupid Yaqui," then was also telling, "Don't you know anything?" She is against Yaqui people because she was calling me Yaqui when she was calling names. I was not paying no attention to what she was saying. She went too far about the Yaqui people. I finally got mad and told her to calm down and quit hating.

Analysis of Steven's writing reveals that although he has a story to share, his message is obscured by poor spelling. His spelling errors reflect weaknesses in phonology (e.g., omitting sounds and confusing similar vowel sounds) and orthography (e.g., *slef* for *self, abowt* for *about, heair* for *her*). When spelling some words, he appeared to listen to the sounds carefully and attend to the movements of his mouth (e.g., *finoley* for *finally*), but was unable to apply the correct English spelling patterns. Steven also has many errors in capitalization and punctuation. Despite multiple errors in syntax and spelling, the general idea of his first draft is clear. He has also clearly expressed his emotions—concern and anger—in regard to this experience. The quality of Steven's written expression is impeded by his deficits in basic writing skills.

Mathematics

Steven's highest academic scores were in mathematics. His standard score on the Math Calculation Skills cluster bridged the Low Average and Average ranges. His RPI indicated that paper/pencil computation and completing a worksheet of math facts would be within his instructional range but difficult. During the Calculation test, Steven commented that math is his favorite subject. He correctly worked multiplication and long division problems; added, subtracted, and divided with fractions; calculated percentages, and multiplied negative integers. His instructional level for calculation is estimated to be beginning eighth grade and fluency of math facts, mid-sixth.

The Math Reasoning cluster is composed of Applied Problems and Quantitative Concepts. Both of these tests were in the Low Average range. Although Math Reasoning appears to be a relative strength for Steven, his RPI suggests that grade level tasks similar to paper/pencil tests regarding practical application; knowledge of mathematical quantities, concepts, and terms; and pattern recognition in numbers would prove very difficult, and be well into his frustration range. His instructional level on both aspects of math reasoning is mid-sixth grade. Test observations and his math teacher's report, however, suggest that Steven's ability to use math in practical situations might be somewhat better than he demonstrated in this evaluation.

DISCREPANCIES

The WJ III provides for the computation of discrepancies between predicted achievement and obtained (actual) scores. Because the tests of the WJ III COG and WJ III ACH tests were normed on the same group of people, statistical regression to the mean does not occur. Results of the discrepancy formulas indicate that Steven is not performing cognitively or academically as expected. The following strengths and weaknesses reported are based on a finding of a statistically significant discrepancy (at least 1.5 standard deviations [SD]) between the predicted score and Steven's

obtained score. It is important to note that the discrepancies used to make determinations of learning disabilities and/or eligibility for special educational services are based on standard scores. Although not considered below, in many cases, Steven's proficiency on a task was considerably more limited than one might assume from the standard score alone.

When comparing Steven's performance in the cognitive abilities measured, he demonstrates a significant strength in Visual-Spatial Thinking (+2.04 SD), and weaknesses in Processing Speed (–1.90 SD) and Comprehension-Knowledge (–1.75 SD).

Based on his oral language abilities, Steven scored significantly lower than expected in the areas of Reading Comprehension (–1.63 SD), Broad Written Language (–1.85 SD), and Written Expression (–1.68 SD). Using the 1.5 SD discrepancy criterion (a generally accepted but arbitrary cut-off point), Steven's Broad Reading score approaches significance at 1.46 SD below the predicted score.

Even when the GIA, which is depressed by specific areas of cognitive deficit, is used for predicting academic achievement, Steven still evidences a significant weakness in Broad Written Language (–1.70 SD) and approaches significance in Written Expression (–1.49 SD).

SUMMARY AND DISCUSSION

Steven is a ninth-grade student with a long history of poor academic performance. Steven acknowledged that he never tried in school and in the past was frequently absent. He identifies one of his main problems as having no confidence in his academic skills. Presently, his greatest academic difficulties are in reading and writing skills, although he is also quite limited in math reasoning, academic knowledge, and general world knowledge.

Steven appears to lack some of the cognitive and academic skills that are prerequisites for developing grade-level word attack, sight vocabulary, reading fluency skills, spelling, sentence construction, grammar, and writing fluency. Prerequisites include more sophisticated phonemic awareness skills (particularly sound segmentation and manipulation), a conscious focus on the orthographic features of words, knowledge and automatic retrieval of phoneme/grapheme correspondences, and a broader vocabulary, including subtleties of meaning.

Test results suggest that Steven has good speech discrimination and, at some time, received training in sound blending. His apparent weakness in auditory closure (suggested by his low score and RPI on Incomplete Words) is of concern as it indicates a possible problem with auditory processing that is not readily trainable. Weakness in auditory processing may obstruct the development of phonemic awareness skills and, possibly, an intrinsic sense of correct sentence structure. Difficulty with auditory closure appears inconsistent with intact speech discrimination in the presence of competing noise; however, Steven may have been aided in the latter task by the pictures and the "multiple-choice" type of response (pointing to the correct picture out of a set of four).

In math, Steven does relatively well with computation skills but lacks automaticity in math facts, mathematical information necessary for practical application, and pattern recognition. Steven's strength in deductive reasoning may contribute to his achievement in computation skills, while a weakness in inductive reasoning may contribute to his difficulty in the practical application of these skills and pattern recognition.

Processing Speed has been identified as a significant weakness. Steven generally did poorly on tests that required speed (Reading Fluency, Rapid Picture Naming) and psychomotor speed (Decision Speed, Visual Matching, Writing Fluency, Math Fluency), although the processing speed tests are constructed to minimize the motor response component. Culturally influenced response style may be a factor contributing to low processing speed; the culture on the Yaqui Reservation approves a slow, casual approach to tasks over a hurried, speed-dependent one. Steven's processing speed deficit is so severe, however, that cultural influence is unlikely to be the sole factor. Culturally influenced or otherwise, slow processing is clearly interfering with Steven's acquisition of academic skills in basic reading, writing, and math. Steven also evidences a weakness in word retrieval, when his choices are restricted by the context and he must come up with a specific word. Also, Steven may be confused by multiple-step oral directions, especially if conveyed in complex sentences incorporating many critical elements to which he must attend.

A significant weakness was also identified in Comprehension-Knowledge, a combination of vocabulary, reasoning with word meanings, and acquisition of information from daily experience. Difficulties in these skills *are* likely to have been caused by limited school attendance, cultural differences, and limited experience. These weaknesses will impede Steven's reading comprehension and restrict formulation of his thoughts in written expression.

Steven demonstrated a significant difference in his performance on memory tasks. He was able to hold unrelated numbers and objects in mind while reorganizing them into categories but had difficulty with seemingly simpler memory tasks of repeating words in the order given or repeating a string of digits in reverse order. It is possible that the very complexity of the harder task challenged him, stimulating more focused attention and effort. In any case, his success in this test indicates that Steven is likely to be successful with memory strategies.

Results of this evaluation indicate that Steven has specific cognitive weaknesses in processing speed, inductive reasoning, certain aspects of memory, vocabulary, phonemic awareness skills, and, possibly, auditory processing, which contribute to his severe deficiencies in academic achievement. Other contributing factors to Steven's academic deficiencies include educational deprivation, poor school attendance, and limited experiences.

A positive outcome of this evaluation is recognition of Steven's significant strength in visual–spatial ability, providing a starting point and focus for career exploration. A second benefit is the identification of other cognitive abilities that are in the Average range in comparison to grade-peers and in which Steven has developed proficiency. These abilities may be exploited in developing strategies to support the weaker areas of learning.

Steven's instructional needs should be addressed to allow him to progress academically, and to help him build a sense of self-confidence in his ability to learn. Steven meets the state and district criteria for classification as a student with learning disabilities. The area of processing speed represents a statistically significant cognitive weakness that is unlikely to be caused solely by cultural influences or lack of formal schooling. His academic achievement in the areas of reading comprehension and written expression are significantly below expectations based on his oral language scores; and his basic reading skills, reading comprehension, basic writing skills, and written expression are considerably more than 2 years behind his current grade placement.

This report will be submitted to the Child Study committee to determine if educational disadvantage and cultural differences can be ruled out as the *primary* cause of Steven's academic weaknesses. The team may also want to consider that unrecognized learning disabilities and lack of appropriate instructional techniques may have caused Steven excessive frustration, and a lack of benefit sufficient to motivate him to continue to come to school, in turn exacerbating his academic difficulties, and continuing a downward spiral.

RECOMMENDATIONS

Accommodations

1. Minimize the amount of copying Steven is required to do and do not require speed when he is copying material from the board or a book. When possible, provide Steven with copies of materials so that he can write on them directly.
2. Permit Steven to take classroom and standardized tests with extended time. Allowing additional time allotment for testing will provide a more accurate reflection of Steven's knowledge and achievement.
3. When possible, administer tests in short sections so that Steven can finish each section at his own pace.
4. Ensure that texts and accompanying materials in content areas are at Steven's instructional level (early 4th grade). If materials are at a frustration level, have Steven listen to tape-recorded texts, and, if possible, read along with the tape.
5. For lectures in which the students are expected to take notes, arrange for a capable student to make a copy of his or her notes for Steven. Provide access to the school copy machine.

Memory

1. Teach Steven a variety of memory strategies and the type of situations/tasks in which each is appropriate. Provide for overlearning in deciding when a strategy is needed, which strategy is best suited to the task, and in practicing the strategy. Examples of memory strategies include: using verbal rehearsal, chunking, making ridiculous visual images composed of items that one has to remember, and creating first-letter mnemonic strategies. An excellent resource for research-supported memory strategies is *Teaching Students Ways to Remember: Strategies for Learning Mnemonically* by M. A. Mastropieri and T. E. Scruggs (1999a). Available from Brookline Books, Cambridge, MA, phone: 800-666-2665, website: www.brooklinebooks.com.
2. Incorporate memory "tricks" into instruction of specific skills. For example, use pictures to help Steven remember phoneme/grapheme associations (e.g., For /aw/, use a picture of a handsaw with the letter *s* incorporated into the handle and the *aw* as part of the serrated edge of the blade). (See: Memory: General Principles for Improvement, attached.)

Reading

1. Steven needs assistance in building his ability to pronounce multisyllabic words. An approach such as *Glass–Analysis for Decoding Only* (Glass, 1976) might be helpful. A summary of this method is attached.
2. To improve reading fluency and automaticity of word recognition, create speed drills in which Steven reads a series of words or word parts based on those he is studying within Glass–Analysis or any other program. The goal is to read all of the words on the page within 60 seconds, with only one or two errors. This technique allows the student to work on fluency at the same time he is developing automaticity on the phonic elements and sight words he is learning, but is time-consuming for the teacher as she or he must decide on the contents and create each worksheet. A research-supported commercial program for developing reading fluency is Great Leaps Reading, providing fluency practice in phonics elements, sight words, sight phrases, and stories. Summaries of both techniques are attached.

Written Language

1. Writing becomes increasingly automatic with practice. Since Steven likes to write, set aside specific time each day for daily writing practice. Emphasize the process of writing (and rewriting) instead of the product. Remember that his instructional level for writing is beginning fourth grade.
2. Because Steven needs to develop correct sentence structure "from the ground up," use a strategy that does not look like it was designed for young children. The *Sentence Writing Strategy* (Schumaker & Sheldon, 1985) assists the student in learning to write grammatically correct sentences of increasing complexity and the related grammatical skills. This strategy, appropriate for middle school-age and above, starts with simple sentences and gradually adds sentence elements until the student is writing compound-complex sentences. Instruction can be done individually or in a group. Available from the University of Kansas Center for Research on Learning, Lawrence, KS 66045, (785) 864-4780, www.ku-crl.org.
3. Use the Six Traits Writing Rubric developed by the Northwest Regional Educational Laboratory (http://www.nwrel.org/assessment). This Rubric provides an excellent approach to teaching and assessing writing skills that can be combined with other writing programs.

4. To help Steven develop an internal sense of what a "good" sentence sounds like, have his tutor read to him from high interest books. Have her read a passage, then go back and read it sentence by sentence, asking Steven why it's a good sentence, if it sounds finished or as if something is missing. Then have her occasionally "read" sentences from passages that she has altered so that they are not complete. Elicit from Steven what is missing and how he could make it better. Eventually, coordinate this activity with the use of the sentence-writing strategy.

5. For taking notes, teach Steven how to use outlines, charts, graphs, maps, and tables rather than writing in narrative form. An excellent software program for creating graphic organizers is Inspiration (http://www.inspiration.com).

6. Reduce the amount of writing required. For example, have Steven write one paragraph rather than an entire essay.

7. Teach Steven how to use a handheld electronic spell-checker and the spell-checker on a computer. Teach him how to use the thesaurus program to make sure that the spelling choice he is selecting is the word that has the meaning he intends.

8. Teach spelling in direct coordination with reading. For example, if using Glass–Analysis for Decoding Only, have him practice spelling the word parts he is learning (e.g., *tion, com*), and incorporate them into speed drills for fluency.

9. Teach Steven a specific method for spelling study. Two outlines are attached. One explains the Fernald Method for Reading and Spelling: Modified; the other, Spelling: General Teaching Principles, lists important principles in effective spelling instruction.

Self-Image

A major problem for Steven is his lack of confidence and his negative self-image as a learner. Steven's academic program needs to provide reasonable expectations and plenty of opportunity for success. Some suggestions are as follows:

1. Provide specific praise to Steven for positive academic behavior (e.g., "Steven, I can hear your voice and the importance of the ideas in this essay you have written").

2. Make learning meaningful to Steven by relating tasks to what he already knows and is interested in. Try to incorporate the history and culture of the Yaquis.

3. Begin to explore career options in which Steven would be able to use his talents.

4. Steven's case manager can help him develop and use positive affirmations describing himself as a successful learner (e.g., "I am able to learn what I set my mind to"). Use Steven's ability to identify his negative thought patterns. Teach him cognitive restructuring techniques to motivate himself to become engaged in the new instructional techniques and supports he will be receiving.

5. The most effective facilitator to self-image change is real and demonstrable improvement in academic skills and, most important, reading. Since Steven's oral language abilities are above his reading skills, development of word attack, sight words, and fluency will improve reading comprehension and enhance his self-image as a learner.

6. Provide opportunities for Steven to use his strength in visual–spatial thinking. Whenever possible, use concrete materials and experiential learning.

Adapted from Ginny Reiss, Ph.D.

The following tables are intended to facilitate comparisons between Steven's standard scores and Relative Performance Indexes on the factors/clusters and tests of the WJ III.

Standard Score and Relative Proficiency Index Comparisons: Cognitive and Oral Language

CLUSTER/Test by Standard Score Ranges	SS (± 1 SEM)	CLUSTER/Test by Instructional Implications	RPI
HIGH AVERAGE (SS 111–120)		**EASY (95/90 to 98/90)**	
VISUAL-SPATIAL THINKING	117 (111–124)	VISUAL-SPATIAL THINKING	97/90
AVERAGE (SS 90–110)		**MANAGEABLE (82/90 to 95/90)**	
AUDITORY PROCESS	95 (90–100)	AUDITORY PROCESS	86/90
L-T RETRIEVAL	93 (88–98)	L-T RETRIEVAL	87/90
Visual-Auditory Learning	100 (93–106)	Visual-Auditory Learning	90/90
Story Recall	101 (94–108)	Story Recall	90/90
Oral Comprehension	94 (89–99)	Oral Comprehension	80/90
Auditory Work Memory	97 (93–101)	Auditory Work Memory	85/90
Analysis-Synthesis	94 (88–99)	Analysis-Synthesis	80/90
Memory for Words	93 (87–100)	Retrieval Fluency	84/90
Rapid Picture Naming	91 (89–93)		
		DIFFICULT (67/90 to 82/90)	
LOW AVERAGE/AVERAGE		Memory for Words	73/90
SHORT-TERM MEMORY	89 (84–94)	Picture Vocabulary	68/90
Numbers Reversed	88 (83–93)	Understanding Directions	70/90
Picture Vocabulary	90 (86–95)		
		VERY DIFFICULT (24/90 to 67/90)	
LOW AVERAGE (SS 80–89)		KNOWLEDGE	28/90
Concept Formation	82 (78–85)	SHORT-TERM MEMORY	65/90
Retrieval Fluency	82 (76–87)	Numbers Reversed	56/90
Understanding Directions	86 (81–91)	Verbal Comprehension	33/90
		Incomplete Words	36/90
VERY LOW and LOW (69 and below)/(70–79)		Rapid Picture Naming	57/90
Verbal Comprehension	79 (75–82)	Concept Formation	32/90
Incomplete Words	61 (53–68)		
KNOWLEDGE	76 (73–79)	**EXTREMELY DIFFICULT (0/90 to 3/90) and IMPOSSIBLE (3/90 to 24/90)**	
PROCESS SPEED	68 (64–71)		
		PROCESS SPEED	17/90

Standard Score and Relative Proficiency Index Comparisons: Academic Achievement

CLUSTER/Test by Standard Score Ranges	SS ± 1 SEM	CLUSTER/Test by RPI Instructional Implications	RPI
HIGH AVERAGE (111–120)		**EASY (95/90 to 98/90)**	
AVERAGE (90–110)		**MANAGEABLE (82/90 to 95/90)**	
Calculation	94 (90–99)	Calculation	82/90
LOW AVERAGE/AVERAGE		**DIFFICULT (67/90 to 82/90)**	
MATH CALC SKILLS	90 (86–93)	MATH CALC SKILLS	79/90
		Writing Samples	72/90
LOW AVERAGE (80–89)		[Punctuation & Capitals]	68/90
MATH REASONING	88 (85–91)	Math Fluency	75/90
Word Attack	82 (80–85)		
Letter-Word Identification	81 (79–84)	**VERY DIFFICULT (24/90 to 67/90)**	
Reading Fluency	83 (81–84)	MATH REASONING	64/90
Editing	88 (84–91)	READING COMP	43/90
[Punct. & Capitalization]	85 (79–90)	BROAD WRITTEN LANG	38/90
Academic Knowledge	84 (80–88)	BASIC WRITING SKILLS	41/90
		WRITTEN EXPRESSION	43/90
LOW/LOW AVERAGE		Sound Awareness	47/90
BASIC WRITING SKILLS	81 (77–84)	Spelling	28/90
		Word Attack	28/90
VERY LOW (<70) and LOW (70–79)		Editing	54/90
BROAD READING	79 (77–81)	Academic Knowledge	46/90
BASIC READING SKILLS	79 (77–81)		
READING COMP.	77 (73–80)	**EXTREMELY DIFFICULT (0/90 to 3/90)**	
BROAD WRITTEN LANG	72 (69–76)	**and IMPOSSIBLE (3/90 to 24/90)**	
WRITTEN EXPRESSION	74 (70–78)	BROAD READING	18/90
PHON.-GRAPH. KNOWL.	72 (69–75)	BASIC READING SKILLS	21/90
Spelling	77 (73–81)	PHON.-GRAPH. KNOWL.	21/90
Sound Awareness	78 (74–82)	Writing Fluency	18/90
Spelling of Sounds	57 (51–62)	Reading Fluency	6/90
Writing Fluency	75 (71–79)	Letter-Word Identification	15/90
Writing Samples	74 (64–84)	Word Attack	28/90
		Spelling of Sounds	14/90

COMPUSCORE VERSION 1.1B: SCORE REPORT

Name: Parker, Steven

Date of Birth: 07/29/1986

Age: 15 years, 8 months

Grade: 9.7

School: Py Charter

Sex: Male

Dates of Testing: 03/29/2002 (COG)

03/30/2002 (ACH)

TABLE OF SCORES: Woodcock-Johnson III Tests of Cognitive Abilities and Tests of Achievement
Norms based on grade 9.7

CLUSTER	RAW	GE	EASY to DIFF		RPI	PR	SS(68% BAND)
GIA (Ext)	—	4.8	2.7	7.8	64/90	13	83 (82–85)
CHC FACTOR/Test							
COMP-KNOWLEDGE (Gc)	—	**3.4**	**2.3**	**4.9**	**22/90**	**3**	**72 (69–75)**
Verbal Comprehension	—	4.0	2.7	5.7	33/90	8	79 (75–82)
General Information	—	2.9	1.8	4.2	15/90	2	70 (66–74)
L-T RETRIEVAL (Glr)	—	**6.1**	**1.6**	**>18.0**	**87/90**	**32**	**93 (88–98)**
Visual-Auditory Learning	9-E	9.4	2.6	>18.0	90/90	49	100 (93–106)
Retrieval Fluency	52	3.7	K.2	>18.0	84/90	11	82 (76–87)
VIS-SPATIAL THINK (Gv)	—	**>18.0**	**10.0**	**>18.0**	**97/90**	**88**	**117 (111–124)**
Spatial Relations	78-D	>18.0	16.2	>18.0	98/90	89	118 (111–125)
Picture Recognition	53-D	>18.0	6.0	>18.0	94/90	69	107 (101–114)
AUDITORY PROCESS (Ga)	—	**7.5**	**2.4**	**12.9**	**86/90**	**38**	**95 (90–100)**
Sound Blending	21	8.4	3.8	12.9	87/90	43	97 (92–103)
Auditory Attention	37	5.8	1.3	13.0	86/90	37	95 (90–100)
FLUID REASONING (Gf)	—	**4.3**	**2.8**	**7.0**	**58/90**	**17**	**85 (82–89)**
Concept Formation	18-D	3.0	2.1	4.5	32/90	11	82 (78–85)
Analysis-Synthesis	24-D	6.9	4.0	11.0	80/90	33	94 (88–99)
PROCESS SPEED (Gs)	—	**4.4**	**3.5**	**5.5**	**17/90**	**2**	**68 (64–71)**
Visual Matching	40-2	5.2	4.3	6.2	18/90	6	77 (73–81)
Decision Speed	24	3.4	2.4	4.6	15/90	2	70 (66–74)
SHORT-TERM MEM (Gsm)	—	**5.6**	**3.6**	**8.2**	**65/90**	**23**	**89 (84–94)**
Numbers Reversed	12	5.0	3.4	7.4	56/90	22	88 (83–93)
Memory for Words	17	6.2	4.0	9.3	73/90	32	93 (87–100)

COGNITIVE PERFORMANCE CLUSTER/Test	RAW	GE	EASY to DIFF		RPI	PR	SS(68% BAND)
COG EFFICIENCY (Ext)	—	**4.8**	**3.6**	**6.4**	**38/90**	**5**	**75 (72–79)**
Visual Matching	40-2	5.2	4.3	6.2	18/90	6	77 (73–81)
Numbers Reversed	12	5.0	3.4	7.4	56/90	22	88 (83–93)
Decision Speed	24	3.4	2.4	4.6	15/90	2	70 (66–74)
Memory for Words	17	6.2	4.0	9.3	73/90	32	93 (87–100)

CLINICAL CLUSTER/Test	RAW	GE	EASY to DIFF		RPI	PR	SS(68% BAND)
PHONEMIC AWARE III	—	**2.5**	**1.1**	**5.8**	**60/90**	**7**	**78 (74–81)**
Sound Blending	21	8.4	3.8	12.9	87/90	43	97 (92–103)
Incomplete Words	11	<K.0	<K.0	1.1	36/90	0.4	61 (53–68)
Sound Awareness	32	2.6	1.7	4.2	47/90	7	78 (74–82)
WORKING MEMORY	—	**6.6**	**4.4**	**9.4**	**73/90**	**27**	**91 (87–95)**
Numbers Reversed	12	5.0	3.4	7.4	56/90	22	88 (83–93)
Auditory Work Memory	24	8.5	5.8	12.9	85/90	41	97 (93–101)
COGNITIVE FLUENCY	—	**4.9**	**3.1**	**7.1**	**52/90**	**9**	**80 (77–82)**
Retrieval Fluency	52	3.7	K.2	>18.0	84/90	11	82 (76–87)
Rapid Picture Naming	112	6.9	5.5	8.4	57/90	28	91 (89–93)
Decision Speed	24	3.4	2.4	4.6	15/90	2	70 (66–74)
KNOWLEDGE	—	**4.1**	**2.8**	**5.7**	**28/90**	**5**	**76 (73–79)**
General Information	—	2.9	1.8	4.2	15/90	2	70 (66–74)
Academic Knowledge	—	5.6	4.1	7.3	46/90	14	84 (80–88)

TABLE OF SCORES (*continued*)

ORAL LANGUAGE CLUSTER/Test	RAW	GE	EASY	to DIFF	RPI	PR	SS(68% BAND)
ORAL LANGUAGE (Ext)	—	**6.3**	**3.6**	**10.7**	**79/90**	**25**	**90 (87–93)**
ORAL EXPRESSION	—	**6.9**	**3.8**	**11.7**	**82/90**	**30**	**92 (88–96)**
Story Recall	—	10.3	2.0	>18.0	90/90	52	101 (94–108)
Picture Vocabulary	27	6.5	4.5	8.9	68/90	26	90 (86–95)
LISTENING COMP	—	**5.7**	**3.5**	**9.8**	**76/90**	**25**	**90 (86–94)**
Understanding Directions	—	4.2	2.3	8.3	70/90	18	86 (81–91)
Oral Comprehension	22	7.1	4.6	10.7	80/90	35	94 (89–99)

ACHIEVEMENT CLUSTER/Test	RAW	GE	EASY	to DIFF	RPI	PR	SS(68% BAND)
BROAD READING	—	**4.9**	**4.0**	**6.1**	**18/90**	**8**	**79 (77–81)**
Letter-Word Identification	52	4.6	3.9	5.5	15/90	11	81 (79–84)
Reading Fluency	47	5.6	4.7	6.5	6/90	13	83 (81–84)
Passage Comprehension	29	4.0	3.0	6.1	48/90	10	81 (76–86)
BASIC READING SKILLS	—	**4.2**	**3.4**	**5.3**	**21/90**	**8**	**79 (77–81)**
Letter-Word Identification	52	4.6	3.9	5.5	15/90	11	81 (79–84)
Word Attack	17	3.3	2.4	4.8	28/90	12	82 (80–85)
READING COMP	—	**4.1**	**3.0**	**6.1**	**43/90**	**6**	**77 (73–80)**
Passage Comprehension	29	4.0	3.0	6.1	48/90	10	81 (76–86)
Reading Vocabulary	—	4.3	2.9	6.1	38/90	7	78 (75–82)
BROAD WRITTEN LANG	—	**4.2**	**3.1**	**5.8**	**38/90**	**3**	**72 (69–76)**
Spelling	32	4.4	3.5	5.6	28/90	6	77 (73–81)
Writing Fluency	14	4.2	3.3	5.3	18/90	5	75 (71–79)
Writing Samples	8-D	3.5	2.0	8.6	72/90	4	74 (64–84)
BASIC WRITING SKILLS	—	**4.8**	**3.8**	**6.4**	**41/90**	**10**	**81 (77–84)**
Editing	14	5.4	4.1	7.5	54/90	20	88 (84–91)
Spelling	32	4.4	3.5	5.6	28/90	6	77 (73–81)
[Punctuation & Capitals	21	6.3	4.4	8.8	68/90	16	85 (79–90)]
WRITTEN EXPRESSION	—	**4.1**	**2.7**	**5.9**	**43/90**	**4**	**74 (70–78)**
Writing Fluency	14	4.2	3.3	5.3	18/90	5	75 (71–79)
Writing Samples	8-D	3.5	2.0	8.6	72/90	4	74 (64–84)
BROAD MATH	—	**7.1**	**5.4**	**9.7**	**75/90**	**23**	**89 (86–92)**
Calculation	24	8.0	6.1	11.0	82/90	36	94 (90–99)
Math Fluency	80	6.6	4.2	9.8	75/90	17	86 (84–88)
Applied Problems	40	6.8	5.5	8.6	66/90	27	91 (88–94)
MATH CALC SKILLS	—	**7.4**	**5.4**	**10.4**	**79/90**	**25**	**90 (86–93)**
Calculation	24	8.0	6.1	11.0	82/90	36	94 (90–99)
Math Fluency	80	6.6	4.2	9.8	75/90	17	86 (84–88)
MATH REASONING	—	**6.5**	**5.1**	**8.3**	**64/90**	**21**	**88 (85–91)**
Applied Problems	40	6.8	5.5	8.6	66/90	27	91 (88–94)
Quantitative Concepts	—	6.1	4.8	8.0	61/90	20	87 (83–92)

OTHER ACHIEVEMENT CLUSTER/Test	RAW	GE	EASY	to DIFF	RPI	PR	SS(68% BAND)
ACADEMIC KNOWLEDGE	—	**5.6**	**4.1**	**7.3**	**46/90**	**14**	**84 (80–88)**
PHON/GRAPH KNOW	—	**2.2**	**1.8**	**3.3**	**21/90**	**3**	**72 (69–75)**
Word Attack	17	3.3	2.4	4.8	28/90	12	82 (80–85)
Spelling of Sounds	13	1.3	1.0	1.8	14/90	0.2	57 (51–62)
ACADEMIC SKILLS	—	**5.3**	**4.3**	**6.7**	**40/90**	**6**	**76 (73–79)**
Letter-Word Identification	52	4.6	3.9	5.5	15/90	11	81 (79–84)
Spelling	32	4.4	3.5	5.6	28/90	6	77 (73–81)
Calculation	24	8.0	6.1	11.0	82/90	36	94 (90–99)
ACADEMIC FLUENCY	—	**5.2**	**4.1**	**6.6**	**26/90**	**8**	**79 (77–81)**
Reading Fluency	47	5.6	4.7	6.5	6/90	13	83 (81–84)
Writing Fluency	14	4.2	3.3	5.3	18/90	5	75 (71–79)
Math Fluency	80	6.6	4.2	9.8	75/90	17	86 (84–88)

(*continued*)

TABLE OF SCORES (*continued*)

ORAL LANGUAGE CLUSTER/Test	RAW	GE	EASY to DIFF		RPI	PR	SS(68% BAND)
ACADEMIC APPS	—	**5.3**	**3.7**	**7.8**	**63/90**	**11**	**81 (78–85)**
Passage Comprehension	29	4.0	3.0	6.1	48/90	10	81 (76–86)
Writing Samples	8-D	3.5	2.0	8.6	72/90	4	74 (64–84)
Applied Problems	40	6.8	5.5	8.6	66/90	27	91 (88–94)
TOTAL ACHIEVEMENT	—	**5.3**	**4.1**	**6.9**	**42/90**	**12**	**83 (81–84)**
Letter-Word Identification	52	4.6	3.9	5.5	15/90	11	81 (79–84)
Reading Fluency	47	5.6	4.7	6.5	6/90	13	83 (81–84)
Passage Comprehension	29	4.0	3.0	6.1	48/90	10	81 (76–86)
Spelling	32	4.4	3.5	5.6	28/90	6	77 (73–81)
Writing Fluency	14	4.2	3.3	5.3	18/90	5	75 (71–79)
Writing Samples	8-D	3.5	2.0	8.6	72/90	4	74 (64–84)
Calculation	24	8.0	6.1	11.0	82/90	36	94 (90–99)
Math Fluency	80	6.6	4.2	9.8	75/90	17	86 (84–88)
Applied Problems	40	6.8	5.5	8.6	66/90	27	91 (88–94)

DISCREPANCIES	STANDARD SCORES			DISCREPANCY		Significant at ± 1.50 SD (SEE)
	Actual	Predicted	Difference	PR	SD	
*Intellectual Ability/Achievement Discrepancies**						
BROAD READING	79	88	−9	16	−1.01	No
BASIC READING SKILLS	79	90	−11	15	−1.03	No
READING COMP	77	88	−11	10	−1.28	No
BROAD MATH	89	88	+1	51	+0.03	No
MATH CALC SKILLS	90	91	−1	47	−0.07	No
MATH REASONING	88	88	0	53	+0.06	No
BROAD WRITTEN LANG	72	89	−17	4	−1.70	Yes
BASIC WRITING SKILLS	81	90	−9	20	−0.84	No
WRITTEN EXPRESSION	74	90	−16	7	−1.49	No
ORAL LANGUAGE (Ext)	90	87	+3	61	+0.29	No
ORAL EXPRESSION	92	89	+3	63	+0.34	No
LISTENING COMP	90	88	+2	56	+0.16	No
ACADEMIC KNOWLEDGE	84	88	−4	34	−0.42	No

*These discrepancies based on GIA (Ext) with ACH Broad, Basic, and Applied clusters.

DISCREPANCIES	STANDARD SCORES			DISCREPANCY		Significant at ± 1.50 SD (SEE)
	Actual	Predicted	Difference	PR	SD	
Intra-Cognitive						
COMP-KNOWLEDGE (Gc)	72	91	−19	4	−1.75	Yes
L-T RETRIEVAL (Glr)	93	88	+5	66	+0.42	No
VIS-SPATIAL THINK (Gv)	117	90	+27	98	+2.04	Yes
AUDITORY PROCESS (Ga)	95	91	+4	62	+0.31	No
FLUID REASONING (Gf)	85	89	−4	36	−0.37	No
PROCESS SPEED (Gs)	68	95	−27	3	−1.90	Yes
SHORT-TERM MEM (Gsm)	89	91	−2	44	−0.15	No
PHONEMIC AWARE	80	91	−11	21	−0.81	No
WORKING MEMORY	91	91	0	50	0.00	No

TABLE OF SCORES (*continued*)

DISCREPANCIES	STANDARD SCORES			DISCREPANCY		Significant at
	Actual	Predicted	Difference	PR	SD	± 1.50 SD (SEE)
Intra-Achievement						
BASIC READING SKILLS	79	84	−5	28	−0.59	No
READING COMP	77	85	−8	19	−0.88	No
MATH CALC SKILLS	90	87	+3	58	+0.21	No
MATH REASONING	88	83	+5	72	+0.58	No
BASIC WRITING SKILLS	81	86	−5	31	−0.50	No
WRITTEN EXPRESSION	74	87	−13	10	−1.29	No
ORAL EXPRESSION	92	85	+7	74	+0.63	No
LISTENING COMP	90	85	+5	68	+0.47	No
ACADEMIC KNOWLEDGE	84	84	0	51	+0.04	No

DISCREPANCIES	STANDARD SCORES			DISCREPANCY		Significant at
	Actual	Predicted	Difference	PR	SD	± 1.50 SD (SEE)
*Oral Language/Achievement Discrepancies**						
BROAD READING	79	95	−16	7	−1.46	No
BASIC READING SKILLS	79	95	−16	9	−1.36	No
READING COMP	77	93	−16	5	−1.63	Yes
BROAD MATH	89	94	−5	33	−0.43	No
MATH CALC SKILLS	90	96	−6	33	−0.44	No
MATH REASONING	88	93	−5	33	−0.45	No
BROAD WRITTEN LANG	72	94	−22	3	−1.85	Yes
BASIC WRITING SKILLS	81	95	−14	13	−1.14	No
WRITTEN EXPRESSION	74	95	−21	5	−1.68	Yes
ACADEMIC KNOWLEDGE	84	93	−9	18	-0.90	No

*These discrepancies based on Oral Language (Ext) with ACH Broad, Basic, and Applied clusters.

Educational Evaluation

Name:	Helen Chapman		Dates of Evaluation:	2/28, 3/9/01
Date of Birth:	6/85		School:	Home-Schooled
Age:	15-9		Referred by:	Special Educator
Grade:	10.6			

REASON FOR REFERRAL

Helen was referred for an educational evaluation to determine her specific learning strengths and weaknesses. Information from this comprehensive assessment process is designed to assist the Evaluation and Planning Team in determining the underlying difficulties that Helen may be experiencing with regard to school learning and appropriate instructional methods to address her academic needs. The Evaluation and Planning Team is also requesting assistance in determining if Helen may be demonstrating specific learning disabilities that are adversely affecting her rate of progress in the development of school skills. This request was made by the special education teacher at the local high school, Dr. Marjorie Tippins. Dr. Tippins is coordinating this evaluation for Helen's local school district, as Helen is currently being home-schooled. Detailed background information may be found in her school record.

BACKGROUND INFORMATION

Helen resides with her family who are considered stable and very supportive. Sociocultural-economic factors are not considered as adverse issues affecting Helen's cognitive, academic, or social development. Helen is an avid reader, loves history and writing, and hopes to have some of her writing published one day. While there is no confirmed family history for learning disabilities, there are indications of possible undiagnosed learning or attention difficulties. Helen's mother notes that she is currently concerned about Helen's younger brother's difficulties with writing.

Referral information suggests that Helen demonstrates adequate social adjustment and the ability to develop interpersonal relationships. She reportedly gets along well with both peers and adults. Earlier concerns were noted in her school records regarding Helen's emotional status and she did work with an in-school counselor during fifth grade. During this time, her family was coping with the deaths of several elderly family members. Helen has long been described as shy, quiet, and withdrawn. Teachers have tried to encourage her to be a more active, vocal participant in class. Helen also noted that she was somewhat apprehensive about being in large settings with lots of people, such as shopping malls.

Helen is presently being home-schooled as a tenth-grade student. She has not repeated any grades. She attended kindergarten at Parsons Elementary, grades 1–3 and grades 5–6 at the Winchester School, grade 4 at the Washington School, grades 7–8 at a Waldorf School, and a Charter School last year for grade 9. Helen currently receives private math tutoring from an instructor from Eastbay College, and has had a number of previous math tutors as well. Review of school records indicates that she received Title I services for math in grade 6. She was also in a group for social skills and participated in an Adaptive P.E. program. School records indicate that concerns regarding Helen's performance were discussed at meetings during grades 5 and 6, and special education testing was considered, but not done. Her reading skills have been described consistently as a strength.

Throughout her school career, math is described as an area of considerable difficulty. Helen still struggles with learning/remembering basic facts, though the use of a calculator enables her to demonstrate math reasoning and conceptual understanding in her work. Her tutor notes that Helen does have great difficulty with basic computation skills, but is showing good progress in other aspects of her math instruction. She is able to use a calculator effectively to compensate for her inability to retain and automatically retrieve facts, enabling her to gain understanding of math concepts and apply these in her work. While Helen is gaining confidence in her math knowledge, her tutor noted that she continues to need specific prompting during instruction to access skills and knowledge that she has acquired.

TESTS ADMINISTERED

Woodcock-Johnson III Tests of Cognitive Abilities
    (WJ III COG) and Tests of Achievement (WJ III ACH)
Test of Mathematical Abilities-2 (TOMA-2)
Informal assessment
Diagnostic teaching activities

OBSERVATIONS DURING TESTING

Helen's evaluation took place over two sessions at Irving High School. She came readily to both sessions and presented herself as a bright, articulate, motivated and mature young woman. She was responsive to the testing process and readily shared her insights into what tasks were easy and what were difficult for her. Helen showed consistent effort and concentration on all tasks presented. She became somewhat frustrated with her difficulties on tasks requiring spatial/sequential processing and did not enjoy tasks with time limits. During informal interview and assessment Helen was able to converse with ease. She commented that she enjoys both reading and writing and has interests in pursuing a career as a writer. On paper/pencil tasks, Helen worked with ease on tests involving writing, but struggled with tasks involving math. Helen seemed to struggle when a lot of visual material was presented on a single page. Helen put forth her best effort on all tasks presented. All current results are considered to be valid and reasonable estimates of Helen's abilities and skills at this time.

TEST RESULTS

Cognitive Testing

The WJ III COG is a comprehensive battery of individually administered tests measuring different intellectual/cognitive abilities. Helen obtained the scores shown in Table 1.

Helen's profile indicates a significant strength in the area of Comprehension/Knowledge, suggesting strong verbal abilities. She also demonstrated strong performance on measures tapping Phonemic Awareness. In contrast, Helen's profile and observation of performance indicate significant weakness in regard to Processing Speed.

A significant difference existed between the tests on the Fluid Reasoning cluster. Helen obtained a score in the High Average range on the Concept Formation test. This test involves categorical reasoning based on principles of inductive logic, and also taps the type of cognitive flexibility required to shift one's mental set frequently. In contrast, Helen had a great deal of difficulty with the sequential deductive reasoning ability tapped by the Analysis-Synthesis test. This task presents logic puzzles that can be solved using a key; the tasks mimic a miniature mathematics system. Helen was able to solve the easier concrete items; however, as soon as the tasks required more complex, multistep procedures, Helen became confused and frustrated. Difficulties with this type of rea-

soning task are consistent with weaknesses in regard to sequential processing, an ability that is inherent in the types of thinking most often associated with math. In addition, Helen became confused with specific items on a verbal analogies task that were related to sequential elements.

Further indications of sequential difficulties are evident when Helen's responses to some memory and automatic fluent processing tasks are analyzed. For instance on the Numbers Reversed test, Helen could recall the digits presented but could not reverse their order. On the Visual Matching test, she was confused when trying to match items that used the same digits but in different sequences (e.g., 16/61, 396/639/369).

Helen also demonstrated difficulties with spatial relationships. While Helen obtained a score on Spatial Relations in the Average range, observations of her performance indicated that this was a frustrating task. The same was true for her performance on the Planning test, a measure of the ability to think ahead and use mental control. Her scores for these tests have more to say about her persistence and determination than they do about the ease with which she manages visual–spatial tasks. Helen had even greater difficulty with the Picture Recognition test. This test required Helen to identify one or more pictures in an array of similar items (e.g., several types of hats), minimizing verbal mediation as a recognition strategy. Helen commented that the task was too hard because there were too many things that were too similar.

While Helen clearly did not like timed tasks, her performance on tasks tapping speed and fluency varied. Across both cognitive and achievement measures, Helen did well on fluency tasks related to language. These included rapidly naming pictures of common objects, ideational fluency (categorical naming within a time limit), and reading and writing fluency tasks (see Table 2). In contrast, Helen had considerable difficulty with both tests within the Processing Speed cluster as well as a measure of math fluency (see Table 2).

Achievement Testing

The WJ III ACH is a comprehensive battery of individually administered tests measuring oral language and the academic achievement areas of reading, mathematics, written language, and general knowledge. Helen obtained the scores shown in Table 2.

Helen was also administered the Test of Mathematical Abilities—Second Edition (TOMA-2) to further examine mathematical competency. Helen's scores for the adminis-

Table 1. WJ III COG Scores

CLUSTER/Test	Age	Easy to Diff		RPI	PR	SS ± SEM)
GIA (Ext)	14-8	11-4	20	87/90	42	97 (95–99)
VERBAL ABILITY (Ext)	>25	19	>25	99/90	93	122 (118–126)
THINKING ABILITY (Ext)	13-7	8-11	>22	87/90	37	95 (92–98)
COG EFFICIENCY (Ext)	10-7	9-3	12-3	40/90	8	79 (75–82)
COMP-KNOWLEDGE	>25	19	>25	99/90	93	122 (118–126)
Verbal Comprehension	21	17-11	>24	98/90	88	117 (112–122)
General Information	>40	23	>40	99/90	95	125 (119–130)
L-T RETRIEVAL	13-10	7-7	>22	89/90	43	97 (93–102)
Visual-Auditory Learning	11-4	7-9	>19	86/90	35	94 (89–99)
Retrieval Fluency	22	7-4	>30	92/90	70	108 (102–113)
VIS-SPATIAL THINK	9-0	6-4	16-5	76/90	16	85 (81–89)
Spatial Relations	10-0	6-10	>25	81/90	28	91 (87–96)
Picture Recognition	8-2	5-10	13-0	69/90	16	85 (81–89)
AUDITORY PROCESS	>25	12-1	>25	94/90	71	108 (103–113)
Sound Blending	>26	14-7	>26	96/90	69	107 (103–112)
Auditory Attention	>20	9-2	>20	92/90	62	105 (96–113)
FLUID REASONING	13-7	10-2	18-3	84/90	38	95 (92–99)
Concept Formation	>21	16-11	>21	97/90	79	112 (107–118)
Analysis-Synthesis	8-6	7-4	10-10	42/90	9	80 (76–85)
PROCESS SPEED	11-2	10-1	12-6	36/90	8	79 (76–83)
Visual Matching	11-1	10-3	12-2	25/90	9	80 (75–84)
Decision Speed	11-3	9-10	13-1	48/90	13	83 (79–88)
SHORT-TERM MEM	9-6	7-11	11-9	45/90	14	84 (79–88)
Numbers Reversed	8-2	7-2	9-10	19/90	7	78 (73–83)
Memory for Words	11-4	9-2	15-4	74/90	33	93 (87–100)
PHONEMIC AWARE	>28	14-5	>28	96/90	78	112 (107–117)
Sound Blending	>26	14-7	>26	96/90	69	107 (103–112)
Incomplete Words	>33	14-2	>33	96/90	84	115 (107–123)
COGNITIVE FLUENCY	13-5	10-11	17-8	82/90	32	93 (91–96)
Rapid Picture Naming	15-7	13-2	19	90/90	49	100 (97–102)
Retrieval Fluency	22	7-4	>30	92/90	70	108 (102–113)
Decision Speed	11-3	9-10	13-1	48/90	13	83 (79–88)
EXEC PROCESSES	16-3	11-11	>20	91/90	54	102 (98–105)
Concept Formation	>21	16-11	>21	97/90	79	112 (107–118)
Pair Cancellation	13-10	11-9	16-4	79/90	33	93 (91–96)
Planning	9-11	4-6	>28	88/90	25	90 (82–98)

Intra-Cognitive Discrepancies	Standard Scores			Discrepancy		
	Actual	Predicted	Difference	PR	SD	Significant at ± 1.5 SEE
COMP-KNOWLEDGE	122	93	+29	99	+2.52	Yes
L-T RETRIEVAL	97	96	+1	56	+0.14	No
VIS-SPATIAL THINK	85	98	–13	16	–1.01	No
AUDITORY PROCESS	108	95	+13	84	+1.00	No
FLUID REASONING	95	96	–1	47	–0.08	No
PROCESS SPEED	79	99	–20	7	–1.46	No
SHORT-TERM MEM	84	98	–14	11	–1.23	No
PHONEMIC AWARE	112	95	+17	91	+1.32	No

Table 2.   WJ III ACH Scores

CLUSTER/Test	Age	Easy to Diff		RPI	PR	SS ± SEM)
BROAD READING	11.5	9.8	13.1	95/90	61	104 (102–106)
Letter-Word Identification	14.1	10.6	>18.0	96/90	70	108 (103–112)
Reading Fluency	11.2	10.3	12.0	97/90	59	104 (102–105)
Passage Comprehension	10.1	6.5	13.0	89/90	48	99 (94–104)
BASIC READING SKILLS	12.6	8.9	17.3	94/90	61	104 (100–108)
Letter-Word Identification	14.1	10.6	>18.0	96/90	70	108 (103–112)
Word Attack	10.2	6.7	15.6	89/90	48	99 (95–103)
BROAD WRITTEN LANG	12.5	8.1	17.4	94/90	66	106 (102–110)
Spelling	12.9	10.0	14.4	97/90	72	109 (105–113)
Writing Fluency	10.1	7.6	13.0	89/90	49	100 (95–104)
Writing Samples	12.9	5.5	>18.0	93/90	68	107 (97–117)
BASIC WRITING SKILLS	12.3	8.9	14.1	92/90	54	102 (98–105)
Spelling	12.9	10.0	14.4	97/90	72	109 (105–113)
Editing	10.8	8.1	13.6	81/90	38	95 (92–99)
WRITTEN EXPRESSION	11.0	7.1	>18.0	91/90	55	102 (96–108)
BROAD MATH	4.8	3.7	6.3	30/90	4	74 (71–76)
Calculation	4.5	3.6	5.7	22/90	3	71 (66–76)
Math Fluency	3.6	1.6	5.8	39/90	1	63 (61–66)
Applied Problems	5.7	4.7	7.1	31/90	16	85 (83–88)
MATH CALC SKILLS	4.2	3.0	5.7	30/90	1	66 (63–70)
MATH REASONING	5.1	4.1	6.4	29/90	10	80 (78–83)
Applied Problems	5.7	4.7	7.1	31/90	16	85 (83–88)
Quantitative Concepts	4.6	3.6	5.8	27/90	7	77 (73–82)

tered subtests and composites are shown in Table 3. TOMA-2 scaled scores have a mean (average) of 10 with a standard deviation of 3. The WJ III standard scores have a mean of 100 and a standard deviation of 15.

Achievement Testing Discussion

In the areas of reading and written language Helen consistently performed at a level that was appropriate for or above her actual grade placement. She clearly demonstrated the ability to manage the typical demands of reading and writing at or above her grade level and would likely be successful with more advanced learning opportunities in these areas.

Table 3.   Test of Mathematical Abilities-2 Scores

Subtest	Grade Equiv.	Scaled Score	Standard Score
Vocabulary	4.2	7	85
Computation	4.2	5	75
General Information	1.2	2	60
Story Problems	2.7	5	75
MATH QUOTIENT			65

Helen's performance on measures of math skills was significantly lower. Helen does not have automatic recall of basic facts and thus was often observed to be working out the answers to simple arithmetic computations. This clearly hindered her performance on the Math Fluency test, in addition to the various computation tasks presented. Helen was able to do multiplication involving the basic facts and can complete whole number addition and subtraction items; however, she was not consistently accurate, particularly when working with larger numbers and when regrouping was required. Helen skipped all division items and did not attempt multiplication items beyond single digits. She used repetitive addition as an alternate strategy when multiplication was required. She appears to have a basic understanding of fraction concepts and correctly added and subtracted fractions with like denominators. Helen had difficulty with items involving number series where she needed to supply a missing number, and had gaps in knowledge of quantitative concepts. Helen's performance on the TOMA-2 also suggests weaknesses related to math vocabulary and typical quantitative information in everyday life. In addition, Helen described her continued difficulty in telling time, especially with analog clocks and watches as opposed to those with a digital format.

Table 4.   Math vs. Other Achievement Areas Scores

Predicted Achievement/Achievement Discrepancies*	Standard Scores			Discrepancy		Significant at ± 1.5 SEE
	Actual	Predicted	Difference	PR	SD	
BROAD READING	104	100	+4	68	+0.46	No
BASIC READING SKILLS	104	101	+3	64	+0.35	No
BROAD MATH	74	97	−23	1	−2.29	Yes
MATH CALC SKILLS	66	93	−27	1	−2.44	Yes
MATH REASONING	80	101	−21	1	−2.19	Yes
BROAD WRITTEN LANG	106	98	+8	80	+0.83	No
BASIC WRITING SKILLS	102	100	+2	55	+0.14	No
WRITTEN EXPRESSION	102	98	+4	64	+0.35	No

*These discrepancies based on predicted achievement scores with ACH Broad, Basic, and Applied clusters.

The scores in Table 4 indicate significant negative discrepancies between Helen's predicted achievement and achievement in all three areas of math. In addition, results from the TOMA-2 indicate that math abilities are significantly lower than other areas of cognitive and academic functioning.

SUMMARY AND CONCLUSIONS

Helen's current evaluation results suggest that she is a student with variability among her cognitive/intellectual abilities. Her cognitive profile indicates that she experiences difficulties in specific areas related to spatial and sequential thinking abilities, and perceptual speed and fluency. In contrast, she has strengths in areas related to verbal abilities and auditory processing, while her ability to store and retrieve linguistic information is in the Average range. The pattern of strengths and weaknesses seen in Helen's cognitive profile is consistent with the strengths and weaknesses seen in her academic achievement performance. Helen is demonstrating skills that are generally at or above her current grade placement in the areas of reading and written language. In contrast, Helen's performance on measures of math indicate significant skill deficits in this area, with grade-level scores approximately 5 or more years below her current grade placement. In regard to the types of issues noted by Helen's teachers in the past, students with spatial and sequential weaknesses may also have difficulties in the social realm, in adjusting to new settings or situations, or in completing academic assignments that require the planning and sequencing of steps.

In planning Helen's comprehensive evaluation the Team has asked whether or not Helen's ongoing math difficulties

are due to the presence of a specific learning disability. The above discrepancy scores suggest that Helen does meet the learning disability eligibility criteria in the State Regulations for special education services.

RECOMMENDATIONS

The following recommendations may help Helen's tutor, her mother, or the staff at her local high school in assisting with planning her home-school program or a program for returning to public school.

1. In teaching math to Helen, place a heavy emphasis on precise and clear verbal descriptions, helping Helen to access a personal understanding of skills and concepts through her strong verbal abilities. This can facilitate Helen's ability to substitute verbal constructions for the intuitive/spatial/relational understanding that she appears to lack. Visual–graphic materials or diagrammatic explanations can be confusing for her and thus will not help to clarify concepts. Repeated use of concrete manipulative teaching materials can be useful (e.g., Cuisenaire Rods, Base Ten blocks), again with the emphasis on developing stable verbal interpretations of the facts, skills, or concepts being learned. Consistent verbal descriptions also need to become internalized regarding when to apply specific math operations and how to complete the correct steps in the correct sequence for written computations. Accompany instruction at the concrete, manipulative level with explicit instruction in how to integrate written numbers and symbols to represent her manipulation of objects (e.g., learning the algorithms). Helen will need to construct strong verbal models in

place of the visual–spatial mental representations that most people develop and draw upon for learning and understanding math.

2. Since Helen is not currently in a formal math class, she does not have the regular opportunity to practice and review math skills and concepts, and observe other students working with math. In considering plans for next year, Helen, her mother, and the team should explore options for Helen to participate in more regular math instruction, such as small group math class in a Resource Room. In this setting, instruction can be better adjusted to Helen's needs and pace, while providing more frequent opportunities for instruction, practice, and interaction with math skills and concepts. Apparently Helen is making good progress in her tutorial at this time, and thus it will be important that she keep using and applying what she is learning so as to help her maintain these gains.

3. A number of instructional components will be important for continuing to build Helen's math skills and knowledge.

   a) Provide frequent interactive practice, review, and opportunities for meaningful application of what she is learning. Distributed practice is best, meaning daily if possible, rather than one weekly session.

   b) Develop her ability to recognize groups, in other words, seeing a group of 5 items and knowing it is 5 without having to count from one.

   c) Help her to strengthen her knowledge of number sequence, ability to compare numbers, and knowledge of how to use tools such as a facts chart or number-line for math work.

   d) Work on small numbers of facts per group for mastery at one time, followed by frequent practice with mixed groups. Place emphasis on "reverses," or "turnarounds" (e.g., 4 + 5/5 + 4, 6 × 7/7 × 6) Teach thinking strategies from one fact to another (e.g., doubles facts, such as 5 + 5, then double-plus-one facts, such as 5 + 6).

   e) Keep in mind that rote memorization of facts is not the primary goal for Helen in math. In fact, her instructional time may be more effectively used by building her compensatory skills (e.g., use of calculator, facts charts) and emphasizing other areas of mathematical concepts, thinking, and problem solving that will be important in daily life. For example, understanding percentage concepts as they relate to discounts, charges, taxes, and tips; time concepts as they relate not only to clocks, but to scheduling, and reading schedules; map reading and using information presented in a key as in a map or chart.

4. Develop and maintain a "Personal Reference Almanac" that will include concepts, procedures, and other important information necessary for Helen's daily work and independent work. This booklet will be an important reference that Helen can use to reinforce her recall of a particular procedure. It will also help establish consistency for learning to facilitate Helen's ability to recall, apply, and generalize from one session or skill to another. Include in this almanac any charts or instructional aids to assist Helen with accuracy in her math facts for basic operations (e.g., multiplication facts grid), formulas, measurement conversions or equivalents, and other important information necessary for Helen's daily work and independence with math. Make and maintain a back-up copy. These accommodations can enable Helen to focus her efforts on the thinking and reasoning demands of her math work while compensating for the impact that spatial and sequential processing issues have on her ability to acquire basic math computation skills.

5. While Helen needs ongoing specialized instruction to address her individual needs in math, ensure that she always has access to a calculator whenever math computations are required. This applies not only to any math class that she may take but to portions of formal tests requiring math computations and in science class as this is a subject area that often requires students to use math in analyzing or comparing information. When using a calculator teach Helen to show, in writing, all steps required to solve a problem and to rework any incorrect solutions.

6. Helen has difficulty with tasks requiring a sequential component. This not only applies to math but to some types of reading comprehension tasks as well, where she may be required to sequence the events or elements of a story, a period in history, or physical changes and observations related to science experiments and studies. Thus, accommodations for extra time will be warranted, especially when her performance is being evaluated, as in exams or standardized tests. As noted above, even with verbal tasks such as analogies, Helen can have difficulties due to spatial and sequential elements inherent in the nature of the task. Thus, it would also be advised that Helen take advantage of the practice materials and programs available in preparation for SATs in verbal areas as well as math.

7. Helen made comments during the testing suggesting that she has feelings of discomfort in large groups and unfamiliar settings. Thus, planning for successful transitions to new settings is recommended. For example, if Helen decides to take classes at her local high school or at any other school setting, have her visit and tour the facility at least one time before her schedule begins, ideally with knowledge of what her schedule will be and where her classes will be located. Perhaps a friend already attending the school can escort her. When it comes time for Helen to select a college, scheduling campus visits and tours will be important.

Adapted from Sheryl Maher, M.A.

Educational Evaluation

Name:	Anjeline Gregg	School:	Washington High School
Date of Birth:	10/27/85	Parents:	Paul and Arlene Gregg
Age:	16 years, 2 months	Date of Testing:	12/16/2001
Grade:	10.4		

REASON FOR REFERRAL

Anjeline was referred for an evaluation by the Glen County School System. The purpose of the referral was to assess current levels of academic performance and to determine appropriate educational interventions. Concerns regarding reading development have been expressed by school personnel and parents. The evaluation was conducted with the consent of Anjeline's parents.

BACKGROUND INFORMATION

Anjeline is the 16-year-old only child of an African-American father, an insurance agent and financial advisor, and a second generation Japanese mother, a flight attendant based in Spokane. English is the language of the home. The Greggs adopted Anjeline at age 5 months. She was healthy and well-nourished but little is known of her biological history.

Anjeline was diagnosed with a reading disorder in second grade and has received school assistance since that time under the category of learning disabilities. A complete review of her educational history is provided in several evaluations in her cumulative file. Anjeline has been evaluated on numerous occasions by many types of professionals (occupational therapist, vision specialist, speech language pathologist, clinical psychologist, neuropsychologist) with the goals of identifying her learning difficulties and planning appropriate interventions to alleviate them. A general conclusion has been that Anjeline has a specific reading disability and requires educational therapy.

To address her difficulties in reading, Anjeline has received 2 years of instruction with the Wilson Reading System, a highly structured, multisensory phonics program. She completed Levels 1–10 but has not yet completed Levels 11 and 12. In addition, she has just finished the first two training disks of the Fast ForWord program. The school has also provided Anjeline with a computer at her home, computers in her classrooms, a scanner, Kurzweil software, and a variety of software programs for home and school use

to assist with reading, as well as to promote writing development.

EVALUATION PROCEDURES

Comprehensive review of prior assessments and school records
Brief interview with Margaret Temple, Assistant Director of Special Education
Brief interview with Arlene Gregg
Brief interview with English and Integrated Science teachers
Oral reading from her classroom text: General Science
Selected tests from the Woodcock-Johnson-III Tests of Cognitive Abilities (WJ III COG) and Tests of Achievement (WJ III ACH)

INTERVIEWS

Prior to the evaluation, a brief interview was conducted with Anjeline's mother, Ms. Arlene Gregg. Similar to school personnel, Ms. Gregg expressed sincere concern about her daughter's present levels of reading and writing performance. She is hoping to find ways to help her improve her reading and writing skills. She noted that Anjeline is able to comprehend textual material when someone reads to her, but does not when reading independently because of difficulties with word identification. Ms. Gregg would like to see Anjeline be at grade level in reading performance and obtain a high school diploma, rather than a certificate. Ms. Gregg stated her belief that Anjeline would benefit significantly from instruction using the Lindamood Phoneme Sequencing Program (LiPS), a highly structured program for teaching phonemic awareness and aspects of reading and spelling, and explained that she has carefully researched the efficacy of this program.

Anjeline is currently participating in all general education courses. Although technology is available in most of her classes (e.g., computer, scanner), both she and her teachers report that she rarely chooses to use it. Current semester results indicate that Anjeline is obtaining an A or B Average in all classes. All teachers indicate that Anjeline does not seem to be experiencing significant difficulties in their courses and that there has been no need for accommodations. Anjeline was described as a cooperative, hardworking student who is well liked by peers and behaves appropriately and responsibly in the classroom.

OBSERVATIONS DURING TESTING

Anjeline was exceptionally cooperative throughout the evaluation. She was attentive to all tasks and no problems were noted in motivation or concentration. She was careful in responding and persisted with difficult tasks. She identified her favorite class as Integrated Science. Asked the reason she likes that class, she said, "The teacher talks a lot." She noted that reading and writing are particularly difficult for her.

ASSESSMENT RESULTS

Anjeline was administered a set of tests from the WJ III Tests of Cognitive Abilities (WJ III COG) and from the WJ III Tests of Achievement (WJ III ACH). The tests were selected based upon the referral question and scored using grade norms. The WJ III ACH is a comprehensive battery of individually administered tests measuring oral language and the academic areas of reading, mathematics, and written language. Because the tests were normed on the same population, direct comparisons can be made among Anjeline's oral language and achievement scores. These comparisons can help determine the presence and significance of any strengths and weaknesses among her abilities. A brief summary and score report are included at the end of this report. The focus of this report will not be on the obtained scores (which only substantiate clinical impressions), but rather on the impressions developed during the assessment process.

Reading and Writing

Anjeline's present scores in reading and writing performance fell in the Low to Low Average range. The most noticeable characteristic regarding her reading is her lack of fluency and accuracy in rapid word identification. When Anjeline was asked to look carefully at words she had mispronounced and to pronounce each of the parts, she was

able to produce the correct pronunciation for many of them. Many of her reading errors showed strong phonological and visual resemblance to the presented word (e.g., "lipids" for *liquids,* "organs" for *organic*). She had little difficulty pronouncing longer content words, such as *monosaccharides,* but then stumbled on small function words, such as *from* and *of.* Similar errors were noted in spelling (e.g., *fourty* for *forty, mite* for *might*).

When asked to correct errors in printed sentences on the Editing test, Anjeline read the word *shoe* and then explained that it was misspelled and should be spelled as *sheo.* These types of mistakes indicated a weakness in recognizing and revisualizing the spelling patterns of English. The spelling patterns of a language are referred to as "orthography."

Anjeline's written responses tended to be short, but had adequate content. Although she made several minor spelling errors, her attempted spellings were all very close to the desired word (e.g., *blue printes* for *blueprints*). In addition, her spellings indicate good knowledge of fundamental English spelling rules, such as when to double consonants or to drop the letter *e* at the end of the word when adding a suffix beginning with a vowel. Of interest is the fact that Anjeline's score on the WJ III ACH Spelling of Sounds test, a measure of the ability to spell nonwords that conform to English spelling patterns, was solidly in the Average range. At her grade level, it would be impossible to perform adequately on this type of task without good phonemic awareness and basic knowledge of phonics and spelling rules. This score illustrates the success of her prior interventions in promoting the mastery of phonic principles and a conscious understanding of English spelling rules.

Mathematics

Anjeline obtained Average scores in the area of mathematics. She solved problems quickly and easily. When presented with word problems, she was able to produce the answer without using paper and pencil. She was confident in responding to math questions and said, "I don't know" when unsure of how to solve a problem. She did note that she had forgotten how to solve some types of problems that she used to know how to do.

Oral Language/Achievement Discrepancies

Anjeline's performance on the Oral Language cluster was within the Average range. In contrast, her performance on the Broad Reading cluster was in the Low range. The magnitude of this discrepancy is such that only 2% of students with oral language abilities similar to Anjeline's would score as low as or lower than she did on reading. As observed by her mother, Anjeline performs at a much higher level when she listens to information than when she reads it. The problem is not due to poor comprehension, limited language abilities, or a lack of knowledge. Instead, it is the result of a lack of automaticity in word identification. Her focus on the content is continually interrupted by inaccuracies in word reading.

DISCUSSION AND DIAGNOSTIC IMPRESSIONS

Results from this evaluation are consistent with many of the findings from past evaluations. To summarize, Anjeline has: (a) superior ability to perform rote visual tasks that require rapid scanning and speed (similar to WISC-III Symbol Search, the WJ III COG Visual Matching test was in the Superior range); (b) above average nonverbal and visual reasoning abilities (documented in prior evaluations); (c) Average to High Average performance in mathematics; (d) Low Average to Average oral language abilities, with receptive language abilities solidly in the Average range; and (e) basic reading and spelling skills in the Low to Low Average range. Past fourth grade, students learn much of their new vocabulary from reading; consequently, in interpreting various measures of oral language, one must consider that weak performance in oral vocabulary may be the direct result of a reading disability.

Anjeline's specific disorder is most aptly described as "surface" dyslexia or "orthographic" dyslexia. Observations that support this conclusion are: (a) she reads and spells phonically regular words (e.g., *market*) more accurately than words with irregular spelling patterns (e.g., *once*); (b) she pronounces longer content-related words (e.g., *dyspepsia*) more easily than simple function words (e.g., *of, from*); and (c) analysis of reading and spelling errors indicates a reliance on phonological features, rather than mastery of correct spelling patterns (e.g., spelling *might* as *mite.*). At this point in her reading and writing development, her basic difficulty is in storing and retrieving letter combinations, not in applying phonic principles and rules.

This finding was also observed by Dr. Emory Robertson, Speech-Language Pathologist, who wrote, "Anjeline's reading disorder is more similar to surface dyslexia than to phonologically based dyslexia. As such, a program focusing mainly on phonological development is highly unlikely to produce the desired results. Intensive and systematic training in an approach with a strong focus on irregular spellings, such as Slingerland, the Spalding method, or the Wilson Reading System, modified to her level, would serve Anjeline's needs more effectively." In addition, his recommendations were appropriate: to increase mastery of irregular rules of spelling, and to increase the ability to recognize and understand the morphological components of the words in order to increase reading speed and word analysis (i.e., prefixes, suffixes, and root words).

Although Ms. Gregg's goal of having her daughter read and write at grade level is certainly understandable, as well as desirable, one must keep in mind that her struggles with the acquisition of reading and spelling skills are not due to poor educational programming or the wrong reading methodology; rather, they are the results of a specific impairment—dyslexia. Individuals with this type of difficulty are slow to acquire basic reading and spelling skills and require intensive therapy and years of systematic instruction, reinforcement, and practice to become proficient and fluent readers. Even with proper help, many individuals with dyslexia have reading and spelling performance substantially below expected levels even into their college years. Because of the intensive instruction that she has received, Anjeline has managed to acquire adequate word identification and spelling skill, and is currently able to pronounce words and sequence sounds accurately. Unfortunately, the types of errors that Anjeline makes (e.g., confusing letter sequences) are highly resistant to remediation and result in slow word recognition and a significant delay in word-reading automaticity (the ability to recognize words instantly). Adults with dyslexia are typically characterized by a slow reading rate and poor spelling.

Both the school district and Ms. Gregg should be commended for their diligence in designing and pursuing appropriate instructional goals for Anjeline. Her good ability to sequence sounds and her explicit knowledge of English spelling rules are clearly related to remedial efforts. It should be kept in mind that there is no magic cure for this type of dyslexia, other than continued therapy and years of hard work. To select appropriate interventions, it is necessary to understand her present level of development and her current needs. Because of appropriate educational therapy, Anjeline has developed sufficient phonological abilities and phonics skills, and now attention has to be directed toward rapid orthographic pattern recognition and reading rate.

Despite the probable difficulties described above, Ms. Gregg's wish for Anjeline to earn a diploma is clearly possible, as long as she is provided with appropriate accommodations in the test setting (such as a reader or the test on tape, and extended time). Anjeline is capable of completing high school, receiving a diploma, and pursuing postsecondary education. She has many good abilities that will help her succeed.

RECOMMENDATIONS

Accommodations

1. Appropriate accommodations, such as shortened reading assignments and/or extended time, should be provided on an as-needed basis in her general education classrooms. Teachers should be informed of Anjeline's slow reading rate and inefficient word recognition so that appropriate adjustments can be made.
2. Until reading performance improves, Anjeline is likely to need a reader for or tape recording of any examinations, including group-administered standardized tests, requiring lengthy reading.

Reading

Ms. Gregg expressed the opinion that the Lindamood Phoneme Sequencing Program (LiPS) would benefit Anjeline. LiPS is a widely used and a reputable program that focuses on relating letters to sounds and sound sequencing. At this point in her development, the LiPS program would just replicate the skills and information that Anjeline has already mastered, thus wasting valuable therapeutic time and doing little to improve her reading rate.

As explained previously, Anjeline is not impaired in phonemic awareness. The focus for remediation needs to be upon increasing her ability to recognize common letter patterns to increase her speed of word perception and her reading rate. The following recommendations are offered as interventions that would be most beneficial for Anjeline at this time:

1. Use techniques specifically designed to increase reading fluency for short periods daily. Take baseline data and document progress. Some suggestions follow. A summary of each program/technique is attached to this report.
   a) *Great Leaps Reading* (Diarmud, Inc., www. greatleapsreading.com): Great Leaps Reading is specifically designed to increase automatic recogni-

tion of letter patterns and reading rate while reinforcing phonics skills and sight word recognition.
   b) Repeated readings: The student reads the same passage repeatedly, the first time into a tape recorder. Between readings, she works out the words that gave her difficulty. Progress is charted based on the percentage of words read correctly and the rate at which the passage was read.
   c) Speed drills: Speed drills are tailor-made for a student based on the phonics rules or patterns, sight words, or word parts the student needs to automatize.
2. If Anjeline is not progressing in accuracy and rate of word recognition after a month of instruction with *Great Leaps Reading* and/or other fluency techniques, consider reviewing Levels 6–10 and completing Levels 11 and 12 in the Wilson Reading System. Continue to work on rate, also.
3. Because Anjeline's listening comprehension is at grade level, but her reading decoding is several years below grade level, provide her with taped copies of all of her textbooks as well as any assigned novels and outside reading. This will enable her to learn the information along with the class and participate in class discussions. Anjeline should be encouraged to follow along with the book as she listens to the material on tape. This process will also help build reading accuracy and speed. Merely listening to the books will not improve her reading performance. Because Anjeline has been identified as having dyslexia, she may register with Recording for the Blind & Dyslexic (RFB&D, 800-221-4792, e-mail: custserv@rfbd.org, website: www.rfbd.org) and secure textbooks from them.
4. Provide Anjeline with many daily opportunities for reading connected text that is between her independent and instructional levels. Although reading is difficult, the more she reads, the more fluent and automatic her reading will become.
5. Consider obtaining a screenreader program for Anjeline to use when she has a great deal of reading to do on the computer, such as when using an on-line encyclopedia, an on-line library, or when reading articles from the internet. Many different types of screenreaders are currently available. Ask the visual impairment specialist for advice on selecting a program or go to http://www. about.com and search "screenreaders."

Written Language

1. Continue instruction in keyboarding skills and use of a spell-checker for editing. Currently, Anjeline's phonetic

accuracy in her spelling will allow a spell checker to detect most of her errors and she will be able to correct them using the technology.

2. Review punctuation and capitalization rules within the context of Anjeline's written assignments.

3. For written expression, continue use of software programs, such as CoWriter, Write OutLoud, and Inspiration (graphic organizers) at school and at home.

Considerations for Postsecondary Education

1. Anjeline should be encouraged to apply to a college that provides services to students with learning disabilities. She is likely to need accommodations, such as extended time, in courses that require extensive reading and writing.

2. Before completing high school, the school should complete a comprehensive evaluation so that Anjeline has current documentation of her disability to present to the postsecondary institution.

3. Anjeline should be encouraged to select a career that will capitalize on her good visual and mathematical abilities. Examples would include computer science, architecture, or a branch of the sciences.

Further Evaluation

No further evaluation is required at this time. Anjeline has completed many lengthy assessments, all with relatively similar conclusions. Further assessment will only frustrate her and contribute to a perception that "there must really be something wrong with me." In addition, her reading disability, orthographic dyslexia, has been clearly documented, as has her need for continued educational therapy. Anjeline has had many excellent evaluations that have all essentially reached very similar conclusions. What is now needed is further attention to her reading and writing development. Care must be taken to ensure that Anjeline understands that her difficulties with reading and spelling are the result of dyslexia, not a lack of ability or poor or limited academic instruction, and that the only way to address this problem is to continue with appropriate therapy.

COMPUSCORE VERSION 1.1B: SUMMARY AND SCORE REPORT

Name: Gregg, Anjeline
Date of Birth: 10/27/1985
Age: 16 years, 2 months
Sex: Female

School: Washington High School
Grade: 10.4
Date of Testing: 12/16/2001

Table of Scores

Woodcock-Johnson III Tests of Cognitive Abilities and Tests of Achievement
Norms based on grade 10.4

CLUSTER/Test	RAW	GE	EASY	to DIFF	RPI	PR	SS (68% BAND)
VERBAL ABILITY	—	**8.2**	**5.9**	**11.1**	**86/90**	**43**	**97 (93–101)**
Verbal Comprehension	—	8.2	5.9	11.1	86/90	43	97 (93–101)
ORAL LANGUAGE (Ext)	—	**6.3**	**3.6**	**10.7**	**81/90**	**29**	**91 (88–95)**
Story Recall	—	4.2	K.6	>18.0	84/90	21	88 (78–97)
Picture Vocabulary	27	6.5	4.5	8.9	73/90	29	92 (87–96)
Understanding Directions		5.9	3.2	11.5	82/90	32	93 (88–98)
Oral Comprehension	22	7.1	4.6	10.7	83/90	38	96 (91–100)
ORAL EXPRESSION	—	**6.0**	**3.1**	**10.2**	**79/90**	**27**	**91 (87–95)**
Story Recall	—	4.2	K.6	>18.0	84/90	21	88 (78–97)
Picture Vocabulary	27	6.5	4.5	8.9	73/90	29	92 (87–96)
LISTENING COMP	—	**6.6**	**4.0**	**11.0**	**83/90**	**35**	**94 (90–98)**
Understanding Directions	—	5.9	3.2	11.5	82/90	32	93 (88–98)
Oral Comprehension	22	7.1	4.6	10.7	83/90	38	96 (91–100)
TOTAL ACHIEVEMENT	—	**5.6**	**4.3**	**7.3**	**55/90**	**17**	**86 (85–87)**
BROAD READING	—	**3.7**	**3.1**	**4.5**	**7/90**	**3**	**72 (71–74)**
Letter-Word Ident.	49	4.0	3.5	4.7	8/90	8	79 (77–82)
Reading Fluency	35	3.7	3.1	4.4	1/90	4	75 (73–76)
Passage Comprehension	26	3.1	2.4	4.3	31/90	4	74 (70–79)
BASIC READING SKILLS	—	**3.8**	**3.1**	**4.7**	**17/90**	**8**	**79 (77–81)**
Letter-Word Ident.	49	4.0	3.5	4.7	8/90	8	79 (77–82)
Word Attack	17	3.3	2.4	4.8	32/90	13	83 (81–86)
BROAD MATH	—	**9.3**	**6.8**	**12.9**	**90/90**	**51**	**101 (98–103)**
Calculation	26	9.7	7.3	12.9	92/90	56	102 (96–108)
Math Fluency	123	13.0	8.6	>18.0	96/90	80	113 (110–115)
Applied Problems	41	7.2	5.8	9.3	77/90	35	94 (91–97)
MATH CALC SKILLS	—	**11.1**	**7.8**	**16.4**	**94/90**	**66**	**106 (103–110)**
Calculation	26	9.7	7.3	12.9	92/90	56	102 (96–108)
Math Fluency	123	13.0	8.6	>18.0	96/90	80	113 (110–115)
BROAD WRITTEN LANG	—	**6.3**	**4.5**	**8.9**	**74/90**	**22**	**88 (85–91)**
Spelling	35	5.4	4.2	7.0	55/90	17	86 (82–90)
Writing Fluency	22	7.7	6.1	10.2	82/90	38	95 (91–99)
Writing Samples	10-D	4.8	2.3	11.6	81/90	14	84 (74–93)
BASIC WRITING SKILLS	—	**5.2**	**4.0**	**6.9**	**53/90**	**15**	**85 (81–88)**
Spelling	35	5.4	4.2	7.0	55/90	17	86 (82–90)
Editing	13	4.9	3.8	6.7	51/90	19	87 (83–90)
WRITTEN EXPRESSION	—	**7.0**	**4.8**	**10.6**	**81/90**	**31**	**92 (88–96)**
Writing Fluency	22	7.7	6.1	10.2	82/90	38	95 (91–99)
Writing Samples	10-D	4.8	2.3	11.6	81/90	14	84 (74–93)

Table of Scores (*continued*)

CLUSTER/Test	RAW	GE	EASY	to DIFF	RPI	PR	SS (68% BAND)
ACADEMIC SKILLS	—	**5.6**	**4.5**	**7.1**	**52/90**	**11**	**81 (79–84)**
Letter-Word Ident.	49	4.0	3.5	4.7	8/90	8	79 (77–82)
Calculation	26	9.7	7.3	12.9	92/90	56	102 (96–108)
Spelling	35	5.4	4.2	7.0	55/90	17	86 (82–90)
ACADEMIC FLUENCY	—	**6.0**	**4.8**	**7.4**	**49/90**	**17**	**85 (84–87)**
Reading Fluency	35	3.7	3.1	4.4	1/90	4	75 (73–76)
Math Fluency	123	13.0	8.6	>18.0	96/90	80	113 (110–115)
Writing Fluency	22	7.7	6.1	10.2	82/90	38	95 (91–99)
ACADEMIC APPS	—	**5.1**	**3.7**	**7.5**	**64/90**	**13**	**83 (80–86)**
Passage Comprehension	26	3.1	2.4	4.3	31/90	4	74 (70–79)
Applied Problems	41	7.2	5.8	9.3	77/90	35	94 (91–97)
Writing Samples	10-D	4.8	2.3	11.6	81/90	14	84 (74–93)
PHON/GRAPH KNOW	—	**4.4**	**2.7**	**7.0**	**63/90**	**19**	**87 (84–90)**
Word Attack	17	3.3	2.4	4.8	32/90	13	83 (81–86)
Spelling of Sounds	31	7.3	3.7	13.0	86/90	39	96 (91–101)
Visual Matching	60-2	>18.0	>18.0	>18.0	100/90	96	127 (121–133)

DISCREPANCIES	STANDARD SCORES			DISCREPANCY		Significant at
	Actual	Predicted	Difference	PR	SD	±1.50 SD (SEE)
Intra-Achievement						
BROAD READING	72	94	–22	1	–2.35	Yes
BROAD MATH	101	87	+14	90	+1.25	No
BROAD WRITTEN LANG	88	90	–2	45	–0.13	No
ORAL LANGUAGE	90	91	–1	49	–0.03	No

DISCREPANCIES	STANDARD SCORES			DISCREPANCY		Significant at
	Actual	Predicted	Difference	PR	SD	±1.50 SD (SEE)
*Oral Language/Achievement Discrepancies**						
BROAD READING	72	96	–24	2	–2.15	Yes
BASIC READING SKILLS	79	96	–17	7	–1.51	Yes
BROAD MATH	101	95	+6	66	+0.42	No
MATH CALC SKILLS	106	97	+9	76	+0.71	No
BROAD WRITTEN LANG	88	95	–7	28	–0.59	No
BASIC WRITING SKILLS	85	96	–11	19	–0.89	No
WRITTEN EXPRESSION	92	96	–4	39	–0.29	No

*These discrepancies based on Oral Language (Ext) with ACH Broad, Basic, and Applied clusters.

Kilmore Country Jail: IEP Review

Name: Donald Ramona
Date of Birth: 9/22/1983
Age: 17-8
Grade: 10.9

Booking Number: B24733
Officer: Toby Ofeish
Date of Testing: 5/17/2001
School: Kilmore County Jail, Juvenile
                 Education

REASON FOR REFERRAL

Donald was referred for an evaluation to develop goals and objectives for his new Individualized Education Program (IEP) as part of the Kilmore County Jail's Education Assessment program. Donald is currently incarcerated in a maximum security setting for juvenile offenders.

BACKGROUND INFORMATION

Records were obtained from Bernald School District. During elementary school, Donald lived with his mother and a younger brother who had a different biological father. In second grade, Donald was described by his teacher as "having difficulty attending to a task, paying attention, and bringing in homework." According to the school records, Donald's mother indicated that his school problems were caused by his asthma medication, and that the medication had given him an "attitude." She described her primary disciplinary procedures as "taking away privileges, yelling, and spanking." She described the methods as not being very effective and the frequency of discipline as "daily."

Medical and developmental history indicated no complications during pregnancy or birth and all developmental milestones were reached within normal limits. During third grade, Donald was hospitalized for asthma. On several occasions during childhood, Donald broke bones from falls. His mother described him as very "accident prone." Teachers during elementary and middle school years described Donald as avoiding schoolwork, frequently lying, sullen, and having temper tantrums. On two occasions, he ran away from home and was returned by the local police.

In fifth grade, Donald was referred for special education. At this time he was referred for carrying a concealed weapon (a pocket knife) to school. His classroom teacher described him as: not following directions, having poor attention, not completing his schoolwork, talking back, losing his school materials, and disturbing classmates. Donald was deemed ineligible for services, but recommendations were made for the mother to obtain an evaluation related to concerns about inattention and to pursue small group counseling. These recommendations were not pursued.

In seventh grade, Donald was referred again for special education. At this time, he was deemed eligible for services under the category of specific learning disabilities. He began receiving resource services with a focus on reading and writing instruction.

During the next few years, Donald had six referrals to the Juvenile Court Center. Complaints included: two charges for vehicle theft, two charges for paint-sniffing, and two curfew violations. When Donald was 14, he was charged with robbery, assault with a deadly weapon (.357 magnum), and unlawful flight. He was sentenced to a 3-year term at Kilmore County Jail Juvenile Education, to be followed by a 3-year term in prison. In 4 months, he will leave Kilmore County Jail and begin his 3-year term at Knoxdale Prison.

Donald is currently receiving instruction in Kilmore County Jail. Donald has attempted to pass the GED two times, but has been unsuccessful. Presently, he is receiving failing grades in his language arts and geography classes for "a lack of effort." He is receiving a passing grade in a science class. During this time he has received several Disciplinary Action Reports (DAR) from teachers. The formal statements of charge on the DARs indicate that that the inmate will not be quiet when given direct orders, talks out of turn, and takes materials from the classroom without approval (e.g., a newspaper).

TESTS ADMINISTERED

Wechsler Adult Intelligence Scale—III (WAIS-III)
Selected tests from the WJ III Achievement Tests
    (WJ III ACH)
Clinical interview

INTELLECTUAL PERFORMANCE

As part of his reevaluation, Donald was administered the WAIS-III. He was cooperative and worked hard during the testing and declined taking any breaks. His Verbal IQ score was 94, within the Average range, at the 34th percentile. His Performance or nonverbal IQ is 109, within the upper portion of the Average range, and at the 73rd percentile. His Full Scale IQ was 100, again within the Average range and at the 50th percentile. The following scaled scores were obtained for Donald:

Verbal	Scaled Scores
Vocabulary	8
Similarities	14
Arithmetic	6
Digit Span	6
Information	7
Comprehension	14
Letter-Number Seq.	(6)

Performance	Scaled Scores
Picture Completion	14
Digit Symbol Coding	11
Block Design	12
Matrix Reasoning	13
Picture Arrangement	7

Donald had strengths in areas measuring attention to visual detail and reasoning using spatial skills. He did particularly well on verbal tasks that involved commonsense judgment and reasoning. Relative weaknesses were noted in areas measuring general information, short-term memory, and the ability to place pictures in a logical sequence. Although Donald speaks quite easily, he lacks much of the information that would typically be acquired through school attendance. Short-term memory for nonmeaningful material is also a weakness, as supported by the low Digit Span and Letter-Number Sequencing tests. Letter-Number Sequencing (9th percentile) requires simultaneously tracking letters and numbers and then manipulating them. Donald showed considerable frustration when attempting this task. Tasks such as taking notes in class while listening to lectures would likely be difficult for him. The results of the WAIS-III suggest that Donald's overall cognitive ability is within the Average range. Because of his experiences, he has not developed the fund of information that most students of his chronological age would have.

ACADEMIC PERFORMANCE

To re-evaluate current levels of academic functioning, Donald was administered six tests from the WJ III Tests of Achievement. A significant difference existed between Donald's performance on measures of basic skills (Academic Skills, Standard Score of 75) and his ability to apply these skills (Academic Applications, Standard Score of 96). As compared to age-peers, Donald had difficulty reading words with ease, spelling words, and performing mathematical calculations. In contrast, his ability to apply these skills was comparable to age-peers. (See Table 1.)

Table 1.   Scores on Woodcock-Johnson III Tests of Achievement

Norms based on age 17-8
Form A of the following achievement tests was administered:

CLUSTER/Test	RAW	AE	EASY to DIFF		RPI	PR	SS (68% BAND)
ACADEMIC SKILLS		11-0	9-8	12-8	22/90	5	75 (73–78)
ACADEMIC APPS		15-10	12-6	>27	86/90	40	96 (93–99)
Letter-Word Identification	55	11-0	9-11	12-3	12/90	8	78 (76–81)
Calculation	20	11-4	10-1	13-0	31/90	5	76 (71–81)
Spelling	35	10-4	9-0	13-2	29/90	8	79 (75–82)
Passage Comprehension	36	15-3	11-7	26	85/90	40	96 (91–101)
Applied Problems	48	16-2	14-0	20	84/90	44	98 (95–100)
Writing Samples	15-D	15-7	9-8	>23	88/90	39	96 (87–105)

CLINICAL INTERVIEW

Donald noted that he felt lonely since his incarceration. He said that he missed seeing his friends. He stated that he really did not want to see his mother as they really did not get along but that he would like to be able to see his little brother. He commented that his father had never been around. He noted that asthma had always been a problem in his life, but that it did not bother him as much now that he was living inside. Donald stated that he had never belonged to a gang. He noted that he was a heavy drinker, had sniffed paint, and had experimented with marijuana and crystal. He stated that when he is released from prison, he would like to work in the computer industry.

Other than missing friends and family members, Donald does not seem to be significantly depressed. He does not report depressive features, such as not sleeping, crying, or ideas of suicide. He is not psychotic and does not suffer from hallucinations. He states that he has a girlfriend, and that his favorite activities are to "go to the movies and the mall." In this clinical interview, he also expressed antisocial tendencies. He stated that he did not trust anyone, that he and his friends were frequently picked up by the police, and that he had taken drugs that were most like speed. When asked if he would rob someone again, he said that he would and the weapon he would choose would be a gun. He noted that "being killed" would not be the worst thing that could happen to him.

DIAGNOSTIC IMPRESSION

Donald's word identification, spelling skill, and math basic skills are significantly below his cognitive and linguistic abilities. In addition, he has a history of learning difficulties and continues to exhibit problems in short-term memory and attention. According to the state's special education guidelines, Donald qualifies for Special Education under the condition of specific learning disability in the areas of basic reading skills and basic math skills. Donald's ethnicity, language, and educational opportunities do not appear to be the primary reason for the continued academic difficulties.

DSM-IV, AXIS I:	312.8 Conduct Disorder, Adolescent-Onset Type
Reading Disorder	315.0
Mathematics Disorder	315.1

RECOMMENDATIONS

1. Donald's history suggests that he has symptoms consistent with a diagnosis of Attention Deficit Hyperactivity Disorder (ADHD). Attentional problems may have also been exacerbated by the asthma medication. A consultation with a physician regarding these issues would be appropriate at this time.
2. Donald should continue to receive special education services to get the help that he needs. Attention should be focused on building reading and writing skills so that he can accomplish his goal of working in the computer industry.
3. Encourage Donald to enroll in Project Hope, a literacy program at Knoxdale Prison.
4. Donald should attempt to complete his GED while in prison and then begin vocational training in computers.
5. Select a mentor for Donald who will help him achieve his goals of completing his GED and beginning vocational training in the computer industry.
6. Provide Donald with extended time on any class examinations.
7. Allow Donald to tape-record lectures or to receive a copy of the instructor's lecture notes.
8. Provide Donald with drug and alcohol counseling while he is in prison.
9. Prior to release from prison, make arrangements for a vocational placement.
10. Donald will be released to the Department of Corrections in 4 months. Due to Donald's current legal status, the ultimate determination of his least restrictive environment will be based upon his safety and the safety of others around him.

Learning Disability Evaluation

Name: Ophelia Jones   Matriculation Number: 5289584
Birth Date: 12-28-81   Grade: College Sophomore
CA: 20   Test Dates: 02/11/02–02/13/02

REASON FOR REFERRAL

Ophelia, a sophomore in pre-medicine, has experienced longstanding difficulties with spelling and reading. Many of her teachers over the years have suggested that she be tested, but she never pursued an evaluation. Recently, a college English professor spoke to her about the many mistakes in her writing and strongly recommended that she contact the University Learning Disabilities clinic for dyslexia testing.

BACKGROUND INFORMATION

Ophelia is a 20-year-old, single, right-handed sophomore who currently resides in a dormitory on campus. She was raised with her older brother, whom she described as a "boy genius," by her mother and father, both of whom are professionals with Master's degrees. Ophelia's father reportedly had difficulty "maintaining focus" in school; otherwise, no learning problems were reported in the family.

Mrs. Jones reported no problems or concerns during her pregnancy with Ophelia. Delivery was by Caesarian section due to lack of labor progress; there were no other reported complications. According to Mrs. Jones, Ophelia was slower than her brother to begin talking but otherwise reached developmental milestones within normal limits.

During her childhood, Ophelia suffered from mild ear drainage problems (during her second and fifth years, no tubes required), chicken pox (age 6), and influenza (ages 9 and 12). No neurocognitive risk factors (e.g., blows to the head, toxin exposure, seizures) were reported. Ophelia described her current health and mood as "good." Her vision and hearing were recently tested and found to be normal.

Ophelia attended public schools throughout her compulsory education. She changed schools three times (before grades 3, 4, and 12) due to family relocations. Ophelia was placed in gifted education classes between grades 4 and 8.

During elementary school, Ophelia had difficulty distinguishing left from right, learning to tell time, tying shoes, learning and recognizing written letters, spelling, reading, and writing cursive. Mrs. Jones noted that reading and writing problems were initially noted during first grade, when her daughter "skipped lines and left out letters and words." Ophelia received an hour of tutoring a day during early elementary school. In junior and senior high school, Ophelia found spelling and in-class composition difficult. Since beginning college, she has struggled with spelling, long reading assignments, and math calculations (when she cannot use a calculator). She noted that she usually "tracks" with her finger while reading and that she has always been confused by written words that "do not follow clear rules."

Ophelia's unweighted high school grade point average was 3.7. A review of transcripts indicated that she earned As and Bs in all classes with the exception of chemistry and French (in which she received Cs during some terms). On the SAT, she obtained scores of 520 (Verbal) and 630 (Math). After her first three semesters at college, Ophelia has a grade point average of 2.91. She has earned A's in all math classes and science labs; B's in English, history, and geography courses; and C's in chemistry and biology classes. She reported that biology and chemistry terms have always been difficult for her.

Ophelia reported no difficulties with concentration and no sources of emotional distress other than struggling in classes in which she wants to do well. She is concerned that if she is unable to improve in classes such as chemistry and biology, she will not be able to go on to medical school. In her free time, Ophelia enjoys mountain biking, being with friends and family, and making stained glass.

INFORMATION FROM TEACHERS

Ophelia provided two letters from teachers. The more recent, written by the English professor who advised her to seek the current evaluation, detailed contrasts between her at-home work (when she can use a word processor with spelling/grammar check programs) and her in-class work (when she cannot). The professor, Dr. Yurkin, described Ophelia's spelling mistakes as "glaring" and "unexpected" given her conscientious nature and the intelligent and creative ideas in her essays. A letter from Ophelia's high school French teacher, Ms. Zelder, was also provided. Ms. Zelder described Ophelia as hard-working and conscientious, but unable to master verb tenses, word endings, and other aspects of written French. She noted that Ophelia would misspell "even basic words that we [had] worked with on a daily basis for months."

TESTING OBSERVATIONS

Ophelia was tested over two sessions. She arrived early for both appointments, dressed in a casual but appropriate manner. She easily established rapport with examiners and remained pleasant and cooperative even when asked to perform tasks that were difficult for her. Ophelia's work style was persistent and efficient, though she was considerably slower on tests related to reading and spelling than she was on other tests. No difficulties with sustained attention, impulsivity, or hyperactivity were noted during the evaluation. Based on examiner observations, the results of the evaluation are believed to be representative of Ophelia's functioning at this time.

CURRENT EMOTIONAL STATUS

Ophelia was asked to complete several measures of social/emotional functioning. Her responses on the Beck Anxiety Inventory (BAI) and the Beck Depression Inventory—Revised (BDI-R) indicated that she was experiencing minimal levels of depressed mood (BDI-R raw score: 2) and anxiety (BAI raw score: 2) during the weeks leading up to the assessment. She endorsed no symptoms as being more than "a little bit" bothersome. Although Ophelia exhibited mild anxiousness when confronted with certain tests related to reading and spelling, nothing in her deportment suggested that she was experiencing global anxiety or depression.

Prior to her testing, Ophelia was provided with self-report and parent checklists related to Attention Deficit Hyperactivity Disorder (ADHD). She filled out one checklist; her mother completed the second (about her). Results indicated that Ophelia is "not likely" to have ADHD.

Behavioral observations suggested that Ophelia was able to maintain a focused level of attention (and a disciplined, careful work style) during the current evaluation. Although she displayed mild fatigue toward the end of the full testing day, she exhibited no symptoms of ADHD. Based on the level of her observed and reported symptomatology, Ophelia does not meet the diagnostic criteria for ADHD.

TESTS ADMINISTERED

Wechsler Adult Intelligence Scale—Third Edition (WAIS-III)
Woodcock-Johnson III Tests of Cognitive Abilities (WJ III COG)
Wechsler Memory Scale—Third Edition (WMS)
Colorado Perceptual Speed Trial III
Speech Sounds Perception Test (SSPT)
Oral and Written Language Scales (OWLS)
Controlled Oral Word Association Test (COWAT)
Beck Anxiety Inventory (BAI)
Beck Depression Inventory—Revised (BDI-R)
Phonological and Orthographic battery (informal)
Oral language and writing samples (informal)

TEST RESULTS

Intellectual Ability

Ophelia's overall cognitive ability was found to be in the High Average range as measured by both the Woodcock-Johnson III Tests of Cognitive Abilities (WJ III GIA: 113) and the Wechsler Adult Intelligence Scale, Third Edition (WAIS-III FSIQ: 115). (See Table 1.) In addition to an estimate of overall ability, the WAIS-III generates four Index scores, which provide additional descriptions of a person's cognitive abilities. Three of Ophelia's Index scores were in the High Average to Superior range:

- The Working Memory (WM) Index includes tests of concentration such as repeating strings of numbers and mentally organizing groups of letters and numbers (SS 113, 81%ile);
- The Perceptual Organization (PO) Index features tests that require attention to visual detail, visual–spatial processing, and organization and manipulation of visual–nonverbal information (SS 111, 77%ile); and
- The Verbal Comprehension (VC) Index measures vocabulary, verbal abstract reasoning, and general fund of crystallized knowledge (SS 124, 95%ile).

Ophelia demonstrated a notable and statistically rare weakness on measures comprising the Processing Speed (PS) Index which features tests of visual discrimination and psychomotor scanning speed (e.g., rapid visual scanning of shapes with a minimal motor response). She scored in the lower end of the Average range (SS 93, 32%ile).

A similar pattern of scores was evident on the WJ III COG. Ophelia's verbal ability (acquired knowledge and language comprehension) was High Average, as was her general thinking ability. In contrast, her cognitive efficiency (automatic processing) was Average.

Brief Attention and Working Memory

Ophelia demonstrated no difficulties on measures assessing short-term memory span, working memory, and attentional capacity. She scored in the Average to Superior range Qualitatively, clinicians observed that Ophelia's abilities to maintain concentration, ignore potential distracters, and sustain focus over long periods of time were consistently strong.

Learning and Memory

Ophelia was administered several subtests that asked her to learn and later recall unfamiliar information. The presented information varied in modality (e.g., visual or verbal) and format (e.g., associative or rote). Ophelia scored in the Superior range in learning the associations between words in pairs. By the end of the first trial, she had encoded all administered word pairs. She scored in the Average range in learning lists of unrelated words and in learning narratives presented orally. Overall, Ophelia's initial auditory/verbal learning was within the range expected. Additionally, her ability to recall this information after delays of 25–35 minutes was consistent with her initial learning. She recalled nearly all of the information she had been asked to learn.

On a variety of measures of visual–nonverbal and mixed-modality learning, Ophelia scored in the Average to High Average range in tests of memory for photographs of faces, details of drawings, and pictograph-word associations. No deficits in visual learning and recall were apparent. Ophelia's recall of visual–nonverbal information after delays of 25 to 35 minutes was Average and commensurate with her initial learning.

In summary, Ophelia's ability to learn and recall novel information was intact across all administered formats and modalities. In general, Ophelia was most effective (High Average to Superior) on associative learning tasks (e.g., linking two seemingly unrelated words or a pictograph to a spoken word).

Visual–Spatial Abilities

Ophelia demonstrated intact visual–spatial abilities across measures of visual–spatial construction and reasoning, scoring in the Average to High range. Additionally, she did not report difficulty using maps, judging distances while driving, or getting lost around campus.

Psychomotor Scanning Speed

As noted previously, Ophelia's scores on measures of psychomotor scanning speed ranged from Low Average to Average. These scores were mildly below expectations based on overall ability. Ophelia was more efficient working with abstract shapes than with clusters of numbers. She reported that she sometimes "flips" letters and numbers while spelling and reading. Notably, Ophelia's ability to name pictures rapidly was High Average and considerably stronger than her ability to scan and respond rapidly to printed symbols such as letters and numbers.

Executive Functions and Reasoning

Ophelia demonstrated an impressive strength on measures of reasoning, scoring in the Average to Superior range. Individuals with good reasoning abilities often solve day-to-day problems with relative ease and can usually generate effective strategies to handle situations or challenges they have not previously encountered. In terms of planning and self-regulation, Ophelia demonstrated problem-solving approaches that were careful, reflective, and effective. She did not exhibit difficulty organizing information and was consistent in her ability to monitor her own performance in order to avoid impulsive or poorly thought-out responses. She demonstrated excellent executive functioning in both structured and unstructured situations.

Oral Language

Ophelia's receptive and expressive language skills were assessed within the contexts of: (a) sounds and single words, (b) sentences, and (c) discourse samples. Informal analyses of fluency and phonological/orthographic processing were also completed. Phonological processing involves working with language sounds such as phonemes, morphemes, and syllables; orthographic processing involves working with the written letters and letter patterns used to represent those sounds.

Phonological Awareness

Ophelia demonstrated intact auditory discrimination abilities, scoring in the High Average range on a test of speech discrimination. No difficulties were apparent on this test, on other tests requiring precise listening skills, or in conversations.

Ophelia's performance on formal and informal measures indicated intact phonological processing abilities.

The tasks included orally segmenting words into syllables and sounds, omitting syllables and sounds from words to make new words, and identifying and changing the placement of sounds in words to create new words. Her performance was average on standardized measures of auditory/phonological processing abilities.

Orthographic Awareness

On language measures featuring orthographic information (i.e., letters, the spelling patterns of written words), Ophelia was slower and less accurate than expected. Compared to others of her overall ability and educational level, she scored particularly low on a variety of tasks requiring perceptual speed and the ability to identify accurate and plausible spelling patterns. She was slow to identify which of two words with the same sound was spelled correctly (e.g., *steam* or *steem*), and to scan rows of numbers (Low Average/Average range) and letter-digit combinations to identify the matching pairs (Very Low range). On the latter test, Ophelia's accuracy was good but her speed was approximately two standard deviations below her peer group. Additionally, she was no faster identifying matching pairs of pseudowords (e.g., *krin*) than unpronounceable clusters (e.g., *f6xp*). According to the WJ III, her awareness of phoneme/grapheme relationships was Low Average. In summary, Ophelia's performance across tasks of orthography and perceptual speed was well below expectations.

Phonological-Orthographic Retrieval

Ophelia demonstrated abilities in the High Average range in formulating definitions for words and rapidly retrieving multiple words within a specified category (e.g., types of clothes). In contrast, when required to consider the spelling of a word within a similar task (e.g., "Tell me as many words as you can that begin with the letter M"), Ophelia's performance was Low Average. Her low productivity on this task likely reflects underlying deficits in orthographic processing.

Discourse Comprehension and Expression

On tests of sentence-level comprehension, Ophelia's scores ranged from Average to High Average. Her ability to understand spoken language appeared to be intact.

During her expressive oral language testing, Ophelia was asked to give two unrehearsed oral narratives: watch a short film and then "retell" the story, and discuss a topic of her own choosing. In both samples, Ophelia demonstrated age-appropriate semantic, morphological, and syntactic skills. She was described as a lively, fluent speaker who easily maintained cohesion and engaged her audience. Across all conversational and narrative situations, Ophelia's expressive language skills were judged to be Average to High Average.

Overall, Ophelia's scores on language measures ranged from Low Average to Superior. A significant deficit was evident in the areas of orthographic processing and perceptual speed. Such deficits are often associated with reading and writing disorders, also called dyslexia.

Academic Testing

Ophelia's academic skills were assessed in reading, writing ability, and math. These areas were assessed using selected tests of the Woodcock-Johnson III Tests of Achievement (WJ III ACH) and qualitative analysis of expository writing samples.

Mathematics

Ophelia's mathematical skills were assessed in three areas: math fluency, math calculation, and mathematical reasoning. She had no difficulty quickly solving simple computation problems in an untimed test and addition, subtraction, and multiplication fact problems under time constraints, and scored within the Average range. On Math Fluency, however, she made several errors that appeared to be the result of misreading signs. Ophelia's score was High Average on an untimed measure of mathematical reasoning. She was able to solve some problems through logic even when she could not recall the expected geometric or algebraic formula.

Reading

Ophelia's reading ability was assessed in the skill areas of basic reading, reading fluency, and reading comprehension. She scored in the Low Average to Average range on the decoding measures of word identification and word attack. On Letter-Word Identification, she was unusually slow to recognize real words out of context, even when they were short and familiar.

Ophelia's decoding skills were significantly below expectations (–1.63 standard deviations) when the predicted score was based on her general intellectual ability (GIA). Only 5% of students her age with the same predicted score in Basic Reading Skills would have obtained a score as low or lower than hers. Her reading rate/automaticity, though

Table 1.   Test Scores on the WAIS-III and WJ III

Factor	Test	Subtest Name	Subtest Score	Converted Score	Descriptor
Gf	WAIS-III	Matrix Reasoning	11	105	High Average
	WJ III	Concept Formation	122		
	WJ III	Analysis-Synthesis	119		
Glr	WJ III	V-A Learning	114		High Average
	WJ III	Retrieval Fluency	114		
Ga	WJ III	Sound Blending	103		Average
	WJ III	Incomplete Words	100		
	WJ III	Sound Awareness	102		
Gv	WAIS-III	Block Design	13	115	High Average
	WJ III	Spatial Relations	105		
Gsm	WAIS-III	Digit Span	10	100	Average
	WAIS-III	Letter-Num. Seq.	14	120	
	WJ III	Num. Reversed	113		
	WJ III	Aud. Work. Mem.	101		
Gs	WAIS-III	Digit Symbol Coding	09	95	Average
	WAIS-III	Symbol Search	09	95	
	WJ III	Visual Matching	90		
	WJ III	Rapid Picture Naming	113		
Gc	WAIS-III	Vocabulary	13	115	Superior
	WAIS-III	Similarities	16	130	
	WAIS-III	Information	14	120	
	WAIS-III	Comprehension	14	120	
	WJ III	Verbal Comprehension	117		
Gq	WAIS-III	Arithmetic	13	115	Average
	WJ III	Math Fluency	101		
	WJ III	Applied Problems	107		
Grw	WJ III	Letter-Word Identification	94		Average
	WJ III	Word Attack	88		
	WJ III	Reading Fluency	93		
	WJ III	Passage Comprehension	109		
	WJ III	Spelling	89		Average
	WJ III	Spelling of Sounds	82		
	WJ III	Writing Fluency	98		
	WJ III	Writing Samples	99		

in the Average range, was also relatively low (WJ III Reading Fluency: 33%ile).

Ophelia's untimed reading comprehension was in the higher end of the Average range and considerably stronger than her decoding and reading fluency. Despite her slow pace, she was generally accurate. The limited speed at which she worked through the passages appeared to be a function of her difficulty recognizing and sounding out individual words. Ophelia's pattern of scores indicated that she is able to comprehend text effectively, but needs extended time to do so. She may have difficulty when encountering words not yet in her oral vocabulary and when higher-level material requires strong cognitive focus on the meaning.

Written Language

Ophelia's written language was evaluated through both standardized tests and qualitative assessment in the areas of spelling, grammar, and written expression. Her scores on spelling tests of both real words and pseudowords were in the Low Average range. On both tests, many of her incor-

Table 2.   Test Scores: on the WMS-III, COWAT, and Phonological/Orthographic Battery

	Standard/Scale Score	Percentile Rank	Confidence Band
WMS-III (Glr subtests)			
Auditory Immediate Index	120	91	79–96
Visual Immediate Index	106	66	37–84
Immediate Memory Index	116	86	68–94
Auditory Delayed Index	111	77	50–90
Visual Delayed Index	103	58	30–81
Auditory Recognition Delayed Index	110	75	39–88
General Memory Index	109	73	50–86
Logical Memory I – Recall	11	63	
Faces I – Recognition	10	50	
Verbal Paired Associates I – Recall	16	98	
Family Pictures I – Recall	12	75	
Word Lists I - Recall Total Score	12	75	
Logical Memory II – Recall	12	75	
Faces II – Recall	10	50	
Verbal Paired Associates II – Recall	12	75	
Family Pictures II – Recall	11	63	
Word Lists II – Recall	12	75	
COWAT			
C/F/L	*T* = 42	21	

	Raw Score	Percent Correct	Descriptor
Phonological/Orthographic Battery			
Segmenting by Syllables	10	83	WNL
Number of Syllables	12	100	WNL
Segmenting by Sounds	7	70	WNL
General Rhyming	11	92	WNL
Phonemic Localization	10	100	WNL
Phonological Segmentation	19	79	WNL
Orthographic Expressive Coding	16	89	low
Orthographic Choice	25	100	WNL (1:34)
Homophone/Pseudohomophone Choice	69	89	low (3:00)
Colorado Perceptual Speed Test			
Part I	15	50	very low
Part II	14	47	very low
Part III	19	63	very low
Orthographic Fluency	16	NA	low

rect spelling attempts were not plausible—that is, they failed to represent accurately all the sounds or syllables in target words (e.g., *obsequs* for *obsequious*), violated phonics generalizations (e.g., *fiegh* rather than *feigh* or *fay*), and reflected poor knowledge of common orthographic patterns (e.g., *strrangk* rather than *strank*).

Ophelia was asked to submit an unassisted writing sample and a "best work" sample for review. She provided a handwritten personal narrative and a word-processed literary analysis. In both papers, she made numerous errors related to sentence structure, basic grammar, word choices, spelling, and punctuation. The combination of these problems sometimes interfered with the clarity of what she wanted to express (e.g., "Most familys would decorate a large plan or a small bush with a couple of lights and maybe a few simple ordaments").

During the evaluation, Ophelia was asked to write an impromptu essay on one of several suggested topics. She discussed several major problems facing U.S. high schools and proposed methods of addressing them. Ophelia began by making a brief outline of her ideas and went on to produce several pages of prose within the allotted 30 minutes (she later indicated that she does not ". . . worry about all the spelling mistakes" she makes as she writes). She introduced her topic, wrote in thematic paragraphs, and provided a conclusion. Unfortunately, her essay contained so many errors in spelling, grammar, and writing mechanics that her ideas were often lost or misrepresented (e.g., "Atheletes' training schedules and practices teach them disiplin and teachers undermind what they learn on the playing field by letting them out certain every day oblicgations"). Her most significant problem area was spelling. She misspelled 30 words, and many of her attempts were not plausible English spellings (e.g., *priveldges, carelessnessness*). Overall, her written expression skills ranged from Low Average to Average and reflected underdeveloped spelling skills, poor attention to orthographic detail, and weak mechanics. (See Table 3.)

Finally, Ophelia scored in the Average range on standardized measures of written expression that do not penalize the examinee for errors in basic writing skills such as spelling or punctuation. Ophelia made numerous spelling mistakes and omitted or misplaced several punctuation marks.

Consistent with clinical impressions, Ophelia demonstrated a writing skills score (Broad Written Language) significantly below expectations (–1.63 standard deviations) when the predicted score was based on her general intellectual ability (GIA). Only 6% of students her age with the same predicted score in Broad Written Language would have obtained a score as low as or lower than hers.

SUMMARY

Ophelia is a 20-year-old, single, right-handed sophomore at Billings University. After years of being advised to seek an evaluation, she has finally done so at the urging of a college English professor who noticed excessive and unusual errors in her writing.

Ophelia presented as a polite, friendly, intellectually curious woman. She does not meet the DSM-IV criteria for a diagnosis of Attention Deficit Hyperactivity Disorder or any other psychological disorder.

Ophelia demonstrated overall intellectual abilities in the High Average range. Her verbal abilities and crystallized knowledge were found to be significantly stronger than her performance abilities. She exhibited intact attentional, learning, visual–spatial, reasoning, phonological processing, and oral language abilities. Her orthographic processing and perceptual speed were found to be well below expectations. These deficits appear to cause functional lim-

Table 3.   Scores on the OWLS and WJ III ACH

Academic Area	Domain	Battery/Test	Test/Subtest	Standard Score	Percentile	Range
Reading	Basic Reading	WJ III ACH	Word Attack	88	22	Low Avg to Avg
			Letter-Word Ident.	94	34	Avg
	Reading Comprehension	WJ III ACH	Passage Comprehension	109	72	Avg
	Reading Fluency	WJ III ACH	Reading Fluency	93	33	Avg
Oral Language	Listening Comprehension	OWLS	Listening Compre.	106	66	Avg
		WJ III ACH	Oral Compre.	117	87	High Avg
	Oral Expression	Informal Samples	N/A			Avg to High Avg
Writing Ability	Spelling	WJ III ACH	Spelling	89	23	Low Avg
		WJ III ACH	Spelling of Sounds	82	12	Low Avg
	Written Expression	WJ III ACH	Writing Samples	99	48	Avg
	Writing Fluency	WJ III ACH	Writing Fluency	98	46	Avg
		Informal Samples	N/A			
Math	Calculation	WJ III ACH	Calculation	107	68	Avg
	Math Fluency	WJ III ACH	Math Fluency	101	54	Avg
	Mathematics Reasoning	WJ III ACH	Applied Problems	113	80	High Avg

itations in reading decoding, spelling, and written expression.

Ophelia's pattern of difficulties point to a notable lack of automaticity when working with orthographic information (i.e., the accurate and automatic identification of printed words and the letter patterns that comprise them). Her basic reading skills were significantly poorer than expected, given her intellectual ability, educational background, and verbal strengths. Her spelling was even further below expectations. Qualitatively, many of her incorrect attempts violated basic spelling principles and/or did not plausibly represent target items. Given Ophelia's intact cognitive and oral language abilities, including phonological awareness and word retrieval, as well as her access to normal instructional opportunities, her underachievement in spelling and reading decoding is best explained by a deficit in orthographic processing.

Because Ophelia is not able to spell and decode nearly as many words as are in her oral vocabulary or as many words as her peers can spell and read, she is slower to complete reading and writing assignments than others of her ability and educational level. In a given text, for example, she must decode more words, in contrast to recognizing them automatically, than her peers. Moreover, her sounding out of unfamiliar or unrecognized words is slow and often inaccurate, taking up cognitive resources that should be available for comprehension and critical thinking. Ophelia's written expression is also problematic. Her unassisted work was notable for word omissions, sentence structure problems, and spelling mistakes. Even when she uses a spell-checker, she is not always able to identify the correct spelling from among the options the computer provides. Finally, although Ophelia demonstrated solid math calculation and math reasoning skills, she sometimes arrived at incorrect answers after "flipping" arithmetic signs and numbers such as 6 and 9.

Despite her compensatory efforts, Ophelia's learning disabilities cause her considerable academic problems. She reported that in an effort to process reading assignments more efficiently, she often "skims" texts, searching only for the main ideas and "skipping" words she does not recognize. Still, she admitted that she has difficulty keeping up with assigned readings. She reported that in lectures, she sometimes does not take notes because the effort and time required to translate spoken words into written ones interfere significantly with her ability to keep up with and comprehend the material presented. Ophelia's written expression, on which a significant percentage of her course grades is based, does not represent her ideas effectively, and often obscures them. In brief, her learning disability limits her access to classroom and textbook information and interferes with her ability to demonstrate what she knows. At present, due to the difficulty she has experienced in undergraduate courses, she is considering abandoning her original goal of attending medical school.

Ophelia has the cognitive ability to succeed during and after college. Professionally, her verbal and pragmatic strength will help her to compensate for areas of weakness. Unfortunately, academic tasks such as advanced reading and writing will prove time-consuming and difficult. Ophelia is encouraged to use all the resources available to her in order to obtain equal access to classroom information, implement supplementary learning strategies (including use of assistive technology), and make the most of her education.

SPECIFIC RECOMMENDATIONS

1. The following modifications would assist Ophelia in her future courses. The reason for each modification is deficient processing of orthographic information.
   a) Extended time (double) for all tests;
   b) Alternate format for exams—oral exams when possible;
   c) Use of a word-processor with a spell-checking program;
   d) During exams, access to a reader and/or proofreader;
   e) Permission to use an instructor-approved word bank during exams;
   f) Permission to use a notetaker and/or tape-recorder during lectures;
   g) Access to textbooks and required readings on tape;
   h) Modifications for foreign language coursework, if applicable;
   i) Access to assistive technology such as voice input software (speech-to-text), voice output software (text-to-speech), scanner, word prediction programs, and hand-held electronic spell-checker/dictionary. The Reading Pen II would be a helpful device in this regard.
2. Ophelia's performance pattern across numerous tests suggests that she is most effective when she can use her verbal, interpersonal, and reasoning strengths. She would benefit from work with a learning disabilities specialist to develop strategies that will allow her to take advantage of her strengths.

Developed by Noel Gregg, Ph.D., and Chris Coleman, M.A.

Learning Disability Evaluation

Name: Gavin Carver

Birth Date: 12/23/76

Chronological Age: 25

School: Tokoma University Law School

Test Dates: 2/15, 2/16/02

REASON FOR REFERRAL

Gavin referred himself for an evaluation because he is concerned about his present performance in law school. Although he understands the concepts of the presented material, he finds that he often does not have enough time to complete examinations. Consequently, he is unable to demonstrate his mastery of the information. He also finds that he spends an inordinate amount of time completing assigned readings. The purposes of the present evaluation were to determine Gavin's present levels of performance, consider eligibility and need for supportive services, and propose appropriate accommodations.

BACKGROUND INFORMATION/
PREVIOUS ASSESSMENT

Gavin was first referred to this evaluator in seventh grade by his parents, who were concerned about his poor progress in both reading and spelling. At that time they revealed that medical and health background were insignificant except for a history of early ear infections. Gavin was having particular difficulty in his Spanish and English classes. School vision and hearing screenings had not found problems requiring follow-up examination.

Results from a diagnostic evaluation indicated that Gavin had auditory processing deficits, a type of learning disability that affects the acquisition and ability to use the sounds of a language. In contrast to other areas, scores in reading and writing were well below grade level. As measured by the Woodcock-Johnson Psycho-Educational Battery—Revised, Gavin evidenced a severe discrepancy between his aptitude and achievement in written language. He evidenced a moderate discrepancy between reading aptitude and achievement.

As part of that assessment, Gavin was given the Goldman-Fristoe-Woodcock Spelling of Sounds test, requiring the subject to spell phonically regular nonsense words. It was noted that Gavin had difficulty pronouncing words when speaking and reading. He also had difficulty distinguishing between letters with similar sounds, particularly voiced and unvoiced consonant pairs, such as /b/ and /p/ and /f/ and /v/. This difficulty with sounds was identified as the major factor hindering Gavin's progress in word identification and spelling.

In contrast to weaknesses in auditory processing, Gavin had above average performance in areas involving reasoning and acquired knowledge. In addition, he worked diligently and was highly motivated to excel. For the next 2 years, Gavin received private tutoring from a specialist in learning disabilities and reading. The central goal of the educational therapy was to help Gavin improve his reading and spelling skills. Although difficulties with word pronunciation and spelling persisted, Gavin was able to complete high school and college successfully, without further support or interventions.

Gavin is currently enrolled in Tacoma Law School. He notes that he rarely has time to finish all the readings for classes or to finish the exams. Although daily meetings with a study group have helped him to master the course content, he feels that his slow reading rate is compromising his performance. The Disability Service Coordinator at Tacoma University advised Gavin to update his evaluation file to help determine if specific accommodations were warranted. Prior to the current assessment, the evaluator requested that Gavin have his hearing tested. The results of pure tone audiological testing were normal bilaterally.

TESTS ADMINISTERED

Wechsler Adult Intelligence Scale—III (WAIS-III)

Woodcock-Johnson III Tests of Cognitive Abilities
   (WJ III COG) and Tests of Achievement (WJ III ACH)

Testing was completed over one 4-hour session and
   one 2-hour session.

OBSERVATIONS

Gavin was a pleasant and cooperative test participant who willingly attempted all tasks. He requested clarifications when necessary and appropriate. He seemed anxious to perform well. When he encountered tasks that were difficult for him, he tended to make self-disparaging comments (e.g., "I'm doing this too slowly because I talk to myself and it slows me down"; "I should know this stuff"; "I am starting to second guess myself"). Gavin maintained good concentration throughout both testing periods and approached tasks in a methodical manner.

During several tests, Gavin talked himself through the task. Although this verbal monitoring tended to slow down his performance, it appeared to help him find the correct solution. Gavin was also aware when his responses were correct or incorrect and made a comment such as: "Well, I know that that isn't right." Occasionally he would apologize for the amount of time he needed to think through a problem. At one point when he was aware of the inordinate amount of time it was taking him to complete a question, he commented, "You ought to see how long it takes me to read my law books."

Difficulties in word pronunciation were also apparent on several occasions. For example, Gavin discussed the "national debicit" then corrected it to "depicit," then reflected: "I'm not sure exactly how you say that word." Gavin also commented that he still has to rely on his "pig/boy" strategy before pronouncing words aloud that contain either the letter *p* or *b*. Before he will ask a question that contains a word with one of these letters, he will check the accuracy of his pronunciation by saying the word "pig" or "boy."

INTELLECTUAL ABILITIES

Gavin's general cognitive ability on the WAIS-III is within the High Average range of intellectual functioning. (See Table 1.) His overall thinking and reasoning abilities exceed those of approximately 79% of adults his age (FSIQ: 112, 95% confidence interval: 108–116). Gavin's verbal reasoning, the ability to think with words, and his nonverbal reasoning, the ability to reason without the use of words, are both within the High Average range, above 77% of his age-peers and 81% of his peers, respectively.

On the Verbal Scale, Gavin achieved his highest performance on the Comprehension subtest, requiring him to provide solutions to everyday problems and to explain the underlying reasons for certain social rules or concepts. This

Table 1. Wechsler Adult Intelligence Scale–Third Edition (WAIS-III) Scores

Verbal Subtests	Scaled Score*	Percentile Rank
Vocabulary	13	84
Similarities	10	50
Arithmetic	11	63
Digit Span	10	50
Information	13	84
Comprehension	14	91

Performance Subtests	Scaled Score*	Percentile Rank
Picture Completion	11	63
Digit Symbol-Coding	10	50
Block Design	15	95
Matrix Reasoning	13	84
Picture Arrangement	11	63
Object Assembly	13	84

*Scaled score Mean = 10; Standard Deviation = 3.

IQ/Index Scores	IQ Score	95% Standard Score Confidence Interval**	Percentile Rank
Verbal	111	106–116	77
Performance	113	105–119	81
Full Scale	112	108–116	79
Verbal Comprehension	110	104–115	75
Perceptual Organization	118	110–124	88

**Standard score Mean = 100; Standard Deviation = 15.

subtest provides a general measure of verbal reasoning, and assesses comprehension of social situations and social judgment. His lowest Verbal scores, albeit still within the Average range when compared to his age-mates, were on the Similarities and Digit Span subtests. Gavin ascertained and explained the similarities between word pairs, indicating the ability to abstract meaningful concepts and relationships from verbally presented material. Gavin's ability to repeat a series of orally presented number sequences, in the order given and in reverse order, indicated average short-term auditory memory. This subtest also requires attention, concentration, and the ability to sequence information correctly.

On the Performance Scale, Gavin scored significantly high on Block Design, better than approximately 95% of his age-mates. The Block Design subtest required Gavin to use two-color cubes to construct replicas of two dimensional, geometric patterns. Results indicated strong abilities in mentally organizing visual–spatial information and analyzing part/whole relationships. Good performance also requires fine-motor coordination and planning.

The WJ III Tests of Cognitive Abilities are a comprehensive set of individually administered tests measuring seven different cognitive abilities. Similar to the results on the WAIS-III, Gavin's overall performance fell within the High Average range (SS: 116; confidence interval: 112–119; see Table 2). Gavin scored in the Superior range on the factor of Fluid Reasoning, the ability to apply logic and reasoning in novel situations. He obtained a score in the High Average range on the factors of Comprehension-Knowledge, a measure of vocabulary and acquired knowledge; Long-Term Retrieval, the ability to store and retrieve

associations; and Visual Spatial-Thinking, the ability to perceive and think with visual patterns. He obtained scores in the Average range on the factors of Processing Speed, the ability to perform simple cognitive tasks rapidly, and Short-Term Memory, the ability to repeat back information that one hears. In contrast to his Average and above scores in the other factors, Gavin obtained a score in the Low range in Auditory Processing. He had difficulty blending a series of sounds to form words and discriminating among sounds against a background of gradually increasing noise. In addition, Gavin's scores on measures of phonemic awareness, the ability to manipulate language sounds, were in the Low Average range.

The WJ III Tests of Achievement were used to assess Gavin's level of achievement. (See Table 3.) This set of tests measures oral language and the academic areas of reading, written language, math, and knowledge. Gavin's scores were based upon age norms. A brief summary of performance is provided for each skill area.

Oral Language

Gavin scored in the High Average range on the Oral Language-Extended cluster. He appeared more at ease on tasks involving expressive language and vocabulary than he did on tasks involving listening and memory. As the number of instructions increased on the Understanding Directions test, Gavin commented: "I really need some paper to follow all this."

Reading

Although Gavin's Broad and Basic Reading scores were in the Low Average range, significant differences existed

Table 2.   Woodcock-Johnson III Tests of Cognitive Abilities Scores

CLUSTER/Test	GE	EASY to DIFF		RPI	PR	SS (68% BAND)
GIA (Ext)	>18.0	14.9	>18.0	96/90	85	116 (112–119)
VERBAL ABILITY (Ext)	>18.0	>18.0	>18.0	98/90	86	116 (112–121)
THINKING ABILITY (Ext)	>18.0	9.7	>18.0	92/90	62	105 (100–110)
COG EFFICIENCY (Ext)	>18.0	>18.0	>18.0	97/90	75	110 (107–114)
COMP-KNOWLEDGE (Gc)	>18.0	>18.0	>18.0	98/90	86	116 (112–121)
L-T RETRIEVAL (Glr)	>18.0	8.6	>18.0	94/90	76	111 (105–116)
VIS-SPATIAL THINK (Gv)	>18.0	16.0	>18.0	96/90	84	115 (108–121)
AUDITORY PROCESS (Ga)	3.4	1.0	9.4	44/90	3	71 (66–75)
FLUID REASONING (Gf)	>18.0	>18.0	>18.0	98/90	94	123 (114–132)
PROCESS SPEED (Gs)	>18.0	14.3	>18.0	96/90	67	107 (103–111)
SHORT-TERM MEM (Gsm)	>18.0	>18.0	>18.0	97/90	78	111 (106–116)
PHONEMIC AWARE III	4.8	2.2	11.0	55/90	8	79 (75–82)
WORKING MEMORY	13.7	11.1	>18.0	86/90	43	97 (94–101)
COGNITIVE FLUENCY	>18.0	10.9	>18.0	92/90	54	102 (99–104)

Table 3.   WJ III Tests of Achievement Scores

CLUSTER/Test	GE	EASY to DIFF		RPI	PR	SS (68% BAND)
ORAL LANGUAGE (Ext)	>18.0	>18.0	>18.0	97/90	87	117 (111–123)
ORAL EXPRESSION	>18.0	>18.0	>18.0	98/90	92	121 (114–129)
LISTENING COMP	>18.0	14.6	>18.0	95/90	73	109 (101–117)
TOTAL ACHIEVEMENT	13.8	11.6	>18.0	84/90	36	95 (92–97)
BROAD READING	10.6	9.0	12.3	32/90	13	83 (81–86)
BROAD MATH	>18.0	>18.0	>18.0	99/90	96	126 (121–130)
BROAD WRITTEN LANG	12.4	8.0	17.2	75/90	21	88 (84–91)
BASIC READING SKILLS	8.8	6.7	12.5	48/90	11	82 (78–85)
READING COMP	>18.0	>18.0	>18.0	99/90	98	132 (126–139)
MATH CALC SKILLS	>18.0	>18.0	>18.0	97/90	78	112 (109–115)
MATH REASONING	>18.0	>18.0	>18.0	100/90	99	133 (127–139)
BASIC WRITING SKILLS	8.9	6.6	12.3	31/90	7	78 (75–81)
WRITTEN EXPRESSION	>18.0	11.8	>18.0	94/90	75	110 (102–118)
ACADEMIC SKILLS	12.9	9.9	16.9	73/90	26	90 (88–93)
ACADEMIC FLUENCY	9.5	7.9	11.3	23/90	10	80 (79–82)
ACADEMIC APPLICATION	>18.0	>18.0	>18.0	99/90	99.5	139 (132–146)
ACADEMIC KNOWLEDGE	>18.0	>18.0	>18.0	99/90	96	127 (119–135)
PHON/GRAPH KNOW	5.0	3.1	8.0	38/90	5	75 (72–79)
KNOWLEDGE	>18.0	>18.0	>18.0	99/90	95	125 (119–131)

among the tests. Gavin scored in the High Average to Superior range on Passage Comprehension, a measure of ability to read and understand passages of one to two sentences, and in the High Average range on the Reading Vocabulary test, requiring the ability to give synonyms and antonyms, and to complete analogies based on printed words. In contrast, he scored in the Low Average ranges on Letter-Word Identification, a measure of word pronunciation skill, and Reading Fluency, a test of reading rate with comprehension. His performance on the Reading Comprehension cluster was significantly higher than on Basic Reading Skills. On several items of the Reading Vocabulary and Letter-Word Identification tests, Gavin stated: "I know the word but I just don't know how to pronounce it." For example, when shown the word "carnivore," Gavin explained that it meant "meat-eating animals" but could not pronounce it, illustrating his good vocabulary knowledge but poor word identification skills.

Gavin's lowest score was on Word Attack, a test requiring pronunciation of phonically regular nonsense words. His strategy was to look at the word, identify a real word with a similar spelling pattern, and then substitute the letter that was different on the target word. For example, when trying to pronounce a word such as "haked," he would say "raked," substitute the /h/ sound, and pronounce it correctly. The pattern of errors in general substantiated Gavin's overreliance on visual cues for word

recognition, as well as his difficulty with applying sounds to aid in pronunciation.

Written Language

Although Gavin's Broad Written Language score fell in the Low Average range, significant discrepancies existed among these tests as well. Gavin's ability to express his ideas in writing was significantly higher than his spelling ability. Although Gavin's spellings were close approximations, he made several errors. On longer words, he tended to misperceive sounds, resulting in the omission or addition of letters. For example, he spelled "omniscient" as *obnishent,* "bizarre" as *bazzar,* and "arrogance" as *arognans.* Gavin's lowest score in writing was on the Spelling of Sounds test, spelling nonwords that conform to English spelling patterns. On several items, he confused the phonemes /b/ and /p/ and /f/ and /v/.

Mathematics

Gavin scored in the Superior range on the Broad Math cluster. On the Calculation test, a measure of basic math skills, and the Applied Problems test, a measure of problem solving, Gavin talked himself through the steps, monitoring the accuracy of his responses. During the Calculation test, he stated that he had not taken math courses for several years and had forgotten how to perform several operations. On the Math Fluency test, Gavin was able to solve simple addition, subtraction, and multiplication problems quickly.

Knowledge

Gavin scored in the Superior range on the Knowledge cluster, which includes General Information (WJ III COG), and Academic Knowledge, a measure of acquired information in the content areas.

In general, Gavin's performance is significantly higher on academic tasks requiring reasoning and vocabulary than it is on tasks involving basic academic skills and speed.

DISCREPANCIES

Ability/Achievement Discrepancies

After correction for regression to the mean, a significant discrepancy exists between Gavin's WAIS III Full Scale score (SS: 112) and his WJ III Basic Reading Cluster score (SS: 82). Based upon his Average to High Average performance in most abilities, one would predict that Gavin

would be performing in basic reading and writing skills at a higher level. In contrast to his High Average language and reasoning skills, Gavin's performance falls in the limited range on tasks requiring word identification or spelling.

Gavin demonstrated significant intra-individual strengths in Reading Comprehension and Math Reasoning. (See Table 4.) Of people his age who had the same predicted score, only 2% would obtain a score as high or higher than Gavin's. In contrast, Gavin demonstrated significant intra-individual weaknesses in the areas of Auditory Processing and Phonemic Awareness, the ability to interpret, analyze and synthesize language sounds. In the area of Auditory Processing, only 2 in 1000 age-peers with the same predicted score as Gavin's (SS 111) would obtain a score as low or lower than his (SS 71). Gavin also has significant weaknesses in basic reading and writing skills. When his actual standard score of 78 on Basic Writing Skills is compared to his predicted standard score of 112, only 2 out of 1000 people would obtain a score as low or lower. Because the WJ III COG and the WJ III ACH were normed on the same group of people, correction for regression to the mean is not necessary.

When Gavin's performance on the Oral Language-Extended cluster is compared to his academic perfor-

Table 4. Intra-Individual Discrepancies

DISCREPANCIES	STANDARD SCORES			DISCREPANCY		Significant at ±1.50 SD (SEE)
	Actual	Predicted	Difference	PR	SD	
Intra-Individual						
COMP-KNOWLEDGE (*Gc*)	116	110	+6	72	+0.59	No
L-T RETRIEVAL (*Glr*)	111	108	+3	56	+0.15	No
VIS-SPATIAL THINK (*Gv*)	115	107	+8	70	+0.53	No
AUDITORY PROCESS (*Ga*)	71	111	−40	0.2	−2.94	Yes
FLUID REASONING (*Gf*)	123	108	+15	87	+1.14	No
PROCESS SPEED (*Gs*)	107	106	+1	53	+0.07	No
SHORT-TERM MEM (*Gsm*)	111	107	+4	61	+0.29	No
PHONEMIC AWARE	80	111	−31	1	−2.22	Yes
WORKING MEMORY	97	107	−10	23	−0.73	No
BASIC READING SKILLS	82	112	−30	0.5	−2.56	Yes
READING COMP	132	107	+25	98	+2.01	Yes
MATH CALC SKILLS	112	107	+5	64	+0.36	No
MATH REASONING	133	108	+25	98	+2.02	Yes
BASIC WRITING SKILLS	78	111	−33	0.2	−2.84	Yes
WRITTEN EXPRESSION	110	109	+1	55	+0.12	No
ORAL EXPRESSION	121	106	+15	87	+1.11	No
LISTENING COMP	109	111	−2	44	−0.14	No
ACADEMIC KNOWLEDGE	127	109	+18	94	+1.58	Yes

Table 5.   Oral Language/Achievement Discrepancies

DISCREPANCIES	STANDARD SCORES			DISCREPANCY		Significant at ±1.50 SD (SEE)
	Actual	Predicted	Difference	PR	SD	
Oral Language/Achievement Discrepancies *						
BROAD READING	83	106	−23	5	−1.69	Yes
BASIC READING SKILLS	82	106	−24	4	−1.75	Yes
READING COMP	132	108	+24	97	+1.87	Yes
BROAD MATH	126	104	+22	9	+1.47	No
MATH CALC SKILLS	112	101	+11	76	+0.70	No
MATH REASONING	133	106	+27	97	+1.94	Yes
BROAD WRITTEN LANG	88	106	−18	9	−1.32	No
BASIC WRITING SKILLS	78	106	−28	2	−2.00	Yes
WRITTEN EXPRESSION	110	105	+5	63	+0.34	No
ACADEMIC KNOWLEDGE	127	112	+15	92	+1.38	No

*These discrepancies based on Oral Language (Ext) with ACH Broad, Basic, and Applied clusters.

mance, he demonstrates significant weaknesses in basic reading and writing skills.

SUMMARY AND RECOMMENDATIONS

Results from past evaluations, history, and the present evaluation confirm that Gavin is a student with phonological dyslexia, a learning disability related to his weakness in auditory processing. Gavin has significant discrepancies between predicted performance, as measured by both the WJ III COG and WAIS-III, and Basic Reading and Writing skills, as measured by the WJ III ACH. Weaknesses in auditory processing and phonology have affected his performance significantly in the ability to pronounce words when speaking and reading, and in the ability to spell words. In turn, these difficulties reduce Gavin's reading and writing rate. He works accurately and thoughtfully, but slowly. Consequently, to have the opportunity to demonstrate his knowledge, he will require accommodations on timed exams requiring reading or writing. In contrast, Gavin is highly successful on tasks that require visual analysis and reasoning. Gavin should be entitled to specific accommodations as an individual with learning disabilities.

Despite the recent normal findings in a pure-tone audiological exam, Gavin should make an appointment with an educational audiologist for an in-depth audiological evaluation including comprehensive testing of speech discrimination. Discuss with the audiologist any new technology that might be helpful.

Gavin will require the following accommodations in graduate school:

1. Extended time, such as double time, on in-class and standardized exams. Ideally, Gavin would be provided with enough time on all exams so that he will have the opportunity to attempt to answer all questions.
2. No penalty for spelling on any in-class assignments or exams.
3. Use of a laptop with a word-processing program and spell-checker for all written work.
4. Provision of taped materials for lengthy reading assignments.

WAIS-III administration and interpretation contributed by Lisa Coyner, Ph.D.

Educational Evaluation

Name: Stacy Lee Alexander

Age: 29

Date of Birth: 3/08/73

Date of Evaluation: 3/7/02

REASON FOR REFERRAL

The disability service provider at Gabrillo Community College recommended that Stacy be evaluated for the purposes of understanding her learning strengths and weaknesses.

BACKGROUND INFORMATION

Stacy attended public school in California and Arizona. She recalls that she was held back in second grade, had emotional difficulties at ages 12 through 14 due to her parents' separation and divorce, and began having serious academic difficulties in high school. Stacy recalls teacher and parent comments similar to "not applying yourself," "not doing your best," and "not trying." In the latter part of high school, she recalls struggling with understanding what she read and with higher-level math courses.

Stacy earned a GED through her high school, entered the police academy, and served as a police officer in California for 4 years. When she moved to Arizona, she worked in hotel management for 4 years while doing volunteer work with a local fire department. Deciding to make a career change, Stacy attended the fire academy but was unable to pass the national fire certification exam. She then turned her attention to Emergency Medical Technician (EMT) work, and successfully passed the certification exam. Stacy is currently employed with the Evergreen Fire Department as an EMT working over 50 hours a week. She initiated an inquiry into the possibility of learning disabilities because she has been having difficulty with her paramedic classes at Gabrillo Community College.

Medical history is positive for childhood asthma. Stacy recalls that at age 13 she was involved in a car accident in which she struck her head (left temporal lobe) against the front windshield of the car and blacked out. Although she was not diagnosed with a concussion at that time, she was treated for a closed head injury. Stacy reports that she has a connective tissue disorder of the lower abdominal area for which she periodically takes medication.

OBSERVATIONS

Stacy was friendly and personable throughout the evaluation. During the assessment, she was observed to use a number of compensatory strategies, primarily talking aloud to herself and using her fingers to remember items. Stacy worked diligently on all tasks. These assessment results are considered a valid indication of overall functioning, information-processing strengths and weaknesses, and academic achievement.

ASSESSMENTS

Selected clusters from the WJ III Tests of Cognitive Abilities and the WJ III Tests of Achievement were administered. In addition, an informal reading inventory was administered and a writing sample was obtained.

Summary of Assessment Results

Strengths

Sustained attention to visual detail, visual processing speed, nonverbal problem-solving and visual-spatial thinking.

Weaknesses

Understanding and using complex sentence structures in speaking and writing, comprehending abstract verbal concepts for reading and listening, following complex directions, solving mathematical problems, expressing ideas in writing, sustaining attention.

INTERPRETATION

In order to document the existence of a learning disability, a significant discrepancy needs to exist between one's overall intellectual potential and one's abilities to process discrete components of perceptual, linguistic, or cognitive information. Perceptual processing involves information received through the senses including visual, auditory, visual–motor, auditory–motor, spatial, and temporal. Linguistic processing involves information transmitted via words and sentences and encompasses one's skills in reading, writing, listening, and speaking. Cognitive processing involves abilities and skills relative to memory capacity, the use of executive monitoring strategies, higher-order problem solving, and visual–spatial thinking.

Attention

Stacy's performance across tasks suggested mild attentional difficulties. She showed difficulty making transitions between activities, difficulty looking at alternatives once a path had been determined, and difficulty working within highly structured activities. She spontaneously talked to herself to keep herself focused. She reported that she often becomes distracted by external stimuli or tangential thoughts, loses her focus, and then has to begin a process again. Subtle difficulties were also noted with executive functioning. Stacy was observed to be able to project two to three steps ahead in a process, but then struggled to remember the sequence of steps to be followed. She noted that she has always had difficulty with long-term planning.

Perceptual Processing

Item analyses of responses on tests of perceptual processing yield a profile of comparative intra-cognitive strengths. Auditory and phonological processing tests were in the Average range when assessed in isolation. Speed of visual processing of symbols was in the Low Average range. Visual–motor processing (the basic eye-hand coordination, as is required for handwriting) was an area of comparative weakness. Stacy prints her written work with a style that combines capital and small letters.

Oral Language

Oral language and language processing abilities were in the Low Average range. When Stacy speaks, her word choice and/or sentence formation are, at times, slow and awkward, and her frustration at not being able to express herself easily and clearly becomes apparent.

Assessment of syntactic abilities (the ability to work with a variety of different sentence structures) reveals weaknesses in both oral and written receptive and expressive language. Difficulties were noted in the spontaneous interpretation and application of spatial concepts (e.g., *on, under*), which will impede her ability to follow directions quickly and accurately. Stacy also has significant difficulties understanding complex sentences with embedded phrases and clauses. She does not reliably interpret the interrelationships among the concepts due to difficulties with cohesive devices (e.g. words such as "therefore" and "otherwise" that signify the relationships among ideas). Whereas Stacy gives the appearance of having understood, she often misses or misinterprets important relationships among ideas when both listening and reading.

Memory

Memory abilities also present as a weakness for Stacy. Short-term memory traces are thought to last for no longer than 30 seconds and short-term memory capacity is believed to be limited to 6 +/–1 items or "chunks" of information. Because of these limitations, information must be manipulated and/or rehearsed in some way to keep it "alive." Stacy performed in the Low range on tasks that required her to repeat what she had just heard.

Working memory represents an individual's ability to hold information in immediate awareness while performing a mental operation on it or using it within another task simultaneously. The integrity of working memory is partially dependent upon memory span and upon the use of strategic thinking abilities. Stacy struggled with tasks requiring her to reorder auditory information (presented orally with no visual support) while holding it in memory, repeating it several times before attempting the task.

Reading

Stacy obtained scores in reading decoding and comprehension in the Low Average range. Although she has mastered basic reading skills, she is hampered in her decoding efforts by her lack of vocabulary knowledge. As she attempted to decode unfamiliar vocabulary, she mispronounced the word unless she was familiar with its meaning. When asked to read short sentences under timed conditions, Stacy's reading speed was in the Low Average range. On an informal reading inventory, when asked to read paragraphs silently and answer the questions that followed, Stacy's difficulties with comprehension became more apparent. Reading comprehension difficulties appear to be language-based rather than reflective of limitations in memory. She was not consistently able to work with pronoun reference, cohesive devices, or complex syntactic constructions. As she reads, she does not automatically monitor her comprehension. As well, she appears inflexible in altering her initial interpretation based upon what is presented in the text.

Writing

Stacy's difficulties expressing her ideas in writing were also apparent. Her performance on tests of written language was in the Low range, largely due to difficulties with syntax. An example provides the best illustration of Stacy's difficulties with sentence structure. When given three target words, such as "cold," "drink," and "my" to use in a single sentence, Stacy wrote, "My cold drink for me."

Although English is Stacy's primary language, she has not mastered basic sentence structure. When asked to compose a paragraph, her response reflects limited vocabulary, reduced sentence complexity, limited knowledge, and little elaboration. The following writing sample is based on a three-frame cartoon depicting the discovery of America.

A long time ago, two ships raced across the ocean to find new land. Both ships landed at the same time. The captains Chris and Leif raced to be the first to claim it. But to there dismay the land was already occupied by Indians.

Mathematics

Stacy's scores on basic math skills were in the Average range but math problem-solving abilities were in the Low range. Stacy relied on paper/pencil computations even on simple problems. She could not recall common measurement concepts (e.g., number of weeks in a year, number of inches in a yard).

SUMMARY AND RECOMMENDATIONS

Stacy is an adult with obvious information-processing strengths and weaknesses when compared to her age-peers. Her low performance on tasks involving linguistic abilities contributes to low performance in reading comprehension, math problem solving, and written expression. The combination of these difficulties poses significant limitations to Stacy's abilities to achieve commensurate with others her age who have comparable intellectual ability. Stacy would profit from instruction at the Gabrillo Learning Center focusing upon improving language comprehension and expression. In addition, Stacy would benefit from:

1. enrollment in continuing education classes for structured instruction in composition skills;
2. use of a tape player to record lectures so that she can review lectures and check her lecture notes outside of class;
3. daily review of key information from lectures;
4. paraphrasing material that she is reading and studying;
5. use of word processing and computer programs for written production;
6. direct instruction in strategies to aid in monitoring comprehension;
7. a study partner to assist with clarification and organization of content to be learned and/or a small study group to assist with preparation and study for classes;
8. shortened oral directions both in academic and vocational settings;
9. an evaluation for Attention Deficit Hyperactivity Disorder.

Adapted from Patricia Tomlan, Ph.D., PST Consultants.

Western State University Psychoeducational Report

Name:	Marcus Gibbons	Post Graduate School:	Doctoral Program
Birthdate:	6/16/52	Evaluation Date:	January 27, 2002
Age at Evaluation:	49 years		

REASON FOR REFERRAL

Mr. Gibbons has completed all coursework requirements for a doctoral degree in vocational rehabilitation counseling; however, he has failed components of his written comprehensive examination twice. The purpose of this evaluation was to provide information regarding Mr. Gibbons' cognitive and academic strengths and weaknesses for the purpose of educational and vocational planning.

BACKGROUND AND INTERVIEW INFORMATION

Background information was obtained in an interview with Mr. Gibbons, his wife, and from a review of transcripts from elementary school, high school, and university programs. The Gibbons' have two sons, ages 23 and 27. They report that their youngest son appears to show signs of Attention Deficit Hyperactivity Disorder although he has never been formally evaluated. Moreover, Mr. Gibbons reports that his father had difficulty learning to read and write and dropped out of high school to join the military.

Mr. Gibbons recalls school as always being difficult. A review of his transcripts, elementary through high school, indicated ongoing reading and spelling problems with grades in other subjects declining also as he advanced through school. He graduated near the bottom of his class. In contrast, examination of postsecondary transcripts found that Mr. Gibbons maintained a GPA of 3.0 in various undergraduate programs and 3.5 in his graduate program at Western State University.

For the past 15 years, Mr. Gibbons has worked as a rehabilitation counselor in the California Department of Vocational Rehabilitation. Reportedly, colleagues respect his opinion as well as his effectiveness in working with clients. For the past 10 years, Mr. Gibbons has devoted much of his nonwork time to earning a doctorate in vocational rehabilitation counseling. In addition to his full-time job, he has regularly driven 3 hours round-trip between home and the university to complete the necessary coursework. Despite his strong commitment, he has twice failed some portion of his written comprehensive exam.

Mr. Gibbons also took the master's exam twice. Mrs. Gibbons worked closely with her husband throughout his college and early graduate courses editing and rewriting his papers, sometimes extensively; she described their content as "talking around the point." She described the personal struggle, long hours of study, and perseverance her husband has demonstrated in pursuing a doctoral degree.

Two faculty members in vocational rehabilitation counseling at Western State provided information regarding Mr. Gibbons' performance in class and written responses on the comprehensive examination. They agreed that Mr. Gibbons has good interpersonal skills, contributes to discussions, and presents himself fairly well verbally. On the other hand, in written expression, he does not seem to be able to "pull out" relevant information to build a strong argument for a cogent point of view, thus failing to demonstrate the facile application of knowledge expected of a doctoral student. The faculty members supported the need for a comprehensive evaluation.

PREVIOUS EVALUATIONS

Mr. and Ms. Gibbons agreed that he showed signs of a learning disability and aspects of an attentional disorder in elementary and high school but at the time, referral for learning problems was not a frequent occurrence. Mr. Gibbons still sometimes transposes numbers and usually needs to write down specific details so as not to forget them, although he recalls faces, people, and interpersonal events with surprising clarity.

Mr. Gibbons reported that he requires a longer than normal period of time to process assigned materials, he must read and re-read material to comprehend it, and he struggles against distraction while studying and during periods requiring prolonged concentration. Based on these concerns, he was evaluated in November 2001 at the Center for Attention Deficit and Learning Disorders by Serena Birch, Ph.D., a licensed psychologist. Dr. Birch diagnosed Mr. Gibbons with Attention Deficit Hyperactivity Disorder, stating that his history indicates "he has struggled with ADHD problems for many years and has exerted much effort in attempting to cope with this disorder." Dr. Birch concluded that with appropriate testing accommodations and academic interventions, Mr. Gibbons would be able to meet the educational requirements for his doctoral degree.

BEHAVIORAL OBSERVATIONS

Throughout testing, Mr. Gibbons was consistent and persistent in his effort despite his obvious struggle with the increasing complexity of the tasks. On several tests, he worked slowly and seemed to require more time than typical for individuals in programs of advanced studies. This was especially apparent on more complex items of tasks involving inductive and deductive reasoning, planning ability, and visual–spatial thinking. The present results are judged to be an accurate reflection of his current abilities.

MEASURES USED

Woodcock-Johnson III Tests of Cognitive Abilities, Standard and Extended Batteries (WJ III COG)
Woodcock-Johnson III Tests of Achievement, Standard and Extended Batteries (WJ III ACH)
Behavioral observations, record review, interviews

RESULTS

Global Intellectual Ability Estimate

Both age and grade norms were used to evaluate Mr. Gibbon's performance. The WJ III COG provides a General Intellectual Ability—Extended (GIA-Ext) score composed of 14 tests, two in each of the seven major cognitive factors.

Age Comparison
Mr. Gibbons' performance on the GIA-Ext cluster earned a standard score (SS) of 101 and a percentile rank (PR) of 53, indicating that his general intellectual ability is equal to or above 53% of adults in his age range. Using this score as a predictor of general academic achievement, no discrepancy exists between his overall intellectual ability and his achievement in reading, mathematics, written expression, or verbal comprehension. His general knowledge is significantly higher than expected.

Grade Comparison
When Mr. Gibbons' performance was compared to a national sample of students just completing their first year in graduate school, his GIA was in the Low to Low Average range (SS 79, PR 8), highlighting the intellectually advanced nature of this group. Graduate students represent the upper percentage of students who have successfully completed their undergraduate studies. When this score is used to predict general ability and is compared with academic achievement among graduate students, Mr. Gibbons performs above expectation in all areas of academic achievement and verbal comprehension. His performance in general knowledge is far above his predicted achievement.

Cognitive Performance Clusters

Age Comparison
When compared with adults his age, Mr. Gibbons' was above average on measures of Verbal/Acquired Knowledge (SS 117, PR 86). Clearly, his years of education have had a beneficial effect—he has amassed an impressive range of practical knowledge about the environment and he can use oral communication effectively. Mr. Gibbons also scored in the Average range in terms of his Thinking Ability (SS 98, PR 44), including measures of long-term retrieval, nonverbal reasoning, fluid intelligence for solving novel tasks, and auditory processing. His Cognitive Efficiency in rapidly processing stimuli in a clerical fashion and holding elements in immediate memory were also similar to adults his age (SS 100, PR 50).

Grade Comparison
When Mr. Gibbons was compared with the graduate school sample, his Verbal/Acquired Knowledge score remained competitive (SS 114, PR 82). He demonstrates well-developed understanding and knowledge of basic concepts in science, social studies, and humanities. In contrast, he scored better than only 6% of graduate students on measures of memory, reasoning, and auditory processing. Mr. Gibbons may experience considerable academic frustration relative to other graduate students who have average ability in these areas.

Clinical Clusters

Test results regarding attentional capacity (i.e., ability to focus on selected stimuli for cognitive processing), cognitive fluency (i.e., ease and speed of performing cognitive tasks), working memory (i.e., holding information in memory while working with it), and executive processes (e.g., strategic planning, proactive interference control, and rule generation) were of special clinical interest in Mr. Gibbons' case. Moreover, performance on these clusters is of particular interest in individuals with suspected or diagnosed attentional deficits with regard to their ability to systematically plan, hold, and manipulate information in immediate memory so that it does not erode. Adequate performance on these tests does not, however, rule out an attentional disorder. ADHD is not necessarily a deficiency in those abilities central to executive processes but in the appropriate, timely, self-initiated, and sustained application of these abilities.

Age and Grade Comparisons

When compared with adults his age, Mr. Gibbons performed well within the Average range in each of the clinically relevant test clusters. In contrast, his scores decreased to the Low range when compared with the graduate school sample (Working Memory SS 75, PR 5; Broad Attention SS 72, PR 2; Cognitive Fluency SS 84, PR 15; Executive Processes SS 67, PR 1). These findings suggest weaknesses relative to other graduate students in abilities such as maintaining information in immediate awareness while working with it, developing strategies to plan certain types of tasks, developing automaticity in frequently practiced tasks, and identifying essential principles in new information.

Academic Achievement

Mr. Gibbons' oral language comprehension and academic achievement were measured in areas of reading, mathematics, written expression, academic knowledge, and academic fluency (speed).

Age Comparison

Results of the WJ III Tests of Achievement indicate that when Mr. Gibbons is compared with adults his age, he has Average to High Average oral language and academic skills. He demonstrated Average ability to comprehend orally presented short passages (SS 100, PR 51). His comprehension of similarly brief text (SS 108, PR 71) and word recognition skills (SS 111, PR 78) were in the Average to High Average range, as was his score in content of written expression (SS 110, PR 75). It is important to note, however, that this task consists of writing one-sentence responses to a variety of task demands, and with no penalty

for errors in spelling or mechanics. Thus, it does not reflect the performance demands of writing a graduate level paper. His spelling skills appear to be Average (SS 102, PR 54). Mr. Gibbons' computation skills (SS 114, PR 82) and mathematical reasoning (SS 104, PR 61) were in the Average and High Average ranges, respectively. Overall, Mr. Gibbons' ability in speed of performing relatively simple academic tasks surpassed 61% of adults his age (SS 104). Consistent with other measures, he demonstrated general world and academic knowledge in the High Average range (SS 117, PR 87).

Grade Comparison

When examining Mr. Gibbons's scores on the WJ III Tests of Achievement, the discrepancy between age and grade comparisons is dramatically less than on the cognitive measures. This is consistent with Mr. Gibbons' relative strength in verbal and acquired knowledge and also suggests that his years in higher education and long hours of personal study have significantly benefited him in these areas.

Mr. Gibbons' reading comprehension, word recognition, content of written expression, writing fluency, math computation, and mathematics reasoning were all in the Average to High Average ranges when compared with other graduate students. His scores in spelling, speed of reading simple sentences, speed of math fact retrieval, and the ability to hold complex oral instructions in mind while following them declined to the Low (Oral Directions) to Low Average range. His acquired knowledge remained competitive and exceeded 92% of the graduate students.

DISCREPANCY DISCUSSION

Although there are many limitations to this procedure, a standard practice is to compare intellectual ability with academic attainments for the purpose of computing whether a severe discrepancy exists between intellectual abilities and achievement. Western State University uses a standard score difference of 15 points to indicate a significant discrepancy. When Mr. Gibbons' academic scores are compared with his GIA within the age comparison, no comparisons produce a difference of 15 points. When the comparison shifts to Mr. Gibbons' academic scores and GIA relative to other graduate students, a far more educationally advanced and restrictive sample, he consistently performs within the Average range in academic skills and far above the predicted scores based on the GIA-Ext standard score of 79. Mr. Gibbons does not present with an ability/achievement discrepancy relative to adults his age or to other graduate students.

SUMMARY AND DISCUSSION

Mr. Gibbons's well-developed verbal intelligence and academic knowledge favorably compare with the majority of adults in his age range as well as with graduate students. Mr. Gibbons' best developed area of abilities is crystallized intelligence, a broad term that includes development of oral language proficiency, acquisition of declarative and procedural knowledge, and use of acquired knowledge in previously established procedures. Compared with his age-peers, Mr. Gibbons has relative weaknesses in memory span, working memory, and in identifying essential elements in new information. Compared with students just starting their second year of graduate school (who have been preselected for these abilities), weaknesses are more pronounced in these areas, and in learning and retrieving new associations, working with information while holding it in memory, planning strategies, and performing simple tasks quickly.

An important difference between Mr. Gibbons and the graduate sample is age. Most students just starting their second year of graduate studies are considerably younger than Mr. Gibbons, who may be experiencing some of the normal, age-related deterioration of certain cognitive skills such as short-term memory. Thus the difference between Mr. Gibbons's obtained scores when compared to his age-peers and when compared to his grade-peers may be due to limited cognitive abilities compared to the latter group and/or due to the normal changes in cognitive functioning related to age. The considerably lower GIA-Ext reflects these differences. Mr. Gibbons's persistence and motivation have, however, been key factors in dealing effectively with this exceptionally high level of competition.

Mr. Gibbons presented previous evaluation results from another psychologist who is of the opinion that he has an attention deficit disorder. A developmental history, review of early school records, and an interview of Mr. Gibbons's wife support that diagnosis. Therefore, it appears to be the case that a mild-to-moderate attention deficit without hyperactivity is a complicating factor. Mr. Gibbons might find benefit from a trial of medication and should consider discussing this with a psychiatrist. Background information also supports the existence of a learning disability (e.g., early struggles with education, family history, difficulty with writing, inconsistent academic performance). Results from this evaluation may be interpreted in different ways. Mr. Gibbons's repeated failures on exams may be due to learning disabilities and ADHD affecting written expression. Or, an alternative explanation is that even though he has attentional and learning difficulties, his overall learning abilities, age-related or not, may be insufficient to allow him to meet the advanced requirements of a doctoral degree.

Mr. Gibbons is a vocational rehabilitation counselor who is a respected professional. He has recently been diagnosed with ADHD and analyses of educational history, as well as marked strengths and weaknesses among his abilities, support the existence of learning disabilities. It is recommended, therefore, that before a decision is made, the faculty in the Department of Vocational Rehabilitation and Counseling have an opportunity to consider these findings, review past educational history, and consider Mr. Gibbons's past successes and potential for future success in the doctoral program. One factor to consider is that Mr. Gibbons has demonstrated that he can achieve in graduate-level classes. The facts that he earned excellent grades in his classes for the most part and completed coursework requirements are testaments to his personal determination, consistent effort, and capability. Although he does not show a significant ability/achievement discrepancy, disability service providers from Western State University will make the final determination regarding whether Mr. Gibbons is eligible for modifications and/or accommodations as a graduate student with a specific learning disability.

SCORE SUMMARIES

Cognitive Abilities

Cognitive Ability Factors	Age Comparison		Grade Comparison	
Cluster/Factor/Test	Std. Score	Percentile	Std. Score	Percentile
General Intellectual Ability	101	53	79	8
Comprehension-Knowledge	117	86	114	82
Verbal Comprehension	111	77	104	61
General Information	120	91	122	93
Long-Term Retrieval	99	47	78	8
Visual-Auditory Learning	97	43	77	6
Retrieval Fluency	107	69	98	44
Visual-Spatial Thinking	107	67	94	35
Spatial Relations	116	85	105	63
Picture Recognition	96	38	84	15
Auditory Processing	98	44	76	5
Sound Blending	102	55	88	21
Auditory Attention	90	25	63	1
Fluid Reasoning	94	36	70	2
Concept Formation	87	19	55	0.1
Analysis-Synthesis	102	56	85	16
Processing Speed	115	84	94	35
Visual Matching	111	78	93	33
Decision Speed	116	86	98	44
Short-Term Memory	90	25	72	3
Numbers Reversed	89	24	77	6
Memory for Words	93	32	79	8

Cognitive Ability Categories	Age Comparison		Grade Comparison	
Factor/Subtest	Std. Score	Percentile	Std. Score	Percentile
Verbal Ability	117	86	114	82
Verbal Comprehension	111	77	104	61
General Information	120	91	122	93
Thinking Ability	98	44	77	6
Visual-Auditory Learning	97	43	77	6
Retrieval Fluency	107	69	98	44
Spatial Relations	116	85	105	63
Picture Recognition	96	38	84	15
Sound Blending	102	55	88	21
Auditory Attention	90	25	63	1
Concept Formation	87	19	55	0.1
Analysis-Synthesis	102	56	85	16
Cognitive Efficiency	100	50	76	6
Numbers Reversed	89	24	77	6
Memory for Words	93	32	79	8
Visual Matching	111	78	93	33
Decision Speed	116	86	98	44

Clinical Clusters	Age Comparison		Grade Comparison	
Cluster/Subtest	Std. Score	Percentile	Std. Score	Percentile
Working Memory	93	33	75	5
Numbers Reversed	89	24	77	6
Auditory Working Memory	99	47	82	12
Broad Attention	97	41	72	2
Numbers Reversed	89	24	77	6
Auditory Working Memory	99	47	82	12
Auditory Attention	90	25	63	1
Pair Cancellation	113	80	99	46
Cognitive Fluency	101	52	84	15
Retrieval Fluency	107	69	98	44
Decision Speed	116	86	98	44
Rapid Picture Naming	93	32	81	10
Executive Processes	98	44	67	1
Concept Formation	87	19	55	0.1
Planning	96	23	89	24
Pair Cancellation	113	80	99	46

Woodcock-Johnson III Tests of Achievement (Form A)

Achievement Clusters	Age Comparison		Grade Comparison	
Cluster/Test	Std. Score	Percentile	Std. Score	Percentile
Listening Comprehension Cluster	97	43	82	11
Understanding Directions	94	34	71	2
Oral Comprehension	100	51	93	33
Broad Reading Cluster	104	62	92	30
Word Identification	111	78	112	78
Passage Comprehension	108	71	104	61
Reading Fluency	99	47	84	14
Broad Mathematics Cluster	110	75	96	40
Calculation	114	82	101	52
Applied Problems	104	61	98	44
Math Fluency	106	66	88	21
Broad Written Language Cluster	110	74	93	32
Spelling	102	54	88	21
Writing Samples	110	75	100	50
Writing Fluency	115	85	100	49
Knowledge Cluster	117	87	121	92
General Information	120	91	122	93
Academic Knowledge	112	79	115	83
Academic Fluency Cluster	104	61	86	18
Reading Fluency	99	47	84	14
Math Fluency	106	66	88	21
Writing Fluency	115	85	100	49

SECTION III

Recommendations

INTRODUCTION

Many excellent techniques and programs are available for teaching individuals with learning and/or behavioral difficulties. For the most part, those offered here are documented as effective in the research literature and/or are widely accepted in clinical use. The recommendations suggested are not meant to be exhaustive but are ones that the authors or their colleagues have used in classrooms and educational therapy or would include when writing reports. Consequently, omission of a specific technique or program should not be viewed as a lack of endorsement. The authors are included for recommended books, and the publishers are included for commercial programs.

This section begins with "CHC Factors: Descriptors, Possible Performance Implications, and Recommendations." This overview of the Cattell-Horn-Carroll (CHC) factors provides a brief description of the factor, keywords that might be used in discussing it, the ways in which a weakness in these abilities might be manifested in academics and daily life, and the focus of therapeutic help.

The recommendations in this section are arranged in categories, such as basic reading skills and math problem solving. Although an attempt was made not to duplicate recommendations, some of the recommendations are appropriate for more than one skill area and so the reader is directed to related sections. As examples, many of the recommendations for reading comprehension are also appropriate for written language or content area instruction, and many of the recommendations under phonological awareness are also appropriate for development of word attack and spelling skills. Wherever possible, the recommendations are ordered in a developmental sequence, progressing from the more elementary to the more advanced requirements of a skill or ability. Depending upon the severity of

the problem, an older student may profit from recommendations at the readiness or beginning level of a skill. Conversely, a student advanced in an area may benefit from higher-level recommendations.

Occasionally, a recommendation has words or phrases enclosed in brackets, exemplifying the *type* of information the evaluator might include. The brackets indicate that the evaluator is expected to substitute wording appropriate to the student for whom the recommendation is intended.

It is often appropriate to write recommendations to address a student's strengths. Placing emphasis solely on difficulties can increase a student's negative perceptions of self and school. The focus of this book, however, is on students who are struggling and need specific educational or behavioral interventions to profit more fully from school experiences. The majority of recommendations, therefore, are written to address areas of need. Specific examples of recommendations to address strengths are presented in the section on Self-Esteem and within the diagnostic reports in Section II. The final report should address both ways to capitalize on areas of strength, as well as ways to remediate or ameliorate academic and behavioral difficulties.

Before writing recommendations, first consider the referral question, review any important background information, analyze the results of diagnostic testing, and assess the specific needs of a student within an educational setting. The goal is to select specific modifications and interventions that will enhance an individual's opportunities for success. For some reports, you may wish to organize the recommendation section by the person responsible for implementation and then adapt the wording accordingly. For example, you may make recommendations directly to a student or client, such as: "You should arrange appointments with each of your teachers at the beginning of each semester." Or, a recommendation may be made to the student's teacher, parents, or counselor, such as: "Help Tobias arrange appointments with his teachers at the beginning of each semester." You may also organize recommendations by the major areas of concern that are addressed (e.g., math, oral language, behavior, self-advocacy). To avoid wordiness throughout this section, the student is referred to as "he" or "she" within subsections.

In some cases, clear distinctions are evident between a general recommendation for instruction and specific activities or programs that support that recommendation, that would be particularly beneficial to the student, and that give the teacher initial direction in carrying out the recommendation. When these distinctions are evident, a general recommendation is provided (e.g., "Teach initial phonics skills using a multisensory approach") followed by a bulleted list of activities and programs. The recommendations in the bulleted lists are written so that they can be used independently, depending on the preference of the evaluator (e.g., "Use a multisensory program to teach phonic skills, such as the Wilson Reading System. Originally designed for older students, this system is also useful for elementary students").

After identifying the areas of concern, read through a section of recommendations and select those appropriate for a particular student. Most of the recommendations have been written for providing individualized instruction, but they could easily be adapted, and sometimes were originally designed, to emphasize small group instruction. Some are appropriate for a whole class. All of the recommendations may be modified, rewritten, or combined, as needed. Based upon assessment results and consideration of the specific circumstances, most evaluators will create additional recommendations specific to the needs of the student.

CHC FACTORS: DESCRIPTORS, POSSIBLE PERFORMANCE IMPLICATIONS, AND RECOMMENDATIONS

The following section provides descriptors and possible performance implications and recommendations regarding the factors in CHC theory represented in the WJ III COG. The intent is to explore the associations between these factors and performance. Some of the relationships are more clearly established than others.

Long-Term Retrieval (Glr)

Involves the ability to store and retrieve information through association. *Glr* is not to be confused with the amount of information available, a *Gc* function. Descriptors: Memorization, fluency, association, retrieval, paired-associate learning, transfer.

Possible Implications
• Learning and recalling information through association (e.g., facts, related ideas/concepts)
• Recalling information on tests through association
• Using associations provided by the teacher to facilitate storage and later retrieval
• Pairing and retaining visual with auditory information
• Retrieving specific words, memorizing poems, speeches, facts

Possible Recommendations
• Provide overlearning, review, and repetition
• Provide immediate feedback
• Provide a list of steps that will help organize behavior and facilitate recall
• Teach memory aids such as verbal mediation or rehearsal, and mnemonic strategies (e.g., Keyword, Method of Loci)
• Provide multisensory learning; use visual, kinesthetic, vocal, and auditory channels as appropriate
• Provide context and meaning-based instruction
• Limit the number of new facts, words, concepts presented in one session

Short-Term Memory (Gsm)

Involves the ability to hold information in mental awareness and use it within a few seconds. May be influenced by attention. Descriptors: Rote, sequential, immediate, attention, auditory, concentration, limited duration, memory span, immediate awareness.

Possible Implications
• Following directions
• Remembering information long enough to process it for understanding
• Recalling sequences
• Memorizing factual information (e.g., math facts)
• Listening to and comprehending lengthy discourse
• Taking notes

Possible Recommendations
• Keep oral directions short and simple
• Ensure directions are understood; have student paraphrase directions
• Provide compensatory aids (e.g., write directions, procedures, and assignments on board or paper, provide lecture notes or arrange for peer-shared notes, provide study guide to be filled out during pauses in presentation)
• Provide overlearning, review, and repetition
• Teach memory strategies (e.g., chunking, verbal rehearsal, visual imagery)

Processing Speed (Gs)

Involves the ability to perform relatively simple cognitive tasks automatically (i.e., quickly and without conscious deliberation), particularly when under pressure to maintain focused attention. May be influenced by attention. Descriptors: Speed, visual scanning efficiency, automaticity, perceptual speed, attention, concentration.

Possible Implications
• Processing information rapidly
• Completing assignments within time limits
• Taking timed tests
• Making rapid comparisons between and among bits of information
• Copying

Possible Recommendations
• Provide more time to complete assignments
• Reduce quantity of work in favor of quality
• Limit or structure copying activities
• Provide activities to increase rate and fluency (e.g., flash cards, speed drills, educational software)

Auditory Processing (Ga)

Involves the ability to analyze and synthesize auditory stimuli (but not comprehend language, which is *Gc*). This ability is important for language development. Descriptors: Phonological awareness, blending, auditory closure, auditory discrimination, phonemic segmentation, musical ability.

Possible Implications
• Acquiring phonics (decoding)
• Learning structural analysis
• Spelling (encoding)
• Speech perception
• Learning foreign languages
• Developing musical skill

Possible Recommendations
• Provide phonological awareness activities (e.g., rhyming, alliteration, imitation, songs)
• Provide specific training in sound discrimination, blending, and segmentation
• Emphasize sound/symbol associations in teaching decoding and spelling
• Provide study guides for listening activities
• Provide assistance with note taking
• Accompany oral information with visual materials

Visual Processing (Gv)

Involves perceiving, analyzing, and thinking with visual patterns, spatial configurations and designs, and spatial orientation. Descriptors: Visual imagery, spatial relations, visual perception, visual closure, visual-pattern recognition.

Possible Implications
• Assembling puzzles • Using patterns and designs in art, geometry, geography • Designing • Building • Sensing spatial orientation • Reading maps, graphs, charts, blueprints • Noting visual detail • Sensing spatial boundaries (e.g., fitting, assembly, and packing) • Organizing, arranging furniture, appliances, equipment, et cetera, for efficient use and visual appeal

Possible Recommendations
• Provide activities with manipulatives • Provide copying, tracing, drawing activities • Provide activities involving construction and design • Verbally describe graphics and visually based concepts • Provide support for tasks requiring spatial organization

Comprehension-Knowledge (Gc)

Involves expressive vocabulary, ability to grasp the relationships among word meanings, and knowledge acquired from general experience within the mainstream culture. *Gc* is often called *crystallized intelligence* and sometimes *long-term memory* in the literature. Descriptors: Prior knowledge, background knowledge, schema, long-term memory, acquired or stored knowledge, vocabulary, comprehension, episodic memory, declarative knowledge, procedural knowledge.

Possible Implications
• Learning vocabulary • Answering factual questions • Comprehending oral and written language • Acquiring general knowledge and knowledge in content areas • Using prior knowledge to perform activities and understand new concepts

Possible Recommendations
• Relate new information to acquired knowledge • Assess prior knowledge before introducing new topics, concepts • Pre-teach relevant vocabulary or background knowledge • Provide specific vocabulary instruction such as the meaning of common prefixes, suffixes, and root words • Incorporate interests and prior knowledge areas into instructional activities • When presenting directions and discussing concepts, use vocabulary that is understood by the individual

Fluid Reasoning (Gf)

Involves the ability to use inductive and deductive reasoning to ascertain commonalities and differences, form concepts, generate rules, and apply rules to solve novel problems. Often called *fluid intelligence*. Descriptors: Creativity, abstract problem solving, transfer, analogical reasoning, inductive reasoning, deductive reasoning, rule generation, inference.

Possible Implications
• Drawing inferences
• Solving abstract problems
• Creating solutions to problems
• Transferring and generalizing information
• Solving unique problems
• Transforming and extending a product or concept (rather than matching or reproducing a stimulus)
• Thinking conceptually
• Problem solving through rule application

Possible Recommendations
• Teach problem-solving strategies
• Provide overlearning, repetition, and review of concepts
• Use real objects and manipulatives to develop concepts
• Teach strategies to increase understanding and retention of concepts (e.g., self-talk, lists of procedures or steps)
• Encourage creativity with solutions
• Teach problem-solving techniques in the contexts in which they are most likely to be applied

Quantitative Ability (Gq)

Involves the ability to comprehend quantitative concepts and relationships and to manipulate numerical symbols. Descriptors: Quantitative reasoning, mathematics application, computation, problem solving.

Possible Implications
• Reasoning with quantitative information
• Understanding math terminology
• Using numeric concepts
• Apprehending numeric relationships
• Using math symbols
• Performing math applications

Possible Recommendations
• Provide math-related instruction in developmental sequence
• Assess knowledge of the concepts underlying weak skills
• Establish a strong understanding of the foundational concepts for new skills
• Use manipulatives or real objects to introduce new concepts and extend known concepts
• Emphasize automaticity with math facts
• Allow use of fact charts, calculators when necessary
• Emphasize problem solving and higher-level skills
• Provide experience with practical math applications
• Introduce new concepts and procedures in the practical situations in which they will be applied

MEMORY

Tests: Auditory Working Memory, Memory for Words (*Gsm*); Visual-Auditory Learning, Retrieval Fluency (*Glr*)

Related Tests: Visual-Auditory Learning—Delayed, Numbers Reversed, Understanding Directions, Story Recall, Story Recall—Delayed

Clusters: Long-Term Retrieval, Delayed Recall, Short-Term Memory, Working Memory

Related Clusters: Listening Comprehension

Related Sections: Oral Language, Homework/Time Management/Organization, Attentional Disorders

Memory
    Further Evaluation
    Accommodations
        Giving and Following Directions
    Instruction
        Repetition and Review
        Comprehension
        Multiple Modalities
    Strategy Use
        General/Simple Strategies
        Mnemonic Strategies

Further Evaluation

Because memory is not a very stable trait, readminister the memory tests at a different time of the day for comparison of performance (e.g., morning rather than late afternoon).

Administer additional assessments to determine if low memory scores are a function of poor memory or a reflection of [limited or poor attention, lack of initial comprehension].

Accommodations

Teach the student how to be a self-advocate and request the specific compensations she needs to compensate for her memory difficulties.

Recognize that the student has difficulty on tasks that require her to manipulate information mentally. Provide strategies and accommodations to reduce the demands placed on working memory.

Because the student has difficulty with tasks involving memory, reduce the amount of information that she is required to memorize. For example, provide her with a calculator to compensate for her difficulty recalling math facts.

The student is more likely to remember the content of a lecture if she can devote her full attention to listening rather than dividing her attention between listening and note-taking. To this end, provide her with a copy of your lecture notes or a copy of the notes of a student who is a particularly good note-taker.

Based upon her difficulties recalling orally presented information, encourage the student to tape-record class lectures. Teach her how to take notes as she listens to the tape. Have her hit the pause button as she writes notes and rewind the tape whenever clarification is needed. Keep in mind, however, that this compensation consumes more time than listening to the initial lecture and so should be used sparingly.

Giving and Following Directions

Limit the length and complexity of all instructions to the student and state them in the same order she is to do them.

When giving oral directions to the student, give only ___ direction(s) at a time. Allow her to complete it (them) before going on.

Ensure that you have the student's attention before speaking to her. If you are giving a series of oral directions, limit them to two or three steps, and ask the student to repeat them. If the directions are lengthy ask the student to write them down (such as the steps for a project).

Prior to giving directions, make certain that the student has secured and is attending to the relevant materials. For example, when explaining the directions on a worksheet, ensure that the student is looking at the assignment.

When giving directions for a task or assignment, write the steps on the board so that the student can review directions as often as needed.

When giving the student directions, incorporate visual illustrations as much as possible. For example, use gestures, draw on the board, or model the steps of a process.

When presenting the student with tasks involving several steps, provide a list of the steps on an index card or have the student write them down. Have the student check off each step as she accomplishes it.

Set up a buddy system for the student. Seat the student next to a responsible peer who will review directions with the student as needed and answer any questions that she has.

Teach the student to count the number of tasks or instructions, tell you the number of tasks, and repeat them as she touches her fingers, one instruction or task to a finger. Continue practice until she is able to repeat the tasks correctly in sequence.

Teach the student specific behaviors that will help her follow oral directions, such as listening carefully, writing down important points, asking questions, and waiting to start a task until all directions have been given.

Instruction

Repetition and Review

Provide intensive repetition, practice, and review in learning activities. To promote retention, provide activities to reinforce the skills or content at frequent and regular intervals, gradually increasing the intervals to less frequent and intermittent.

In each teaching session, before introducing new information to the student, review previous information from the last lesson and check for mastery.

When teaching the student new skills, provide frequent opportunities for practice and review. Provide systematic review within a few hours and for the next few days and then slowly fade review. Check retention after a week has passed without review, then 2 weeks, then a month.

Whenever possible, use a game format for learning (e.g., reviewing for a test by playing Jeopardy with the target information). The student will find it easier to attend to the information and hold it in mind long enough to process it more effectively.

Comprehension

Understanding facilitates memory. Ensure that the student understands the concept underlying any new information or skill, as well as how each aspect of the new information is related to every other part.

Due to the possibility of a weakness in memory, the student will find it easier to work with data mentally if she has a strong understanding of the related concepts.

Recognize that difficulties in memory and listening comprehension compromise the student's performance in all subjects taught in a lecture-discussion format. Provide visual outlines, class notes prior to the lecture, and a study guide to fill out during the lecture.

Because the student processes spoken language in meaningful contexts more effectively than in isolation, provide instruction in meaningful contexts and de-emphasize tasks involving rote memorization.

Multiple Modalities

When introducing new information and skills, provide the student with pictures to look at or a way to visualize and form associations regarding what she is learning.

Use graphic organizers to teach new concepts and information. When the student can picture how the ideas are interrelated, she will be able to store and retrieve them more easily.

As much as possible, provide the student with multisensory learning experiences. Present content and skill instruction using combinations of visual, auditory, tactile, and kinesthetic input or experience.

Present all types of verbal information accompanied by visual stimuli that clearly illustrate the concept being taught. Examples are: pictures, charts, graphs, semantic maps, and videotapes. Simultaneous visual–verbal presentation will improve comprehension and retention of information.

Provide experiential approaches to learning to enhance memory.

Strategy Use

General/Simple Strategies

To activate her awareness of strategy use, discuss with the student what strategies she uses to help her recall information. Then, suggest and teach other strategies to enhance recall.

Teach the student specific memory strategies and how to recognize which strategy may be most useful in a variety of situations, such as taking notes versus memorizing factual information for a test. Examples include: using verbal rehearsal, chunking, making ridiculous visual images composed of items that one has to remember, and creating first-letter mnemonic strategies.

Have the student put a colored rubber band on her wrist or tie a string around her finger as a reminder of a task that she is supposed to do. Have the student remove the rubber band or string as soon as she has completed the task.

Organization facilitates memory. Teach the student strategies for organizing all types of information and tasks, including [the content of reading material, school-related materials and notes, information for a test, tasks she has to accomplish over the month.]

Teach the student how to use index cards to review and memorize information. Write the information on the card and review the cards several times a day. Information can be categorized by color. For example, when studying a particular biological class (e.g., reptilia), the orders, families, genera, and common names can each be written in a different color.

Teach the student how to break down information to learn into smaller chunks. As she learns one piece of information, have her add in another piece, and then review the material that was previously learned.

Teach the student to make a list of tasks she wishes to accomplish by [drawing a simple picture, writing one keyword] for each task. For example, if she wants to remember to return a book to the library, she would [draw a simple picture of a book, write the word "book"].

Train the student to use verbal rehearsal for information or instructions that she has to remember for only a short time. For example, when trying to remember a phone number long enough to dial it, have the student repeat the number over and over until she is finished dialing.

Mnemonic Strategies

Note: Mnemonics are memory techniques that help the learner alter the information to be learned in some way (recode), relate it to something familiar (relate), and recall it later (retrieve). Research demonstrates that students who use mnemonics remember information more effectively than students who were not trained in these techniques. At times, when using a mnemonic technique, you may choose to create the mnemonic yourself rather than take the time to have the student do so. Although devising the mnemonic would be a helpful skill for the student to develop, it cuts down on the time available for teaching content and skills.

Teach the student a simple strategy to aid in recall. One example is the PAR formula, *P*icture it, *A*ssociate it, and *R*eview it. This may be combined with the USA formula guide for clear visualization: *U* = *U*nusual, unforgettable; *S* = *S*ee the picture as vividly as you can using as many senses as possible; *A* = *A*ction, see the item happening with action (Herold, 1982). Provide systematic practice using this strategy for storing and retrieving information.

To recall multiple items, such as a shopping list or the parts of the body that are considered organs, teach the student the technique of forming associative images to recall information. Have the student create a visual scene that depicts strange or ridiculous interactions among the specific items to be remembered. Encourage the student to use as many senses as possible to create vivid pictures. Have the student practice retrieving the relevant information.

Teach the student how to use a first-letter mnemonic strategy, using acronyms and acrostics, to help her remember and recall facts and information. For first letter mnemonics to be effective, the information to be recalled must be familiar and meaningful to the student.

- To use an acronym, the student forms a word from the first letters of the words to be remembered. Some well-known acronyms are HOMES for the Great Lakes (Huron, Ontario, Michigan, Erie, Superior) and FOIL for the order of operations when multiplying two binomials (First terms, Outer terms, Inner terms, Last terms). If she cannot make an acronym out of the first letters, the student could use the first letter of the first word, the second letter of the second word, and so on, but must remember that she did so.

- To use an acrostic, the student takes the first letters of the words to be remembered and makes up an easy-to-remember sentence using words that have the same first letters as the words to be remembered. For example, the first letter of "Every Good Boy Does Fine" represents the names of the lines in the treble clef music staff, "Kings Play Chess On Fancy Green Soft Velvet" help recall the order of classification in the animal kingdom— Kingdom, Phylum, Class, Order, Family, Genus, Species and Variety.

- Acronyms and acrostics can also be used as memory aids for more complex information such as a list of rules, biographical information, or the causes of a war by using keywords as links. In this case, the student selects a keyword from within each element of information and makes up either an acronym or an acrostic. The acronym/acrostic evokes the keyword, which is then used to recall the information. For example, the acrostic, "In Fact, Rhinos Can Eat Many African Apples," helped a student recall the Eight Examples of Poor Integrity that she had to recite as part of her test for advancement in taekwondo. The words "In" and "Fact" were linked to the keywords "improper" and "fixing," reminding her of the examples, "The instructor who misrepresents himself and his art by presenting *improper* techniques to his students because of lack of knowledge or apathy," and "the student who misrepresents himself by *'fixing'* breaking materials before demonstrations."

Teach the student how to use substitute words to evoke images for memorizing individual words. When she thinks she may have difficulty remembering a word, have her think of words that sound like, or remind her of, the word and can be easily pictured in her mind. For example, she may remember the state, Minnesota, as a "mini soda." Teach her how to form a link, or another association, with the next word or concept that she is trying to remember.

Teach the student how to use the method of loci to remember lists of items or key elements in an oral report, particularly when the elements must be recalled in a particular order. The student is to imagine traveling a familiar route (e.g., from home to school, around her bedroom) and choose a place on the route for each thing she must remember. She then imagines placing the first item in the first place, the second item in the second place, and so on. When she has to recall the items, she simply travels the route and retrieves each item in order. A critical element of this technique is for the student to create a strong mental link between the location and the item by creating a vivid mental image of the item interacting with the location. For example, if the student is giving a report on Arizona, and has the state's major product as her fourth topic and a tree as her fourth location, she can picture the tree with leaves of copper. For different lists of items, have the student use different routes and locations.

Teach the student how to use a pegword (number–rhyme) system when she has to remember the order in which the items occur. Each number from 1 to 12 has a specific rhyme, a pegword, associated with it. Have the student memorize the numbers and their rhymes or make up and memorize her own keywords: 1-bun, 2-glue, 3-tree, 4-door, 5-dive, 6-bricks, 7-heaven, 8-gate, 9-wine, 10-tent, 11-elephant, 12-shelf (Herold, 1982). The pegwords should be something concrete and easy to visualize. Then, for each item, the student creates a vivid image in which the item and the pegword related to its number interact. For example, Figure III.1 shows the pegword mnemonic for the reason earthquakes happen and the order of events.

One advantage of the pegword mnemonic is that the student does not have to go through each item in the series to get to the one she wants. The item's number will allow her direct access to it.

1. Plates get stuck: As one plate slides past another, it locks. (A bun—1—sits stable atop the plates.)

2. Stress builds in the rocks on both sides of the fault line as the force that was moving the plate continues to exert pressure. The rocks begin to crack. (A shoe—2—pushes one plate forward.)

3. The stress overcomes the strength of the rocks and the rocks break. The sudden movement of the rocks at the fault line is an earthquake. (A tree—3—falls over in the earthquake.)

Figure III.1. Illustration of a Pegword Mnemonic: Why Earthquakes Happen

Teach the student to use the keyword technique when she has to remember unfamiliar information, such as foreign words, facts and their referents, scientific terms, or content-related vocabulary. First the student thinks of a word (keyword) that sounds like the word or a part of the word she must remember (target word). The keyword should represent a familiar, easily pictured, tangible object. Second, the student creates a strong association between the keyword and a picture that will recall the meaning of the target word or term. Finally, to retrieve the target word, the student thinks of the keyword, which triggers recall of the mental image into which it has been integrated, which triggers recall of the target word (Mastropieri & Scruggs, 1999a). For example, to remember the definition of igneous rock, the student might decide on "pig noose" as the keyword for igneous and picture a pig hanging by its leg from a noose over a small erupting volcano. As the lava flows down the mountain, it solidifies into igneous rock. Thus, when asked the definition of "igneous," the student thinks of "pig noose," recalls the image of the pig over the solidifying lava, and retrieves the definition of igneous rock as solidified molten rock. To remember the capital of Peru, the student thinks of a keyword for Peru—parrot—and for Lima—lima beans. The student then creates a mental image of a parrot, perhaps wearing a Peruvian shawl, eating lima beans. When a test asks for the capital of Peru, the student thinks of the parrot eating lima beans, and remembers Lima.

To help the student remember how to use the keyword technique, teach her IT FITS (King-Sears, Mercer, & Sindelar, 1992).

*I*dentify the term.

*T*ell the definition of the term.

*F*ind a keyword.

*I*magine the definition doing something with the keyword.

*T*hink about the definition doing something with the keyword.

*S*tudy what you imagined until you know the definition.

Teach the student to use a body-file system to help in remembering information. This technique is related to the method of loci. Retrieval cues for this mental filing system are body parts and locations. Have the student begin with the first six cues, body parts, from the top of the head to the tip of your toes: hair, nose, mouth, hands, pocket, foot. Have the student repeat and touch each place, until she can mentally visualize the six places without any touching. The next six places are spaces around the body that make an uncompleted circle: left, front, right, back, above, and below. Have the student memorize and practice the body spaces. Make sure that the student can visualize the 12 file places in the correct sequence. As she associates information, teach her to create vivid images in which the item or action to recall interacts with the ideas she is trying to associate with each of the body-file places. For example, an item she is trying to remember could be stuck in her hair or blowing her hair around (Herold, 1982).

FLUID REASONING

Tests: Concept Formation, Analysis-Synthesis
Related Tests: Verbal Comprehension
Clusters: Fluid Reasoning
Related Clusters: Thinking Ability

Fluid Reasoning
   Strengths
   Accommodations
   Instructional Approach
      Problem-Solving
      Reasoning

Strengths

Help the student learn to use his excellent reasoning skills and conceptual ability. Provide him with meaningful activities that will involve finding solutions to problems, understanding and applying rules, and predicting logical conclusions.

The student's strength in fluid reasoning suggests that he has good aptitude for higher-level mathematics. Encourage him to develop these abilities and to pursue advanced math courses.

Accommodations

Help the student select courses in high school that emphasize practical and experiential learning and do not require a high level of abstract reasoning.

Even when the final solutions or answers are incorrect, provide the student with encouragement and praise for persistence in problem solving and attempts to discover a solution.

Instructional Approach

Due to the student's apparent preference for deductive learning and reasoning over inductive, he will probably benefit more from explicit and systematic teaching than from a discovery learning type of approach.

Explain the concept of inductive reasoning to the student. Guide the student to examine several specific situations and formulate a general rule that applies for each case. Help him to develop an understanding of this concept by providing many situations in which to use it. Activities might include guided discovery, searching for patterns, and making comparisons and contrasts.

When teaching the student any new process or skill, provide slow, step-by-step instruction. Use manipulatives and concrete objects whenever possible to illustrate the concepts.

Because the student appears more adept at inductive than deductive reasoning, when teaching new concepts and skills, do not expect him to memorize and use theorems, rules, and codes to guide his work or to accept procedural information at face value. He needs to understand how the theorems, rules, or codes came about; how they are related to the function they are serving; and the associated concepts. The student needs to know "why" before he can understand and remember "what."

The student is having difficulty with conceptual level skills, especially in the areas of math and science, due to limited abilities in recognizing similarities and differences as a basis for forming new concepts. Provide explicit instruction in the development of categorization skills, moving from concrete to abstract materials and from simple comparison to contrast based on multiple attributes.

Help the student develop the concept of categorization so as to increase his ability to relate objects, events, components of problems, and other concepts by similarities and to apprehend the critical differences.

Problem Solving

When teaching problem-solving strategies, present problem situations in areas where the student possesses expertise so that he can draw on his background knowledge as he learns the strategy.

Provide the student with practice in using problem-solving strategies that can be generalized to a variety of situations. Include the following steps: deciding what the problem is and what you would like the outcome to be; brainstorming possible solutions; considering which solutions are feasible; considering the positive and negative outcomes of each of the solutions; choosing the solution that seems best; trying it; asking if it is working; modifying it or selecting a different solution if the strategy does not work, and generalizing the use of the strategy so that it is self-initiated in multiple situations.

Teach the student a specific strategy to use for solving problems, such as one that includes defining the problem, task analysis, brainstorming alternative solutions, considering possible outcomes, choosing a solution, etc. Provide practice in application of the strategy in a variety of situations.

Reasoning

Guide the student in his development of reasoning skills by using the Hilda Taba Critical Thinking Strategies. These group-oriented, highly interactive strategies raise students' level of thinking and problem solving from dealing with concrete information to making valid and supported generalizations. An updated, organized description of these strategies may be found in *A Comprehensive Approach to Teaching Thinking* (Schiever, 1991).

Teach the student how to analyze tasks into their component steps and then to sequence the steps. Directly teach generalization to a variety of tasks such as writing a research paper or planning a trip.

Integrate higher-level thinking skills into daily lessons. Three good resources for activities that foster self-directed thinking are *Catch Them Thinking: A Handbook of Classroom Strategies* (Bellanca & Fogarty, 1986), *Creating the Thoughtful Classroom: Strategies to Promote Student Thinking* (Udall & Daniels, 1991), and *A Comprehensive Approach to Teaching Thinking* (Schiever, 1991). These books present strategies that may be used to teach thinking skills in all classes.

VISUAL–SPATIAL THINKING/VISUAL DETAIL

Clarification. Because the effects of problems in visual–spatial thinking, in comprehending two-dimensional visual information as representing three-dimensional information, and perceiving visual detail are sometimes difficult to differentiate, these recommendations are placed into one section. The evaluator is advised to read through both subsections when looking for recommendations for students who have difficulty with visual skills.

Visual–Spatial Thinking
Tests: Spatial Relations, Picture Recognition
Related Tests: Planning
Clusters: Visual–Spatial Thinking
Related Clusters: Fluid Reasoning

Visual Detail
Tests: Visual Matching, Decision Speed
Related Tests: Rapid Picture Naming, Pair Cancellation, Reading Fluency
Clusters: Processing Speed

Related Recommendations: Basic Reading Skills, Basic Writing Skills, Handwriting/Visual–Motor, Mathematics

Visual–Spatial Thinking/Visual Detail
    Further Evaluation
    Strengths
    Accommodations and Modifications
        General
        Visual–Spatial
        Visual Detail
            Copying
            Worksheets and Textbooks
            Student Self-Management of Adaptations
            Writing
            Math
    Instruction and Activities
        Visual–Spatial
        Visual Detail

Further Evaluation

Conduct further assessments that require the use of manipulatives and real objects.

Conduct further assessments that evaluate visual–spatial thinking abilities in a timed format.

Conduct further assessments that require the ability to reproduce patterns or designs, both two- and three-dimensional, and then to reproduce them from memory.

Conduct further assessments that require the ability to recall designs and patterns.

Because the student frequently has such difficulty with [keeping her place when reading, her eyes tiring and/or tearing while doing close work, seeing letters and numbers as double or fuzzy as her eyes tire, visual discomfort in normal light], recommend that she have a comprehensive vision examination from a qualified vision specialist.

Strengths

Because the student is superior in activities involving visual–spatial thinking, allow her to substitute projects (such as building a model) for more language-based assignments, such as presenting an oral book report.

To take advantage of the student's strong awareness of visual details, use visual displays in the classroom when illustrating key points.

Provide the student with activities and/or classes that will allow use of her excellent visual–spatial and mechanical skills.

Consider the student's superior visual–spatial processing ability when providing career and vocational counseling.

Accommodations and Modifications

General

In planning instruction for the student, consider how her difficulty with spatial organization and her inattention to visual details will affect performance. Think of ways to modify assignments and tasks so that the student can be successful.

For art assignments, relax standards of production and accept approximations of expected criteria.

Ensure that the student clears her desk completely before she begins any task. She should remove all extraneous materials from her desk. Attempt to reduce visual clutter from the area of the classroom in which she works.

Visual–Spatial

As far as possible, explain new skills and concepts to the student orally.

Do not ask the student to use any visual strategies that she finds confusing. Examples are webs, diagrams, and schemas for math operations.

Recognize that manipulatives, drawings, diagrams, and charts may overwhelm and confuse the student. Reduce the number of visual displays and instead provide clear verbal descriptions.

The student will have trouble interpreting and gaining meaningful information from visual displays, such as models, graphs, maps, diagrams, charts. Instead, emphasize sequential verbal approaches and provide explicit outlines and study guides to help to structure the student's learning. [See Strategies: Study Guides.]

Visual Detail

When the students are doing seatwork, periodically pass the student's desk to make sure she has not inadvertently skipped items. If she has, point out the missed items.

Copying

The student is likely to experience extreme difficulty in copying material from chalkboards or textbooks and completing tasks that involve aligning information, such as writing basic math problems. Provide the student with a copy of notes from the board, as well as textbooks that she can write in.

Limit near- or far-point copying activities. When copying is necessary, do not require speed or accuracy.

Do not require the student to copy problems from her math or other textbooks. Instead, provide her with clear worksheets that contain only a few problems and plenty of white space.

Teach the student to use verbal mediation when she copies material from the chalkboard. Have her say each letter, word, or phrase as she copies it from the board to paper.

Worksheets and Textbooks

Find some quiet time and a private place to sit with the student and experiment with adaptations that would make it easier for her to do the classroom work. Try a variety of adaptations to see which seem to be most helpful and which ones she likes. Be creative with adaptations and view them as an ongoing project as they are likely to change as the type of work and materials change.

Provide the student with extra visual structure on worksheets and assignments. For example, arrange problems in numbered boxes or columns.

Do not penalize the student for placing information incorrectly on a page. Instead, provide graph paper and lined paper that will help the student organize her work. [See Strategies: Math Computation Forms.]

Adapt worksheets for the student's use. Examples include clean copies, ample blank space between sections and items within sections, cutting pages into sections and enlarging each section, having the student cover all sections except the one on which she is working, color coding.

Make all worksheets clear and clean looking. Keep visual information to a minimum and portions of it well separated.

To clarify the organization of a worksheet, border each section in colored highlighter. Items that are part of the same task comprise a section.

Use colored highlighting to indicate the order in which the student is to work on the sections. Choose a different color for each step and use them consistently. For example, green indicates the first part the student is to do, yellow the second, and red, the last. For example, instructions might be bordered in green, the reading passage bordered in yellow, and questions about the passage bordered in red. A section requiring a task unrelated to the passage would be cut off, enlarged, and presented separately.

Because the student has severe difficulty keeping her place and her eyes tire easily, she might prefer to use a window card, a large index card with a window cut out large enough to see one or two lines of print. White cards can cause glare; dull green or buff are better.

To reduce visual "busyness" of a page of print or numbers, make enlarged copies of the pages to be worked on or read. If creating worksheets on the computer, use large print with ample space between lines of print. Use a sans serif font with ___ point typeface.

The following are suggestions for reducing or eliminating the perception of visual clutter in any printed material:
- Cut the worksheet into sections and work on one at a time;
- Cover the sections on which the student is not working with a thin mousepad with a spongy back, cut to the cor-

rect size. Mousepads won't slide around like paper templates do.
- Make enlarged copies of the material. Allow the student to decide what size print is best.
- Cut materials into sections and provide the student with only one section at a time.

When the student is working on a worksheet with different sections and activities, enhance the spatial organization of the page by using colors and frames. Use the following suggestions separately to avoid adding to the visual confusion:
- Draw a frame or border around each major section with a marker or highlighter;
- Highlight or draw frames around the different steps or components of a task, assigning a role to each color, such as (a) consistent colors to show the order in which to do the task (e.g., green is always first, yellow is second, and red, third), or (b) consistent colors to indicate the type of task component (e.g., blue for instructions, orange for examples of the task, green for the task items).
- Place boxes on the paper in the places where the student will write her name and the date.
- For tasks that require left-to-right work across the page, a green line on the left margin and a red line on the right margin will help the student stop at the end of a line and find the place to start on the next line. The student may need to verbalize: "Start on green, stop on red, go back to green."
- Number the items, in a different color, on the worksheet in the order in which the student is to do them.

If possible, modify the light over the student's desk to minimize glare or provide her with a slant board, which will accomplish the same purpose.

Student Self-Management of Adaptations
For any adaptation that the student has learned to do herself, make sure that the materials she might need are easily accessible and organized. Examples are highlighters or markers for color-coding, ready-made templates and the materials to make templates, line guides and cardstock in dull colors, scissors, and a slant board.

Teach the student how to analyze a worksheet herself by finding the separate sections, the instructions for each task, restating the task, and identifying the section of the worksheet it requires. Teach this skill using enlarged worksheets in different styles. Teach the student how to highlight or color-code sections herself.

Teach the student how to interpret the organization of a page of text that has an unusual format, such as a number of windows interspersed with columns of text and pictures. Also, help her by numbering the sections in the order in which she should read them.

To help the student keep her place in reading, teach her to use a large index card down the page, either under or over the line she is reading. White cards can cause glare; dull green or buff are better. As an alternative, show the student how to track along a line with her finger.

Writing

To help the student with spatial orientation when writing, cue her to write from left to right and to observe the margins with a green line down the left margin and a red line down the right (green-go, red-stop). To help her write on the line, provide raised-line paper so she can feel where to place the letters on the line. To increase motor control in letter formation, have the student write with a fine-point felt-tip marker in the color of her choice. Raised-line paper is available from PRO-ED: phone: (800) 897-3202, website: www.proedinc.com.

To help the student learn to space letters evenly and to leave a space between words, have her write on graph paper, one letter to a square with an empty square between words and two squares between sentences. Try out different size grids to find one that feels comfortable to her. Many teaching supply stores sell books of grids and charts for copying.

Math

The student's difficulty in ordering her numbers in rows and columns causes her math papers to be messy and disordered, increasing her errors due to visual confusion. To help the student keep her numbers orderly, have her use graph paper with squares of a comfortable size for her to write in. Teach her to write only one number to a square. [See Strategies: Math Computation Forms.]

To avoid the visual busyness that adds to the student's frustration and increases her errors, have her fold her paper into 4 or 6 sections, unfold it, and use the creases as borders for each section. She is to place only one problem in each section, ensuring plenty of space around each. To prevent her mistaking the item number for part of the problem, have her number each section in the upper left corner and draw a circle around the number or write it with a colored marker.

When the student is copying math problems onto her paper, have her write the problem itself with a colored, fine-point marker but work the problem in pencil. The color contrast will help her distinguish between the digits in the problem and her own computation.

Teach the student to use verbal mediation to reduce her errors in copying math problems onto her paper from the board or from the textbook. Tell her to say the numbers of the problem she is to copy from, then say them again as she writes them on her paper. Teach her to chunk numbers to increase the number she can hold in memory. For example, for 2972, instead of saying, "two thousand, nine hundred and seventy-two or two-nine-seven-two," she would say "twenty-nine, seventy-two."

When copying problems from a book, the student can avoid losing her place if she puts a piece of sticky paper over the last problem she copied. She looks at a problem in the book, writes it on her paper, moves the "sticky" over one problem (covering the item she just copied) and looks at the next problem. If using verbal mediation to help her remember the numbers, the procedure would be: look and say, say and write, move the "sticky," (next problem) look and say, and so on.

For timed math fact drill, use flashcards instead of worksheets and test the student individually. Consider a fact automatic if she responds correctly within 3 seconds. Alternately, run through the math facts orally (e.g., teacher: "six plus seven," student: "thirteen").

Instruction and Activities

Visual–Spatial

Teach the student how to use the concepts of "same" and "different" to categorize real objects and manipulatives. Gradually move to two-dimensional stimuli such as pictures, shapes, letters and numbers, and designs. Provide the student with activities that require classification. For example, have him sort a variety of objects by different attributes, such as size, shape, or color.

After initial instruction, in a pull-out setting, in interpreting a variety of visual formats (e.g., worksheets, books) have the student practice verbally describing the relationships of text to pictures, maps, graphs, charts, diagrams, and directions.

Provide the student with direct instruction in reading and interpreting maps, graphs, charts, and diagrams.

Encourage the student to participate in activities that have elements of visual problem-solving and manual manipulation, such as chess, designing and building, and art projects. It will be necessary to provide both guidance and support.

Encourage the student to talk himself through tasks that are visually based, such as reorganizing the furniture in his room or drawing a map of the school playground.

Visual Detail

Teach the student strategies that will help her attend to visual detail. For example, have her interpret and describe the elements of a picture. First have her name all of the things that she sees and tell you what, if anything, is happening. Then teach her to divide the page mentally any way that is easiest (quarters, columns). Have her trace slowly in a systematic way through the section with her finger. Direct her to stop each time she sees something she has not yet named and name it. When finished with a section, ask her to try and find the same things without using her finger. Practice until she is able to look at a visual field and scan it visually in an organized way. Work with this type of task using different types of visual fields until the student can scan a small environment, such as a room, and find specific objects. Use practical tasks.

VISUAL PROCESSING SPEED

Tests: Visual Matching, Decision Speed, Pair Cancellation, Rapid Picture Naming
Clusters: Cognitive Fluency, Processing Speed
Related Clusters: Academic Fluency
Related Sections: Reading Fluency, Math Fluency

Visual Processing Speed
    Further Evaluation
    Accommodations
        Shortened Assignments/Extended Time
        Instruction and Activities

Further Evaluation

Administer additional processing speed tests. Attempt to determine if slow performance results primarily from poor scanning speed or poor attention.

Administer processing speed tasks that do not involve a motor component.

Due to her extremely slow visual processing speed, refer the student for a vision exam to rule out or confirm inefficient functioning related to the eyes.

Accommodations

[See Recommendations: Visual–Spatial Thinking/Visual Detail, Basic Reading Skills, Basic Writing Skills, Basic Math Skills, Testing/Test-Taking.]

Shortened Assignments/Extended Time

Do not require the student to work under time pressure. Place the emphasis in evaluation on accuracy rather than speed.

Replace timed tests with alternative assessment procedures.

Because the student has difficulty performing tasks rapidly under pressure, provide her with ample time to complete her work or shorten assignments so that they can be accomplished within the period.

The student may need extra time to complete reading, math, or writing tasks. Make sure she is allowed this time in a way that does not bring negative attention to her.

Shorten drill and practice assignments that include visual information or require visual–motor skills, such as the repeated writing of spelling words.

Instruction and Activities

Slow visual processing of symbols could reduce the student's reading speed to a degree that is significantly slower than her oral language and reasoning abilities, causing poor comprehension, frustration, and boredom. Provide instruction to increase her processing speed specifically within the task of reading. Skills to train are reading fluency, ability to recognize common letter sequences automatically when used in print, and sight vocabulary.

Provide the student with activities designed to increase her rate of production, such as recording the starting and stopping times on an assignment or using a stopwatch or timer to increase response rate.

Provide various timed activities, such as having the student read a list of high-frequency words or calculating simple math facts as fast as she can. Chart daily performance.

Have the student estimate the amount of time that it will take to complete a task. Have her write down the starting and finishing times.

NONVERBAL LEARNING DISABILITIES (NLD)

Related Tests: Concept Formation, Spatial Relations, Picture Recognition, Decision Speed, Planning, Pair Cancellation, Quantitative Concepts, Calculation
Related Clusters: Visual–Spatial Thinking, Oral Language, Processing Speed

Nonverbal Learning Disabilities (NLD)
    Further Evaluation
    General
    Social
        Organization
        Visual–Spatial
        Language/Instruction

Further Evaluation

Provide the student with a comprehensive evaluation to confirm or rule out the existence of a nonverbal learning disability. The evaluation should include: (a) developmental history, (b) neuropsychological testing, (c) a speech and language evaluation, (d) an occupational therapy evaluation, and (e) an academic evaluation.

Refer the student for a speech/language evaluation to assess the student's ability to use language for social purposes (pragmatics).

Refer the student to an occupational therapist to evaluate both fine- and gross-motor skills.

General

For educational planning, review and determine appropriate recommendations and interventions from the book *The Source for Nonverbal Learning Disabilities* (Thompson, 1997). This resource provides many strategies for assisting the student in the classroom.

Recognize the profound effect that NLD can have upon academic achievement. The student is likely to experience difficulty in aspects of reading comprehension, motor co-ordination, mathematics, and visual–spatial organization.

Recognize that students with NLD often demonstrate severe difficulties in subjects that involve complex problem solving and concept formation. Structure and adjust the difficulty level of tasks so that the student can be successful.

Although the student's excellent rote memory will help her succeed with tasks in the lower grades, she will experience increasing difficulties as the academic demands shift to more complex applications.

Consider that nonverbal learning disabilities will impact both academic and social functioning. Consult with a specialist to develop individualized interventions that will meet the student's needs.

Remember that nonverbal learning disabilities is a complex syndrome and that no student is likely to exhibit all of the common, associated characteristics.

Social

[See Recommendations: Social Skills/Self-Esteem.]

The student needs to be taught social skills directly, as she will not learn them easily through observation. Select a social skills training program that provides direct, practical training. The components of a structured learning curriculum are modeling, role playing, feedback, and transfer of training.

Recognize that the student will have trouble understanding subtle cues inherent in nonverbal communication. Teach the student how to recognize situations where nonverbal cues are used, such as interacting with people. Help her learn to interpret facial expressions, body language, and gestures through role playing, observation, and modeling.

Traditional behavior modification techniques will be ineffective with the student because many of the inappropriate behaviors are a result of a neurological impairment. Instead, employ verbal strategies that will help the student learn more appropriate behaviors (Thompson, 1997).

The student will have difficulty interpreting facial expressions, understanding body language, moderating her tone of voice, and observing personal space. Engage in role playing and modeling that focus upon teaching interpretation of nonverbal cues and appropriate social conventions (e.g., not standing too close to someone when speaking).

The student has difficulty interpreting novel stimuli and adapting to new situations. Prepare the student ahead of time for any changes in the schedule or routine that will occur during the day.

The student is likely to have difficulty interpreting gestures, facial expression, and tone of voice. Using pictures and videos, discuss the meaning of certain expressions and gestures. Help the student learn to recognize the implications and how nonverbal language is used to communicate and convey emotions.

Model social learning strategies through discussion and role playing.

Assume the role of a positive coach with the student. Help her figure out what is going on in various social settings and how to deal with new situations.

Use the following techniques to enhance the student's social skills: (a) verbally discuss and teach social skills because the student will not pick up nonverbal cues; (b) prepare the student for new situations before they arise; (c) offer alternative behaviors when the student responds inappropriately; (d) explain and help the student learn to respond in an appropriate way to common questions; (e) provide clear and explicit responses to appropriate and inappropriate responses; (f) avoid ultimatums; (g) assist the student in complex social situations; (h) recognize and reinforce effort; (i) discuss unacceptable behaviors in nonjudgmental ways; and (k) consider social skills training groups and professional counseling (Thompson, 1997).

Organization
[See Recommendations: Attentional Disorders, Homework/Time Management/Organization.]

Provide the student with a daily assignment book. Until organizational skills improve, have the teacher record the assignments, rather than the student.

Break down assignments into manageable components. As the student becomes more proficient with tasks, gradually decrease the amount of structure provided.

As much as possible, attempt to maintain a consistent daily schedule that is written on the board.

Help the student learn how to organize her notebook, desk, and locker. Discuss the reasons for arranging materials in certain ways. [See Strategies: Organization of Materials and Assignments.]

Visual–Spatial
[See Recommendations: Visual–Spatial Thinking.]

Recognize that the student with NLD will have tremendous difficulty with temporal concepts (organizing time) and spatial perceptions (coordinating physical space). Organize the classroom environment to facilitate performance (Thompson, 1997).

Language/Instructions
[See Recommendations: Oral Language.]

To the extent possible, provide step-by-step explanations for tasks. Have the student complete one step in the task and then proceed and review the next step.

When speaking to the student, breakdown lengthy instructions into several steps. Verbally number each step of the direction (e.g., first, second, third).

Explain homework and assignments in a linear, sequential format. The student will be able to follow instructions if they are presented step-by-step in a numbered list.

Avoid complicated and lengthy instructions and directions.

Encourage the student to ask questions when new material has been presented.

The student has well developed expressive and receptive language skills in regard to rote information. She may be able to memorize information easily, but will have limited understanding of what she has memorized. Help her develop an understanding of words and concepts by explaining them in simple terms.

When explaining graphic material, use simple, clear language and be aware of the complexity of spatial terms you are using.

Do not ask the student questions that involve abstraction and inference, such as why something happened. Instead, base questions on concrete, real-life experiences, such as "who" and "what happened."

Provide direct, explicit instructions for all teaching. Do not expect the student to understand figurative language, or complex instructions.

The student with NLD is likely to interpret language literally. Help the student learn to develop meaningful connections between words and concepts and to become more flexible in interpreting linguistic relationships. For example, teach the student how to interpret words or phrases with multiple meanings, figurative language, and ambiguities by using the context in which they are presented. [See Strategies: Context Clues.]

Although the student will be able to recall specific details, she will have trouble on tasks that involve open-ended questions or making inferences.

When modeling tasks, provide detailed verbal descriptions and precise explanations. Do not expect the student to infer procedures from modeling or nonverbal demonstrations.

After teaching a task, ask the student to explain the concepts in her own words to make sure that the ideas have been understood.

The student will benefit from teaching approaches that promote the development of self-talk. Reveal and discuss inner thoughts that aid in comprehension. Help the student learn to ask and answer questions as an aid to evaluating and monitoring comprehension.

Use the following five-step method to help the child learn to improve decision-making skills: (a) define the issue (e.g., no lunch money for school); (b) verbalize available options (e.g., call home, borrow money, skip lunch, share another's lunch); (c) identify the best option; (d) take that action; and (e) review action and decide if the plan was effective (Thompson, 1997).

In teaching a task, use the following four-step strategy with the student: (a) model the entire task as you provide a verbal description of what you are doing; (b) break down the task sequentially and, using concrete terms, describe the component parts; (c) guide the student through the task and help her to talk herself through it; and (d) have the student complete the task on her own as she talks herself through it (Thompson, 1997).

ORAL LANGUAGE

Tests: Story Recall, Understanding Directions, Picture Vocabulary, Oral Comprehension
Clusters: Oral Language, Oral Expression, Listening Comprehension
Related Tests: Verbal Comprehension, General Information, Story Recall—Delayed, Auditory Attention, Sound Blending, Incomplete Words, Sound Awareness, Academic Knowledge
Related Clusters: Comprehension-Knowledge, Phonemic Awareness, Phonemic Awareness 3, Short-Term Memory, Long-Term Retrieval
Related Sections: Sensory Impairment: Hearing, Knowledge/Content Areas/Study Strategies, Phonology

Oral Language
  Further Evaluation
  Accommodations
  General Recommendations
  Teaching Approaches
    Teaching Principles
    Multimodality Instruction
    Lectures
  Language Remediation
    Instructions
    Vocabulary
    Linguistic Concepts
    Word Retrieval
    Sentence Formulation/Generation of Ideas
    Sentence Structure
    Inference/Prediction
    Cohesive Devices
    Narrative and Expository Discourse Structures
    Verbal Reasoning
    Figurative Language
    Pragmatics

Further Evaluation

The student needs a comprehensive language evaluation by a speech/language pathologist that will include the assessment of receptive and expressive language skills, and a language sample.

To evaluate the severity and nature of the student's language difficulties more specifically, provide diagnostic therapy with a speech/language pathologist experienced in working with [preschool children, school-age children, adolescents, adults]. The therapy should focus on [specify area of concern].

Refer the student for a language evaluation specifically to assess possible difficulties in the area(s) of [specify area of concern]. Areas for the evaluator to consider include: vocabulary (including antonyms, synonyms, multiple meanings), question words (e.g., *who, what, why*), word retrieval, following instructions, language concepts (e.g., temporal, spatial, ordinal, same/different, familial, exclusion), generation of ideas, sentence formulation, sentence structure (e.g., embedded clauses, passive voice, negatives, length and level of complexity), cohesive devices (i.e., transition words), discourse/text structures (e.g., stories, narratives, different expository structures), conceptual level of language interpretation (literal, inferential, critical, figurative language, ambiguous statements), and rate of language processing.

Determine whether or not the language level of the student's textbooks is above the student's receptive language level. Select a variety of passages from the textbook in question; establish a purpose for listening; introduce the vocabulary; read the passage to the student; ask him to retell the passage, then ask him comprehension questions.

Evaluate further the student's ability to follow complex oral and written instructions in the classroom setting.

Through diagnostic teaching or informal testing, evaluate further the student's ability to comprehend the structure of expository discourse and text compared to his ability to comprehend narrative discourse. See if the student comprehends certain types of expository structures better than others.

Further evaluate the student's ability to generate ideas in a variety of circumstances, such as making conversations, retelling a movie or book, describing a familiar topic, creating a story from a picture stimulus, or creating a story without a visual stimulus.

Using diagnostic teaching, further evaluate the extent to which problems in word retrieval and/or sentence formulation interfere with the student's ability to express his ideas clearly.

Accommodations

Seat the student near the teacher and away from environmental noises.

When teaching or speaking to the student, face him, speak slowly, pause between phrases for processing time, and limit sentence length and complexity. If the student can count on you to do this consistently, he is more likely to listen to what you say with intent to understand. Give the student an opportunity to request repetitions or clarifications.

Be aware of the linguistic complexity of the language you use in instructions, questions, and test items. Encourage the student to ask you to restate and clarify instructions and questions that he found difficult to understand.

Be aware of when the student has become inattentive or looks confused. Repeat what you have said or attempt to clarify and simplify instructions.

Directly teach the student to request repetition or rephrasing of instructions, questions, or statements when necessary. Additionally, encourage the student to ask you to paraphrase test questions when needed. He may know the content but not understand the question.

If, when called on, the student does not appear to know the answer to a question, repeat it verbatim. If the student still does not appear to know the answer, rephrase the question using simpler language.

To increase classroom participation, let the student know prior to a discussion that you will be calling on him and asking him this particular question. He can then rehearse the answer.

Call on the student soon after posing a question but not first, unless you are sure he knows the answer. Hearing another student's response may give him needed clues to the nature of the question or type of answer expected; however, if a few students answer before him, one of them is likely to give the only answer he knows.

Call on the student soon after posing a question. In a long wait period, the student is likely to forget the question and/or the answer he had wanted to give.

Never assume that the student has prior knowledge or previous experience of the words or information you are using to teach new concepts.

Modify assignments to accommodate the student's language impairment. For example, to accommodate his weakness in [specify area, such as sentence formulation], [specify accommodation, such as reduce the length of an assigned report].

When grading the student's papers, make allowances for the errors related to linguistic difficulties. [Give examples based on assessment results.]

Waive the foreign language requirement for the student.

General Recommendations

Use a collaborative approach for teaching language and academic skills. In this model, the speech/language pathologist shares with the teacher the current focus of therapy and ways to integrate work toward the language objectives into classroom activities. The teacher shares the current units or skills being presented in class. Together, they can decide on modifications in activities, instructional techniques, or presentation style that can be instituted in class and content-related vocabulary and concepts for the SLP to integrate into therapy activities. Such collaboration is most likely to facilitate the student's comprehension of classroom material and success in classroom tasks.

Establish a system of communication between the school and home so that the vocabulary and language forms the student is learning or beginning to use will be mutually encouraged and reinforced.

Request that the speech/language pathologist discuss with the student's teacher(s) the nature of his language impairment and how it affects him in academic, social, and general classroom functioning. Include discussion of his learning strengths and ways to capitalize on them for instruction.

Explain to the student in simple terms the nature of his language difficulties as well as his strengths, whether linguistic or in other areas. Explain also what will be done to help him with regard to therapy and accommodations.

Identify and encourage development of areas of strength or talents in nonlinguistic areas such as mechanical skills, music, art, or sports.

Place the student in a classroom in which the students are given maximal opportunity to participate in small- and large-group discussions in a noncompetitive environment.

Provide the student with daily specific opportunities to discuss subjects he knows well, such as events that he has experienced, a hobby or sport he engages in frequently, and people with whom he has close relationships.

Arrange for the student to spend time with an adult who will expose him to wide a variety of experiences, explain what is happening, name objects and actions, and answer questions.

Teaching Approaches

Teaching Principles
Introduce activities and tasks by explicitly stating the focus and purpose, what the student is supposed to learn and why.

Provide ample examples of a new concept or skill and relate the new information to what is already known.

Help the student organize and relate new and known information by using cognitive strategies such as the adapted KWLS Strategy and activities for activation of prior knowledge. [See Strategies: KWLS Strategy, Anticipation Guide, Semantic Feature Analysis: Concepts.]

When teaching any new process or skill, provide systematic, sequential instruction, ensuring mastery of each skill before moving on to a more complex level or a new skill.

When introducing new concepts or information, use simple sentence structures and familiar vocabulary as much as possible so that the student can focus attention on the new content.

Draw the student's attention to new concepts, words, or constructs by placing stress on them when speaking.

When initially presenting new concepts, present the information more slowly than you would when speaking about familiar concepts.

Provide redundancy and repetition in teaching the student any new concept. Repeat important statements verbatim and explain the concept in a variety of ways.

As much as is feasible, teach new concepts and vocabulary within thematic units so that new learning is interrelated conceptually. The thematic unit provides a consistent framework and familiar context to introduce new concepts and vocabulary.

Multimodality Instruction
Present all types of verbal information accompanied by visual stimuli that clearly illustrate the concept being taught. Examples are pictures, charts, graphs, semantic maps, and videotapes. Simultaneous visual–verbal presentation is necessary for the student's comprehension and retention of the information.

If the student is unable to take in auditory and visual information simultaneously, direct the student to look at the complete visual display, then direct him to the portion of it about which you will be speaking. When he has had adequate time to look at the illustration, give a brief oral explanation. Then, direct him to look at the visual again.

As much as possible, involve the student in concept or skill-learning, tactile–kinesthetically or experientially.

Teach the student to create a visual image of what he hears and reads so that he can provide for himself visual input to supplement verbal information.

Be aware that the student's ability to benefit from any activity that is purely auditory, such as round-robin reading, listening to an oral presentation, or listening to a story tape, is extremely limited.

Lectures

When lecturing, present ideas in an organized and logical sequence. Keep the points as simple as possible and group related information.

When presenting lectures, use an overhead projector to highlight the important points. If the technology is available, use computer presentation programs, such as PowerPoint, to provide colorful and descriptive visual information simultaneous with the oral information.

Prior to beginning a lecture, write on the board the important points to be covered and review the major points at the end of the lecture. This will help the student recognize and retain the critical information.

Provide the student with an outline of questions to follow during a lecture. Go over the questions before beginning the lecture and guide a discussion of the answers after the lecture.

For increased comprehension of lectures, provide the student with a study guide that identifies the critical information. Encourage the student to complete the study guide. Alternatively, stop at natural breaking points during the lecture and allow the students to respond to the questions on the study guide that are related to the material just covered. Students can then use the completed guide to study for exams.

Language Remediation

Instructions

Use barrier games to develop the awareness that careful listening is necessary for following instructions. Using the barrier, the student may be asked to give or receive instructions for building objects, drawing designs, or writing information. Tape-record the instructions given by the teacher and the student so that, if needed, the exact wording may be played back.

Teach the student to monitor his understanding of instructions so that he recognizes when he needs to ask for clarification.

- In order to teach the student when to recognize the need for clarification of instructions, present instructions in which information is either missing, unclear, or incompatible with another statement. Teach the student how to ask specific questions for clarification.

Teach the student to comprehend the sequence of instructions, the terms used to denote sequence, and a strategy to remember more than two steps. Provide practice in following instructions containing temporal terms, such as *before, after,* and *at the same time.*

Teach the student to comprehend and follow directions using spatial terms such as *below, above, on the right,* and terms that can be both temporal and spatial, such as *first, next to last,* and *before.* Provide practice in following spatial directions, such as moving around a familiar place or maps with familiar landmarks.

Vocabulary

Work directly on vocabulary development in reading, writing, and oral discussions. Ensure that oral vocabulary continues to develop and that the student pronounces and uses new words correctly.

- Help the student correct mispronunciations by repeating his mispronunciation, giving the correct pronunciation, then writing his pronunciation and the correct spelling. Point out the differences. Have him look at the proper spelling and pronounce the word correctly.

Expose the student to multiple repetitions of new words in many different contexts and settings.

Directly teach the concepts of antonyms and synonyms and provide many activities for practice in finding antonyms and synonyms for given words. Ascertain the student's comprehension of "same" and "different" before doing so.

To handle the tasks of school and adult life effectively, the student must greatly increase both the breadth of his vocabulary and the depth in terms of related meanings (e.g., antonyms, synonyms, multiple meanings). Teach new words and their meanings explicitly and in context. Explain and use them in relation to familiar situations, and within categories so that the words taught together are meaningfully related to each other.

- Arrange some activities around certain themes with which the student is familiar, such as medical offices, plants, transportation, or various ethnic groups within the class. Teach and reinforce vocabulary for each of the themes.
- Introduce new vocabulary by expanding and clarifying the student's statements. For example, if the student

says, "The house is old and ugly," the teacher might say, "Yes, that house looks *dilapidated*."

- Use interesting pictures to foster and reinforce vocabulary development. The book *Animalia* (Base, 1986) presents numerous objects and activities in detailed pictures. Each page represents a letter; all of the pictures on the page begin with that letter.
- Play games that focus on word meanings. These include naming members of a given category, thinking of words that go together, making collages of pictures that go together, and discussing how the words or pictures are related. Later, incorporate the concept of opposites.

When teaching vocabulary, help the student learn to consider what he already knows about the meaning of the word or engage his interest in finding out the meaning by using vocabulary teaching strategies such as Semantic Feature Analysis and the Directed Vocabulary Thinking Activity. [See Strategies: Semantic Feature Analysis: Vocabulary, Directed Vocabulary Thinking Activity.]

When teaching vocabulary, use a variety of activities that involve active learning. Avoid passive learning activities, such as asking the student to look words up in the dictionary and then memorize their definitions as the student is unlikely to retain words learned out of context.

Directly teach the student that words can have more than one meaning. Teach multiple meanings (e.g., *prompt* can mean on time or a cue) and provide practice in using them.

Use all possible situations to teach the student words for feelings. Ask what he is feeling during or after specific activities and conflicts. Supply more precise words for the student. For example, if he says, "I'm sad," say, "I understand, and are you also feeling a little ashamed of hitting your friend? Ashamed means sorry and knowing that it wasn't the right thing to do." Use a poster of pictures of facial expressions captioned with the depicted emotion to help the student identify emotions.

Linguistic Concepts
Teach/reinforce positional (e.g., *first/last*), directional (e.g., *right/left*), and quantitative (e.g., *more, fewer*) concepts by using them in a variety of experiential contexts. For example, when the students line up, count them from the first child in line, then describe their positions with positional terms or ordinal numbers (e.g., "Jimmy, you're *first*. Alicia, you're *second*. Tina is *last* today, but she might be *first* tomorrow").

Teach the student how to categorize everyday objects, manipulatives, and pictures, working toward categorizing more abstract elements such as words, letters, numbers, and designs. Use these activities as a vehicle for familiarizing the student with the concepts of *same* and *different* at increasingly complex levels. Have the student explain his rationale for grouping things and label the groups accordingly.

- Play games with the student that will require him to categorize words. For example, you may say, "Tell me everything you see that looks like a circle" or, "Tell me everything you see that is a machine." Follow up by listing all of the objects that the student named previously and ask how they are all alike. ("They're machines.")

Teach the student the meanings of question words (e.g., *what, when, where, why,* and *how*).

- During play activities, ask questions using these words and guide the student to the appropriate answer. Later, use the question words in less experiential settings, such as before, during, or after a story is read (e.g., "Look at the picture. What is happening? Why do you think the boy is doing that?").

Teach the student the meaning of ordinal words and words denoting temporal/sequential order.

- Devise activities to develop the idea of sequence in daily events, the different parts of one event, and in the events within a story. Use words that denote temporal, sequential, and ordinal order (e.g., *before, finally, third*) to describe the events and set up situations in which the student demonstrates comprehension of these words (e.g., "What did we do *before* we ate lunch?").
- Plan experiences with the student in which he helps to decide the necessary sequence of activities (e.g., in building a sand castle, he might decide to get the bucket, shovel, and water, make a pile of sand, shape it, and jump on it). Within these situations, teach comprehension and expression of temporal and ordinal words (e.g., *first, fifth, meanwhile, later, last*).

Help the student increase his sense of time. Teach him the meanings of terms like *today, yesterday, tomorrow, last week, next week, in November*. One technique is to use a calendar, put events on it, mark off each day and note events for that day and the next day. The next day, look at the calendar and discuss the events in terms of *yesterday, today, tomorrow,* then branch out to longer periods of time. Use representative pictures whenever possible (e.g., turkey and Pilgrim for November, party hats and horns for January).

Word Retrieval

As the student's word-retrieval problem interferes with the fluency of his oral reading, do not require the student to read aloud in the classroom. Call on the student if he volunteers.

Due to the student's word-retrieval difficulty, structure oral comprehension questions so that the question contains the keywords he is likely to need without giving the content of the answer. This relieves him of the burden of accessing the words from long-term memory. For example, the question, "What is the latitude of Peru?" provides the word, *latitude,* so the student can focus on answering, "Which one?" rather than, "What's that thing called?"

Provide activities to reinforce integration of recently learned and familiar words within a strong conceptual framework. Well-established associations with known words and concepts will help alleviate word-retrieval problems. [See Strategies: Semantic Feature Analysis: Vocabulary, Semantic Maps: Evaluating/Activating Prior Knowledge.]

Teach the student to recognize when he is having difficulty retrieving a word so that he may use a retrieval strategy.
- Teach the student to visualize the object or the spelling of the word to prompt recall of the verbal label.
- Teach the student to think of a category for the target word and mentally list associated objects to try and prompt recall. For example, if the student is trying to retrieve the word *thief,* he could list *crook, robber,* and *bad guy.*
- Teach the student to visualize a different context for the word and mentally describe it with a sentence. Example: For *blocks,* the student would think, "Children build with."
- To facilitate word retrieval, encourage the student to try to recall and say the first sound of the word.
- To facilitate word retrieval, teach the student to "talk around the word," describing its appearance, function, and/or category.
- If the student cannot recall a word, encourage him to use a synonym.

Sentence Formulation and Generation of Ideas

When calling on the student in class, provide him with as much time as necessary to organize his thoughts and formulate a response. He may know the answer but need extra time to find the words. Privately, alert the student to this plan so that he does not feel pressured to come up with answers quickly.

Teach the student how to sequence his ideas mentally so that he can state them in an organized fashion. For example, before speaking, he should ask, "What is the beginning of what I want to say? The middle? The end?"

Use elaboration to model how the student might add details and information to his statements.

Facilitate the student's ability to generate ideas by using a variety of techniques including: (a) story starters, (b) expansion of one sentence by using reporter questions (i.e., *who, what, when, where, why, how*), (c) story structures with specific questions to facilitate each element, and (d) brainstorming, retaining only those sentences that can be related to each other, adding details or story elements as needed.

Use story or movie retellings to facilitate generation of ideas for speaking or writing.

To facilitate generation of ideas, provide the student with an outline of a story or report on a familiar topic. Have the student fill in missing information, gradually decreasing the amount of information given in the outline.

Sentence Structure

Teach the student strategies for interpreting the following sentence structures: [Specify types of sentence structures].

Provide visual cues for teaching morphological markers. For example, to highlight the concept of plural *s,* you could use a picture of two cats with an *s* after the second cat. To illustrate the concept of *er,* use a picture of a can of paint with *er* written after it followed by an equal sign and a picture of a person painting a house.

When correcting the student's syntactic errors and modeling correct word order, speak slowly and change as little as necessary to make the sentence correct. Say the sentence as he said it, say it correctly, write the sentence as he said it, and write your correct sentence. Have him read or say the sentence correctly.

Use [pictures, written sentences or phrases] to accompany activities in oral sentence comprehension.

Repeatedly expose the student to complex sentence structures in stories, preferably supported by pictures, before introducing these sentence structures out of context for instructional activities.

Teach the student to understand the ways in which cohesive devices add critical meaning to sentences by referring to another word or concept. [See Strategies: Cohesive Devices: Types.]

Specifically teach the student the meaning of transition words and how they signal the relationship between main and subordinate clauses. Teach the student to write complex sentences and then to use them in his expressive language.

Provide a variety of activities in which the student combines given phrases and selected transition words into complex sentences.

Provide extensive oral [and written] practice with sentence-combining exercises. Present the student with several clauses or short sentences and have him generate as many sentence patterns as he can by using a variety of connecting words. As an alternative activity, provide the student with a specific word or words to use in joining several clauses or sentences.

Teach the student to comprehend passive voice by constructing active sentences out of word cards. Show the student how to resequence them, adding cards for *was* and *by*, to create passive sentences or omit *was* and *by* to create active sentences.

Teach the student to interpret sentences in which the order of mention does not match the order of events.

Inference/Prediction
Use techniques to activate prior knowledge before introducing new concepts, reading material, or oral information. Directly teach the student the necessity of using his own prior knowledge and experience to help understand the information. [See Strategies: PreReading Plan, Semantic Maps: Evaluating/Activating Prior Knowledge.]

Teach the student how to use prior knowledge to infer information and relationships that are not stated in instructions, stories, and factual information.
- Give the student practice in determining what materials, tools, or pieces of information are missing in given situations. First, use actual situations. Later, have the student consider situations that are familiar but are not actually happening. Finally, use situations that are less familiar, requiring more generalization from what he already knows.
- Use pictures and devise activities to give the student practice in inferential thinking—inferring the middle event when told the first and last event (e.g., Show a picture of a boy in his swimsuit about to dive into a swim-

ming pool and a picture of the boy drying off with a towel. Ask, "What happened in between?").

While reading stories, watching videotapes, or conducting simple science experiments, encourage the student to predict the outcome. Afterwards, ask him to evaluate the prediction.

Use predicting strategies in listening and reading activities to increase the student's comprehension and retention of implied information. [See Strategies: Directed Reading-Thinking Activity.]

Cohesive Devices
Through diagnostic teaching or informal testing, determine which types of cohesive devices the student can interpret, such as reference, lexical, conjunction, substitution, and ellipsis, as well as any difficulties within these categories. [See Strategies: Cohesive Devices: Types.]

To increase the student's awareness of the importance of cohesive devices, demonstrate how terms denoting linguistic relationships in text and in oral language help to clarify relationships among events, objects, and people. Use examples from social studies, science, and literature.

Teach the student to interpret and use cohesive devices in oral and written language to improve the coherence of his communication. [See Strategies: Cohesive Devices: Types.]

Narrative and Expository Discourse Structures
Teach the student a strategy for understanding, retelling, and generating narratives. For example, the student might use the STORE the Story strategy as a reminder of the elements: setting, trouble, order of events, resolution, ending. [See Strategies: STORE the Story.]

Teach the student to recognize the structure of the type of discourse and text you are using in the classroom. For example, if working with stories in a narrative structure, teach the student to recognize the elements of a story grammar. For expository discourse or text, teach structures such as comparison/contrast, cause/effect, and enumeration.

Teach the student different ways expository information might be organized. Use graphic organizers to illustrate each. The following illustrations are examples of graphic organizers for contrast (Figure III.2a), description (Figure III.2b), and cause–effect (Figure III.2c).

Trait	Toad	Frog

Contrast

Figure III.2a Graphic Organizer for Expository Text Structure: Contrast

Figure III.2b Graphic Organizer for Expository Text Structure: Description

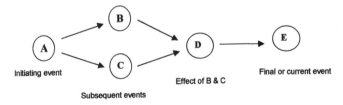

Figure III.2c Graphic Organizer for Expository Text Structure: Cause–Effect

Subsequently, teach the student to recognize these patterns in reading material and orally presented information and to use these patterns to organize information for writing.

Use simple semantic mapping to help the student organize information for a short oral report. First the student can base the report on notes written from the semantic map; later he should learn to organize thoughts into a mental semantic map to guide expression of ideas.

Verbal Reasoning

Ask the student to provide a rationale for statements or opinions he offers in the classroom (e.g., "And what do you think is the reason that happened?"). Provide prompting and guiding questions.

Tell or have the student read absurd statements or brief stories. Ask him, "What's wrong with this sentence/story?" Direct him to identify and correct the absurdity. If necessary, guide him (e.g., "Do cows eat chocolate?") Occasionally, include a sentence that makes sense.

To improve verbal reasoning, use the Request Procedure when reading stories or textbooks. You may also use this strategy with short portions of taped stories or textbooks. [See Strategies: ReQuest Procedure.]

Use the Directed Reading–Thinking Activity as an oral activity to help the student increase his understanding of content area textbooks. Read aloud to the student and stop at certain points to have him predict what might happen next. Read on to confirm the predictions. [See Strategies: Directed Reading–Thinking Activity.]

Use the Directed Reading–Thinking Activity as an oral activity to increase the student's ability to listen actively to a story or explanation of an event. Tell the student a portion of the story and ask him to use information from the story and his own experience to guess what will happen. Make sure that he can support his prediction. [See Strategies: Directed Reading-Thinking Activity.]

Figurative Language

Teach the student to understand and use figurative language such as metaphors (e.g., "The teacher watched him with an eagle eye"), similes (e.g., "The teacher watched him like a hawk"), idioms (e.g., "He threw away a wonderful opportunity"), and proverbs (e.g., "Necessity is the mother of invention").

Help the student to understand humor such as jokes and riddles. Use direct explanation, many examples, and pictures, where appropriate.

Pragmatics

To teach pragmatic language skills, use a combination of modeling, direct teaching, watching other people, videotaping, and monitored practice in authentic contexts.

Teach the student how to consider the existence or lack of a shared context and/or information when speaking to someone else. For example, teach him to explain who the people are that he refers to in describing an experience.

Teach the student how to change his manner of speech depending on the person to whom he is speaking (e.g., a teacher vs. a friend).

Teach the student to interpret the social language of his peers and how to use social language in a variety of situations.

Teach the student how to take turns in a game, discussion, or conversation.

Help the student learn how to maintain the topic in a conversation, recognize when he does not understand and ask for clarification, and recognize when his conversation partner doesn't understand and provide clarification.

PHONOLOGICAL AWARENESS

Tests: Incomplete Words, Sound Blending, Auditory Attention, Sound Awareness
Related Tests: Word Attack, Spelling of Sounds, Spelling
Clusters: Auditory Processing, Phonemic Awareness, Phonemic Awareness 3
Related Sections: Basic Reading Skills, Basic Writing Skills, Sensory Impairments: Hearing

Phonological Awareness
    Clarification: Phonological Awareness and Auditory
        Processing
    Further Evaluation
    Accommodations
    General
    Sample Programs
    Instruction in Phonological and Phonemic Awareness
        Rhyming
        Segmentation
        Sound Blending
        Phonemic Manipulation (addition, deletion, substitution, transposition)

Clarification: Phonological Awareness and Auditory Processing

Phonological awareness is the recognition that the ongoing stream of spoken language can be broken down into smaller units, such as sentences, words, syllables, and phonemes. It includes the ability to segment sentences into words and words into syllables and sounds; to blend syllables and sounds into words; and to delete, add, and substitute sounds in words to make other words. Phonological awareness is a necessary foundational skill for reading decoding and spelling but is unnecessary for comprehension and expression of spoken communicative (primary) language. Although a deficit in phonological awareness may be secondary to a central auditory processing disorder (CAPD), it is not the same.

CAPD is a perceptual disorder that causes a person to miss or misperceive the sounds of words as they hear them and/or have difficulty directing attention to auditory input. These difficulties are exacerbated in the presence of poor acoustic conditions such as background noise, a reverberant room, and speaking from room to room or across dividers. A CAPD also interferes with perception of speech that is altered in some way, such as rapid speech, accented speech, dialectical variations, or articulation errors. It may also cause misperception of speech in optimal acoustical conditions. Although CAPD cannot be diagnosed in the presence of a hearing loss, many of the recommendations for accommodations are the same or similar to those for students who are hard-of-hearing and students with specific language disorders. The recommendations in this section address the development of phonological awareness that may or may not be secondary to a CAPD. The broader range of recommendations related to CAPD are addressed in the sections Oral Language and Sensory Impairments: Hearing.

Phonemic awareness plays an important role in learning skills related to word identification and spelling. Good phonemic awareness suggests that the student will learn to read and spell easily. Poor phonemic awareness suggests that the student will struggle to learn to read and spell and is likely to require explicit instruction in decoding (word reading) and encoding (spelling).

Further Evaluation

Refer the student to the reading specialist or speech/language pathologist for a more comprehensive evaluation of phonological awareness.

Refer the student to an audiologist for a more comprehensive assessment of hearing acuity and speech discrimination.

Refer the student to an educational audiologist for evaluation of central auditory processing abilities.

Assess phonological awareness in depth. Use an informal assessment tool to determine the student's proficiency in the following tasks:
- rhyme recognition (e.g., Tell me the two words that rhyme: "cat," "dog," "hat");
- rhyme production (e.g., Tell me all the words you can think of that rhyme with "cat.");
- phoneme matching (e.g., Which word starts with a different sound? "ball," "bat," "tree");
- word counting (e.g., Tap out the number of words you hear in each sentence);
- syllable counting (e.g., Tap out the number of syllables you hear in each word);
- compound word deletion (e.g., Say the word: "cowboy" without the "cow");
- syllable blending (e.g., Tell me the word I am trying to say: "tur . . . tle");
- phoneme blending (e.g., Tell me the word I am trying to say: "m . . . a . . . t");
- sound counting (e.g., How many sounds do you hear in the word "toy");
- sound segmentation (e.g., Tell me the sounds you hear in the word "sock")
- phoneme deletion (e.g., Say the word: "hat" without the /h/ sound);
- phoneme manipulation (e.g., Change the /t/ in tip to /r/).

Because phonemic awareness skills appear weak, administer a standardized measure that assesses phonemic awareness and rapid automatized naming in more depth.

Because the student has severe weaknesses in English phonology, conduct additional assessments to determine whether or not the student will require a waiver for the foreign language requirement.

Accommodations

Modify the classroom instruction in phonemic awareness so that it more clearly matches the student's developmental level.

Because the student lacks phonemic awareness skills, she will not be able to keep pace with the phonemic awareness activities that are provided in the classroom. Provide individualized instruction so that activities and materials can be adapted to her developmental level.

General

Because the student has limited phonemic awareness, a critical set of skills for developing strong reading and spelling, provide instruction that is explicit and systematic in introduction, practice, and reinforcement of phonemic awareness skills. In a systematic program, skills are presented in graduated steps, from simple to complex, with students achieving mastery in the current skill before the next is introduced. Continuous practice and reinforcement in previously learned skills will allow the student to develop automaticity.

Help the student develop phonological awareness abilities as a foundation for basic reading and spelling skills. The general order of development of these skills is:
- preschool: segmenting sentences into words;
- preschool to kindergarten: rhyming;
- kindergarten: segmenting words into syllables and deleting syllables from words to make new words;
- grade 1: blending phonemes into words, segmenting words into phonemes, deleting phonemes from and adding phonemes to words to make new words;
- grades 1–2: manipulation—substituting one phoneme for another in a word, and transposing phonemes in words to make new words.

(Many children are not able to perform the types of phoneme manipulation tasks measured in the WJ III Sound Awareness test until the end of second grade.)

When providing instruction in phonemic awareness, consider the findings from the National Reading Panel (2000): (a) emphasize and teach to mastery only one or two phonological skills at a time, (b) provide letters when teaching phonemic manipulation tasks, and (c) provide instruction in small groups.

Many phonological awareness tasks require a series of words, syllables, and sounds to be held and manipulated in memory. Due to the student's significantly weak memory span and short-term memory, she may have more difficulty than anticipated when working on some of these tasks and will require modifications. Because she has some knowledge of letter/sound correspondence, ease the burden on memory by incorporating the use of letters to represent sounds.

Many phonological awareness tasks require a series of words, syllables, and sounds to be held and manipulated in memory. Due to the student's weak memory skills, teach her strategies such as verbal mediation and verbal rehearsal, and how to use them during phonological awareness activities.

As the student has some knowledge of letter/sound correspondences, use the letter/sound associations that she knows in phonemic awareness training. As she becomes more proficient in a phonemic skill, such as sound blending, teach a new grapheme/sound association and incorporate it into practice of the phonemic skill. (A grapheme is a letter or combination of letters that represents only one sound.) For example, when she has become reasonably fluent in blending three-phoneme words, introduce /ch/ and incorporate it into the types of sound blending activities she has been doing.

Keep in mind that children differ in the amount of time that they need to acquire phonological awareness. Adjust the amount of time and instruction based upon the student's needs.

Use materials that are age-appropriate. A variety of commercial materials are available for older students, but materials readily available in the classroom can also be used, such as plastic disks or paperclips to represent words, syllables, and sounds; interlocking cubes to represent syllables and sounds; and pictures in magazines or sets of picture cards.

To help the student increase phonological awareness, play games that focus on the sounds of words. Examples include rhyming games and songs, thinking of words that start with a particular sound, and counting the "beats" (syllables) of words.

Use a variety of classroom activities for promoting phonological awareness. These activities should be interactive and game-like, involving singing, rhyming, clapping, and movement. The goals of these activities are to draw the student's attention to the sounds of spoken language and increase ability to analyze speech sounds.

Choose one of several carefully developed commercial programs and compilations of classroom activities for promoting phonological awareness to ensure that all skills in the developmental progression are addressed.

When teaching new vocabulary, reinforce specific words by using them in phonemic awareness activities. Use words from a story that has just been read or words related to an instructional unit.

Explain to the student how speech sounds relate to printed words, how the skills you are working on relate to reading and spelling, and how developing competency in the skills will help her improve her reading and spelling. Develop activities or demonstrations that will allow the students to experience these connections.

To promote phonological awareness, use literature that plays with language sounds. Read texts that emphasize rhyming patterns, alliteration, and the manipulation of phonemes. These types of books will increase the student's awareness of the phonological structure of language.

Do not limit instruction in phonemic awareness only to oral activities. Incorporate activities that include letters. [See Recommendations: Basic Reading Skills.]

Make sure the student knows the difference between letter sounds and letter names. Some students are helped by the analogy that just like animals have a name (e.g., "lion") and a sound (e.g., /roar/), so do letters (e.g., "A" and /a/).

When incorporating letters into phonemic awareness activities, use only the letters and letter combinations for which the student has already learned the sounds.

For reinforcement of direct instruction in phonological awareness, incorporate computer programs into practice sessions. Because the student's age level far exceeds his phonological skill and reading level, be careful to choose programs that are age-appropriate.

Sample Programs

Follow a program such as those outlined in *Road to the Code* (Blachman, Ball, Black, & Tangel, 2000) or *Phonemic Awareness in Young Children: A Classroom Curriculum* (Adams, Foorman, Lundberg, & Beeler, 1998). Both programs provide a sequence for instruction in phonological awareness. Both are available from: Paul H. Brookes Publishing Company, P.O. Box 10624, Baltimore, MD 21285-0624, (800) 638-3775, www.brookespublishing.com.

Because the student has such severe difficulty perceiving speech sounds, use a program that stresses the oral–motor characteristics of speech. One carefully designed, intensive program for developing phonemic awareness is the Lindamood® Phoneme Sequencing Program for Reading, Spelling, and Speech (LiPS®). This program addresses the development of phonemic awareness as a base for accurate reading and spelling and provides explicit instruction about the articulatory dimensions of speech. The program progresses from sounds in isolation, to sequences of sounds in nonwords and then real words, to reading in context. LiPS requires specific instructor training. The Lindamood Phoneme Sequencing Program for Reading, Spelling, and Speech, products and training are available from: Gander Educational Publishing, 412 Higuera St., Ste. 200, San Luis Obispo, CA 93401, phone: (800) 554-1819, website: www.lindamoodbell.com/gander.

To build phonological awareness, use a software program aimed at helping students develop phonemic awareness skills, such as *Earobics*. The program charts performance and prints progress reports for up to 25 users. *Earobics* Step 1 (ages 4–7) and Step 2 (ages 7–10) are available from: Cognitive Concepts, Inc., P.O. Box 1363, Evanston, IL 60204-1363, phone: (888) 328-8199, website: www.cog-con.com.

Reinforce explicit instruction in phonological awareness skills with a variety of active and interactive games. A good source of activities is *The Sounds Abound Program: Teaching Phonological Awareness in the Classroom,* which includes a book and videotape describing and demonstrating the activities and picture cards. Available from: LinguiSystems, 3100 4th Avenue; East Moline, IL 61244, phone: (800) 776-4332 (voice), (800) 933-8331 (TTD), website: www.linguisystems.com.

In remediating phonemic awareness with older students, use activities and materials appropriate to their ages, such as *The Phonological Awareness Kit: Intermediate.* Available from: LinguiSystems, 3100 4th Avenue; East Moline, IL 61244, phone: (800) 776-4332 (voice), (800) 933-8331 (TTD), website: www.linguisystems.com.

LinguiSystems has a wide variety of instructional programs and materials for teaching phonological and phonemic awareness appropriate for a range of age levels. Additionally, some well-designed, research-based, comprehensive language arts programs, such as Scholastic Literacy Place and SRA Open Court, begin with programs for teaching phonological awareness. LinguiSystems, 3100 4th Avenue; East Moline, IL 61244, phone: (800) 776-4332 (voice), (800) 933-8331 (TTD), website: www.linguisystems.com; Open Court Collections for Young Scholars, SRA/McGraw-Hill, 1221 Farmers Lane, Suite C, Santa Rosa, CA 95405, (888) SRA-4KIDS, website: www.sra-4kids.com; Literacy Place, Scholastic, 555 Broadway, New York, New York 10012, phone: (800) SCHOLASTIC, website: www.scholastic.com.

Instruction in Phonological and Phonemic Awareness

When introducing new phonological or phonemic awareness concepts, use real objects or manipulatives, and then pictures, before starting oral activities without the support of visual aids.

As the student is considerably older than most students learning phonemic awareness skills, explain and demonstrate to her the connection to decoding and spelling skills and importance of developing mastery in this area.

Collaborate with the student's speech therapist to integrate phonemic awareness activities into speech instruction and to reinforce speech objectives within phonemic awareness activities in the classroom. Use letters to allow the student to "see" the sounds that are supposed to be pronounced in target words. Color all of the letters that have sounds, or just the letters that represent the sounds targeted for development.

Use a variety of computer programs to reinforce and develop mastery in phonemic awareness skills for which the student has demonstrated understanding and initial ability. Monitor her progress in the program to guard against wasted time and the reinforcement of erroneous concepts. Some computer software allows the teacher to adjust the tasks and to audiotape instructions in the program according to the needs of specific students. The student's responses are saved for later review by the teacher who can then decide how to program the next session.

To improve phonological awareness, provide tasks that involve the active manipulation of phonemes represented by tangible objects such as disks or cubes. Keep in mind that tasks involving larger units (e.g., syllables) will be easier than tasks involving the manipulation of phonemes.

Rhyming
Before introducing direct instruction in rhyming, familiarize the student with rhyming by reading poems to her with simple rhyme patterns (e.g., AABB, ABAB) and singing songs that emphasize rhyme (e.g., "Willoughby Wallaby Woo" by Raffi). Choose some to read/sing repeatedly and encourage the student to say/sing the words with you. Eventually, have the student say/sing the last word of the rhyming phrase without you.

Read predictable books aloud to the student that emphasize rhyming words, such as the Dr. Seuss books. Have the student say back or read back the rhymes.

Provide instruction in rhyming. Start with teaching the student to recognize rhyming versus nonrhyming word pairs (e.g., "Do '*cat*' and '*hat*' rhyme? Look at the three pictures, say their names, and circle the two that rhyme"); progress to the student providing a word to complete a given rhyme (e.g., "Jack and Jill went up the ___"); and, finally, teach the student to provide several words that rhyme with a given word (e.g., "Tell me three words that rhyme with '*far*'").

When teaching rhyme recognition, show the student pictures, tell her the names, and ask her to point to the words that rhyme. Have her repeat the rhyming pair aloud. Once she can do the task with picture support, give words orally and ask her to identify the rhyming pair. Provide both instances (e.g., "*star/car*") and noninstances (e.g., "*cat/shoe*") of the concept. Once the student can do rhyme identification tasks, introduce rhyme completion, then rhyme production tasks.

Play games with the student that reinforce rhyme production. Give her a clue and then have her generate a rhyming word. For example, you might say: "I'm thinking of what you check out at a library that rhymes with the word '*took*'" or "I'm thinking of a bird that rhymes with the word '*truck.*'"

Teach the student to grasp the concept of rhyming. Use visual representations to help the student envision the sequence of sounds in rhyming words. To develop the understanding that rhyming words start differently but end the same, use colored interlocking cubes to represent three-phoneme words, such as *ram* and *ham*. Show *ram* as a blue block interlocked with two red blocks, then show *ham* directly under it as a green block with two red blocks. Emphasize that the first sound changes but *am* stays the same, as represented by the colors. Continue building a column of "words" that rhyme with *ram* so that the colors of the first cube in each word differ but all of the others are the same. When the student demonstrates understanding, show how changing the last sound in a rhyming word pair would spoil the rhyme as the final colors/sounds would no longer be the same.

Segmentation

Before introducing the concept of segmentation of words into syllables, ensure that the student understands that words have parts. One way to introduce this is to use compound words along with pictures formatted as addition sentences. Figure III.3 illustrates the "equation," *butter + fly = butterfly.*

Figure III.3   Illustration of the Use of Pictures to Explain Compound Words

The explanation is that when we put the pieces together, *butter* and *fly,* we get *butterfly.* Each word retains its sound but when we put the two words together, they make a new word with a new meaning.

Teach the student how to segment sounds (isolate the sounds in a word by pronouncing each one in order) to promote reading and spelling acquisition.

When teaching segmentation, start with dividing sentences into words, then words into syllables, then one-syllable words into individual sounds.

To help the student develop the concept of segmenting words into sounds, use interlocked cubes to represent whole words, then "break" them into pieces.

When first teaching segmentation, use visual cues and manipulatives, such as saying a word slowly, while pushing forward counters on a table.

When teaching segmentation of words into individual sounds, teach the student first to identify and say the initial sound in words (sound isolation). When initial sound isolation is mastered, proceed to final sounds, and finally, to medial sounds in three-phoneme words.

Use games to make sound-isolation practice engaging. One game with many adaptations is Sound Bingo. Each student receives a chart with pictures on it. The teacher says a sound and the students place tokens on the pictures whose names begin with that sound. Alternately, the teacher may say a word and direct the students to cover the picture that starts with the same sound. The same game may be used for final and medial sounds, and later, for letter/sound correspondence (e.g., The teacher says a sound and the students cover the corresponding letter).

When teaching segmentation of words into individual sounds, start with two-phoneme words composed of a consonant and a long vowel sound such as *ape, eat, knee,* and *toe.* Long vowel sounds are easier to perceive than short vowel sounds. Use consonants with "stretchy sounds" (sounds that can be elongated, such as /m/ and /s/) as these are easier to articulate in isolation. Progress to consonant–vowel–consonant words such as *soap* and *rain.* Be careful not to use final consonant sounds, such as /l/ that change the sound of the preceding long vowel.

Use the following sequence to assess or teach segmentation. Begin with tasks that require the student to segment sentences into individual words. The student can clap the number of words or push forward markers to represent each word. Next, progress to compound words (e.g., *raincoat*). Then progress to syllables. When the student has learned to break words into syllables, teach her how to segment short words into onsets and rimes (the first part and then ending part of a syllable), and then into individual phonemes.

When teaching segmentation, if the student has particular difficulty segmenting words into syllables try the following techniques: Have her place her hand under her chin and then say the word aloud. The number of syllables is equal to the number of chin drops. Alternatively, she can put her hand in front of her mouth and feel the number of puffs of breath. Be aware that some words have syllables that are not discernible by chin movements or breath so preselect words for which they will work. As the student learns to "hear the beat" of words, she will no longer need this technique.

Use onsets and rimes to teach segmentation through word families. The onset is the initial consonant or consonants of a one-syllable word that change the meaning of the rime (*m*at). The rime is the ending part of the syllable that remains constant (e.g., m*at*).

When working with counting the number of words in sentences, or of syllables/sounds in words, use visual representations, such as colored tiles or poker chips. As an alternative activity, have the student move a token along a sequence of squares that represents the correct number of words, syllables, or sounds. Have the student pronounce the corresponding word, syllable or sound, while she pushes forward each token or moves it along the squares.

Use the adapted Elkonin Procedure to teach sound segmenting, progressing into using letters to represent sounds and, finally, the concept of silent letters. [See Strategies: Elkonin Procedure: Adapted.]

Integrate instruction in segmenting and blending. Going back and forth between tasks involving synthesis and analysis will result in the greatest benefits for reading and spelling acquisition.

Sound Blending

The central ability related to word pronunciation is blending. Teach the student how to blend sounds to pronounce unfamiliar words.

When introducing the concept of blending, start with blending two words into a compound word, then syllables into words, and finally individual sounds into one-syllable words.

When teaching sound blending initially, start with letters that make continuous sounds, such as /s/ and /f/, rather than those that make stop sounds, such as /p/ and /k/. The continuous sounds are easier to glide together.

Because an awareness of onsets and rimes seems to develop earlier than an awareness of phonemes, teach the student how to blend the initial sound(s) of a word with the remainder of the word (e.g., *m-at*).

As the student is having particular difficulty learning to blend sounds, use the following sequence of sound combinations, developing facility at each step before moving on to the next: (1) vowel + consonant; (2) consonant–vowel + final consonant; (3) onset + rime; (4) consonant + vowel; (5) consonant + vowel + consonant. From step (3) on, use initial consonant sounds that can be elongated without distortion, such as /m/. When the student has developed some proficiency at step (5), introduce initial sounds that cannot be elongated. The easiest sounds to pronounce (elongated) are: /m/, /n/, /f/, /v/, /sh/, /zh/, /s/, /z/, /th/, and /th/ (unvoiced). The following are slightly more difficult to pronounce: /t/, /p/, /k/, /ng/, /l/, /ch/, /w/, /wh/, and /h/. The most difficult sounds to pronounce in isolation for blending are: /d/, /b/, /g/, /r/, and /j/.

Provide the student with direct instruction in sound blending using the following steps: (a) have the student say the word, (b) present the word with prolonged sounds but no break between the sounds and ask the student to say the word, (c) present the sounds with a short break between them and ask the student to say the word, (d) present the word with a quarter-second, then half-second, then 1-second break between the sounds, with the student saying the word after each presentation (Kirk, Kirk, & Minskoff, 1985).

When the student understands the concept of sound blending and has developed initial ability, develop mastery using the following three-step sequence: (1) Encourage the student to blend sounds together as quickly as possible, rather than stopping between the sounds; (2) Have the student sound out each sound in the word and then pronounce the whole word rapidly; and (3) Encourage the student to sound out words in her head.

Teach the student how to blend three sounds into a syllable or word. Add sounds until she is able to blend a consonant-blend–vowel–consonant-blend pattern.

Teach the student how to blend sounds into a word and then segment the word back into sounds. Say the word phoneme-by-phoneme and ask the student to say the whole word. Then, have the student break the word back into phonemes.

Provide visual cues to help the student learn how to blend. For example, write a word on a piece of paper with the letters spaced evenly apart. Draw a line under the word. Glide your finger under the word slowly as the student blends together the sounds of each grapheme.

Use manipulatives to accentuate the idea that when blending sounds, we are moving them closer together. Use interlocking cubes, each one representing a sound. Interlock the cubes and tell the student the word they represent (e.g., "*sun*"). Then break the cubes apart, explaining that you are breaking the word into its sounds. Space the cubes a few inches apart, and point to each cube, saying its sound, with a pause in between. Move the cubes closer together and say the sounds with shorter pauses. Continue until you have pushed together and locked the cubes, say the whole word, and lift the interlocked cubes as a unit to show that you now have a whole word.

Provide the student with direct instruction in sound blending. If she cannot develop skill in sound blending, even after using techniques developed for students with excessive difficulty, select a nonphonics approach for beginning reading instruction, such as linguistic patterning (i.e., word families).

Phonemic Manipulation

Sound Sequencing

Prior to teaching sound sequencing, ensure that the student grasps the concept of using objects in a visual–spatial order to represent sounds, which occur in temporal order. Once this has been established, use manipulatives to represent the sounds in words.

Integrate instruction in sound sequencing with instruction in sound isolation so that as the student learns to listen for an individual sound in a certain position, she is also able to point out its position in a row of cubes representing the sounds of the word.

To practice sound manipulation, place a row of blocks down on a table. Say the word slowly and then pronounce one sound. Have the student point to the location of the sound within the row of blocks. Alternatively, after saying the word, you point to a block and the student says the sound.

Once the student has demonstrated facility in identifying the position of sounds in words using visual aids, pronounce pairs of words that differ in only one phoneme (e.g., "*gold*," "*goal*") and have the student identify what sound is different in the two words and its position.

Provide the student with additional practice in listening to and identifying medial vowel sounds. Start with long vowel sounds (e.g., "*comb*," "*bean*") as they are the easiest vowel sounds to hear within words. Have the student say the vowel sound in isolation and then pronounce the whole word.

Sound Insertion and Deletion

Use colored blocks to demonstrate to the student how changing the color of a block, deleting a block, then adding in a block will alter the sounds of a word. Use a color for each sound. For example, the sound /g/ could be represented with a red block (R), /ā/ with a green block (G), and /m/ with a white block (W). The word *game* would be represented as RGW, the word *maim* as WGW. Set up a word, such as *game* and have the student pronounce it. Take the first (R) block away and ask what the word says now (*aim*). Place another white block in front of the green block and ask what it says (*maim*). Continue taking away and adding blocks/sounds until the student is comfortable with the task. Then work on final sounds, then a combination of initial and final sounds. Since a word cannot exist without a vowel, the vowel cannot be deleted but can be manipulated.

When providing instruction in sound deletion, begin with compound words and provide picture support. When the student is able to delete parts of compound words, provide instruction in onsets and rimes. Counters or blocks may be used to demonstrate how to delete the initial part of the word (the onset) and then the final part (the rime).

When teaching the student how to manipulate and delete phonemes, follow Rosner's (1979) sequence: (a) delete one part of a compound word, (b) delete one syllable from a word, (c) delete the initial consonant from a word, (d) delete the final consonant from a word, (e) delete the initial phoneme in a blend, (f) delete the final phoneme in a blend at the end of a word, and (g) delete the second consonant in an initial blend.

Because phonemic deletion of middle sounds is more difficult and places demands on working memory, target only initial and final sounds in words.

Sound Substitution and Transposition
(By the time students are practicing activities at this level, they will be using letters a good deal of the time.)

When providing instruction in tasks that involve the manipulation of phonemes in words, begin with manipulating the initial phoneme. When the student is able to isolate and manipulate the beginning sounds of words, provide instruction in identifying and manipulating sounds in the final position.

To increase the student's flexibility in reading words, help him to develop fluency in substituting one sound for another in words. (Insertion and deletion may be incorporated into this activity to provide reinforcement and develop automaticity in those skills.) Use only grapheme/phoneme correspondences that the student knows. If including two-letter graphemes, have both letters printed on one letter tile. Lay out letter tiles for a four-sound word and have the student read it (e.g., "*hand*"). Replace a letter with a different one and have the student read the new word (e.g., "*band*"). Continue to add, delete, or exchange letters, asking to the student to read the new word each time. So as to develop encoding as well as decoding, alternate between the teacher moving the letters and the student reading it, and the teacher saying the new word and the student moving the letters accordingly.

Give the student practice in reordering the sequence of sounds in a word. Select three sounds [letters] that can be combined in multiple ways to produce a pronounceable word—real or nonsense. Use [letters with] sounds that can be easily perceived no matter what their position in the word (e.g., students with undeveloped phonemic awareness skills would have difficulty "hearing" the /p/ in the word *apt*). Avoid using sounds [letters] that alter the sounds around them, such as /r/ and /l/ in the final position. Lay out three cubes and give each one a sound. Have the student repeat the sound for each cube. Put the cubes in order. Tell the student the word they make (e.g., "This says *pam*"), and ask her to repeat the word. Then change the order of the cubes and ask the student, "What does it say now?" If her answer is correct (e.g., *map*), rearrange the cubes and ask again (e.g., *amp*). Alternatively, you can say the "word" and have her move the cubes. Either method reinforces listening for

and identifying the sequence of sounds. As the student learns grapheme/phoneme associations, use letter tiles to represent the sounds in this activity.

BASIC READING SKILLS

Tests: Letter–Word Identification, Word Attack, Reading Fluency
Related Tests: Incomplete Words, Sound Blending, Auditory Attention, Sound Awareness
Clusters: Basic Reading Skills (Letter–Word Identification and Word Attack), Phoneme–Grapheme Knowledge (Word Attack and Spelling of Sounds), Academic Skills, Academic Fluency
Related Areas: Phonological Awareness, Spelling

Basic Reading Skills
    Further Evaluation
    Support
    Accommodations and Modifications
        Instructional Level
        Assignments
        Taped Books
        Technology
    Interest, Motivation, Self-Esteem
        School
        Home
    General
    Letter Identification
    Letter/Sound Associations
    Phonological Awareness to Print
    Phonics
        General
        Synthetic Phonics
        Analytic Phonics
        Embedded Phonics
    Multisyllabic Words
    Sight Word Identification
        Further Evaluation
        General
        Survival Sight Vocabulary
    Reading Practice in Decodable Text
    Reading Fluency
        Further Evaluation
        Accommodations and Modifications
        Methods
    Altering Rate
    Fluency/Comprehension

Further Evaluation

Informally test the student on the following skills: differentiating between letters and numbers, reciting the alphabet, naming letters presented in random order (upper- and lowercase), and writing letters dictated in random order (upper- and lowercase).

Administer an informal reading inventory to evaluate reading skills in more depth. Tape-record the student's oral reading of the passages for later review to obtain a baseline measure of reading speed and fluency.

Listen to the student read several short passages from a classroom textbook aloud. (Choose passages from three different sections of the book as readability levels can vary widely within a book.) Record mispronunciations and substitutions verbatim. Analyze the types of errors he makes regarding letter/sound correspondence, phonics rules, and immediate identification of whole words (sight words) and common word parts (e.g., *re, com, tion*). Plan appropriate instruction to assist the student with the development of decoding and word identification skills.

Before beginning the intervention program, tape-record the student reading several graded passages from an informal reading inventory. Keep the taped readings for error analysis and as a way to document reading improvement.

Further evaluate the student's reading performance using the classroom reading series. Identify an appropriate level for instruction.

Determine if the classroom materials are too difficult by using the "rule of thumb." Count out 100 words and ask the student to read the passage aloud. Put a finger down for every error made. If your thumb is put down before the passage is completed, the text is too difficult.

Ask the student what she finds difficult about learning to sound out printed words, instantly recognize printed words, and/or read fluently. Use her response to help inform instruction.

Use a phonic skills checklist to evaluate further the student's letter/sound knowledge. Attempt to identify which phonic elements the student knows and which ones she needs to be taught. [See Strategies: Phonics Check-Off Chart.]

Attempt to determine whether the student's difficulties are more related to problems in phonology or orthography. Compare his performance on reading and spelling phonically regular nonsense words (more related to phonology) to his performance on reading and spelling irregular words (more related to orthography). (Irregular words are words that contain an element that does not conform to English spelling rules. These words are often taught as sight words, such as *the* and *what.*)

Support

Based on the student's present level of reading achievement, he would benefit from individual or small group [intensive, daily] instruction from a [qualified tutor, reading specialist, learning disability specialist].

Provide the student with as much individualized instruction as possible. Use volunteers, peers, or cross-age tutors to provide additional support.

To promote generalization of newly learned skills and strategies to other situations in which they should be used, remind the student to use the skill or strategy during the occurrence of these situations, or ask her which strategy or skill she should be using at that time. Give other teachers a list of the skills and strategies the student has learned and request their help in reminding her to use them at the appropriate times. Monitor the frequency and accuracy of use of the skill or strategy.

Accommodations and Modifications

Instructional Level

Ensure that the student is given reading materials at the independent level for seatwork and homework and at the instructional level when support is provided. Classroom instructional materials should be at approximately the [ ]-grade level.

Place the student in reading materials at the [ ]-grade level. Use reading texts other than the classroom series.

Match the readability of all classroom materials to the student's independent or instructional reading levels, depending on whether the related assignment is intended to be done independently or with support and guidance.

Ensure that all assigned readings are at the student's independent level so that she can read the material without assistance. If material is too difficult, provide the student with a reading partner or the material on tape.

Assignments

Reduce the length of the reading assignments so that the student can complete them in the allotted time.

Because the student reads slowly, base assignments on the amount of time spent reading rather than the number of pages.

When assigning reading to the student, base the number of assigned pages on his reading rate and skill.

Assign the student short passages at his reading level so that he can complete the reading without difficulty.

Break reading assignments into smaller, more manageable units of text (e.g., one chapter, sections within a chapter, or paragraphs within a section).

Taped Books

Because the student has been identified as having a reading disability or dyslexia, help the student register with Recording for the Blind & Dyslexic (RFB&D) and secure textbooks on audiotape from them. This national, nonprofit organization provides textbooks for individuals unable to read standard print because of a visual, physical, or learning disability. The master-tape library has educational books that range from kindergarten through postgraduate level. If a book is unavailable, and is deemed to fit within the scope of the collection, the book will be recorded upon request. In early 2002 RFB&D will make available a library of digital textbooks on CD-ROM, allowing students to navigate the book/disk by page, chapter or heading. [See Strategies: Taped Books.]

Provide the student with information regarding free sources for taped books (e.g., Recording for the Blind & Dyslexic, public library, university library, local school or agency for the visually impaired) and how to obtain them. [See Strategies: Taped Books.]

Because the student's listening comprehension is at approximately the (higher) grade level, but his reading decoding is at approximately the (lower) grade level, provide the student with taped copies of all of his textbooks as well as any assigned novels and outside reading. This will enable him to learn the information along with the class and participate in class discussions.

Before the end of this school year, ascertain what textbooks and novels the student will be required to read next year, complete an application to register him with Recording for the Blind & Dyslexic, and place an order for any books that he will need. [See Strategies: Taped Books.]

Provide the student with a list of the outside readings that will be required next year so that he can get them on tape from the library and listen to them over the summer. Once he is familiar with the story or information, it will be easier for him to read along with the tape when the reading is assigned in class.

If a reading selection is too difficult for the student to read independently, have a peer read it with him or have the student listen to a tape of the book as he follows along with the print. Provide earphones to avoid drawing attention to the student and to avoid disturbing other students.

Technology

Provide the student access to and training in using a computer with a screenreading program and voice synthesizer designed for students with learning disabilities (rather than visual impairments). Desirable qualities in screenreaders for students with learning disabilities include a simple, intuitive command interface; phonetic accuracy in speech production; visible display of each word as it is read; consistent command interface; ability to read in linguistic units (word, sentence, paragraph); ability to read an entire text file; simple ways to set technical aspects (speech speed, text); ability to support keyboard and word echo functions; speech activated on demand only; and a cursor track toggle (Norris, 1992).

Provide the student access to and training in using a computer with a screen magnifier that will allow him to manipulate the size, font, and color of text, and the spacing between lines of text. Check to see that the software will not conflict with the screenreading program if one is installed in the computer.

To aid with word pronunciation, provide the student with a talking pen. Two examples follow:
- The Quicktionary II scans any word from printed text, displays the word and definition in large characters, and reads the word aloud through a built-in speaker or earphones.
- The Reading Pen II was designed specifically for people with reading or learning disabilities. It contains the American Heritage dictionary, displays a definition of the scanned word or line of text, and reads the word and definition aloud. Words may be spelled out or broken into syllables.
  Available from: Wizcom Technologies, Inc., 257 Great Road, Acton, MA 01720, phone: (888) 777-0552, website: www.wizcomtech.com.

For independent reading, provide the student with an electronic speaking dictionary, such as the dictionaries developed by Franklin Learning Resources, 122 Burrs Road, Mt. Holly, NJ 08060, phone: (800) 525-9673, website: www.franklin.com.

Employ engaging software programs that are designed to promote early literacy. These programs can reinforce skills and enhance student motivation.

Use computer programs only for reinforcement of and development of mastery or fluency in the skills in which the student has a sufficient level of ability that he will make few errors. If the student is making frequent errors, he is not benefiting from use of the software and requires direct instruction.

Use a variety of software programs designed to build accuracy in decoding and sight words.

Teach the student how to use the program *Read, Write, & Type*. This software program, designed for ages 6 to 8, teaches typing, as well as beginning literacy skills. The sequential curriculum provides instruction and games with all 40 speech sounds while students learn to use the keyboard. The program involves several steps: (a) learning each sound; (b) identifying beginning, middle, and ending sounds in words; (c) building words by typing sounds; (d) reading and writing simple stories; (e) creating stories; and (f) writing messages. Companion CDs and additional materials are also available. Talking Fingers, One St. Vincent Drive, San Rafael, CA 94903, phone: (888) 839-8939, website: www.talkingfingers.com.

Interest, Motivation, Self-Esteem

School

For independent reading activities, provide the student with a selection of high-interest, low-vocabulary readers so that he will spend time in independent reading, increase speed of sight word recognition, and discover that reading is enjoyable.

Read and discuss high-interest material with the student to increase willingness to spend time reading.

Select or have the student choose materials to read that are related to his interests.

Set aside 15–30 minutes each day for recreational reading. Help the student to choose books and periodicals that are of interest to him and that are at his independent reading level.

Until the student's basic reading skills improve, do not ask him to read aloud in class unless he volunteers.

The student requires intensive instruction to learn to read. Because it would be difficult and embarrassing to the student to provide this type of assistance within the general education classroom, schedule daily sessions in the resource room.

If planning a time that students will read aloud in class, give the student at least one day's warning. Give him a copy of (or show him in his book) the passage that he will be asked to read so that he can practice the material several times before he reads it aloud in class. Plan a time to help him practice or make arrangements with another adult or the student's parents to do so.

Encourage and reinforce independent reading. For example, let the student select an activity that he enjoys after reading for a specified amount of time.

Discuss with the student how daily silent reading will help him improve reading skill. Review the benefits of being a good reader for scholastic and/or occupational success.

Establish a system using reinforcers to increase the amount of time the student spends in daily reading. For example, provide the student with a sticker for every [ ] pages read or a poster for each book that is completed.

Establish a contract with the student that identifies the minimum number of pages to be read each day. Let the student trade the number of pages for points that may be exchanged for a specified reward when the contract has been completed. Ensure the student's reading selections are at the independent reading level.

Integrate literacy instruction with meaningful classroom activities.

Use a variety of reading materials in the classroom to help the student recognize the need for reading in daily life. Examples include: cookbooks, board games, magazines, newspapers, menus, directions on food and medicine packages, game instructions, catalogues, the Yellow pages, a TV schedule, and a driver's manual.

Provide the student with reading materials directly related to his career or vocational goals.

For the weekend, arrange with the student's parents for him to watch "Reading Rainbow" (Public Broadcasting System) or choose a similar television program that enhances interest in reading. Then bring the book read on the show to class for the student to read, for paired reading, or for you to read with the student.

Allow the student to read "books" on computer software programs. Many programs have a voice that reads the text, highlighting the word as it is read, allowing the student to listen or to read along. Many books also contain animations, increasing a student's interest in reading the story. Reading material on software is available at a wide range of reading and interest levels.

Home

Read with your [son, daughter] for about 15 minutes every night. Enlist the help of the children's librarian at the public library to select interesting books that are at the instructional reading level (slightly above the child's present level of reading development). At [his, her] instructional reading level, your [son, daughter] should be able to read 95 to 97 words in a 100-word passage without difficulty.

As a pleasurable activity, select a high-interest book or magazine at your child's independent reading level to read in the evenings. Stop at certain points and encourage your child to discuss the pictures and ideas presented in the story. Ask your child questions that will enhance interest and stimulate understanding of the story.

Schedule weekly trips to the library so that your child can select books for recreational reading and for informational interest. Request help from the children's librarian in selecting books and magazines related to his interests.

Watch "Reading Rainbow" (Public Broadcasting System) with your child and then borrow from the library and reread the books that he finds interesting.

Watch "Reading between the Lions" (Public Broadcasting System) with your child. This program will help build reading and spelling skill.

To increase interest in reading, encourage your [son, daughter] to read simple stories to younger siblings. Patterned language books, in which phrases and lines from the story are frequently repeated, would be appropriate. These types of books may be found in the children's literature section of the public library.

When reading with your [son, daughter] at home, provide as much assistance as needed. Take turns reading sentences, paragraphs, or pages. Initially, you may need to read a larger portion of the text. For example, you will read three sentences and then your will child read one.

When reading with your [son, daughter] at home, let him read any words that he recognizes easily and tell [him, her] words that [he, she] has difficulty identifying. Too much time spent trying to figure out unknown words may detract from comprehension, as well as from the enjoyment of reading with a parent.

Play games at home that require simple reading and spelling, as sounding out words for spelling will reinforce sounding out words for reading. Adapt the rules according to the needs of your child or the (learning) object of the game. For example, in playing Scrabble, tell the child that he can make up any "word" as long as it follows a [consonant-vowel-consonant, consonant-vowel-consonant-final e] pattern and he can read it correctly.

Spend time with your child using educational computer software designed to promote reading development. When you are sure that your child can handle one or more of the activities independently, with almost no errors, encourage [him, her] to play without your help, but check in to make sure that he is using the program appropriately or he will not benefit from it. [See Strategies: Software Selection Tips.]

Help your [son, daughter] select and order one or two magazines of interest with a readability level at or below his instructional reading level.

Encourage discussions in the home about any books or magazines that your [son, daughter] is reading independently.

Provide opportunities and guidance for functional reading, such as reading recipes, directions, catalogues, or television guides.

Use an assisted reading method to help your child increase reading readiness or fluency. Read your child a phrase or sentence and then have him read it back. Move your finger along the line of print to help him focus on the word. Reread the passage several times. When your child recognizes the words, have him read independently. Provide assistance with words on which he is having difficulty.

When reading with your child at home, if he is having difficulty keeping his place, point to the words with your finger or hold an index card under the line being read.

Provide a time each evening for reading. Encourage your [son, daughter] to read at least 20 minutes each night.

Use the Reading Reflex program with your child at home (McGuinness & McGuinness, 1998). This program was designed for young children or elementary-age children who are struggling to learn to read. The program provides a child with systematic instruction in the alphabetic code. The book includes simple diagnostic tests, lesson plans, word exercises, and games. Additional support materials are available that can be used in conjunction with the book. Available from: Reading Reflex, The Free Press, 1230 Avenue of the Americas, New York, NY 10020, phone: (800) 732-3868, website: www.SimonSays.com.

General

Provide the student with an instructional approach that is intense, explicit, and provides direct instruction in how to apply alphabetic knowledge to word recognition.

The student needs an instructional program in basic reading and spelling skills that is systematic in introduction, practice, and reinforcement of phonemic awareness skills, phoneme/grapheme relationships, sight words, syllabication rules, structural analysis, and spelling rules. In a systematic program, skills are presented in graduated steps, from simple to complex, with students achieving mastery before the next skill is introduced. Practice assignments on the current skill incorporate previously learned skills, providing opportunities for the student to develop automaticity.

The student will do best with a multisensory instructional program for basic reading and spelling skills, such as Lindamood® Phoneme Sequencing Program for Reading, Spelling, and Speech (LiPS®) or the Wilson Reading System, which is somewhat less intensive. Other programs, which are not multisensory, such as Saxon Phonics or Scholastic Phonics and Scholastic Spelling, might be successfully used with the addition of multisensory activities and extra reinforcement activities.

As the current reading program is highly structured and well-developed (e.g., Success for All, Saxon Phonics, Open Court), do not change programs but use it as the skeleton of a more intensive program. Start from [insert appropriate skill level or lesson in program, depending on the skills the student has mastered] with the student. Teach [letter recognition, names, sounds, and formation]. At every step, supplement the recommended techniques with other multimodality techniques to reinforce his understanding and ability to use each skill.

As you teach basic skills, ensure that the student learns the names and meanings of the related reading terminology, such as: letter name, letter sound, syllable, word, sentence, and paragraph.

Discuss with the student how improvement in basic reading skills will make reading easier and more enjoyable. Show him the types of daily living activities and recreational activities that require reading (e.g., reading street signs while driving, prescription warnings, internet website, game instructions, menus, movie guide). Obtain a commitment from him that he wishes to improve his basic reading skills and agree on a specific short-term goal.

Since the student has a tendency to overrely on picture clues, use high-interest books with few pictures so that he will pay more attention to graphophonic clues.

Provide ample practice with basic reading skills in context. Directly teach the student to recognize when and how to apply skills.

Provide the student with systematic instruction in basic skills, as well as extensive opportunities to read decodable and authentic texts.

Provide the student with the opportunity to teach any reading skill that is close to mastery to a peer or younger student who needs that skill.

Create situations where the student can tutor children with lower performance levels in basic reading skills. Teaching these skills to another child will help reinforce and strengthen phoneme/grapheme connections.

Integrate instruction in reading decoding with instruction in spelling. For example, when teaching the student how to read phonically regular, three-letter, closed-syllable words (e.g., *tag, lip*), teach him how to segment the sounds in the same types of words, writing the letter corresponding to each sound in order. Teach any related phonics generalizations (e.g., closed syllables contain only one vowel and end in a consonant; the vowel in a closed syllable typically has its short sound). Provide ample practice in recognizing the syllable pattern and applying the generalization to reading and spelling real words and nonsense words. [See Strategies: Six Syllable Structures.]

If the student is unable to learn sound blending and sound segmenting skills after explicit instruction within a systematic phonological awareness and synthetic phonics program, introduce [a word family approach to decoding, such as Merrill Linguistic Readers; a sight word approach to decoding, such as Reading Milestones; an analytic approach incorporating words parts, such as Glass Analysis for Decoding Only.]

At this point, do not spend time on strategies for reading comprehension. As the student comprehends and can express himself adequately in oral language, limited decoding skill is the major impediment to his reading comprehension. The level of language that he can read without undue effort should not present any comprehension difficulty. Spend all reading instructional time focused on reading decoding and spelling skills. Reading comprehension strategies can be taught as oral comprehension strategies that can later be applied to more fluent and higher-level reading.

Letter Identification

Teach the student the names of the letters. Due to his particular needs, try the following activities:

- Before teaching the names of the letters, give the student the opportunity to become familiar with the shapes of the letters by incorporating three-dimensional letter models into games and activities. Some ideas for doing this include:
  - —Make up games for small groups of students to play using letter models, matching letter models to each other, and matching them to bold, colored drawings of letters.
  - —Create activities in which the students make three-dimensional letters, such as making letters out of clay then decorating and baking them, or making letters out of dough, baking, and eating them.
  - —Provide alphabet puzzles that have large, thick rubber or wooden letters that come out with their shapes intact. Have students both match letters with each other and fit letters back into their spaces.
- Teach only one to three letter/name associations a day, depending on the student's ability to retain them. At least once a day, review *all* previously learned letter/name associations through recognition (teacher says the name and student points to the letter) and identification (teacher points to the letter, student names it). Incorporate review into games when possible, such as playing Go Fish or Old Maid with letter cards. If the student has forgotten any, reteach them using an instructional technique that creates a stronger letter/name association than in the previous instruction.
- When teaching letter identification, start with uppercase letters. These are easiest for young children to discriminate and to learn to write. Introduce lowercase letters only after the uppercase letters have been mastered.

- When teaching the student the alphabet, begin with the letters in his first name, and then his last name. Use these letters to demonstrate how to create and write simple words.
- Because the student is an older nonreader with more mature visual perceptual and fine-motor skills than most beginning readers, introduce lowercase letters first so that he may begin working with text as soon as possible.
- Because of the student's extremely poor short-term memory, it will probably be easier for him to learn the letter names in conjunction with their shapes rather than by rote in the alphabet song.
- Teach the student to sing the alphabet song. Prior familiarity with the letter names will make it easier for him to learn the association between the names and the letter shapes. When teaching the song, however, make sure that the student knows where the breaks are between letter names. For example, he needs to be thinking, "L, M, N, O, P" rather than "elemenopee."
- Use gross motor movements to help the student visualize and remember letter forms. For example, have the student stand up straight and stick both arms out to form the letter *T*.
- If the student has difficulty learning some of the letter names, make drawings out of those letters to strengthen the association between shape and name. For example, make a bee out of an uppercase B; and draw the D *deep* under the ocean.
- Use a simple electronic speller so that the student can key in a letter and hear the letter name or choose a key, guess the name, and check himself. Alternatively, the student can use a Language Master.

Provide multisensory instruction to aid in letter learning. When teaching the student to associate letters with their names, teach only one letter name at a time. To promote retention and attention, incorporate tactile–kinesthetic activities into instruction. Activities may include having the student trace glitter letters while saying the letter name, put letter forms into their proper place in a puzzle jig while reminding himself of its name, or, working with another student, making the shape of the letter with their bodies while saying (shouting, singing) its name.

As the student is unclear as to the difference between upper- and lowercase letters, provide matching and sorting activities. At first, provide upper- and lowercase alphabet strips for him to use as a reference, then have him work from memory. A suggested sequence is:

- Using letter cards, have the student practice matching upper- and lowercase letters.
- Mix up uppercase and lowercase letter cards. (You may include numbers if you want the student to differentiate letters from numbers.) Have the student sort them into [2, 3] piles. If he can, have the student put each letter pile into alphabetical order, then match up the upper- and lowercase letter pairs.
- When the student is ready for workbook-type activities, provide sheets of letter outlines with combinations of upper- and lowercase letters. Have the student color in only the uppercase. Do not have him color uppercase with one color and lowercase with another as instruction is still focused on working with uppercase letters only.
- Move to more advanced activities such as having the student circle all of the uppercase letters on a page of text.

Guide the student to activate, organize, and increase knowledge of the relationship between letters and words. Games are particularly helpful in this regard. For example, play games requiring students to come up with words starting with specified letters, such as Grandmother's Trip (go through the alphabet but do not require the student to recall all previous items named) or games wherein the student has to name objects within a given category and starting with a particular letter (e.g., "My family owns a pet store and they sell something that begins with the letter C."

With the student's help, brainstorm as many words as you can generate. Continue the game with another letter).

As the student continues to confuse graphically similar letters, such as *b* and *d,* provide clues and "tricks" to differentiate between them. "Tricks" for distinguishing *b* from *d* include:

- A story: Bob wants to play baseball. If he has a ball, he can play lots of games, but to play baseball, *first* you have to have a bat (begin to draw a *b,* making the *bat* or stick), then the ball (complete the *b* with the loop). Have the student memorize, "B. *First,* you have to have a bat."
- Teach the student to print *b* and *d* according to D'Nealian style or Handwriting Without Tears. The *b* and *d* start in different places (*b* – top, *d* – middle) and use different strokes.
- Make a *b* with the left hand and a *d* with the right (forefinger straight up, circle with thumb and other fingers). Making sure the student understands reading from left to right, tell him that the *b* comes first in the alphabet so check the left hand for *b;* the *d* comes after it, so look at the right hand.

- Make a picture of a bed (with headboard and footboard) out of the word *bed.* Teach the student to think of the picture and the sounds of the word when confused. The first sound is /b/ so the first letter is *b;* the last sound is /d/ so the last letter is *d.*

Letter/Sound Associations

Help the student understand the reason for learning letter/sound associations and how letters and sounds are applied in beginning reading to determine unfamiliar words.

Teach the student that letters have both names and sounds. Using an analogy to animals is helpful. For example, show the student a picture of a lion and say: "His name is lion but his sound is /roar/." To build understanding of this concept, use only one sound per letter, and short sounds for vowels. Provide ample practice differentiating between them by creating activities in which the student (or group of students) says a letter name or sound in response to the teacher (or other student) holding up a letter card and asking for *name* or *sound,* and activities in which the teacher holds up a letter card and says either its name or sound and the student has to say, in response, *name* or *sound.*

When introducing letter/sound instruction, help the student to create associations by using pictures or picture cards (keywords) that represent the letter shape and sound. For example, present the letter *o* as a drawing of an octopus, the letter *m* as two mountains, the letter *e* as an egg, and the letter *s* as a snake. When practicing with alphabet cards, have the student say the letter name, the keyword, and the associated sound. Model the sounds of the consonants with as little subsequent vowel sound as possible and ensure that students practice it that way (e.g., /b/ not *bŭ*).

When the student is familiar with many of the consonants and vowels, point out to him how the letters are put together to make up words and how the words go together to make sentences. Build in the concept that letters and words are the building blocks of reading and writing.

Use language clues for teaching the sounds of frequently confused letters, such as *m* and *n.* For example, a short verbal cue could be: M has many mountains and N does not.

If the student has difficulty retaining new phonic elements, add a tactile component, such as tracing and saying the sounds of the new letter/sound combinations as they are learned. Reinforce this association by having him say the sound(s) while he writes the letter(s) from memory. The student will require extra reinforcement to commit the letter/sound associations to memory.

As the student is having difficulty retaining letter/sound correspondences, play games specifically focused on their reinforcement. One such game, "Tongue Twister," is also useful for phonological awareness. Each student is given a card and tokens. On one side of the card is an array of nine pictures and on the other, an array of nine letters. The object is to cover all of the pictures or letters. The taped voice says an alliterative phrase (e.g., "itchy insects in igloos") and the student places a token on the picture that matches or the letter that corresponds to the initial sound of each word (e.g., *i*).

Once the student has learned the sound of a letter or phonogram, give frequent practice reading it and spelling it in nonsense words as well as real words.

Phonological Awareness to Print

Guide the student in moving from phonological awareness into the use of print through a program of activities such as *Road to the Code: A Phonological Awareness Program for Young Children* (Blackman et al., 2000). Available from: Paul H. Brookes Publishing Company. P.O. Box 10624, Baltimore, MD 21285-0624, phone: (800) 638-3775, website: www.brookespublishing.com.

Help the student to visualize the relationship between speech sounds and printed letters, while emphasizing sound segmenting and sequencing, through use of the adapted Elkonin Procedure (Elkonin, 1973). [See Strategies: Elkonin Procedure: Adapted.]

As a basis for the acquisition and development of fluency with letter/sound knowledge, integrate phonics with phonemic awareness instruction by including activities using letters. Provide activities that require blending sounds into words, breaking words into individual sounds, and sequencing and resequencing sounds. An example of one [or more] such activity is: [Include any of the following activities that are appropriate to the student's needs.]

- Use *Making Words* (Cunningham & Cunningham, 1992) to help the student develop phonemic awareness and discover how our alphabetic system works by increasing his understanding of sound/letter relationships. This series of 15-minute activities is to be used along with regular writing activities. Each student is given letters that he uses to make 12 to 15 words. The activities begin with short, easy words and end with a big word that uses all of the letters. Available from: Good Apple, Inc., A Division of Frank Schaffer Publications, 23740 Hawthorne Blvd., Torrance, CA 90505, (800) 421-5565, website: www.frankschaffer.com.

- Use *Easy Lessons for Teaching Word Families* (Lynch, 1998) to help the student increase letter/sound knowledge. This K–1 instructional program, adapted from *Making Words* (Cunningham & Hall, 1994), is designed to teach the student how to sequence letters and sounds. Scholastic, 2931 East McCarty Street, Jefferson City, MO 65102, phone: (800) 724-6527, website: www.scholastic.com.

- To encourage the use of letter/sound correspondence, using magnetic letters or letter tiles, show the student a word, say the word, scramble the letters, and ask the student to rebuild and pronounce the word.

- Use letter tiles to teach the concept of sound sequencing and blending. Arrange a given set of tiles and have the student attempt to pronounce real or nonsense words. Resequence, omit, add, or substitute one letter at a time and have the student pronounce the new word. For a change of activity, and to reinforce sound segmenting, pronounce a word and have the student arrange the letters to match the sequence of sounds. Modify the pronunciation slightly and have the student rearrange the letter tiles. Be careful to present only syllable patterns that the student has learned and not to include letters that change the sound of the letters around them (e.g., *lad* to *lard*).

- Play games to increase phonological awareness and knowledge of sound/symbol correspondences. For example, number a paper from 1 to 10 (or any other number). Write a short, phonically regular word. Pass the paper to the student and ask him to form a new word by just changing one letter. Letters may be inserted, omitted, or rearranged. If the student cannot think of a word, provide as much assistance as needed. After he writes a word, he returns the paper to you. Continue until ten words are written. When finished, have the student read the list of words.

As letter patterns are learned, incorporate them into fluency and text-reading activities.

Prior to reading passages, ask the student to find and attempt to pronounce words in the reading materials that include one or two of the phonics elements he is learning.

Phonics

General

To help the student improve his ability to use phoneme/grapheme relationships, discourage reliance on pictures as aids for word recognition.

Since the student tends to overrely on the use of context clues for word recognition, directly teach him how to use phoneme/grapheme relationships.

Presently, the student overrelies on semantic and syntactic cues which results in inaccurate word identification. Provide the student with extensive practice in using graphophonic cues.

Because the student lacks knowledge of the alphabetic system, teach phonics explicitly, rather than incidentally (instruction within text).

Praise the student for any attempts he makes at pronouncing unknown words when reading aloud. Encourage him to try and identify words rather than guessing or skipping over words.

When the student is reading independently, do not encourage him to skip words. Instead, teach the student to examine the word carefully and then reread the sentence in which the word appears. Discuss with the student how attempting to pronounce unknown words, when he is reading independently, will improve his word attack skills.

When teaching the student phonics skills, be sure to provide additional time for activities involving oral language development and reading comprehension.

In all reading and spelling instruction, make sure to point out the letter patterns. Incorporate activities to draw the student's attention to these such as color coding, circling, or searching for specific letter patterns in text.

Use computer programs (e.g., Reader Rabbit, Kid Phonics), card games (e.g., The Phonics Game), and board games for drill and practice of reading and spelling skills and sight words.

Make games out of word attack practice by using game boards such as Chutes and Ladders for small groups of students to play. In the following example, the students are working on recalling and blending sounds in closed-syllable words. Make a stack of cards with CVC words, both real and nonsense. Write a number on the face of each of the cards. Using their markers on the Chutes and Ladders board, the students progress along the path by picking a card, sounding out the word, and moving according to the number on the card. As soon as the student gains some fluency in blending sounds to make a word, the word cards can be written at the next level of skill development (e.g., CCVC and CVCC words, following instruction in consonant blends). Older students prefer more mature-looking games such as Parcheesi.

Synthetic Phonics

Use a synthetic phonics approach to teach the student reading skills. With synthetic phonics instruction, the student is taught explicitly the relationship between letters and sounds. After sounds are taught in isolation, he is then taught how to blend the letter sounds together to pronounce words. Once the student can blend single phonemes, additional graphemes are introduced and emphasis is placed on learning to chunk or break words into their basic parts. For many disabled readers, research has shown synthetic phonics to be the most effective of the phonics methods.

Use a program such as the Stevenson Language Program, a language skills program that teaches students language rules by connecting them to images that can be readily visualized. This sequential system provides lessons in reading, vocabulary building, spelling, penmanship, grammar, comprehension work, and typing. At the beginning level, decoding and spelling are emphasized. Materials are available from Stevenson Learning Skills, Inc., 85 Upland Road, Attleboro, MA 02703 or through the Guide Line, (800)-343-1211.

Teach the student phonic skills by using a highly structured synthetic approach. Examples include the *Phonic Remedial Reading Drills* (Kirk, Kirk, & Minskoff, 1985), the *Spalding* method (Spalding & Spalding, 1986), *Angling for Words* (Bowen, 1972), *Reading Mastery* (Engelmann et al., 1983–1984), and *Corrective Reading* (Engelmann et al., 1988).

Due to the student's difficulty with [memory, processing speed, language], teach basic reading skills through a highly structured, multisensory, synthetic phonics program that will help the student to form a strong association between letters and their corresponding sounds, and to blend, segment, sequence and manipulate sounds as represented by letters.

Teach the student phonics skills using a highly structured synthetic program that incorporates a strong tactile–kinesthetic component, such as the *Slingerland* method (Slingerland, 1971), the *Orton-Gillingham* approach (Gillingham &

Stillman, 1973), or the *Lindamood Phoneme Sequencing Program for Reading, Spelling, and Speech.* Available from: PRO-ED, 8700 Shoal Creek Blvd., Austin, TX 78757-6897, phone: (800) 897-3202, website: www.proedinc.com.

Use a multisensory program to teach phonic skills, such as the Wilson Reading System, that was designed originally for older students. Available from: Wilson Language Training, 175 West Main Street, Millbury, MA, 01527-1441, (800) 899-8454, www.WilsonLanguage.com.

Use a program with the student such as Visual Phonics, a system of 46 hand signs and written symbols that suggest how a sound is made. This program can be used in conjunction with any reading, literacy, speech, or ESL program. More information is available from: International Communication Learning Institute (ICLI), 7108 Bristol Blvd., Edina, MN 55435, (612) 929-9381.

Provide explicit instruction in phonic elements. The focus of phonics instruction should be to help the student see how letters relate to sounds, and then how letters and sounds are used to read and spell words.

To teach the student phonic skills directly, use the resource *Words* (Henry, 1990), which presents 50 lessons based on word structure, and *Patterns for Success in Reading and Spelling: A Multisensory Approach to Teaching Phonics and Word Analysis* (Henry & Redding, 1996), which includes 40 lessons in each of three books. Available from: PRO-ED, 8700 Shoal Creek Blvd., Austin, TX 78757-6897, (800) 897-3202, www.proedinc.com.

Analytic Phonics

Use an analytic phonics program to teach the student basic reading skills. This type of approach begins with familiar letter patterns (e.g., *at*) rather than single letters and sounds. Make sure the student automatically recognizes each letter pattern taught and can use it to pronounce unfamiliar words in other types of reading material. Begin with the most commonly used rimes (e.g., *at, an, it*). Sample activities include:

- Using manipulatives, teach the student a common cluster, such as *at.* Form new words by changing the initial consonant. Have the student attempt to pronounce the new words.
- Write a familiar word on a piece of paper. Have the student say the word. Without changing the word, alter various letters, both consonants and vowels, and ask the student how the new word would be pronounced. For example, you may write the word *sank,* and ask the student

what the word would be if you changed the *s* to *t,* or the *a* to *i,* or the *n* to *c,* and so on. If necessary, have the student write the new word to aid in pronunciation.

Teach the student new words in word families. Select common word patterns, such as *at* or *am* and then identify and practice common words in the family. Help the student learn to identify the patterns rapidly and automatically.

Use the words in the student's sight vocabulary as a basis for building phonic skills. For example, start with a word that he automatically recognizes, such as *run,* and then show him how that pattern can help him identify a new word, such as *fun.* Help promote generalization of common patterns by frequently pointing out similarities in words.

Embedded Phonics

Provide the student with practice in word attack skills using high-interest reading materials. When the student comes to a word that he does not know, provide phonic clues (such as the initial sound) to help him identify the word.

Teach phonics instruction within meaningful text reading. Highlight specific phonic elements when they appear in text.

Integrate phonics instruction into daily reading and writing activities. Provide opportunities for the student to use his knowledge of letter/sound relationships.

Multisyllabic Words

Teach the student the six most common syllable structures. [See Strategies: Six Syllable Structures.] Show him how recognizing the syllable structure will aid with word pronunciation and help him know how to pronounce the vowel sound.

A good supplementary activity for practicing recognition of the syllable structures and their most common pronunciations is *Syllable Plus: A Game to Teach Syllable Types.* Available from: Educational Tutorial Consortium, 4400 South 44th, Lincoln, NE 68516, (402) 489-8133.

Teach the student how to use structural analysis to decode multisyllabic words. Ensure that he "overlearns" these skills so that he begins to see unfamiliar words as a sequence of recognizable word parts. Teach him to identify both meaning parts (prefixes, suffixes, and root words) and pronunciation parts (common clusters and syllables).

Some activities and programs that might be helpful in this regard are:

- Reinforce the student's pronunciation and knowledge of the meaning of affixes and root words by providing the student with the most common prefixes, suffixes, and root words printed on index cards, one to a card. Have the student build and then pronounce both real and nonsense words by rearranging the cards (e.g., *subductable*—able to be taken under; *transportation*—the act of carrying across).
- Reinforce the student's recognition and pronunciation of affixes and root words by using activities in game format, such as *Intermediate Syllable Plus* and *Advanced Syllable Plus*. In these activities, students categorize a wide variety of the most common prefixes, suffixes, and roots by syllable type and pronunciation. Available from: Educational Tutorial Consortium, 4400 South 44th, Lincoln, NE 68516, (402) 489-8133.

Focus the student's decoding and spelling instruction on content area words while teaching syllabication and structural analysis. One program specifically addressing the needs of older learners is *WORDS: Integrated Decoding and Spelling Instruction Based on Word Origin and Word Structure* (Henry, 1990). This program, intended for grades 3–8 and older students with learning disabilities, includes activities such as organizing letter/sound correspondences, studying syllable patterns, learning about word origins, and practicing decoding and spelling multisyllabic words taken from math, social studies, and science textbooks. The manual contains tests, content area word lists, nonphonetic word lists, and spelling rules. Available from: PRO-ED, 8700 Shoal Creek Blvd., Austin, TX 78757-6897, (800) 897-3202, www.proedinc.com.

Teach structural analysis by cutting apart words into common clusters. Keep the letters of the words you are working with large. Combine the word parts in a variety of ways to make pseudowords or real words to pronounce. Let the student then scramble the letters to make new words for you to pronounce.

Make a chart with several suffixes listed down the side, such as *ing, er,* and *ed.* Write root words across the top. Have the student determine which endings can be added to form new real words. When he has completed the chart, have him pronounce all the words.

Use high-interest materials, such as magazines or newspaper articles to reinforce pronunciation of multisyllabic words. Before reading, have the student scan the passage, underline, and attempt to pronounce words containing three or more syllables.

Have the student engage in activities that will develop his automatic recognition of any affixes, specific letter patterns, and morphemes on which the student is working, such as *ing* or *cious.*

To develop automatic recognition of the word part on which the student is working, prior to reading a passage aloud, have him color code or highlight it each time it appears in the text.

To familiarize the student visually with affixes, introduce him to a short list of prefixes and suffixes with their most common meanings. Provide practice pronouncing these affixes with a variety of root words.

To teach immediate visual recognition of common affixes, have the student scan for them in his school texts or the newspaper.

Prior to having the student read a passage, underline any multisyllabic words that he may have difficulty pronouncing. Review pronunciation of the words. Have the student then practice reading the words fluently in context.

When pronouncing multisyllabic words, have the student slide his index finger slowly under the word parts as he pronounces them.

Teach syllabication and structural analysis through a highly structured and sequential program that highlights the visual aspect of the word parts and reinforces a strong association with their corresponding sounds. One such method is *Glass Analysis Method for Decoding Only* (Glass, 1973, 1976). [See Strategies: Glass Analysis for Decoding Only.]

Teach the student a learning strategy such as DISSECT (Lenz, Schumaker, Deshler, & Beals, 1984) to use when she encounters unknown words.

Sight Word Identification

Further Evaluation
Use diagnostic teaching to determine the most effective method for helping the student to learn sight words.

Use informal evaluation and diagnostic teaching to determine the reason for the student's difficulty in recognizing and retaining sight words.

General

Teach the student to recognize and pronounce common exception words (e.g., *once*). Discuss with the student that some words are not consistent in sound/symbol correspondence and that these irregular or exception words must be memorized or learned as sight words.

Teach sight words from one of the lists of words most frequently used in reading materials, such as the 220 words of the *Dolch Basic Sight Word List* (Dolch, 1939) or *1,000 Instant Words* (Fry, 1994). Available from: Teacher Created Materials, 6421 Industry Way, Westminister, CA, 92683, (800) 662-4321. [See Strategies: Instant Words 300.]

Teach the student to recognize the 300 Instant Words (Fry, 1980). These words make up approximately 65% of written material. [See Strategies: Instant Words 300.]

Have the student develop a word box, such as a recipe box with letter tabs or a shoe box with envelopes as dividers. Print sight words on index cards, one to a card, and in uniform color and print style (or typeface) so that he will use the letter patterns to identify the word rather than incidental characteristics such as color, cursive versus print, or a smudge on the card. Have the student place known words into the box and arrange them alphabetically or create categories by level of mastery, such as Known Words (words mastered), New Words (words to study next), Review Words (studied but not quite mastered), and Problem Words. Provide the student with many and varied opportunities for review of the sight words in his word box. [See Strategies: Word Bank Activities.]

Do not give the student separate sight word and spelling lists to learn. The student is unable to handle that amount of material and is confused by the separate requirements. Practicing the spelling of the sight words will reinforce the student's recognition of the words and the letter patterns within the words as well as the recall of their sounds.

Have the student learn no more than [appropriate number] sight words at a time. To document his mastery of words studied and to know when to assign new words, use a flow chart. The flow chart has a column in which to list the words to be studied and boxes across from each word in which to record if the student read the word correctly or incorrectly, if he restudied the word, and the date. After the student has demonstrated mastery of a word, it can be crossed off the list (or marked as needing periodic reinforcement) and

a new one added. [See Strategies: Flow Chart—Sight Words/Spelling.]

Assign the same list of words for reading and spelling. Have the student write, read, or read and write his sight/spelling words every day. Several times a week, he needs to see them in his reading assignments and use them in writing activities such as sentence dictation. When the student has read and spelled the word correctly for five consecutive days, fade practice to twice, then once a week, and eventually to once a month. Once the student has studied the word, subsequent writing of the word must be from memory. If he cannot write the word from memory correctly, the student needs additional practice.

Prior to reading, introduce and practice any unknown words with the student.

To promote automatic recognition of sight words, practice with rapid exposure. This may be done with brief exposures of words on index cards, a simple tachistoscope, or a computer. Expose the word for progressively decreasing periods of time.

To help the student generalize sight word recognition to text, have him scan printed material and name and cross out target sight words he recognizes. *Word Tracking: High Frequency Words* (Kratoville, 1989), a book of tracking worksheets using the Francis-Kucera list of the 1,092 most frequently used words in English, is appropriate for this type of activity (Kucera & Francis, 1967).

Strategies for Sight Word Instruction

Use the spelling study strategy Look-Spell-See-Write to teach the student sight words. [See Strategies: Look-Spell-See-Write.]

Use the Sight Word Association Procedure (SWAP) (Bos & Vaughn, 2001) as an activity for reinforcing sight words. [See Strategies: Sight Word Association Procedure.]

Because the student has difficulty with memory, teach sight words using the Fernald method (Fernald, 1943) or the modified Fernald method. Important elements of these methods are repeatedly tracing the word while saying it, then writing it from memory. [See Strategies: Fernald Method for Reading, Fernald Method for Reading and Spelling: Modified.]

If the student continues to have difficulty recognizing and spelling sight words within an instructional program using decodable text and controlled vocabulary, use a modification of the Fernald method for initial instruction. Provide the word printed neatly in large bold letters (1½ to 2" high) on a strip of rough paper, such as a grocery bag. Have the student repeatedly trace the letters of the word as he says each sound (not the letter name). When the student is positive that he can write the word from memory with no mistakes, he writes it 5 times, checking his spelling against the model each time, and covering up his previous attempts. If he makes a mistake at any point, he goes back to tracing. [See Strategies: Fernald Method for Reading and Spelling: Modified.]

When teaching sight words, directly teach the student to recognize common letter patterns within the word (e.g., *ight* in *sight, oo* in *look*). Reinforce automatic recognition of the letter pattern by giving practice finding it in other words and in discriminating it from similar patterns. For example, given a page of words containing *oo,* have him track across each line, circling *oo.* Later, have him circle *oo* on a similar worksheet composed of words that incorporate *oo,* as well as vowel combinations similar to *oo* such as *ou.*

Use a modified letter cloze procedure to help the student with word identification. Write the whole word on the front of an index card and then rewrite the word on the back of the card, deleting all the vowels. After showing the student both sides twice, have him identify the word and the missing vowels.

To increase the student's word recognition, use patterned language books that repeat words and phrases. If the student does not retain the words introduced in these books, provide additional practice with flash cards. If he continues to have difficulty with retention, incorporate a tracing component.

Use a modified language experience approach (Bos & Vaughn, 2001) to help the student establish a positive attitude toward reading, reinforce his understanding that printed words represent spoken language, and increase sight vocabulary. [See Strategies: Language Experience for Sight Words: Modified.]

Select words to teach the student that will be used in his particular vocation or avocation. Teach the student to use technological devices, such as the Reading Pen II or an electronic talking dictionary, to help him read printed information in his daily life. When the student scans a word (or line of print) with the Reading Pen II, a voice synthesizer reads the word (line) aloud and displays it in large print. It can also provide a spoken definition. Available from: Wizcom Technologies, Inc., 257 Great Road, Acton, MA 01720, phone: (888) 777-0552, website: www.wizcomtech.com.

Talking dictionaries are available from Franklin Learning Resources, 122 Burrs Road, Mt. Holly, NJ 08060, phone: (800) 525-9673, website: www.franklin.com.

Survival Sight Vocabulary

Teach the student survival sight words, such as exit, entrance, danger, men, women, and yield.

Provide the student with practice reading informational signs in the environment.

Select words to teach the student that will be used in his particular vocation or avocation. Teach the student to use technological devices, such as the Quicktionary Reading Pen II or a talking dictionary, to help him read printed information in his daily life.

Reading Practice in Decodable Text

Provide daily reading practice in decodable text (text based on a controlled vocabulary with many presentations of the sight words and reading/spelling patterns taught and in the same sequence). The student must read decodable text to integrate new and previously learned subskills into meaningful and connected text as well as to develop automaticity in word attack and sight word identification in multiple contexts. Regular basal texts or trade books are not effective for this purpose as they do not provide a controlled vocabulary with sufficient presentations of specific reading and spelling patterns in a specific sequence.

Combine phonics instruction with a reading program that uses decodable text. Decodable text is reading material that is composed primarily of words with regular sound/symbol correspondence. Reading decodable text provides the opportunity for application of newly learned skills and generalizing skills learned in isolation to practical use.

Set aside at least 15 minutes every day for the student to read decodable text. Decodable text is reading material composed of the phonics and sight words he has already learned. Reading decodable text provides the opportunity for application of newly learned skills, reinforcement of sight words, and transitioning skills learned in isolation to practical use. At his current skill level, reading aloud is best.

Supplement the student's phonics instruction with additional decodable books that he can read during free reading time and at home. Examples of the series available from educational publishers are the Steck-Vaughn Phonics Readers

(Steck-Vaughn), SRA Reading Series (SRA/McGraw-Hill), Decodable Books (The Wright Group), J & J Language Readers (Sopris West), Phonics-Based Chapter Books (High Noon), and Scholastic Phonics Readers (Scholastic).

Use direct instruction for teaching phonics and then have the student apply the skills in decodable text formats. The use of controlled vocabulary will help the student practice the skills that he is learning.

Set aside at least 15 minutes every day for the student to read decodable text. At his current skill level, reading aloud is best.

- Use paired reading to provide practice in reading decodable text. Pair up the student with another student at a similar reading level. Both may take turns reading aloud to each other. Each student is responsible for making sure that what his partner reads makes sense and for stopping him if it does not.

Reading Fluency

Further Evaluation
Obtain a baseline measure of the student's reading fluency. Tape-record the student reading several graded passages at his instructional reading level. Record the number of words in the passage, the amount of time that it took the student to read it, and the number of errors. Divide the number of words read correctly by the total amount of reading time to find the number of correct words read per minute. Keep the taped readings and the record to document progress in reading fluency.

Calculate the student's reading rate by dividing the number of words read correctly by the total amount of reading time. Count out 100 words in a passage and then time the student as he reads the passage.

Use a series of graded textbooks or an informal reading inventory to establish the reading level at which the student is able to read fluently. Note both rate and expression.

Use a speed drill and a 1-minute timing to assess reading accuracy and rate. Use the following general guidelines: 30 correct words per minute (wpm) for first- and second-grade children; 40 correct wpm for third-grade children; 60 correct wpm for mid-third-grade; and 80 wpm for students in fourth grade and above (Fischer, 1999). To conduct a speed drill, have the student read a list of words for 1 minute and record the number of errors. You may use a high-frequency word list or sample speed drills from Concept Phonics, Ox-

ton House, P.O. Box 209 Farmington, ME 04938, (800) 539-READ.

Accommodations and Modifications
Because the student has a slow reading rate, provide extended time on tests involving reading and shorten classroom reading assignments.

Because of the student's slow reading rate, as an alternative to assigning the student a specific number of pages to read in class or for homework, specify a certain amount of time for the student to read. Have the student keep a record of the number of pages completed within the time period.

Presently, the student's lack of automaticity interferes with higher-order reading skills. Because his decoding is slow and effortful, most of his attention is directed to trying to read words accurately rather than trying to understand what he is reading. Be sure to provide the student with necessary support in the classroom. This may include taped books, peer readers, extended time, and modified instructional materials.

Methods

General
Because the student reads accurately but slowly, use a variety of methods to increase reading fluency. Effective fluency methods include repeated readings, choral reading, speed drills, practicing with taped books, and reading decodable text. Provide short, frequent periods of practice and concrete, visible measures of progress (e.g., charts, bar graphs). [See Strategies: Repeated Readings, Neurological Impress Method, Great Leaps Reading, Speed Drills for Reading Fluency and Basic Skills.]

Provide the student with many daily opportunities for reading connected text (e.g., partner reading and choral reading). These activities will improve word identification abilities and fluency.

Help the student develop proper phrasing in his oral reading by modeling appropriate expression and prosody, and supervising the student's practice. Prosody is composed of pitch or intonation, stress or emphasis, tempo or rate, and the rhythmic patterns of language.

Speed Drills
As the student has particular difficulty with reading fluency, provide a program specifically designed for this purpose. *Great Leaps Reading* (Campbell, 1996) is used to in-

crease reading speed and fluency while reinforcing phonics-skills. One-minute timings are done that employ three stimuli: phonics, sight phrases, and short stories. Chart performance on graphs so that the student can see his progress. A K–2 version of this program provides a phonological awareness instruction component (Mercer & Campbell, 1998). [See Strategies: Great Leaps Reading.]

Use a Rapid Word Recognition Chart to improve speed and accuracy for pronouncing irregular words (Carreker, 1999). The chart is similar to a rapid serial-naming task. It is a matrix that contains five rows of six exception words (such as "who" and "said"), with each row containing the same six words in a different order. After a warm up or brief review of the words, students are timed for 1 minute as they read aloud the words in the squares. Students can then count and record the number of words read correctly. Once the student can read all words easily and quickly, new words can be written in the chart.

To help automatize decoding skills and sight word recognition, as well as to increase reading fluency, create reading speed drills using sight words, syllable structures, word patterns, and phonic elements on which the student needs practice. The same six items (e.g., six sight words, six words representing the silent e syllable pattern) are printed in random order over ten rows. The goal for each page is for the student to read 60 items within 60 seconds. Given the student's current [phonics, sight word, etc.] needs, items to work on are [VC and CVC word patterns, CVC–silent e, a combination of both, and sight words.] [See Strategies: Speed Drills for Reading Fluency and Basic Skills.]

Repeated Readings and Choral Reading
Use guided repeated oral reading to improve word recognition and fluency. Have the student read the same passage several times orally. Provide him with systematic and explicit feedback and guidance.

Used paired reading with the student in the classroom (or home) to help him increase fluency. In the classroom, select a peer with whom the student enjoys working. Use the following steps: (a) the student and tutor read aloud together; (b) when the student wants to read independently, he taps the tutor to stop reading; (c) the student reads aloud independently until he does not know a word or makes an error; (d) the tutor provides the word, the student pronounces the word, and the pair resumes choral reading. Use the procedure five times a week for a minimum of 5 minutes for a period of 6 to 8 weeks (Topping, 1987a, b).

Use the Presenting Technique (Heckelman, 1986) as a pre-reading method to familiarize the student with the language and content of the reading passage, enabling a more fluent reading of the text or better participation when choral reading with the teacher. [See Strategies: Presenting Technique.]

Use the Repeated Readings Procedure (Samuels, 1979) to help the student improve reading speed. [See Strategies: Repeated Readings.] Tape the student's first and final reading of the passage to document progress and so that he can hear himself reading in a fluent manner. Chart his performance.

Use the Neurological Impress Method (Heckelman, 1966, 1986) with the student for 10–15 minutes daily. You may have a volunteer, a peer, a cross-age tutor, or the parents read with the student. Provide training to the person working with the student. [See Strategies: Neurological Impress Method.]

To improve reading fluency, have the student practice reading a short, predictable story or book (repeated words and phrases) until he is able to read it with ease. Have him read the book to someone else. Tape his first and final readings to document progress and so that he can hear himself read in a fluent manner.

Reading with Taped Books
Use taped books to help build reading skill. One program designed to build fluency in students from mid-first through sixth grade is called *Read Naturally*. Instruction is individualized and involves three main steps: (a) reading along with an audio tape of a story that provides a model of fluent reading; (b) intensive, repeated practice to build speed and accuracy; and (c) monitoring and evaluating performance through graphing. To use the program, students are placed into an appropriate level based on their oral reading fluency. The sequenced reading levels range from beginning reading to sixth-grade level, with 24 stories available for each level. In addition, the lower-level materials have been rewritten into Spanish. Available from: Read Naturally, 2329 Kressin Avenue, Saint Paul, MN 55120, (800) 788-4085, READNAT@aol.com.

Use the Carbo Method (Carbo, 1989) for recording books for the student. [See Strategies: Carbo Method.]

Have the student listen to a taped passage or a short book several times as he reads along with the tape. When he has mastered the passage or book, have him read it to someone else.

Altering Rate

Teach the student how to alter reading rate depending upon the purpose for reading. For example, he may want to scan for specific information, skim to see if an article is appropriate for a report, read a technical manual or history text slowly, or read at a fast pace for pleasure.

Teach the student how to slow down his reading when he encounters difficult material and to reread passages when the meaning is unclear.

Teach the student how to skim a passage to obtain the general idea. This skill is necessary in selecting appropriate reading materials for reports and for pleasure reading.

Teach the student how to scan a passage for specific information, such as answering questions in a text, taking an open-book test, or looking for information on a specific topic for a report.

Demonstrate how to adjust reading rate for varied purposes. Use the analogy of adjusting reading speed to the shifting of gears in a car. Lower gears, Gear 1 and Gear 2, are the slowest, yet most powerful gears. First gear is used to memorize materials. Second gear is used to learn material. Third gear is the normal typical reading rate. The fourth gear, skimming, and the fifth gear, scanning, are the fastest but least powerful gears. These gears are useful when you are trying to locate a specific piece of information or trying to get the general sense of a passage without reading every word (Carver, 1990).

Fluency/Comprehension

Combine a fluency method with a method for increasing comprehension. For example, read aloud several paragraphs with the student and then stop to discuss the story. Before resuming choral reading, have the student predict what he thinks will happen next.

Give the student a study guide or a cloze passage to complete as he listens to the text. Have him hit the pause button or turn off the tape recorder whenever he needs to write in information. Encourage him to rewind the tape and listen to the passage several times.

Use choral repeated reading with the student to increase both fluency and comprehension. Select a high-interest book that is one or two levels above the student's instructional level. Establish a purpose for reading by skimming the book. Encourage the student to make predictions about the content. Read the book using this three-step process: (a) read a short passage from the book as the student watches, running your finger smoothly under the text; (b) read the same section together with the student as many times as needed so that he feels comfortable reading independently; and (c) have the student read the passage independently. After each section, discuss how the content related to your predictions and set new purposes for reading (Bos & Vaughn, 2001).

Have the student use the *Timed Readings in Literature* series by Jamestown Publishers (Spargo, 1989) to increase reading speed and comprehension. Each book contains short passages followed by questions. The student practices reading at a slightly faster-than-normal speed and then answers questions about the passages. Charts are provided to record performance.

READING COMPREHENSION

Tests: Passage Comprehension, Reading Vocabulary
Related Tests: Oral Comprehension, Verbal Comprehension, Reading Fluency
Cluster: Reading Comprehension
Related Areas: Oral Language, Academic Knowledge/Content Areas, Written Expression, Writing Evaluation Scale

Reading Comprehension
    Further Evaluation
    Accommodations
        Instructional Level
        Color Coding
        Taped Books
    General Recommendations
    Reading Materials
    Vocabulary
    Context Clues
        General
        Cloze Procedure
    Prereading Activities
        Activating/Evaluating Background Knowledge
    Skill Instruction
    Strategies
    Self-Monitoring Comprehension
        Predicting/Making Inferences
        Retelling/Paraphrasing/Summarizing
        Questioning
        Study Guides
    Text Structures
        Narrative
        Expository

Further Evaluation

Because the student's reading decoding and reading fluency skills are so much better than her comprehension of the same material, refer the student for a language evaluation to confirm or rule out a primary oral language disorder as the major contributing factor to poor reading comprehension.

Further evaluate the student's reading comprehension using classroom texts. Have her read several passages silently and then retell the major points. See if the number of major concepts and those that she chooses are sufficient for adequate comprehension based on current standards.

Use an informal reading inventory to further assess basic reading skills, reading fluency, reading comprehension, and listening comprehension. For both reading comprehension and listening comprehension, request that the student retell the passage before asking questions. Note key points and organization of ideas and details. Compare the student's retellings and response to comprehension questions in relation to having read the material and having the material read to her to determine if her oral language level is higher than or the same as her reading level.

Administer an informal assessment to ascertain whether the student's difficulty with retelling expository reading material is related to an initial lack of understanding or to weak recall. Prepare a passage at the student's word recognition instructional level, noting the most important ideas, events, and details. Have the student read and retell the passage. Record the key elements she included. Then test her comprehension of the material using a multiple-choice, true/false, or other test format that does not require free recall. Repeat with two other passages. Compare the results.

Determine if the student is able to monitor her own comprehension and recognize when a breakdown in understanding occurs. Provide her with a short text that contains some type of inconsistency. Ask her to retell that passage and see if she notes or detects the contradiction.

Accommodations

Instructional Level

Because the student's listening and speaking vocabulary are considerably higher than her present instructional level in word identification, teach reading comprehension skills orally, based upon her oral language level. As her word identification increases, guide her to apply the comprehension skills she learned orally.

Provide a set period every day for the student to engage in sustained silent reading. Provide a variety of materials at the independent level and allow the student to select the reading materials.

When providing instruction in reading comprehension, ensure that the student's instructional materials are at the independent reading level in word recognition. Materials at the independent level will allow the student to devote her full attention to the comprehension activities.

Place a student in a reading group based on her present performance level in language and reading comprehension, rather than her performance in word identification skills.

Provide the student with daily readings of text that are at the independent or instructional reading levels. When text at the frustration level is unavoidable (e.g., entire class reading an on-grade level book), provide supported reading (e.g., partner reading, taped books).

Color Coding

Before the student reads a textbook, color-code with a yellow highlighter the sections that are most important to read.

Using different color markers, highlight specific types of information in the text that the student should know. For example, highlight important vocabulary words in pink, important concepts in yellow, and important names and dates in green. The use of color will draw the student's attention to the most important information.

When the student is reading, teach her how to use highlighters to color-code specific types of information for easy review. For example, she can color vocabulary words as pink, definitions in yellow, and important concepts in green.

Taped Books

Because the student can comprehend the vocabulary and information in textbooks that are at or above grade level, but is unable to read them due to difficulty with basic skills, provide her with tape recordings of her textbooks.

Make tape recordings of the student's textbooks in a way that will help her learn to think strategically about the material that she is reading. Use the following procedure: (a) preread the chapter and mark the portions of the text that should be read verbatim, those that can be paraphrased, and those that can be skipped; (b) prepare questions or a study guide to accompany the text; (c) determine actions for the student to complete while working through the text (e.g., "Stop and answer question 1 on the study guide" "Stop the tape and write a paraphrase of the title in your own words"); (d) provide the student with a marked text that shows what paragraphs are read verbatim, what material is paraphrased, what material is omitted, and where specific learning activities will occur; and (e) summarize the key information on the tape (Schumaker, Denton, & Deshler, 1984).

General Recommendations

Praise the student for using any new skills and strategies in reading.

Present meaningful reading assignments to motivate the student's intent to understand the reading material. For example, within text have the student locate and take notes on information that she will provide to her cooperative learning group or use to lead a discussion.

To increase reading comprehension, provide many oral language activities, particularly those designed to build vocabulary and increase listening comprehension.

Reading Materials

Suggest that the [student purchase, parents purchase for the student] a second set of textbooks so that the student can mark them up while reading and studying. Good readers often write comments, questions, or summary statements in the margins, highlight topic sentences and new vocabulary, and mentally organize parts of the text by writing keywords (e.g., relating the information to a main idea) in the margin.

For comprehension activities, do not exclusively use "decodable" reading materials that are highly dependent on word families and specific phonic elements (e.g., "The dog hopped on the log in the bog"). This type of text is intended to provide practice and develop automaticity of decoding skills rather than comprehension skills. Because the student's oral language ability is considerably higher than her decoding skills, teach comprehension skills orally. Apply learned comprehension skills to reading material as soon as the student's reading improves sufficiently that the material

warrants discussion of concepts and organization of information.

When choosing reading comprehension materials for the student, evaluate the books on decoding level and sentence cohesiveness. Be aware that high-interest, low-vocabulary books may obstruct comprehension rather than facilitate it. The major criteria for many readability formulas are sentence length and number of syllables. Although the individual words may be easier for a student to identify, the truncated sentences are more difficult to comprehend. This is because the cohesive devices (e.g., transition words) in complex sentences provide important syntactic and semantic clues to meaning. The student depends on her good oral language skills to make use of context clues, which are reduced when sentences are arbitrarily forced into simpler structures to meet the criteria for readability formulas.

Schedule time daily for reading authentic texts. Read texts to the student that will help increase her knowledge base and vocabulary, and encourage her to read a variety of different types of text.

Help the student improve her reading comprehension skills using texts that will be required or are similar to the types that will be required in her college courses.

Vocabulary

[See Recommendations: Oral Language, specifically Vocabulary, Linguistic Concepts, Cohesive Devices, Figurative Language; Memory, specifically Mnemonic Strategies.]

Because the student's vocabulary is presently limited, she is likely to experience difficulty making sense of text. Keep in mind that vocabulary development and word knowledge play a key role in the understanding of what has been read. Emphasize learning new vocabulary in the classroom. Before assigning reading on new topics, use prereading activities that are appropriate to the student's age and abilities to familiarize the student with the meanings of the critical vocabulary.

Attempt to teach vocabulary that is appropriate to the reader's abilities. When discussing difficult words, relate them to easier words to enhance vocabulary development and understanding.

Do not teach vocabulary from lists unrelated to classroom context. Select new vocabulary directly from the student's reading, your lecture, or classroom projects. Ensure her ability to understand and use these words in context before presenting new words.

Teach new vocabulary in the student's reading selections by using synonyms or short phrases. Simplify dictionary definitions.

Help the student relate new vocabulary words and their meanings to her own experiences. Elicit from the student any associated words that she knows. This will aid in retention and alert you to misinterpretations of word meaning.

Use Semantic Feature Analysis (Johnson & Pearson, 1984) to help the student relate new concepts or vocabulary to her prior knowledge. [See Strategies: Semantic Feature Analysis: Vocabulary.]

Use the Directed Vocabulary Thinking Activity (Cunningham, 1979) to engage the student's interest and to help her learn how to infer the meaning of unknown words from context. [See Strategies: Directed Vocabulary Thinking Activity.]

To enhance vocabulary retention, after introducing new vocabulary, provide the student with repeated and multiple exposures to the words. This direct instruction will enhance vocabulary acquisition.

Use a variety of methods to build vocabulary. Provide different types of instruction, such as teaching words prior to reading, discussing words in the context of reading texts, playing games with new vocabulary, and using new vocabulary in writing assignments.

Provide systematic instruction in the meaning and pronunciation of root words, prefixes, and suffixes as this will help the student understand new words independently as well as helping her recall the meanings of newly acquired vocabulary words that contain previously learned word parts.

- For an activity that stimulates both study and retention of these word parts, give the student a root word, attach affixes to create real or nonsense words, and have the student determine a possible meaning. For example, the nonsense word *circumcessable* could mean "able to go around." Similarly, the student can make up nonsense words in this manner for you or other students to decipher.
- Provide the student with lists of common prefixes and suffixes. Have her locate examples of words using these affixes in her textbooks.

To encourage learning of new vocabulary, use a computer program that provides hypertext definitions and synonyms (highlighted text that, when clicked, "jumps" to further information).

Teach the student to recognize sentences that signal a transition from one subtopic to the next and the meanings of keywords that signal the transitions (e.g., *then, but, however, yet, meanwhile, consequently*).

Help the student increase her awareness of terms denoting linguistic relationships in text (such as *temporal, spatial, cause/effect, analogous, exceptions, comparison/contrast*) to help clarify relationships among events, objects, people. Use specific illustrations of these words and phrases from social studies, history, science, and literature textbooks.

Teach the student how to recognize and understand "signal words" (e.g., *although, but, however, therefore, nevertheless*) or words that imply that the author is going to qualify, extend, or provide exception to the information presented. Encourage the student to stop when she encounters such a word, think what has gone on before, and then form a hypothesis about what the author will say next.

Context Clues

General
[See Recommendations: Oral Language.]

Teach the student additional ways to use her good reasoning and language skills to identify unfamiliar words. One suggestion is to have her look at the first few letters or any part of the word that she recognizes, read to the end of the sentence for clues about what word would make sense, and then go back and try to identify the word. Keep in mind that the use of context clues for decoding (rather than meaning) is a "back up" skill and indicates that the student requires additional instruction in decoding.

Teach the student how to use context to monitor her decoding. As she reads, she should actively work on understanding the concepts. If she comes to a word that does not make sense or sounds strange, that's a signal to stop and take a closer look.

Teach the student how to recognize and use a variety of context clues within the text. Examples include: direct explanation (within an appositive, signaled by "that is," or explained later in the paragraph); explanation through example; synonym or restatement; summary; comparison or contrast; words in a series; and inference (Thomas & Robinson, 1972). [See Strategies: Context Clues.]

Use the Directed Vocabulary Thinking Activity (Cunningham, 1979) to engage the student's interest and to help her learn how to use context clues to infer the meaning of unknown words. When creating sentences to use in the activity, incorporate the context clue that you intend to teach, for example, "explanation through example." Then, after the student has guessed at the meanings, ask her how she tried to figure it out. Point out the context clue and guide her to understanding how it points to the actual meaning of the word. Then provide guided and independent practice in using that type of context clue. [See Strategies: Context Clues, Directed Vocabulary Thinking Activity.]

Cloze Procedure

As a prerequisite for using the Cloze Procedure to aid in reading comprehension, teach the student how to respond to this procedure. Begin by using an adaptation of Cloze called the Maze procedure. Provide a passage of text and delete some of the words that you would expect the student to be able to guess from the context. Provide a list of the deleted words at the bottom of the page from which the student chooses the word that fits in the blank space. As the student's skill increases, add several distracters to the list. As a final step, do not provide words from which to choose.

When teaching sentence structure or parts of speech, provide practice using a modified Cloze Procedure. For example, if you are teaching the student to use transition words to build complex sentences, you could provide two clauses and direct the student to add the transition word that would make sense in the context (e.g., "Mary wanted to go to sleep; _____ John continued to play his music"). If focusing on state-of-being verbs, you could provide a written passage in which all of the state-of-being verbs and auxiliary verbs have been omitted and direct the student to fill them in.

Use a modified Cloze Procedure to help the student increase her ability to use semantic clues. Provide a passage with blank lines in the place of some of the content words. Direct the student to read the passage and write in a word that makes sense in the context. Initially, delete words at the end of the sentence and then, as her skill increases, randomly delete words.

Prereading Activities

Activating and Evaluating Background Knowledge
[See Recommendations: Knowledge/Content Areas/Study Strategies.]

[See Strategies: Content Area Instruction: Components of Effective Lessons.]

Before assigning reading selections, make sure that the student has the necessary vocabulary and background knowledge to understand the content. If she does, guide her to relate any new information to her own experiences; if she does not, provide activities and instruction that give her the foundation necessary to understand the material.

Follow these guidelines to help the student develop prior knowledge: (a) build upon what the student already knows, (b) provide much of the background information through discussion, (c) provide real-life experiences, (d) explain parts of the passage before the student reads it, (e) help the student expand her knowledge, and (f) encourage wide reading (Devine, 1986).

Teach strategies to help the student link new information with background knowledge. Help the student learn to summarize and paraphrase materials, generate questions, and predict what will happen based upon her knowledge and experiences.

Prior knowledge has been established as one of the most important factors contributing to students' comprehension or lack of comprehension of reading materials. Before assigning reading selections, assess the level of knowledge and experience the student has regarding the major concepts and most important vocabulary. Use of the [write in name of strategy] (descriptions attached) will also activate the student's prior knowledge, bringing to conscious awareness what she already knows about the topic. [See Strategies: Anticipation Guide, KWLS Strategy, PreReading Plan, Semantic Feature Analysis: Concepts, Semantic Maps.]

After the student has read the assignment, repeat the prereading activity as a postreading assessment. Compare the type and number of correct responses the student can produce after the reading to the level of knowledge she demonstrated in the prereading activity.

Before assigning independent reading, provide a preview of all new concepts and vocabulary in the assignment. List them on the board and provide ample opportunities for discussion.

Teach the student to use the KWLS (Know–Want to Know–Learned–Still Need to Learn) strategy (Ogle, 1986) to help her organize her knowledge of a topic both before and after reading a passage. [See Strategies: KWLS Strategy.]

To activate prior knowledge and engage the students' interest in a discussion related to a new topic, use the Anticipation Guide activity before assigning the reading material. Create a set of statements regarding key concepts in the material to be read. The content of the statements must include information that is sufficiently familiar that the students will have an opinion about it. Guide the students in a discussion regarding their agreement or disagreement on each statement. Then direct the students to read the assignment to find out more about the topic and to continue the discussion following the reading. [See Strategies: Anticipation Guide.]

When eliciting background knowledge from the student, try to organize the information in a semantic map (Pearson & Johnson, 1978). The final diagram should visually present the information in such a way that the relationships are evident. Seeing her own information organized in this way will help her create a framework to accommodate new information.

As a prereading activity to activate prior knowledge and set a purpose for content area reading, use Semantic Feature Analysis: Concepts (Anders & Bos, 1986; Bos, Anders, Filip, & Jaffe, 1989). Based on the upcoming reading assignment, the teacher creates a chart listing the key concepts across the top and most important vocabulary down the side. The student considers whether or not particular words and concepts are related and fills out a chart (+ for *yes*, – for *no*, and *?* for *don't know*). She is then directed to read the assignment with the intention of correcting or confirming her predictions. This procedure is particularly effective in a group setting as students discuss their reasons for choices both before and after reading. [See Strategies: Semantic Feature Analysis: Concepts.]

Integrate reading assignments with Internet applications. To facilitate this, help the student learn how to locate different sources of information related to varied topics.

Skill Instruction

[For recommendations regarding comprehension of sentence structure, see Recommendations: Oral Language, Sentence Structure.]

Teach the student the importance of punctuation for understanding the meaning of a passage. Add impact to the lesson by presenting examples of sentences and sentence combinations that have very different meanings depending on where the punctuation is and what punctuation is used.

Teach the student critical reading skills such as recognition of fact vs. opinion, objective vs. persuasive language, supported vs. unsupported generalizations, and valid vs. invalid arguments.

Teach the student the difference between the topic of a reading selection (what it's about) and the main idea (what the author says about the topic), while increasing her active involvement in the reading process (Longo, 2001). The topic can usually be summed up in a word or phrase, while the main idea is usually a sentence. To find the topic, the student asks herself, "What is the selection mostly about," responds in one or two words, and rereads the introductory paragraph and bold subtitles to confirm. To find the main idea, the student asks herself, "What is the writer saying about this topic," reads the first paragraph to find the main idea statement, skims the rest of the selection to see how each relates to the topic, and writes a sentence stating the writer's most important idea.

The ability to paraphrase requires active, conscious processing of information in order to extract and restate the meaning without changing it. Teach the student how to paraphrase what she reads for note-taking, summarizing, and oral and written reports. When teaching the student how to paraphrase begin with short sentences. Gradually progress to more complex sentences, paragraphs and then longer passages.

Teach the student how to make mental images of any material she is reading. Visualization improves comprehension by helping the student to retain the information read (as images) in memory as she assimilates the meaning, associate the new information with information she knows already, and recognize when she does not understand.

Develop sequential lessons to teach the student how to visualize what she is reading. Begin by stating short phrases that represent easily visualized, familiar images, and gradually increase the verbal information in length, complexity, and concept level. For some students, it helps to "set the stage" for each lesson by having them visualize themselves walking into an empty theater, choosing the best seat, seeing the lights dim, and seeing the screen light up with images as you begin presenting the oral information. Following each visualization, have the student describe exactly what she pictured. Ask her questions to elicit more specific details. As soon as the student appears comfortable with visualizing sentences, alternate between oral and written presentation.

Teach the student to attempt to visualize or make a "mental movie" of what she reads. As she reads each passage, have her describe in detail the images that she created. Initially, ask the student detail and inferential questions about the images and passages. As skill increases, allow her description of images to progress without interruption.

Strategies

Help the student improve her reading comprehension. A variety of strategies for teaching reading comprehension may be found in *Reading Strategies and Practices: A Compendium* (Tierney & Readence, 1999).

Integrate instruction in reading comprehension with instruction in written expression. Many reading comprehension strategies can be used for enhancing the organization and quality of a student's writing. For example, teach the student how to recognize compare-and-contrast formats when reading and then teach the student a strategy for planning and executing compare-and-contrast paragraph writing (Deshler, Ellis, & Lenz, 1996).

The student would benefit from a strategy that stimulates more active involvement with expository material and focuses attention on the most important information. The Center for Research on Learning at the University of Kansas has developed a number of strategies to promote reading comprehension as well as specific steps for strategy instruction that have been proven effective with adolescents with learning disabilities. Information on the Learning Strategies Curriculum is available from: Center for Research on Learning, University of Kansas, 1122 West Campus Road, Lawrence, KS, 66045, (785) 864-4780, www.kucrl.org. Information on these strategies is frequently available on the website: www.ldonline.org.

To enhance the student's reading comprehension, provide explicit instruction in several types of comprehension strategies such as paraphrasing, summarizing, and formulating questions from subtitles and answering them after reading the passage.

Teach the student reading comprehension strategies using a research-validated model of strategy acquisition (Schu-

maker & Deshler, 1992) incorporating these steps: (a) administer a pretest to assess the student's current level of performance; (b) obtain a commitment from the student to learn the strategy; (c) describe the strategy—the steps, the purpose, and the situations in which to use it; (d) model the steps of the strategy, thinking aloud as you apply it to the material to be learned; (e) have the student practice it verbally, using a mnemonic to help memorize the steps (provide a cue card if necessary); (f) provide controlled practice in materials at the student's independent performance level, gradually applying it to more challenging material; (g) administer a post-test to evaluate the student's ability to apply the strategy and his improvement in the target skill, as well as to validate, for the student, his success; and (h) plan for and facilitate the generalization of the strategy into other academic and nonacademic settings.

Because the student has difficulty with sustained attention to the reading material, as much as possible, involve him in activities that will stimulate active reading and discussion throughout the assignment. Examples of activities are Directed Reading–Thinking Activity and Reciprocal Teaching. [See Strategies: Directed Reading–Thinking Activity, Reciprocal Teaching.]

Self-Monitoring Comprehension
Teach the student to check/reinforce her own comprehension at the paragraph level by paraphrasing the main idea and at least two supporting details orally or in writing. Teach the student to include a clear statement of the relationship among ideas.

Teach the student to monitor her comprehension. Direct her to stop at the end of each sentence and ask herself, "What did I just read?" If she can picture it or paraphrase it, she continues to read. If not, she rereads with a stronger focus on understanding the information. As skill improves, increase the number of sentences between self-checks.

Predicting/Making Inferences
To develop critical and active reading, either involve the student in an individualized or group Directed Reading–Thinking Activity (DRTA). The DRTA has students predict what a selection will be about based on the title, then make other predictions about what will happen in the story or text at other stopping points. Students discuss their predictions and support them with reasons based on text-based information and/or prior knowledge (Stauffer, 1969;

Tierney & Readence, 1999). [See Strategies: Directed Reading–Thinking Activity.]

When reading a story to the student, stop at specific points and ask her questions about the story events. Ask her to predict what she thinks will happen next and give a reason for her prediction that is based on her own knowledge and what has been read to that point.

Prior to reading, assign the students to groups of two or three, and provide them with a list of prediction questions or possible outcomes. Have the students discuss these questions within their group and then read to find the answers. Alternatively, before reading, designate specific stopping points in the text and provide questions for each. The questions should refer to the next section rather than the section that has been read. At each point, the students will discuss whether their answers to the previous question were correct and discuss possible answers to the question for the next section. Predictions must be supported by reasons based on prior knowledge and information in the text.

When reading with the student, make a prediction map on the board or paper. Stop at appropriate points and have the student predict what she thinks will happen next. Record the prediction on the map and then read to find out if it is correct. If the answer is incorrect, revise the map.

Retelling/Paraphrasing/Summarizing
Help the student improve her reading comprehension and ability to recall and retell textual information in three ways. (1) Provide frequent opportunities to practice. When students expect to be asked to retell what they have read, they begin to prepare for it while reading; (2) Provide explicit instruction in recognizing expository text structures and ample practice in analyzing text to ascertain the structures (e.g., *comparison, contrast, sequence, cause/effect*); and (3) Have the student reread before retelling. To facilitate the retelling, you can supply prompts that cue the student as to the text structure (e.g., "Retell the passage and include the differences between . . ."). Additionally, you can teach the student other memory and comprehension strategies to aid him in acquiring, storing, and retrieving the information (Carlisle, 2001).

In nonfiction materials, teach the student to use paraphrasing of the main idea and supporting details to help her draw a semantic map of the structure and content of the material.

Use a strategy such as the Paraphrasing Strategy (Schumaker, Denton, & Deshler, 1984) developed at the University of Kansas. The strategy uses the acronym RAP to remind students to Read the paragraph (or a limited section of text), Ask: "What was the main idea and the details" (at least 2), and Put the information into their own words. This strategy is designed to improve comprehension by focusing attention on the important information of a passage and by stimulating active involvement with the passage.

When teaching the student how to paraphrase, ensure that the materials are at the independent reading level so that the student can fully attend to understanding the text, rather than shifting energy to word identification.

Encourage the student to be a more active reader by teaching her to summarize what she has read using a four-step strategy described by A. M. Longo (2001).
1. Get information: (a) Write the topic in one or two words; (b) List the main ideas (c) List some important details that go with the main idea.
2. Reread and check information: Cross out information that is unimportant or redundant.
3. Write sentences: Write a sentence stating the topic, one stating the main idea, and a sentence for each detail. Put them in order.
4. Write a summary using the sentences: (a) Include words that indicate the organization of the information; (b) Combine sentences into more complex sentences.

Teach the student to ask two questions after reading a paragraph: (a) Who or what was the paragraph about, and (b) What was happening to them (Malone & Mastropieri, 1992)? Place a blank line after each paragraph and have the student write a summary sentence for each paragraph. Write the steps on a self-monitoring card so that the student can check her application of the strategy.

Teach the student how to take notes in the margin to summarize information while she is reading to enhance her comprehension. Have her place question marks by any sections in the text that she does not understand and ask a parent, teacher, or friend to explain it.

Questioning
Provide the student with questions to answer while she is reading. Have her read the questions before she reads the selection to establish a purpose for reading. After she has read the passage and answered the questions, have her write a brief summary that includes the main ideas and important details.

Prior to reading, provide the student with a set of questions to answer. Create some questions that require factual recall to be answered and others that may be answered using prior knowledge. Before the student reads the material, have her attempt to answer as many questions as she can.

Help the student set a purpose for reading by presenting her with a picture, title, segment of text, or a combination of these. Have her generate as many different questions as possible, then read to find the answers.

When reading stories or content area textbooks, teach the student to read the questions at the end of the chapter first so that she knows what information is important and can look for the answers as she reads.

When introducing a new chapter, have the student write the questions from the chapter on an index card and refer to the card while she is reading the chapter. Have her check off each question when she locates the answer.

Teach the student how to set a purpose for reading by turning chapter subheadings into questions and then reading to find the answer.

Teach reading study skills, such as surveying a chapter in a textbook prior to reading it, to establish a framework for understanding the information.

Teach the student how to create and answer the reporter questions for each subsection of content area reading material (*when, where, who, what, why,* and *how*).

Use the language experience approach to reading instruction with the student but place an emphasis on comprehension activities. After the student has written a story, demonstrate and provide practice in forming questions, paraphrasing the story, and using context clues to identify words.

Teach the student to recognize when a question cannot be answered based solely on the information given in the reading selection. Teach her to use prior knowledge as well as the information given in the text to make inferences.

In reading for key ideas and critical details, ask the student to underline or note elements that she would expect to be covered on a test.

After the student learns how to recognize key ideas and critical details, reinforce this skill by having her make up test questions for the teacher or other students on a literature or content area selection.

Teach the student how to apply SQ3R (Survey, Question, Read, Recite, Review; Robinson, 1970). This technique is used to help the student create a framework for the context to be read, set a purpose for reading, and learn to monitor comprehension. [See Strategies: SQ3R.]

Use the ReQuest procedure (Manzo, 1969; 1985) to increase the student's ability to ask questions actively when reading. Read a story together with the student. Take turns asking questions of each other. When first learning the procedure, ask questions about factual material. As soon as possible, ask questions that will promote higher-level comprehension skills. [See Strategies: ReQuest Procedure.]

Use a modified ReQuest procedure with the student (Alley & Hori, 1981) to develop verbal reasoning and active reading. [See Strategies: ReQuest Procedure.]

With any questioning strategy that the student learns, provide her with many opportunities to practice and apply the selected technique in school reading assignments.

Use Collaborative Strategic Reading (CSR), an intensive classroom or group-based reading comprehension strategy, that is designed to be used with expository text (Vaughn & Klingner, 1999). [See Strategies: Collaborative Strategic Reading.]

To improve her reading comprehension, the student needs to learn how to read actively. An effective activity to teach self-questioning, comprehension monitoring, and to promote active involvement with the reading process, is the Reciprocal Teaching procedure (Palinscar & Brown, 1986). This procedure is taught in small groups and includes the following four skills: questioning, summarizing, clarifying, and predicting. The first two skills, questioning and summarizing, help students learn to identify and paraphrase the most important information in the text. To begin, students may read a paragraph or passage together. After the passage is completed, they generate questions together about what has been read and then summarize the content in a sentence or two. For clarifying, students discuss any difficult or hard to understand sections and review the meaning of any new vocabulary. For the final skill, students predict what will happen in the next passage. The process of making predictions helps students link background knowledge with the new information. As students practice these procedures, they can take more responsibility for developing questions, summarizing the content, and making predictions about the next section. [See Strategies: Reciprocal Teaching.]

Teach the student a self-questioning strategy to use while reading content area information. Teach the student to: (a) Ask yourself: Why am I studying this passage? (b) Locate the main idea in the paragraph and underline it. (c) Think of a question about the main idea. (d) Read to learn the answer. (e) Look back at the question and answer for each paragraph to determine a relationship (Wong & Jones, 1982).

Teach the student how to ask questions about the text as she is reading. For example, she may ask whether or not she agrees or disagrees with the author, or how the information relates to her own world experiences. As a modification of this technique, the student may write down the answer to her main idea question in a complete sentence (Wong & Jones, 1982). Teach the student how to create a structured overview of a selection based on her written answers to main idea questions generated by use of the self-questioning strategy.

Study Guides
To encourage interaction with the text, provide the student with study guides in a variety of formats for her reading assignments.

Teach the student how to summarize important information from a chapter on a one-page or two-page study guide that she can then use to prepare for tests.

Provide the student with a structured study guide that provides specific questions and the page number and paragraph in the text where the information is located. As skill in locating information increases, eliminate these prompts.

After the student recognizes or is guided to recognize, the passage structure, provide an outline, based on the passage, in which she can record content. These summaries will aid retention and then may be used as study notes. Ensure that the student has prior knowledge of the concept of main idea and adequate summarization skills (Slater, Graves, & Piche, 1984). Figure III.4 illustrates a sample guide for a passage with a cause-effect structure.

Insert questions into the text for the student to answer while she is reading. To minimize writing in the textbook, make a study guide with numbered questions pertaining to specific information in the text. Record the question number in pencil in the margin next to the related information.

Before the student reads an assignment, provide her with questions that highlight the most important points. Have the student answer the questions as she locates them in the text. After reading, discuss the questions with the student.

a. Cause: _____
    Support:_____
    Support:_____
    Support:_____

b. Related Topic:_____
    Support:_____
    Support:_____
    Support:_____

c. Effect: _____
    Support:_____
    Support:_____
    Support:_____

Figure III.4 Sample Guide for Summarizing a Passage with a Cause–Effect Structure

To set a purpose for reading and help the student understand the structure of information in the text, provide her with a study guide that will direct her to the key ideas, most critical details, and/or the organization of the information. [See Strategies: Study Guides.]

Provide the student with a study guide or student workbook that is produced by the publishers of the textbook. This will help the student to recognize and prioritize the information that is to be learned. Prepare exams that focus on the material covered within the study guide.

Text Structures

Make sure that the student is able to understand both narrative and expository text. Provide many opportunities for reading stories and factual accounts.

Narrative
Teach the student how to recognize the sequence of events, ideas, steps, times, and places in stories and literature selections.

Teach the student a simple story grammar to use when reading and discussing stories, such as that all stories have a beginning, middle, and end. As proficiency develops, introduce a more complex story grammar.

Teach the student a simple story grammar that includes these four questions: (a) Who is the story about? (b) What is she trying to do? (c) What happens when she tries to do it? (d) What happens in the end? (Carnine & Kinder, 1985)

Teach the student a story grammar, the underlying structure of stories, so that she has a framework for understanding new stories that she reads. Elements of a story grammar include: setting (time, place, situation), major characters, problem (and problems within the problem), resolution of the problem, and an ending (Thomas, Englert, & Morsink, 1984).

Teach the student a strategy that will familiarize her with the common elements of stories; help her to comprehend, recall, and retell stories; and facilitate her writing of stories. STORE the Story uses a mnemonic that represents setting, trouble, order of events, resolution, and ending (Schlegel & Bos, 1986). [See Strategies: STORE the Story.]

When reading short stories, teach the student to: (a) identify the main problem or conflict, (b) draw inferences from the text about the personalities and motivations of the main characters, (c) identify how the main problem is solved, and (d) determine the theme or what the author was trying to say (Gurney, Gersten, Dimino, & Carnine, 1990).

Teach the student the following seven categories of story elements (Montague & Graves, 1993):
1. Major setting: the main character is introduced.
2. Minor setting: the time and place of the story are described.
3. Initiating event: the atmosphere is changed and the main character responds.
4. Internal response: the characters' thoughts, ideas, emotions, and intentions are noted.
5. Attempt: the main character's goal-related actions are represented.
6. Direct consequence: the attainment of the goal is noted; if the goal is not attained, the changes resulting from the attempt are noted.
7. Reaction: the main character's thoughts and feelings in regard to the outcome are specified, along with the effect of the outcome on the character.

Expository

To help the student increase her understanding of how ideas are organized, separate the paragraphs in a report or article. Have her read the paragraphs, and then reassemble them into a logical sequence.

Encourage the student to discuss with others the materials that she has read. Provide structured activities for these types of discussions within the classroom.

Teach the student that the main idea is the sentence that holds the paragraph together. When the main idea sentence is deleted or covered, the paragraph loses its meaning. The student can check her choice of a main idea by reading the paragraph without that sentence to see if it does, in fact, diminish the paragraph's meaning (Wong, 1985).

Teach the student how to tell the difference among main ideas, supporting details, and tangential information in both fiction and nonfiction material.

Teach the student to recognize different patterns for the organization of information within a paragraph or within a longer selection. Examples include: sequential, comparison/contrast, or cause/effect.

Directly teach the student different ways that information in textbooks can be organized (e.g., listing, sequential, comparison/contrast, hierarchical, main idea and details, description, cause/effect).

Teach the student how to read the introduction of an article or a content area textbook chapter to find the general topic, what the author wants to say about the topic, the key points of the selection, and how the key points will be related to each other and the central idea. Then have her read the conclusion of content area text to find a restatement of the central idea, the key points, and the organizational pattern of the chapter.

Teach the student to categorize information from a reading selection to aid recall. Examples include: Major battles fought in Europe during World War II, or the effects of the lack of light on cave-dwelling animals.

Teach the student to use semantic mapping to clarify the key ideas and supporting details in a selection and the structure by which they are interrelated. After the student reads the selection, she might: (a) brainstorm everything that she can remember, categorize this information, and depict the organization of this information on a semantic map; or (b) use the headings and subheadings in the chapter to create a preliminary map and fill in the critical details from the text.

Directly teach the student to recognize and understand the different structures of expository material. Use graphic organizers to illustrate them. Examples of expository structures include: sequence (main idea and details which must be given in a specific order), enumerative (topic sentence and supportive examples), cause/effect (topic sentence and details telling why), descriptive (topic sentence and description of attributes), problem-solving (statement of problem followed by description, causes, solutions), comparison/

contrast (statements of differences and similarities), and position/opinion (statement of opinion on a specific topic and argument for that position). The figures exemplify the expository text structures of chronology (Figure III.5a), main ideas and details (Figure III.5b), and description (Figure III.5c).

When working with text ordered chronologically/sequentially, such as history or literature, teach the student to place events on a time line. This visual depiction will help her visualize the temporal relationships, as well as any cause/effect relationships.

Help the student increase her understanding of how expository text is structured. The title often describes the subject. The subject is organized into a series of paragraphs. The first paragraph usually explains the subject. Each paragraph has a main idea with supporting details that provides

Figure III.5a　Graphic Organizer for Expository Text Structure: Chronology

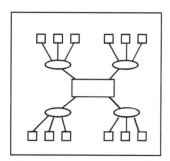

Figure III.5b　Graphic Organizer for Expository Text Structure: Main Ideas and Details

Figure III.5c　Graphic Organizer for Expository Text Structure: Description

important information about the subject. Sometimes the main idea must be inferred. The last paragraph summarizes or explains the author's viewpoints (Greene & Enfield, 1994; Smith, 1999).

HANDWRITING/VISUAL–MOTOR

Tests/Procedures: Handwriting, Handwriting Elements Checklist
Related Tests: Spelling, Writing Samples, Writing Fluency

Handwriting/Visual–Motor
   Further Evaluation
   Accommodations: Visual–Motor
   Accommodations: Handwriting
   Feedback
   Sample Programs/Software
   Readiness
   Materials
   Writing Posture
   Grip
   Practice
   Reversals
   Format
   Spacing
   Slant
   Alignment
   Letter Formation
     Manuscript
     Cursive
   Rate
   Self-Monitoring/Evaluation

Further Evaluation

Refer the student to an occupational therapist to assess and provide therapy for hand strength, flexibility, and dexterity.

Based upon the severity of his fine-motor problems, refer the student to an occupational therapist who is skilled at dealing with visual–motor and handwriting problems.

Refer the student to an educational occupational therapist to evaluate hand skills, muscle tone, and general coordination to help ascertain the reasons for his apparent motor skills deficiencies.

Develop a writing portfolio to document growth in handwriting. Date all handwriting samples so the student can see concrete evidence of progress.

To determine handwriting rate, ask the student to write a memorized sentence over and over as many times as possible within a 2-minute period. Obtain the handwriting rate, the average number of letters written per minute (lpm), by dividing the total number of letters written by the total number of minutes.

Use the Zaner-Bloser scale of handwriting proficiency (Barbe, Lucas, Wasylyk, Hackney, & Braun, 1987), to determine if the student has the expected writing speed for his grade. Have the student copy the following sentence that contains all of the letters of the alphabet: "The quick brown fox jumps over the lazy dog." Have the student practice the sentence one time and then ask him to copy the sentence as quickly as he can in 3 minutes. Count the total number of letters that he has written in the 3-minute period, and then divide this number by 3 to get the total letters per minute (lpm). Compare the student's proficiency level to the following scale:

Grade 1: 25 lpm
Grade 2: 30 lpm
Grade 3: 38 lpm
Grade 4: 45 lpm
Grade 5: 60 lpm
Grade 6: 67 lpm
Grade 7: 74 lpm

To evaluate the formation of specific letters, have the student copy a sentence that contains all of the letters of the alphabet, such as: "The quick brown fox jumps over the lazy dog." Have him write the sentence using uppercase and then lowercase letters.

Identify the specific patterns of illegibility in the student's handwriting and provide corrective work.

Because the student's handwriting is characterized by illegibility, slowness, tension, and fatigue, assess keyboarding skills to plan for further development.

Accommodations: Visual–Motor

Exempt the student (or allow the parents to do so) from assignments requiring visual–motor skills that are not directly related to academic learning (e.g., making thank-you cards, creating a pictorial cover for a book report).

For all assignments requiring visual–motor skills (e.g., map drawing, picture drawing, cutting, constructing), discuss with the student if a lesser standard of neatness, accuracy, and organization will be accepted without penalty or if she should be given an alternative assignment.

Provide the student with a word-processing class until she masters typing and the use of a specific word-processing program.

When tasks require visual–motor coordination (e.g., drawing a picture of an event in a book), substitute a language-based task (e.g., oral explanation, writing on the computer).

Provide the student with support in any classroom activity that involves cutting or motor planning (e.g., pasting pictures on a chart).

Provide ample work space for the student when she is asked to write or solve problems. Recognize that inconsistent letter size and spacing are the result of a neurological difference, rather than a lack of effort.

Accommodations: Handwriting

Shorten writing assignments and encourage the student to supplement his work with illustrations, clip-art, and verbal explanations.

For note-taking activities, provide the student with a partially completed outline so that he can fill in specific information under major headings.

Provide more time for all writing assignments, including note-taking, copying, and taking exams.

Because of a compromised writing rate, the student will complete writing tasks at a slower pace than others. Reduce the amount of required writing so the student can finish tasks within the allotted time frame or allow the student extra time.

Reduce the amount of copying required. For example, in math, provide the student with a worksheet with the problems, rather than asking him to copy the problems from a book.

When students are copying homework assignments from the board, check to see if the student is having difficulty. He is likely to be slow in finishing, have more difficulty than other students with the actual writing, write illegibly, or forget to write some or all of it. Offer to give the student paper with the assignments written on it or write the assignment yourself in his book.

Encourage the student to take a keyboarding course as an elective.

For taking notes, have the student use an AlphaSmart. The AlphaSmart 2000 model has a keyboard with an LCD screen, eight files for organizing different classes or school subjects, and a built-in spell checker. The student can then print out notes at a later time. Available from Intelligent Peripheral Devices, 20380 Town Center Lane, Suite 270, Cupertino, CA 95014, www.alphasmart.com.

To increase the speed and legibility of written work, teach the student how to type and to use a word processor. Allow him to use it for all writing assignments.

Given the student's dysgraphia, ensure that he is allowed to write all standardized essay tests using a word processor. His motoric difficulties will also influence typing speed, so provide extra time on written assignments as needed.

On tests and assignments, do not penalize the student for handwriting and letter formation errors.

(Progressive neurological impairment) The student needs to become proficient in typing and using a word-processing program well before he can no longer use writing implements due to loss of hand strength and fine–motor skills. Provide the student with instruction in keyboarding and using a word-processing program with daily instruction and practice. Along with manual writing in the classroom, the student should have a word processor, such as the Alpha-Smart, and daily support to do some assignments on it.

For students with fine-motor difficulties, typing is easier than writing. Use various technological tools to assist with writing. Text production processes can be supported by using voice recognition software and word prediction programs.

Because of his extreme difficulty with handwriting, have the student dictate responses to a scribe or into a tape recorder, whenever writing is required. Encourage the student to develop handwriting skill, but only in ungraded and untimed situations.

Feedback

Although development of legible handwriting should be one instructional goal, do not respond critically to poor handwriting. Remember that the student's poor handwriting stems from limited motor control, not from a lack of effort.

Reinforce the student for properly formed letters. For example, let the student select a sticker whenever he carefully completes an assignment.

Because writing is difficult for the student, do not use "neatness" as part of the grading criteria. Evaluate written responses without attention to handwriting.

When working with the student on visual–motor activities or handwriting, provide ample positive reinforcement for effort as well as for improvement or quality of the product.

Sample Programs/Software

Use the program *Handwriting Without Tears* (HWT) to help the student improve legibility. Developed by an occupational therapist, this program is designed to reduce student frustration in developing a legible writing style. The program teaches letter formations in groups based on their formation, which facilitates memorization and production of the letter forms and reduces letter reversals. HWT incorporates prewriting skill development for young learners, supports visual–motor development, and incorporates visual–spatial cues. Available from: Jan Z. Olsen, 8802 Quiet Stream Ct., Potomac, MD, 20854, (301) 983-8409, www. hwtears.com.

Use the *D'Nealian Handwriting* program. This program teaches letters in groups based on their formation, facilitating memorization and production, and eliminating letter reversals. The program incorporates auditory, visual, and tactile cues in teaching letter formation. Students begin writing words almost immediately. The letter style provides for a quick and easy transition to cursive. A computer disk allows the teacher to created individualized worksheets. Available from: Scott Foresman-Addison Wesley, 1 Jacob Way, Reading, MA 01867, (800) 552-2259, www.sf.aw.com.

Develop individualized handwriting practice sheets for the student so that he can improve handwriting skill. Computer software programs that can be used to develop personalized practice sheets for manuscript, manu-cursive, or cursive are available from the following sources: Start Write: Handwriting—The Right Way, Idea Maker, Inc., 80 South Redwood Rd., Suite 215, North Salt Lake, UT 84054,

(801) 294-7779, www.startwrite.com and Fonts4Teachers, Downhill Publishing, PO Box 516, Hermosa Beach, CA 90254, www.Fonts4Teachers.com.

Readiness

Because the student has not yet developed the muscular control or visual–motor skill needed for beginning handwriting, focus on readiness skills before beginning specific handwriting instruction.

- To develop hand and finger coordination and strength, provide the student with activities such as consecutively touching each finger to the thumb, opening clothes pins, and squeezing rubber balls.
- Provide the student with lots of opportunities to use writing implements and scissors so that he can plan and execute movements using the small muscles of his hand. If necessary, directly teach the student how to visualize where the pencil, marker, or scissors should be at the end of each stroke or cut.
- Provide the student with many opportunities for use of fine-motor skills in activities consistent with his current ability level. Such activities may include: simple paper folding; cutting paper across a bold line; cutting out large simple shapes with bold borders and tracing them; and copying large, simple shapes on the chalkboard. Use a variety of fun and interesting mediums, such as finger paints, watercolors, and glitter-on-glue designs. Also provide activities where the goal is not recognizable figures, but simply free-form designs.
- Use activities such as tracing using templates, and coloring within simple, bold-line drawings, before asking the student to copy forms and draw pictures.
- When providing practice with copying or tracing shapes, gradually decrease the size of the shapes as the student's performance improves and the tasks become easier. Do not decrease the size of the shapes until he has mastered the current size.

Use finger painting with the student to let him practice forming straight lines, curved lines, and circles. Play around with formation of a variety of shapes. When simple shapes are mastered, begin to teach uppercase letters. After letters are mastered with finger paint, provide practice with a pencil or a felt-tip pen.

Since the student is highly motivated to write, explain to him how spending time doing fine-motor activities will make handwriting easier.

Materials

Provide the student with paper with a dotted middle line to use for handwriting practice and for writing assignments.

The student needs a tactile reinforcer to enhance his awareness of the line on which he is supposed to write. Make a thin line with white glue over the baselines on the paper (if using paper with guidelines). When the glue dries, it will leave a clear, raised line. Raised line paper, in a variety of styles, is also commercially available from: PRO-ED, 8700 Shoal Creek Blvd., Austin, TX 78757-6897, (800) 897-3202, www.proedinc.com.

As a reminder to help the student keep his letters on the line, trace over the baseline with a red felt-tip pen.

To increase the friction of the pen against the paper and fine-motor control, have the student use a black felt-tip pen on lined paper.

Let the student sample a variety of writing implements and select the one that he likes best for handwriting practice.

If assignments must be written in ink, permit the student to use an erasable ballpoint pen.

Writing Posture

Make sure the student's desk and chair fit him properly. Make sure that the chair height allows his feet to be planted firmly on the floor (90° angle at hips and knees) and the desk comes to 2 inches below his elbow when he is sitting on the chair.

Grip

Teach the student how to hold a pencil. Have him hold the pencil between the index finger and thumb, resting the pencil on the middle finger and slanting the pencil at a 45° angle.

Use a special pencil grip to help the student position the hand so that the pencil rests on the first joint of the middle finger and the thumb and index fingers hold the pencil in place. Various grips are available from: Handwriting Without Tears, 8802 Quiet Stream Court, Potomac, MD, 20854, (301) 983-8409, www.hwtears.com. These grips promote more efficient/functional grasps, and provide a visual/tactile cue for correct finger placement.

Provide the student with a variety of pencil grips and have him try them over a period of time to see which feels most comfortable and helps most with fine-motor control. Pencil grips are available at most educational supply stores and office supply stores.

Use modeling clay around the pencil to help the student develop a more relaxed pencil grip.

Place a rubber band right above the shaved area of the pencil to help the student remember where to place his fingers on the pencil.

Teach the student an alternative grip, such as the D'Nealian grip (Thurber, 1988), that does not require much fingertip pressure to hold the writing instrument. Have the student position the pencil between the index and middle fingers with about a 25° slant.

Practice

Help the student become motivated to improve his handwriting. [Discuss practical reasons for improving legibility. Have him participate in meaningful writing activities. Help him understand how his handwriting may affect how someone evaluates his school papers or his job applications.]

Because the student has difficulty with fine-motor control, keep fine-motor activities short and intersperse them with activities that are fun, interesting, or active, such as listening to a story or playing on the playground.

Until legibility improves, include 10 minutes of handwriting practice as part of the student's daily routine.

As the student has a tendency to begin making errors in letter formation after the first few correct productions, provide supervision or frequent monitoring until he has demonstrated correct production of the letter he is learning multiple times consecutively. Immediately, assign practice in using the letter in words, then sentences to facilitate generalization and automaticity.

When the student is concentrating on handwriting instruction, provide exercises that require little thinking so that he can devote his attention to legibility. As his handwriting improves, increase the conceptual level of the task.

Have the student concentrate on neat handwriting only when he is preparing the final drafts of papers.

Because of the severity of the student's fine-motor problems, do not devote much time to handwriting instruction.

Instead, help him improve his keyboarding and word-processing skills.

Reversals

At the student's [age, developmental level], reversals are common. Provide cues to help her remember the orientation of letters and numbers but do not be concerned about a developmental weakness at this time.

Because the student has become anxious about her letter reversals in writing, do not bring attention to them. Treat reversals as spelling errors that will be corrected during the editing stage of writing.

Provide the student with a visual cue for recalling the orientation of frequently confused letters.

- To help the student distinguish between *b* and *d,* draw an association between the letter *b* and the word baseball. Tell the student, "If you want to play baseball, *first* you need a bat." Draw an upright bat and then the loop as a ball. Have her memorize, "*First,* you need a bat." Otherwise, you can only play catch.
- Show the student that the letter *b* can be formed with the fingers of the left hand and *d* with the right. Teach her that since the alphabet is written from left to right and *b* comes first in the alphabet, *b* is the letter made with the left hand. Since the letter *d* comes after *b,* it is made with the right hand. Give her practice in using this trick so that the differentiation becomes automatic.
- Provide the student with cards that include keywords containing frequently reversed letters, such as *dog* for *d,* that she may keep at her desk and refer to when writing.
- Teach the student how to form the letter *b* using a forward circle (clockwise) and the letter *d* using a backward circle (counterclockwise).
- Show the student how to check her papers for *b/d* reversals. By turning the paper to the right, a correctly formed *b* will look like the start of a pair of glasses.
- Help the student recall the orientation of letters by using language clues.
- Remind the student that a lowercase *b* is just a capital *B* that has lost its top.
- Draw a bed made of the letters *b, e,* and *d,* with the *b* as the headboard and the *d* as the footboard. When the student says the word "bed" and either looks at or imagines the picture, she will recall that the first letter has the /b/ sound and the last letter has the /d/ sound. (See Figure III.6.)

Figure III.6 Picture of a Bed to Aid in Recalling the Correct Orientation of b and d

Figure III.7 Clock Face Overlaid with a Number 2 as a Cue to Number Orientation

After identifying the letters that the student reverses, have her practice one letter daily in different applications. For example, have the student trace the letter and write it from memory, write several keywords that contain the letter, and circle as many of the letter that she can find in a magazine or newspaper article. At the end of the week, check to see that the student is able to recognize and write the specific letters that she has been practicing.

Provide the student with practice of letters that she frequently reverses. Present a model of the correctly formed letters, followed by the letter formed several times with a series of dots. Gradually fade out the dots so that the student forms the letter independently.

To reduce reversals in writing, have the student describe aloud the movement pattern she makes when writing a frequently reversed letter. For example, when forming the letter *b,* she may say: "start high, line down, back up and around."

Based upon her frequent letter reversals, teach the student cursive writing. Provide oral cues as you teach letter formation.

To help the student recall the direction of numerals, relate their orientation to an analog clock face. Show her that 2, 3, 4, and 7 always start at 11:00. Figure III.7 shows an example using the number 2.

Teach the student how to position her paper correctly. [For a right-handed writer, the bottom left-hand corner should point at his navel. For a left-handed writer, the paper runs parallel to the writing arm like a railroad track.]

Show the student how to hold her paper steady with the alternate hand when writing.

Provide the student with a clipboard to use in writing activities. This will make writing easier because the paper will remain in a consistent position.

Format

Provide visual cues to help the student remember to use margins and left-to-right progression.
- Glue stars on the paper to show the student where to start and stop writing.
- To help the student learn to use margins, fold the paper along the side to make a crease down the vertical line to remind him where to stop writing.
- To help the student remember to use margins, have him use a ruler and felt-tip pens to "format" a stock of blank composition paper. Use a green pen to draw in the left margin and a red pen to draw the right.
- To help the student remember to observe margins, place a piece of Scotch tape along the right side of the paper as a reminder to go to the next line.
- To help the student visualize the format of a well-organized piece of writing, provide him with some samples of page formats. For example, demonstrate how to format the paper with name, date, title, three indented paragraphs, and equal margins. Show him samples of papers that are neatly formatted. Figure III.8 depicts a format for a simple composition.

Show the student how to use margins and indentations when formatting a paper.

Place a dot about 1 inch in from the margin to remind the student to indent paragraphs. Have him make a dot before starting each new paragraph.

Spacing

Show the student how to reduce the spacing between his words and letters to improve legibility. Explain to him that letters are written next to each other and a small space about the size of his letter *o* should be left between words.

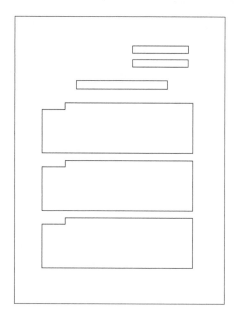

Figure III.8   An Example of a Page Format for Writing a Simple Composition

To provide additional practice with spacing between letters, have the student practice writing words on graph paper, placing one letter in each box. The sets of lines will help him with spacing, size, and alignment.

Slant

Since regularity of slant is affecting legibility, use lightly drawn slant indicators (//////) on the paper to remind the student to form letters consistently.

Show the student how altering his paper position and then maintaining a consistent position can make it easier to produce letters with a consistent slant.

Provide opportunities for the student to evaluate the regularity of slant in his writing. Model forming letters with a consistent slant and provide practice for mastery.

As long as the student's letters are parallel, allow their "slant" to be either straight up and down, to the right, or to the left.

Alignment

Discuss with the student how he can remember the proper heights of the letters by thinking of the following story: All letters start out living on the ground. Some, the short letters, stay there. Other letters stick their heads up into the sky, and still others hang their bottoms into the ocean. If letters who don't belong in the sky stick their heads up there, they'll blow away. If letters who don't belong in the ocean hang their bottoms in the ocean, they'll drown. At first, to reinforce this image, you may color-code the ocean, ground, and sky.

Use pictures to reinforce the height of letters. For example, a giraffe for tall letters, a dog for short letters, and a cat (or mermaid) with her tail hanging down for letters that have a tail below the baseline. Cut out pictures to match against the letters for instructional purposes.

Show the student how to place the base of each letter on the writing line. To encourage him to place each letter on the line, color-code the line, used raised-line paper, or make a raised line with white glue.

Letter Formation

Provide the student with handwriting instruction that includes the following sequence of components: modeling, copying, feedback, correction of errors, and positive reinforcement. Watch the student's letter formation and reteach those formed incorrectly (sequence and direction of strokes). Monitor his practice until you are sure he will continue to write it independently in the correct [manuscript, cursive] style used in the classroom. Provide continued practice, in isolation and incorporated into other tasks, until he has established the pattern in memory (i.e., can write it correctly without thinking).

Have the occupational therapist or learning disabilities specialist work with the student individually, outside of the classroom, to teach proper letter formation within one style of writing, such as D'Nealian. Have him practice tracing large letters and writing from memory to integrate the proper sequence as well as formation of strokes within a letter. To increase interest, provide practice making letters on different surfaces (e.g., shaving cream, white board, wet sand, chocolate pudding on a cookie sheet) and using different writing implements (e.g., finger paints, colored markers, glitter pens). Simplify letter formations as much as possible, such as dropping the tails off D'Nealian lowercase letters.

Show the student a letter on a card and have him trace it in wet sand or cornmeal.

Have the student make raised letters with glue sprinkled with dry colored gelatin, cornmeal, or sand. Have him trace the letter and say either its name or sound. After repeated tracings, have him turn over the card and attempt to write the letter from memory. With guidance, have him check the letter against the model for accuracy.

Demonstrate proper letter formation to the student. Provide systematic practice with one letter before introducing another.

Use the following progression to teach the student letter formation. Have him: (a) trace the letter, (b) complete a dot-to-dot pattern of the letter, (c) copy from an index card, (d) write the letter after seeing it briefly on a flash card, and (e) reproduce the letter from memory.

Show the student a letter on a card and have him trace it with his finger as he says the letter name. Have him then trace the letter with a crayon or felt-tip pen and then with a pencil. When the student is able to trace the letter accurately, have him copy the letter while looking at a model. When he can copy the letter accurately, have him turn over the card and attempt to write it from memory.

To teach letter formation, use the following steps: (a) write the letter on the board, modeling and describing how to form the letter; (b) have the student say aloud how to make component strokes and features and describe each step explicitly; (c) have the student say aloud how to make each letter as he forms the letter on his own paper; (d) have him compare his productions with model letters on letter strips or transparent overlays and describe how they differ and make necessary corrections; and (e) have him select examples of his best work.

Manuscript

Introduce letter shapes to the student with manipulatives, such as plastic letters. Before beginning paper-and-pencil tasks, have the student practice forming letters out of clay.

Roll out a slab of clay and have the student practice forming letters with a pencil or wooden stylus. Initially, provide a light etching for the student to trace more deeply.

Because of the student's fine-motor difficulties, introduce uppercase manuscript letters first because they are easier to form.

To help the student learn the motor pattern associated with each letter, have him use his whole arm, making large letters in the air while naming the letter out loud.

Use a handwriting method that transitions from manipulatives to uppercase letters before introducing lowercase letters. Handwriting without Tears incorporates this process.

When teaching the student how to write letters, first guide his hand to show proper formation. Keep practicing until he feels that he can imitate the pattern independently.

When teaching the student how to form letters, provide a verbal description of the sequence of the strokes. When the student is forming the letters, have him verbalize the sequence of strokes while he writes the letter. Some handwriting programs, such as D'Nealian (Thurber, 1983, 1984), provide specific audio directions.

Teach the student lower and uppercase D'Nealian letters. This method: (a) provides audio descriptions for letter formation, (b) reduces the number of strokes needed to form letters, (c) eliminates component parts, and (d) provides a natural transition into cursive writing.

Verbalize the directions for producing a letter as you trace it on the student's hand, back, arm, or finger. This will help him associate the oral directions with the kinesthetic/tactile formation of letters.

Have the student verbalize his movements as he forms large letters on the chalkboard. For example, to form the letter *n*, he would say: down, up, make a hump, and back down. Initially, encourage the student to make the letter as large as he can.

Use colors, arrows, and dots as cues to help the student remember the proper direction of strokes in letter formation.

To help him recall letter forms, place an alphabet strip at the top of the student's desk and on the inside cover of his notebook.

Permit the student to use manuscript or cursive writing, whichever is the most legible.

Do not require cursive writing, since the student's manuscript is legible and easier for him to write.

Do not require the student to learn cursive writing. Instead, help him focus efforts on improving the legibility of his printing.

Because the student is having extreme difficulty with the rhythmic movements required for cursive writing, allow him to print on all writing assignments.

Cursive

Have the student concentrate on improving the legibility of his cursive writing.

To help the student perceive words as units and reduce the frequency of letter reversals, teach cursive writing.

Teach the student cursive writing. Cursive writing minimizes spatial and directional confusion of letter forms. D'Nealian (Thurber, 1983) and Handwriting Without Tears are two of the easier forms of cursive writing to learn and to use. The student will need specific instruction in the formation as well as the direction of each stroke.

When introducing cursive writing, provide the student with as much practice as he needs with one letter before introducing another. As you teach him to join letters together, use real words to work simultaneously on spelling.

When introducing new letter forms to the student, follow a developmental sequence based on the similarity of motor patterns used to form each letter. For example, introduce formation of the lowercase cursive letter *e* with letters that are formed with a similar stroke, such as *l, f,* and *k*.

Use the following sequence for teaching the student lowercase cursive letters: The *e* family (*e, l, h, f, b, k*); the *c* family (*c, a, d, o, g*); the "hump" family (*n, m, v, y, x*); tails tied in the back (*f, q*); tails tied in the front (*g, p, y,* and *z*); the *r* and *s* (Hanover, 1983).

Check formation and joining of all cursive letters in writing. Provide practice in the correct formation of the letters that cause the student difficulty. Those that require a "bridge" or "handle" (*b, o, v,* and *w*) are often difficult.

Rate

To develop automaticity, fluency, and speed in cursive writing without losing legibility, provide directed and supervised handwriting practice at least once daily, preferably twice. Do not emphasize speed, only legible letter production. Speed will increase with mastery. While the student is concentrating on handwriting practice, provide exercises that require little thinking so that she can devote her attention to accurate and legible production. As she develops mastery, increase the conceptual level of the task. Once a week or so, date and keep a handwriting practice sheet so she can see concrete evidence of her progress.

Request consultation from an occupational therapist with expertise in handwriting skills for ways to make handwriting easier for the student and practice techniques to help automatize the motor act of letter formation.

In order to increase automaticity with letter formation and speed of writing, do daily timed writings. Encourage the student to write as many (letters, words, or sentences) as he can during a 2-minute period. Keep a graph that displays the daily numbers of letters per minute (lpm).

To build writing speed, have the student copy printed material as fast as he can for a 2-minute period. Have him set a goal for the numbers of letters to be produced within a minute.

Discuss with the student how his slow rate of writing is affecting classroom performance. Design a program to increase writing speed.

To build writing speed, have the student do daily timed writings. Count the number of letters or words that he is able to copy from a book in a 1- to 3-minute period. Chart performance daily so that he is able to see his progress.

Encourage the student to increase keyboarding speed. Provide daily practice using software designed to improve typing speed.

To reduce the mechanical challenges of writing, have the student use speech synthesis, word prediction, and word bank software. This will help the student produce a more legible product.

Self-Monitoring/Evaluation

Teach the student how to evaluate his own handwriting in relation to letter formation, spacing, alignment, slant, and line quality.

Teach the student how to use self-corrective feedback by comparing his own productions to correct models to monitor progress and needed improvements.

After handwriting practice, have the student evaluate his own writing. Ask him to circle his best production of the target letter and to explain why it is best. Provide immediate feedback. Have him practice the specific letters that need correction or improvement.

Provide frequent opportunities for the student to evaluate his own handwriting. Conduct brief conferences to help the student set appropriate instructional goals.

BASIC WRITING SKILLS

Tests: Spelling, Spelling of Sounds, Editing, Punctuation and Capitalization
Related Tests: Letter–Word Identification, Word Attack
Clusters: Basic Writing Skills, Phoneme-Grapheme Knowledge, Academic Skills
Related Areas: Phonological Awareness

Basic Writing Skills
    Spelling
        Further Evaluation
        Accommodations
        General Recommendations
        Word Lists
        Spelling Tests
        Rules
        Sample Programs
        Spelling Strategies and Approaches
            General
            Phonology to Phonics
            Orthography
            Morphology
    Punctuation and Capitalization
        Further Evaluation
        Instruction
    Editing
        Further Evaluation
        Feedback
        Assistance
        Strategies
        Checklists

Spelling

Further Evaluation

Conduct a careful error analysis of the student's spelling to aid in selecting an appropriate remedial strategy. Evaluate several writing samples to determine any patterns of spelling errors. Attempt to determine if the student sequences sounds correctly.

Attempt to determine the specific strategies (phonological, orthographic, and morphological) that the student uses when spelling by analyzing errors to determine which are sound-based and which are orthographic/morphological (e.g., letter sequences and word endings).

Informally assess the student's knowledge of phoneme/grapheme relationships by analyzing his attempted spellings on classroom writing assignments.

Use diagnostic teaching to ascertain an effective spelling study strategy for the student.

Determine exactly which words the student knows and does not know how to spell from a high-frequency word list, such as the 300 Instant Words (Fry, 1980). Establish a program to help the student master the spellings of these common words. [See Strategies: Instant Words 300.]

Dictate to the student a 100-word paragraph from a story in his reading series. Determine the percentage of words spelled correctly. Analyze the frequency and types of spelling errors. Save the sample to use to evaluate progress. In several months, dictate the same passage again and analyze the spellings for growth.

Accommodations

Provide the student with a poor spellers' dictionary. This is a book with words listed according to many possible misspellings with the correct spelling after each listing.

Praise the student for systematic and logical attempts to spell words even when the words are spelled incorrectly. For example, if he spells the word "rain" as "rane" that would be considered a good English spelling.

Do not penalize the student for misspellings in written work. Provide assistance as needed with correcting spelling for final drafts.

Do not draw attention to spelling errors until the student is ready to edit the final drafts of papers.

Provide the student with a pocket-sized, electronic spelling checker and teach him how to use it.

Help the student learn to use a spell checker on a word-processing program to edit his work.

As an aid to spelling, have the student use word prediction software that will provide suggestions of words and spelling based upon the first few letters.

Based upon his severe difficulties with spelling, teach the student how to use voice-activated word-processing programs or voice recognition software. The student speaks into a microphone and the text is then translated into a word-processing format on the computer. Although this procedure is not error-free, it will significantly reduce the demands on spelling, allowing the student to concentrate more fully on expressing and organizing his ideas.

General Recommendations

Integrate instruction in spelling and word identification so that the student sees the connections between phonemes and graphemes as well as between graphemes and phonemes.

Until the student's willingness to write improves and his confidence about spelling increases, de-emphasize the need for correct spelling. Immerse the student in frequent, purposeful writing activities. As skill develops, provide formal spelling instruction.

Discuss with the student the difference between "invented" or temporary spelling and conventional spelling. Explain to the student how learning to spell words correctly will help him increase knowledge of English spelling patterns and make it easier for others to read his writing.

Emphasize the functional use of spelling. Demonstrate the importance of correct spelling in practical and social situations.

Have the student spend 10 to 15 minutes daily studying and practicing spelling words. Make sure that the study method he is using is effective.

Use a variety of spelling games and exercises to build interest and to reinforce correct spelling and the acquisition of spelling generalizations.

Reinforce spelling skills within the context of stories. The following game, adapted from Forte and Pangle (1985), may be used to practice words from a spelling list, an individualized spelling list, or a high-frequency list. To begin, write the words to be practiced on index cards. Follow these steps: (a) Pair students together to play the game. Provide students with a pencil and sheet of lined paper. Place the stack of word cards between them. (b) The first student draws a word card and then writes the word in a sentence to begin a story. Before the student writes the spelling word, he looks at the card, turns it over, and attempts to write the word from memory on a separate piece of paper. The spelling is then checked and the procedure continued until the word is written correctly. The student reads his sentence aloud. (c) The second student draws a word card and writes the next sentence in the story, studying and writing his spelling word from memory. The second student then reads the two sentences. (d) The players continue to draw word cards and write and read the sentences until all cards are used and the story is completed. (e) As a final step, the students may want to edit their story, illustrate it, and/or read it aloud to the class.

Give the student practice using his spelling words in written compositions and letters.

Play a board game but use spelling accuracy instead of dice to move ahead. Dictate a word that the student should be able to sound out based on the letter/sound association. If he writes the word with all of the appropriate sounds and no others, he can move ahead. The exception is sight words. Those must be spelled correctly. When the student has a list of five words that he has written, have him read the list of words aloud.

Word Lists

Do not use separate lists for reading and spelling. The student's spelling words should come from within the reading/spelling rules and his reading sight words.

Provide the student with a reduced list of spelling words. Begin with [five] words a week. As performance improves, increase the number of words on the list.

Because of the student's difficulties with spelling, do not use the basal spelling program. Instead, have the student create his own spelling list, selecting words that are frequently misspelled in his writing. Alternatively, you select words that he frequently misspells in writing.

Do not assign the student any spelling words that he cannot read easily, does not know the meaning of, or does not use in his writing.

Present the student with just three or four new spelling words at a time at three intervals throughout the week, rather than 10 or 15 words all at one time. Provide study time when the new words are presented.

Because the student has difficulty with spelling, use a spelling flow list with daily testing rather than a fixed list with weekly testing (McCoy & Prehm, 1987).

Focus on mastery of the spelling of commonly used words and teach only a few spelling words at a time. Have the student identify from three to six words that he uses in his writing, but spells incorrectly. Write the words on a spelling flow list form. Have him study the words and then test him daily on the words. Mark each correctly spelled word with a "+" and each incorrect word with a (−). When a word is spelled correctly 3 days in a row, cross it off the list and add a new word. File all correct words alphabetically into a word bank. One week later, review the words in the bank. If a word is incorrect, add it back to the list. [See Strategies: Flow List-Spelling.]

Select specific spelling words for the student to master, such as words with phonically regular spelling patterns. Remind the student that if he listens closely to the sounds in the words he will spell them correctly.

Have the student select words that are misspelled in his writing for extra credit spelling words.

Have the student develop his own spelling dictionary that includes words he frequently misspells in his writing. Use these words as the basis of his spelling program.

Have the student enter words that he has trouble spelling into a pocket notebook. Encourage him to use his personalized dictionary when he edits his writing.

Select spelling words from Instant Words (Fry, 1980), a list of the 300 most common words used in writing. Have the student keep a chart that displays the words that have been mastered. [See Strategies: Instant Words 300.]

Select words from "Instant Words—The 1000 Most Used Words in the English Language" and "Frequently Misspelled Words" (separate lists for elementary and high school students) from *The Reading Teacher's Book of Lists* as the basis of the student's spelling lists. Pretest before assigning words (Fry, Kress, & Fountoukidis, 2000).

Spelling Tests

When assigning the student a list of words to study, be sure to give him a pretest to identify the words that he knows. Replace these with other words so that he is continually learning new words.

Dictate to the student words with phonically regular spellings, one at a time. Pronounce the sounds of the word separately and slowly in sequence. Remind him to write each letter sound as he hears it.

When dictating spelling words to the student, say each word slowly and pause between syllables. Repeat the word several

times so that the student has time to listen to, write, and check the word. This procedure will help the student learn to sequence sounds.

Provide corrective feedback to the student immediately after completion of a spelling test. Have the student touch each letter of the word with his pencil as you spell the word out loud. Have the student correct each word that has an error.

Use a developmental scale to evaluate spelling tests. Instead of scoring responses as correct or incorrect, assign point values based upon the number of correct letters:

0 points: no correct letters
1 point: one correct letter
2 points: two correct letters
3 points: three correct letters (and so on).

Use a developmental scale to grade spelling tests. A spelling rating scale is more sensitive to measuring growth than use of dichotomous scoring (correct or incorrect). This type of scoring system will help you monitor a student's progress in sequencing sounds correctly. Use the following scale, adapted from Tangel and Blachman (1992) and Kroese, Hynd, Knight, Hiemenz, & Hall, (2001), to evaluate performance on spelling tests.

0 points: random letters
1 point: one phonetically related letter
2 points: correct initial phoneme
3 points: two correct phonemes (does not have to be correct grapheme)
4 points: correct number of syllables represented (only used for multisyllabic words)
5 points: all phonemes in the word are represented
6 points: all phonemes in the word are represented with possible English spellings (e.g., rane for rain)
7 points: correct spelling.

Rules

Use a systematic approach to teach the student common spelling rules that he has not mastered. Keep track of rules that have been introduced and those that are mastered. [See Strategies: Spelling Rules: 43 Consistent Generalizations.]

Teach the student only the most common spelling rules (e.g., when a word ending in *y* is made plural, drop the *y* and add *ies; u* always follows *q;* when adding an ending starting with a vowel, double the final consonant to maintain the short vowel sound). Reinforce generalization to words in classroom writing.

Teach the student that each syllable within a word must contain at least one vowel. Reinforce the student for including a vowel in every syllable.

Do not have the student rote-memorize spelling rules. Instead, build his knowledge of the alphabetic system by teaching him how to segment spoken words into phonemes, how to match up graphemes with the phonemes, and how to spell common English spelling patterns.

Sample Programs

Help the student improve his spelling by using a highly structured program based on spelling rules and structural analysis, such as *Spelling Through Morphographs* (grades 4–adult) and *Spelling Mastery* (grades 1–6) (Dixon & Engelmann, 2000). Available from: SRA/McGraw-Hill, 220 East Danieldale Rd., DeSoto, TX 75115-2490, (888) 772-4543, www.sra4kids.com.

An effective way to teach spelling is to use a spelling program that is integrated with an explicit and systematic reading decoding program. Some programs that are integrated in this manner are Scholastic Phonics and Scholastic Spelling, the Wilson Reading System, Open Court Phonics, and Saxon Phonics: An Incremental Development. [See Strategies: Wilson Reading System.] Available from: Scholastic, 555 Broadway, New York, New York 10012, (800) SCHOLASTIC, www.scholastic.com; Wilson Language Training, 175 W. Main Street, Millbury, MA 01527-1441, (508) 865-5699, www.wilsonlanguage.com; Open Court: SRA/McGraw-Hill, 1221 Farmers Lane, Suite C, Santa Rosa, CA 95405, (888) SRA-4KIDS, www.sra-4kids.com; Saxon Publishers, 2450 John Saxon Blvd., Norman, OK 73071, (800) 284-7019, www.saxonpub.com.

Use high-interest activities to help the student build his spelling skill. One book that contains a wide selection of classroom games and activities to reinforce spelling skill is *Selling Spelling to Kids* (Forte & Pangle, 1985).

Use daily dictations to help the student master the spelling rules that he is learning. An example of a manual that provides dictations that review spelling rules, word building, and word patterns is *The Spell of Words* (Rak, 1984).

Use a systematic program to teach the student morphology within the context of reading decoding and spelling. WORDS (Henry, 1990) is a program designed for students in grades 3–8 and students with learning disabilities. In structured lessons using a discussion format, students learn about letter/sound associations, syllable patterns, the three major language origins in English (i.e., Anglo-Saxon, Latin, and Greek), morpheme patterns (compound words, prefixes, roots, and suffixes), and practice decoding and spelling multisyllabic words taken from math, social studies, and science textbooks. WORDS can be used effectively by teachers, instructional aides, or parents. Available from: PRO-ED, 8700 Shoal Creek Blvd., Austin, TX 78757-6897, (800) 897-3202, www.proedinc.com.

Spelling Strategies and Approaches

General

Discuss with the student the strategy that he is presently using to study his spelling words. Determine whether or not the present technique is effective. If not, teach the student a new strategy to try.

Teach the student how to use a specific spelling study strategy. A variety of techniques can be found in many texts on teaching students with learning difficulties and on many educational websites, such as www.ldonline.org. Make sure that any spelling strategy selected includes multiple writings of the word without copying from a model.

Teach spelling through direct instruction, rather than expecting the student to learn how to spell words through reading or by looking up difficult words in a dictionary. Provide opportunities for the student to practice a spelling strategy independently.

Regardless of the selected spelling strategy, provide opportunities for the student to write the word correctly without a model and then to self-check his accuracy.

Have the student use a spelling method that involves visual, auditory, and kinesthetic modalities and places an emphasis on recall.

Teach the student how to use the Fernald method (Fernald, 1943) for studying spelling words. If the student continues to have difficulties, use a modification that increases tracing, writing from memory, and reinforcement. [See Strategies: Fernald Method for Spelling Instruction, Fernald Method for Reading and Spelling: Modified.]

Teach spelling and reading patterns simultaneously so that they are mutually reinforcing (e.g., teach the CVC pattern and have the student read and spell words that have this pattern).

Provide opportunities for the student to practice his spelling words on the computer.

To reinforce sound segmenting and sequencing, as well as spelling of sight words, incorporate games. The following is an example: The teacher makes word cards that correspond with the phonics skills the students are learning and which include sight words. The students play a board game in which they each write (on paper or a small white board) the word that the teacher dictates. If the student who has the turn spells the word with all of the appropriate sounds and no others, even if misspelled, he may move ahead. If he has spelled it incorrectly, play passes on to the next student. The exception is sight words. Those must be spelled correctly.

Phonology to Phonics

As spelling skill develops, encourage the student to listen to the sounds in words and then try to write the sounds that he hears in order. This will help him increase understanding of the relationships between spoken and written words.

Give the student daily practice in sounding out words for spelling. Using only phonically regular words, dictate words and sentences for him to write. Accept phonically correct misspellings. As he learns spelling patterns, expect him to use them where appropriate. Any parts of the words that have patterns he has not yet learned may be spelled as they sound.

To improve spelling, help the student learn to determine the number of syllables that he hears in a word and then the number of sounds. Have him pronounce the word slowly as he makes a mark or pushes out a tile or marker for each sound. As skill improves, have the student write the sounds that he hears. [See Strategies: Elkonin Procedure: Adapted.]

Have the student study his spelling words using a tape recorder. Use the following steps: (a) have the student look at the word while hearing it pronounced; (b) have the student look at the word while hearing it spelled letter by letter; (c) have the student repeatedly spell the word aloud with the tape until he can write it from memory; and (d) have the student write the word from memory three times, checking for accuracy after each attempt.

Dictate short words with regular sound/symbol correspondence for the student to write. Pronounce words slowly so that the student can hear the separate phonemes. Have him pronounce each sound as he writes the letter or letter combinations.

Dictate simple spelling words to the student that he can rebuild with magnetic plastic letters or letter tiles. Have the student form the word with the letters, cover the word, write the word, and then check the word for accuracy. Have the student repeat the procedure until he can spell the word correctly three consecutive times.

Have the student sort words with common phonic elements and spelling patterns (e.g., beginning or ending letters, double letters, medial vowel sounds, etc.) into groups and tell how each set is similar. Have him then practice spelling the words in categories.

Use color to highlight regular word parts. For example, when helping the student analyze a word, write the phonically regular parts in green and the irregular parts in red.

When studying the spelling patterns of words with the student, use a three-part classification with color coding: (a) predictable (green), (b) unpredictable but frequent (yellow), and (c) unpredictable and rare (red) (Venezky, 1970). Draw a comparison to a stop light. Green words mean "go"; yellow words mean "pause and think"; and red words mean "stop and think."

Help the student learn to generalize the words that he is learning to other words with the same phonemic element. For example, if he is learning to spell the word *night,* introduce and have the student practice other common words that share the *ight* spelling pattern.

Teach the student how to sequence sounds in correct order when spelling. Have him pronounce a word slowly as he writes each sound. Although this strategy will not always produce correct spellings, it will enable the student to use a spell checker or a poor speller's dictionary when he wishes to verify the spelling of a word.

Orthography

Because most of the student's spellings represent phonetically accurate spellings, provide an intervention that will focus upon the visual recall of words.

Because of a weakness in orthographic knowledge, the student has trouble memorizing specific letter sequences in words. Provide extensive review and practice to build orthographic awareness.

Discuss spelling demons with the student. Show him words that contain problem letters, including silent letters and uncommon spelling patterns. Explain to him that special strategies are often needed to memorize these words. [See Strategies: Spelling: General Teaching Principles.]

Have the student practice high-frequency "spelling demons," commonly used words that contain an irregular element. Discuss with the student the part of the word that has the irregular spelling pattern. Then suggest some strategies to help him remember the spelling. Strategies to suggest include: color-coding (marker, highlighter) only the tricky part of the word; creating a visual image that would be a clue to the spelling (e.g., *antelope:* two ants in wedding clothes, carrying suitcases, running away); and pronouncing the word out loud the way it is spelled.

Have the student use the Look-Spell-See-Write strategy to highlight the visual image of a word for spelling. Print the word to be learned on a piece of paper or index card for the student. Make sure that the word is one that the student can read easily. The student then looks at the word while reading it aloud, says each letter, tries to create a mental picture of the word, and writes it three times, each time checking it against the card for accuracy. If he makes an error at any point during the three trials, he goes back to the original study-steps. [See Strategies: Look-Spell-See-Write.]

Use a letter cloze procedure to practice spelling. Give the student an index card that has a word written at the top and then, underneath, the word written several times with different letters deleted. Gradually, reduce the number of letters provided in the targeted word. On the last trial, have the student turn over the card and write the entire word from memory. This method can be adapted by omitting specific word parts, such as vowels, consonants, consonant blends, prefixes, suffixes, or the irregular element of the word.

Teach a spelling study strategy to help the student master words with unusual spellings. One such strategy is Alternate Pronunciation, in which the student pronounces the word he is learning in a way that all letters can be heard (e.g., "lab-o-rat-ory" or "Wed-nes-day") (Ormrod, 1986). The purpose of this spelling strategy is to help the student recall the correct spelling of a word although the letters may not carry their most common sounds or may be silent. Use the following steps: (1) break the word up into parts in such a way that any difficult letters to remember will be pro-

nounced; (2) memorize the alternate pronunciation; (3) write the word according to the alternate pronunciation without looking at the model, (4) check the spelling; (5) if correct, repeat step 3 two to four times more; and (6) if incorrect, devise a new pronunciation that will help the student correct the error.

Use an adaptation of the Simultaneous Oral Spelling method (Bradley, 1981; Gillingham & Stillman, 1973) to have the student practice his spelling words. Use the following steps: (1) the student proposes a word that he wants to learn; (2) the word is written for the student or made with plastic script letters; (3) the student pronounces the word and says the letter names; (4) the student covers the word as soon as he thinks he can write the word from memory, saying the alphabetic name of each letter of the word as it is written; (5) the student says the word and checks to see that it is written correctly; (6) the student repeats Steps 2–5 twice more; and (7) the student practices the word in this way for 6 consecutive days.

To practice spelling with the student, write a word on the chalkboard (a whiteboard does not work for this). Give the student a tiny piece of wet sponge. Have him say the word, then trace over the letters you have written, erasing them with the sponge. Give him the chalk and have him write over the lines he has erased. Give him a card with the word written on it so he can check his spelling each time. When he knows he can write the word without a model, have him do so on the cleaned chalkboard, on a whiteboard, or on paper. Provide frequent, then intermittent reinforcement.

Present a spelling word to the student using a tachistoscope, flash card, or computer. Expose a word for several seconds and then ask the student to write the word from memory. Decrease exposure time and increase the length of the word as skill develops.

As the student is studying irregularly spelled words, have him underline the parts of the word that are not predictable from the pronunciation. Have the student use the following steps for practicing spelling: (a) pronounce the word slowly while looking carefully at each word part, (b) say the letters in sequence, (c) recall how the word looks and say the letters, (d) check recall by looking at the correct spelling, (e) write the word from memory, and (f) compare the written word with the correct spelling. Repeat these steps until the word is spelled correctly (Horn, 1954).

Morphology

Use WORDS (Henry, 1990) to provide an integrated program of reading decoding, spelling, and morphology.

Assign the student one spelling word a week, such as the word *friend*. Teach him how to spell all of the derivations of the word (e.g., *friends, friendship, unfriendly, friendliest*). Discuss how the addition of morphemes alters word meaning. For practice, provide a sentence for each of the derivations, with a blank where the word should be. Based on the context, have the student fill in the blank with the appropriate word.

Teach the student how to spell common prefixes and suffixes and then to add these common affixes to root words. For fun, have the student put together root words and affixes to make meaningful nonsense words. For example, *hypermortation* means the state of excessive death (*hyper*–excessive, *mort*–death, *ation*–state or quality).

To help with spelling, teach the student about inflectional and derivational morphemes. Inflectional morphemes (e.g., past tense or plurals) provide additional information about time or number without changing word meaning or part of speech. Derivational morphemes (e.g., prefixes and suffixes) alter the meaning or the part of speech (e.g., *teach–teacher*). Provide practice with adding both inflections and derivations.

Punctuation and Capitalization

Further Evaluation

Analyze several samples of the student's writing to determine errors in punctuation and capitalization. Make a list of the most common errors to target for instruction.

Provide the student with a short passage that does not contain punctuation. Have him add in the correct punctuation and capitalization. Review any errors and target these rules for instruction.

Analyze several unedited writing samples. Attempt to determine the punctuation and capitalization rules that the student knows and uses, knows but does not always apply, and does not know.

Instruction

Teach the student punctuation and capitalization rules sequentially, one rule at a time, with practice in a variety of situations (e.g., worksheets, finding the use of the rule in reading, writing sentences and paragraphs, and editing his own or a peer's work).

Introduce punctuation and capitalization rules to the student as he needs them for writing. Do not teach a new skill, such as the use of quotation marks, until he is ready to incorporate it into writing.

Make sure that the student masters one punctuation or capitalization rule before introducing another. For example, teach the student how to use a period at the end of a sentence. When this rule is mastered, introduce the use of a question mark. As the student is learning a new rule, incorporate tasks requiring use of previously learned rules.

Choose one error made by the student in writing and discuss it. Illustrate correct usage. Have the student practice using this skill correctly until it is mastered.

Teach the student how to recognize and write complete sentences, including starting each sentence with a capital letter and ending each sentence with the appropriate punctuation mark.

Have the student keep a list of the punctuation and capitalization rules that he is learning on an index card. Have him use the card as a reference when editing.

Editing

Further Evaluation

Further evaluate the student's proofreading skill by having him edit several of his rough drafts. Ask the student to mark and attempt to correct all errors. Perform an error analysis to see the types and percentage of mistakes that he is able to correct.

Provide the student with papers to proofread that list the number of errors to be located on the top of the paper, or in the margin by each line, if necessary. Perform an error analysis to identify how many and what type of errors the student was able to identify and correct.

Use the following pretest (Schumaker, Deshler, Nolan, Clark, Alley, & Warner, 1981) to assess editing skills. Follow these steps: (1) Give the student a list of expository writing topics from which to choose. Ask him to write at least six lines. Allow at least 20 minutes. (2) Ask the student to read the composition, circle the errors, and correct them. (3) Ask the student to rewrite the composition, corrected. (4) Repeat Steps 1–3 in the next session with a new topic. (5) If the student has identified less than 80% of the errors, teach the Error Monitoring Strategy. [See Strategies: Error Monitoring Strategy.]

Feedback

Use a consistent set of proofreading symbols when editing the student's work. Make sure that he understands the meaning of all the symbols.

When editing the student's paper, do not mark every error. Instead, select a few errors for him to correct.

After the student has proofread a paper, praise him for both identifying and correcting any errors.

Discuss with the student the types of errors that he makes frequently in writing, such as omitting word endings. Demonstrate and provide practice in checking word endings carefully when proofreading papers.

Assistance

Make sure that the student receives additional help from someone (teacher, parent, peer) in proofreading papers before he turns in a final draft. Consider setting up a buddy system for peer editing in class.

Prior to having the student edit a paper, underline all misspelled words so that he can correct the spellings.

Have the student proofread his paper for spelling errors, underlining all words he thinks may be spelled incorrectly. Teach him how to use a spell checker to make the needed changes.

Provide opportunities for the student to help younger students proofread and correct their papers. In addition to building his self-esteem, he will gain additional practice with editing.

Strategies

Teach the student a specific strategy for proofreading and editing his papers. One strategy is the Error Monitoring strategy which uses the acronym COPS (*C*apitalization, *O*verall appearance including sentence structure, *P*unctuation, and *S*pelling) (Schumaker et al., 1981). [See Strategies: Error Monitoring Strategy.]

Teach the student a modification of the Error Monitoring strategy (Schumaker et al., 1981), using the mnemonic SH! COPS! [*S*pelling, *H*andwriting, *C*apitalization, *O*verall appearance, including visual format (e.g., margins, indentations, poor erasures), *P*unctuation, and *S*entences (structure, sentence boundaries)]. [See Strategies: Error Monitoring Strategy.]

To avoid the problem of seeing what one expects to see or meant to write when proofreading for spelling, have the student start from the bottom of his paper and check the spelling of the words while "reading" backwards. The student may find it easier to spot the errors when the words are out of a meaningful context.

Encourage the student to read his paper aloud when proofreading. This will help him detect usage errors.

Have the student read his rough draft into a tape recorder. Have him play back the tape and listen to the material before rewriting sections.

Checklists

Give the student a checklist to use when he proofreads his paper. Make sure that the student understands how to use all of the rules on the list. Alternatively, make a list of the student's most frequent writing errors and have him use this list when he proofreads his papers.

Proofread the student's paper before he corrects it. Count, but do not mark, his errors in spelling, punctuation, capitalization, and usage. Give the student a card on which you have written the number of each type of error. Challenge him to find all of the mistakes (or a percentage) of the mistakes you found. He could correct each type of error in a different color and, if he does not know how to correct it, underline the error to show that he found it. Give credit for the percentage of errors found, regardless of correction, as well as credit for corrections.

Instead of marking the specific errors in the student's paper, put a check in the margin by any line that contains an error. If there are two mistakes in the line, place two checks. Have the student try to find and correct the errors in each line.

WRITTEN EXPRESSION

Tests: Writing Fluency and Writing Samples
Related Procedures: Writing Evaluation Scale
Related Tests: Spelling, Spelling of Sounds, Editing, Punctuation and Capitalization
Cluster: Written Expression
Related Areas: Oral Language, Reading Comprehension

Written Expression
 Further Evaluation
 General Recommendations
 Accommodations
  Computers/Typing
 Motivation
 Journal
 Grammar/Syntax/Morphology
 Vocabulary
 Prewriting
  Topic Selection
  Background Knowledge
  Semantic Maps/Graphic Organizers
 Story Structure
 Paragraphs
 Report Writing
 Compositions/Essays
 Revising
  Feedback
  Revising versus Editing
  Rewriting
 Outlining
 Note-Taking

Further Evaluation

Conduct a more intensive evaluation of the student's writing skill. Collect and evaluate at least four samples of classroom writing. Determine appropriate goals and objectives for enhancing writing performance.

Use the Writing Evaluation Scale to evaluate the student's writing skill in more depth (WJ III Tests of Achievement: Examiner's Manual). Have the student keep a writing folder that contains samples of her work. Conduct frequent evaluations to assess progress and establish new objectives.

Before developing a specific instructional program for writing, conduct a careful and complete assessment of writing ability. The purpose of this assessment is to identify the specific factors that are affecting writing performance and to determine the student's strengths and weaknesses.

Have the student develop a writing portfolio or a showcase of her best work. Use the writings in the portfolio to measure and monitor her growth over the school year or, if possible, several years. Have the student be responsible for selecting the pieces to go in the portfolio. Meet with the student to discuss growth, strengths, and goals.

Analyze several samples of the student's spontaneous writing. Particularly assess her [specify skills that appeared weak or skills in which the student's competence was not clear].

Compare the student's apparent competence in a piece of writing that she has handwritten to writing she has done on the computer to determine whether or not writing improves when the motoric demands are reduced.

Evaluate various examples of the student's written expression according to the Six Traits + One of the Writing Rubric. This approach to evaluating students' writing categorizes the many components of written expression into six traits, plus one. These are ideas (content), organization, voice (the writer's personality or adopted persona coming out through the writing), word choice (rich and precise vocabulary usage), sentence fluency (rhythm and flow of the language), and conventions (basic writing skills)—plus presentation (the "look" of the finished piece). Each trait is evaluated on a 6-point scale according to specified criteria. Use of the Six Traits teaches student writers to analyze their own writing and that of others in a workshop atmosphere while maintaining a clear focus on what they need to do to improve. Training and materials are available from: Northwest Regional Educational Laboratory, 101 SW Main, Suite 500, Portland, OR 97204, (503)-275-9500, www.nwrel.org/sixtraits/sixtraits.html.

General Recommendations

Analyses of the student's oral language and writing abilities document her difficulties expressing her ideas in both speaking and writing. Consult with the speech/language pathologist (SLP) for specific recommendations. The SLP and the general education teacher(s) should have ongoing communication in regard to procedures for reinforcing newly developing language skills in the classroom. The SLP can integrate vocabulary and concepts introduced in the classroom into therapy sessions. The selected procedures and techniques would be designed to enhance both oral and written formulation.

Provide daily guided discussions that will help the student increase her awareness of the strategies that she uses when writing. Use brief teacher–student conferences to help the student understand how she approaches writing tasks and then how she can use alternative strategies.

Use the instructional/evaluation approach advocated by the Northwest Regional Education Laboratory (NWREL) to help the student become aware of what good writing looks and sounds like. NWREL provides training in teaching the Six Traits of Writing + One. Northwest Regional Educational Laboratory, 101 SW Main, Suite 500, Portland, OR 97204, (503) 275-9500, www.nwrel.org/sixtraits/sixtraits.html.

Use the writing process approach with the student for writing assignments (Flower & Hayes, 1980; Graves, 1983). Within this approach, help her to understand the purpose of each stage of the writing process. Explain that writing is a recursive activity that usually involves multiple drafts and revisions, prior to publishing. [See Strategies: Writing as a Process.]

Consider using a direct instruction approach, such as Expressive Writing to teaching basic written expression skills. Within the framework of a highly structured, teacher-directed process, students learn to integrate sentence writing, paragraph construction, and editing skills. Level 2 includes more sophisticated and conversational writing with complex sentences and more advanced punctuation. Expressive Writing is intended for grades 4 and above. Available from: SRA/McGraw-Hill, 220 East Danieldale Rd., DeSoto, TX 75115-2490, (888) 772-4543, www.sra4kids.com.

Make sure that the student spends at least 30 minutes daily on writing activities.

Before writing, have the student consider the purpose, her point of view, and the audience who will be reading her paper.

Teach the student the differences between narrative and expository styles. As a basis for discussion, give the student a paragraph written in narrative style and another written in expository style, but with similar information. Discuss with the student the stylistic differences.

Accommodations

Adapt all writing assignments to match the student's present level of oral language skill. Adjust the grading criteria accordingly.

Provide the student with [sufficient time to complete, extended time] on all writing assignments.

Reduce the amount of writing that the student is expected to complete, both in the classroom and for homework.

When an assignment requires a large amount of writing, allow the student to dictate answers to an instructional/par-ent aide or, at home, to her parent. Depending on the situation, a peer could take dictation, if it would not cause the student embarrassment.

Allow the student to take [written exams, content area exams] orally. If necessary, she can go to a quiet room and dictate her answers to an aide or into a tape recorder for grading at a later time.

On some assignments, provide a scribe or typist for the student. Have her dictate her thoughts to another who will write them or type them on a word processor. Have her then read the printed copy and [discuss, make] revisions.

Help the student become an advocate for herself by discussing the possible accommodations that she may require on written language assignments to be successful in both school and vocational settings.

Computers/Typing

Provide specific instruction in how to use technology as a substitute for writing. For example, teach the student how to use a tape recorder to complete different types of assignments. Provide practice in taking oral examinations and preparing and giving oral reports, essays, and short stories.

Provide the student with instruction and daily practice in using a word-processing program until she is proficient at typing and using the program functions that she will need most often (e.g., spell checker, moving and revising text, saving, setting up files, printing).

Because the student has such difficulty expressing her ideas in writing, provide her with and teach her how to use voice recognition software. For written assignments, she can dictate her first draft, and revise it using the keyboard. [For students with severe reading difficulties, incorporate into this recommendation a screenreader and voice synthesizer to read what has been translated into print on the screen to facilitate revisions.]

Allow and encourage the student to write her letters and school assignments on a word processor.

Provide the student with good quality computer programs that are designed for creating and publishing stories.

Provide the student with a portable word-processing device, such as the AlphaSmart, or a laptop computer to use in her classes for recording notes, taking exams, and writing papers. Available from: AlphaSmart, 20400 Stevens Creek

Blvd., Suite 300, Cupertino, CA 95014, (888) 274-0680, www.alphasmart.com.

Motivation

Develop an incentive program to motivate the student to increase the quantity of her writing. Establish a set of rewards and set criteria for the amount of writing expected for each assignment. You may want to develop specific criteria for a minimum level of quality and discuss these with the student. Gradually fade the reinforcement as the student's competence, and hopefully, her motivation increase. [See Strategies: Token Economy Systems, Mystery Motivator, Positive Reinforcers.]

As a service to younger students, have the student write short summaries of lower-level books and attach them to the inside jacket covers. The younger students can then read the summaries to see if they are interested in the books.

Based upon her interest and talent, provide the student with activities that include opportunity for both artistic and written expression. For example, have her write and illustrate a story or book, or a brief description of a picture she has drawn. Provide opportunities for her to share her written work with others.

Have the student work in cooperative learning groups to write stories. Ensure that she participates in the writing activity by assigning her a specific role, for example, during the prewriting activity, recording the ideas generated by the students in her group.

Have the student engage in meaningful writing activities that emphasize the communicative and interactive nature of writing, such as writing letters or postcards to friends.

Identify the types of writing that the student may be required to perform in vocational and other settings in the future, such as applications for jobs, college, or a bank loan. Assign a variety of relevant writing assignments.

Journal

Have the student keep a daily journal. Allow her to select her own topics and provide topics if she cannot generate any ideas. Set time limits or designate the quantity of writing (e.g., two sentences, a page). When reviewing the journal, write specific and legitimate positive comments about the content.

Encourage the student to keep a journal or diary on all trips and during summer vacation.

Start the student writing a daily journal. Invite her to ask questions of you in her journal, if she has specific topics to which she would like a response. When she turns in the journal, ask her to turn down the corner or bookmark any pages to which she would like a response.

Select an interesting journal entry the student has written and ask her if she would be willing to read it to her classmates. Secure her prior agreement in private.

Have the student select entries from her journal that she could use to develop into stories.

Grammar/Syntax/Morphology

Do not require the student to participate in grammar exercises, such as memorizing and identifying the parts of speech. Instead, concentrate on methods that will improve the quality of her writing, such as providing models, direct feedback, or sentence-combining exercises.

Provide practice writing paragraphs in different verb tenses: present, past, and future. During the editing stage, help the student check to ensure that she maintains consistency with verb tense.

Because the student's visual–spatial abilities are so much stronger than her language abilities, consider using Manipulative Visual Language (MVL) to teach grammar and sentence structure. Developed by teachers of the deaf, MVL is a hands-on program that provides students, deaf or hearing, with a visual, manipulable model of English grammatical elements. The program utilizes two-and three-dimensional forms—variously shaped, colored, and coded—to represent different parts of speech. Concepts of nouns, verbs, verb tenses, prepositions, and other parts of speech are introduced through the use of these shapes. Once the concepts are understood, English sentence structure is introduced, and ultimately, literature is incorporated. MVL is recommended for elementary students to establish an early, strong foundation in English grammar and is also appropriate for use with older students still struggling with these skills. MVL can also be used to teach the syntax of American Sign Language. Instructional materials and training in using the system are available from: Jimmy Challis Gore, (520) 744-2168 (TTY or use Relay Service), e-mail: JGore3312@aol.com or from Robert Gillies, 23

Bridge Street, Yarmouth, ME 04096, (207) 846-8937, e-mail: caitnor@mac.com.

Because the student needs to develop correct sentence structure "from the ground up," use a strategy that does not look like it was designed for young children. The *Sentence Writing Strategy* (Schumaker & Sheldon, 1985) assists the student in learning to write grammatically correct sentences of increasing complexity and the related grammatical skills. This strategy, appropriate for middle school–age and above, starts with simple sentences and gradually adds sentence elements until the student is writing compound–complex sentences. Instruction can be done individually or in a group. Available from: the University of Kansas Center for Research on Learning, Lawrence, KS 66045, (785) 864-4780, www.ku-crl.org.

Use sentence starters to give the student practice in different ways to expand sentences (e.g., "That is the man who _____" or "The movie got exciting when _____"). Provide practice with a variety of sentence patterns. Use this activity to complement teaching specific sentence types.

Use sentence-combining exercises to help the student write longer, more complex sentences. Present the student with a set of simple sentences to combine. Begin teaching sentence combining with just two sentences and gradually progress to more complex transformations. Specific patterns may be taught, for example, by asking the student to use the word "who" to combine the sentences. Use this technique several times a week for 10 to 15 minutes.

Teach the student to combine sentences into more complex structures by using transitional words (e.g., continuation, sequence, conclusion, causal, conditional, comparison/contrast). Directly teach transitional words to introduce subordinate clauses and to clarify the meaningful relationship among sentences. A good list of transitional words is "Signal Words," in *The Reading Teacher's Book of Lists* (4th ed.) (Fry, Kress, & Fountoukidis, 2000).

Use graphic organizers to demonstrate the relationships among prefixes, suffixes, and root words. Write the root word in the middle of the map with prefixes and suffixes extending from the side. After completing the map, have the student attempt to write all of the words that can be formed through the addition of various affixes. You can put the root word in the middle so that the student can read across from prefix to root word to suffix, creating various derivations of the word. Or, as an alternative, a prefix or suffix can be placed in the center of the map.

Ask the student to expand orally on a sentence that she has written, adding descriptive words and phrases, additional details or more explicit adjectives. Have the student then rewrite her sentence incorporating her new expansions.

Use a slotting technique (Poteet, 1987) to help the student expand sentences. Take a story that the student has written and put in blanks where the sentence can be expanded. Have her add adjectives, adverbs, phrases, and/or clauses to make the writing more mature.

Vocabulary

Help the student increase her vocabulary by having her work with a peer or a small cooperative learning group to generate as many words as they can, related to a current topic of study, and explain how the words are related to the topic. As a second step, to clarify the conceptual or grammatical relationships among the words, have the group design a semantic map to connect them.

Because her oral vocabulary is more mature and extensive than the words she uses in writing, encourage the student to use more of her oral vocabulary in writing by assuring her that she will not be penalized for spelling mistakes, and praising her when she uses more precise vocabulary.

Help the student eliminate overused or redundant words in her writing, such as *good* and *nice.* List the target words at the top of the paper before she begins writing a story to remind her that she must think of substitutes for these words. You may also generate with the student, or a group of students, words and phrases with strong, definite meanings, categorizing them by part of speech. Then, when stuck on an overused word, the student would check the adjective list for an alternative word with a more precise meaning, such as *virtuous.*

Use a five-step strategy (Harris & Graham, 1985) to help the student expand vocabulary in her compositions. Target a certain type of word, such as nouns, adjectives, or verbs. To begin, select a picture and present the following five steps on a chart:

1. Ask the student to look at the picture and write down a list of the type of targeted word, such as adjectives or describing words.
2. Have the student think of a story that will use the selected words.
3. Ask the student to write a story that makes sense and uses as many of the words as possible.

4. Have the student read the story and ask these questions: Did I write a good story? Did I use the selected words?

5. Have the student edit the story and try to use more of the type of words selected.

Prior to writing, have the student set a goal for the number of describing words to be used in the story. After completion of the story, have the student count the number of targeted words used and chart this number on a graph. Students can also do this type of activity in pairs or small cooperative groups. The additional dialogue with peers can help students expand their own word knowledge.

To build awareness of the importance and power of word choice for a writer, read short stories and essays to the student that are rich in the use of words that evoke clear ideas, vivid images, and emotions in the reader. Brainstorm and list the words and phrases that she found particularly effective or which were used in an unexpected way. Define words that are new to her. For comparison, read stories and essays in which the word choices are mundane and brainstorm and list the words that are overused. Compare strong and weak word choices, their effect in communicating the intent of the writer, and the response they evoke in the reader. Have the student start a list of "strong words" to refer to when she writes, and to add to it whenever she finds a word or phrase that she particularly likes.

Use a synonym cloze procedure to help the student increase her writing vocabulary. After a draft of a story is complete, underline words that could be more descriptive. Delete each word to be changed and then write it under the line. Have the student, or help her, determine other words that would make the story more interesting.

Teach the student how to use a thesaurus to locate more precise vocabulary for her papers and themes.

Have the student review her paper and underline all words for which she would like a synonym. Teach her how to use a thesaurus or a pocket-sized, computerized spelling checker with a thesaurus to find and select alternative words.

To increase vocabulary, demonstrate how words can be grouped into a superordinate system. As an example, the superordinate structure of *animals* would include *cows, horses,* and *zebras.* Or, students can practice grouping words into semantic categories, such as things to eat or drink.

Prewriting

Help the student increase her sensitivity to and interest in the purpose and communicative functions of writing. When making assignments, provide clear, concise reasons as to why a given writing activity is important so that the student views writing as a meaningful activity.

In the prewriting phase, provide the student with a variety of activities that will involve her in thinking about and discussing the topic in detail.

Just prior to teaching language and thinking skills in writing, such as using descriptive language, organizing information, or using introductions or conclusions, read with the student and have the student read many examples of writing that illustrate both good and poor use of the skill. Ensure that any reading she does is at her independent reading level.

For prewriting, encourage the student to jot down all of the ideas and details she can think of about the chosen topic without regard to spelling or handwriting. Then, help her put together all of those that are related in some way and throw out those that do not seem to fit. Guide her in using this rough organization to develop a simple outline, a chart, or a graphic organizer. Putting each detail on a piece of paper from a sticky pad will allow her to try out and change arrangements easily.

Use a colorful action picture to elicit oral details from the student or choose music for her to listen to. Have her record her thoughts about the picture or the music, then create a composition or story based on her thoughts and the notes.

Have the student generate and then answer a series of questions that she will be able to use to organize the writing assignment. Have the student locate and learn the answers to the questions before writing.

Prior to writing, brainstorm with the student any words or phrases that she thinks she may want to use in her paper. List all the words on the board or a piece of paper. As skill improves, you may designate specific categories of words, such as action or descriptive words.

Topic Selection

For writing assignments, let the student select topics that are familiar and interesting to her. You might also allow her to discuss a chosen topic with several peers to get their information, record it, and incorporate it into her writing.

To improve motivation and provide support for skills and idea generation, have the student pair up with a peer and select a topic to write about in which they are both interested. Have them work together to collect data and organize the information that they acquire about the topic.

Help the student learn to narrow her topic so that she can "write more about less" to draw the reader in. Help her to select a topic, event, or experience, discuss it, and choose only one part to write about. Have her look at that one piece as though through a microscope—all aspects are magnified and more are evident. Read to her or have her read many pieces of writing in various genres that illustrate this approach and, for contrast, many that just say a little about a lot of things. Discuss the differences and what makes one more interesting than the other. For example, if her topic is her trip to Disneyland, rather than just listing all of the rides she went on, she could select one, Space Mountain, and describe it as a total experience—the boredom of waiting in line, her anticipation as she moved closer to the launch pad, the feeling and sights of "entering space," the motion of the car and her fear or exhilaration, and so on.

Have the student keep a writer's notebook where she can record any ideas that she may have for future writing topics.

Background Knowledge

Prior to presenting writing assignments, make sure that the student has the background knowledge required to write about the topic. If not, provide the necessary instruction.

Before writing an assignment, encourage the student to answer several questions, such as: What do I know about the topic? What experiences have I had with it? What do I want to say about this topic? Have her record her ideas on paper before she starts to write.

Have the student write about an interesting picture. Before she begins, have the student describe all the things she sees, relate the picture to her own experiences, and tell what seeing the picture makes her think about. List her responses on a paper. When the student cannot think of anything else, help her to categorize the ideas. Once the student's ideas are organized, have her write a story about the picture.

To help the student and her classmates generate ideas for writing, use a prereading technique. For example, to generate ideas for a position paper, you might use the Anticipation Guide. Write a few statements about a controversial topic; have the students consider, individually, if they agree or disagree (and to what extent); and conduct a discussion. Before starting, tell the students to write down their thoughts as they consider the statements and to continue to write down ideas, theirs or others', throughout the discussion. Stop the discussion while the students are still quite involved and much information has been shared. Direct the students to write a statement of their opinion about the topic and use their notes to provide well-considered reasons. [See Strategies: Anticipation Guide.]

Semantic Maps/Graphic Organizers

When teaching the student text structure strategies, such as semantic mapping, provide sufficient practice with the technique for her to feel competent before assigning writing. For example, draw semantic maps on the board when lecturing or have students work in groups to create maps based on the lecture.

Work on prewriting strategies using graphic organizers. Teach the student how to organize her ideas and details into topic areas or generate subtopics related to the main topic and add details. Help her to recognize information that does not belong to any of the subtopics and to omit it.

The ability to visualize a variety of text structures will help the student to organize her ideas in any writing assignment for which she can envision a structure. As you teach different types of text structures, match each to a graphic organizer and explain how they are related. For example, as depicted in Figure III.9a, contrast may be depicted as a three-column table. If contrasting frogs and toads, the first column would have a list of the traits to be considered (e.g., skin); the second column, a description of a toad's skin

Trait	Toad	Frog

Contrast

Figure III.9a   Graphic Organizer for Expository Text Structure: Contrast

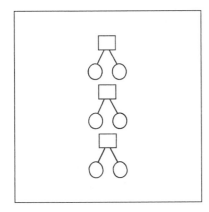

Figure III.9b Graphic Organizer for Expository Text Structure: Compare–Contrast

(bumpy); and the third column, a description of a frog's skin (smooth). If one wanted to compare and contrast, emphasizing that for each difference there is a similarity, she might use a graphic organizer similar to the one illustrated in Figure III.9b. There, a trait to be considered would be in each box and the difference between the toad and frog in the circles right below. For example, both have skin but the toad's is bumpy and the frog's is smooth.

When using a structured overview or semantic map, after the map has been created, have the student verbalize the relationships among the ideas and details before writing.

In the instructional program, place an emphasis on prewriting activities, such as brainstorming followed by semantic mapping, so that the student's ideas will be organized prior to beginning a writing assignment.

Teach the student to use graphic organizers, semantic mapping, and/or structured overviews to organize her ideas and clarify the relationships among her ideas prior to writing.

Use graphic organizers to help the student improve her vocabulary. For example, have her place a word in the center of the map and then generate synonyms or antonyms for the word in the outside circles. Or have her write a word in the center of the map, and then generate all the derivations of that word (e.g., *friend—friends, friendly, friendship, unfriendly, befriended,* etc.)

Use an adaptation of the KWLS (i.e., what I *Know,* what I *Want* to know, what I've *Learned,* what I *Still* need to learn) strategy that adds mapping and summarization (Carr & Ogle, 1987). To add the mapping component, have the student categorize the information listed under L. The topic forms the center of the map. For example, if the student were learning about the planet Saturn, she would write "Saturn" in the center of the map. Lines are then added to show the relationship between the main topic and the facts that have been learned. For the summarization component, the student can use the map that depicts the organization of the information. The center of the map becomes the title of the essay and each category is used as the topic for a new paragraph. The student may then add supporting details to expand the paragraph or explain the topic further.

Use maps, webs, or frames to assist with writing. Initially, teacher modeling and cueing are necessary until the student learns to use the strategy independently. Begin mapping with the brainstorming of ideas. The purpose of brainstorming is to increase background knowledge and help the student retrieve prior knowledge. During the brainstorming or free association stage, place emphasis upon divergent thinking and the rapid production of ideas. Write one- or two-word cues to represent concepts or ideas as they occur. When the student is not able to generate any more ideas, return to each cue, elaborating upon the idea within. Color-code ideas that can be grouped or categorized together, and/or write the ideas on a graphic organizer developed for the text structure (e.g., compare/contrast). Develop paragraphs for each category, expanding upon the ideas already formulated.

As the student becomes more familiar and confident with the use of cognitive mapping and graphic organizers, help her learn to categorize the ideas as they are generated. Once she can construct her own organizers, she will be likely to benefit from explaining her organization and ideas to others.

Story Structure

Provide a variety of oral language activities that will help the student develop the characters, plot, and outcome of her stories prior to writing. Use organizational strategies that emphasize oral development of the story prior to writing.

Teach the student simple questions to use when writing stories. For example, write on an index card: Add additional questions as the student's skill increases.

Who?
Did what?
And so?

Teach the student a simple story grammar to help her organize her stories. Teach her that all stories have a beginning (setting, main characters), a middle (a problem), and an ending (resolution to the problem). Have her complete a story chart prior to writing.

Teach the student to use a story structure to identify the elements most stories share. Having a framework into which to set the elements of a story as she hears or reads them, makes it easier to store and retrieve the content. Knowing the structure and the critical elements also facilitates the generation of ideas for stories, their internal organization, and elaboration of the elements. STORE the Story (Schlegel & Bos, 1986) is a relatively simple strategy for teaching story structure; the acronym stands for *S*etting, *T*rouble, *O*rder of events, *R*esolution, *E*nding. The teacher explains and guides discussion of the elements, demonstrates and models the strategy, and provides guided practice and independent practice. For writing, this strategy is easily integrated with the Writing Process Approach. [See Strategies: STORE the Story, Writing as a Process.]

Give the student practice with story structure using a macro-cloze technique. Delete specific information from the story, such as the setting, description of the main characters, or the ending. Help the student reconstruct the missing story part. Have her check to make sure that the missing story part is consistent with the other information in the story.

Use the mnemonic strategy, W-W-W, What = 2, How = 2 (Graham & Harris, 1989) as a prewriting strategy for narrative text. Prior to writing, have the student answer the following questions:
1. Who is the main character? Who else is in the story?
2. When does the story take place?
3. Where does the story take place?
4. What does the main character do?
5. What happens when he or she tries to do it?
6. How does the story end?
7. How does the main character feel?

Paragraphs

Teach the student that a paragraph expresses one main idea and the topic sentence introduces the idea. Details are provided to support the main idea, and final sentences are used to summarize the main idea or provide a transition to a related idea.

Review with the student the major purposes of a topic sentence: introduction of the type of paragraph or essay that is being written and clear specification of what the paragraph or essay will contain. Have the student develop a variety of topic sentences to introduce different types of paragraphs or essays. The student would benefit from activities, such as those provided in *Writing Skills 2* (King, 1993) and *Writing Skills for the Adolescent* (King, 1985).

Teach the student how to write short paragraphs that follow a narrative sequence. Give her a series of pictures that illustrate a sequence of events and have the student write a sentence about each card. Show her how to use sequence words, such as *first, then, next,* and *finally.*

Teach the student different cohesive ties that can be used in reports organized by chronology (e.g., *first, then, later, finally*). Show her how to write a transition sentence between paragraphs.

Teach the student how to write a variety of formula paragraphs including: expository or enumerative, contains the main idea and supporting details; sequential, describes an event in chronological order or in a number of ideas; and compare/contrast, describes similarities and differences between two things. Provide sufficient opportunities to master one type of paragraph before introducing another.

Teach the student how to organize expository paragraphs by using statement-pie (Hanau, 1974). The statement is the main idea of the paragraph and the "pie" includes the *p*roof, *i*nformation, and *e*xamples. Model how to write a main idea statement and then develop several related supporting sentences (the *pies*). Provide systematic practice with multiple examples until the student is ready to use this format to write paragraphs.

Use the strategy presented by Sparks (1982) to help the student develop expository writing skills. Teach the student that main ideas are the first power (1st power), and that the details are second powers (2nd power). Additional details are placed under the second power sentences (3rd power). The student can indent details under higher powers to illustrate subordination.

1st Power: Main idea statements
   2nd Power: Major details or subtopics
      3rd Power: Minor details.

Begin by teaching a three-sentence paragraph and progress to seven-paragraph reports.

Report Writing

To facilitate writing in a more literate style, teach the student to differentiate between oral and literate language. After reading many examples of oral and literate language and discussing the differences, a sequence of activities requiring increasing skill may include: (a) dividing pairs of sentences into categories of style (oral and literate), (b) labeling a given sentence as oral or literate in style, (c) rewriting sentences from oral to literate style based on previous practice in complex sentence structures and cohesive devices, and (d) rewriting passages in a variety of styles (e.g., letter to a close friend, news article) (Wallach & Miller, 1988). As much as possible, include practice using the student's language.

Provide the student with and teach her how to use educational software designed to facilitate research, the use of reference materials, organization of reports, and access to reliable information on the Internet. An example is the *Microsoft Encarta Reference Suite,* which includes an encyclopedia, a globe, reference materials, and a research organizer. The encyclopedia articles have associated pictures, sounds, videos, and links to related websites. The globe allows the user to magnify any area, see different types of geographical boundaries (e.g., political, climate), mark geographic points, and filter out cities by population levels. Reference materials include a thesaurus, a dictionary, famous quotations, a style guide, a dictionary of computer terminology, and an almanac. The Research Organizer facilitates the organization of electronic "notecards," proper citation of resources, incorporation of graphics, and putting the report together. An option enables the user to have the built-in speech synthesizer read the text aloud: Available from: Microsoft Corporation, One Microsoft Way, Redmond, WA 98052-6399, (888) 218-5617, (U.S., Canada) or (716) 871-2915, www.encarta.msn.com/products/info/refsuite.asp.

The World Wide Web is an extraordinary resource for information of virtually every type and the student needs to become a proficient and savvy user of this tool. Teach the student how to use the Internet as one of her sources of information for reports, how to judge the veracity of the information she finds, how to cite Internet references, and how to copy text and pictures (with proper citations). Incorporate lessons on Internet safety covering a wide range of risks (e.g., believing whatever she comes across, chatting with Internet acquaintances, providing personal information, giving out a credit card number on an unsecured site).

Help the student learn to differentiate major topics from minor details as she is collecting and organizing facts for a report. Have her list all the information that she thinks is important (or provide her with a list of information) and then help her think of ways to categorize the major and minor points.

Teach the student how to use a variety of reference books both to obtain information and to find out where to go to obtain information. Also, teach her how to use the public library computers to search for and put a hold on all types of library materials and how to use her home computer to log on to the library's system so that she can "search the stacks" from home.

Teach the student how to organize index cards to gather information for writing a report. Teach her to write keywords for the major topics in the upper right-hand corner, and how to sort and organize the cards prior to beginning the first draft.

Compositions/Essays

Help the student improve expository writing skill by providing assignments that will help her develop confidence as a writer. Provide intensive feedback and several opportunities for revision.

Teach the student a simple and systematic method of building and organizing compositions by using Kerrigan's Integrated Method of Teaching Composition (Kerrigan, 1979). [See Strategies: Kerrigan's Integrated Method of Teaching Composition.]

As the student's discussion of topics in her expository writing appears disjointed, focus writing instruction on clear introductions, transition sentences, and conclusions.

Revising

Feedback
Help the student improve her attitude toward writing by increasing the amount of attention and positive feedback she receives on drafts of assignments.

In helping the student with her writing, always stress meaning first; then teach any skills that she needs in the context of meaning.

Make sure that the student receives specific and legitimate feedback on her writing assignments so that each one she hands in is an opportunity to find out what she did well and what she needs to work on. Try to avoid handing back a paper with a grade and no comments, as the effort that writing exacts from the student requires acknowledgement.

Have a brief revision conference with the student before she attempts to revise a paper. Discuss specific ideas and suggestions that will help the student improve the paper. If needed, write these down so that the student can refer back to this information when revising her work.

Revising versus Editing

When revising her work, encourage the student to focus upon the meaning of the text, not on the detection and correction of errors in basic writing skills.

Help the student understand that when she is revising and organizing her ideas, she should not simultaneously attempt to edit for spelling, punctuation, and sentence structure. Although some revision strategies provide an editing step, the focus of revision activities is upon organization, clarification, and elaboration of content. Errors of mechanics can be corrected on the final draft.

Rewriting

Teach the student how to use the word processor to revise her work. Due to her difficulty with [visual–motor skills, sentence formulation, organization of ideas, frustration tolerance, sustained attention], she will be unwilling and, probably, unable to handle paper-pencil revisions without a high level of anxiety and a feeling of being confronted with an overwhelming and undoable task. Since revision on a computer is so much easier, she is more likely to put more effort into it.

Always have the student write her first drafts on every other line on the paper so that when she revises, she has room to rewrite and make marks indicating relocation and deletion of material.

Help the student learn how to revise her papers. Make a short list of questions to provide a purpose for reading through her draft and to help her focus on specific aspects of writing. Questions might include: Are there any sentences that are difficult to understand? Where can I make this sound better with more details? Do I have any words that are boring? Have the student focus upon content and communication, not upon mechanics such as spelling or capitalization errors.

Show the student various editing techniques that are used for revision, such as cutting up parts of a paper with scissors to reorganize sections or circling blocks of text and drawing an arrow to show where they should be inserted.

Show the student how to use a cut-and-paste revision process. Have her locate the best passages in her writing and cut them out. Have her arrange them in different orders. Have her reassemble the pieces in the best order and then write the necessary transitions.

Have the student work with a peer who will help her organize and revise her papers.

Outlining

Teach the student how to take notes in an abbreviated outline format when reading and then to use the notes for studying for tests.

After the student has taken notes during a lecture, have her rewrite the notes in a more organized format, such as an outline or graphic organizer.

Teach the student how to create an outline of a chapter using several steps. Have the student: (a) skim the chapter, (b) write down headings and words in bolded type, (c) take notes on important points, (d) draw lines and arrows from additional notes to the headings and bolded type, (e) put Roman numerals by the headings and bolded type, (f) put capital letters next to additional notes, (g) review items, (h) cross out unnecessary information, (i) renumber and reletter, and (j) create an outline.

Note-Taking

Teach the student a strategy for active listening and note-taking, such as listening for keywords, specific verbal cues that indicate sequence (e.g., *first, then*), a change of ideas (e.g., *but, nevertheless*), and importance (e.g., *more important, listen to this*). Taped lectures from the student's classes are effective practice materials. Provide explicit systematic instruction. Include guided, then independent practice. Monitor the quality of the student's notes.

Teach the student how to organize her class notes into a semantic map or graphic organizer.

Help the student to increase her awareness of the key points of a lecture. Listen to a lecture with her while you both take notes. After the lecture, encourage her to develop and organize her notes. Then, compare and contrast both sets of notes by looking for and discussing the key points you both wrote down and important information that she has omitted.

Teach the student how to take notes from a textbook using the two-column note-taking strategy. The student folds her paper in half length-wise to make two columns. She titles the first column, "Names, Numbers, Terms, Topics," and the second column, "Definitions, Explanations, Information." As she reads, the student writes any important proper names, numbers or dates, and new vocabulary in the first column, one item to a row. As textbooks are divided into sections by subtopic, after reading each section, the student is to take the subheading, make it into a question, and write it in the first column. If it is already a question, she creates a topic statement out of it instead. For each item she writes in the first column, she writes associated information in the second: for names—the importance of the person or place; for numbers or dates—what they refer to; for terms—the definition; and for the question—a brief answer, which should state the main idea. Have the student skip a line or two, and go on to reading and taking notes in the same fashion on the next subsection. To study, the student folds the paper so that only the first column is visible, uses a card to cover all but the first item, reads the first item, and recalls the related information from the second column. She continues, each time covering the items below the one on which she is focused. When she completes the first column, she turns the paper over so that only the second column is visible and repeats the procedure, this time mentally reviewing the related information in the first column (Rooney, 2001).

MATHEMATICS

Tests: Calculation, Math Fluency, Applied Problems, Quantitative Concepts
Clusters: Basic Math Skills, Math Reasoning
Related Clusters: Fluid Reasoning

Mathematics
    Further Evaluation
    Resources and Programs
    Instructional Approaches
    Technology in Mathematics Instruction
    Terminology
    Accommodations and Modifications
        General
        Homework
        Visual Format

Basic Math Skills
    General
    Self-Monitoring
    Noting Process Signs
Number Sense, Numeration, Place Value
    Concept Development
    Classification: Creating Sets
    From Sets to Numbers
    Counting and One-to-One Correspondence
    Using Numerals
    Number Patterns and Ordinal Numbers
    Recognizing and Writing Numbers
    Place Value
Basic Facts
    General
    Using Strategic Organization to Memorize Facts
    Other Memorization Methods
    Motivation
    Fluency
Algorithms
    Teaching Concepts with Manipulatives
    Teaching Algorithms
Application
    Word Problems: Primary School and Above
Higher-Level Mathematics
    Problem-Solving Instruction
    Problem-Solving Strategies
Computer Software
Measurement & Estimation
    General
    Time
    Money
    Calendar
Life Skills Mathematics

Further Evaluation

Use a standardized diagnostic math test to assess in depth the student's understanding and mastery of math concepts and skills.

Use diagnostic teaching to evaluate the student's mastery of the prerequisite skills necessary to learn the skills currently presented in the curriculum. Plan a program to teach the necessary skills.

Informally assess the student's understanding of the Piagetian concepts that are critical foundations of mathematical concepts and relations: object permanence, conservation of matter, reversibility, seriation, one-to-one correspondence, and classification.

Evaluate the student's understanding of the concepts underlying addition and subtraction in a variety of situations and with a variety of materials. Make sure she understands that numbers represent the quantity of any type of entity within a set, that addition is the combining of sets, and that zero also represents a set that has nothing in it (the null set). Before the student will be able to make sense of the value of money and equivalencies in money (e.g., the number of nickels in a quarter and the reason) and measurement (e.g., time: seconds, minutes, hours, days, weeks, months, years), she must understand sets and how they can be combined.

Before teaching math facts, give the student [a timed test to see what facts she can complete correctly within 2 minutes, an oral test using flashcards to see which facts she can answer within 3 seconds]. Use the results to develop a program for fact learning. Have the student chart her progress as she masters new facts. [See Strategies: Addition Fact Chart, Multiplication Fact Chart.]

To assess the student's conceptual understanding of basic computation, give her a worksheet with a few addition, subtraction, multiplication, and division problems. Have her work out the problems using concrete objects, such as beans or marbles. Ask her to think out loud as she sets up and works the problems.

When it is unclear why the student is missing specific computational problems, conduct an oral interview with her. Ask her to talk through the steps as she solves the problems.

When the student makes errors on word problems or computations, analyze the errors to find the component skills or prerequisite information she is missing and/or the rules she misunderstands. Without intervention, the student will continue to make the same types of errors.

Use task analysis to help the student master computational algorithms. Identify the algorithm to be learned. List and arrange all the prerequisite skills and the steps needed to perform the algorithm into a logical teaching sequence. Determine exactly which steps the student cannot perform through informal testing and then teach the steps in sequence.

Assess the student's comprehension of algebra word problems by providing problems accompanied by tables representing the variables involved in each problem. Ask the student to fill in the values of the variables based on the information given in the problem. The student's ability to associate the variables and values indicates her comprehension of the problem.

Resources and Programs

For a valuable resource for teaching mathematics from readiness skills through algebra and geometry, especially in developing conceptual foundations, the teacher is referred to *Today's Mathematics: 10th Edition: Part 1: Concepts and Classroom Methods* (Heddens & Speer, 2000a), and *Part 2: Activities and Instructional Ideas* (Heddens & Speer, 2000b). These companion books provide comprehensive and detailed information regarding national math standards, a graded scope and sequence for curriculum expectations, developmental levels within strands of mathematics, explanation of and instructional approaches in developing mathematical concepts and procedures from readiness through beginning high school math, and integration of technology, as well as specific activities and suggestions for classroom instruction.

For specific suggestions for teaching mathematics to students with special needs, the teacher is referred to *Teaching Mathematics to Students With Learning Disabilities, Fourth Edition* by Carol A. Thornton and Nancy S. Bley (PRO-ED, 2000) and *Windows of Opportunity: Mathematics for Students With Special Needs* edited by Carol A. Thornton and Nancy S. Bley (National Council of Teachers of Mathematics, 1994).

The following websites are excellent for checking out the Principles and Standards for School Mathematics (National Council of Teachers of Mathematics, 2000) for instructional principles, ideas, and examples (National Council of Teachers of Mathematics, 2000): www.nctm.org and www.illuminations.nctm.org.

A valuable on-line resource for teachers in mathematics education, from research summaries to lesson plans, is AskERIC. The website is http://ericir.syr.edu/.

One source of videodisks that provide visual representations of math concepts and practice in problem-solving, and that may be used to supplement the existing math program, is Optical Data School Media, a subsidiary of SRA/McGraw-Hill, 220 East Danieldale Road, DeSoto, TX 75115-2490, (888) 772-4543, SRA: www.sra4kids.com, Optical Data Corporation: www.opticaldata.com.

As the student is having difficulty memorizing math facts and the steps of the basic operations, supplement her current math program with a multisensory program, such as Touch Math. Touch Math is available from: Innovative Learning Concepts, 6760 Corporate Drive, Colorado Springs, Colorado, 80919-1999, (888) TOUCHMATH (or 868-2462), www.touchmath.com. [See Strategies: Touch Math.]

As the student needs a highly structured, multisensory, incremental approach to learning the language of math for comprehension of word problems, use the Touch Math Story Problems Kit. This program provides for reinforcement of the concepts of each operation, instruction in the related language, and application to practical problems. Touch Math is available from: Innovative Learning Concepts, 6760 Corporate Drive, Colorado Springs, Colorado, 80919-1999, (888) TOUCHMATH (or 868-2462), www. touchmath.com. [See Strategies: Touch Math.]

Use a highly structured, sequential program for teaching basic math skills that includes teacher-directed instruction, hands-on activities for concept formation, continuous review and integration of previously learned skills, and ongoing evaluation. Many excellent programs are currently available.

Instructional Approaches

For effective math instruction, develop a program for the student with the following components: a high level of academic response rate, mastery of the skill/procedure, corrective feedback, behavioral reinforcement, modeling, imitation, prompting/cueing, and guided and independent practice (Bryant & Dix, 1998).

Before you introduce new skills, ensure that the student has full mastery of the prerequisite skills. In addition to teaching the new skill/concept and its relationship to known skills/concepts directly, engage the student in activities that guide her to build a bridge between the new and the known.

Teach all new concepts and extensions of known concepts first with concrete materials, making sure that the student has a chance to experiment with the materials and understands the new concept before moving to the next level of abstractness. For example, when teaching simple fractions, use a variety of materials (e.g., tiles, pizza, Cuisenaire rods) to represent the whole and the fraction. Make sure she un-

derstands or learns the related terminology (e.g., *numerator, denominator*) by having her talk about what she is doing with the materials. Provide plenty of practice in manipulating the materials to solve problems. Then present similar types of problems using pictures and requiring her to draw pictures to represent the problems posed. When she has mastered this step, associate these materials with numbers. If necessary, tallies may be used as a level between pictures and symbols. The last step is to use numbers alone to represent new concepts. [Adapted from Principles and Standards for School Mathematics, National Council of Teachers of Mathematics, 2000.]

The student is unlikely to learn new concepts, extensions of concepts, or procedures at the symbolic level until she has experienced it multiple times with concrete objects or, at least, pictures.

Because the student appears to have a strength in inductive reasoning, use a guided discovery approach to teaching new concepts and extensions of new concepts. Guide the student to solve problems and then to generate a rule based on her observations. Then have her test the rule in further examples.

Because the student appears to be stronger in deductive reasoning than in inductive reasoning, use a rule-based approach in teaching new concepts and extensions of new concepts. Explain the concept/extension to the student, demonstrate how it works, state the rule governing it, ask questions to assess understanding, and have the student practice its application.

Teach all new math concepts and processes through direct instruction, not a discovery method. The student will benefit most from instruction that is structured and step-by-step, and rules that are clearly stated.

Despite the student's difficulty memorizing math facts and learning the algorithms, do not hold her back from learning more advanced mathematics concepts and skills. With her excellent reasoning and problem-solving skills, she will be able to acquire higher-level mathematical concepts. Keep in mind that basic math skills are just a small part of mathematics.

The student has difficulty understanding procedures in math activities and does not intuit mathematical relationships. Spell them out explicitly and repeatedly, gradually asking her what she is to do next until she can verbalize the procedure. Then have her practice the procedure until it is memorized.

When introducing new concepts and skills, use modeling and demonstrations. Have the student watch you perform the task as you talk yourself through it and then have her perform the task as you talk it through.

Supplement the student's basal math textbook with additional examples and practice exercises. Allow the student to move on in the text only when she has demonstrated mastery of the current skills.

As the student requires more vivid models as well as supplementary explanation and practice of the concepts and procedures taught in the classroom, investigate computer software that will be compatible with the current curriculum. Use of videodisk programs has been shown to be effective in improving ability to solve algebra word problems for college students with learning disabilities. Important components of the software program were elaborate visual representations and program adherence to principles of effective instruction (i.e., review of previously learned material, remedial instruction as needed, direct instruction format including modeling and guided practice, response feedback, and ongoing assessment).

Immerse the student in an integrative, collaborative problem-solving approach to mathematics. She will reflect on and integrate new concepts and procedures more thoroughly when collaborating on problems with a partner or small group. Before using this approach, however, the student and her partners will need training in how to work as a group so that all students fully participate.

Avoid involving the student in competitive games and drills. Instead, emphasize cooperation among students in mathematics activities.

The student will require systematic reinforcement of acquired math knowledge, concepts, procedures, and strategies. Before providing reinforcement, however, make sure that the student has developed a solid understanding of the targeted topic.

The student requires frequent review and reinforcement of concepts and procedures learned. Begin each lesson with a review of the mathematical skills and concepts covered the previous day and, additionally, provide weekly and monthly reviews.

Frequent communication between the student's math teacher and educational therapist or tutor would be particularly helpful. As much as possible, the educational therapist should teach new concepts and procedures before they are presented in the classroom. Provide the educational therapist with a copy of the class math book to prepare lessons.

Technology in Mathematics Instruction

Integrate the use of calculators into the instructional program to give the student practice in reasoning through problems involving arithmetic that would be too complex or time consuming to do with paper and pencil. Using numbers taken from facts about the world adds a motivational and real-life component. Examples include finding the number of seconds it would take to go to the moon if you travel at x seconds per mile, or the difference between the number of steps it would take you to walk around the earth at the equator compared to crossing the poles.

Teach the student how to use a calculator and its various processes.

Give assignments incorporating the use of a calculator to guide the student in exploration of mathematical concepts. For example, the student may be assigned to find the square root of a number by successive approximations based on the square roots (moving into decimal places) of the numbers above and below it.

Incorporate use of the calculator into assignments that will reinforce the student's use of math processes. For example, to reinforce rounding numbers, the teacher may provide a list of numbers and their sum *if* they had been rounded. The student's task is to round the numbers, consecutively entering them into the calculator using addition. If she rounded correctly, the cumulative sum will match the teacher's.

Use hypermedia when creating or selecting computer programs for the student to use. Hypermedia incorporates links within a program to other types of media or instructional components such as pop-up menus, definitions, sounds, explanatory or descriptive visual images, and the choice of doing remedial, on-level, or advanced problems. One such program is HyperStudio, available from: Roger Wagner Publishing, 1050 Pioneer Way, Suite P, El Cajon, CA 92020, (800) 497-3778.

Incorporate the use of digital cameras to provide a practical understanding of how math is applied. For example, students can take pictures of geometric shapes or angles that they see in their environment and incorporate them into creation of a computer program or report on architecture.

Based on her interest and high aptitude in mathematics, teach the student how to use computers as mathematical tools. For example, teach the student how to use electronic spreadsheets, numerical analysis packages, and/or computer graphics.

Have the student use computer programs that build problem-solving skills in an applied context.

Terminology

While teaching classification skills, use each attribute that the student identifies as a springboard for teaching quantitative terms such as *big, small, narrow, wide, tall, short, thick,* and *thin*. Also teach the terms for comparative concepts such as *big, bigger,* and *biggest*.

Encourage the student to notice and compare attributes of objects in her environment. Ask questions such as, "Which is the tallest piece of equipment on the playground? Which is the shortest?"

Use manipulatives to teach the student and provide practice with the concepts of *bigger than, equal to,* and *smaller than*.

Teach the student that several terms can indicate the same process. For example, *adding, plus,* and *all* can refer to the operation of addition. Other related terms would include *sum, total, more than,* and *greater than*.

As you and the student move into working with numbers and number sentences, introduce all new terminology using concrete objects and manipulatives. Make sure that she uses the terminology expressively. For example, you might ask, "How does the number of boys in the class compare with the number of girls?" so that she will answer, "There are more boys than girls." You can then ask her to express the same concept in other ways, such as "There are fewer girls than boys" and "There are not as many girls as boys."

Teach the student to be flexible with the math vocabulary used to express number relationships. Teach it in concert with the skill or operation for which it is used. For example, teach *minus, subtract from, less than, how much more,* and *what is the difference* when using manipulatives to teach the concept of subtraction.

When the student is familiar with the concept of joining two sets to create a third set, introduce the vocabulary of addi-

tion (e.g., "Four stars added to three stars is the same as seven stars"). When the student is familiar with verbalizing the operation of removing one subset from a set, teach her the terms for subtraction.

Have the student develop a written file of math vocabulary. On a 3×5 index card, have her write the word, the definition, and make a picture to illustrate meaning. Have the student file the words alphabetically. Provide opportunities for review.

Provide the student with clues that will help her to recall specific math terminology. For example, to differentiate between the terms *numerator* and *denominator,* she can remember that the denominator is down.

Using the student's math textbook or a list of math terminology, identify and then teach specific math vocabulary that she needs to know. Provide review, as needed.

Accommodations and Modifications

General

Be aware of the linguistic complexity of all word problems that the student is expected to answer. Rephrase or rewrite the problems as needed.

Due to the student's difficulty with language comprehension, when asking her to solve story problems that are presented orally, use concrete objects or visual diagrams to illustrate the problems.

Include the following [accommodations, modifications] in the student's individualized educational plan (IEP). [Include any appropriate accommodations and modifications.]

Accommodations and instructional procedures for the student should focus on relieving the burden on working memory by automatizing lower-level skills [and alleviating anxiety].

When working with the student on math problems, spread the practice time over short periods. Have the student complete six to eight problems rather than an entire page.

Before calling on the student in math class, make sure that she will be able to respond successfully to the question. If necessary, provide or review a question with her before class begins.

Do not have the student do timed tests, written or oral. Provide her as much time as she needs to complete a test. If extra time cannot be made available, reduce the number of problems she is expected to do.

Avoid the use of timed math tests with the student. Do not emphasize speed or rapid recall of math facts, but instead accuracy, persistence, and understanding.

When grading the student's papers, give her partial credit for parts of problems solved correctly. For example, give some credit for correct reasoning even if the computation is incorrect.

Do not penalize the student for errors on math worksheets. (If necessary, simply record the number of problems correct.) Instead, attempt to determine the reason for the errors and then provide appropriate instruction.

Because the student has not developed automatic recall of math facts and algorithms, provide her with a calculator to use in all activities focused on mathematical reasoning. This will allow her to concentrate on the reasoning process without diverting attention to the more mechanical aspects of the task.

After completing problems, have the student use a calculator to check calculations and then rework any incorrect solutions.

Due to the student's specific disabilities in [mathematical procedures, retrieval of math facts] allow her to use a calculator on any standardized group-administered achievement test.

Do not have the student copy problems from books or the board as she is likely to either copy incorrectly or have difficulty reading her own handwriting. It would be far better to write the problems using a colored marker on grid worksheets, one digit to a square. Have the student work the problems in pencil to provide for good contrast between the problem and her work. [See Strategies: Math Computation Forms.]

Before the student works a page of math computation problems, have her highlight the process signs. Help her decide on colors for each of the four signs and consistently highlight each in its own color.

Keep a supply of the student's special graph paper [3/8" squares with bold lines dividing the paper into quadrangles] in the classroom. This paper will help her line up her numbers correctly and keep her work on different problems widely separated from each other and easier to read. [See Strategies: Math Computation Forms.]

Remind the student to use scratch paper (the grid paper), even when the problems being done would normally not require it. Encourage her not to save space on her paper. She should leave plenty of space around any problem on which she is working.

Ensure that all assigned word problems are presented at the student's independent reading level.

Since the student has difficulty reading the story problems in her math textbook, develop taped readings that she can listen to as she reads along in the book. Teach her how to recognize the end of a problem and use the pause button to stop the tape.

To discourage the student's tendency to attempt all word problems mentally, regardless of the complexity, always make sure that she has scratch paper to use, even when the problems being done would normally not require it.

Homework

Before the student takes home math assignments, make sure that she understands the directions and process for solving the problems. Work the first few problems with the student at school.

Reduce the student's homework and classroom assignments so that she can complete her work in the same amount of time as do other students. Start by cutting her work by [50%] but in such a way that she attempts each type of assigned problem (e.g., all the odd numbers).

To encourage flexibility, when assigning practice on a new operation (e.g., multiplication of fractions), incorporate problems involving previously presented operations (e.g., addition and subtraction of fractions) throughout the assignment.

Make sure that the student has one or two review problems on each homework assignment.

Place a limit on the amount of time the student is to work on math homework. Grade her work on a percentage basis, using the number of items she has completed as the total number of possible points.

Request that the student's parents put a check mark next to those items completed with their assistance. In this way, the teacher can monitor the types of problems with which the student is having difficulty.

Provide homework assignments that will help the student improve her skill in using a calculator. For example, when she is assigned 10 problems, have her solve the problems and then use a calculator to check for accuracy.

Visual Format

Accommodations and instructional procedures for the student should focus on alleviating the visual confusion caused by her handwriting and enhancing orderliness on the worksheet.

The student perceives math worksheets and textbook pages as visually confusing. Focus accommodations and instructional procedures for the student on enhancing the visual structure and appearance of orderliness on the page.

Make sure worksheets are visually clear with only a few problems on each page.

To enhance visual clarity and prevent the student from becoming confused, the student requires a strategy. Use the following suggestions:

a) Use special computation paper with squares sufficiently large for one digit per box and with bold lines segmenting the paper into compartments to separate problem solutions. [See Strategies: Math Computation Forms.]

b) Fold the paper in fourths or sixths to have "frames" to outline each problem before copying computation problems onto a sheet of paper. Copy/write only one problem in each frame.

c) Use graph paper with squares of [one] centimeter to keep rows and columns of numbers in order. Show the student how to write only one digit in each square.

d) Turn the paper sideways and use the lines to delineate columns.

To help avoid errors, teach the student to use verbal mediation to aid in accurate copying of problems from text to paper. Teach the student to double up long numbers, rather than say every digit. For example, 5234 + 874 would be said as "fifty-two thirty-four" (write) "plus eight seventy-four" (write).

Do not require the student to copy math problems from a chalkboard or math textbook. Instead, provide all practice problems clearly printed and aligned on worksheets.

Teach the student to circle the item number so that she does not confuse it with digits in the problem.

Use a 5" × 8" index card, a folded piece of paper, sticky pad, or thin mousepad to mask the half of the page on which the student is not working. A mousepad will stay in place until moved deliberately.

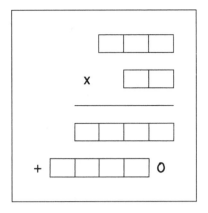

Figure III.10   Format for Multiplication Algorithm

Teach the student to use a template with a cut-out square made of poster paper. The square should be large enough so that it will expose one computation problem and block out distracting visual information on the page.

Provide worksheets with formats already written for the type or types of problems the student is expected to work. Figure III.10 is an example of a multiplication format.

Basic Math Skills

General

Immediately after the student has demonstrated what appears to be true understanding of a process or concept, ask her if she would be willing to teach it to someone else. Teaching forces one to clarify one's own understanding of a process. Make sure the teacher is available to help if she needs help.

Teach the student how to use a number line, counting forward and backward, to solve addition and subtraction problems.

Concentrate on teaching the student the supporting concepts and algorithms of addition and subtraction. She is not ready for multiplication until she has mastered these operations.

When reviewing the four basic operations, explain and demonstrate to the student the relationship between addition and multiplication and between subtraction and division. For example, demonstrate how $8 \div 2 = 4$ means that 2 can be subtracted from 8 exactly 4 times.

When reviewing the four basic operations, explain and demonstrate to the student the relationship between addition and subtraction and between multiplication and division. Create examples to demonstrate these principles, such as if $2 + 2 = 4$, then $4 - 2 = 2$, or if $4 \times 3 = 12$, then $12 \div 3 = 4$.

Review the concept of zero as used within all the basic mathematical operations. For example, teach the student why one cannot subtract a number from zero (unless using negative numbers), but can add any number to zero. Teach the student why any number multiplied by zero is zero and that zero then becomes the place holder in the answer.

When reviewing computations with the student, place the emphasis on how she solved the problems, rather than on the accuracy of the solutions.

Teach the student how to interpret problems set up horizontally as well as problems set up vertically.

Self-Monitoring

Help the student develop self-monitoring skills by estimating answers to math calculations. Have her estimate the answer and write it by the side of a problem before she calculates the answer.

After the student has learned to estimate, teach her to ask herself, "Does this answer make sense?" after solving a problem.

Teach the student to talk through the steps of computation problems as she attempts to solve them.

Have the student work with a peer or a small group to check each other's answers on an assignment. When they find an answer that is dissimilar, have them review the problem step-by-step to discover the error and then correct the missed problem.

Teach the student how to check her answers to problems with all types of operations by using the reverse operation. As examples, teach the student to check her division answers by multiplying the divisor by the quotient to get the dividend; check for ratio equality by using cross multiplication of terms.

Noting Process Signs

Before the student works a page of math computation problems, have her color-code the operation signs. Help her decide on a color for each of the four signs and consistently highlight or trace each in its own color.

Enlarge the operation signs on math worksheets, draw them with heavy lines, or highlight them so that the student is more likely to notice them.

Teach the student to look at and say the process sign aloud, before she begins to solve a problem.

To reduce the student's tendency to overlook operations signs, in all assignments, include a mixture of problems rather than just one operation, such as a page of addition problems.

Number Sense, Numeration, Place Value

Concept Development

Use concrete objects and manipulatives to teach all new concepts and to extend previously presented concepts. Then, if the student is ready, provide similar work with pictures, then tallies, and finally numbers.

Provide the student with discovery-oriented activities that will promote understanding of mathematical relationships including object permanence, conservation of matter, reversibility, seriation, one-to-one correspondence, and classification.

Provide the student with mathematical puzzles and patterns that will allow her to discover varying relationships based on quantity, order, size, and shape. Integrate instruction in the related language, such as comparative (e.g., *big, bigger, biggest*), shape names, and ordinal numbers.

Classification: Creating Sets

Introduce the concept of sets and develop classification ability by teaching the student to sort objects, first using familiar objects, then pictures.

To teach the concept of sets and develop classification ability, provide sorting activities such as the following. Using many physical objects, ask the student to sort through them to find all those that match an object shown by the teacher (e.g., "all the balls," "like this," "on the toy shelves"). Subsequently, have the student find sets of orally described objects (e.g., "all the balls in the room," "all the tools that may be used for drawing"). Gradually work with more abstract objects and attributes of objects such as pictures, then shapes.

The student is having difficulty with number concepts because she has not yet developed flexibility in working with classification and multiple attributes of sets (groups). Provide guided exploration in classification activities. Once she understands the concept of grouping according to similarities and differences, extend the concept to flexibility of classification (i.e., grouping objects/pictures based on similarity of attribute, then regrouping the same objects/pictures based on a different attribute).

Use activities to develop the concept of classification that are based on finding similarities and differences between and among objects. Examples include:

- Using a variety of objects, such as small toy chairs, cars, people, and food, place one of each kind in each of two or more shoeboxes. Have the student sort through the pile of objects provided to find similar items and sort them into the appropriate boxes. Do the same activity using pictures cut from magazines.

- Using manipulatives such as Attribute Logic Blocks, Cuisenaire Rods, and flannel boards, guide the student to discover a variety of attributes by which these materials may be sorted. Attributes include color, shape, size, thickness, width, height, and use.

- To provide practice in classifying and creating sets, create experiments in which the students participate. Examples of sets amenable to experimentation are objects that float/sink, those that feel heavy/light, and those that can be seen through/those that cannot.

To guide the student in developing flexibility in classifying objects:

a) Take a set of objects and divide them into groups based on a particular attribute (tools and cooking utensils). Have the student explain the basis on which you separated them. (What are the differences between groups and what are the similarities within groups?)

b) Reassemble the objects into one group, then ask the student to group them on some other basis (e.g., metal and wood) and discuss the attribute on which she made the distinction (in this case, what they are made of).

c) Continue taking turns classifying objects in different ways.

d) When the student appears to have a solid understanding of this concept, extend the concept by using two attributes to differentiate between groups (e.g., height *and* function).

e) Progress to more complex relationships (e.g., color *or* function).

f) Gradually move to more abstract materials such as Attribute Logic Blocks, Tangrams, and Cuisenaire Rods, and eventually to number and letter patterns.

From Sets to Numbers

Engage the student in guided activities to develop the concept of sets, including what makes a set, the empty set, naming sets by attributes (classification), and representing sets by the amount of items (number). Related objectives and activities include:

- Teach the student that the members of a set may or may not contain objects/pictures that have a common attribute. For example, a star, a ball, and a tree may all share membership in a set just because they are described as such.

- Provide activities to develop the concept of the empty set, the idea that a set may have no members. For example, give four students boxes with three, two, one, and no crayons in them, respectively. Have each student describe the contents of their box, ending with the student who has no crayons. Explain that her box contains the empty set. Or, ask questions for which the answer is "none," such as the number of members in the set of zebras in the classroom.

- Teach the student that sets in which members have a common attribute may be named for that attribute. For example, a group of colored objects may be sorted into a red and a green set.

- Help the student to develop conceptualization of sets at the semi-concrete level by representing groups of physical objects by pictures. When the student clearly understands the representation, introduce new concepts with pictures. Assess comprehension by asking questions about the relationship among objects in the environment.

- Help the student to develop conceptualization of sets at the semi-abstract level by teaching her to represent each member of a set with a tally, such as a Popsicle stick. This will encourage her to consider the number properties of sets rather than other characteristics of the objects.

Counting and One-to-One Correspondence

When the student is counting small items, teach her to separate each from the group as she counts it so that she does not miss any or count the same item twice. Provide systematic practice until the procedure is automatic.

Teach the student to count to [appropriate number] and provide practice in activities that will highlight their use in daily living. For example, have the student count the students ordering milk, pass out a certain number of books, or play board games that involve moving a marker according to a number on a chosen card or spinner.

Give the student practice in counting and recognizing cardinal numbers by activities such as counting buttons into numbered compartments of an egg carton.

Teach the student that when a number represents a set, it refers to the amount of objects in the set, not the nature of the objects.

Teach the student that when items are counted, the order in which the numbers are counted does not matter and the last number named represents the number of the set.

Engage the student in activities to develop the concept of one-to-one correspondence. This is a prerequisite to understanding addition and subtraction.

Teach the student to use one-to-one correspondence to compare quantities; teach the associated vocabulary. For example, have her match each member of one set with a member in another set. Help her verbalize if one set has the same number as the other set or not. Gradually, introduce comparative terms such as *more, less, same, equal* and have her use these terms in statements describing the relationship between the sets (e.g., "There are more shoes than stars;" "There are the same number of shoes as stars").

The student does not count on because she is still unsure that the quantity of a group of objects is invariable (if nothing has been done to it). Students who count on assume that 6 is really 6 so they do not have to count it. To help the student understand the process of counting on, have her count all the objects in two sets and write the answer. Then guide her in counting on and in comparing the answers. She may need to practice this many times to understand the validity and efficiency of the latter approach.

While working on comparing the number of items in two sets, work on developing the concept of conservation of matter. Help the student to see that if one has the same number of objects, no matter how they are arranged, the same number of objects is still present. Engage the student in activities to experience conservation of other attributes, such as volume and length.

Using Numerals

Do not introduce numerals to the student until she is developmentally ready to use the symbolic representations. Make sure that she understands one-to-one correspondence by providing appropriate readiness experiences, such as counting objects and matching or comparing one set of objects to another.

Use a variety of activities to guide the student to associate number symbols with the amount of items within a set, such as matching large models of numbers (e.g., plastic, rubber) with cards according to the number of pictures on each.

Use games to reinforce the idea of numbers representing a set and rapid recognition of the number of items in a set. For example, play a version of Bingo in which the teacher holds up a card with a set of dots on it and the students cover the corresponding number on their Bingo cards. To reinforce rapid recognition of item amounts up to [3, 5], the teacher can show the cards for decreasing intervals of time.

As a conceptual basis for addition, using manipulatives or pictures, teach the student how to join two sets so that all members of the first set and all members of the second set are combined to form a new set. When this concept is mastered, have the students give each of the sets a number (in writing or with number tiles).

Use objects or pictures to teach the student that sets may be broken up into a variety of subsets. For example, a set of five objects contains: five subsets of one member each; one subset of two and one subset of three; one subset of four and one subset of one; or one subset of five and one subset of zero.

As a conceptual basis for subtraction, using manipulatives or pictures, teach the student that one subset of a set may be removed from the set, leaving the other subset(s).

Number Patterns and Ordinal Numbers

Help the student develop the concept of pattern recognition using familiar objects in simple patterns, such as fork, spoon, fork, spoon, fork, spoon. Guide the student to describe the pattern. Very gradually, increase the complexity of the pattern and the abstractness of the items in the pattern (e.g., from objects to colored beads to pictures to amount of items in pictures). Eventually, move to recognition of simple number patterns. At each level, when the student is able to identify the pattern, have her complete similar patterns.

Help the student develop the idea of number sequence. Use a number line to answer questions such as: "What number comes just before . . . ?" "What number comes just after . . . ?" Work with segments of numbers and fade use of the number line as each segment is mastered. Provide a wide range of activities so that the student learns that *before, after,* and *between* relate to the sequence of numbers in general (abstract) not just on the number line.

Introduce the concept of ordinal numbers by using terms for numbers during activities throughout the day in the classroom. For example, when getting ready to go outside, specify who should line up first, second, and so on.

Reinforce the use of ordinal numbers with gross-motor activities such as having a few students stand on a number line on the floor. After each one says the cardinal number, tell the student the corresponding ordinal number (e.g., "Joel is first in line, Desiree is second"). Then, using ordinal numbers instead of names, give each student an instruction (e.g., "Will the second child clap her hands two times?").

As the student learns to recognize numbers, color-code the repeating patterns of the numerals in the units column, then the tens columns, and the hundreds column.

Recognizing and Writing Numbers

Provide the student with many opportunities to form a stable visual image of numbers before she is asked to write them. Suggestions include playing with number puzzles; placing number models in sequence; matching number tiles, cards, or models; and feeling a number model with eyes closed and naming it.

At home or at school, use games to reinforce number recognition and counting skills. For example, play board games that require moving a marker a specified number of squares, card games such as "21," or dominoes with a peer or parent who will encourage accurate counting with comments such as, "See if you have a domino with three dots just like this one."

Teach the student to recognize the cardinal numbers by their names. You may use gross-motor activities to reinforce number recognition by writing the numbers to 10 on a long sheet of butcher paper and having the child count her paces, simultaneously stepping on each square and looking at the number. Alternatively, you may use numbers on steps.

To help the student get ready to start writing numbers, provide multisensory experiences to help familiarize the student with the form. For example, the student may copy a model to make numbers out of clay, make cookies in the shape of numbers, trace numbers in wet sand or on tactile number cards.

Teach the student to write numbers within the framework of the classroom handwriting program. If necessary, supplement the program with a variety of tracing activities and writing from memory. Provide supervision to ensure that the student traces or produces the letter in the proper formation and with the correct sequence of strokes.

Motivate the student to produce the numbers correctly by having her practice writing them in a tray of chocolate pudding. If she writes the number correctly, she may lick her finger clean or use a washcloth.

When the student reverses numbers on a math worksheet, do not count the answers as incorrect. Instead, provide cues to teach and reinforce the correct orientation of those numbers.

Place Value

Ensure that the student has developed a solid understanding of place value before introducing regrouping (borrowing and carrying).

When teaching place value, tell the student a story with pictures to help her understand that no more than 9 of any set may go in one column. The following is an example of a place value story with related pictures (Figure III.11).

> Once there was a person who moved into a house. Although the landlord had told her that no more than 9 people could live in the house, eventually a tenth person moved in. The landlord said, "Only 9 people can live in that house," and he evicted all of them. So, they became one family (of 10 people) and moved into an apartment house. The apartment house had room for 9 families just like theirs—10 people each. But families kept moving into the apartment house and before they knew it, there were 9 families there. Eventually, a tenth family (of 10) moved in. When the landlord found out, he said, "Only 9 families can live in that house." And he threw them all out. So the 10 families formed a community (How many families are in that community now? How many people?). The community then moved into a huge, brand-new apartment complex. This new landlord told them, "Only 9 communities can live in this complex." And they said, "OK," but, eventually, other communities (of 100) moved in. Finally, when the tenth community moved in . . .

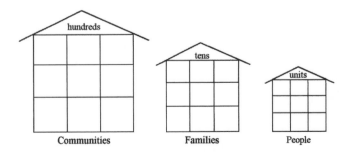

Figure III.11   Illustrations for Story of Place Value Houses

Using manipulatives (e.g., Unifix cubes, Base Ten Blocks), teach the student the concept of place value. Teach her how to "trade up" (regroup) for the next largest set and how to use a place value mat. If you use a dry erase board for the mat, she can write the digits corresponding to the blocks in each column. Write the resulting number on another piece of paper. Try to guide her to discover and verbalize that the value of each digit within the number is related to its position on the board and the way it is represented by the objects (e.g., small blocks, sticks equivalent to ten blocks, flats equivalent to 100 blocks or 10 sticks).

When the student has learned the concept of place value, show her how reading printed numbers relates to the place value of the digits. Write the number, have the student place the corresponding number of blocks on the mat, and have her read it. Point out that the digit with the highest value is named first. When she understands this, reverse the process so she learns to write multidigit numbers.

When the student understands the connection between the place of the digits comprising a number and the value of the digits, extend the concept to working with expanded notation.

Review or reteach place value using manipulatives to clarify the function of zero as a place holder and as representing an empty set. Use a place value mat or a box divided into parallel compartments. Represent multiple-digit numbers on the mat/box and practice reading them. Start with no zeros in the number, then one zero, then two. Transfer the activity to reading numbers written on paper.

Review the rule of one digit to a column and make sure the student understands and can explain the reason for the rule. Use manipulatives to illustrate this concept.

Explicitly connect regrouping on the place value board with regrouping using numbers on paper. Have the student work the printed problems by doing them on paper and on the board. When she moves a "ten-stick" (or any manipulative representing a group of ten) over into the tens column on the mat, she puts the one it represents in a box above the tens column in the printed problem. Give the student lots of practice in verbalizing what she is doing as she works the problems both on the board and on the paper.

Basic Facts

General

Do not require the student to memorize facts until her understanding of the process is firmly established.

Have the student overlearn the math facts for all operations.

Continuously reinforce previously learned facts interspersed with practice of more recently learned facts. Continue fact practice even when the student seems to know them automatically.

Rather than drill the student on math facts at this point, find out what strategies she is using and help her become more efficient in those that are reasonable.

Do not have the student compete with other students when practicing math facts. Instead, have her keep her own private performance chart. Draw an analogy to a runner's "Personal Best."

Once the student understands mathematical operations, shift the focus to memorization of facts. Make adequate provisions for overlearning by using games, language masters, tape recorders, computer software, tracing activities, and peer tutoring.

Have the student participate in selecting a method that she will use to learn her facts. After using the approach to study for several days, have the student evaluate whether or not the method seems effective. If not, have her select another approach to try.

As the student has great difficulty memorizing and retrieving math facts, use TouchMath, a systematic instructional program for teaching computation skills. TouchMath uses dots on each number to represent its value, emphasizes use of the Touchpoints as a bridge to conceptualizing and memorizing the facts, and provides visual prompts to help students learn the algorithms. TouchMath is available from: Innovative Learning Concepts, 6760 Corporate Drive, Colorado Springs, CO, 80919-1999, (888) TOUCHMATH (or 868-2462), www.touchmath.com. [See Strategies: Touch Math.]

For now, do not spend time trying to get the student to learn facts that she has historically been unable to recall. Instead, for computation problems, give her pocket-sized charts with addition and multiplication facts. Teach her how to use the addition chart for subtraction and the multiplication chart for division. If she has difficulty finding the number at the intersection of the row and column for the fact she is checking, provide a template made from strips of colored transparency material in the shape of a reversed L. At the juncture of the two strips, cut out a square through which the answer can be seen. The student may use the chart any time she wants for the answers to math facts but encourage her to guess the answer before looking. That way, she gets immediate reinforcement if she is right and immediate correction if she is wrong. Also, eventually, visualizing the location of the answer may help in retrieving it. When a fact has become truly automatic, she should black it out. This will continue to strengthen her ability to recall the fact as well as allow her to see how many facts she has left to learn.

Using Strategic Organization to Memorize Facts

The student creates elaborate strategies for reconstructing the answers to simple math fact problems because she has not memorized basic math facts. As she has demonstrated understanding of the concepts underlying [addition, subtraction, multiplication, division], organize the facts for easiest learning and recall, then provide daily drill and practice. Use a systematic plan for practice so that previously learned facts are reinforced along with more recently learned ones. [See Strategies: Addition Fact Memorization: Organizational Structures; Math Facts-Instructional Sequence.]

Mental organization of math facts reduces memory demands and facilitates retrieval. Teach math facts in a sequence and using an instructional approach in which each new set of facts is related to facts or processes the student already knows. Suggestions for instructional sequences are attached to this report. [See Strategies: Addition Fact Memorization: Organizational Structures; Math Facts-Instructional Sequence.]

To reduce memory demands, teach the student strategies to use to solve computation problems based on facts she already knows. Some multiplication examples follow:
a) use skip counting and hatch marks (e.g., for 5×4, count by fives, stopping when you have made 4 hatch marks);
b) use repeated addition for the lower multiplication tables;
c) split one factor in half and add the products (e.g., $4 \times 7 \rightarrow 2 \times 7 = 14$, and $14 + 14 = 28$, so $4 \times 7 = 28$);
d) lower one factor by 1, multiply, then add one more set (e.g., $4 \times 7 \rightarrow 3 \times 7 = 21$, and $21 + 7 = 28$, so $4 \times 7 = 28$);
e) for the nines table, teach the "magic 9s" trick.
  - Start with any number times nine (e.g., 6×9). Reduce the number by one ($6 - 1 = 5$) and put it in the tens place ($5-$). Ask: "That number (5) plus what (x) equals 9 ($5 + x = 9$)?" Put the answer in the units column. Thus, the product is 54. The sum of the two digits in the product will always equal 9.
  - Hold both hands up, palms out, thumbs adjacent. Imagine a number on each finger, from one to ten,

starting with the left little finger. To multiply 6 times nine, count on your fingers from the left until you reach 6. Turn finger 6 (right thumb) down. The number of fingers to the left of this finger (5) represents the tens column. The number of fingers to the right (4) represents the units column. The answer is 54.

While teaching [addition, multiplication] facts, help the student to develop flexibility and a deeper understanding of number relationships by working with [addition, multiplication] sentences (e.g., $2 + 5 = 7$). This will reinforce the [addition, multiplication] facts while increasing readiness to learn the [subtraction, division] facts. Provide a variety of guided activities with addition [multiplication] sentences in which one of the numbers or relational signs is omitted. Have the student figure out the number/sign that would make the sentence true and explain how she did so. Use the fact groups the student is studying for the arithmetic sentences. As she develops facility in filling in the missing element, she will be able to come up with the related [subtraction, division] facts. The ability to complete $6 + 2 = \square$, $6 + \square = 8$, $\square + 6 = 8$, and $2 \square 6 = 8$, facilitates comprehension and acquisition of $8 - 2 = 6$ and $8 - 6 = 2$.

Try teaching addition facts as "families" centered on sums. For example, the "3 family" has 4 "brother/sister pairs:" $0 + 3$, $1 + 2$, $2 + 1$, $3 + 0$. Given three blocks and two empty frames, the student can practice making different brother/sister pairs and matching them to number cards (as above) and then to addition fact cards. This type of structure may be easier for her to learn than the usual +1, +2, +3. One advantage to teaching facts in this way is that in any subtraction fact, the higher number is the family name and the other number is one of the brother/sister pairs. The answer is the missing brother/sister pair.

Other Memorization Methods

Provide peer tutoring to help the student learn basic math facts and whole-number computation. The success of this program depends on a high degree of tutor competency in the skill addressed, training and monitoring the tutor, and the tutor's use of principles of effective instruction.

Have a peer or parent provide practice sessions with flash cards so that the student can become automatic with her math facts. Additionally, using flash cards that have the answer recorded on the reverse side, have the student practice facts for several minutes daily. Provide frequent review of the newly mastered facts.

Teach particularly difficult multiplication facts by using a rhyme with a picture clue. These may be made by the student or class.

Have the student use computer math games that provide immediate feedback to reinforce facts and operations she has mastered. Provide time for the student to practice independently.

Use a write-say procedure to help the student memorize her multiplication facts. Give the student a worksheet of problems with answers. Have her cover the row of answers with an index card. Have her look at the problem, say the answer, and then move the card to check the answer. If the answer is incorrect, have the student look at the problem and answer, cover it with a finger, and then write it from memory several times, checking for accuracy each time. Assign only a few facts at a time.

Record a set of number facts on tape at a slow pace, repeating each one twice. Have the student hold a flash card in her hand as she listens to each fact being said. Encourage the student to repeat the fact aloud with the taped presentation. As an alternate activity, have the student say, then write, each math fact. Present only a few at a time. Provide daily practice for 5 minutes until all facts are mastered.

Motivation
Set up a reinforcement program for the student for improving retention of math facts. For example, she could earn a sticker or a set number of points for each new fact learned.

To increase motivation, teach the student how to monitor her progress in automaticity of math facts by using a chart with a math fact in each square. As she learns each fact to an automatic level, allow her to highlight the square. If she understands the commutative property, she may fill in 2 squares for each fact learned. [See Strategies: Addition Fact Chart, Multiplication Fact Chart.]

Use computer programs to motivate drill and practice but do not let it replace regular monitoring of fact knowledge through [oral response to flashcards, written timed tests.]

Fluency
To help the student increase her speed in math operations, drill her on math facts using visual stimuli such as flash cards, computer programs, and, when she can respond to a math fact within 3 seconds, worksheets. Eventually, move to timed tests.

Administer daily timed multiplication tests to see how many facts the student can complete within a minute. Record and monitor her progress.

Use Precision Teaching to help the student memorize her math facts. Have her complete daily timed drill activities in which she competes against her own best score. [See Strategies: Precision Teaching.]

Use the Great Leaps Math Program (Mercer, Mercer, & Campbell, 2002) to build fluency in the basic facts, including addition, subtraction, multiplication, and division.

Algorithms

Teaching Concepts with Manipulatives
For any skill or operation, allow the student to use manipulatives as long as necessary. Prematurely shifting her to numbers alone may interfere with conceptual mastery.

Make sure the student understands the concept underlying each new algorithm that is introduced. Use manipulatives, such as Cuisenaire Rods (Davidson, 1969), beans, or money to introduce all new concepts.

Use visual aids and manipulatives to illustrate new ideas and extensions of previously learned concepts. Use real objects first (e.g., food, measuring liquid, wood for building, crayons), then pictures. Later, move to Cuisenaire Rods, Unifix Cubes, tokens, and other semi-concrete materials.

When teaching the student concepts of fractions and decimals, use tangible objects, such as money or food. For example, demonstrate cutting a pizza into pie-shaped pieces.

Use manipulatives that are already compartmentalized to teach fractions. For example, an empty egg carton may be used to teach fractions with a denominator of 12.

Teaching Algorithms
In teaching the student computational algorithms, ensure that she understands the underlying concepts so that the procedures and the sequence of steps make sense. For example, one must understand place value to understand regrouping.

Provide opportunities for the student to teach the math algorithms and concepts that she has recently learned to other students. Have her assume the role of instructor and teach the concept using her own words.

Reteach the concept of fractions, including what the numerator and denominator represent, the reason for needing a common denominator, the methods for finding common denominators, the procedures for reducing fractions, and the meaning of improper fractions and mixed numbers.

Before introducing decimals, make sure that the student understands fractional concepts so that she can see the relationship between the two and acquire an understanding that decimals are an easier and more consistent way to express fractions.

To provide a basis for higher-level math, help the student develop concepts and skills with percents, decimals, fractions, and negative numbers.

Reminders for Algorithm Sequences

Make flowcharts for the student that illustrate the sequence of steps required for any particular operation that she is learning. Have the student keep the flowcharts clipped inside her math textbook and/or workbook to refer to whenever necessary.

Provide the student with an index card that contains clear verbal explanations of questions to ask herself as she works math problems. For example, when learning regrouping techniques for subtraction, write the question, "Is the top number larger than the bottom number?"

   If yes—subtract   If no—regroup (borrow)

Analysis of the student's errors indicates that she understands that the procedures are rule-governed but that she misunderstands or misapplies them, or has made up a rule for herself. To help her use and remember the correct rules, provide her with memory aids such as a decision map. Figure III.12 represents a decision map for subtraction with regrouping.

Teach the student memory strategies for performing new math algorithms in the correct sequence. For example, for long division, teach her to write the symbols representing the steps at the top of her paper; to recite, "Divide, multiply, subtract, check, bring down"; or make a tune for it and sing it. Figure III.13 shows a visual cue for long division.

Provide tape-recorded instructions for solving computation processes. Fade use of the tape gradually as the student memorizes the steps.

Use color-coding to: (a) identify starting and stopping places within a problem; (b) code the units, tens, hundreds,

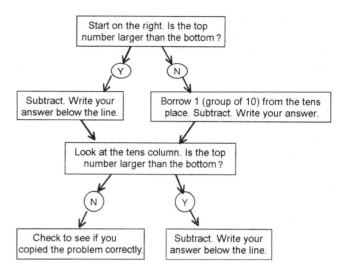

Figure III.12   Math Decision Map

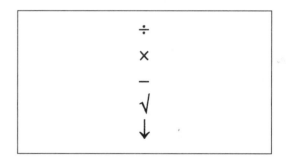

Figure III.13   Mnemonic for the Steps of the Division Process

and thousands place; (c) indicate where the final answer should be written; and (d) highlight important features, such as operation signs, the question being asked, or the key information provided in the problem.

Remind the student that reading starts on the left and moves right, whereas the math computations of addition, subtraction, and multiplication start on the right and move left. If she requires a visual cue to remind her, place a green dot or arrow over the units column and have her place her pencil point on the dot or arrow before beginning the problem.

Consider using the TouchMath instructional approach and materials to teach the basic algorithms. As the student is not having difficulty with math facts, do not teach the touchpoints. The computational algorithms are taught systematically, with visual and auditory cues, self-talk, and ample practice. The materials can be used along with the classroom math program. TouchMath is available from: Innovative Learning Concepts, 6760 Corporate Drive, Colorado Springs, Colorado, 80919-1999, (888) TOUCH-MATH (or 868-2462), www.touchmath.com. [See Strategies: TouchMath®.]

Application

Word Problems: Primary School and Above

Problem-Solving Instruction
Do not teach the student "tricks" for solving math problems, such as identifying cue words (i.e., "how many" or "altogether" means addition). Instead draw attention to understanding the language of the problems.

Ensure that when the student is asked to solve story problems, the computation involved is not difficult. This will allow the student to concentrate on understanding the language of the problem.

Before teaching word problems, set up practical situations in the classroom that would be described in a word problem. Have students work collaboratively to verbalize the situation, the numbers involved, and what has to happen. Then have the student create word problems that represent the situation they just experienced.

Have the student and several peers physically act out word problems. For example, the students could count up and divide a set of blocks or demonstrate making change for a purchase in a grocery store. Guide them to talk about what they are doing in mathematical terms.

To ensure that the student understands the different types of story problems that she is expected to solve, have her solve them first using manipulatives.

Provide the student with a mixture of story problems that require different mathematical operations. Have her determine what operation(s) are appropriate for each problem.

As the student appears to misinterpret word problems, have her restate the problem in her own words and identify the givens and the problem goal before planning the solution.

The student is more likely to understand word problems and find solutions if she can relate to their content. As much as possible, make problems relevant to the student's life. This will also increase her motivation.

When introducing word problems to the student, present concrete situations that she will be able to visualize or draw.

Provide the student with extensive guided practice in reading [multiplication, addition] word problems, setting them up with manipulatives and then as computation problems, and solving them. Use problems that incorporate many types of objects (e.g., eggs, nickels, miles, minutes). Try to use situations that would be familiar to her as well as practical (e.g., paying for her family to see a movie at $7.50 each).

Present the student with a very simple [addition] oral story problem. Teach her how to make pictures of the problem or to set it up with real objects (e.g., cookies). Make the connection between this and the activities she did using the place value board. Transition to having the student write math statements to represent the story problem.

When the student has become comfortable with representing simple, brief word problems, provide longer narratives that describe real-life situations and that include more information and events. Provide a series of math-related questions about the story that are not necessarily more complex but that require careful consideration to identify the required information and operations. At times, include questions that cannot be answered with the data given and/or ask the student to list information that is not required to answer any of the questions posed.

Teach the student to recognize the number of steps (operations) involved in a word problem, what they are, and how to sequence them correctly.

Have the student work with a partner or in a cooperative learning group to write or solve word problems. Provide a variety of activities such as creating problems for a set of objects, writing problems for a given equation, or solving problems written by a peer or from another group of students.

Teach the student how to recognize when she does not have all of the information needed to solve a problem. Some example activities are:
- Give the student word problems in which specific information needed to solve the problem is missing. Have the student identify what is missing, provide the information, and then solve the problem.
- Have several teams of students create story problems that cannot be solved because information is missing.

Have them exchange problems and discuss why they cannot be solved. Have the students then rewrite the problems so they can be solved.

Help the student learn to identify extraneous information in word problems. With a marker, have her cross out any extraneous information before she attempts to solve a problem.

Teach the student how to interpret what is asked in a math problem as well as how to use resource material to find the data needed to solve the problem. Several suggestions follow:

- If you use familiar objects to create problems and generate questions, the student's interest level will be higher. Additionally, the student will have the objects to help solve the problem.
- Combine math and content area learning. For example, use data in reference books to create math problems and teach the student to use the reference books to find the answer. An example would be, "If everybody in the world gave you a penny, approximately how much money would you have?"
- Provide easy-to-read reference books for each student or cooperative group and challenge them to create math problems using information in the book. Examples of reference books are encyclopedias, atlases, the Guinness Book of World Records, or books on the human body.
- Create problems for the student that require experimentation or that combine experimentation with use of a reference book. Examples would be, "How many tablespoons of liquid equal a cup?" or "If you leave Tucson on foot for Yuma, can you make the trip in less than 1,000,000 steps?"

Problem-Solving Strategies

When the student has difficulty with the computation involved in a story problem, have her substitute smaller numbers so that she can understand the operation(s) involved and then calculate the problem a second time using the original numbers.

Teach the student how to plan what she needs to do to solve a problem. Different techniques, such as the following, may be called for by the type of question asked:

a) Decide what operation(s) to use (e.g., Harry weighed 250 pounds. He weighed 72 more pounds than James. How much did James weigh?)

b) Make a table, graph, or chart of the information provided (e.g., Hansel and Gretel went to the witch's house every day except Sunday. On Mondays and Thursdays, Hansel went twice. On Wednesday, Gretel went in the morning, at noon, and once after Hansel was in bed. Who traveled to the witch's house more times in a month?).

c) Make a drawing of the information provided (e.g., Mehitabel planted a square garden with 12 garlic plants on each side to keep the snails away. How many garlic plants did she plant?)

d) Make inferences and logical deductions (e.g., The Carsons went to Jack-in-the-Bag and spent $20.75 for lunch. An adult meal costs $4.95 and lunch for a child costs $2.95. How many people are in the family? How many of them are children?)

Teach the student a simple strategy to use for solving story problems. For example, teach her to: (a) read the problem, (b) reread the problem to identify what is given (What do I know?) and to decide what is asked for (What do I need to find out?), (c) use objects to solve the problem and identify the operation to use, (d) write the problem, and (e) work the problem (Smith & Alley, 1981). Write the strategy on an index card for easy reference.

Teach the student a specific math problem strategy to use for solving story problems. [See Strategies: Math Problem-Solving Strategy.]

When teaching the student any problem-solving strategies, use the following sequence. First, teach the steps to the strategy, have the student memorize them (or, if necessary, provide a cue card), and then work with the strategy until she has mastered its use. Second, teach a self-questioning strategy that will prompt the student to use the strategy when appropriate to the task. Third, provide follow-up training to ensure retention and use of the strategy.

Teach any problem-solving strategies as directly and explicitly as you would any academic skill, providing for instruction and ample guided and independent practice, monitoring for misunderstandings and errors. Incorporate instruction and practice in when to apply the strategy.

When choosing a strategy, consider both the procedures or information targeted for instruction and the particular strengths of the student. Select from the following strategies those you think would be most beneficial to the student: restating the problem; acting out the problem; estimating the answer; using a model; guessing and checking; making a drawing; working backward; solving a simpler, related problem; constructing a table or graph; looking for a pattern; applying a formula; and writing a mathematical sentence.

Higher-Level Mathematics

Problem-Solving Instruction

Because the student has not automatized many procedures commonly applied in algebraic problems, the cognitive attention necessary to reason through the problem is diverted to the steps in the procedures. To overcome this problem, she requires far more practice with a variety of problems addressing each new concept and procedure taught, and extensions of those previously taught. This will necessitate moving through the curriculum at a slower pace and periodically reviewing material covered previously.

Teach the student how to differentiate among assignment propositions, relational statements, and questions.

As the student appears to have difficulty converting relational statements (e.g., a plane travels 10 times faster than a car, Tia's grade is 17 points higher than Robin's) into mathematical expressions, focus instructional time on interpreting and paraphrasing a wide variety of relational statements and then representing them in mathematical form.

To help the student recognize the mathematical structure of word problems, provide direct instruction in comparing a group of word problems and identifying those with the same mathematical structure by drawing representations of the problem structures (i.e., equation network), for example, with a chart or diagram (d'Ailly, 1995).

When presenting a new type of problem or equation, in addition to instructing the student in how to work it, give her examples that have already been worked. Give her time to study them, answer any questions she has, and have her use them as models while working problems with the same structure. This strategy should help her recognize the problem structure at a later time and facilitate the solution.

The student's difficulty with comprehending word problems increases along with level of abstraction. She will have more success if, within each procedure or concept presented, concrete factual problem types are introduced first, concrete hypothetical second, abstract factual third, and abstract hypothetical, the most difficult, last. Examples of each problem type follow:

- *Concrete Factual:* A farmer has eight more hens than dogs. Since hens have two legs each, and dogs have four legs each, all together the animals have 118 legs. How many dogs does the farmer own?
- *Concrete Hypothetical:* There are four more girls in an English class than boys. If there were six times as many girls and twice as many boys, there would be 136 pupils. How many boys are there?
- *Abstract Factual:* The value of a given number is six more than the value of a second number. The sum of two times the first number and four times the second number is 126. What is the value of the second number?
- *Abstract Hypothetical:* A given number is six more than a second number. If the first number were four times as large and the second two times as large, their sum would be 126. What is the second number? (Caldwell & Goldin, 1987).

Problem-Solving Strategies

To help the student learn to analyze and then reintegrate the information in a problem, teach her to create a situational model (e.g., picture, diagram) of the problem before trying to set up a quantitative representation such as an equation. Research indicates that inclusion of this intermediate step (the situational model) is positively related to correct solutions (d'Ailly, 1995).

Teach the student that if a problem looks too complex, she should substitute lower or simpler values, figure out the solution, then use the solution to solve the more complex problem.

As the student is confused by problems that contain many variables, the following strategy may be helpful. Teach her to construct a different problem, similar to the one that is given but with fewer variables, and solve it. This may help her to clarify her understanding of the given problem using all of the variables and allow her to solve it by adapting the solution she used in the simpler problem (d'Ailly, 1995).

Teach the student that when a problem appears too confusing even to start, to try and find part of the answer and see if she can proceed from there. Alternatively, she can try to break the problem into smaller or simpler questions, solve them, and combine the results (d'Ailly, 1995).

To aid the student in organizing her approach to algebraic word problems, teach her to use the following 6-step procedure: (1) Read the problem carefully; (2) Decide what question the problem asks and choose a variable to represent the unknown; (3) Consider the other information given in the problem and how it relates to the unknown; (4) Write an equation or equations expressing the given relationships; (5) Solve the equation or equations; (6) Check the answer (Bassler, Beers, & Richardson, 1975).

Help the student learn to: recognize the problem, identify the steps to follow, determine what numbers are needed to solve the problem, draw a picture if possible, write a number equation, sequence the computation steps, estimate the answer, check the answer for reasonableness, self-monitor the entire process, and investigate alternate ways to solve the problem.

Teach the student the following strategies to try when she is having difficulty proving a logic statement:

- Contrapositive: When the statement that must be proven is positive (e.g., If X is true, then Y must be true), instead try to prove the equivalent negative statement (e.g., If Y is false then X must be false). Either is a sufficient proof.
- Contradiction: Assume that the statement that must be proven is false. Using this assumption, the student tries to prove either that one of the conditions given in the problem is false, that something she knows to be true is false, or that what she wishes to prove is true. If she can do any of these, she has proved the original statement (Schoenfeld, 1979).

Guide the student to consider how she tried to solve a problem. Comment on what she did well and how she could improve her performance. Ask questions such as:

- How did you do this problem?
- I noticed you had some trouble with _____. How did you proceed?
- How could you solve the problem in another way?

Use the following types of self-questioning strategies to help the student learn how to represent algebra word problems (Hutchinson, 1993):

- Have I read and understood each sentence? Are there any words whose meaning I need to ask about?
- Have I gotten the whole picture of the problem?
- Have I written down my representation of the problem on my worksheet? (goals; unknown(s); known(s); type of problem; equation)
- What should I look for in a new problem to see if it is the same kind of problem?

For solving algebra number problems:

- Have I written an equation?
- Have I expanded the terms?
- Have I written out the steps of my solution on the worksheet? (collected like terms; isolated unknown(s); solved for unknown(s); checked my answer with the goal; highlighted my answer)

- What should I look for in a new problem to see if it is the same kind of problem?

For algebra instruction, engage in modeling, provide guided practice activities, and check students' responses (Maccini, McNaughton, & Ruhl, 1999). Maccini et al. recommend that instructors employ the following principles to help students succeed in higher-level mathematics courses: Before beginning instruction:

a) Administer a daily quiz of previously learned skills.
b) Give a general orientation to introduce the strategy; explain the rationale for self-questioning strategies.

During instruction:

(1) Provide a clear and precise presentation of the skill or concept with a range of examples as well as non-examples.
(2) Make use of manipulatives and computer-assisted instruction when possible.
(3) Teach students self-questioning strategies.
(4) Provide guided practice, reinforcing instruction with structured worksheets.
(5) Provide feedback and reinforcement by offering opportunities for monitoring student level of understanding and providing corrective and positive reinforcement.

Maccini et al. also recommend requiring a level of mastery, using set criteria, providing independent practice, and assessing students frequently using a variety of measures, such as oral and written responses.

Computer Software

Use educational software to encourage the student to reflect on new concepts and practice new procedures. Select software with care, however, to ensure that it matches the teaching objectives and is well designed. [See Strategies: Software Selection Tips.]

Use tutorial computer software to reinforce word problem-solving strategies, representations, and solutions, but make sure that the student is able to transfer the ability demonstrated when using the program to paper/pencil tasks.

Measurement and Estimation

General

When the student has to memorize rote information, such as units of measurement, help her to create visual or auditory associations to help her remember them. For example, 12 inches in a foot could be drawn as a footprint of a bare foot with 12 inchworms end to end crawling across it. To add in that there are 3 feet in a yard, 2 more feet could be drawn, toe to heel with the first foot (without the worms) tightly bordered by a fence filled in with grass to represent a "yard."

Help the student learn to differentiate situations where an exact answer is needed from those where an estimate is more appropriate.

Teach the student to estimate length in terms of familiar objects. For example, a regulation baseball bat is 1 meter in length. A notebook is approximately a foot in height.

Time
Use a strategy to teach the student to state the time on an analog clock. [See Strategies: Telling Time: Instructional Strategy.]

Teach the student how to read both a digital clock as well as an analog clock. Have her practice setting the hands on a clock to match the time on the digital clock.

Teach the student how to tell time to the hour, half hour, and quarter hour. Teach her the different ways to express these times. For example, 8:30 might be referred to as eight-thirty, half-past eight, or thirty minutes past the hour.

Money
When teaching the student money concepts, use actual money or realistic facsimiles. Have the student perform problems that involve actual manipulation of the money.

Teach the student the value of coins and bills. Provide practice in exchanging coins and bills while maintaining equal value.

Provide opportunities for the student to practice making change. Discuss money in relationship to things that the student wishes or needs to purchase. Use a catalog of merchandise for ideas.

Provide daily opportunities for the student to increase her skill with money. For example, have her purchase lunch or budget daily spending.

To increase the student's flexibility in making change, provide her with practice matching equal value of coins. For example, using real money, ask her to show you as many ways as she can think of to give someone 50 cents in change. Ex-

plain to the student why the combination with the fewest coins is usually returned.

Teach the student how to use a cash register. Help her increase her speed and accuracy in making change.

Teach the student the skills needed for money management, such as how to set up a bank account, balance a checkbook, determine interest on a loan, and/or use a credit card.

Calendar
In order for the student to develop a better sense of time sequences (days, weeks, months), give her a calendar to use to keep track of important events. Cross off each day as part of the daily classroom routine or if used at home, before bedtime. Mark the end of the month by turning the page. Use a calendar that has a holiday or seasonal picture for each month.

Use a yellow highlighter to draw a line separating the weekend days from the weekdays or color the weekend days yellow.

Teach the student how to obtain information from a calendar. Make sure that she can name the month, day of the week, and the date. As exercises, have her count the number of Tuesdays in a month and identify any holidays in the month. Have her identify yesterday's date and tomorrow's date.

Life-Skills Mathematics

Identify and teach the student the basic math skills that she will need for adult independent living.

Encourage the student to enroll in a consumer mathematics course.

Provide opportunities for the student to apply math in real situations, such as getting change at a laundromat, finding the correct bus fare, or determining the cost of clothing on sale.

Provide extensive practice in practical application of all new math skills that the student has learned or is learning, both in story problems and real life (e.g., measuring for cooking, deciding on one shirt over another depending on budget considerations, building a bookshelf).

Teach the student the survival math skills that she is missing and incorporate them into independent living situations (e.g., balancing a checkbook, determining interest on a car loan, budgeting her salary, measuring for cooking).

Teach the student to read simple maps, using a highlighter to follow along a route and a different color marker to mark key points along the way. Gradually increase the complexity of the maps.

Before the student begins employment, determine the on-the-job demands for mathematical literacy. Make sure that the student is sufficiently prepared to meet these requirements.

Devise a variety of real-life situations/simulations in which the type of operation you are teaching is used. Teach students how to write down computation problems as they arise and use calculators to solve them.

KNOWLEDGE/CONTENT AREAS/STUDY STRATEGIES

Tests: Academic Knowledge, General Information
Clusters: Knowledge
Related Sections: Memory, Oral Language, Reading Comprehension, Written Expression

Knowledge/Content Areas/Study Strategies
    General
    Accommodations
    Instructional Approaches
    Background Knowledge
    Multimodality Instruction/Experiential Learning
    Learning and Study Strategies

General

Identify the student's special interests and hobbies. Find ways to use her present knowledge to enhance learning of new situations.

Suggest that the parents spend time with the student or have other adults do so, specifically to expose her to a wide variety of experiences, explain what is happening, name objects and actions, and answer questions. They may also watch videotapes together to introduce historical events, give a sense of time periods in history, and introduce abstract concepts.

The World Wide Web is an extraordinary resource for information of virtually every type and the student needs to become a proficient and savvy user of this tool. Teach the student how to use the Internet as one of her sources of information about the world and how to judge the veracity of the information she finds. Browse the web with her to show her how to find interesting information about places, people, and events. Teach her how to use the web to shop, find out medical information, communicate by e-mail, and a myriad of activities that have the potential of opening the world to her. Incorporate lessons on Internet safety covering a wide range of risks.

Teach the student how to use interactive educational software as much as possible to facilitate her ability and enhance her interest in working with certain information. An example is the Microsoft Encarta Reference Suite which includes an encyclopedia, a globe, reference materials, and a research organizer. The encyclopedia articles have associated pictures, sounds, videos, and links to related websites. The globe allows the user to magnify any area, see different types of geographical boundaries (e.g., political, climate), mark geographic points, and filter out cities by population levels. Reference materials include a thesaurus, a dictionary, famous quotations, a style guide, a dictionary of computer terminology, and an almanac. The Research Organizer facilitates the organization of notes, proper citation of resources, incorporation of graphics, and putting the report together. An option enables the user to have the built-in speech synthesizer read the text aloud. Available from: Microsoft Corporation, One Microsoft Way, Redmond, WA 98052-6399, (888) 218-5617, http://encarta.msn.com/products/info/refsuite.asp.

Accommodations

Ensure that all content area textbooks are adjusted to the student's level of language and reading competence.

Introduce junior encyclopedias to the student as reference material for general information.

Permit the student to tape-record all class lectures so that she may play them back at a slower pace later and take notes.

Have the student arrange with another student, who takes good class notes, to make a copy of her notes for each class session. This will allow the student to listen carefully to the lecture and to participate in class discussion. If needed, the student may arrange this through the instructor.

Defer grading of content area tests until you can meet with the student and discuss her responses in private. This will ensure that unanswered questions, incomplete responses, and accidental omissions caused by limited [attention, basic skills] do not compromise assessment of the content the tests were designed to assess.

For classroom lectures, provide the student with an outline or study guide so that she can follow along, fill in missing information, and have a complete outline for studying and review.

Develop a clear scope and sequence for the student based upon the objectives she can master within a specific time frame. If the content is covered too rapidly, the student will not have time to learn the information.

Instructional Approaches

[See Recommendations: Oral Language, specifically Multi-modality Instruction and Lectures.]

When introducing new concepts, information, and procedures, activate and evaluate prior knowledge of the topic. If necessary, preteach key vocabulary and foundational concepts before beginning the instructional unit.

When introducing new concepts, information, and procedures, use pictures and nonsymbolic visual information along with any other input—oral, sign, or print.

Use learning strategies where appropriate to strengthen the student's ability to hold information in short-term memory while working with it and to help him retrieve the steps of procedures.

Provide a study guide well before a test. Include questions for key concepts and events. Give this to the special education teacher so she can teach the student strategies for how to find the answers and study them, then guide him in using the study techniques in the material to be tested.

To help the student work independently but more successfully in a study guide or open-book test, organize the questions by where they are found in the book. Draw a vertical line with a highlighter down the left side of a section of questions, then write the numbers of the pages on which the answers can be found next to each section of the test/guide.

To help the student comprehend the concept of history, develop a timeline with the student for the specific country the class is studying. Use pictures as a reminder of famous events, along with the dates and number of years between events. Make sure the student understands what the timeline represents. Try to relate the number of years between events to a length of time that could have meaning in his experiences. Use the timeline as a framework for the student to understand when an event happened. Use videotapes to get a sense of different time periods.

To enhance student learning, activate the student's prior knowledge, teach key vocabulary, provide an advance organizer, present a reasonable amount of material, help students keep track of where you are in the presentation of the material, and reinforce and evaluate concept learning. [See Strategies: Content Area Instruction: Components of Effective Lessons.]

Reduce the amount of content presented to the student at any one time. Make sure that she has mastered the material before introducing new material.

Before starting class, list on the board what you are going to do in class that day (e.g., go over homework, discuss answers to yesterday's question sheets, watch a video on geysers, answer question sheet, assign homework). Review it with the class. During class, check off activities/items as they are started and cross them out as they are completed.

For content area instruction, begin each lesson with a review of the content covered previously, introduce relevant objectives for new material, activate student knowledge about the present lesson, present the lesson, encourage discussion, and provide guided practice activities (Scruggs & Mastropieri, 1992).

In content area classes, do not expect the student to learn any formula by rote. Using familiar concepts and information, teach her the general concepts and variables relating to the formula. Then, introduce the formula, provide many examples of its application, and explain why it is applied in that context.

Use graphic organizers to help the student organize known information. Select a topic that has several subordinate ideas and is familiar to the student. Write the topic in the middle of the map. Place the related concepts in circles around the main topic and draw lines to the main concept. Then write a summary statement based on the graphic organizer.

To help promote comprehension and recall of text, use familiar, concrete analogies that are easy to picture. "Far analogies" that contain few obvious links between topics (e.g., soccer and math) appear to promote learning better than "near analogies" that have high surface similarity (e.g., soccer and rugby). Far analogies require the reader to process information at deeper levels (Halpern, Hansen, & Riefer, 1990).

Use a five-step process to teach the student concepts: (a) decide what concepts and related vocabulary to teach, (b) assess the student's knowledge of the concepts and related vocabulary, (c) use pre-learning or pre-reading activities to facilitate learning, (d) conduct the learning or reading activity, and (e) provide post-learning activities that further reinforce the concepts and information learned (Bos & Vaughn, 2001).

Remember to incorporate four critical concepts in teaching: (a) activate prior knowledge, (b) relate new information to information the students already know, (c) organize the information to be presented, and (d) show the organizational framework.

Have the student work on projects or assignments in collaborative groups so that the students have an enhanced opportunity to share general knowledge about the topic. Make sure that all of the students have and perform specific roles within the group (e.g., facilitator makes sure everyone has a chance to offer ideas, courtesy clerk makes sure that everyone acts with respect to each other, timer keeps the discussion on topic and keeps track of time, scribe takes notes).

Background Knowledge
[See Recommendations: Reading Comprehension, specifically Prereading Activities.]

Provide periodic reviews of previously learned information to help the student maintain acquired knowledge.

Discuss pictures in the text with the student. Have her discuss what is happening in the picture and predict what the outcome will be. Introduce new vocabulary as you discuss the picture.

Use the Pre Reading Plan (PReP) strategy (Langer, 1981, 1984), a three-step procedure, to activate and increase the student's background knowledge. This strategy is most effective when done with a group. In the first step, have the student(s) brainstorm or free-associate any key words or concepts related to the topic that come to mind. In the next

step, have them evaluate their responses by answering the question: "What made you think of . . . ?" In the third step, encourage the students to form new questions based on the discussion. [See Strategies: PreReading Plan.]

Before beginning a new unit in any content area class, evaluate and activate the student's prior knowledge of the topic, using a well-established activity such as the PreReading Plan, Semantic Mapping, Semantic Feature Analysis for Key Concepts, or Anticipation Guide. If necessary, preteach background knowledge, vocabulary, and key concepts before introducing the unit. [See Strategies: PreReading Plan, Semantic Feature Analysis: Concepts, Anticipation Guide, Semantic Maps: Advance Organizers.]

Because the student's environment and cultural knowledge are, for the most part, [Navajo, Chinese, Mexican], a critical aspect of introducing all new content area instruction to her will be to evaluate prior knowledge and spend whatever time is needed to fill in missing concepts and experience.

To activate prior knowledge and help the student incorporate new material into her knowledge base, guide a small group discussion prior to having her read content from textbooks. Keep the sessions to about 10 minutes and have the students summarize what they already know about the topic and what they think they will learn.

Multimodality Instruction/Experiential Learning
[See Recommendations: Oral Language, specifically Multimodality Instruction.]

When presenting lecture content or new information, use visual aids (e.g., pictures, maps, charts, graphs) [and manipulatives] to help the student visualize the concepts or information being presented.

In planning units, incorporate films and videos that will reinforce or introduce textbook content or help to enhance the knowledge required as a foundation for the next unit.

To help the student increase her knowledge of [science, social studies, humanities], encourage the parents to have her watch educational television programs, such as [Reading Between the Lions, Sesame Street, Reading Rainbow, Nova, National Geographic] and a wide variety of educationally oriented, interesting videotapes, such as [animal habitats, functions of the body, prejudice, crafts, legends, and conservation].

Encourage the student to watch movies on the topics that she is studying.

Show the student how to review material through various sensory modalities (e.g., type it on the computer, listen to it on tape, read the information aloud, and tell it to someone else) and explain the value to her in doing so.

Organize field trips for the student to provide direct experiences related to the information that she is or will be learning about.

To build background knowledge, supplement instruction with nonwritten sources of information, such as videos, computer simulations, simulation games, field trips, guest speakers, storytellers, and music.

Provide the student with varied experiences to expand cultural and world knowledge (e.g., ballet performances, library and museum visits, observances in a variety of religions, visits to historic places). Before going, tell the student about your trip, the purpose, and what she can expect to see and do there before going. Guide discussion and elicit questions before, during, and after the experience.

Invest in one or two magazine subscriptions for the student. Select magazines at her independent reading level that will introduce new information about the world and expand her current knowledge. The reference librarian at the local library may be able to suggest magazines to review.

Learning and Study Strategies
[See Recommendations: Memory, specifically Mnemonic Strategies.]

Use learning strategies where appropriate to strengthen his ability to hold information in short-term memory while working with it and to help him retrieve the steps of procedures.

Teach the student a variety of study strategies that will enhance content area learning. Teach her how to: (a) use mnemonic strategies to improve memory of specific information, (b) review prior tests to determine why errors were made and how to correct the mistakes, (c) summarize sections of the text with an outline or using a tape recorder, and (d) prepare index cards to help memorize factual information.

When reading content area textbooks, encourage the student to identify the main points, paraphrase orally what has been read, take notes while she is reading, and reread sections of the text when needed.

To improve understanding of text, teach the student how to generate questions by identifying the main idea of a passage and then formulating a question about the main idea.

Teach the student a variety of cognitive strategies so that she can actively monitor her comprehension. Teach her how to summarize a passage, paraphrase a passage, create visual representations, and generate questions.

Because she has difficulty determining what is important in passages, do not have the student underline material as a strategy for selecting the important information. Instead, provide the student with an outline or study guide that highlights the important vocabulary and concepts and have her fill in the details.

Because the student has difficulty deciding on what is important in the text, discuss the important ideas prior to assigning reading.

Provide a study guide well before a test. Include questions for key concepts and events. Give this to the special education teacher so she can teach the student strategies for how to find the answers and study them, then guide him in using the study techniques in the material to be tested.

To help the student work independently but more successfully in a study guide or open-book test, the teacher can organize the questions by where they are found in the book, draw a vertical line with a highlighter down the left side of a section of questions, then write the page numbers of the book on which the answers can be found next to each section of the test/guide.

Help the student learn when, where, and how to apply strategies, and to evaluate the efficacy of the strategy. Provide guided practice and feedback as the student learns to use a new strategy.

Provide guided practice with all strategy instruction. Work with the student so that she learns how to apply the strategy. As the student gains more competence, have her practice the strategy with materials that are at or slightly above her instructional level. Help the student learn to modify the strategy based on the task demands. Check periodically to ensure that the student is using the strategy.

Help the student learn to summarize information. Teach her how to delete unimportant information, delete repetitive information, and identify a topic sentence or the main idea for each paragraph. Provide the student with feedback about the quality of her summaries.

Encourage the student to enroll in a course that teaches study strategies, efficient methods for studying, time management, note-taking, and strategies for improving organization.

Whenever it is possible, use a game format for learning (e.g., reviewing for a test by playing Jeopardy with the target information). The student will find it easier to attend to the information and hold it in mind long enough to process it more effectively.

Play the Twenty Questions game with the student to activate background knowledge or review/reinforce previously studied material. The "responder" thinks of a person, place, thing, or event and says, "I am thinking of . . . ," adding a clue to give the "questioner" a place to start. Examples include: a famous explorer, a period in history, a discovery that changed medical thinking, a type of animal that lived 200 million years ago and is still living. The questioner may only ask "yes/no" questions and must guess the answer within 20 questions. Exchange roles with the student in thinking of a topic and asking questions. Use your turn as responder to model how to move from broader (category) questions to more detailed ones. If necessary, teach the student how to use this strategy. Playing this in a small group may enhance the quality of questions asked and information shared.

HOMEWORK/TIME MANAGEMENT/ORGANIZATION

Related Sections: Attentional Disorders [Class Placement and Class Schedules, Increasing Attention and Time on Task, Task Completion]; Behavior Management and Interventions [Behavioral Interventions]

Homework/Time Management/Organization
  General
  Assigning Homework
  Communicating with Parents
  Making Homework Meaningful
  Modifying Homework Assignments
  Organizing Assignments and Materials
  Long-Term Assignments/Tests
  Completing Assignments
  Turning in Assignments
  Indirect Teacher Support of Student Organization

General

Remember that students with learning problems experience significantly more difficulties completing homework

than do their peers. These children are more likely to forget their assignments, lose their homework, and make careless mistakes. The problems may be caused by the fact that the child is easily distracted, overly dependent on others for assistance, or poorly organized. Increased discipline or withdrawal of privileges are not the ways to address incomplete schoolwork. Attempt to determine a successful homework plan that meets the needs of the child and his or her family.

Provide the student with after-school tutoring so that he can get extra help with homework.

Stress the importance of nightly review of class notes. This will help the student prepare for tests and also give him a chance to fill in missing information or ask questions the next day about confusing information.

Assigning Homework

When you make assignments, provide the student with clear instructions. State the purpose of the assignment, the date it is due, the format required, materials that are necessary, and the criteria for good performance.

Establish a routine for assigning homework. Always assign it at the same time (beginning or end of class), have it written or write it on the board, have everyone write it down in an assignment book, and circulate through the room to ensure that the student (and others who may need monitoring) has written it down.

Establish a routine for assigning homework. At the beginning of the period, write homework assignments on the board in a specified place. Explain the assignment, ask for questions, direct the students to write it in their assignment book, and give sufficient time for them to do so before starting classwork or talking about any other subject.

Before the student leaves class, check his assignment book to make sure that he has taken down the assignment correctly, legibly, and completely—and in such a way that his parents will be able to understand what is required.

Communicating with Parents

Refer the parents to the following sources for specific suggestions about improving homework for their child: Zentall, S. S., & Goldstein, S. (1999). *Seven Steps to Homework Success: A Family Guide for Solving Common Homework*

Problems. Plantation, FL: Specialty Press (800-233-9273); or *Handwriting without Tears* (Canter, 1993).

Ask the student's parents whether they are satisfied with the type and amount of homework their child receives, how much time the child is spending, how much assistance is needed, what kinds of problems are encountered, and what suggestions they could offer to improve the homework policies for their son.

Ensure that the student and his parents understand the [class, school] homework policy.

Keep the parents informed about the student's homework assignments, as well as problems with homework completion. Focus the communication on problem solving and creating a realistic homework plan for the student.

Set up a system by which the teacher and parents can communicate on a daily basis. This may include the use of e-mail, faxes, telephone, the assignment book, or a separate notebook sent between school and home daily. Issues to communicate include missed or incomplete assignments, lost materials, and difficulty with certain assignments. When communicating about behavior and emotional stability, use a method of communication that the child cannot access.

To ensure that the student and his parents can always discover what the homework assignment is, establish telephone homework hotlines (updated daily), send homework assignments through e-mail, or post assignments on a website.

Making Homework Meaningful

Before assigning the student homework, ask yourself if the purpose of a homework assignment is to develop skill or knowledge. If knowledge is emphasized, do not allow weaknesses in reading or writing to interfere with activities. For example, make sure that the child can read the history homework or provide the reading on tape.

To increase interest in homework completion, select assignments to reinforce what has been learned, alternate math and reading homework on different nights, keep repetition to a minimum, and encourage the student to begin homework in class to ensure that he understands the process.

Review and provide feedback to the student on all homework assignments. Include positive along with corrective comments.

Ensure that all homework provides practice and review of material that was covered in class and that the student has the skills to complete the work with minimal parental involvement.

Assign work that is interesting and relevant to the child's age level. Provide choice, when possible. Help the student understand how his school work relates to his own skills and experiences.

Match the student's homework assignments to the goals and objectives in his individual education plan (IEP).

Ensure that all homework assignments are at the student's independent level of performance. The student should understand what to do and have the skills necessary to perform the task.

Use homework to provide independent practice and reinforcement of skills that the student has been taught, understands, and does correctly. Keep the assignments short.

Use homework to provide practice in application of skills or knowledge in which the student has demonstrated basic competence.

Do not penalize the student for errors made on homework. Instead, confer with him regarding the errors to attempt to determine why they were made. Use this information to design appropriate instruction and/or to revise the homework assignments.

If possible, assign homework near the beginning of the class period and explain to the student how to complete it. Give the student some time to start the homework so that you can check for understanding before he leaves class.

Do not use homework assignments as punishment or failure to complete assignments as a basis for denying participation in school activities, such as field trips. When assignments become part of a behavior management system, the student's attitude toward these assignments will become negative.

Do not make homework part of the class behavior management system. This will reduce motivation and encourage the student to develop a negative attitude toward homework assignments.

Modifying Homework Assignments

Because the student [has trouble sustaining attention, reads slowly], modify the amount of work that he is required to do at home.

Based upon the present circumstances, do not assign the student homework. Instead, provide a time for all homework assignments to be completed and handed in during or after school.

Attempt to reduce the amount of homework for the student without changing the purpose of homework. For example, have the student complete only the odd-numbered problems on the page.

Modify the amount of homework so that the student can spend increased time in positive nonacademic pursuits, such as time with family, sports, music lessons, or socializing with friends.

Help the student obtain the phone numbers of at least two students in each of his classes so that he has someone to call after school if questions arise regarding a homework assignment.

Reduce the amount of work the student is required to do during independent in-class assignments so that he is more likely to complete his work in school. When figuring the grade for in-class or homework assignments, the reduced amount assigned is considered as 100%. Do not send unfinished class work home for homework.

Reduce the amount of work in each area assigned for homework so that the student can complete his assignment in approximately the same amount of time other students are expected to spend. Examples of modified assignments are: solving the odd-numbered math problems instead of all the items, studying 10 spelling words instead of 20, and writing a half-page report instead of a whole page.

Due to the student's attentional problems, he is less efficient than his peers with comparable academic ability and takes considerably more time to complete his assignments. Provide the student with some flexibility in assignment deadlines. Give him some passes at the beginning of the semester that will allow him one or two days, or an extra weekend, to complete and turn in an assignment and some "The dog ate my homework" passes that allow him to skip an assignment altogether, without penalty.

Instead of assigning a certain number of pages to read or a certain number of problems, assign the amount of time that the student should work on the homework (e.g., 15 minutes). Have the parent sign the homework when the student has worked for the specified time.

For each assignment, have the student record the amount of time it took him to complete the assignment. Have the parent sign next to the recorded time. This will allow you to monitor the quantity of homework assigned to the student.

Provide the student with a certain number of excused homework assignments.

Allow the parents to help decide which homework assignments should be reduced or modified. Accept their requests for extended due dates.

When assigning homework that does not have obvious academic application, such as coloring a picture, doing word searches, or making cards, make the assignment optional for the student. His [general work pace, inefficient attention, struggle with basic skills, academic tutoring] will continuously require more time than other students will have to put in.

Hand back all of the student's assignments with specific comments about what he did well and what he needs to improve. Comments such as "Nice job" are too general to help him improve his skills.

Organizing Assignments and Materials

Teach the student specific study skills to help him approach homework tasks more efficiently and effectively.

Have a tutor, resource teacher, or academic coach teach the student how to (a) organize homework and assignments, (b) complete the work, and (c) turn in the work on time.

Help the student develop a notebook for organizing class notes and assignments. Use a binder notebook that is divided into several sections and has pockets that may be used for completed assignments.

Provide the student with a separate folder that he may use to transport homework to and from school. Have him place new assignments on one side of the folder and completed assignments on the other side to be handed in on the next day. [See Strategies: Organization of Materials and Assignments.]

Provide the student with an assignment book in which to write his homework for each class. Check it for legibility and accuracy and sign it. If there is no homework, have the student write "none" and have it signed. At homework time, have the parent check their child's assignment book, help him prioritize the assignments, check the completed homework, and sign his book for each completed assignment.

Before the student goes home, check his assignment book to ensure that all homework assignments are legible, accurate, and complete.

Ensure that the student has an assignment book that he brings home from school every day. Have the teacher or a responsible peer check his assignment book to ensure that he has the needed materials.

Encourage the student to write down all homework assignments as they are given. If he is confused about an assignment, have him meet with the teacher after class or during office hours.

Help the student set up an assignment notebook to organize assigned tasks and materials. [See Strategies: Organization of Materials and Assignments.]

Have the student read a book entitled *Becoming a Master Student* (Ellis, 2000) that provides numerous study strategies, planning techniques, and time management strategies.

Do not penalize the student for errors made on homework. Instead, confer with him regarding the errors to attempt to determine why they were made. Use this information to design appropriate instruction and/or to revise the homework assignments.

Because the student requires more assistance, structure, and supervision than most [ninth-graders] of comparable ability to get started on assignments and to carry them out to completion once begun, program into his schedule a time at the beginning and the end of each week with [each of his teachers; one designated teacher; his counselor] to develop a written schedule for working on assignments.

Long-Term Assignments/Tests

Do not assign more than one long-term project at a time. The student needs support to manage the organization of just one such project.

Teach the student how to plan for long-term assignments. For example, he could establish intermediate, sequential deadlines on each assignment within a unit of work and place each completed piece in a special folder on the "due date." The next-to-last date would be the due date for the last assignment and the final date would be when the entire contract is due. The intervening time would be used for final proofreading and editing. Alternatively, record progressive due dates on the assignments within the contract and have the student hand in each assignment as he completes it.

For long-term assignments, have the student break the assignments into steps, schedule a deadline for each step, and schedule time in his assignment calendar for him to actually work on that step. Have the student hand in each step of the assignment before going on. If needed, tape a month-long calendar on the back of the student's homework folder so that he may keep track of the steps of the project.

Notify the student's parents as far in advance as possible of any major project that the student will need to work on at home. Examples include research reports, book reports, map drawings, timelines, science fair projects, and upcoming tests. Provide written instructions to the parents that include all of the requirements for the project and the grading criteria.

Whenever the parent is notified of a long-term project, encourage the parent or a tutor to help the student break it into stages and write deadlines for the completion of each stage on a large wall calendar. Set aside a certain amount of time nightly or weekly to work on the project.

Teach the student specific organizational skills to use with homework. These may include: (a) learning how to keep an assignment book, (b) learning how to task-analyze assignments, (c) allocating appropriate amounts of time to complete assignments, (d) identifying and locating required materials and information, and (e) planning the steps leading to completion of extended assignments, such as term papers.

Teach the student to record information concerning upcoming tests on a special Test Information page immediately following his regular assignment calendar sheet. Or, the student may designate a special section in the assignment book for test information.

Teach the student how to record information regarding tests as follows: (a) the date of the test (on the Test Information page and in his regular calendar), (b) the chapters to be covered, (c) the dates of lecture notes to be included, (d) additional information such as field trips or movies, (e) the type of questions to be asked (e.g., essay, multiple-choice), and (f) the point value of the test. Have the student note any information that the teacher states will not be on the test.

Teach the student to ask his teachers periodically about upcoming test dates. Some teachers announce tests only a few days ahead of time and the student needs additional time to prepare for tests.

Teach the student to include on his assignment book or calendar specific days and times to study for an upcoming test. Have him note what information to study in each session and the method he is going to use.

Maintain and post on the wall a master list of in-class assignments, homework assignments, and tests. This will help the student self-monitor what assignments are currently due and which have not yet been completed.

Completing Assignments

Review homework assignments and take-home tests to ensure that the student has completed all sections and items. Return any incomplete assignments/tests to the student for completion, without penalty.

Provide the student with homework excuse slips when he completes a certain number of assignments.

Develop a school schedule for the student in which one class (e.g., elective, foreign language) is replaced with a study hall or a second study hall to allow for tutorial support and in-school homework time. This alleviates the problem of the student doing homework after school when he is cognitively exhausted and is without the benefit of medication.

Have the student graph the number of completed homework assignments for the week or the month. Have him make three columns: homework completed (color a green square); homework late or partially completed (color a yellow square); homework not started (color a red square). Provide a reward when the student achieves a predetermined number of green squares.

If the student fails to complete a homework assignment, talk to him about why the assignment was not completed and assist him in developing a system to make sure certain assignments are completed. Consider specific adaptations in assignments and whether too many assignments are being made.

Request that the student's parents help him create a clean, quiet, organized space for nightly homework.

Request that the student's parents set aside a regular period of time each day for homework and that one parent be available during that time to provide help, as needed.

Before the student begins each night's homework, ensure that he understands what he is required to do and then encourage him to complete the homework independently.

Before beginning nightly homework, help the student review all assignments, estimate the time each will take, prioritize them, and then list them in order on an index card. As the student finishes an assignment, have him cross it off the list.

Encourage or help the student to remove unnecessary papers from his backpack or notebook periodically. Help the student learn how to keep the notebook organized.

Set a specific amount of time for the student to work on homework and include short breaks. Have the parent sign the paper when the student has completed the pre-established amount of time.

Encourage the student to estimate how long a task will take and the time needed to complete the task. Trying to meet his estimated time will help the student sustain attention and increase his accuracy in estimating the necessary time.

To involve the student in self-monitoring homework completion and accuracy, have him correct and evaluate his own assignments.

Turning in Assignments

As the student often completes his homework and then forgets to turn it in, remind the student daily to turn in his homework and specify that he is to do it right then. Make sure he does so.

Regardless of the classroom routine for turning in homework, have the student hand his directly to the teacher. The teacher is then aware of whether or not he has done so and can remind him if necessary.

Indirect Teacher Support of Student Organization

Maintain a consistent schedule. Have daily activities planned in a consistent, and thus, predictable sequence. A consistent schedule facilitates classroom routines, daily reinforcement of skills and information, independence in getting ready for and starting activities, feelings of control and competence, and the ability to recall and discuss daily activities.

Keep the physical environment organized. Maintain the room with the appearance of orderliness and tidiness. Have materials categorized and placed by function, frequency of need, and who needs to get them. Have materials put away when not in use.

While explaining activities and tasks, tell students the purpose of the activity or the objective of the lesson, and what they are supposed to know or be able to do when it is completed.

In planning lessons: (a) Know your specific teaching objective. What are the students supposed to be able to do when they complete the activity? (b) Plan how you are going to present the material or lesson; (c) Plan the steps through which you will take the students to achieve your teaching objective; (d) Have the materials ready and immediately accessible; (e) Plan what the students will do on their own based on what they have learned.

Explain your expectations for behavior during transitions between activities. Teach transition behavior the same as you would any other skill. Provide practice.

TESTING/TEST-TAKING

Accommodations are based on the student's daily instructional needs, not used only on tests or assessments. Each accommodation should be related to the individual student's needs and reduce or minimize the impact of the student's disability on accessing the general curriculum and demonstrating knowledge and skills. Accommodations must be reasonable as well as documented on the current 504 Plan or the IEP. Use of normative scoring is appropriate for most testing accommodations, such as extended time.

Modifications are designed to support and enhance learning so that the student may progress academically. Modifications may include out-of-level testing and non-standardized procedures. In many cases, these modifications will preclude the use of normative scoring. As with accommodations, modifications must be supported by diagnostic evaluation and documented on the IEP.

Testing/Test-Taking
    Test Instructions
    Test Format Modifications
    Strategies
    Extended Time on Standardized Tests
    Testing Environment

Test Instructions

When administering [classroom, standardized tests], [select any that are appropriate]
- Speak directly to the student; make eye contact.
- Ask the student to repeat or paraphrase the instructions.
- Read the instructions to the student.
- Paraphrase the instructions for the student using simpler

language. Alternatively, give the instructions in smaller increments.
- Highlight the keywords or elements in the instructions so that the student is more likely to attend to them.
- Draw a border around the instructions to separate them from the rest of the printed information.
- Use oral cues or prompts to remind the student, at key points, what he is supposed to do.
- Monitor the student's work periodically throughout the testing to ensure that he has not forgotten the instructions and is doing the test correctly.
- Encourage the student to ask for clarification of the instructions before starting the test and during the test, as needed.

After giving the instructions to the group, reread the instructions individually to the student, page by page or section by section.

Test Format Modifications

Permit the student to take open-book exams.

Reduce the number of questions the student will be required to answer on a test.

Instead of having one comprehensive test at the end of a chapter, provide the student with short, daily quizzes to monitor progress.

Sequence the questions on the exam from easy to difficult. Either assign the student a certain number of questions to complete or just the questions at his present performance level.

Review exams and identify the questions appropriate for the student. On the exams, circle each question you would like him to complete. Inform the student to start with the circled questions and then to complete any other questions if he has enough time.

Because of difficulties with writing, when assessing the student's knowledge of content areas, keep writing requirements to a minimum. On tests, provide him with multiple choice, matching, true-false, or sentence completion questions, rather than essay questions.

In content area classes, allow the student to take oral examinations so that you can accurately assess what he has learned rather than what he is able to read or write.

In content area classes, have the student take the written test along with the other students. Tape-record the test and provide him with earphones so that he will not have difficulty understanding the questions. Schedule a time to meet with him after the test so that he can respond to the questions orally. Compare his written and oral answers and give credit for accurate content contained in both.

On math tests with word problems, tape-record the word problems for the student. Say the number of the item, pause (giving the student time to pause the tape recorder while he finds the problem), read the problem slowly, pause, and read it again. The pauses allow the student time to find the problem and when he needs more time, to pause the tape recorder without losing information.

On timed examinations, only review and score the items that the student was able to complete.

Because of his difficulties in maintaining his place while reading, provide the student with large-print format on all test materials. Allow the student to mark responses directly on the test rather than using an answer sheet or bubble key.

Provide study questions for exams that demonstrate the test content as well as the type of test format. Provide several illustrations of what constitutes an *acceptable* and a *good* response.

Encourage the student to find out from instructors prior to examinations what format will be used (e.g., short answer, essay, multiple choice). Ask the instructors if practice exams or sample exams are available for additional practice.

Teach the student how to adjust his studying for the kind of test that will be given. Use practice tests as a means for practicing the type of test format.

Test formats have different implications for studying. Ensure that the student knows the types of questions that will be on the exam. For an essay exam, the student needs to be prepared to write about general principles and concepts. For a multiple choice exam, the student needs to be able to identify, rather than produce information (Scruggs & Mastropieri, 1992).

Prior to exams, provide the student with practice tests that have a similar format and question type. Exposure to the test format will reduce test-related anxiety and improve performance.

Teach the student the following pointers for answering multiple-choice questions: (a) Make sure you know the meaning for "All of the above" and "None of the above," (b) Read the question stem, (c) Underline any keywords (e.g., *not, unless, except, incorrect, false, never, always*), (d) Read the stem of the question along with each answer choice, (e) Cross out each incorrect answer choice. If more than one choice is left when you are done, read the stem with each of the answer choices remaining. Choose the best, (f) Do not change an answer unless you are sure it is incorrect. Generally, your first answer is correct.

Teach the student the following pointers for answering true/false questions: (a) Assume an answer is true unless the statement can be proven false, (b) Be sure that all parts of the statement are correct before marking it true, (c) Watch for negatives such as *not* or prefixes such as *in* (e.g., *infrequently*), since these can completely change the meaning of a statement, (d) Simplify statements that contain a double negative (e.g., "Birds that are not black cannot hunt at night" becomes "Only birds that are black can hunt at night"), (e) Assume that absolute statements are false, and that qualified statements are true.

When answering questions on a bubble response sheet, have the student mark the row he is to write his response on with a small and lightweight mousepad. It can be moved down to the next line easily but is less likely to move accidentally than an index card or paper.

When the student takes a test using a bubble response sheet, provide an enlarged copy of the response sheet to make it easier for the student to keep his place.

Because the student has difficulty keeping her place and moving her eyes efficiently from one paper to another, do not require the student to use bubble sheets for standardized tests. Instead, permit her to circle her answers directly on the test.

To accommodate for her deficiencies in the rapid processing of symbols, ask the student to mark her answers in the booklet rather than on the scantron sheet.

On all tests, use a format that provides ample white space between lines of print and between other print or graphic information on the page. Increase the spacing between items.

On tests, draw a border around the instructions with one color highlighter and separate other clusters of items by different color borders (e.g., questions, graphics).

Strategies

Teach the student that on all tests he should use his time wisely, read all directions and questions carefully, attempt to answer every question, and ask for clarification any time he is uncertain or does not fully understand a question (Putnam, 1992, p. 20).

Teach the student specific test-taking strategies, such as reading over the entire test before starting, outlining the answers to essay questions, and reading all multiple-choice answers with the stem sentence before selecting a response.

To help the student represent his knowledge on tests, teach him the following steps: (a) Read the test instructions before starting, (b) Ask for clarification of any instructions that you do not understand clearly, (c) Look through the test to get an idea of how much you need to do in the time allowed, (d) Decide how much time you should use to answer each item, (e) Answer easy or known items first, then go back to the hard ones, (f) Answer all items unless there is a penalty for guessing.

Teach the student how to eliminate answers on multiple-choice tests, and then to select one of the remaining items.

Teach the student to preview a test before starting to write and to circle any items with which he will have difficulty. Then the student should take the test, answering all of the items for which he knows the answer. If the student skips a question, he should write its number down after the last question to remind himself to go back to answer it.

Teach the student how to read test questions carefully. Have him underline the verb that describes what he is to do and then follow the directions exactly.

Teach the student how to employ prewriting strategies, such as brainstorming, writing down thoughts, and then organizing the key ideas before answering an essay question.

Teach the student how to estimate the amount of time he will need to complete specific questions on exams composed of several short essay questions.

For tests with lengthy reading passages, teach the student how to skim the information briefly and then proceed directly to the questions.

On multiple-choice tests, teach the student to read the stem and then attempt to think of the correct answer before reading the choices, then consider all answer choices, use elimination strategies, consider specific determiners (e.g., *always* or *never,* which are often false), and consider which question stem bears the most logical relationship with the answer (Scruggs & Mastropieri, 1992).

Teach the student to prepare for tests so that his stress and anxiety will be reduced.

Have the student practice the SNOW strategy (Scruggs & Mastropieri, 1992) to answer all essay questions. *S*tudy the question, *N*ote important details, *O*rganize the information, and *W*rite directly to the point.

Teach the student the PIRATES Test Taking Strategy (Hughes & Schumaker, 1991) for answering objective tests. [See Strategies: PIRATES Test-Taking Strategy.]

For short answer questions, encourage the student to: read each question carefully, be brief but complete, ensure that the response answers the question asked, and use information from the rest of the test to help confirm answers.

To answer essay questions, encourage the student to: read the directions carefully, read each question carefully, outline a response, get to the point quickly, and respond to all parts of the question.

Prior to taking essay exams, encourage the student to anticipate the questions and to write out answers for these questions.

Encourage the student to ask instructors for clarification when he does not understand what a question means.

Help the student learn to read test directions carefully. Have him underline the verb that tells what you are supposed to do and then follow the directions precisely.

Teach the student how to turn essay questions into the topic or main sentence for the essay. By rephrasing the question into a statement, and by rereading the topic sentence, the student will be able to ensure that he is maintaining the topic.

Teach the student the following strategies to use when she is required to use separate answer sheets or bubble sheets: (a) fold the test booklet so that only one page is showing, (b) ensure that the subtest matches the numbers on the answer sheet, (c) check the page number each time the page is turned, (d) note whether the answer sheet has one or two sides, and (e) mark answer choices clearly (Scruggs & Mastropieri, 1992).

Teach the student one or two relaxation techniques that he can use during tests to alleviate his anxiety.

Extended Time on Standardized Tests

Provide the student with extended time for tests, including standardized tests. In coordination with the student, prior to giving the test, establish a time and place for him to complete any items he does not finish. The absence of time constraints will allow him to work more carefully and with less anxiety, and allow him to check his work before turning it in, without feeling that he must rush through to make sure he can finish.

Provide extended time on tests. Because of the student's difficulty with [sustained and focused attention, speed of information processing, and work production under time constraints], it is critical to differentiate between lack of sufficient knowledge and lack of sufficient work time.

Because of his slow reading rate and processing style, the student needs additional time to read, comprehend, and analyze material.

Because of his slow reading rate, permit the student to take untimed exams.

As the student's processing speed and reading rate are significantly low, provide extended time on all in-class tests and exams, as well as standardized examinations.

The student's processing speed, short-term memory, and long-term retrieval are all significantly lower than his verbal abilities. The student will require additional time on tests so that he can accurately demonstrate his knowledge and abilities.

Given the student's difficulty with [retrieving and producing information within a time-limited frame], provide the student with a [50%] increase in time allotment on all [standardized, classroom] tests.

Provide the student with untimed administration of all group-administered, standardized tests. Test results under time constraints would not allow the student to demonstrate his current skill and achievement levels.

The student possesses superior oral language abilities. His difficulties with [insert areas related to low performance] do not let him demonstrate his potential on tests that have stringent time limits. Provide the student with extended time on examinations so that he can demonstrate his capabilities.

Because he requires more time to process linguistic information, administer all standardized tests with extended time. This will allow for a more accurate assessment of the student's abilities.

Given that the student's weakness is in formulating ideas for written expression, extended time is not necessary for multiple choice or reading comprehension tests, but is rec-

ommended for all tests requiring lengthy writing, such as essay tests.

Based upon the type of task, the student may need extended time on certain assignments and exams. Decisions and arrangements will need to be made in conjunction with the class instructor.

Remove the time constraints from all exams so that the student is able to demonstrate his knowledge.

Encourage the student to request untimed or extended time on exams that are designed to assess his knowledge, such as college entrance exams. Have him meet with the school counselor who will provide the appropriate forms and application materials for seeking accommodations.

Whenever possible, eliminate time constraints on written work. Additional time will help the student organize, write, and monitor her work without the anxiety of a time limit.

Remind the student that extended time is not the same as unlimited time and that he will still be required to pace himself during testing.

Discuss with the student the maximum amount of time he can focus optimally in the test situation, and break up testing sessions so as not to exceed that length of time.

Shorten test sessions and either provide frequent breaks or spread out the sessions over several days.

Testing Environment

Administer all tests in a separate, quiet environment.

Because the student has difficulty concentrating, permit him to take exams in a quiet room without other students present.

Allow the student to take his tests in a private setting so that he does not get distracted by noise and frustrated when other students finish more quickly.

To enable the student to dictate responses into a tape recorder, administer his test in a room separate from other students.

Because the student will have a reader for all testing, provide him with a separate, quiet setting.

Administer tests to the student either individually or in a small group setting.

Within the testing room, seat the student so as to minimize distractions. This may be a specific area of the room (e.g., away from windows, door, air conditioning unit), a study carrel, close to the administrator, or away from particular students.

ATTENTIONAL DISORDERS

Related Sections: Organization/Homework/Time Management; Behavior Management and Interventions; Reading Comprehension: Study Strategies; Content Area Instruction/Strategies; Short-Term Memory; Executive Functioning; Social Skills/Self-Esteem; all achievement sections

Attentional Disorders
    Further Evaluation
    Service Delivery and Documents
    Parent as Advocate, Educating School Staff, Case
        Managers
    Maintaining a Reality Perspective
    Class Placement and Class Schedules
    Environmental Accommodations
    Giving Instructions
    Helping the Student Follow Through on Instructions
    Maintaining Routines, Departures from Routines
    Teaching Approaches and Modifying Task Character-
        istics
    Beginnings and Transitions
    Increasing Attention and Time On-Task
    Task Completion
    Improving Academic Performance
    Directing/Controlling Activity Level
    School/Home Communication
    Developing Self-Advocacy in Older Students
    Building/Maintaining Self-Confidence and Self-Esteem
    Noneducational Treatment Considerations
        Medication Usage
        Counseling, Parent Training, Educational/Support
            Groups

Note: In accordance with the *Diagnostic and Statistical Manual of Mental Disorders IV* (DSM IV), disorders previously referred to as Attention Deficit Disorder with and without hyperactivity will be referred to as Attention Deficit Hyperactivity Disorder (ADHD). Students may fit any of the three types: Impulsive-Hyperactive, Inattentive,

or Combined. Students with ADHD typically require behavior management techniques—often the same techniques as those recommended for a broader range of students with behavior disorders unrelated to or comorbid with ADHD (e.g., Oppositional Defiant Disorder, Conduct Disorder, Antisocial Personality Disorder, Depression, Tourette Syndrome). These techniques are found in a separate section: Behavior Management and Interventions. Many of those recommendations are critical to the improved functioning of students with ADHD and were developed for and researched with students with ADHD. Other related sections are listed above. When choosing recommendations from any section for a student with ADHD, it is important to differentiate between a skill deficit (not knowing the skill) and a performance deficit (not using a known skill), and between problem behaviors that are intentional and within the control of the student and those that are secondary to weak self-regulation. As with other sections of Recommendations, an evaluator must use specific information about a student's unique characteristics and needs to determine which recommendations are likely to be most the appropriate and effective.

Further Evaluation

Because the student has noticeable difficulty staying on task, working carefully on mildly challenging tasks, and sitting reasonably still, consider consulting a [behavioral pediatrician, psychiatrist, psychologist] about the possibility of Attention Deficit Hyperactivity Disorder.

Provide a questionnaire/checklist specific to ADHD to the teacher(s), parent(s), and student. An example of one such scale is the Conners' Rating Scales—Revised and, specifically, the DSM-IV Symptoms scale and the ADHD Index within the CRS-R. Subsequently, interview the respondents individually to follow-up responses of concern. Be aware that the respondents' interpretation of the questions, and thus their responses, may differ substantially from the evaluator's.

During the next month, monitor the individual's behavior for characteristics of Attention Deficit Hyperactivity Disorder. Conduct several classroom observations to document the percentage of time he is on or off task, have teachers complete standardized questionnaires, and establish a behavioral program addressing the most problematic behaviors. If a structured behavior management program does not produce the desired changes, suggest that his parents schedule an appointment with [their pediatrician, a behavioral pediatrician, a psychiatrist, a psychologist] who has expertise in ADHD.

Meet with the student's parents to discuss further concerns about Attention Deficit Hyperactivity Disorder. Refer them to their pediatrician [or a behavioral pediatrician, a psychiatrist, a psychologist with expertise in ADHD] to investigate this condition, to rule out other behavioral or medical disorders that may present as ADHD, to educate the parents and child, and, if a diagnosis is made, to establish a treatment plan.

The student's behaviors suggest a need for a [psychological, psychiatric] evaluation to diagnose or rule out a psychological or behavioral disorder and, if appropriate, to suggest treatment.

If the student's parents are reluctant to pursue the possibility of an ADHD diagnosis with their physician, have the school assessment team conduct a comprehensive evaluation and, if findings warrant, classify the student, for educational purposes, as having ADHD.

After the student has been stabilized on medication, reevaluate his cognitive and academic performance.

Service Delivery and Documents

Due to the deleterious effect of his ADHD on his ability to benefit from the instruction offered in the classroom, his ability to demonstrate his knowledge in classroom productions, and his ability to develop age-appropriate social relationships, provide the student with resource services and accommodations in accordance with the provisions of Section 504 and the Individuals with Disabilities Education Act (IDEA: Other Health Impaired).

As the student has been diagnosed with ADHD as well as [learning disabilities], write behavioral objectives, modifications, and accommodations addressing his ADHD-related [educational, organizational, and social] needs into his Individualized Educational Plan along with those for his [learning disabilities.]

As the student's ADHD symptoms disrupt his learning, as well as the learning of others, to a significant degree, assemble a team to write a Functional Behavioral Assessment and Behavioral Intervention Plan.

Parent as Advocate, Educating School Staff, Case Managers

Seek a multimodal treatment approach for the student that includes parent training in relating to and managing the behavior of a child/adolescent with ADHD, a systematic behavioral intervention that is implemented consistently, and medication, the effects of which are closely monitored by the school staff with frequent feedback to the parents and the prescribing physician.

Meet with the school [principal, appropriate agent] to request initiation of procedures to evaluate [or establish] the need for an accommodation plan (under Section 504 of the Rehabilitation Act of 1973) or an Individualized Education Plan (under the Individuals with Disabilities Education Act) to facilitate the student's success in the school setting. Follow up with a written request.

Before the beginning of the school year, meet with the student's teacher(s) to explain Attention Deficit Hyperactivity Disorder [or other conditions/disorders], how this condition is manifested in the student's behavior, and the situations in which the problem behaviors are most likely to occur. Discuss with the general education teacher(s) his or her key role as a member of the treatment team and solicit cooperation in working with the [psychologist, counselor, pediatrician] in establishing accommodations and interventions as needed.

Help the student's teacher learn more about Attention Deficit Hyperactivity Disorder by providing reading material, videotapes, suggestions as to helpful technological devices, and a list of informational websites.

When considering the student's negative classroom behaviors, attempt to differentiate between a skill deficit (not knowing the skill) and a performance deficit (not using a known skill), and between problem behaviors that are intentional and within the control of the student and those that are secondary to weak self-regulation. Do not punish the student for behaviors that are symptoms of the disability (e.g., poor self-regulation, impulsive actions, lack of organization, poor listening) until you have established a behavioral program that delineates and supports expected behavior and clearly spells out the consequences for infractions of the rules.

All staff working with the student need to be educated about ADHD and how this disorder affects the student's behavior and performance.

Shortly before the end of the current school year, schedule a meeting with the school principal and this year's teacher and/or counselor to discuss the instructional style and behavior management system to which the student responds best. Use that information to decide on next year's class placement.

At least [four times a year], request a meeting with the teachers in which they can show you the materials they are using with the student, how they are being used, how the student is progressing, the skills with which he is having particular difficulty, and how you can help.

Educate the school bus driver (e.g., small pamphlet, lend a videotape) about ADHD in general, the problematic behaviors the student is likely to display on the bus, and ways to prevent or handle them.

Assign the student to a case manager [or designate the student's counselor as case manager] to coordinate the multiple services the student is receiving, to ensure that the requirements of the accommodation plan [or the accommodations listed on the IEP] are being met, and to act as a facilitator between the school staff and the student, his parents, physician, and his outside counselor.

Help ensure that the student is receiving optimal benefit from his medication by notifying the case manager immediately if the student starts demonstrating hyperactive, impulsive, or inattentive behavior in excess of that expected for other students of his chronological age.

Maintaining Reality Perspective

Ensure that the parents and teachers understand that the behaviors the student exhibits relative to ADHD are neither caused by poor parenting nor lack of effort and caring on the student's part but by the student's neurological makeup.

Keep a perspective about the nature of a chronic disability. Remember that the student did not choose this condition and probably won't grow out of it. ADHD is managed, not cured.

When setting up a behavioral intervention for a child with ADHD, ensure that the adults involved understand that external support for maintaining the target behaviors (e.g., attention to task, not bothering others) may be ongoing. For most children with ADHD, behavioral changes are not maintained after the support has been faded.

When establishing accommodations and modifications in the school setting, adjust expectations and remain focused on the goal. For example, because of his disability, the student may be having difficulty remembering to write down his assignments and, consequently, does not complete his homework. Decide which goal is most immediate and achievable. If it is completing homework so he can participate in class and keep his grades up, he must have help in writing down his assignments. Without support in the latter, he will fail in both.

Do not personalize the student's problems or see the negative behaviors as a lack of respect for you and your authority. Recognize that the student is not in a power struggle with you, he is "stuck" within his disability and is unable to take a different perspective at the time.

Class Placement and Class Schedules

Schedule the classes most likely to be difficult for the student in the morning and electives in the afternoon.

Develop a school schedule for the student in which one class (e.g., elective, foreign language) is replaced with a study hall or a second study hall to allow for tutorial support and in-school homework time. This alleviates the problem of the student doing homework after school when he is cognitively exhausted and is without the benefit of medication.

Students with ADHD generally do well with calm and well-organized teachers who use daily routines and positive, consistent behavior management techniques, who are comfortable accommodating individual needs, who can correct without being critical, and are knowledgeable or willing to learn about the behavioral characteristics associated with ADHD [or other behavioral disorders.]

The student requires a class placement incorporating the following components:
- a highly organized teacher with a structured and systematic teaching style and calm, respectful manner of interacting with students;
- a behavioral program with clear rules, frequent and immediate positive reinforcement for target behaviors, and immediate consequences for specified negative behaviors;
- a consistent daily schedule so that areas of academic instruction, recess, and routines (e.g., passing out daily work, assigning homework) are done in the same manner and order daily;

- a morning review of each day's schedule (with the student given a copy of his schedule for that day);
- a minimum of classroom noise and confusion (visual and auditory);
- a system in which students are aware that a transition is coming, when the current activity will end, what will happen next, and what they are expected to do to be ready; and
- an emphasis on interactive and participatory instructional activities in which students have little or no wait time.

Environmental Accommodations

Place the student in as small a class as possible.

Keep classroom noise to a minimum. The Classroom Noise Monitor senses the noise level of the classroom and at a preset level sounds a buzzer and displays a red light.

Seat the student away from possible distractions, such as the air conditioner, the window, or a talkative student.

Provide a visually quiet, nondistracting place in the classroom where the student can go when he needs or wants to work in a more isolated environment.

Have a portable study carrel available for the student to either put on his desk or have a permanent study carrel available, separated from most of classroom activities. Allow the student to move to that desk when he feels that separating himself would help him to focus his attention.

Seat the student close to the teacher so that she may help him to remain on task or to return to task. The proximity of the teacher will help the student stay involved in teacher-directed and interactive tasks and make it easier for the teacher to make frequent contact and provide feedback during independent work.

Circulate through the classroom, in a random path, between the tiers or pods of desks, during all types of activities. This facilitates more frequent contact with the student while at the same time increasing the frequency of your physical proximity to other students. Moreover, teacher movement helps students remain on task by heightening their awareness that you are likely to be at any student's desk next.

Arrange desks in a multitiered horseshoe pattern or pods of 4 desks to provide easy access to each desk. Figure III.14 illustrates these seating arrangements.

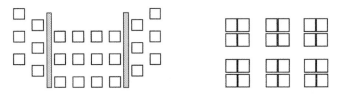

Figure III.14   Classroom Seating Arrangements for Facilitating Teacher Circulation

Schedule more cognitively demanding classes in the morning, leaving electives, more active classes, or classes that hold special interest for the student in the afternoon.

To preclude pushing and touching, avoid situations in which students are in close proximity (e.g., lining up, seats crowded around a table).

Giving Instructions

Encourage the student to ask for clarification and repetition of instructions.

Make sure you have eye contact with the student before speaking to him or giving oral instructions.

When giving instructions for an activity, provide enough time for the student to accomplish each step before going on. For example, wait until the student has found the correct page in a text before explaining the task.

Make oral instructions clear and concise. Simplify complex instructions and avoid multiple commands.

Explain all the instructions clearly before allowing the student to start any assignment. Methods for helping to clarify the instructions for the student and the group include: having the student or another student repeat the instructions to the group; modeling the activity before having students start; or pretending to model the activity and asking the students to try and catch you in mistakes. Make mistakes deliberately, and, when caught, ask, "What did I do wrong? What was I supposed to do?"

Before speaking to the student, come within 3 feet of him and say, "___, look at me." Once he has made eye contact, continue with what you wanted to say. Do not do this in such a way or in situations (e.g., large group interactions or lecture) in which attention will be drawn to the student.

Always write homework assignments on the board or on a handout for the student to take home.

For whole-group instructions, the following sequence is helpful:

1. Decide on a signal to let students know you want their attention. Use the same signal consistently. Examples are ringing a bell, tapping a triangle, turning the lights off and on, turning on a music tape, and saying, "Attention please." Another way of getting students' attention is to tell them to make some physical movement (e.g., "Put your hands on top of your head"). The students who are not paying attention notice the others doing this and look to see what is happening. Signals other than voice are easier for students to differentiate from background noise.
2. Do not speak until all students are quiet and looking at your face. (Be aware that in some cultures, making eye contact with an elder or authority figure is considered rude.)
3. Establish helping behaviors to guide students in helping each other to turn their attention to you. [See Strategies: Behavioral Interventions for the Whole Class.]
4. Give instructions briefly, clearly, and in the same sequence as they are to be followed.
5. Write instructions on the board as backup or for students who process information more slowly or have poor memory.
6. If a transition will follow the instructions, teach students that nobody moves until all instructions have been given and the teacher gives the transition signal. [See Strategies: Transitions Between Activities.]

Helping the Student Follow Through on Instructions

To counteract the student's tendency to forget to follow the second and third instruction within a set of worksheets, have him highlight each instruction in a different color. Each time he completes one, he checks it off.

Talk the student through a set of multiple instructions so that he can break the task down into doable steps. Help him write down the steps on an index card, or do it for him, so he has a visual reminder.

With the student's prior permission, set up a buddy system by selecting a student who will repeat or explain instructions to the target student at his request.

To offset the student's difficulty holding multiple instructions in mind, always write instructions on the board. If possible, do so before giving and explaining them orally.

Maintaining Routines, Departures from Routines

Keep the daily schedule consistent. Routine sets up a structure in which the student can develop a sense of inner organization and control rather than feeling as if the day's activities and schedule happen arbitrarily.

Within the classroom routine, vary types of tasks, shorten work periods, and provide frequent reinforcers for staying on task or working carefully.

As children with ADHD often respond poorly to changes in routine, warn the student ahead of time, privately if possible, about any upcoming change and how it will affect him.

When planning situations that will depart from the normal routine (e.g., field trips, assemblies, parties), think ahead to the problems the student may have in this situation as well as preventive techniques to avoid them. For example, on a lengthy bus ride, you may ask the student to act as your helper and sit next to you. On a trip through the planetarium, you could pair him with a well-behaved student and have them lead the line. Provide frequent positive feedback for good behavior.

Teaching Approaches and Modifying Task Characteristics

Shorten classroom activities and provide frequent change. This may be done while maintaining the focus on the same academic topic.

Incorporate instructional techniques that allow for hands-on work or activities that allow for experiential learning.

Do not assign more than one long-term project at a time. The student needs support to manage the organization of just one such project.

Be careful to keep material and tasks at the student's instructional level or, depending on the task, his independent level. Materials that are too easy encourage boredom, those that are too hard produce frustration. Either increases the likelihood of acting out behaviors or giving up.

Allow the student to work at his own pace. Time pressure interferes with reflective thinking and problem solving.

During instructional time, rather than using the chalkboard or whiteboard, use an overhead projector. This allows you to face the class while writing, maintain interaction more effectively, as well as demonstrate certain skills (e.g., math) with materials made for overhead instruction.

On easy or repetitive tasks, increase stimulation through the addition of shapes, colors, and textures.

Use as many games, hands-on or interactive activities, and interesting, colorful materials as possible to sustain the student's attention and make learning fun.

When planning academic skill and concept instruction, try to incorporate activities that show their functional and pragmatic use—how they are necessary for life outside of school.

Use interactive teaching approaches. The student may find it easier to attend to task when involved in cooperative learning groups, guided student discussions, and activities with a high level of teacher/student interaction.

The student is more likely to benefit from instructional approaches that promote active student involvement and emphasize understanding of ideas and concepts, with less emphasis on rote memory and retrieval of facts. Encourage active discussion and debate of ideas and their real-life implications and applications.

While lecturing, help the student maintain focus or return to focus by incorporating verbal cues to alert him that something important is coming. This may be done by changing your voice inflection, or stating a warning such as, "This next information will be on the test," "Listen. This is important," or "OK. Now we are done with . . . and are changing topics. The next topic is. . . ."

Prior to a lecture, write an outline on the board and review it with the class. Not only does this provide a vital framework for the information that will be presented, it also allows the student to reorient himself if his attention wanders during the lecture.

Wherever possible, *contextualize* new information by relating it to real-life examples or applications. Also, teaching scientific, literary, or historical events with stories (emphasizing the human challenges, conflicts, decision points, and drama) will increase the student's interest and attention, thereby facilitating his retention of new information

In cooperative learning groups, make sure that each student has a well-defined role or task and that the student knows what is expected of him.

Use a carefully established system of peer tutoring to increase attention to specific skill study as well as to self-esteem. Peer tutoring, if set up correctly, can be effective and highly motivating as a supplement to teacher instruction. *The Tough Kid Book: Practical Classroom Management Strategies* (Rhode, Jenson, & Reavis, 1995) provides a good explanation of how to set up and use an effective peer-tutoring system. Available from: Sopris West, 4093 Specialty Place, Longmont, CO 80504, (303) 651-2829, www.soprizwest.com.

Alternate teaching approaches. Alternate sessions of paper/pencil seatwork with more hands-on or interactive tasks, as well as tasks that require students to be out of their seats. Also, alternate difficult tasks with those with which the student is more competent.

Observe the student's attention span during a variety of teaching contexts and activities (e.g., working independently, cooperating in group activities, writing, doing math worksheets). Use your observations about contexts/activities in which he has most success to help you modify contexts/activities in which he has less success.

To increase and sustain interest, incorporate technology such as videotapes, camcorders, tape recorders, and stopwatches into skill practice.

Beginnings and Transitions

Help the student start each day in an organized fashion. For example, if a student typically needs to be reminded to turn in his homework and put his backpack away, you might greet him by saying, "Good morning, ___. Homework and backpack."

When the student enters the classroom (middle or high school), hand him a "Rules for Readiness" card or have it on his desk. The card should have written on it the few things the student has to do to be ready to begin class (e.g., 1. Get book from shelf; 2. Get notebook, pencil, and compass from backpack; 3. Sit down and look at teacher).

Keep informal transitions between activities to a minimum. Provide extra structure during transitions and positive reinforcement if the student is ready for the next activity on time. [See Strategies: Transitions Between Activities.]

Help the student transition from one activity to another by giving instructions in the following manner: (a) Require all students to stay seated and quiet until you have given all instructions and have said, "Go ahead"; (b) give all instructions in the same order as they are to follow them; and (c) limit the number of instructions.

Increasing Attention and Time On-Task

Require the student to keep unnecessary objects off his desk.

Within the classroom seating arrangement, surround the student with model students who will not distract him and who will respond to any attempts at socializing only at appropriate times.

With the student's prior permission, set up a buddy system whereby the student's neighbor agrees to give him an unobtrusive signal when his attention wanders.

When the classroom or environmental noise level is particularly distracting, or at any time it might be helpful, allow the student to listen to quiet music or white noise (e.g., water sounds, Native American flute music, classical guitar) with a headset.

Incorporate movement into instructional activities. For example, before presenting information on a new topic, activate students' prior knowledge by asking questions requiring agree/disagree responses. Instead of having them write *agree* or *disagree,* have them show thumbs up or down or hold up a card with their response on it. Other responses may include pointing, clapping, standing up, or (starting from a sitting position), sitting down.

Ask parents to provide materials that the student enjoys using—a special type of pen (e.g., roller point) with preferred color ink (green, black, purple); pastel colored, lined paper rather than white; high-lighters in preferred colors).

Increase the student's attention span in challenging tasks by providing rewards for gradually increasing the amount of time he works in a focused and reflective manner.

Praise the student for good attention while he is on task, or drop a note on his desk saying, "Good attention to work," or something similar.

Each morning, write the day's schedule of activities on the board and review it with students. Cross off activities as you complete them, making sure students see you do so. The student may need his own copy to keep on his desk.

Divide the student's in-class assignments into smaller, more manageable chunks. Give him one chunk at a time with instructions to hand each in as it is completed and pick up the next. Each time the student hands in a portion of the work, provide reinforcement for completed work and for time on task. Examples for dividing the work are: cut apart the ma-

jor sections of a worksheet and give the student one section at a time to complete, place a piece of "sticky" paper over the bottom half of a worksheet; put a sticker on the bottom of every two pages of a story.

Work periods with pre-established time limits prevent the student from feeling overwhelmed by difficult or seemingly lengthy tasks. Set a limit on the amount of time the student will work on the task. When the time is up, you can accept the amount of work completed or give him a short break followed by another preset work period. Place the timer where he can see it (but not touch it) so he can monitor his time and see his work period continuously decreasing.

The use of technology such as videotapes, audiotapes, computer software/images, and computer speech programs that can read the on-screen print to the student will enhance the student's engagement in academic tasks.

Teach the student to use a beeper tape to remind him to stay on task. This tape provides a sound at varying time intervals, cueing the student to ask himself, "Am I on task?" If he is, he places a check on a chart. If not, he resumes work. Build in positive reinforcement for increasing the number of checks he accumulates within a work session. You might set a lower number of checks necessary for a reward in tasks in which his attention is significantly challenged (e.g., writing a paper) and raise the limit in tasks in which his attention is not so challenged (e.g., watching a video).

Use a beeper tape program to guide the student to gradually increase his time on task. Before starting the program, observe the length of time that the student generally remains on task. Start the program with a tape on which the tones are sounded at slightly longer intervals. For example, if the student generally stays on task for 3 minutes, start with beeper tones at 31/2 or 4 minutes. Set a definite period in which to use the tape so that you can establish the maximum number of points he can earn. Explain to the student that each time the beep sounds, if he is on task, you will award him a point. The student must be on task at the time the beep sounds. Intermittent reinforcement, such as is incorporated into this system, is effective in increasing behavior. At the end of the period for which you are using the tape, if he has earned 85% of his points, he will earn a reward. Each time the student earns a point, verbally praise his attention to task. This sets the stage for fading out the beeper tapes and points, while maintaining a response to verbal praise. When the student earns a reward 3 days in a row, use a tape with slightly longer intervals between beeps up to 15 minutes. If the student does not earn a reward after

3 days with a particular tape, consider whether or not the student understands what behavior is expected, change the reward to something more motivating, decrease the percentage of points required to earn a reward, or drop back to a tape with shorter intervals.

Incorporate computer-assisted instruction into the student's academic schoolwork. Look for software programs that: (a) the student will find interesting and stimulating; (b) provide frequent and immediate feedback; (c) allow the teacher to adapt the program and rate of task presentation to the student's needs; (d) allow the teacher to adapt the length of each lesson to the student's attention span; and (e) allow the teacher to control the frequency and type of reinforcement provided.

To enhance the usefulness of computer-aided instruction, specify the educational objective ahead of time, employ tasks that are integral components of the classroom skill instruction, supervise the student's use of the program, monitor his work to provide supportive instruction as necessary, and provide on-going assessment of skill development.

Provide the student with a device such as the WatchMinder, a watch that signals the wearer to do certain activities at preset times (e.g., GO BATHRM, MEDS, COPY HMWK, DO CHORES) throughout the day. As a training device, the WatchMinder may also be programmed to vibrate at regular intervals to signal the student to do certain behaviors such as ask himself if he is actively working. Watch-Minder available from: PMB #278, 5405 Alton Pkwy #5A, Irvine, CA 92604, (800) 961-0023, www.watchminder.com.

Help the student to develop a heightened awareness of his attention to task by using an audiotape or vibrating device. Whenever the student hears or feels the signal, he considers whether or not he was on task and marks a chart. A variety of such devices are available, including *Get 'Em on Task: A Computer Signaling Program to Teach Attending and Self-Management Skills; Listen, Look, and Think: A Self-Regulation Program for Children;* MotivAider; and Watch-Minder. *Get 'Em on Task* is available from: Sopris West, 4093 Specialty Place, Longmont, CO 80504, (800) 547-6747, www.sopriswest.com. Listen, Look, and Think and MotivAider are available from: A.D.D. WareHouse, 300 Northwest 70th Avenue, Suite 102, Plantation, FL 33317, (800) 233-9273, www.addwarehouse.com.

Set up a system whereby the student and other students chart/graph their performances in a certain area of classroom functioning (e.g., number of math problems done in 5 minutes, number of consecutive minutes on task) and post them on the wall. For effectiveness, the data recorded must be related to meaningful behaviors or skills, be recent, and be posted immediately.

Task Completion

Help the student obtain the phone numbers of at least two students in each of his classes so that he has someone to call after school if questions arise regarding a homework assignment.

Reduce the amount of work the student is required to do during independent assignments so that he is more likely to complete his work in school. When figuring the grade, the reduced amount assigned is considered as 100%. Do not send unfinished class work home for homework.

Reduce the amount of work in each area assigned for homework so that the student can complete his assignment in approximately the same amount of time other students are expected to spend. Examples of modified assignments are: solving the odd-numbered math problems instead of all the items, studying 10 spelling words instead of 20, and writing a half-page report instead of a whole page.

Review tests and assignments to ensure that the student has completed all sections and items. Return any incomplete assignments/tests to the student for completion, without penalty.

As the student's difficulty with sustained attention interferes with his efficiency, allow him extended time to complete tests and in-class assignments. Inform him ahead of time that this will be allowed so as to reduce anxiety while he is working on the test or assignment.

Teach the student goal-setting strategies and ways to use visualization to enhance success (before he starts a task, creating a mental image of how he will carry out and complete it).

Due to the student's attentional problems, he is less efficient than his peers with comparable academic ability and takes considerably more time to complete his assignments. Provide the student with some flexibility in assignment deadlines. Give him some passes at the beginning of the semester that will allow him one or two days, or an extra weekend, to complete and turn in an assignment, and some "The dog ate my homework" passes that allow him to skip an assignment altogether without penalty.

Improving Academic Performance

Prior to giving complex verbal instructions, write them on the board. This will avoid the need for repetition as the student needs to see the organizational structure to grasp it.

After giving instructions for certain activities (e.g., lining up, taking turns in presenting oral reports, handing in papers, getting materials for a project), have one or two students model the correct way to do this. Seeing it done correctly will make it more likely that the student will do it correctly. When possible, have the student participate in modeling, providing guidance as needed.

To avoid confusion and enhance accuracy of work, make sure that worksheets have plenty of space between items and that different activities are clearly delineated as such.

Use color to highlight any areas of academic tasks that the student appears to be overlooking (e.g., the teacher highlights the bolded words in a text or the vowel digraphs in a page of text, or draws a colored box around instructions; the student highlights math operation signs, one color for each sign, before doing a page of problems).

Because of the student's difficulty with sustained and divided attention, he is unable to listen and take notes simultaneously. Free him from taking notes during classroom lectures and discussions by providing him with a copy of another student's notes (make provisions for use of a copy machine or use NCR paper) or teacher lecture notes, if available.

Tape, or allow the student to tape, lectures and classroom discussions, so that he can listen to them in shorter time blocks and play back parts that he may have missed in the classroom.

When presenting notes on the board for copying, enhance the organization of the written information by using different colors, numbers, and clear separations between sections. When discussing certain ideas based on the printed information, use colored markers to highlight or circle the phrases you are addressing.

When presenting information, use language that cues students as to its organization or importance. This includes sequencing terms such as *first, next, last,* and direct statements such as, "This is important," "Listen," or "This will be on the test."

When presenting information, use accompanying visual images such as pictures, graphics (e.g., webs, charts, graphs), and videotapes. Enhancing auditory information may be as simple as drawing a sketch on the board or standing easel to illustrate concepts such as contrasts, similarities, levels of importance, and cause/effect. Use numbers and/or color to differentiate sections of information.

Teach the student organizational skills, such as time management and materials management, directly and explicitly, with modeling, guided practice and reinforcement, and independent practice and monitoring.

Computer programs that help the student organize information for papers and research will not only aid in organization but will enhance his interest in the project, his willingness to work on it, and will promote better writing. One such program is Microsoft Encarta Research Organizer, part of the Microsoft Encarta Reference Suite. Available from: Microsoft Corporation, Redmond, WA, (800) 426-9400, www.microsoft.com.

Use interactive software as much as possible to enhance the student's interest in working with certain information. An example is the Microsoft Encarta Reference Suite which includes a globe that allows the user to magnify any area, see different types of geographical boundaries (e.g., political, climate), mark geographic points, and filter out cities by population levels. The encyclopedia articles have associated pictures, sounds, videos, and links to websites. An option allows the user to hear the articles read aloud. This program is also linked to reference materials (e.g., thesaurus, dictionary, quotations) and a program to aid in organizing research. Available from: Microsoft Corporation, Redmond, WA, (800) 426-9400, www.microsoft.com.

At the end of the year, request that the student be given the textbooks that will be used in his classes the following year and a reading list for any class that will require outside reading. The student will be able to handle the requirements of school with far less stress if he can become familiar with the materials ahead of time and get some of the reading accomplished during the school break.

To help the student store and retrieve new information efficiently, provide explicit instruction specifically in planning, organization, time-management, and mnemonic strategies.

Teach the student cognitive strategies for studying, memorizing, and learning content area material. An excellent series of resource books on strategy teaching and strategic learning is available from Brookline Books (Cambridge, MA, www.brooklinebooks.com, 1-800-666-BOOK). Some of the titles in this series are: *Cognitive Strategy Instruction*

That Really Improves Children's Academic Performance (2nd Ed.) (Pressley & Woloshyn, 1995), *Helping Students Become Strategic Learners: Guidelines for Teaching* (Scheid, 1999), *Cognitive Strategy Instruction For Middle And High Schools* (Wood, Woloshyn, & Willoughby, 1999), *Teaching Students Ways To Remember: Strategies For Learning Mnemonically* (Mastropieri & Scruggs, 1999a), and *Teaching Test Taking Skills: Helping Students Show What They Know* (Mastropieri & Scruggs, 1999b).

Directing/Controlling Activity Level

Find ways for the student to take frequent breaks from seatwork or, if needed, from the classroom. For example, give him an errand to do, have him hand out materials, or send a note to another teacher in a sealed envelope. The note can simply say, "The student needed a break from the classroom. Please just thank him and send him back to class."

Provide occasional breaks in the work schedule for exercise (e.g., using light weights for 2 minutes when work is completed, jump on small trampolines, stretch Therabands). The student may do exercises individually when he completes a task, taking turns with equipment, or the teacher may direct a whole class exercise break.

Allow the student to move in and around his seat as long as he is not disruptive to others.

Provide the student with a "fidget toy," such as a Koosh ball, a balloon filled with flour, or a string of paperclips to keep his hands busy in a nondisruptive manner when a task does not require the use of his hands. Make sure the student understands the rule that if the toy becomes a distraction in itself, you will take it back.

Provide the student with a chair that allows his feet to be planted firmly on the floor (90° angle at hips and knees) and a desk that comes to 2 inches below the student's elbow when he is sitting on the chair. A body that feels unstable (e.g., feet swinging above the floor, writing surface too high or too low) may increase the tendency to fidget and lose focus.

When the student's activity becomes distracting, redirect it. For example, remind him to tap his pencil on his arm or leg rather than on his desk or other object that produces noise.

Some students find that extrasensory stimulation helps them to sit more comfortably for brief periods of time and in doing so, allows them to attend more effectively to their work. Examples include wearing a weighted vest or lap pad, sucking on hard candy or salditos, or chewing gum. This method, called "sensory diet," is a supplement to treatment, not a treatment in itself.

To help the student remember to wait until he is recognized before responding to a question, immediately after asking the class a question, look at him and use a previously agreed-upon gesture to remind him to wait.

School/Home Communication

Set up a system by which the teacher and parents can communicate on a daily basis. This may include the use of e-mail, faxes, telephone, the assignment book, or a separate notebook sent between school and home. Issues to communicate include missed or incomplete assignments, lost materials, and difficulty with certain assignments. Behavior and emotional stability are best communicated in a such a way as to prevent the child from reading the message.

Developing Self-Advocacy in Older Students—For the Student

Learn as much about [ADHD] as possible from reliable sources and consider how it affects you. [Attach a list of resources that the student may borrow and where he can obtain the materials, preferably from a teacher, the school counselor, or the school library. Students with ADHD are more likely to watch a videotape than read a book.]

Schedule private meetings with your academic teachers once every [   ] weeks to check on your academic status and to discuss any accommodations you might need at that time. This arrangement will help you stay on top of your course work as well as demonstrate to your teacher that you are motivated.

Request a meeting with any teacher who assigns multiple, simultaneous assignments or who has them listed on the course syllabus. Explain your difficulty with this type of assignment and suggest an alternative arrangement to complete them sequentially.

When given the grading criteria for a class, figure out exactly how many and what type of assignments you can miss and still come out with a [B] average. Put a chart containing this information where you can see it easily as a reminder.

Building/Maintaining Self-Confidence and Self-Esteem

Put special effort into establishing a personal relationship with the student. Complying with classroom expectations such as paying attention, cooperation, and putting his best effort into his work will be much easier for him if he knows that you like and respect him.

Build rapport with the student. Greet him by name when he enters the classroom and in the halls. Ask how he is and listen to his answer. Ask his opinion when the opportunity arises.

Do not have students grade each other's papers. This practice makes public knowledge of the student's academic difficulties as well as the fact that his assignments are modified. Many students who need modifications will refuse them in such circumstances. Moreover, the student graders may make errors that remain undiscovered and the teacher does not become aware of the skills and concepts with which the student is having difficulty.

When the student fails at a task or interaction, structure an opportunity for him to try again and succeed. This will prevent him from developing a sense of helplessness and lack of interest and motivation toward school and learning.

Send periodic notes home with the student praising specific behaviors related to effort, attention, and social interactions.

Noneducational Treatment Considerations

Medication Usage
Explain to the student the reason medication has been prescribed, what effect it is expected to have (e.g., allow him to pay attention if he tries), what it cannot do (e.g., make him pay attention if he does not try), and the possible side effects. Involve him as much as possible in the decision to take the medication and in monitoring and discussing how it is working.

Be sensitive and respectful of the student's privacy in taking medication. Provide scheduling information that will help the physician to set dosage times during natural breaks in the day or create a reason for the student to be out of the room at the time he must get his medication. Remind him privately, by voice or signal.

Remind the student privately when it is time to take his medication.

If the student is on medication, ask the parents or physician what behavioral changes to expect, at what time(s) during the day the student should exhibit optimal behavioral control, how long the effects of the medication should last, and side effects to look for. If the student is still displaying off-task behavior, impulsivity, hyperactivity, or disruptive behavior—or if you notice side effects—notify his parents or the physician.

Schedule a conference for (date) to include the student's parents, the teacher(s), and the school psychologist or counselor. If, at that time, the student has not made considerable progress in the behavioral manifestations of ADHD, consider the use of medication to allow him to benefit from the other interventions that have been established.

Due to the inconsistency of the student's behavior in the classroom, combined with his apparent continued impulsivity and lack of attention, the parents should discuss the adequacy of the dosage of the student's current medication with his doctor.

Discuss with the student's pediatrician the need for the student to continue taking medication during non-school hours, such as afternoons, weekends, and vacations. This recommendation is made to allow the student to control his own behavior, learn from modeled behavior, and minimize possible negative feedback he may receive from staff and other children in the summer program. As others may not understand ADHD, they may not be tolerant of the student's inattention, social insensitivity, overactivity, and impulsivity.

It is the responsibility of the school staff to make sure that the student receives his medication on time and in the proper dosage, as prescribed by his doctor.

Notify the case manager immediately if the student starts demonstrating hyperactive, impulsive, or inattentive behavior in excess of that expected for other students of his chronological age. These behaviors indicate the need for a review of medication.

Make sure that the student has a steady level of medication throughout the day, to include homework time, after school or extracurricular sports, and social time with friends. Using feedback from the teachers, request your doctor's help in establishing the optimal medication, medication schedule, and dosage.

Monitoring Medication Effects
Before the student starts a trial of medication, initiate teacher/staff completion of a rating chart composed of a few behaviors that are problems in the classroom and are likely

to respond to medication (e.g., pays attention while teacher is talking, socializes only when appropriate, ignores mild distractions, work shows appropriate level of thought, stays in seat without excessive fidgeting), a question about time of the day when medication benefits appear to have worn off, and comments. Have the teacher and other school staff continue to chart behaviors, sharing results with the student's parents (for consult with the physician) until the optimal dosage and dosage times are established. [See Strategies: Behavior Rating Chart.]

If the student is on medication, observe him carefully throughout the day to determine the time of day when the beneficial effects of the medication appear to be wearing off. Help the parent or physician work out the amount of time that the medication is effective and the efficacy of different dosages.

Since the student is unsure how much he benefits from his medication, ask Dr. _____ about the advisability of taking a planned drug holiday. Plan it for a week during the [   ] quarter of school after the student has become used to the routine of the new [school year, quarter.] Each of his major teachers should complete a simple questionnaire documenting a few medication-related characteristics (e.g., pays attention during lecture and instructions, completes work in class, stays on task during in-class assignments) for one week before, during, and after the drug holiday. Inform the teachers that the student will be without medication for some time during the 3-week period but do not tell them which week. [At the end of the school day, the student may rate himself on his own chart so that he has a record of his own perceptions as to the effectiveness of medication and can participate in the discussion.]

Counseling, Parent Training, Educational/Support Groups

Parents of children with ADHD often benefit from training in parenting skills specific to the needs of the child. Encourage the student's parents to seek further education about ADHD and parenting training from a mental health professional who specializes in this area.

Many families of children with ADHD find family counseling helpful. Often, the goals of counseling are to help set up a consistent behavior management system in the home, help the child deal with the sense of failure and frustration that often accompanies this condition, and help siblings cope with the child's behavioral differences and need for special attention. Also, counseling can provide support and education for the parents in a frustrating and puzzling situ-

ation, while helping them to develop realistic expectations for their child.

Provide counseling to ensure that the student understands the nature of ADHD, how it affects him, and the reason for medication. Counseling also provides an opportunity for the student to discuss his feelings about having this condition, ask questions as they arise, and learn how to handle problem situations.

For information about joining a support group for parents of children with ADHD, contact: CHADD, 8181 Professional Place, Suite 201, Landover, MD, 20785. Phone: 800-233-4050, Website: www.chadd.org/findchap.htm.

The student may benefit from a group for children/adolescents with ADHD led by a mental health professional or teacher with expertise in this area. The focus should be on education about ADHD, importance of the child's participation in the treatment, social relationships, and effective problem solving.

Involve the student in an education and support group of children/adolescents in his age range to facilitate his understanding of ADHD and how it affects him, to teach him how to advocate for himself and set up situations for success, and to help him recognize that he is not unique in having this condition.

BEHAVIOR MANAGEMENT AND INTERVENTION

Related Sections: Test Session Observations Checklist; Attentional Disorders; Social Skills/Self-Esteem

Behavior Management and Intervention
    Further Evaluation
    Behavior Management
        Proactive Strategies for Avoiding Classroom Problems
    Behavioral Interventions
        Setting Up a Behavioral Intervention
        Parenting Skills Training
        Negative Interventions and Consequences
        Positive Reinforcers
        Increasing Compliance to Requests and Directives
    Recess and Physical Education: Preventing Behavior Problems
        Calm-Down Time
        Relaxing Recess
    Emotional Disorders

Further Evaluation

Due to the [disruptive] nature of the student's behavior, conduct a Functional Behavioral Assessment and develop a Behavioral Intervention Plan.

Interview the general education teacher(s) and/or parents to obtain more information about behaviors affecting school performance.

Consult with staff who work with the student throughout the school day to find out what types of behaviors interfere with the student's school performance and/or social interactions. Make a referral to the school psychologist or counselor to further evaluate these behaviors.

Interview the student's parents regarding his behavior at home and in nonschool situations. Compare this with his behaviors in school to establish whether or not the behaviors are situational in nature and whether they require further evaluation.

Perform several systematic classroom observations, taking on-task and off-task interval data, to determine the extent to which the student's behavior interferes with his learning and the learning of others. Note off-task behaviors.

Conduct several classroom observations. Select classes/subjects that the student enjoys and ones in which the student has difficulty. Record the student's positive and negative behaviors, the teachers' responses, and consequences for both types of behaviors. Note the teacher's instructional style and classroom management system, as well as the subject and the time of day. Analyze the data to see which factors appear most highly related to the student's behavior.

Have the teacher(s), parent(s), and the student [depending on age] complete a comprehensive behavioral questionnaire such as the Behavior Assessment System for Children, Conners' Rating Scales—Revised (CRS-R), or the Achenbach Child Behavior Checklist. (If one of the diagnostic considerations is ADHD, include a questionnaire/checklist specific to ADHD, such as the items comprising the DSM-IV Symptoms scale or the ADHD Index from the CRS-R.) Subsequently, interview the student to follow-up responses of concern. Be aware that the teacher's, parent's, and student's interpretation of the questions, and thus their responses, may differ substantially from the author's intent.

Interview the student in a comfortable setting to explore how he perceives the behaviors others have noted as problematic and the factors he sees as contributing to those behaviors.

Discuss with the parents the need to make an appointment with a licensed, clinical child psychologist [psychiatrist, pediatric neurologist] to further investigate the behaviors of concern and/or to recommend treatment.

Behavior Management

Proactive Strategies for Avoiding Classroom Problems
Develop a behavioral program for the student that is proactive in helping him to attend to task and refrain from bothering other students, rather than reactive to the problematic behaviors.

Before starting any activity, remind all students of the critical behaviors needed for participating in the activity. Make eye contact with the student.

As the student often gets into trouble during periods of waiting, plan lessons and structure activities to minimize or eliminate waiting time.

Teach the student and the rest of the class the expected behaviors for transitions between activities and maintain a consistent structure for transitions. Always give a 2-minute warning before ending an activity or assignment. [See Strategies: Transitions Between Activities.]

As often as possible, provide a special motivation for the student to [any target positive behavior such as completing assignments, coming to class on time, achieving 75% correct out of items completed]. The motivator may be any activity or privilege that the student truly enjoys (e.g., 10 minutes use of the computer, errand for teacher, reduction in a homework assignment, note home to the parent).

Classroom Rules
Limit classroom rules to four or five, make sure they clearly specify the behaviors expected in the classroom, that the behaviors are observable and measurable, and list the positive and negative consequences for following or breaking each rule (the consequences may vary by rule). Include a rule that directs the students to comply with your requests and directives. [See Strategies: Classroom Rules: Guidelines.]

When teaching classroom rules to your students, explain the reason for each rule, give examples and nonexamples of each rule, and describe the specific consequence for breaking it. Create skits that allow the students to identify the rule in question, to role-play its use, and to role-play the consequence.

Give students daily or weekly assignments to remember and recite one of the classroom rules on request. If there are four rules, choose four students for the week and choose four different students the next week. Assign the student the rule he breaks most often.

Before activities in which the student typically has behavioral difficulties, meet with him privately and review the rules for that particular activity (e.g., recess, school bus, field trip). Then have the student restate the rules.

Monitoring Behavior

Have the teacher complete a behavior-rating chart at specified intervals to monitor the student's response to medical or behavioral interventions. The chart should list the following behaviors of concern: [Specify behaviors, such as pays attention during teacher instructions, attends to assignment until completion, refrains from socializing except at appropriate times, sits in chair without excessive fidgeting]. State behavioral items positively to facilitate consistency in rating. Each day (segment of day, period) the teacher assigns one to five points for each behavioral item. Send a copy of the behavior chart home on a daily or weekly basis. If the parents so desire, you (or they) may send charts on a regular basis directly to the physician. [See Strategies: Behavior Rating Chart.]

In any home/school communication, consider using e-mail rather than sending a note, point paper, or behavior chart home with the student. E-mail avoids the possibility of the student losing the paper or forgetting to give it to his parent. Before doing this, set up an agreement that teacher and parents will check their e-mail daily. One advantage of this arrangement is the ability to share, save, and print out communications for record-keeping purposes.

The student's parents should speak with the teacher(s) at least once every 2 weeks and ask specifically about the student's academic progress and behaviors of concern (e.g., activity level, ability to stay on task, level of fatigue, impulsivity, social interactions, the quality and completeness of his work, academic progress).

Reinforcing Behavior (apart from a behavioral intervention)

Make all praise specific and legitimate. Clearly state the behavior to be reinforced and only praise behaviors that matter (e.g., "Good job" may be legitimate but is not specific.

"You're the best pencil sharpener in the class" is specific but not legitimate).

Praise specific behaviors in the student that you want to encourage. For example, stop by his desk and say quietly, "You're concentrating well on this assignment," or, after the activity, say to the class, "Many of you really stayed focused on this assignment," with a smile at the student so he knows he is included. This technique will help make him aware of the behavior and encourage him to continue it and repeat it at a later time.

Give at least three positive comments for each correction or criticism.

Keep a pad of paper and pen handy. When the student displays a behavior you want to encourage, immediately write a brief note to his parents, show him what it says, and have him put it in his homework folder to bring home. This procedure is most effective when done intermittently.

Make it a point to call the student's parents periodically to tell them something positive that he did that day. To ensure that the tone of the conversation remains positive, make the call brief and do it on a day when you do not have to report any problem behaviors.

Watch the student carefully during the day for times he demonstrates the target behavior. Immediately describe and praise his use of the behavior. Be specific (e.g., "You told Hank you were angry with him, you explained why, and you stayed calm. That was mature behavior").

Enlist the aid of other students to provide approval when the student exhibits the targeted behavior. So as not to single out the student, all students in a group could choose behaviors they would like to improve. Train all students to reinforce the chosen behavior in others verbally and to ignore negative instances of the behavior.

Set up a group reward program to encourage the student to increase a specific behavior that he knows how to perform but forgets or, perhaps, refuses. Setting up a group contingency avoids singling out the student. Explain to the class that each time any student (or all students) in the class exhibit the target behavior (e.g., raises hand and waits to be called on, complies immediately with the teacher's request, hands in homework), you will mark their progress toward the goal. (It may be necessary to teach the students how to do this.) Set up a system by which students can monitor their progress visually (e.g., coloring in floors on a picture of a skyscraper or dropping marbles in a jar with a "finish line" drawn near the top). As soon as the markers reach the finish line, the class is given a pre-established reward, such as a popcorn party with a video or a night (or more) off from homework. This program works only if students remind, encourage, and praise each other regarding demonstration of the behavior.

Correction and Redirection

Correct the student's negative behavior by reinforcing positive behavior in another student. For example, when the student is looking around, say, "I see that Ginger and Kai are concentrating on their work."

State corrections and redirections in a positive, nonhumiliating manner. State what you would like the student to do rather than what you want him to stop doing (e.g., "Mike, we're returning to our desks now to take out our social studies books").

When correcting a behavior or redirecting the student to task, remain calm. If the student perceives anger or disapproval, he will react with an emotional response and be unable to process the content of your statement.

Whenever possible, use humor to correct or redirect a specific behavior.

When reprimands for inappropriate behavior are necessary, give them immediately, concisely, and to the extent possible, privately. Stand near the student and obtain eye contact. Be calm and firm.

For both praise and reprimands, keep statements brief and specific to the behavior.

In cooperation with the student, make up and use a private signal, such as a hand signal or touch on the shoulder, as a reminder to return to task. This allows you to redirect him without interrupting teaching. Alternatively, alert him by saying his name, and asking him a question you know he can answer.

Do not allow or become engaged in lengthy verbal discussions regarding inappropriate or disruptive behavior. Redirect or give consequences calmly, firmly, and immediately.

Help the student recognize how his actions affect others. Immediately after a negative behavior, discuss with him how others may interpret his behavior, the reason for your concern, and a solution. Guide the student to devise a solution. Example:

> I know you were just playing but the rule is, "Keep your hands to yourself." That means no pushing, hitting, or grabbing.

Other students don't realize that you're playing when you push them and they will probably get angry. Or, they may bump into something or fall down and get hurt. How can you remind yourself about not pushing when we come in from recess this afternoon?"

Behavioral Interventions

Setting Up a Behavioral Intervention

Before instituting an intervention to reduce noncompliant behavior (i.e., responding to a teacher request or directive by refusing, negotiating, arguing, or otherwise avoiding the task), obtain baseline data regarding the number of times the student demonstrates this behavior in a specified period of time.

Set up a behavioral program based on a token reinforcement system. Based on the information provided by [the teacher, the parents] and the results of this evaluation, consider _____ as the first behavior to target. [See Strategies: Token Economy Systems.]

Set up a school/home cooperative behavioral program based on a token reinforcement system. In this system, the student is awarded points at school for demonstrating specific behavior; a note, point paper, or behavior chart is sent home daily; and rewards or mild negative consequences are provided at home. A home-based reinforcement system widens the scope of possible rewards to activities (e.g., baking cookies, playing a video game, borrowing the car) and tangible items (e.g., trading cards, accessories for a bike, money toward car insurance). As well, it can make available more meaningful consequences for the student (e.g., missing a favorite TV show, not earning a video game for the day). A home/school program must be planned and carried out with the same consistency and attention to rules as an in-class program. Regular communication between the teacher and parents is critical. [See Strategies: Token Economy Systems.]

Increase the student's ability to maintain behavioral control by using a self-management intervention program. In this program, the student learns not only how to monitor specific behaviors but also how to evaluate and reinforce his own performance. [See Strategies: Self-Management Strategy for Improving Adolescent Behavior.]

Establish a program of rewarding behaviors that are incompatible with the problem behavior. For example, if the student tends to have temper outbursts when frustrated by an assignment, set up a program in which he is rewarded each time he maintains control and asks for help.

Parenting Skills Training

Explain to the parents the benefits of taking a class in parenting children with difficult behaviors. Help the parents find a class offered in the community and, if possible, provide them with informational materials.

Children with [ADHD, Tourette Syndrome, Oppositional Defiant Disorder] require a different type of parenting and behavior management than do children without such syndromes. The student's parents are encouraged to take a class in behavior management strategies for children with difficult behaviors. The introduction and consistent follow-through of a program that clearly ties privileges to meeting responsibilities and obligations will ease the current dynamics within the family. [Provide the names of agencies at which such training is available.]

Negative Interventions and Consequences

To reduce the student's tendency to [refuse class assignments, use disrespectful language, blame others], use a system of response-cost. The student starts out the day or period with a specified number of tokens (e.g., chips, checks) or primary reinforcers (e.g., M&Ms, nickels); then, each time he demonstrates the (negative) targeted behavior, he loses one. At the end of the time period, he is allowed to keep the primary reinforcers he has left or trade in his remaining tokens for a primary reinforcer. [See Strategies: Response-Cost.]

Develop a behavioral intervention program that combines positive reinforcement with a response-cost component. [See Strategies: Response-Cost.]

When using response-cost, as the negative behaviors diminish, make sure the student recognizes the positive aspect(s) of his behavior and develops an internal locus of control. For example, if you are trying to reduce the number of times he refuses in-class assignments, document the increases in the number of assignments completed, number of times he has accepted classwork agreeably, or list his improved grades. Emphasize that he is responsible for the positive results and that the response-cost system is only a reminder to help him maintain control.

Use time out in increasing levels of exclusion. Remember that time out only works when a student is being removed from an environment that he feels is positive and in which he wants to remain. Set the duration of the time out just long enough to have an impact on the student, depending on his age and the level of exclusion. The level of exclusion, but not the duration, is related to the severity of the problem. Levels of exclusion include: (a) Keep the student at his desk but remove work materials and ignore behaviors, (b) Move the student to a chair situated away from the group but allow the student to watch, (c) Place the student in a class that is a grade or two higher (placement in a lower grade is humiliating) with an academic assignment to do, or (d) Place the student in a time-out room with supervision, devoid of objects he could damage. Plan procedures for exclusionary time out ahead of time with the staff working with the student, the parents, and the school counselor or private mental health professional. Explain the system to the student and answer any questions before initiating it.

Whenever the student earns less than [choose a number] time outs [or any other negative consequence] in [period of time], reward him with a tangible reinforcer or privilege.

Identify the behaviors that the student typically displays before [a temper outburst, an argument, aggressive behavior]. Plan a course of action or consequence to intervene at the first level of behavior to diffuse the situation.

As the student displays behaviors that are unsafe for him and/or other students, he must be provided with a one-to-one aide in the classroom and/or all situations in which structure and supervision are relaxed (e.g., passing time, lunch, going to or from other classrooms, the bathroom, the bus).

Positive Reinforcers

Do not make rewards time-dependent (e.g., a previously scheduled field trip). The student must have the ability to earn the reward. The unknown element should be when, not if, he will receive the reward.

Effective positive reinforcers are the keys to a successful behavioral intervention. Check with the student to ensure that the selected reinforcers are highly motivating. Ask the student what he would like to earn, provide a list of possible reinforcers from which he may choose, or provide a menu of reinforcers with different "items" at varying "prices." To set up a menu, give the student a list of possible reinforcers (make sure that all of the items on the list can be made available) and ask him to prioritize the items in order of preference and to add to the items on the list. The teacher may veto added items. Items that are higher in monetary value or in preference may be given higher "prices" on the menu. [See Strategies: Positive Reinforcers.]

Use novel delivery systems for reinforcement of targeted behaviors such as chart moves, spinners, mystery motivators, grab bags, and lottery tickets.

Increasing Compliance to Requests and Directives

Tell, do not ask, the student what you want him to do. Use precision requests and do not repeat yourself. [See Strategies: Precision Requests.]

Enhance the efficacy of precision requests by using the "Sure I Will" program. [See Strategies: "Sure I Will" Program: Increasing Compliance.]

Make only one request at a time. Wait until the student has completed what you have asked before making the next request.

Stand within 3 feet of the student and obtain eye contact before giving him a request or directive. Speak in a quiet voice.

Make a request or give a directive no more than twice. If the student does not comply the second time, immediately institute a preplanned consequence. When this has been completed, make the request or directive again. Have an established set of backup consequences increasing in severity for repeated noncompliance. [See Strategies: Precision Requests.]

When making a request of or a directive to the student, be specific in describing what you want him to do. State important details.

Socially (nonverbally) acknowledge the student's compliance with requests (e.g., verbally, smile, wink, and pat on shoulder).

Let the student know you like him. Students are much more willing and able to perform and produce in situations in which they feel valued and feel they are treated fairly.

Recess and Physical Education: Preventing Behavior Problems

Make the rules for recess (or Physical Education) clear. The general education teacher should review them with the class once a week or more frequently depending on the need. If the student requires more reinforcement, meet with him privately before the first recess of the day. Make it clear that the purpose of adhering to rules is so that he may have a more enjoyable time on the playground. If the student has behaved appropriately, as he comes in from recess, praise him for the specific positive behaviors.

Reinforce positive behaviors frequently. Look for them. Each time the student has a successful experience on the playground, comment upon the positive behaviors he is dis-

playing. Such comments might be, "Passing the ball to Jimmy to take that shot was good teamwork. I'll bet it made him feel good." "Keeping your temper when Amanda yelled at you took self-control. I hope she learned from you." On occasion, send home a positive note to the student's parents, such as "Missy played kickball with her classmates, followed all of the rules, and had a good time." Give the student the opportunity to be a monitor-aide by providing him with special duties. Possibilities are helping to go and get sports equipment from storage, spot possible problems, or blow the whistle to end recess. Select activities that will serve to shorten any unstructured time the student has on the playground.

In games, place the student in a position that will force constant physical and mental involvement, such as playing catcher during a softball game.

Calm-Down Time

Discuss calm-down time out with the student. Ensure that he understands that this time is not a punishment but an opportunity to regain control away from the middle of the problem, without consequences. If a student loses control on the playground, ask him to come and stand by the teacher or monitor. After a preset interval (e.g., 2 minutes), if the student feels calm, he may choose to return to play or to stay near the monitor. Provide the student with positive reinforcement during the calm-down time for cooperating with the monitor and for regaining self-control, even if he has done this only minimally.

Relaxing Recess

If a student demonstrates violent or particularly dangerous behaviors on the playground a predetermined number of times in a week, assign him to an inside recess. Instead, the student goes to the office, a supervised room (not a classroom in which the class is in session), or, if supervision can be arranged, the library. Have available age-appropriate and pleasurable activities and materials, such as coloring books and crayons with good points, puzzles of varying levels of difficulty, board games (that can be completed within the period), Etch-A-Sketch, interesting books, and clay. Each day during recess, the student will go to this room for "relaxing recess." When the student is ready to try outside recess again, he stays in "relaxing recess" for most of the period and comes outside for the last 10 minutes. If his behavior is appropriate, his time in outside recess increases by 5 or 10 minutes per recess period until he has earned back the whole recess period. Notify parents ahead of time regarding this plan so that they do not turn it into a negative experience by penalizing the student for having "relaxing recess." For the student (and others), this might fulfill the intent of recess far more effectively than becoming overstimulated and out of control on the playground. Parents may be asked to reward their child for increasing time spent on the playground successfully. Alternately, the student may be given the choice to continue "relaxing recess" rather than return to the playground.

Emotional Disorders

Put special effort into establishing a personal relationship with the student. If he feels that you like and respect him, he will be able to confide in you any discomfort or problems that affect him during the school day. As well, this rapport will make it easier for the student to comply with classroom expectations such as paying attention, cooperating, and putting his best effort into his work.

Seat the student within a group of students with good attention and social behavior so as to maintain his emotional comfort and, concomitantly, his focus on learning.

In the case that the student may be questioned regarding disciplinary issues or possible infractions of school rules, ensure that his counselor will be present. If this is not possible, ensure that a counselor who is knowledgeable about [anxiety, bipolar, depressive] disorders will be present.

When the student feels the need, allow him to leave class (with/without asking for permission) to go to a pre-established place to calm himself.

The [school counselor, case manager] will maintain ongoing communication with the student, his parents, and the outside [counselor, psychiatrist] for the purpose of monitoring his emotional status as to how it may affect his academic functioning, classroom performance, and social interactions.

Request that the student's tutor and [indicate subject] teacher communicate with each other frequently. The teacher can alert the tutor to any problems she has noticed and the tutor can help the student master new concepts and processes. To lower the student's level of anxiety, the tutor can teach a new concept or process before it is presented in the classroom so that the information is not new when the teacher introduces it.

Schedule the student for appointments at least weekly with a school counselor, and develop a plan that will give him access to the counselor whenever he is in crisis.

The student clearly benefits from his [daily physical therapy activities] to help him maintain emotional and behavioral control throughout the school day. This program should be continued on a daily basis.

A neuropsychological evaluation and a pediatric neurological evaluation may provide valuable insight into a more comprehensive view of the student's psychological, emotional, and cognitive problems; identify specific areas of neurological damage; rule out seizure activity that may be presenting as dissociation; and suggest treatment and remedial options that have not yet been considered.

To help with the student's behavior outside of school, the parents might want to consider seeking consultation from a psychologist or social worker with expertise in behavioral management of children with [mental illness and low cognitive functioning.] Additionally, they might want to contact [any mental health organization providing education and support for families] to obtain support and share experiences with other parents in similar circumstances.

The student is at risk for developing learned helplessness, a condition in which a child is not able to function competently in the school setting because she has come to believe that she cannot learn on her own. Support intended to foster independence can sometimes create dependency instead. Rather than have [a private tutor, instructional aid, cross-age tutor] sit with her, provide her with appropriate accommodations that will allow her to function effectively in class without highlighting her learning problems.

SOCIAL SKILLS/SELF-ESTEEM

Test Observations Checklist
Related Sections: Attentional Disorders, Behavior Management and Intervention

Social Skills/Self-Esteem
Social Skills
    Further Evaluation
    Instruction/Training
    Promoting and Modeling Social Behavior in the School
        Setting
    Activities

Self-Esteem
    General Recommendations
    Development and Appreciation of Strengths
    Understanding Weaknesses/Self-Advocacy
    Assignments
    Class Discussions
    Home

Social Skills

Further Evaluation

Refer the student for a comprehensive social skills evaluation. This would include (a) a social skills rating scale to assess general skill areas (e.g., cooperation, self-management, aggression, disruption); (b) a more specific social skills rating scale to ascertain and prioritize the particular behaviors of most concern in a variety of settings and by a variety of respondents; (c) social skills interviews with the parents, teachers, and student; and (d) direct observations. The assessment may also include a sociometric rating to ascertain the student's social standing among her peers.

To ascertain whether or not a more in-depth social skills assessment is warranted, have the student's teachers, parents, and the student complete a social skills rating scale and share the results with the school counselor or psychologist. One well-recommended rating scale is the Social Skills Rating System (Gresham & Elliott, 1990), which provides forms for preschool, elementary, and secondary students and questionnaires for teachers, parents, and the student herself. Available from: American Guidance Services, 4201 Woodland Road, Circle Pines, MN 55014-1796, Phone (800) 328-2560, website: http://www.agsnet.com.

Refer the student for a social skills training program that will specifically address the social skills she is lacking. A social skills assessment will be necessary to ascertain the target behaviors.

Instruction/Training

Students' preferences regarding help with social problems frequently differ from those chosen by teachers (Pavri & Monda-Amay, 2001). Accordingly, before taking action to help the student in social interactions, conduct a private conference with the student in which you ask about her social concerns and perceptions of social problems at school. Ask guiding questions to help her generate strategies that might be useful in improving or resolving these situations.

As the student has not improved her social functioning just by inclusion in a general education classroom, she requires explicit instruction and intervention in social skills. Continued placement in the general education classroom will provide her with the social context in which to observe and practice the social skills she learns.

Provide a program to teach problem-solving in social situations including specific training in (a) identifying and defining the problem, (b) generating a variety of alternative solutions, (c) identifying the most likely outcomes of each alternative, and (d) selecting and implementing the appropriate solution.

Teach the student the SLAM strategy (McIntosh, Vaughn, & Bennerson, 1995) for responding to negative feedback or comments from others. The components of the strategy are:

- Stop whatever you are doing when someone is trying to give you feedback,
- Look the person in the eye when he or she is speaking to you even if you don't like what he or she is saying,
- Ask the person a question to clarify what he or she is saying, and
- Make an appropriate response to the person to indicate how you intend to change or what you want him or her to understand about your situation.

This strategy incorporates practice and rehearsal regarding the problems students are experiencing and may be taught in a small group.

Use a structured learning curriculum to teach the social behaviors identified as problematic for the student. The components of a structured learning curriculum are modeling, role playing, feedback, and transfer of training.

Help the student improve social appropriateness by imagining how other people will react to her words and behavior. Teach the student to consider another person's possible reaction before she speaks or acts.

Teach the student how to maintain eye contact with a person when speaking. Provide structured situations for practice.

Teach the student how to notice and interpret facial expressions and body language when she is conversing with people.

Provide the student with practice in rehearsing what she will say in a situation before it occurs. For example, if the student wants to join a group of students on the playground, have her think of exactly what she will say, before walking over to the group.

Use live demonstrations, films, and videotapes of other students spontaneously using the behaviors targeted for intervention. Use videotapes of the student behaving in ways that illustrate the behavioral problem and, during training, videotapes of the student demonstrating the target behavior.

Discuss problematic social situations and brainstorm with the student different ways to resolve the problem. For example, draw a semantic map on the board with the problem in the center. Connect and write each proposed solution in an outside circle. Discuss how different solutions are related to each other and any underlying concepts (e.g., respect).

Promoting and Modeling Social Behavior in the School Setting

Establish classroom rules for social interactions. Discuss and provide examples of appropriate and inappropriate comments. Make sure that the students understand the importance of respecting others. Post the rules on the wall along with the pre-established consequences.

Help prevent social problems from arising by establishing rules regarding respect and acceptance in student interactions within the classroom. Promote this behavior among students by modeling it and by facilitating discussions about respect, acceptance, and individual differences.

Each time the teacher witnesses the student making an attempt to cope with a social problem in a positive way, provide verbal reinforcement and encouragement. When appropriate, ask the student what actions appeared to be most effective and what actions were less effective, and the student's perceptions of the reasons for the differences.

Engage the whole class or small groups of students in problem-solving sessions regarding social situations. Encourage the student to participate so that you can ascertain her perspective.

Praise the student for behaviors such as helping, sharing, or saying something nice to another person. Through role modeling, teach her how to compliment other people sincerely.

Have the student work on a project with a peer who will model positive social interactions.

Activities

To help the student become more accepted by other students, tailor some classroom activities to fit her specific strengths. Ask the student's parents to provide a list of the student's specific skills, interests, or areas of knowledge. For example, if you are planning a science project, identify an aspect of the topic in which the student has expertise and could present information or lead a group discussion. Help her organize and practice any presentation so it is successful.

Create situations that allow the student to have successful social experiences. For example, select a peer who would like to play a game with the student on the playground during recess.

Use highly structured cooperative learning groups to help the student participate in positive social interactions. Make sure that all students in the group know their responsibilities and how to accomplish them.

Encourage the student to join and participate in a school club or organization in which she is interested.

Teach the student or ask the physical education teacher to teach the student the rules and skills of a game. Select a game that the student will be able to participate in during recess or after school.

Improve the student's social skills by having her participate in a team sport with a coach who is aware of the student's behaviors and is able to provide a supportive, positive learning experience.

Use the student's involvement in athletics to train socially acceptable behaviors. If possible, enlist the aid of the physical education teacher. Provide regular feedback to the student about how her behavior and actions in physical education or on a team were received. When negative behaviors occur, brainstorm alternative behaviors with the student.

Self-Esteem

General Recommendations

The student will need support for improving her self-concept. A good resource for ideas is *100 Ways to Enhance Self-Concept in the Classroom,* Second Edition (1994) by J. Canfield and H. C. Wells. Available from: Allyn & Bacon, 75 Arlington Street, Suite 300, Boston, MA 02116, phone (800) 666-9433, website: http://www.ablongman.com.

The student's instructional needs must be addressed immediately to ensure that she does not quit trying and that she progresses academically. With a highly structured teaching situation and with appropriate activities and materials modified to her performance levels, she should make progress, regain self-confidence and self-esteem, and renew her interest in learning.

An intensive program of academic intervention must begin soon to reduce the student's frustration regarding her lack of learning, to increase her self-esteem, and to resolve attitudinal concerns regarding self and school.

One of the strongest factors in improving a student's self-concept and effecting the personal changes secondary to improved self-concept is a strong, positive relationship with a teacher who likes and enjoys the student as a person. Ideas for showing acceptance are: demonstrate to the student that you like and approve of the student by providing frequent positive reinforcements, such as a smile, a hug, a positive comment on a paper, special privileges, or rewards.

Watch for situations where the student is doing something correctly or behaving appropriately. Make a positive comment to the student in front of others regarding the behavior.

When providing daily feedback to the student, be sure to make five positive comments to one negative or corrective comment.

Assign the student a classroom task that she would enjoy, such as watering the plants or collecting homework assignments. Express gratitude after she has completed the task.

Create opportunities to ask the student what she thinks about certain things. Make it apparent that you are sincerely interested in her opinion.

Development and Appreciation of Strengths

Recognize and comment upon the student's unique talents. When you acknowledge a student's strengths, you provide an opportunity for other students to make positive comments as well.

Help the student become better in whatever she already does well. For example, because she is struggling with reading, but not having difficulty in math, be sure to direct attention to increasing skills in both reading and math.

Help the student develop her strengths. The student should participate in enrichment programs that will enhance her abilities in [write in appropriate area]. Two examples might be: [(a) an advanced hands-on science program that emphasizes discussion and activity rather than reading and writing or (b) classes or discussion sessions that use questioning strategies designed to encourage and develop critical thinking skills].

Encourage the student's parents to help her become involved in individual sports rather than team sports. In sports such as swimming or martial arts, she can be physically active, progress at her own pace, and develop self-confidence.

Encourage the student to participate in well-supervised, competitive activities, such as team sports, in which she has demonstrated a particular affinity and skill.

Capitalize on instructional activities in which the student is successful. For example, have the student participate in a cross-age tutoring program in a structured setting where she teaches a younger student the skills that she has recently mastered.

To help build self-esteem, provide opportunities for the student to teach something she knows or skills she knows how to perform to another student or small group of students.

Help the student develop specialty areas where she can be an expert. Encourage her to study topics of interest in depth. Provide opportunities in the classroom so that she can share her expertise.

Place value in the classroom on nonacademic strengths, such as mechanical, musical, or athletic abilities. Provide opportunities for the student to demonstrate her knowledge or abilities to classmates.

The student has many strengths that are not highly related to academic performance. Attempt to determine ways to integrate these abilities (e.g., motor skills, artistic skills) into the curriculum.

Ask that the physical education teacher or parents help the student develop skill in a one-to-one sport, such as tennis or handball. Provide opportunities for the student to play with others.

Understanding Weaknesses/Self-Advocacy
Teach the student about learning disabilities in general—what they are, how many people have them, their hereditary nature, and their lack of correlation to general intelligence. Explain the student's specific learning disabilities, discuss the fact that other people have similar differences, and explain how the techniques you or the resource teacher use can strengthen the problem areas. Discuss also the student's areas of cognitive, academic, and social strengths.

Include the student in a learning disabilities education and support group composed of peers with learning disabilities and facilitated by an adult who has specific expertise in learning disabilities, who can engage the students in discussion-generating activities, and who is skilled in guiding discussions.

Explain to the student the reasons that she is struggling on certain tasks in school. Tell her how specific accommodations will help her to be more successful. Encourage her to ask teachers for accommodations, such as extended time on assignments, whenever she feels that they are needed.

Discuss with the student how all people are unique and have areas in which they excel and areas in which they struggle. Help the student understand her own individuality so that she is able to make an accurate, noncritical, and honest self-appraisal.

Help the student learn to become an advocate for herself. A clear understanding of strengths and limitations will enable her to share information about her instructional needs with others. Help her learn how to explain her areas of difficulties and strengths to someone else, the accommodations and modifications she needs, and how these will help her to accomplish the tasks assigned.

Help the student develop a clear understanding of the types of tasks that are easy for her versus those that are difficult. Help her explore the types of courses and career options that are most in line with her unique talents.

Assignments

Do not assign the student work that is too difficult for her to complete independently. If additional instructional support is required, such as a peer tutor or parent volunteer, be sure to provide it. Reinforce the student based upon the amount of work she completes successfully.

Reduce the amount of work the student is required to do during independent seatwork assignments so that she completes her work successfully in school. Comment upon how diligently she has worked on the assignment.

When the student has difficulty with an assignment or project, provide the student with an opportunity to redo the work for a higher grade.

Remember that a student will become successful by having successful experiences. Initially, ignore the student's errors and mistakes and praise her effort. As effort improves, help the student understand that mistakes are just part of a learning process and that they help inform the teacher about whether or not the material has been learned.

Consistently praise the student for sincere effort rather than accomplishment. Increases in effort will result in improvement of the final product.

Keep a folder with the student's schoolwork. Occasionally, meet with the student, review past work, and discuss progress and development.

As the student's confidence increases, teach her strategies for coping with failure. For example, if she fails an assignment or a test, brainstorm alternative methods of handling the situation. Help her to understand that low grades are not a reflection of self-worth.

Class Discussions

When the student provides correct responses in class, make a positive comment. Commenting upon the right responses will increase confidence and, as a result, help the student develop a more positive attitude toward school.

When the student is uncertain about answers, encourage risk taking. Even if a response is incorrect, make a positive comment that acknowledges the student's willingness to express ideas.

Until her confidence increases, when calling on the student in class, only ask her questions that you know she will be able to answer successfully. You may want to let her know ahead of time that you will be calling on her and asking her to answer this specific question. If necessary, review the correct answer with her.

Help the student organize thoughts and knowledge about a topic prior to a class discussion. Call on the student when you know she will be able to answer a question correctly. If needed, let the student know the question you will ask her before class begins.

Home

Encourage your child to participate in extracurricular and recreational activities in which she will be successful.

Have your daughter be responsible for completing several chores at home. Have her make a list of duties and check off the tasks as they are completed.

Encourage your daughter to participate in some type of volunteer program, such as at a local hospital or nursing home. Make sure that the job expectations are clear.

Ensure that your child develops an island of competence (Brooks, 1991). She needs to have one or more areas where she is accomplished, admired, and rewarded for her knowledge and talents.

SENSORY IMPAIRMENTS

Related Sections: Most of the recommendations provided in the other sections of Section III are appropriate for students with sensory impairments, in some cases with minor adaptations. The recommendations in this section primarily address needs and problems of students with hearing or visual impairments.

Sensory Impairments
    Hearing
        Primarily Oral Communication: Hard of
            Hearing/Auditory Processing
            Phonological Awareness, Phonics Approach for
                Basic Reading and Spelling Skills
        Primarily Signed Communication: Deaf
        Hard of Hearing, CAPD, Deaf: Oral or Signed
            Communication
    Vision
        Further Evaluation
        Consultation, Collaboration, and Resources
        Accommodations
        Inclusion
        Instruction

Hearing

For the purposes of this section, students who are hard of hearing are those who depend on speech as their primary mode of communication; deaf students are those who use some form of manual communication and little or no speech. Evaluators writing recommendations for students who use a communication mode that incorporates sign and speech, may want to read through the recommendations for both groups.

When choosing a recommendation, consider the type of training and expertise that would be required of the professional providing the service. In the area of hearing impairment, a student may be served by a general education teacher, a certified teacher of the hearing impaired, a speech-language pathologist (SLP), and/or a learning disabilities specialist. A recommendation that depends on interpretation of an audiometric report might best be addressed by the certified teacher of the hearing impaired, whereas the development of phonological awareness skills may be addressed by the general education teacher, the SLP, or the learning disabilities specialist, depending on the hearing abilities and learning needs of the student.

Although the etiologies are different, the problems presented by students who are hard-of-hearing and students with central auditory processing disorders (CAPD) are similar in many ways. CAPD is a perceptual disorder that causes a person to miss or misperceive the sounds of words and/or have difficulty directing attention to auditory input, even in optimal acoustic conditions. These difficulties are exacerbated in the presence of poor acoustic conditions such as background noise, a reverberant room, or extended distance from the teacher or speaker. A CAPD also interferes with perception of speech that is altered in some way, such as rapid or accented speech. While CAPD cannot be diagnosed in students with hearing impairments, many of the accommodations and instructional recommendations are the same or similar. Consequently, the authors have chosen to include Auditory Processing here rather than duplicate many recommendations.

Recommendations that may apply to students who have any level of hearing impairment, regardless of mode of communication, or CAPD, are listed under the last major subheading in this section, *Hard of Hearing, CAPD, Deaf: Oral or Signed Communication.* The oral language problems secondary to CAPD are addressed in the Oral Language section of Section III: Recommendations.

Primarily Oral Communication: Hard-of-Hearing/Auditory Processing

Further Evaluation
Because the student has particular difficulty with tasks involving auditory processing, he should have a comprehensive audiological examination to rule out a hearing loss. The examination should measure hearing acuity levels at different sound frequencies and discrimination of speech sounds.

Request that the student be evaluated for a central auditory processing disorder by an educational audiologist who specializes in this area. The audiologist should rule out a hearing impairment as part of this examination.

Accommodations
TECHNOLOGICAL
Consult the school's educational audiologist about using an assistive listening device system (e.g., personal FM systems,

sound-field amplification) for the student to increase the signal-to-noise ratio and, thus, improve perception of the teacher's voice. (Students with CAPD may benefit from these systems.)

The student should use the best possible amplification during the lesson and during the rest of the day so that the language sounds he hears are as accurate as possible. Check his amplification system [hearing aids, FM system, cochlear implant] for proper functioning at the start of each day and just prior to instruction in phonological awareness/reading and speech. High malfunction rates are common in systems that are not routinely monitored.

Provide opportunities for the student to use taped materials (e.g., audio books, Language Master) along with printed materials in the classroom. Hearing the words as he looks at them will help to increase the student's oral and reading vocabulary.

ENVIRONMENTAL

Because the student has difficulty [hearing, perceiving] speech sounds clearly, provide him with preferential seating in any educational setting. Place him near the teacher or major source of instruction. He should have full view of the teacher's face, have his better ear toward the teacher, and be seated away from noisy areas (e.g., hallway, air conditioner).

Attempt to reduce distracting sounds and minimize background noise by seating the student away from noisy hallways, ventilation ducts, windows near playgrounds, or other obvious noise sources. Use rubber tips on chair legs, unless the room is carpeted, and plant thick shrubbery outside windows that face noisy streets.

Attempt to minimize reverberation effects by using carpeting, drapery, acoustical ceiling tile, sound-absorbing bulletin boards, and sound-absorbing room dividers to separate work areas.

INSTRUCTIONAL

Even though the student's hearing may be improved by use of a hearing aid, it is still not corrected. Provide special classroom adaptations, as needed.

For group discussions, develop a system for indicating which student is about to speak so that the student who is hard of hearing does not lose the content of what is said while trying to locate the source of the voice. The teacher may call on a student by name while pointing to him, or the

student who is to speak may raise his hand or stand. Explain to the class the reason for doing this and that it is a matter of courtesy.

Discuss with the [teacher of the hearing impaired, resource specialist] ways you can regularly reinforce skills that the student is learning.

Because the student has difficulty [hearing, processing] oral information, provide visual outlines and graphic organizers for tasks involving listening. Resource or itinerant personnel may assist the general educator with pre-teaching concepts and providing instruction that increase prior knowledge and background to facilitate better processing of the classroom instruction.

Encourage the student to tape-record important lectures so that he may listen to and write down the significant points at a later date.

The student may have difficulty listening to lectures while taking class notes. Provide him with your lecture notes or a note-taker.

Because of [poor auditory processing, distorted detection] of sounds, the student is likely to struggle with the phonology of foreign languages. Allow the student to use American Sign Language to meet the foreign language requirement or consider a waiver or course substitution.

When speaking to the student, stand within 2 to 6 feet, use a normal voice, face the individual, and speak slowly. Do not exaggerate mouth movements.

When the student needs clarification of something you have said, paraphrase or reword your statement instead of repeating it. Move to within 2 to 3 feet of the student at his eye level.

Phonological Awareness, Phonics Approach for Basic Reading and Spelling Skills

Provide the student with a systematic and explicit program of instruction in phonological and phonemic awareness prior to and integrated with instruction in basic reading and spelling skills. Due to the student's limited hearing, he may lack incidental experiences in verbal communication and language play (e.g., alliteration, rhyming) that typically provide significant foundation for developing phonological and phonemic awareness. [See Recommendations: Phonological Awareness: Sample Programs for suggestions and descriptions of specific programs.]

Directly teach the student how to use verbal mediation and verbal rehearsal to enhance his short-term memory. As many phonological tasks are facilitated by oral or subvocal repetition of sentences, words, or sounds (e.g., repeating words to see if they rhyme, repeating sounds to blend them), verbal rehearsal and mediation are necessary skills. When you assign a task, model and talk through the process, including repeating the oral stimulus. Provide a variety of activities for practice, then guide the student to generalize the use of verbal rehearsal into other tasks.

• A game to promote verbal rehearsal that is used in a small group of students who are hard of hearing, is motivating to students of any age, and focuses on teamwork, is "telephone." The teacher writes down a sentence that is short and syntactically simple enough for everyone in the group to repeat accurately and, if possible, with consideration to the frequencies that most of the students can hear. The teacher and one student move to a place where their faces cannot be seen by the group, and the teacher (the "teller") tells the student the sentence. (If the group uses an FM system, the "teller" should use the mike and all students except the "listener" turn off their hearing aids.) The "listener" becomes the "teller," chooses another student, and passes on the sentence. Students repeat this procedure until each has told another. The last "listener" says the sentence aloud and the teacher checks it against the written sentence. If correct, all of the students receive a reward (e.g., point on board toward free time). This game may also be played with teams competing against each other. Gradually, increase the complexity, length, or conceptual level of the oral stimuli or decrease the context (e.g., word lists, sounds).

Because the student's oral vocabulary is limited, instruction in phonemic awareness and basic reading and spelling skills should incorporate words already in the student's oral vocabulary. This is important because (a) familiar words are easier to hold in short-term memory, (b) the student is able to focus on the task itself without trying to learn the pronunciation and meaning of a new word at the same time, and (c) when the student is practicing blending individual sounds to make a word, he must be able to find a match for the resultant word in his oral vocabulary.

Accurate speech production is important in tasks that depend on sound awareness. The student is more likely to pronounce words accurately if he can hear the sounds; consequently, when planning initial instruction in any phonemic, reading, or spelling skill, request help from the audiologist to identify words and sounds that will be audible to the student based on his audiogram and speech discrimination ability. Words that the student has learned to pronounce correctly, even if he cannot hear all of the sounds, may also be used.

Because the student demonstrates severe difficulty perceiving speech sounds, use a program that stresses the oral–motor characteristics of speech. One carefully designed, intensive program for developing phonemic awareness and reading skills is the Lindamood Phoneme Sequencing Program for Reading, Spelling, and Speech (LiPS®), which incorporates training in the oral–motor aspect of the sounds and cues for remembering them. LiPS requires specific instructor training. Products and training are available from: Gander Educational Publishing, 412 Higuera St., Ste. 200, San Luis Obispo, CA 93401, (800) 554-1819, www.lindamood-bell.com/gander.

Due to the student's difficulty in learning new sight words and spelling words, teach him to use multisensory study methods that depend on revisualization of the word without a model (no copying). One such method is the adaptation of LSFW (Look-Sign-Fingerspell-Write) for students who use both sign and speech, including signing and saying the word, fingerspelling and saying the letters, and then signing and saying the word, before correctly writing from memory and checking five consecutive times. If the student continues to have difficulty, include a tracing component or use the Modified Fernald Method for Reading and Spelling. [See Strategies: Look-Sign-Fingerspell-Write, Fernald Method for Reading and Spelling: Modified.]

Primarily Signed Communication: Deaf

General Recommendations
The student should be provided with educational opportunities to work with age-peers who are deaf and to receive instruction directly from a teacher using American Sign Language.

The student requires an active, experiential approach to language and concept development that is delivered within [an American Sign Language, a simultaneous communication, other communication system] environment. Language development should be infused and supported throughout the school day.

The student can communicate with few people in the school other than his sign interpreter. Provide opportunities for other students in the classroom to learn to sign. An easy way to begin is to teach fingerspelling, the hand positions for individual letters of the alphabet, to the entire class. If possible, invite a person experienced in teaching sign to work with your class several times weekly.

The visual contrast between the interpreter's clothes, and her hands and face can make it easier or more difficult for the student to understand her sign. Help the student to consider this and, if he has a preference (e.g., dark clothes, no stripes or bold print), communicate it to the interpreter.

When students are expected to take notes, provide the student with a note-taker, as he cannot take notes while watching the interpreter.

Although the student may be able to speechread to some extent, remember that this is not a viable method of communication for any information of importance. Only about 30% of English speech sounds are visible on the lips and 50% of speech sounds look like other sounds (e.g., "maybe," "baby," "pay me").

Teach the student how to use verbal rehearsal in sign to help himself hold information in memory while working with it.

Reading Programs

Select a basic reading program that controls the introduction of sight words and English syntax so that the student receives direct instruction in vocabulary and syntactical structures before they are presented in text, and previously introduced vocabulary and syntax are repeatedly incorporated into subsequent reading and writing activities so that they are continually reinforced, to move the student from new learning to automaticity.

Use a reading/spelling program that incorporates many high-frequency words, that introduces English syntax systematically, that continuously reinforces previously learned sight words, spelling words, figurative language, and syntax in connected text and writing activities while introducing new ones, and that progresses slowly enough for the student to gain mastery before moving on. One such program is *Reading Milestones,* Third Edition. Available from: PRO-ED, 8700 Shoal Creek Blvd., Austin, TX 78757-6897, (800) 897-3202, www.proedinc.com.

As soon as the student has acquired sufficient sight vocabulary and understanding of basic English syntax, incorporate trade books and books of higher interest into classroom reading but do not have the student read above his instructional level.

Basic Reading and Spelling Skills

Because the student's sight vocabulary is quite limited, he will need to focus on building a strong base of sight words. Use the same words for sight word and spelling study, rather than using separate lists. Learning to spell his words will reinforce his reading recognition and provide a solid base for learning words with similar spelling patterns.

Use reading materials with carefully controlled vocabulary so that as the student learns new sight words, he encounters them in text repeatedly.

Within his reading program, the student will benefit from a strong emphasis on increasing sight vocabulary, learning similar two- and three-word verbs (e.g., *look up, look out, look for, look out for*), dual meaning words and phrases (e.g., "*look up*" has at least four meanings), common idioms, and survival words (e.g., *Do not enter, Poison*).

Guide the student to develop orthographic awareness by helping him to recognize the letter patterns that are frequently seen in written English. The object is for the student to perceive common letter patterns as *chunks,* rather than as a string of individual letters. For example, once the student automatically recognizes *pr, ea,* and *ch,* he is likely to perceive the word *preach* as having only three elements rather than six. As his inventory of chunks increases, he will perceive new words as having fewer, and more familiar, elements, facilitating both recognition and retrieval. Provide instruction and reinforcement of letter patterns until recognition and retrieval are automatic. [See Strategies: Phonogram Activities.]

- When teaching sight words, directly teach the student to recognize common letter patterns within the word (e.g., *igh* in *sight, oo* in *look*). Reinforce automatic recognition of the letter pattern by having the student find it in other words and differentiate it from similar patterns. For example, given a page of words containing *oo,* have him track across each line, circling *oo.* Later, have him circle *oo* on a similar worksheet composed of words that incorporate *oo* as well as vowel combinations similar to *oo* such as *ou.* [See Strategies: Phonogram Activities.]

As the student needs to focus on letter patterns in order to improve his reading and spelling skills, do not use word searches or words with scrambled letters in instructional or reinforcement activities. Instead, use activities that emphasize the correct letter sequences.

Teach the student the difference between vowels and consonants, and what syllables are. Generally, except for final, silent *e,* each vowel or vowel combination separated from another vowel/vowel combination by consonants represents a syllable. The ability to recognize the number of syllables in a word gives a clue to its length and facilitates chunking the words for easier recognition of word parts. Make sure that the student learns that there are no words without vowels in English and that all syllables have at least one vowel. (Exceptions do not require discussion at this time.)

To learn new sight words and spelling words, teach the student to use LSFW (Look-Sign-Fingerspell-Write) or other study methods that depend on revisualization of the word without a model (no copying) after initial study. [See that he practices his fingerspelling with a pause between word parts (e.g., cr-ab) to reinforce kinesthetically his recognition of common letter combinations.] If the student continues to have difficulty retaining the words, use one of the modifications, such as incorporating a tracing step. [See Strategies: Look-Sign-Fingerspell-Write.]

Teach the student reading-decoding skills using a multisensory program such as See the Sound (formerly Visual Phonics), a system of 46 hand signs and written symbols that suggest how a sound is made. Learning sight words through See the Sound gives the student a way to link specific gestures and oral–motor cues, representing sounds, to letters and combinations of letters. Within this system, students learn to recognize letter patterns, such as vowel-consonant as contrasted with vowel-consonant-silent *e,* thus facilitating the development of a student's orthographic awareness. More information is available from: International Communication Learning Institute (ICLI), 7108 Bristol Blvd., Edina, MN 55435, (612) 929-9381.

Due to difficulty recognizing and retaining sequences of visual symbols, the student will benefit from instructional techniques that highlight the critical features of the symbols while compelling attention to task. For reading, use multisensory techniques to teach the student to recognize common letter patterns as well as whole words. For math, use TouchMath, as a supplement to the classroom math program, for basic computation skills and for comprehension of word problems. Available from: Innovative Learning Concepts, 6760 Corporate Drive, Colorado Springs, CO, 80919-1999, (888) TOUCHMATH (or 868-2462), www.touchmath.com.

Create multiple opportunities for the student to encounter new words and previously learned words in a variety of reading materials and to write them many times within meaningful but structured writing assignments.

Use computer programs whenever possible for drill and practice to enhance the student's attention to the principle or skill being reinforced. Make sure, however, that the programs used directly address the skill he is learning and that the auditory components of the program are not necessary for him to benefit from its use. [See Strategies: Software Selection Tips.]

If the student repeatedly missequences letters while practicing the fingerspelling component of word study and cannot resolve his confusion quickly with guidance, have him stop studying that particular word and come back to it later so that he does not learn the missequence.

Reading Comprehension

As the student's primary language is American Sign Language (ASL), teach him the difference between ASL and English. Initially, for reading comprehension, he needs to be able to translate what he reads into his primary language. You might start with a picture and ask him to sign what is happening. If necessary, help him to sign it in proper ASL, not English. Then show him how it is written in English. Help him to understand that ASL is how it would be signed when directly communicating with another person but English is how it is written. Gradually, move him toward reading a simple English sentence first and then signing it in ASL.

When teaching any reading comprehension skill, teach the concept first in [American Sign Language, primary communication mode]. For example, when teaching main idea, present stories or expository information in ASL or on a videotape (with the characters signing or teacher interpreting the captions), and conduct activities and discussion regarding the main idea in ASL. When the student can watch an ASL presentation and sign the main idea, provide reading passages at his independent reading level, and practice expressing the main idea.

Content Area Instruction

The student depends on visual learning. When planning lessons, think in terms of replacing sound with vision. Make every effort to provide visual representations of concepts and information that he needs to learn. This includes the use of videotapes and computer software. For example, computer software is available that provides explanations along with three-dimensional views of geometry concepts, photosynthesis, and historical events. Make frequent use of graphic organizers, such as using a timeline to show events in temporal relationship or a two-column table to show comparison/contrast.

As the student has particular difficulty understanding question words, encourage him to take particular notice of these words and motivate him to consider their meaning more carefully by giving credit for paraphrasing a question correctly, in sign, even if he cannot answer it. For example, in response to the question, "Why did the settlers keep moving west?" the student would receive partial credit for signing, "Reasons for move west."

When using a video in content area classes, increase comprehension and retention of the important information using some supportive techniques: (a) write on the board and briefly explain the key concepts you want the student to get from the video, (b) give the student a study guide containing questions he will answer either during or after the videotape presentation. Explain the questions and clarify the type of information that constitutes an acceptable answer, (c) interpret the entire videotape, simplifying the language when necessary. Do not depend on the student reading the captions, and (d) using the remote, stop the tape when you need more time to interpret and explain the information being given in the captions—especially when the video answers one of the questions you have asked.

Teach the student a study technique for learning and recalling conceptual information using index cards as study materials. On one side of the index card, print the word for the target concept. On the other side of the card, provide examples of the concept using pictures, pictures of the signs, or printed words. For example, if *photosynthesis* were printed on one side of the card, a diagram of the process could be drawn on the other; if *attitude* were written on one side, the other could have pictures or signs illustrating willing, cheerful, angry, and rude. The student can read the word on the card, try to explain the meaning to himself, and then check by turning the card over. Conversely, he can look at the picture/sign side of the card and sign or spell the word that names the concept.

Behavior/Social Skills

Teach the students how to gain someone's attention appropriately, such as tapping on the table top with the flat of the hand, tapping a person lightly on the shoulder, or waving a hand from a few feet away.

When writing classroom rules and behavioral intervention objectives, keep in mind the differences between deaf and hearing cultures. For example, "Keep hands to yourself" may prohibit a student from requesting attention in expected and acceptable ways. Model what you mean.

Hard of Hearing, CAPD, Deaf: Oral or Signed Communication

Further Evaluation

Consult an educational audiologist to obtain a comprehensive hearing evaluation for the student that measures the degree of loss and the individual's level of hearing at various sound frequencies as well as his ability to discriminate speech sounds. The evaluation should include unaided and aided hearing levels and speech discrimination.

Resources

In planning the student's educational program, consult with a specialist in education of the hearing impaired who can recommend necessary classroom modifications, provide resource help, and identify community resources.

Consult with the audiologist or teacher of the hearing impaired regarding the type of hearing loss the student has. Realize that a conductive hearing loss can be assisted by amplifying sound, whereas a sensorineural hearing loss may or may not be helped by amplification since the distortion of sound is also amplified.

Schedule regular communication with resource personnel so that information in classroom lessons can be reviewed in individual therapy.

Identify the local, state, and national resources that can help you develop a program for a student with a hearing impairment.

Two websites that provide a wide range of valuable information regarding issues related to deafness and hearing impairment, including education, are http://www.nad.org, sponsored by the National Association of the Deaf and http://clerccenter.gallaudet.edu, sponsored by Gallaudet University.

Technology

Amplification systems (e.g., different types of hearing aids, cochlear implants, auditory trainers, classroom FM systems, sound-field systems) differ widely in their use and in the type of benefit they provide to the people wearing them.

Request information from the teacher of the hearing impaired or the educational audiologist regarding the type of amplification system the student has, its features, the most effective way to use it, and when he should take it off (e.g., for swimming, certain PE activities).

[Many deaf students who use sign language predominantly depend on their personal amplification systems to alert them to environmental sounds, emergency situations, and, in many situations, to assist in perceiving oral communication.] Have the school audiologist or speech-language pathologist teach you how to [operate, test] the student's amplification [system, device]. Check daily to see if the equipment is turned on and switched to the proper setting. Keep spare batteries in your desk and know how to change them.

Make sure that the student who cannot use the telephone has access to a telecommunication device (TTY), enabling him to send and receive typewritten messages over telephone lines. Also, teach him how to use the relay system so that he can use his telecommunication device (TTY) to communicate with people who do not have a TTY.

Seating Arrangements

Use seating arrangements that allow the student to see other students (e.g., horseshoe, circle). This type of arrangement is particularly important during group activities.

Because the student requires more intensity, repetitions, and a different technique than his classmates, he should always have the option to study in a place out of the view of other students but where he can be easily monitored periodically by the teacher. A study carrel would serve this purpose.

General Instruction

The student requires an educational program designed for the hearing impaired and administered by a certified teacher of the hearing impaired. [American Sign Language, simultaneous communication, or other language system] should be the primary language of instruction within an instructional setting with a small student-to-teacher ratio.

Due to the student's learning disabilities, he requires instruction that is explicit and systematic. Present all [insert skill area] skills to the student in a developmental and logical sequence, provide direct instruction, assess his understanding, provide drill and practice, assess mastery, and teach generalization. Review and reinforce previously learned skills and concepts by incorporating them into practice of more recently learned skills.

Use films and videotapes with open captions so that the student will be able to read the same information that other students are hearing from the soundtrack. Films and videotapes may borrowed, rent-free, from a catalog of over 4,000, from Captioned Media Program, National Association of the Deaf, 1447 E. Main Street, Spartanburg, SC 29307, phone: (800) 237-6213 (voice); (800) 237-6819 (TTY); website: www.cfv.org, e-mail: info@cfv.org.

To enhance learning, provide relevant visual stimulation such as videos, pictures, graphic organizers, and computer software to help the student form associations for new concepts.

Help the student expand his vocabulary by providing field trips to a variety of locations accompanied by [signed] discussions of what you are seeing or experiencing.

Lectures and Content Area Information

Because students who are deaf or hard of hearing miss vast amounts of information that hearing children learn incidentally, their background knowledge is often critically limited. Consequently, it is imperative to assess the student's prior knowledge in any area of study before starting a new unit. It is likely that he will need supplementary information to establish the same level of readiness as his classmates to begin the new unit.

Preteach difficult or important words and concepts before presenting them in class. Resource teachers, itinerant teachers of the hearing-impaired, teaching assistants, and parent volunteers can assist in this area.

Have the student prepare ahead for topics that will be discussed in class. For example, the student may read the chapter before it is introduced in the class. This will help the student to participate more fully in class discussions.

Encourage the student to ask questions when he does not understand what has been said. Rephrase the information to convey the intended meaning.

Students with hearing impairments gain particular benefit from well-organized lessons in content areas. Some guidelines are: activate students' prior knowledge, preteach key vocabulary, provide an advance organizer, present the material, and reinforce and evaluate concept learning. [See Strategies: Content Area Instruction: Components of Effective Lessons.]

When you are introducing a new subject, give some indication to the student that you are changing the topic. For example, write the new topic on the board or, if you have written an outline on the board, cross out the topic you have just completed.

Write homework assignments on the board—if possible, at the beginning of the period—and provide quiet time for all of the students to copy it down. The student is less likely to understand the assignment, and may not know there is an assignment, if it is explained only orally or if he must copy it down in a hurry.

Reading Instruction

When teaching sight vocabulary, teach the words most frequently used in print in English. For the 300 Instant Words, the first 25 make up about 30% of all printed material, the first 100 words make up 50%, and the first 300 words comprise 65%. [See Strategies: Instant Words 300.]

Teach the student to use context clues primarily as a way to infer the meaning of a word but only as a supportive strategy for word recognition. Generally, in educational materials used in grades 4 through 8, students are 40% accurate in using context to guess function words (e.g., articles, prepositions) and 10% accurate in guessing content words (e.g., nouns, verbs), which carry the most important meaning. Instead, focus on the development of a sight vocabulary covering many concepts, multiple meanings, and figurative language. [See Strategies: Context Clues.]

Specifically teach the student the morphological structure of words, including Greek and Latin word parts, to help the student develop both orthographic recognition of words as well as clues to their meanings.

English Grammar and Syntax

Use a hands-on, visual program to teach the student to understand and use English grammar correctly for reading and writing. One such program is Manipulative Visual Language (MVL), developed by teachers of the deaf to provide students, deaf or hearing, with a visual, manipulable model of English grammatical forms. This program utilizes two- and three-dimensional forms—variously shaped, colored, and coded—to represent different parts of speech. Concepts of nouns, verbs, verb tenses, prepositions, and other grammatical elements are introduced through the use of these shapes. Once the concepts are understood, English sentence structure is introduced, and ultimately, literature is incorporated. MVL is recommended for elementary students to establish an early, strong foundation in English grammar and is also appropriate for use with older students still struggling with these skills. MVL can also be used to teach the syntax of American Sign Language. Instructional materials, the teacher's manual, and training in using the system are available from: Robert Gillies, 23 Bridge Street, Yarmouth, ME 04096, phone: (207) 846-8937, e-mail: caitnor@mac.com, or Jimmy Challis Gore, phone: (520) 744-2168 (TTY) or use Relay Service, e-mail: JGore3312@aol.com.

Social-Emotional Competence

The student would benefit from participation in a program to increase emotional and social competencies. The PATHS (Promoting Alternative THinking Strategies) Curriculum is one such program, designed for elementary school-aged children, and research-validated with classes of deaf and hard-of-hearing children as well as with children in general education settings. A key objective of the PATHS Curriculum is to prevent or reduce behavioral and emotional problems. Documented outcomes included an increase in children's ability to understand social problems and develop effective alternative solutions, and a decrease in aggressive or violent solutions. Additionally, children demonstrated increased understanding and recognition of emotions and frequency of prosocial behaviors. PATHS was selected by the Center for the Study and Prevention of Violence as one of 10 model programs (out of 450 reviewed) based on effectiveness in violence prevention. Available from: Developmental Research and Programs (subsidiary, Channing L. Bete Co.), 200 State Road, South Deerfield, MA 01373, phone: 877-896-8532, e-mail: custsvcs@channing-bete.com, website: www.channing-bete.com. PATHS website: http://www.prevention.psu.edu/PATHS

Vision

Further Evaluation

Obtain a complete, clinical vision evaluation from an ophthalmologist. The evaluation should provide information on visual acuity, visual fields, use of binocular vision, visual disorders (if any), and prognosis for visual functioning.

Obtain a functional vision assessment, which provides specific information on how the student uses his vision in typical activities and recommendations for how to optimize his use of his vision. If additional information is needed, a low vision evaluation can provide suggestions for optical and non-optical aids and materials to enhance visual functioning.

Obtain an evaluation from a behavioral optometrist to assess the student's ocular–motor functioning, or ability of the eyes to work together efficiently, including skills such as convergence sufficiency (combining the image from each eye into one clear image), accommodative efficiency (quickly changing focus between far and near objects), and tracking (moving the eyes smoothly along a line of print or down a column).

Request that the vision specialist conduct a learning media assessment to ascertain the student's most effective modes of learning and literacy—tactile, visual, or auditory—and, based on the results, to make recommendations on best methods of working with the student.

Request that the vision specialist evaluate the benefit of colored, nonglare transparent overlays. Try them with different materials, with different size print, on different colors and compositions of paper, and in all of the lighting environments in which the student might read in the school and, if possible, at home. Document his responses and try to determine if he receives any benefit from the overlays.

Although the student appears to have difficulties that would indicate the presence of a learning disability, before classifying him as such, the multidisciplinary team is advised to review the student's educational history and determine if the student has been receiving instruction and accommodations for his visual impairment that are both appropriate and sufficient to his needs; if the consistency of provision of services met his needs; and if he has been provided with the services of a certified teacher of the visually impaired who is both knowledgeable and competent.

Consultation, Collaboration, and Resources

The classroom teacher, vision specialist, and learning disabilities specialist should meet to decide what role each will take in providing the student the multiple services he needs, how to reinforce what the others are teaching, and how to communicate problems as they arise. Set up meetings at regular intervals to review his progress.

Consider asking the vision specialist to provide inservice training for all staff working with the student to explain how he sees his world, how his visual impairments affect his learning, and the importance of providing the accommodations she has recommended.

In planning the student's educational program, consult with a vision specialist who can clarify or explain information regarding the student's visual abilities and recommend necessary classroom accommodations and modifications, provide resource help and appropriate instructional materials, and identify community resources.

Obtain help from the vision specialist on ways to adapt lessons and materials so that the student can participate fully in the activities of the class.

Read the student's ophthalmologic, functional vision, and/or low vision evaluations and consult with the vision specialist to ensure that the student has the visual devices, accommodations, and modifications required for him to benefit from his educational experience to the same extent as his normally sighted peers.

The teacher may find it helpful to obtain additional information regarding visual impairment. The following websites provide a wide range of information regarding blindness and low vision.

- Lighthouse International: www.lighthouse.org
- National Association for Parents of Children with Visual Impairments: www.napvi.org
- About.com, The Human Internet: www.blindness.about.com

Accommodations

Environmental Accommodations

Keep classroom supplies and materials organized, in the same place, and easily accessible so that the student may locate them easily.

At all times, make sure that the student is seated so that he has an unobstructed view of the target of attention such as the board, the teacher, overhead projector screen, or demonstration materials.

Since the classroom is not organized traditionally, rather than seating the student at the front of the room, include him in the "pod" arrangement of desks with his CCTV at right angles to his desk. Make a desk available to him near the front of the room to which he can move when the overhead projector is being used or when other activities are happening there.

Make sure that the illumination in the classroom is appropriate for the student and that he is not in a position to look at direct light or into the glare of direct light on surfaces.

Avoid moving large pieces of furniture/equipment without first bringing it to the attention of the student. Teach all of students in the class to push their chairs in whenever they get up so they are less likely to obstruct the student's passage.

Specify a place in the classroom, such as near the door, for the student to store his cane. Make sure that other students understand clearly that they are not to touch it.

Technological Accommodations and Special Materials
Read the reports of the student's [ophthalmological, functional vision, low vision, behavioral optometric] evaluations and consult with the vision specialist regarding the materials and technology that would be beneficial for the student.

- Specialized materials may include soft pencils or black felt-tip pens to increase contrast when writing, raised-line paper to enable the student to identify writing guidelines tactually, reading materials and writing paper printed on off-white or light-colored paper to reduce glare and increase contrast, and large print (print size must be specified) [or smaller print, for reduced visual fields] in sans serif fonts;
- Specialized devices may include special lenses for glasses, magnification and/or telescopic devices, and slant boards;
- Lighting accommodations may include dimmed lights, indirect light, or a lamp focused directly on the student's work;
- Technological accommodations may include books on tape to compensate for slow reading or delayed reading skills; a CCTV (closed-circuit television) to magnify print and graphic materials or small objects; a screen magnifier program to magnify print and graphics on a computer monitor to any chosen size; a screen reader program to read all printed and graphic information on the computer screen; talking calculators, spell checkers, and thesaurus/dictionaries; and a speech recognition device to convert voice input to print on the computer.

Read the reports of the student's vision evaluations and consult with the vision specialist to ensure that the student has the accommodations and modifications required for him to benefit from his educational experience to the same extent as his normally sighted peers. As the student does not have residual vision usable for instructional purposes, ask about technological accommodations such as books on tape; Braille materials and a Braille Writer; a Braille note-taker (the user types Braille notes into the device and it reads them back); a screen reader program that will read aloud all printed and graphic information on the computer screen; a speech recognition device to convert voice input to print on the computer; an abacus; and a talking calculator, spell checker, and thesaurus/dictionary.

Investigate the possibility of providing the student with a computer Braille display—software and board of Braille cells that allow the user to use Braille to interact with the computer screen. The board displays refreshable Braille (Braille cells with pins that rise up out of the base or retract to represent Braille symbols). The user can move up or down rows of Braille cells or lines of print by use of rocker keys on the board. The cursor is indicated by a "blinking" (continuous up and down movement) pin just below the Braille cell, which the user can move to insert or delete text, as one would in a word-processing program. This technology transforms the print on the screen into Braille on the display and converts the user's braille-writing on the display into print on the screen. One such device is the Power-Braille, available from Blazie, a division of Freedom Scientific, BLV Group, LLC, 2850 SE Market Place, Stuart, FL 34997, (800) 444-4443, www.blazie.com.

Task Accommodations
When writing notes on the board, write large, neatly, and in a clearly organized format. Erase nonessential information and keep boards clean to eliminate visual distractions and clutter.

While writing notes on the board, read them aloud or, with the student's permission, appoint another student or an instructional aide to read them to the student.

Do not require the student to copy from the board. As much as possible, provide this material preprinted for him. When not possible, provide a note-taker.

Whenever you use visual displays in the classroom, remember to describe the diagrams or illustrations in detail as well as the relationships between parts.

Provide the student with a printed copy of the [DOL sentences, "Fast Five" math problems, or other daily tasks that students copy from the board], so that he can do the work directly on the paper rather than having to copy the [sentences, problems, other stimuli] before doing the task.

Allow the student to record all class lectures on an audio tape.

Provide the student extra time to accomplish visual tasks such as reading, writing, math computation, drawing, and pulling information from pictures.

Remember that a student using Braille or large print will typically read at a rate two or three times slower than the average reader. Be sure to allow him/her sufficient time to complete readings or shorten the assignments.

Ensure that the student's reading materials are clear, well-spaced, and easy to read.

Teach the student how to take notes verbally for a paper or report, using a tape recorder. Later, the information can be transcribed into [print, Braille].

Provide the student with appropriate modifications for testing, ranging from extension of time limits to provision of oral examinations. [See Recommendations: Testing/Test-Taking.]

Be aware that the student may not interpret pictures accurately, especially line drawings or sketches.

Allow the student to have frequent rest periods from near-point, visually demanding tasks.

Inclusion

Encourage the student to participate in as many classroom activities as possible. If an activity is inappropriate for the student, arrange an alternative activity.

To ensure that the student is a full participant in the class, have him perform the same types of tasks as other children, such as watering plants, erasing the chalkboard, or collecting lunch money. You may choose those that are less dependent on vision or appoint a buddy to guide the student, but not to do it for her.

Work closely with the physical education teacher to develop an appropriate physical education program. Try not to exclude the student from typical activities, unless indicated by the ophthalmologist.

Instruction

Orientation

Help the student devise a system to keep his materials organized in the classroom.

Obtain the services of a certified orientation and mobility specialist to help the student [with very limited vision] learn to move about the classroom and school environment safely and independently.

Request that the vision specialist make labels and signs in Braille to post around the classroom. Explain to the students how Braille is another system of communication.

Social Skills

Because of the student's visual impairment, he is [severely, moderately, somewhat] limited in the type of social information that normally sighted children acquire through incidental learning, including reading body language and facial expressions in social contexts, knowing when to offer his hand to shake, making or simulating eye contact, and developing conversational pragmatics. Use opportunities throughout the school day to explain these social conventions to him and provide him the opportunity to practice when you are able to observe and give feedback.

Cognitive and Academic Strengths

Despite the student's significant visual impairment, he demonstrates a strength in his ability [to note critical details in pictures and remember them later]. Thus, the use of [pictures] will be an important instructional device in helping him to learn new concepts and remember rote information.

Braille

Help the student use his remaining vision to learn to recognize the spatial orientation of the dots comprising Braille symbols. For example, use half of an egg carton as a Braille cell and 6 ping-pong balls as dots. Paint 3 balls in one color and the other 3 in a contrasting color, for example, red and yellow. Teach the student that the left side of the cell is always yellow and the right is red. Give the student practice in using the color-coding along with the placement of the balls to recognize and construct Braille letters. When the student masters a letter or contraction, continue to practice it with all white balls. Then practice with eyes closed. Gradually, reduce the size and tactile contrast of the materials.

As the student is experiencing severe difficulty recognizing the spatial layout of the dots comprising Braille symbols, introduce letters represented by larger cells, more pronounced tactile contrast, and increased spatial information. For example, teach a letter on a swing cell on which the student will be able to feel the holes ("nondots") as well as the dots. For spatial orientation, knowing where dots are not is just as important as knowing where dots are. The ability to feel all six positions provides more information as to the spatial layout of the symbol than feeling only the raised areas. Using different materials, gradually reduce the tactile contrast between the dots and nondots (e.g., a mouse pad with a row of cells represented by 6 punch-holes for each and ball bearings for dots). Practice recognition and construction of Braille symbols, gradually reducing the size, tactile contrast, and nondots as the student masters them in each medium. Continue, ensuring mastery at each step, until the student is able to recognize normal Braille symbols.

Because the student confuses reversible Braille letters, such as lowercase *i* and *e*, help him to devise tactile–kinesthetic or oral mnemonics to help him distinguish between them. Example: Tactile-kinesthetic mnemonic: To distinguish between *i* and *e*, teach the student to simultaneously say "*Ice—i-c-e*" while he Braille-writes *i-c-e* until the movements are automatic. Then, the next time he experiences *i*/*e* confusion, he can use the spelling of *ice* to remind him. Example: Verbal mnemonic: To distinguish between *m*/*sh*, teach the student to use the phrase, "*m* and *sh* are meshed," noting that /*m*/ is at the beginning of the word and /*sh*/ is at the end. Correspondingly, when two dots are on the left (or beginning) side of the cell, the letter is *m*, when the two dots are on the right side (the end) of the cell, it is the *sh* contraction.

Reading

Help the student register with Recordings for the Blind & Dyslexic (RFB&D) and secure textbooks on audiotape from them. The master-tape library has educational books that range from kindergarten through postgraduate level. If a book is unavailable, and is deemed to fit within the scope of the collection, it will be recorded upon request. In late 2002, RFB&D will make available a library of digital textbooks on CD-ROM, allowing students to navigate the book/disk by page, chapter, or heading. [See Strategies: Taped Books.]

Provide the student with information regarding free sources for taped books (e.g., Recordings for the Blind & Dyslexic, public or university library, local school or agency for the visually impaired) and how to obtain them. [See Strategies: Taped Books.]

Before the end of this school year, ascertain what textbooks and novels the student will be required to read next year, complete an application to register him with Recordings for the Blind & Dyslexic, and place an order for any books that he will need. [See Strategies: Taped Books.]

Ensure that the student has a taped copy of any book that the class is reading. Provide headsets and encourage the student to listen to the book during silent reading time.

Document the student's reading rate before he begins to use a new visual device and periodically as he uses it to ensure that his reading rate returns to baseline or higher. Be aware that when a student first starts using a new visual device, his reading rate is likely to decrease. As he becomes familiar with the use of the device, his rate should increase again (Smith, 1999).

As the student needs a highly systematic multisensory decoding and spelling program, consider becoming trained in the Wilson Reading System and adapting it for the student and others with visual impairments needing a similar program. Originally designed for older students with reading disabilities, the program does not depend on pictures for any of the exercises, making it uniquely adaptable for students with visual impairments. [See Strategies: Wilson Reading System.]

To reinforce reading recognition, build automatic retrieval of [letter sounds, sight words], and increase reading fluency, create speed drills from the [phonics skills, sight words] the student has learned but which have not become automatic. The goal is for the student to read a page of 60 words within 60 seconds. Given his current achievement, [phonics elements, sight words] to include would be [write in specific phonics elements and sight words]. This technique works well with large paper and print. The field on a CCTV, however, is too restricted to allow for uninterrupted reading across a line and a smooth return to the left side of the line below. [See Strategies: Speed Drills for Reading Fluency and Basic Skills.]

To reinforce reading recognition, build automatic retrieval of [letter sounds, sight words], and increase reading fluency, create speed drills from the [phonics skills, Braille contractions, sight words] the student has learned but which have not become automatic. The goal for each page is for the student to read ___ words within 60 seconds. [Write in a number that would represent a reasonable increase in rate based on the baseline measurement.] Given his current level of achievement, [phonics elements, contractions, sight words] to include would be [include those on which the student needs practice.] Develop speed drills using the attached method but prepare materials in Braille. [See Strategies: Speed Drills for Reading Fluency and Basic Skills.]

Math

Ensure that the student learns to use both an abacus and a talking calculator for math functions. The abacus is the blind person's "paper and pencil" for solving math problems. The use of this device requires the development of problem-solving skills that the calculator does not. Additionally, the student needs to have a device, at least as a backup, that is unlikely to break.

As the student is having so much difficulty transferring his knowledge of foundational math concepts to the use of numbers and numerical operations, teach him Touch-

Math®. If the student has difficulty seeing the dots clearly, use fuzzy dot stickers. TouchMath® is available from Innovative Learning Concepts, 6760 Corporate Drive, Colorado Springs, CO, 80919-1999, (888) TOUCHMATH (or 868-2462), www.touchmath.com.

Content Area Learning

Due to the student's visual impairment, his oral vocabulary is considerably more limited than that of most normally sighted age-peers. Even when events or objects are described to him, he may not have an adequate concept with which to match the description. For example, if he has never seen a cloud, a description of the difference between cumulus clouds and thunderheads would have little meaning. Consequently, it is imperative to provide the student with as many direct experiences as possible, in varied situations, especially those that allow touch and physical involvement. Simultaneously, describe what he is experiencing and touching, verbally expand upon the experience, relating it as much as possible to other information that is familiar to him.

Allow the student to explore materials and equipment tactually that will be used in classroom demonstrations or projects, such as science experiments or models, before the activity begins.

In the classroom, provide the student with concrete objects to accompany a lesson and encourage exploration of the environment. Explain relationships between objects and encourage the student to touch and manipulate objects.

Provide concrete systematic experiences to help the student master science and social studies concepts. Investigate content area programs designed specifically for students with visual impairments which include hands-on activities.

At home and at school, provide the student with general information about the world. This is best done throughout direct experience and touch, audiotapes, [videotapes], discussion, and reading materials that introduce new subjects at very basic levels.

Always assess prior knowledge before introducing a new unit or topic. The student is likely to need some compensatory instruction to keep pace with the class in learning the new material.

Check the student's comprehension during class discussions, lectures, and instructions, using open-ended questions.

Teach listening skills and use verbal cues to alert the student to upcoming important information or to highlight the organization of a lecture or instructions. Words such as, "OK-

new topic," "the first thing you need to know," "first, finally," "now this is interesting," and "remember" serve this purpose.

TRANSITION

Transition
   Further Evaluation
   Elementary to Middle School
   Secondary to Adult Living: General
   Secondary to Vocational/Adult Living
   Secondary to Postsecondary Education
   Self-Advocacy
   Accessing Community Resources

Further Evaluation

Schedule a comprehensive educational evaluation to include a thorough assessment of cognitive abilities, including receptive/expressive language abilities, and achievement areas. The central goal of the evaluation should be to identify specific strengths and weaknesses to aid with educational and vocational planning.

Schedule an evaluation of the student that includes cognitive abilities, oral language skills, academic achievement, adaptive behavior skills, and vocational aptitude and interest.

Have a vocational specialist evaluate the student's interests and aptitude for suggestions as to possible vocational directions.

Provide a functional vocational evaluation to estimate the student's current levels of functioning and to develop necessary transition services.

Using an adaptive behavior scale, assess the student's ability to function independently in nonacademic areas, such as personal living skills, community orientation, work-related skills, social communication skills, and motor skills. Identify specific goals and objectives that will help him develop independent living skills.

Assess the student's functioning levels related to transition. Areas for assessment should include work behaviors, as well as social, independent living, and vocational skills.

Assess the student's ability to function independently and age-appropriately in the following areas: current vocational skills, vocational training, independent living or residential placement, transportation, finances, recreation/leisure, social relationships, and sexual awareness.

To help the student explore career options, locate a career counselor who will provide aptitude, interest, and personality testing.

Elementary to Middle School

As the student begins middle school, consult a vocational specialist to design and involve him in a structured program of career exploration. As the student moves toward one broad vocational path, select high school courses that will provide the prerequisite skills.

At the beginning of the school year, schedule periodic conference dates for the parents, school personnel, and the student, if appropriate, to discuss the student's progress and suggest changes in the educational plan, if necessary.

To help the student move smoothly into school next year, obtain a list of academic and behavioral skills expected of the average student entering ___ grade. Use these to create teaching objectives and a plan for transition.

As middle school places more demands on a student to be organized and responsible, consider the student's special needs in setting up a class schedule and selecting teachers for next year. Include accommodations and behavioral objectives on his [IEP, Section 504 accommodation plan] to provide support and help him develop the skills he needs in these areas.

At the end of the school year, take the student on a tour of the middle school, arrange for him to observe the classes he is likely to take next year. Introduce him to some of the teachers, counselors, and office staff. If possible, arrange for him to shadow a sixth-grade student who will be friendly and helpful and introduce him to other students.

Arrange for a staff member, such as a teacher or counselor, to serve as an advocate and contact person for the student in middle school. The advocate should schedule regular check-in times, at least once a week, to provide support, help solve problems and straighten out confusions, and assist the student in new situations.

Secondary to Adult Living: General

Teach the student about his rights under [Section 504 of the Rehabilitation Act of 1973, the Americans with Disabilities Act of 1990] regarding his disabilities and [support services in school, rights to reasonable accommodations in the workplace], and the right to reasonable access in businesses open to the public.

Develop a program in independent living skills including components related to daily living, employment, leisure and recreation, community involvement, home and family, personal development, and health. Teach and practice daily living skills within the settings in which they are to be used.

Help the student contact a rehabilitation counselor, for example through Vocational Rehabilitation, for referral to an independent living center for a postsecondary program in independent living skills.

Help prepare the student for independent living by teaching him organizational skills, such as using a calendar, a time planner, and a "to do" list. Help him set up a file drawer with files for various kinds of papers to which he will need access, such as renter's insurance, car insurance, car repair receipts, receipts for purchased items, medical records, bank statements, and credit card information.

Focus on helping the student develop interpersonal skills expected of adults in the workplace or in college such as using good posture, using a pleasant tone of voice, paying attention, asking questions during conversation, active listening, and maintaining eye contact.

Help the student and other students develop poise and state information confidently and concisely. As each student enters the classroom, have him shake your hand firmly, summarize how the previous day went, how today is going so far, and what he will accomplish in class today.

Have the student make a personal and professional data card on which he writes information normally required on job applications. The card can be tri-folded and kept in his wallet for immediate access.

Currently, the student is lacking the social skills necessary for successful functioning in the workplace or in postsecondary education. Write social skills goals into the student's Individualized Educational Plan and develop a social skills training program for him to include [problem solving, goal setting, relaxation techniques, self-evaluation].

Due to the student's nonverbal learning disabilities and resultant limits in social perception, he is likely to have difficulties in the workplace or in postsecondary education. Develop a program of social skills training specifically in areas such as recognizing and interpreting nonverbal communication, such as facial expression, body posture, and gesture; recognizing and respecting personal space; appropriate touching; and interpreting suprasegmental language cues such as voice pitch, tone, volume (Minskoff, 1982).

Secondary to Vocational/Adult Living

As part of the student's IEP, write an Individualized Transition Plan (ITP) for the transition into adult life. Begin this process 4 years prior to the student's proposed graduation and include instruction in career options, experience in the community, development of employment-related skills, adult living objectives, daily living skills, and a functional vocational evaluation. Update the ITP annually.

Ensure that the following components are included in the student's transition plan: (a) individualized goals, reviewed annually, addressing residential living, vocational or post-secondary education, and independent living skills; (b) integration into normalized/mainstream settings; (c) acquisition of a work history through paid work experience; (d) active family involvement for support; (e) coordination between the school and adult services; (f) specific instruction in locating and obtaining employment; and (g) ongoing evaluation and feedback regarding progress toward transition goals (Rojewski, 1992).

As part of the student's IEP, write an Individualized Transition Plan (ITP) for the transition into adult life. Focus on vocational education programs, instruction in community-based environments, and paid, part-time employment. Ensure that the ITP includes long-range plans, specific objectives related to expected outcomes and activities, the person responsible for each objective, and timelines.

Help the student gain the skills necessary for obtaining and maintaining employment: (a) completing a personal inventory of interests and skills (technical and adaptive), (b) matching the results to vocational interests, (c) learning to view one's self from the employer's perspective, (d) writing a resume, (e) completing and following up on an application, (f) practicing job interview skills, and (g) developing work ethics and character traits important for maintaining employment (e.g., promptness, hard work, following rules, interpersonal skills).

Refer the student to the guidance counselor to assist him and his parents in planning an appropriate academic schedule.

Work with the student's parents in prioritizing transition goals. Some considerations include current therapy, opportunities for mainstreaming in school, community-based instruction, and technical training.

To facilitate the transition from school to independent living, obtain information from the parent regarding the child's medical history and needs, family history, independent living skills, and social/emotional development.

Help the student to develop clear, realistic vocational goals that will provide the direction for educational planning and support services throughout high school.

As part of transition services, provide the student with personal and career development counseling that will help him clarify his interests and consider academic and professional goals.

Request that the student's parents complete a questionnaire regarding their plans and expectations for their son after graduation, the level of involvement they expect to maintain, and areas in which they foresee him needing assistance.

Assist the student in acquiring the skills needed for transition, including appropriate work behaviors, as well as social, independent living, and vocational skills.

Ensure that the student understands that most employers consider traits such as being on time and getting along with co-workers more important than initial skill on the job.

Educate the student and his parents about options for future vocational placements and the requirements for entering and being successful in those placements.

Suggest vocational training to the student as an alternative to college. He may be more willing to devote energy to learning skills that have more immediate and practical applications.

Assist the student in exploring vocational training programs at the community college and local technical schools.

Assist the student's parents in developing a plan for encouraging and training independent responsibility in their son over the next ( ) years. Particular areas of focus include helping the student: (a) do financial planning, (b) obtain a social security number, (c) make a will, (d) apply for Supplemental Security Income, (e) set realistic goals, and (f) develop self-advocacy skills. Other areas include: (a) monitoring good grooming habits; (b) encouraging and facilitating social activities with peers; (c) providing sex education; (d) reinforcing good work habits; (e) encouraging and supporting the student in a job in the community; (f) teaching daily living skills such as cooking, cleaning, and doing laundry; (g) teaching and monitoring money management such as budgeting and saving; and (h) developing leisure time skills such as participation in sports, daily exercise, hobbies, or acquiring computer skills.

Provide consultation from a vocational transition specialist regarding equipment modifications that may be necessary when the student pursues a job.

Because current academic skills and skills related to successful adult living are age appropriate, specialized transition services are presently not necessary.

Secondary to Postsecondary Education

Help the student request [appropriate accommodations such as extended time, private testing area, responding in test booklet rather than on response sheet] for standardized examinations such as the [name of exam student will take for college entrance or eligibility].

Upon completion of the secondary program, help the student find a 2-year or 4-year college that provides support services for students with disabilities.

In exploring college options, encourage the student to review institutions that have well-established programs for students with disabilities.

Help the student identify an appropriate college program using a collaborative effort that involves his family, his teachers, and the guidance counselor.

Help the student select a college program that will provide the necessary compensations and accommodations the student requires to succeed.

Prior to applying to college, help the student understand the difference between meeting the minimum requirements and taking challenging courses that will help prepare him for college-level work. Competitive colleges expect students to go beyond the typical high school course load by taking advanced placement courses.

Ensure that the student has updated testing prior to transitioning to college. Most colleges will require documentation of a disability that has been completed within the last 3 years.

Because the student has a documented disability that impacts the academic areas of [specify area(s)], request course substitutions. These requests are evaluated on a case-by-case basis and require approval from the college. The decision will be based on the information provided in the student's assessment report, primarily the testing reflecting the individual's achievement in the area(s) in question. In most instances, course adaptations or accommodations are considered before a substitution is granted.

For the first semester of college, the student should consider taking a reduced course load. This will allow him to adjust to the postsecondary setting without being overwhelmed with the amount of work and to have adequate study time.

If the student chooses a field in which a considerable amount of reading and writing are involved, have him consider taking two or three courses per semester rather than a full course load. This will provide him with enough time to complete assignments.

Suggest that the student request help from the center for students with disabilities just prior to the start of the first semester to engage a tutor for [area of need such as algebra, writing papers, study skills, organizational skills].

During his junior year (high school), set up a program in which the student will explore postsecondary options, evaluate learning disabilities services provided at colleges and universities, prepare for the college entrance exam (e.g., SAT, ACT), organize a personal transition file, and begin to narrow down postsecondary alternatives (Brinkerhoff, 1996).

Find out what courses the student will be required to take during the next year. Help him learn reading, writing, notetaking, study, and learning strategies that are directly applicable to these courses. If possible, obtain a syllabus prior to the beginning of class and use the course material to teach study strategies.

Whenever possible, encourage the student to obtain his textbooks in the summer prior to the academic year so that he can begin reading and reviewing the material prior to taking courses.

Help the student understand that the accommodations that he received during high school or college may or may not be available in certain courses and/or on certain exams. Oftentimes, for more advanced exams, such as those required by licensing agencies, officials review documentation to ascertain if specific accommodations will be approved and granted.

Develop a program of skills training that specifically addresses the skills that are necessary for successful functioning in college such as understanding of one's areas of cognitive and academic strengths and weaknesses, self-advocacy, learning strategies, listening and memory strategies, time management skills, note-taking strategies, test preparation, test-taking strategies, and use of a variety of computer applications including word processing, spreadsheets, and presentation programs (e.g., Powerpoint).

Explore psychological and emotional supports available to students with learning disabilities at the colleges and universities the student is considering. Help him to connect with the chosen support (e.g., counselor, facilitated support group) within the first week of school.

Self-Advocacy

Help the student develop a self-advocacy plan for either work or school, including a list of accommodations or modifications he will need. In preparation for this, help the student prepare to run his own Individualized Educational Plan (IEP) meetings. Part of the preparation should include a self-evaluation of academic and personal strengths, areas to improve, and vocational or educational goals. The student should also set the date for his IEP meeting and send out notices. Subsequent to the IEP meeting, help the student monitor his progress toward the behavioral objectives.

Help the student become a self-advocate. Help him understand what compensations he needs in a classroom and how to request them.

Help the student learn to appreciate that all people have their own rates and styles of learning. Self-understanding can be obtained through appreciating that all people have both strengths and weaknesses and that an understanding of learning and behavior is necessary for self-advocacy.

Ensure that the student understands clearly the nature of his difficulties. Teach ways that he may use his strengths to compensate for weaknesses.

Teach the student how to explain his learning difficulties to another person, such as a teacher or employer, as well as how to request modifications that will help him succeed in the particular situation. For example, have the student role-play asking an employer to give a set of instructions slowly enough so that he can write them down.

Given that the student is reluctant to ask others for help, provide him with an advocate at school who is familiar with his needs and can monitor progress and accommodations.

Help the student set up appointments to meet with teachers individually at the beginning of each semester to introduce himself and explain his needs. Encourage the student to meet with each teacher during office hours at least every 2 weeks to check on progress.

Help the student and his parents to understand that colleges and universities will ask the student to indicate if he has a disability and, if so, to provide documentation that supports requests for accommodations. The college disabilities support services provider will interact directly with the student, not with the parents, so that student will be responsible for obtaining services and legal protections.

Help the student learn how to apply compensatory strategies; express needs to faculty and staff; and independently access essential services in the postsecondary setting.

Encourage the student to consult on a regular basis with an academic advisor who will help him to set goals and develop appropriate strategies for meeting these goals. Goals can include improvement in the areas of time management, self-advocacy, study strategies, as well as personal issues affecting social and academic success.

In order to become an advocate for himself, the student will need continuous support and encouragement from supportive adults, both parents and teachers, who will help him develop both academic and vocational goals.

Accessing Community Resources

Provide the student and his parents with information regarding community services available to adults with disabilities.

Obtain information from agencies and services for adults with disabilities regarding eligibility requirements. Help the student apply to the appropriate services.

Educate the student and his parents about the procedures within the school system and community service agencies for accessing services.

Help the student's parents with advocacy and case management so that they can effectively secure services for their son and coordinate the services and information from professionals working with him.

Help the student locate community services and resources for further education, recreation, leisure, and work opportunities.

Provide consultation from a vocational transition specialist to coordinate school services, related services, and adult services in the community.

Assign the student an advisor or case manager who can help coordinate the accommodations and recommendations into his academic program, as well as help the student learn how to locate the necessary people on campus who will provide and implement the services.

Help the student learn to take advantage of the resources that are available in the university setting, including computer labs, study groups, and any tutorial services.

SECTION IV

Strategies

INTRODUCTION

Diagnostic reports usually include recommendations that address the educational and behavioral concerns that were noted in the referral, as well as those that were observed in the evaluation. Teachers who are asked to implement the recommendations may not, however, be familiar with a suggested method or technique. Because writing descriptions of methodology is time-consuming, short summaries of methods and interventions that have been mentioned in the Reports and Recommendations sections are provided here. These summaries may be attached to a report or shared with a teacher at a school staffing. As these are summaries, the teacher, resource specialist, or diagnostician may want to go to the source of the material, listed in the citation, for more detailed information. Additionally, the Strategies section includes examples of forms, such as charts, graphs, and contracts, to facilitate use of these and other methods. As with other sections of this book, the purpose of this section is to reduce the time associated with writing a comprehensive, practical assessment report.

ADDITION FACT MEMORIZATION: ORGANIZATIONAL STRUCTURES

Purpose

Memorization is easier when the information to be memorized is organized and when new information is related to information already known. The following structure builds on those two principles to facilitate memorization of basic math facts.

Procedure

Ensure that before introducing math facts, all students have a solid understanding of the concept underlying the corresponding operation and can represent the facts using physical objects as well as numbers. Additionally, ensure that they understand the basic properties of the operation, such as commutative property, associative property, and distributive property.

Keeping track of how many facts they have learned and how many remain to be learned is motivating for students and may be done by filling in or highlighting the sums on a table as facts are learned. As an illustration (Figure IV.1), each square of this table contains the letter of the fact set as explicated below (e.g., a = 0 + x and x + 0 facts). In the classroom, the sum corresponding to the math fact would be written in.

Prerequisite Skills

Before learning the addition facts, students should be able to count by 1 and count by 2 using both odd and even numbers. Before or during instruction, students must learn the principles of commutative property ($x + y = y + x$) and place value.

a) Teach $0 + x$ and $x + 0$. Help students discover the commutative property. Fill in the columns on the chart corresponding to 0 (**a:** 19/100 facts are learned).

b) Teach $1 + x$ and $x + 1$. Help the student to discover that when adding 1 to a number, the sum is always the next number in the number counting sequence. Prerequisite skill: Counting by ones (**b:** 36/100 facts are learned).

c) Teach $2 + x$ and $x + 2$. Help the student to discover that when adding 2 to any number, the sum is the next number up when counting by 2s. Prerequisite skills: Counting by 2s by even and by odd numbers, from 0 to 11 (**c:** 51/100 facts are learned).

+	0	1	2	3	4	5	6	7	8	9
0	a	a	a	a	a	a	a	a	a	a
1	a	b	b	b	b	b	b	b	b	b
2	a	b	c	c	c	c	c	c	c	c
3	a	b	c	d	e					f
4	a	b	c	e	d	e				f
5	a	b	c		e	d	e			f
6	a	b	c			e	d	e		f
7	a	b	c				e	d	e	f
8	a	b	c					e	d	e
9	a	b	c	f	f	f	f	f	e	d

Figure IV.1   Math Fact Chart to Aid in Memorizing Addition Facts

d) Teach the doubles facts (x + x). Students rarely have difficulty learning the doubles facts but you may facilitate this by using visual clues such as 5 fingers on each hand makes 10 and 9 tires on each side of a truck makes an 18-wheeler (**d:** 58/100 facts are learned).

e) Teach the related doubles, two for each double except for 9 + 9 (e.g., 3 + 3 → 3 + 4 and 4 + 3). The sum of each related double is one more than the sum of the double, so the student just has to remember the double fact for the lower number and count up one number, e.g., (3 + 4) = (3 + 3) + 1. Prerequisite skills: doubles facts (**e:** 70/100 facts are learned).

f) Teach the 10's-related facts. Demonstrate how "9 +" facts are related to "10 +" facts. Place 9 objects inside a frame (e.g., circle drawn on paper, embroidery hoop) and 6 objects inside another. Move one object from the 6-group to the 9-group, thereby building a group of 10 and reducing the 6-group to 5. The sum will always be a group of 10 plus 1 less than the other number—or 10 + (x − 1). Students will learn to automatically reduce by 1 the number that is not the 9 and put a 1 in front of it. Prerequisite skill: Place value to the 10's place (**f:** 80/100 facts are learned).

Although 20 facts remain to be learned, use of the commutative property reduces them to 10. These are normally the most difficult for students to learn and need to be memorized. Present them one or two a day using a variety of practice activities.

For similar suggestions for teaching subtraction, multiplication, and division facts as well as for extending the facts using place value, see: Heddens, J. W., & Speer, W. R. (2000a). *Today's mathematics: Part 1. Concepts and classroom methods* (10th ed.). New York: Wiley.

ANTICIPATION GUIDE

Purpose

The Anticipation Guide is a prelearning strategy used to activate students' prior knowledge about a topic to be studied, to arouse students' interest in the topic, and to evaluate the students' current level of knowledge. Simultaneously, the agree/disagree statements alert the students to the key concepts of the lesson or unit. The Anticipation Guide can also be used at the end of the lesson or unit to evaluate how much students have learned and to reinforce the new learning.

The Anticipation Guide can be used for any grade level and is compatible with almost any method of presenting information, including lecture, reading, videotape, and field trip.

Procedure

1. *Identify key concepts.*

Review the material to be presented with careful attention to the most important concepts that the students are expected to understand. Write a statement for each key concept.

> Example: Topic: Civil Rights Movement
> Concepts: Separate is not equal
> Sometimes laws are wrong or unfair
> Groups of people, working together, can change unfair laws.

2. *Consider your students' familiarity with the key concepts.*

As the statements are intended to promote discussion, the students must have enough prior knowledge of and experience with the concepts to understand your statements but not so much that there is little left to learn. Be aware of factors that may influence students' prior knowledge such as culture, socioeconomic level, maturity, and intellectual ability. The factors to consider will change depending on the topic and the way you word the questions.

Mather, N., & Jaffe, L. (2002). *Woodcock-Johnson III: Reports, Recommendations, and Strategies.* New York: John Wiley & Sons.

3. *Write a statement addressing each of the key concepts.*

Phrase the statements in such a way that they lend themselves to opinion supported by knowledge. Statements of fact do not lend themselves to discussion; one either knows the answer or does not. Example:

- It wouldn't matter if children of different races had to go to different schools. The quality of education would be the same.
- Even in a democracy, some of the laws can be wrong or unfair.
- If a law is unfair, there's really not much regular citizens can do about it.

4. *Decide statement order and presentation mode.*

Often, the order in which the concepts are to be presented in the instruction determines the order in which to present the statements. Depending on the topic, however, you may alter this sequence. Statements may be written on a form and handed out to the class, as shown in Figure IV.2, presented on an overhead projector, or written on the board.

5. *Present the Anticipation Guide.*

After presenting the guide, read the directions and the statements aloud. Explain that the students need to decide if they agree or disagree with each statement and will be ex-

pected to support their decision. Allow time for students to consider their answers and complete the guide. Students might also work in small groups and present a group answer (allowing for dissenters).

6. *Discuss the statements.*

Ask students for a response indicating agreement or disagreement with each statement (e.g., hands up, thumbs up or down, stand up or stay seated). Record the number of students who agree and disagree with each statement. Facilitate a brief discussion regarding each of the statements and require students to explain the reasons for their responses.

Argument from other students is encouraged. Putdowns are not allowed.

7. *Present the lesson.*

Direct students to think about the statements as the lesson is presented (e.g., listen to the lecture, read the materials, watch the video) and then to ask: "What did I decide? Do I want to change my opinion? How does this information relate to the discussion we just had?"

8. *Follow-up discussion.*

Direct the students to think about the statements again in light of what they have learned and to complete the guide again. They are free to change their responses. Again, you may lead a whole-class discussion or allow students to discuss the statements in small groups. Students' rationales must be at least partially based on information presented in the lesson but, depending on the information, they do not have to agree with the author's point of view.

Take a recount on agreement and disagreement with each statement and compare the results to the original count. Ask students to discuss why there is or is not a change in the count.

The follow-up discussion will allow you to evaluate if the students increased their knowledge and understanding to the expected level or if you need to provide more information about and experiences regarding the topic.

Adapted from: Tierney, R. J., & Readence, J. E., (1999). *Reading strategies and practices: A compendium* (5th ed.). Boston: Allyn and Bacon.

Anticipation Guide

Directions: Read each statement. Think carefully about what it means and decide if you agree or disagree; then check the appropriate box. Be ready to explain why you agree or disagree with each statement.		
Statements	Agree	Disagree
It wouldn't matter if children of different races had to go to different schools. The quality of education would be the same.		
Even in a democracy, some of the laws can be wrong or unfair.		
If a law is unfair, there's really not much regular citizens can do about it.		

Figure IV.2 Example Anticipation Guide Chart

Mather, N., & Jaffe, L. (2002). *Woodcock-Johnson III: Reports, Recommendations, and Strategies.* New York: John Wiley & Sons.

ADDITION FACT CHART

Name _____

0 + 0	1 + 0	2 + 0	3 + 0	4 + 0	5 + 0	6 + 0	7 + 0	8 + 0	9 + 0	10 + 0	11 + 0	12 + 0
0 + 1	1 + 1	2 + 1	3 + 1	4 + 1	5 + 1	6 + 1	7 + 1	8 + 1	9 + 1	10 + 1	11 + 1	12 + 1
0 + 2	1 + 2	2 + 2	3 + 2	4 + 2	5 + 2	6 + 2	7 + 2	8 + 2	9 + 2	10 + 2	11 + 2	12 + 2
0 + 3	1 + 3	2 + 3	3 + 3	4 + 3	5 + 3	6 + 3	7 + 3	8 + 3	9 + 3	10 + 3	11 + 3	12 + 3
0 + 4	1 + 4	2 + 4	3 + 4	4 + 4	5 + 4	6 + 4	7 + 4	8 + 4	9 + 4	10 + 4	11 + 4	12 + 4
0 + 5	1 + 5	2 + 5	3 + 5	4 + 5	5 + 5	6 + 5	7 + 5	8 + 5	9 + 5	10 + 5	11 + 5	12 + 5
0 + 6	1 + 6	2 + 6	3 + 6	4 + 6	5 + 6	6 + 6	7 + 6	8 + 6	9 + 6	10 + 6	11 + 6	12 + 6
0 + 7	1 + 7	2 + 7	3 + 7	4 + 7	5 + 7	6 + 7	7 + 7	8 + 7	9 + 7	10 + 7	11 + 7	12 + 7
0 + 8	1 + 8	2 + 8	3 + 8	4 + 8	5 + 8	6 + 8	7 + 8	8 + 8	9 + 8	10 + 8	11 + 8	12 + 8
0 + 9	1 + 9	2 + 9	3 + 9	4 + 9	5 + 9	6 + 9	7 + 9	8 + 9	9 + 9	10 + 9	11 + 9	12 + 9
0 + 10	1 + 10	2 + 10	3 + 10	4 + 10	5 + 10	6 + 10	7 + 10	8 + 10	9 + 10	10 + 10	11 + 10	12 + 10
0 + 11	1 + 11	2 + 11	3 + 11	4 + 11	5 + 11	6 + 11	7 + 11	8 + 11	9 + 11	10 + 11	11 + 11	12 + 11
0 + 12	1 + 12	2 + 12	3 + 12	4 + 12	5 + 12	6 + 12	7 + 12	8 + 12	9 + 12	10 + 12	11 + 12	12 + 12

Mather, N., & Jaffe, L. (2002). *Woodcock-Johnson III: Reports, Recommendations, and Strategies.* New York: John Wiley & Sons.

BEHAVIOR RATING CHART

Name: _____Date: _____   Respondent: _____

Compared with typical age-peers, please rate the student on the following behaviors:

1. Better than most
2. Average

3. Somewhat less than average
4. Much less than average

	M	T	W	Th	F
Stays on task in independent work					
Pays attention when teacher is talking					
Stays in seat w/o excessive fidgeting					
Transitions efficiently between activities					
Classwork indicates sufficient focus and care while working on the task.					

COMMENTS _____

_____

_____

_____

_____

Please keep a copy and send the original home on Friday afternoons

Adaptations for Behavior Charts

To document response to medication or response to behavioral interventions, or for use in rotating classes, charts may be developed to accommodate shorter intervals.

Self-Contained Class

If chart is to be filled out each class period, teacher(s) uses a new chart each day:

	Per 1 Reading	Per 2 Math	Per 3 Writing	Per 4 Hist/Sci	Per 5 Elective
Stays on task in independent work					

Mather, N., & Jaffe, L. (2002). *Woodcock-Johnson III: Reports, Recommendations, and Strategies.* New York: John Wiley & Sons.

If chart is to be filled out before lunch and at the end of the day, the teacher(s) uses the same chart throughout the week, sending it home with the student, faxing it, or mailing it on Friday.

	M		T		W		Th		F	
	am	pm	am	pm	am	pm	am	pm	am	pm
Stays on task in independent work										

Rotating Classes

For rotating classes, the chart is to be filled out each class period. Each teacher has a chart and uses it throughout the week, sending it home with the student on Friday or giving it to the home liaison staff person (e.g., counselor, homeroom teacher).

	M	T	W	Th	F
Stays on task in independent work					

BEHAVIORAL CONTRACTS

A behavioral contract may be the next step if the student becomes accustomed and responds well to a token economy intervention. A behavioral contract is an agreement between the student, teacher, and sometimes the parents. The contract delineates the behaviors or tasks a student is to perform, the criteria for an acceptable level of performance or completion, the reinforcement (i.e., activities, privileges, or tangible items he/she will receive in exchange), and any quantifiers of the rewards. A system of record-keeping must be developed to document the student's progress toward fulfilling the contract.

Typically, children are less frequently reinforced in a contract system than in a token economy system; consequently, the time interval between demonstration of (or refraining from) the target behavior and reinforcement is longer. Contracts may not be sufficiently motivating to allow younger students and students with a moderate or more severe level of ADHD to sustain behavioral improvements. Delay between behavior and reinforcement must be attuned to the child's maturational level. Children under 6 years of age are unlikely to benefit from behavioral contracts as they are frequently unable to delay gratification or understand the contract rules (e.g., that they do not receive a "reward" after just one demonstration of a particular behavior).

Initially, as with any behavioral intervention, the behav-ioral criteria for earning rewards must be well within the ability of the student and reinforcers must be highly motivating to the individual child as well as appropriate to his/her developmental level. As the student demonstrates consistent success with one level of behavioral criteria, the criteria for earning rewards, the period of time between rewards, or the delay between behavior and rewards, can be gradually increased. To sustain interest in the program, reinforcers may need to be reviewed and changed frequently.

In the initial stages of establishing a behavioral contract, including the following elements in the contract will ensure failure: targeting too many behaviors at one time, targeting multiple-step tasks, and setting excessively high criteria. The child must experience success, strictly within the boundaries of the contract, from the start.

Sample Behavioral Contract

Goal: _____ (student) will complete his homework each night and come to class ready and able to participate in assignments and activities based on the homework.

Student and Teacher Responsibilities
I, _____ (student), agree to:

1. write down my assignments in my assignment book at the end of each day and ask the teacher to initial them.

If no homework is assigned for a specific subject, I will write "NH" in the box. Criteria: At least 75% of the assignments for the week.

2. bring home the books and materials necessary to do my homework each day. Criteria: At least 75% of assignments for the week.

3. put my homework in the homework box each morning.

I, _____ (teacher), agree to:

1. write the assignments on the board at the end of each day and remind _____ to write them in his book;

2. remind _____ to put materials in his backpack, helping _____ to check each assignment on the board as he does so;

3. remind _____ to hand in his homework when he enters class each morning.

School-Based Rewards

Each day that _____ hands in his homework in the morning, has his assignments written down from the day before, and has brought home the correct materials for the previous day's homework, he will be allowed to choose one of the following:

1. spend 15 minutes before lunch using a computer program of his choice;

2. leave 5 minutes early for lunch;

3. treat the whole class to popcorn at snack time. (Ms. Smith will make it.)

Parent Responsibilities

I, _____ (parent), agree to:

1. remind _____ to do his homework before or immediately after dinner;

2. review _____'s assignment book with him to make sure he understands the tasks assigned;

3. provide quiet during homework time;

4. be available for help as needed.

Home-Based Rewards

If _____ meets his obligations for the entire week, he may choose to:

have a friend stay overnight at his house;

have pizza for dinner and rent a movie on Friday or Saturday night; or

have his mom/dad take him to a movie, skating, bowling, or other special activity.

I agree to carry out my responsibilities as stated above. Signed:

_____   _____
Student   Teacher

_____
Parent

_____

Documentation Form for Behavioral Contract

Name	Mon	Tues	Wed	Thurs	Fri
Write assignments	Y N N/A	Y N N/A	Y N N/A	Y N N/A	Y N N/A
Bring home materials	Y N N/A	Y N N/A	Y N N/A	Y N N/A	Y N N/A
Hand in homework	Y N N/A	Y N N/A	Y N N/A	Y N N/A	Y N N/A

Adapted from DuPaul, G. J., & Stoner, G. (1994). *ADHD in the schools: Assessment and intervention strategies.* New York: Guilford.

BEHAVIORAL INTERVENTIONS FOR THE WHOLE CLASS

Teaching the Behavior

Decide on the behavior (termed here "target behavior") you most want to develop within your class. Brainstorm a few and prioritize by choosing the behavior that would help you most in your teaching and help the class most in their learning. The target behavior will usually be the behavior that causes the most disruptions, such as going from one activity to another quickly and quietly, staying on task during independent seatwork, listening to instructions quietly while looking at the teacher, and being quiet during independent seatwork except when asking for or giving help.

Mather, N., & Jaffe, L. (2002). *Woodcock-Johnson III: Reports, Recommendations, and Strategies.* New York: John Wiley & Sons.

Plan to spend time teaching the behavior just as you would a specific reading skill. Concentrate on one new behavior until it is mastered, even if it takes a month. Incorporate practice every day and throughout the school day, whenever the appropriate situation arises. Define the target behavior. List the specific actions the students would do from beginning to end. See below for examples.

Teaching the Target Behavior

1. Define the Target Behavior for the class. List and explain the specific actions you have determined are integral components.
2. Put up a sign labeling the Target Behavior to be learned.
3. Ask for examples and nonexamples of the behavior. List and role-play both. For nonexamples, ask the students to decide how the actor *should* have behaved.
4. Provide frequent opportunities for the students to practice the behavior with teacher guidance. After each occasion, briefly tell them what went well and what can be done better the next time.
5. Set up a reward system to motivate students to practice the Target Behavior. A reward system also enhances their ability to *remember* to use it. See below for a whole class reward system to help build team consciousness and helping behaviors.

Example of Target Behavior for Whole Class Training: Efficient Transitions

1. Definition: moving from one activity to the next
2. Specific actions:
   a. Stop current activity.
   b. Put materials away.
   c. Take out materials for new activity.
   d. Move to new place in the room (e.g., other table, line up at door).
   e. If you have a question, ask a friend or raise your hand to ask the teacher.
   f. Show readiness by sitting/standing quietly, hands in specific position.
3. Set a specific time limit for transitions and tell the students what it is. Three minutes is a good place to start. Shorten or lengthen the transition time according to what the students have to do (e.g., put away/get new materials and move to new tables vs. line up at the door).
4. Establish a specific signal. Transitions start and end at prearranged signals. For example, the teacher may ring a bell, say "go ahead," or use a timer. If using a timer, get one with pause capability in case of interruptions. Try not to allow transitions to be interrupted.

5. If all of the students are ready when you give the signal to end the transition, give the class credit (e.g., points, marble in the jar) toward their reward. Make sure they know they have earned the credit for their behavior.

Establishing a Whole Class Reward System

The following will remind and encourage students to practice the Target Behavior, as well as build a team consciousness in the classroom.

1. Explain to the students that they will be working for some type of reward (e.g., popcorn party; daytime pajama party; sodas or juice boxes for the whole class; field trip; magician coming to perform; grab-bag prizes). You may ask the class to brainstorm a list of rewards but give them certain limits (e.g., has to fit within a certain budget, cannot take longer than one school day), but the teacher has the final decision. The reward chosen must be something they can win at some time but does not have to be accomplished by a specific time. If they choose a trip to the circus and do not earn it before the circus leaves town, they will lose faith in this system. The question must be *when,* not *if,* they will earn the reward.
2. Each time the class as a whole demonstrates the behavior, the teacher drops a marble in a jar. When the marbles are up to a premarked level, the prize has been earned. Provide the reward within a few days. *As soon as* the marbles have reached the mark, empty the jar, choose another reward, and start to fill the jar again. If the Target Behavior has been mastered, you may choose to teach and reward a new Target Behavior. Do not go on to a new Target Behavior until the previous behavior is well established. Never stop praising individuals and the class as a whole for using the previously learned Target Behaviors.
3. Teach helping behaviors to aid the class in mastering the Target Behavior. Teach helping behaviors directly.

Teaching Helping Behaviors

Using a group reward system can help the students focus not only on their own behaviors but on the behaviors of others as well. The faster the students "get with the program," the faster the whole class earns the reward. Frequently, however, students who do not already have a group consciousness must be taught *how* to help others to "get with the program."

Mather, N., & Jaffe, L. (2002). *Woodcock-Johnson III: Reports, Recommendations, and Strategies.* New York: John Wiley & Sons.

1. Teach what helping behaviors are. The actions that constitute a helping behavior will depend on the type of target behavior you are trying to develop (e.g., efficient transition; working quietly; staying on task; sharing).
2. Explain the specific helping behavior you are trying to help them develop and how it will help them to learn the target behavior. Write the target behavior on the board.
3. Ask students to suggest ways they could help each other to accomplish the target behavior. You may want to provide limits, such as not hurting someone else's feelings or using a gentle touch. List these. Ask for and make a separate list of actions that one would not use (e.g., put downs, hitting).
4. Role-play examples and nonexamples of helping behaviors for the target behavior.
5. Reinforce the use of helping behaviors. For example, each time the target behavior is used (e.g., efficient transition), ask: "Who received a helping behavior?" After responses, ask: "Who offered a helping behavior?"

Rule: Reports of helping behaviors are not to be accompanied by complaints about the other student or reports that the helper was ignored. (These may be reported to the teacher privately or discussed in class problem-solving meetings.)

If necessary, helping behaviors may be further encouraged by dropping tokens into a cup on the student's desk, making a tally mark on a card on the student's desk, or putting a star on a wall chart. Marks/tokens/stars may be used to buy small rewards from the class treasure chest.

CARBO METHOD

Purpose

The Carbo method (Carbo, 1989) is a procedure for recording books for students to listen to on tape. The purpose is to help students achieve maximum gains in fluency.

Procedure
Follow these steps to record books:

1. Decide which pages you will record on each cassette side.
2. Since every tape cassette has about 5 to 8 seconds of "lead time," let the tape run for that amount of time before starting to record.

3. Speak into the microphone from a distance of approximately 6 to 8 inches.
4. Convey your interest in the book through your voice.
5. Begin by reading the story title, providing a brief introduction, pausing, and then tell the student which page to turn to. Pause long enough so that the reader will have enough time to turn pages and look at pictures.
6. Tell the student when to turn the page. When stating a page number, soften your voice so that you will not distract the student from the content. Pause before reading the next page.
7. Read the story in logical phrases, slowly enough so that most students can follow along, but not so slowly that they will become bored.
8. End each tape with, "Please rewind the tape for the next listener. That ends this recording." This will prevent students from continuing to listen to the blank tape.

As general guidelines, record 5 to 15 minutes at a normal pace for instructional level material and have the student listen to the tape once. For difficult material, record no more than 2 minutes at a slow pace with good expression and have the student listen to the passage two to three times. After listening, have the student read the passage aloud.

Adapted from: Carbo, M. (1989). *How to record books for maximum reading gain.* New York: National Reading Styles Institute.

CLASSROOM BEHAVIORAL INTERVENTIONS: ISSUES IN DESIGN

1. *Situational analysis:* Identifying the problem behavior and the situation in which it most commonly occurs provides direction in the type of intervention to develop as well as the components and procedures to include. To begin, make a list of the student's behaviors that interfere with learning (the student's or the class's) and/or social interactions (e.g., disturbing other students, limited attention) as well as the situations in which these most frequently occur (e.g., independent seatwork, lunch). Teacher interviews, behavior rating scales, and classroom observations facilitate this process. Prioritize these behaviors according to the severity of disruption they cause, and target the most disruptive behavior.
2. *Positive reinforcement:* Generally, the primary components in behavioral programs for students with

ADHD should be frequent feedback, specific to the target task or behavior, and positive reinforcement, given immediately after the student demonstrates the behavior. Delay reduces the effectiveness of the reinforcement.

3. *Mild negative consequences:* It is sometimes necessary to supplement positive reinforcement with mild consequences for negative behavior, such as mild reprimands and/or redirection to task-related behavior. Reprimands and redirection must specify the behavior the teacher expects; be expressed during or immediately after the problem behavior occurs; and be stated briefly, calmly, and, to the extent possible, privately.

4. *Consistency:* A critical component in carrying out any behavioral intervention is that the program be adhered to exactly as described to the student. The student must know ahead of time what he will earn for each demonstration of the targeted positive behavior and what he will lose for each targeted negative behavior. For example, if a student who has already met the criteria for a chosen reward misbehaves, it would be unfair and counterproductive to withhold it. Assign an appropriate consequence, consistent with the behavioral program, for the new infraction. For example, if a student had earned the right to attend a special event and then cut class, assign an immediate consequence for cutting class but allow him to attend the event.

5. *Target behaviors:* To be most effective, interventions should target academic products and performance (e.g., work completion, accuracy) rather than task-related behaviors (e.g., paying attention). In this way, the attention of the teacher and the student is focused on academic outcomes and organizational skills, and, in the process, promotes independent learning and academic achievement. Moreover, as improving academic outcomes is incompatible with inattentive and disruptive behaviors, such a focus reduces negative behaviors. In choosing behaviors to target for intervention, do not set unrealistic expectations, such as asking a student to sit perfectly still or to never call out an answer.

6. *Reinforcers:* Social praise from teachers is not as effective as stronger reinforcers such as earned privileges or activities (e.g., computer time) or tangible rewards (e.g., candy) in producing behavioral change in students with ADHD. The use of activities and privileges as reinforcers is preferable to tangibles. Additionally, for the reinforcers to provide sufficient motivation for behavioral change, they must be uniquely interesting to the student.

Thus, in choosing reinforcers, request suggestions from the student as well as note the activities he chooses himself. Regardless of the reinforcers chosen, as their novelty wears off, their motivating power will diminish, and with it, the student's interest in the program. To avoid this, create a menu of rewards, some "cheap" (requiring few tokens) and some more "expensive," allowing for variety and change.

7. *Immediate success.* Initially, the criteria for earning reinforcers must be set at a level the student can achieve immediately. Immediate success is necessary to activate the student's interest in the program and desire to meet the criteria.

8. *Priming:* Before the student begins a classroom task, review with the student the possible rewards and the behaviors necessary to earn them, and have him or her choose one as an immediate goal.

9. *Ongoing program evaluation:* Monitor and evaluate the integrity with which an intervention program is implemented. Results may suggest a need to change some components or procedures of the program, indicate and justify the need for additional resources, and/or guide additional staff training. Conduct simple evaluations. An observer may check off the procedures on a checklist as they occur as well as record elements of the student's present behaviors.

Adapted from: DuPaul, G. J., & Stoner, G. (1994). *ADHD in the schools: Assessment and intervention strategies.* New York: Guilford; and Lindsley, O. R. (1991). From technical jargon to plain English for application. *Journal of Applied Behavior Analysis, 24,* 449–458.

CLASSROOM RULES: GUIDELINES

Use classroom rules to specify your expectations for student behavior in the classroom with a focus on maximizing benefit from the educational opportunities offered and promoting mutual respect. Before the first day of school, decide what rules are necessary and post them. On the first day of school, explain them to the students. Allow students to question the reason for and fairness of a rule but not at a time when a rule has been broken. Set aside times for discussion of the rules but retain the right to determine the acceptability of any changes.

Mather, N., & Jaffe, L. (2002). *Woodcock-Johnson III: Reports, Recommendations, and Strategies.* New York: John Wiley & Sons.

Characteristics of Good Proactive Rules

1. Keep the number of rules to a *minimum*—about five rules for each classroom.
2. Keep the wording of rules *simple*—pictures or icons depicting the rules will help younger students remember.
3. Have the rules logically represent your *basic expectation* for a student's behavior in your classroom.
4. Keep the wording *positive* if possible.
5. Make your rules *specific.* The more ambiguous (i.e., open to several interpretations) the rules are, the more difficult they are to understand. Students with behavioral problems can take advantage of nonspecific "loopholes" in poorly stated rules.
6. Make your rules describe behavior that is *observable.* The behavior must be observable so that you can make an unequivocal decision as to whether or not the rule has been followed.
7. Make your rules describe behavior that is *measurable.* That is, the behavior must be able to be counted or quantified in some way for monitoring purposes.
8. Post the rules in a prominent place in the classroom (e.g., in the front of the classroom, near the door). Make the lettering large and block-printed.
9. Tie following the rules to *consequences.* Explain what happens positively if students follow the rules, and what they lose if they do not follow the rules. Frequently, teachers forget to state the positive consequences.
10. Always include a *compliance* rule, such as "Do what your teacher asks immediately."

Reprinted with permission from Sopris West Educational Services, *The Tough Kid Book: Practical Classroom Management Strategies* by Ginger Rhode, Ph.D., William Jenson, Ph.D., & Ken Reavis, Ed.D., Copyright 1992–1996 (6th printing).

CLOZE PROCEDURE

Purpose

The cloze technique may be used for informal assessment or as an instructional strategy. Use this strategy to help students increase their understanding of text. Typically, in this procedure, every *n*th word is deleted and replaced with a blank of uniform length. The number of words deleted is based upon the level of conceptual difficulty of the material and the competency of the reader.

Steps

Use the following three-phase teaching procedure as a basic framework to implement the cloze technique:

Phase 1: Presentation and Preparation
Use prereading activities, such as developing a purpose for reading, to motivate the student and build background information. Provide short practice sessions. Work with the student and model how the exercises are completed. Select materials at the student's independent reading level.

Phase 2: Preview and Completion
Have the student read the passage three times. During the first reading the student gains an overview of the material and fills in the blanks mentally. In the second reading, the student fills in all of the blanks. For the third reading, the student checks to see if the responses make sense. During the second and third readings, students may work in pairs or small groups.

Phase 3: Follow-up
The most important step is the follow-up conference. Discuss with the student(s) their choices, review other acceptable alternatives, and ask the student(s) to explain why they chose a particular response. If needed, discuss specific context clues that are found around the blank and assist in word selection. As a final step, have student(s) compare their responses with the original.

Adaptations

Use adaptations of this procedure based upon the purpose of the instruction. The following applications were field tested by Thomas (1978).

1. Context/Content Clues
Delete the specific terms that complete the key ideas in the passage. The reader then focuses on these essential ele-

Mather, N., & Jaffe, L. (2002). *Woodcock-Johnson III: Reports, Recommendations, and Strategies.* New York: John Wiley & Sons.

ments. This adaptation is particularly appropriate for content-area material.

Example: The largest state in the United States is _____.

2. Process Strategies/Combined Clues

Provide different graphophonic clues to help the student identify the word, such as the initial consonant, several letters, or the ending of the word.

Example: The little girl loved to ride her b___.

3. Specific Phonic Elements

Select specific phonic elements to delete from words, such as consonant blends or digraphs or short vowel sounds. This adaptation requires the student to use context clues as well as phonic skills and may be used to reinforce specific phonic elements that the student is learning.

Example: The b_g d_g r_n to the house.

4. Specific Morphemic Elements

Delete root words, prefixes, or suffixes. If necessary, the specific elements to use can be listed for the student.

Example: The ___school teach__ was sing___ the children's favorite song_.

5. Relationships: Function Words

Delete function words, such as prepositions, articles, conjunctions, or auxiliary verbs, from various types of syntactic structures, or delete a particular part of speech. The purpose is to help the student attend to language structure.

Example: Sally __ leaving ___ school __ the morning.

6. Relationships: Pronouns and Pronoun Referents

Delete pronouns, selected pronoun referents, or both.

Example: Mary had helped Jim all year. ___ had treated ___ kindly.

7. Relationships: Organizational Patterns

Delete the keywords and phrases that signal the organizational pattern of a passage, such as the words *first, next,* or *finally.* This variation can also be used with words signaling time order, such as *before, after,* or *when;* words signaling a comparison/contrast organizational pattern, such as *however, but, although,* or *yet;* or words signaling a cause/effect organizational pattern, such as *because, therefore,* or *consequently.*

Example: When you start any project, _____ plan the steps and ____ decide what materials you will need.

Adapted from: Thomas, K. (1978). Instructional applications of the cloze technique. *Reading World, 18,* 1–12.

COHESIVE DEVICES: TYPES

Purpose

Speakers and writers use a variety of cohesive devices to link or clarify the relationships among ideas. Instruction in cohesion is aimed at helping a student grasp (when listening or reading) or express (when speaking or writing) the relatedness of meaning between words or clauses within a sentence and across sentences. Many students can benefit from direct instruction in how to use words that signify a variety of types of semantic relations. Examples of several types of cohesive devices follow.

Reference

Cohesion is formed by a word (or words) that refers to information, found elsewhere in the text, that is necessary for comprehension of the statement. The *exact* identity of the referent is stated elsewhere.

Pronominal: Hansel took some bread crumbs. *He* put them in his pocket.
Demonstrative: Their parents took them to the *forest* and left them *there.*

Lexical

Textual cohesion between one word and another is created by repetition of the word or use of a synonym, a superordinate word, a more general word, or an associated word.

Same word: The *darkness* of night came swiftly. The children were afraid of the *darkness.*
Synonym: Hansel and Gretel huddled together to wait for *daybreak.* Oh, when would *dawn* come?

Mather, N., & Jaffe, L. (2002). *Woodcock-Johnson III: Reports, Recommendations, and Strategies.* New York: John Wiley & Sons.

Superordinate word: Mice and raccoons snuffled closer to investigate the intruders. The *animals* were curious.

General word: Finally, the tired children snuggled down in the *leaves and pine needles* of the forest *bed* and went to sleep.

Associated word: As the *dawn* broke, *sunlight* filled the forest.

Conjunction

A conjunction represents a semantic relation that expresses how a clause or statement is related in meaning to a previous clause or statement; it is signaled by a specific connecting word or phrase. Following is a variety of types of semantic relations with examples of words that typically signal each.

Additive: and, also, in addition
Amplification: furthermore, moreover
Adversative: but, however, in contrast, nevertheless
Causal: if/then, because, due to, as a result
Conclusion: therefore, accordingly, consequently
Temporal: after, meanwhile, whenever, previously
Sequence: first, second, then, lastly, finally
Spatial: next to, between, in front of, adjacent to
Continuative: after all, again, finally, another
Likeness: likewise, similarly
Example: for example, as an illustration
Restatement: in other words, that is, in summary
Exception: except, barring, beside, excluding

Substitution

A word is substituted for the referent that is not identical in meaning or carries some differentiation, but performs the same structural function.

Nominal: The witch wanted a bigger *pot.* She ordered Gretel to go and get *one.*

Clausal: Could Gretel *save Hansel?* She thought *so.*

Ellipsis: A word, phrase, or clause is left unsaid, but is understood.

    Verbal: "Are you coming?" called the witch. "I am (coming)," answered Gretel.

    Nominal: Gretel looked for a sharp tool, but she knew she would take whatever (tool) she could find.

    Clausal: I know I can kill the witch. I'm sure I can (kill the witch).

Adapted from: Wallach, G. P., & Miller, L. (1988). *Language intervention and academic success.* Boston: Little, Brown, and Company.

COLLABORATIVE STRATEGIC READING

Collaborative Strategic Reading (CSR) is an intensive classroom or group-based reading comprehension strategy designed to be used with expository text. This strategy is most effective when implemented within an elementary or secondary class structure so that students can practice it several times with different teachers. In this method, teachers model the strategies, provide ongoing examples and opportunities, and guide and provide feedback over an extended period of time. CSR integrates the following four specific reading comprehension strategies to teach students how to become active, effective readers:

1. *Preview:* The first step, previewing, develops students' interest in what they are reading, activates background knowledge, and encourages students to make predictions about what they will read.

    To review the concept of previewing, use a discussion about movie previews to illustrate ways in which the viewer begins to develop expectations and interest in the upcoming movie. Once students understand the concept, model the steps of previewing: read the title; look at pictures, graphs, diagrams, etc.; read the headings and try to anticipate what they mean; look for keywords (words that are underlined, italicized, in bold or set off); and read the first and last paragraphs. As a final step, predict what you think you will learn from the reading. After this procedure has been demonstrated, have the class practice the preview step several times over the next few days, providing feedback and support.

2. *Click and Clunk:* In the second step, students learn to monitor their reading, determining what they already know about and what causes difficulty. A "click" occurs when the reader identifies something she knows (it "clicks" because it makes sense). A "clunk" is a word or point that the student does not understand. For this step, model "clicks" and "clunks" and then ask students to write down their own "clunks" after reading a short assignment. If students are using consumable materials, they may note the "clunks" right in the text or in the margin. Once students learn to recognize clunks, teach strategies to address them. Strategies might include use of a glossary or a dictionary, rereading, or discussion with a peer. Students are asked to identify the strategy they use to address the clunk so that they learn which strategies to apply in different situations.

Mather, N., & Jaffe, L. (2002). *Woodcock-Johnson III: Reports, Recommendations, and Strategies.* New York: John Wiley & Sons.

3. *Get the Gist:* For the third step, ask each student to summarize the main idea of a paragraph in 10–12 words and then ask students to discuss and offer different versions. Ask students to provide evidence to support their summary and to exclude unnecessary details. Have students vote on which summary is best and explain why.
4. *Wrap-Up:* During wrap-up, the student reviews the reading and what has been learned by asking and responding to questions. Depending on the age group, provide question stems, such as:

How would you compare and contrast . . . ?
How were _____ the same or different?
How would you interpret . . . ?

Eventually encourage students to write their own questions. To improve students' abilities to ask higher-level questions, assign values to questions. A $10.00 question is one where the answer is located in the text and requires a short response; a $20.00 question is located in the text but requires more than two or three words to answer; a $30.00 question is found in the text but in order to respond, students need to reread the text and compose an answer based on the reading. A $40.00 question requires inference and generalization. Students have to integrate responses with previous knowledge and/or experience.

Have each group generate questions. Place questions on one side of color-coded index cards and answers on the reverse side. Use the cards for review, as the basis for questions on future tests, and as a resource for students learning to ask good questions. The cards can also be used in a game in which members of one group quiz members of other groups or create a simulated quiz show, such as Hollywood Squares or Jeopardy.

To make the collaborative groups successful, a variety of reading levels (including both a good and poor reader) need to be present in each group and at least one student member should have leadership skills. Assign the following roles:

- Leader: focuses the group on using the four strategies;
- "Clunk" expert: reminds the group of strategies for figuring out a clunk;
- "Gist" expert: reminds the group about steps to use to figure out the main idea;
- Announcer: calls on students to read or share an idea and reports back to the entire class.

Adapted from: Vaughn, S., & Klingner, J. K. (1999). Teaching reading comprehension through collaborative strategic reading. *Intervention in School and Clinic, 34,* 284–292.

CONTENT AREA INSTRUCTION: COMPONENTS OF EFFECTIVE LESSONS

Purpose

The purposes of using the lesson structure described below are: (a) to enhance students' learning by activating their intention to learn, (b) to help them understand the organization and key concepts of the lesson, (c) to increase their understanding of the content, and (d) to reinforce their new learning through evaluation. This framework may be adapted for any presentation format including lecture, reading, video- or audiotape, or a field trip.

Procedure

1. *Activate students' prior knowledge* regarding the key concepts of the lesson while evaluating their readiness to understand the content. Vary your use of questioning techniques.
    Suggestions: Anticipation Guide, PReP (PreReading Plan), Brainstorming and Semantic Mapping, KWLS (Know, Want to know, Learned, Still need to learn), and Study Guides.
2. *Teach key vocabulary.* After deciding on a limited number of vocabulary words necessary for comprehension of the key concepts, use interactive techniques for teaching them.
    Suggestions: DVTA (Directed Vocabulary-Thinking Activity), Semantic Feature Analysis.
3. *Provide an advance organizer.* List the key concepts and/or sections of the lesson on the board in order of presentation. Review the list and provide a brief (2 or 3 minutes) overview of the lesson.
4. *Present the material.*
    a) Ensure that each section has a clear beginning and end.
    b) When introducing a new section, mark its position on the board. When completing it, cross it out (but leave it up so students can see the whole outline).
    c) If lecturing, use keywords or actions to help students perceive important points (e.g., pause for a few seconds, then use such phrases as: "This next point is important and will be on the test") and the organization of the information (e.g., "In the beginning"; "First, second, last"; "At the same time"; "OK, now. We have to back up. *Before* that happened . . .").

Mather, N., & Jaffe, L. (2002). *Woodcock-Johnson III: Reports, Recommendations, and Strategies.* New York: John Wiley & Sons.

d) Use visual materials to make instructional information more interesting and to illustrate the key concepts.

5. If time permits, *provide an instructional or reinforcement activity* for each section of the lesson, covering only the information included in that section.

   Suggestions: Have students: Fill in the corresponding part of the study guide or KWLS sheet; mark their opinion on the Anticipation Guide based on the new information and discuss the changes; pair up to use the Reciprocal Teaching procedure (a question/answer strategy); work in small groups to make up a test on the key concepts covered; complete a worksheet focusing on comprehension of the key concepts; or engage in a DRTA (Directed Reading-Thinking Activity).

6. *Help students to stay on track* while they are working independently or in small groups. Circulate, make positive comments about their work, and provide clarifications, as needed.

7. *Limit the lesson* to a reasonable length and depth of information. This depends on the students' abilities to attend and their readiness to learn the content as well as, of course, the teacher's presentation. Short lessons are more effective than long lessons.

8. *Reinforce and evaluate concept learning.* Go back to whichever prior knowledge technique you used initially and do it again. Facilitate a discussion of how and why the information has changed. For example, if using a semantic map (web), ask the students how they would change the constellation of ideas based on what they learned. Require them to support their responses, even if opinions, with factual information.

CONTEXT CLUES

Purpose

The use of context clues to derive the meaning of new words from text is the most effective way for students to increase vocabulary independently. Furthermore, it frees students from overreliance on looking up words in the dictionary, a method that is cumbersome and interrupts the flow of meaning in reading.

The following explanation of context clues is provided as a guide for the teacher in introducing them to their students. Teaching context clues within a variety of activities, such as the Directed Vocabulary Thinking Activity (Cunningham, 1979), will facilitate learning and retention of the clues.

1. Direct explanation
   a. Appositive: The writer provides the definition, as an appositive, immediately following the word it defines.

      Example: An *environmentalist,* a person devoted to protecting the ecological balance of the earth, opposes the destruction of vast tracts of rain forest.

   b. That is: The phrase "that is" alerts the reader to an explanation for the word preceding it.

      Example: The *descrambler*—that is, the device for decoding scrambled messages—did not prove to be an effective tool for the Axis powers, as the Allied messages were being sent in the Navajo language.

   c. Placed at a distance from the word to be explained.

      Example: Life on the *kibbutz* was hard but rewarding. They had awaited this life of communal living on a collective farm.

2. Experience clue: The use of past experience to infer the meaning of a word from the situation depicted in the text.

   Example: Arriving home to find his rare and most precious classical records shattered on the floor *infuriated* Mr. Witherspoon beyond reason.

3. Mood or tone: The reader finds the clue to the unknown word's meaning in the general mood or tone of the passage.

   Example: The small *disheartened* group trudged slowly through the sultry, dusty, streets, burdened with the tiny casket.

4. Explanation through example: The reader may find an example of the meaning of the unfamiliar word in the same or the next sentence.

   Example: An undiagnosed learning disability may have serious emotional *ramifications.* An adolescent who has consistently tried, but has had difficulty learning, may assume that "good grades" are beyond him and drop out of school as soon as age and the law permit.

   Example: Eyes sparkling, doing little dance steps through the crowded market, and flashing her smile at the vendors and patrons alike, Jillian was surprised by her own *vivacity.*

5. Summary: The unknown word sums up the situation described in the passage. The word may be placed either before or after the situation.

Mather, N., & Jaffe, L. (2002). *Woodcock-Johnson III: Reports, Recommendations, and Strategies.* New York: John Wiley & Sons.

Example: Through the beveled panes of the leaded glass windows, the sunlight splintered into kaleidoscopic hues. The effect was *prismatic.*

6. Synonym or Restatement: The reader must infer the relationship between the word and a previously stated idea.

Example: The exercises to improve his binocular coordination were time consuming. He had to admit, however, that the *orthoptics* were helping.

7. Comparison: A comparison clue allows the reader to infer a similarity between the new word and another idea in the sentence or passage.

Example: The sweet and gentle voice of the cello drifted through the halls of the building like the *mellifluous* tones of an angel.

8. Contrast: The meaning of the new word is clearly meant to be dissimilar from another word or idea.

Example: Almost to a fault, Maura was *conscientious* and meticulous about her obligations; Brandon, on the other hand, was as unreliable as the weather in Dublin.

9. Familiar Expression or Language Experience: This type of clue is rather like a restatement/synonym, except that the clue words are idioms or everyday expressions.

Example: As the eye of the hurricane passed, it rained buckets. The *torrent* seemed to hit the ground in waves.

10. Words in Series: The reader can glean some idea of the meaning of a strange word if it is listed in a series of others.

Example: Her dress was in shockingly poor fashion. Flowers of pink, purple, red, and *puce* fought with each other against a yellow background.

11. Inference: Many types of context clues share characteristics with the inference clue.

Example: He was a short, wiry, aggressive little boy who had a propensity for fighting. Who would have expected a *pugilist* in such a little package?

Comment: To evaluate a student's ability to use a variety of context clues, the teacher may construct a test with all 10 types of clues. Ensure that all words except the new vocabulary are at the student's independent reading level.

Adapted from: Thomas, E. L., & Robinson, H. A. (1972). *Improving reading in every class: A sourcebook for teachers.* Boston: Allyn and Bacon.

DIRECTED READING-THINKING ACTIVITY

Purpose

The purpose of the Directed Reading-Thinking Activity (DRTA) is to improve reading comprehension by promoting critical thinking in the reading process. Students are expected to learn to set a purpose for reading, read to prove or disprove a hypothesis, and evaluate the accuracy of their hypotheses based on the textual information. Students' active involvement in the reading process improves comprehension and retention of information. Other expected outcomes include increased ability to make logical predictions and support decisions based on given information.

DRTA may be used individually or in groups of 8 to 10 students. It is appropriate as a developmental reading activity or for students who have adequate decoding ability but below-average comprehension. DRTA was originally developed for use with basal readers; initial teaching of the activity is done with literature, but may be adapted later to content area material as the students gain familiarity with the process.

Preparation

Choose a high-interest reading selection and divide it into parts. The first part includes just the title and possibly an introductory picture. The last part includes the final portion of the reading selection. The remainder of the selection may be divided into two or three segments. The segments are selected on the basis of events in the story rather than number of pages.

Procedure

1. Direct the students to the title of the selection and introductory picture (if there is one) and ask the following questions:

   Based on the title (and picture), what do you think this story will be about?
   What do you think might happen in this story?
   Why?

   Lead a discussion wherein students state and give reasons for their predictions. Each student's prediction forms the basis for further reading.

2. Direct the students to read to a predetermined point for

the purpose of verifying or disproving their predictions. Have the students close their books and ask questions to help them evaluate their predictions:

Were you correct? (Partially correct? Incorrect?)
What will happen now?

a) Require students to provide support from the text (e.g., state events from the text, read relevant sentences) in discussing the accuracy of their previous predictions.
b) Encourage the students to use evidence given by other students to make or refine their subsequent predictions. As students repeat the predict, read, evaluate cycle, their diverse hypotheses should tend to converge.

Guidelines

1. All students must have instructional reading levels that permit adequate decoding of the material.
2. The teacher's role in DRTA is as a facilitator, helping students to clarify and refine their responses and asking students open-ended questions.
3. The teacher must maintain neutrality in responding to students' statements.
4. To keep the momentum, the teacher should not paraphrase student responses, but should encourage students to state their predictions and explanations clearly and in a sufficiently loud voice for the group to hear.

Modifications

1. Slow readers may be paired up with a partner who will read the selection aloud.
2. All students may be divided into teams of two, read to each other, and discuss predictions prior to whole-group discussion.
3. To develop listening/thinking skills, this procedure may be conducted orally, with the teacher reading the selection to the class or telling a story.
4. DRTA may be individualized for one-to-one teaching of reading-thinking skills. In this case, the teacher may provide more questions to help the student clarify and support his/her predictions.

Adapted from: Stauffer, R. G. (1969). *Directing reading maturity as a cognitive process.* New York: Harper & Row; and Tierney, R. J., & Readence, J. E. (1999). *Reading strategies and practices: A compendium* (5th ed.). Boston: Allyn and Bacon.

DIRECTED VOCABULARY THINKING ACTIVITY

Purpose

Use this procedure to introduce a unit on the use of context clues or to introduce keywords before reading. The purpose is to build awareness of how one can use context to infer the meaning of unknown words.

Preparation

Choose a few keywords from the selection that are likely to be unfamiliar to the student(s). Write a sentence for each word. Each sentence should incorporate one of the types of context clues that will be included in the unit (e.g., direct explanation, contrast, synonym, restatement).

Procedure

1. Write the words, without their definitions, on the board or copy and hand out the list of words. Have the student(s) guess the definition of each word. Either the teacher or a student may record the guesses.
2. Show the words within the sentences you have created. Have the student(s) guess definitions again and record them.
3. For each word, have the student(s) discuss how other words in the sentence helped them to come up with the new definitions.
4. Look up each word in the dictionary or provide a paraphrased definition appropriate to the student's language level.

Adapted from: Cunningham, P. M. (1979). Teaching vocabulary in the content areas. *NASSP Bulletin, 613*(424), 112–116.

ELKONIN PROCEDURE: ADAPTED

Purpose

The following procedure, adapted from Elkonin (1973), moves the student gradually from counting speech sounds to recording these sounds as letters.

Mather, N., & Jaffe, L. (2002). *Woodcock-Johnson III: Reports, Recommendations, and Strategies.* New York: John Wiley & Sons.

Procedure

1. Select a simple line drawing representing a one-syllable word.

2. Place a rectangle under the drawing. Divide the rectangle into one row of sections equal to number of sounds in the word, as depicted in Figure IV.3. Begin with words where the number of phonemes (speech sounds) matches the number of graphemes (letters). Words that have sounds that can be elongated, such as /s/ /f/ /l/ and /m/, are easiest for students who are just beginning to learn to segment words into sounds.

3. Ask the student to say the word slowly and push a marker forward for each sound. Use blue and red poker chips or colored tiles. Once a student is able to segment words with confidence, introduce vowel sounds. Color-code markers for vowels and consonants (e.g., blue for consonants and red for vowels). Teach the student how to differentiate orally/aurally between the vowel sounds and the consonant sounds. Once a student can identify and differentiate vowel and consonant sounds, introduce letters.

4. Substitute movable letters (e.g., letter tiles, magnetic letters, letter cards) for markers. To facilitate this step:

   a. Determine what letter/sound associations the student already knows;

Figure IV.3 Picture of a Sun for the Elkonin Procedure: Adapted

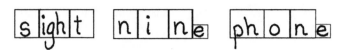

Figure IV.4 Illustration of Ways to Box Different Spelling Patterns in the Elkonin Procedure: Adapted

   b. Teach the difference between the vowels and consonants.

   c. Create a list of words in which
      (1) there is a one-to-one correspondence between letters and sounds;
      (2) each consonant has its most common sound and each vowel its short sound (e.g., "sun," "lip," "jam," "mop"); and
      (3) the student already knows the letter/sound correspondences.

5. When a student is proficient with the tiles, have him write the letters rather than using letter tiles.

6. Gradually introduce additional graphemes that are spelled with more than one letter, such as *sh* and *oa*) and less predictable spelling patterns (e.g., long vowel-silent *e*). Explain the concepts that two or more letters can be combined to make one sound (digraphs) and that letters can be silent in a word. Figure IV.4 illustrates how some spelling patterns are boxed.

As these words are introduced, the number of boxes will not match the number of speech sounds. Plan your word list before drawing the boxes in preparation for the lesson. Since each digraph has only one sound, it will be written in only one box. When introducing letter patterns in which a silent letter is not part of a digraph, draw small boxes for the silent letters to emphasize that they have no sound but must still be included in the spelling of the word. Discuss with the student the difference between what you see when a word is written and what you hear.

This type of instruction improves both decoding and encoding ability due to the emphasis on segmenting and blending sounds.

Adapted from: Elkonin, D. B. (1973). U.S.S.R. In J. Downing (Ed.), *Comparative reading* (pp. 551–579). New York: Macmillan.

ERROR MONITORING STRATEGY

Purpose

The Error Monitoring Strategy is a technique used to help students develop proofreading skills and improve basic writing skills. The final goal is self-monitoring with independent use of the strategy.

Steps in the Error Monitoring Strategy

1. Write a draft of a composition on every other line.
2. Write COPS on the top of the page.
3. Read through the composition once for each type of error you are trying to locate, marking each error with a colored pencil. When you have checked the entire composition for a specific type of error, check off the cue letter on the top of the page.
4. Optional: Ask someone to double-check your paper.
5. Look up spelling words; ask for help with corrections.
6. Recopy composition neatly. Use every line.
7. Reread and proofread.

Mnemonic

Cue	Error	Correction
C	CAPITALS	Write over error
O	OVERALL APPEARANCE	
	Fragments & Run-ons	Line out and write new sentence above
	Paragraph indent	→
	Margins	Draw lines down the side of page
	Note marks, rips	
P	PUNCTUATION	Circle each incorrect mark or position for omitted marks
S	SPELLING	Write SP above word

Procedure

Introduce Error Monitoring
1. Explain to the student that if he/she is able to identify the errors in compositions, his/her papers will be better and his/her grades will improve.
2. Administer a pretest, using a copy of a handwritten sample passage, in which the student is asked to mark any errors found. Show the student the percentage of errors he/she identified and the percentage he/she did not identify.
3. Explain that you will teach the student a strategy that will help with proofreading. Make sure he/she understands why proofreading is necessary.
4. Obtain a commitment from the student to learn the strategy.
5. Describe the steps in the strategy.

Model the Strategy
1. Have available a short composition, written on every other line, with a variety of errors in capitalization, punctuation, paragraph indentations, margins, spelling, and sentence construction.
2. Using the cue card, model the steps and think aloud.

Provide Guided Practice
For practice, use copies of a variety of prepared handwritten passages, on which the student just marks and corrects the errors.

1. Have the student memorize COPS, the type of error each letter represents, and the proofing mark. If needed, provide a cue card.
2. Have the student practice the Error Monitoring Strategy on passages starting at the student's independent reading level, moving up to more advanced levels. Mastery at each level is 80%.

Independent Practice
When the student has attained 80% mastery on passages slightly higher than his/her own writing level, have the student use COPS on his/her own writing. At this point, include Step 7: Reread and Proofread.

Posttest and Commitment to Generalize
1. When the student is familiar with the procedure and is using it well in the student's own writing, give a posttest similar to the pretest.
2. With the student, compare the posttest with the pretest results. Ask the student to tell you what he/she has learned.
3. Explain the importance of generalization and obtain the student's commitment to use the strategy in the classroom and at home.
4. Give the student a cue card to remind him/her of the basic steps.

Promote Generalization
1. Talk with the student's other teachers. Ask them to remind the student to use Error Monitoring and, if needed, to provide a cue card.

Mather, N., & Jaffe, L. (2002). *Woodcock-Johnson III: Reports, Recommendations, and Strategies.* New York: John Wiley & Sons.

2. Possibly, offer to teach Error Monitoring to the student's entire class or to the teacher.
3. Collect the student's writing from other classes to see if he/she is using the strategy. Provide incentives to do so.

CUE CARD	
C CAPITALS	First word in each sentence
	Names of people & places
	Dates
O OVERALL APPEARANCE	Fragments & Run-ons
	Paragraph indent
	Margins
	Marks, rips
P PUNCTUATION	Ends of sentences marked
	Commas
S SPELLING	Correct

Adaptation

For students who need to have skills more clearly delineated, you may use the acronym: SH! COPS!

Cue	Error	Correction
S	SENTENCE	Line out and write new sentence above it.
H	HANDWRITING	Underline poorly written or illegible words
C	CAPITALS	Write over error
O	OVERALL APPEARANCE	
	Paragraph indent →	
	Margins	Draw lines down the side of page
		Note marks, rips

CUE CARD: SH! COPS!	
S SENTENCE	Fragments & run-ons
H HANDWRITING	Neat
C CAPITALS	First word in each sentence
	Names of people & places
	Dates
O OVERALL APPEARANCE	Paragraph indent
	Margins
	Marks, rips
P PUNCTUATION	Ends of sentences marked
	Commas used
S SPELLING	Correct

P	PUNCTUATION	Circle each incorrect/omitted mark
S	SPELLING	Write SP above word

Adapted from: Schumaker, J. B., Deshler, D. D., Alley, G. R., Warner, M. M., Clark, F. L., & Nolan, S. (1982). Error monitoring: A learning strategy for improving adolescent performance. In W. M. Cruickshank & J. Lerner (Eds.), *Best of ACLD: Vol. 3* (pp. 170–182). Syracuse, NY: Syracuse University Press; and Schumaker, J. B., Deshler, D. D., Nolan, S., Clark, F. L., Alley, G. R., & Warner, M. M. (1981). *Error monitoring: A learning strategy for improving academic performance of LD adolescents* (Research Report No. 32). Lawrence, KS: University of Kansas Institute for Research in Learning Disabilities.
    Adaptation by the authors.

FERNALD METHOD FOR READING

The Fernald Method is a systematic, multisensory instructional approach that incorporates use of the visual, auditory, kinesthetic, and tactile (VAKT) modalities simultaneously. The association of sensory and perceptual cues reinforces the mental image of words as well as the association between printed words and their oral representations. Use of this approach also improves memory for printed words and word parts. The Fernald Method is intended for individual or small-group instruction.

Purpose

The Fernald Method improves sight word acquisition and word identification skill in students who have failed to learn to read through other instructional methods or who have particular difficulty learning exception or phonetically irregular words (e.g., *once*). Using this method, students are expected to retain reading recognition of the words learned. A different procedure is used to teach the written spelling of words for long-term retrieval.

Procedure

The Fernald Method consists of four stages through which the student progresses as reading and writing proficiency increase.

Mather, N., & Jaffe, L. (2002). *Woodcock-Johnson III: Reports, Recommendations, and Strategies.* New York: John Wiley & Sons.

Stage I

1. *Solicit the student's interest and involvement.* Tell the student that you will be showing him or her a new way to learn words. Explain that while the method requires concentration and effort, it has been successful with students who have had problems remembering words.

2. *Select a word to learn.* Have the student select a word to learn. Discuss the meaning of the word.

3. *Write the word.* Sit beside the student and model these steps: (a) say the word, (b) use a crayon or marker to write the word in large manuscript or cursive (depending upon which the student uses) on a 5" × 8" index card, and (c) say the word again as you run your finger underneath the word.

4. *Model* word tracing for the student. Say: "Watch what I do and listen to what I say." Use the following steps: (a) say the word; (b) trace the word using one or two fingers, saying each part of the word as you trace it; (c) say the word again while underlining it with the tracing fingers in a fluent motion; and (d) have the student practice tracing until the process is completed correctly.

5. *Trace the word until learned.* Have the student continue tracing the word until the student is sure he or she can write the word from memory with no errors.

6. *Write the word from memory.* When the student feels ready, remove the model and have him or her write the word while saying it. If at any point the student makes an error, stop the writing immediately, cover or erase the error, and have the student use the tracing procedure again before proceeding.

7. *File the word.* After the student has written the word correctly three times without the model, have the student file it alphabetically in a word bank.

8. *Type the word.* Within 24 hours, type each word the student has learned that day. Reading the typed word will help the student establish the link between handwritten and typed words.

As soon as a student can write words, begin story writing. The student selects a topic. Have the student trace any words that he or she does not know how to spell. Type the story within 24 hours so that the student has an opportunity to read newly learned words in context.

Important points. During stage one instruction, observe the following:

- Finger contact is important in tracing.
- After tracing, the student should write the word without looking at the model.

- The word should always be written as a unit from the beginning. In the case of an error, cover or remove the mistake and start over from the beginning.
- Always use words in context to provide meaning.
- Encourage the student to say each part of the word while tracing and writing.

Stage II

During Stage II the student no longer needs to trace words to learn them and the stories increase in length. The student learns a word by looking at it, saying it, and writing it. The teacher writes requested words, saying each part of the word while writing it while the student listens and watches. The student looks at the word, says the word, and then writes the word without looking at the copy.

As in Stage I, select the words to be learned from the stories that the student is writing. Continue to file the learned words.

Stage III

By Stage III the student learns directly from the printed word without having it written. Pronounce the word for the student, have him or her look at the word and pronounce it before writing it. At this stage, introduce books. Select interesting books and tell the student any unknown words. After reading, have the student review and write the new words.

Stage IV

At this stage, the student recognizes known words in print and also begins to notice the similarities between parts of unknown words and known words. The student begins to recognize many new words without being told what they are. Provide enough assistance with unknown words at Stage IV so that reading proceeds smoothly.

One helpful technique at this stage is to have the student glance over a paragraph and lightly underline any unknown words. Tell the student the words and have the student write them before beginning to read. Using this technique, the student can read the new material smoothly without interruption.

Adapted from: Cotterell, G. C. (1973). The Fernald auditory-kinaesthetic technique. In A. W. Franklin & S. Naidoo (Eds.), *Assessment and teaching of dyslexic children* (pp. 97–100). London: Richard Madley; Fernald, G. (1943). *Remedial techniques in basic school subjects.* New York: McGraw-Hill; and Mather, N. (1985). *The Fernald kinesthetic method revisited.* Unpublished manuscript, University of Arizona, Department of Special Education, Rehabilitation, and School Psychology, Tucson.

FERNALD METHOD FOR SPELLING INSTRUCTION

Purpose

This spelling method is appropriate for students who have difficulty retaining spelling words and learning to spell exception words. Select words that the student uses frequently in writing.

Procedure

1. Write the word to be learned on the chalkboard or on paper.
2. Pronounce the word clearly and distinctly. Ask the student to look at the word and pronounce the word with emphasis on correct pronunciation.
3. Allow time for the student to study the word to develop an image of it. Depending upon the learning style of the student, different senses are emphasized. A student who learns visually tries to picture the word; a student who learns auditorially says the word; and the student who learns kinesthetically traces the word with a finger. The student studies the word until a picture of the word can be formed in his/her mind.
4. When the student indicates that he/she is sure of the word, erase the word and have the student attempt to write the word from memory.
5. Turn the paper over and ask the student to write the word a second time from memory.

In daily writing, any misspelled words are marked out entirely and the correct form is written in its place. When a student asks how to spell a word, the teacher writes the word, while pronouncing it. Students are encouraged to make their own dictionaries from words they have learned or words that are especially difficult for them.

Adapted from: Fernald, G. (1943). *Remedial techniques in basic school subjects.* New York: McGraw-Hill.

FERNALD METHOD FOR READING AND SPELLING: MODIFIED

Purpose

To provide an independent study method for students who have extreme difficulty retaining sight words and their spelling. This procedure may be integrated into other reading/spelling methods for students who do not seem to be able to revisualize words for writing or who do not retain the association between printed words and their spoken equivalents.

Materials

Strips of paper bag or other rough paper cut to about 3" × 8"
Wide black magic marker
Tape
Writing instrument preferred by the student (e.g., pencil, black felt tip pen)
8" × 11" sheets of lined paper cut in half vertically

Procedure

1. Tell the student you have a new way to teach him/her to read and spell words that has been very successful with other students.
2. Using the wide, black marker, write the word to be learned neatly and large on a strip of rough paper in either manuscript or cursive, depending on the writing form the student uses (cursive is easier to trace).
3. Tape the word strip to the table so that it will remain stable while you and the student trace over the letters.
4. Model the following, impressing on the student that each step has to be done exactly as you are doing it. If the student makes a mistake at any point in the process, he/she will start the study process from the beginning.
5. Warn the student that if he/she makes a mistake at any point while writing the word, you will stop him/her immediately by covering his hand and/or the word so that the student cannot see the wrong spelling.

Study Procedure

1. The student looks at the printed word throughout the next three steps. The student:
   a. says the whole word while underlining the printed word with his/her finger;
   b. traces (using the top of the pads of both forefinger and middle finger) each part of the word while saying the sounds of the word, matching sound to letter as closely as possible without distorting the pronunciation; and
   c. says the whole word again while underlining the printed word with his/her finger.
2. The student repeats this sequence of steps until he/she has formed a clear mental image of the word and is *positive* that he/she can write it five times in a row without looking at the model and without making even one mistake. It does not matter if the student has to trace the word 100 times; the student must be sure he/she can write it without errors. The number of times required to learn and retain a mental image will diminish as the student gains experience with the procedure.
3. The student untapes the word card from the table and turns it face down. The student says the word and writes it at the top of the half-sheet of paper, turns the word card over and checks his/her spelling. Have the student check the spelling of the whole word at once rather than letter by letter so that the word is seen as a whole unit.
4. If the student has written the word correctly, he/she turns the card over and either uses it to cover the word just written or folds down the top of the paper so that he/she cannot see the word just written. The student then repeats the previous step, saying and writing the word, and checking it against the word card.

Do not allow the student to check his/her spelling against his/her previous spelling. The student must always check it against the word card, which is neatly written and has the correct spelling. When the student starts using this study process independently, if the student is in the habit of correcting his/her spelling against the previous spelling, and the student has made a mistake on the previous spelling, he/she will learn the word incorrectly.

5. When the student has written the word correctly and checked it five times, the instructor or student types the word on an index card. If the student types it, the instructor checks to see that it is typed correctly. The student reads the typed word, then places it, alphabetically, in a card file for future activities.

Important Points

- For the initial teaching of the technique, allow the student to choose a word that he/she cannot read but wants to learn. (Longer, more distinctive words, such as *dictionary,* are sometimes easier to learn than shorter words, such as *what.*)
- The success of this technique depends on frequent review (flash cards for reading, writing from dictation for spelling), then distributed practice, to prevent the student from forgetting the word. Incorporate the word into reading and writing activities.

Adapted from: Fernald, G. (1943). *Remedial techniques in basic school subjects.* New York: McGraw-Hill.

FLOW LIST-SIGHT WORDS

Purpose

The purpose of using a sight word flow list is to provide systematic instruction and review. The additional practice and repetition promote automatic sight word recognition. The list changes (flows) as the student learns each word, instead of being fixed.

Procedure

1. Identify three to six words that the student continuously fails to recognize in reading or new sight words being introduced in the instructional program.
2. Write the words on the flow list form.
3. Have the student study the words and then test the student on the words. Write the date at the top of the column in the flow list form and write an S for each word studied.
4. Mark each correctly read word with a + and incorrectly read words with a 0.
5. Provide daily testing and practice with the words.
6. When a word is read correctly 5 days in a row, cross it off the list and add a new word.

Mather, N., & Jaffe, L. (2002). *Woodcock-Johnson III: Reports, Recommendations, and Strategies.* New York: John Wiley & Sons.

Sight Word/Spelling Flow List

Dates of Study or Review

Study Words																		

S   studied
+   correct
0   incorrect
0_s incorrect and restudied

Mather, N., & Jaffe, L. (2002). *Woodcock-Johnson III: Reports, Recommendations, and Strategies.* New York: John Wiley & Sons.

Study Words	September												
	1	1	1	1	1	2	2	2	2	2	2	2	3
~~against~~	S	+	+	+	+	+		+		+	+		
usually	S	0s	+	0s	0s	0s	+	+	+	+	0s	+	+
heard	S	+	+	+	+	0s	+	+	+	+	0s	+	0s
measure						S	+	+	+	+	+	+	0s
~~listen~~						S	+	+	+	+	+		+
because											S	+	+
enough													

S   studied
+   correct
0   incorrect
0s incorrect and restudied

Figure IV.5 Example of Sight Word/Spelling Flow List with One Student's Responses Recorded

7. File mastered words alphabetically into a word bank.
8. To ensure retention, provide review and reinforcement of the words that have been crossed off the list, fading gradually.

A sample flow list chart, representing the data for one student, is shown in Figure IV.5.

Adapted from: McCoy, K. M., & Prehm, H. J. (1987). *Teaching mainstreamed students: Methods and techniques.* Denver: Love.

FLOW LIST-SPELLING

Purpose

The purpose of using a spelling flow list is to provide systematic instruction and review. The additional practice and repetition promote the mastery of spelling words. The spelling list changes (flows) as the student learns each word, instead of being fixed, as in a weekly spelling test.

Procedure

1. Identify three to six words that the student uses but misspells in writing.
2. Write the words on the spelling flow list form.
3. Have the student study the words and then test the student on the words. Write the date at the top of the column in the flow list form and write an S for each word studied.
4. Mark each correctly spelled word with a + and incorrect words with a 0.
5. Provide daily testing and practice with the words.
6. When a word is spelled correctly 3 days in a row, cross it off the list and add a new word.
7. File mastered words alphabetically into a word bank.
8. To ensure retention, provide review and reinforcement of the words that have been crossed off the list, fading gradually.

A completed sample flow list and a blank list are presented for use.

Adapted from: McCoy, K. M., & Prehm, H. J. (1987). *Teaching mainstreamed students: Methods and techniques.* Denver: Love.

GLASS-ANALYSIS FOR DECODING ONLY

Purpose

Glass-Analysis for Decoding Only is a technique for improving students' ability to analyze the structure of printed words to aid in pronunciation.

Procedure

1. Individual words are presented to the student on cards.
2. The student is asked to look at the whole word. Do not cover parts of the word.
3. Train only letter clusters that can be generalized to other words.
4. Select words for practice from the student's reading materials.
5. Use the method for one or two 15-minute sessions daily.

Steps

Follow these five general steps for presenting each word:

1. Identify the whole word.

   For example, present the word *carpenter* on an index card and say: "This word is 'carpenter.'" Review with the students which letters and letter clusters make which sounds.

Mather, N., & Jaffe, L. (2002). *Woodcock-Johnson III: Reports, Recommendations, and Strategies.* New York: John Wiley & Sons.

2. Pronounce a sound in the word and ask the student to name the letter or letters that make that sound.

   Say: "In the word 'carpenter,' what letters make the '/car/' sound? What letters make the '/pen/' sound?," "What letters make the '/ter/' sound?"

3. Ask for the sound that certain letters or letter combinations make.

   Say: "What sound does /e/r/ make? What sound does the /t/e/r/ make?" Ask about each part of the word.

4. Take away letters (auditorily, not visually) and ask for the remaining sound.

   Say: "In the word 'carpenter,' if I took off the /c/ sound, what would the word say?" Ask the same question omitting different word parts.

5. Identify the whole word.

Adapted from: Glass, G. G. (1973). *Teaching decoding as separate from reading.* Garden City, NY: Easier to Learn. New York: Adelphi University; and Glass, G. G. (1976). *Glass-Analysis for decoding only teacher guide.* Garden City, NY: Easier to Learn. New York: Adelphi University.

GLASS-ANALYSIS FOR SPELLING

Purpose

Although developed primarily for teaching reading decoding skills, the Glass-Analysis method can be modified easily to teach and reinforce spelling skills (Mather, 1991).

Procedure

1. Identify and discuss the visual and auditory clusters in the word. For example, in the word "consideration," you would discuss *con, sid, er, a* and *tion.*
2. Ask students to write the letter(s) that make the /con/ sound, then the /sid/ sound, then the /er/ sound, then the /a/ sound, and finally the /tion/ sound.
3. Have students write the word *consideration* while pronouncing each part slowly: "con-sid-er-a-tion."
4. Have students turn their papers over and write the word *consideration* from memory while saying the word as it is written.
5. Have students write the word from memory (cover the model and previous writings of the word) two more times.

When using this adapted method for spelling, place emphasis upon ordering the sounds of a word in the correct sequence. This can be accomplished by presenting and practicing the visual and auditory clusters of a word in the order that they appear.

INSTANT WORDS (300)

First Hundred

___ 1. the	___ 26. or	___ 51. will	___ 76. number
___ 2. of	___ 27. one	___ 52. up	___ 77. no
___ 3. and	___ 28. had	___ 53. other	___ 78. way
___ 4. a	___ 29. by	___ 54. about	___ 79. could
___ 5. to	___ 30. word	___ 55. out	___ 80. people
___ 6. in	___ 31. but	___ 56. many	___ 81. my
___ 7. is	___ 32. not	___ 57. then	___ 82. than
___ 8. you	___ 33. what	___ 58. them	___ 83. first
___ 9. that	___ 34. all	___ 59. these	___ 84. water
___ 10. it	___ 35. were	___ 60. so	___ 85. been
___ 11. he	___ 36. we	___ 61. some	___ 86. call
___ 12. was	___ 37. when	___ 62. her	___ 87. who
___ 13. for	___ 38. your	___ 63. would	___ 88. oil
___ 14. on	___ 39. can	___ 64. make	___ 89. now
___ 15. are	___ 40. said	___ 65. like	___ 90. find
___ 16. as	___ 41. there	___ 66. him	___ 91. long
___ 17. with	___ 42. use	___ 67. into	___ 92. down
___ 18. his	___ 43. an	___ 68. time	___ 93. day
___ 19. they	___ 44. each	___ 69. has	___ 94. did
___ 20. I	___ 45. which	___ 70. look	___ 95. get
___ 21. at	___ 46. she	___ 71. two	___ 96. come
___ 22. be	___ 47. do	___ 72. more	___ 97. made
___ 23. this	___ 48. how	___ 73. write	___ 98. may
___ 24. have	___ 49. their	___ 74. go	___ 99. part
___ 25. from	___ 50. if	___ 75. see	___100. over

Second Hundred

___ 101. new	___ 126. great	___ 151. put	___ 176. kind
___ 102. sound	___ 127. where	___ 152. end	___ 177. hand
___ 103. take	___ 128. help	___ 153. does	___ 178. picture
___ 104. only	___ 129. through	___ 154. another	___ 179. again
___ 105. little	___ 130. much	___ 155. well	___ 180. change
___ 106. work	___ 131. before	___ 156. large	___ 181. off
___ 107. know	___ 132. line	___ 157. must	___ 182. play
___ 108. place	___ 133. right	___ 158. big	___ 183. spell
___ 109. year	___ 134. too	___ 159. even	___ 184. air
___ 110. live	___ 135. mean	___ 160. such	___ 185. away
___ 111. me	___ 136. old	___ 161. because	___ 186. animal
___ 112. back	___ 137. any	___ 162. turned	___ 187. house
___ 113. give	___ 138. same	___ 163. here	___ 188. point
___ 114. most	___ 139. tell	___ 164. why	___ 189. page
___ 115. very	___ 140. boy	___ 165. ask	___ 190. letter
___ 116. after	___ 141. follow	___ 166. went	___ 191. mother
___ 117. thing	___ 142. came	___ 167. men	___ 192. answer
___ 118. our	___ 143. want	___ 168. read	___ 193. found
___ 119. just	___ 144. show	___ 169. need	___ 194. study
___ 120. name	___ 145. also	___ 170. land	___ 195. still
___ 121. good	___ 146. around	___ 171. different	___ 196. learn
___ 122. sentence	___ 147. form	___ 172. home	___ 197. should
___ 123. man	___ 148. three	___ 173. us	___ 198. America
___ 124. think	___ 149. small	___ 174. move	___ 199. world
___ 125. say	___ 150. set	___ 175. try	___ 200. high

Mather, N., & Jaffe, L. (2002). *Woodcock-Johnson III: Reports, Recommendations, and Strategies.* New York: John Wiley & Sons.

Third Hundred

___ 201. every	___ 226. left	___ 251. until	___ 276. idea
___ 202. near	___ 227. don't	___ 252. children	___ 277. enough
___ 203. add	___ 228. few	___ 253. side	___ 278. eat
___ 204. food	___ 229. while	___ 254. feet	___ 279. face
___ 205. between	___ 230. along	___ 255. car	___ 280. watch
___ 206. own	___ 231. might	___ 256. mile	___ 281. far
___ 207. below	___ 232. close	___ 257. night	___ 282. Indian
___ 208. country	___ 233. something	___ 258. walk	___ 283. real
___ 209. plant	___ 234. seem	___ 259. white	___ 284. almost
___ 210. last	___ 235. next	___ 260. sea	___ 285. let
___ 211. school	___ 236. hard	___ 261. began	___ 286. above
___ 212. father	___ 237. open	___ 262. grow	___ 287. girl
___ 213. keep	___ 238. example	___ 263. took	___ 288. sometimes
___ 214. tree	___ 239. beginning	___ 264. river	___ 289. mountain
___ 215. never	___ 240. life	___ 265. four	___ 290. cut
___ 216. start	___ 241. always	___ 266. carry	___ 291. young
___ 217. city	___ 242. those	___ 267. state	___ 292. talk
___ 218. earth	___ 243. both	___ 268. once	___ 293. soon
___ 219. eye	___ 244. paper	___ 269. book	___ 294. list
___ 220. light	___ 245. together	___ 270. hear	___ 295. song
___ 221. thought	___ 246. got	___ 271. stop	___ 296. leave
___ 222. head	___ 247. group	___ 272. without	___ 297. family
___ 223. under	___ 248. often	___ 273. second	___ 298. body
___ 224. story	___ 249. run	___ 274. late	___ 299. music
___ 225. saw	___ 250. important	___ 275. miss	___ 300. color

The first 100 words make up 50% of all written material. The 300 words make up 65% of all written material.

Fry, E. (1977). *Elementary Reading Instruction.* McGraw-Hill. Reprinted with permission from the author.

Mather, N., & Jaffe, L. (2002). *Woodcock-Johnson III: Reports, Recommendations, and Strategies.* New York: John Wiley & Sons.

GREAT LEAPS READING

Great Leaps Reading is a program designed to assist individuals of all ages who are at risk for or have significant reading problems. Different versions are available for adults as well as for students in primary (K–2), intermediate (3–5), middle (6–8), and high school (9–12). The purpose of the program is to build reading accuracy and speed. Students work individually with an instructor and the materials for less than 10 minutes per day (3 days per week minimum). Depending on the severity of the reading problem, 1 to 2 school years is the average length of intervention.

One-minute timings are taken for each of three stimuli: phonics, sight phrases, and the oral reading of short stories. The Phonics section is focused on developing and mastering essential sight/sound relationships and/or sound awareness skills. This section takes students from identifying sounds in isolation to being able to sound out CVC, CVCC, and CVCE patterns. The Sight Phrases section focuses on accurate word identification and fluent reading of sight words in phrases. Students practice and review common sight words such as: *these, them, of, off,* and *from.* The stories for all levels are designed to build reading fluency. The Great Leaps K-2 Reading Program is designed for the young beginning reader and provides an instructional component in phonological awareness.

Each program comes with all necessary materials and instructions. Before beginning the program, the teacher assesses the student's present reading level. Instruction begins at the level within the program where reading speed is slow and the student makes several errors. The teacher reviews the errors with the student and discusses strategies that he or she can use to improve performance. Performance is charted on graphs so that both the student and teacher can keep track of progress. The charting also provides a strong behavioral, motivational component for the student.

All Great Leaps programs begin at a very low reading level and work progressively toward more difficult material. Manuals are selected based upon the social functioning level of the student rather than the reading level. For example, the stories in the high school program begin at the Primer level. All the programs contain charts and assessment forms that may be duplicated.

The stories are also presently available in the two Great Leaps Stories Collections, one for elementary students and one for all students. The Stories Collections are intended for instructors who want to provide additional oral reading/fluency practice for their students. Every story is designed to be read in 1 minute at the age and reading level indicated. These collections contain the published stories from each binder as well as additional stories.

Great Leaps Math is now available, focusing on building fluency in the basic facts, including addition, subtraction, multiplication, and division. It features concrete lessons (using manipulative objectives) and representational lessons (using student drawings) to help the student understand math operations. The program consists of three instructor manuals and three student workbooks, and includes placement tests and instructional games.

Further information is available from Diarmuid, Inc., P.O. Box 357580, Gainesville, FL 32635, phone (toll free): (877) GRLEAPS (475-3277); Canada: (352) 271-9720, website: www.greatleaps.com

KERRIGAN'S INTEGRATED METHOD OF TEACHING COMPOSITION

Purpose

This method for essay writing takes the beginning writer step-by-step through the process of theme organization and the actual writing of the composition.

Procedure

1. Write a short, simple declarative sentence that makes one statement and that more can be said about.
2. Write three sentences about the sentence in Step 1 that are clearly and directly about the whole of that sentence, not just something in it. These three sentences will then become the topic sentences for the paragraphs.
3. Write four or five sentences about each of the three sentences in Step 2.
4. Make the material in the four or five sentences in Step 3 as concrete and specific as possible. Go into detail and give examples. Do not introduce new ideas into the paragraph.
5. Write a concluding sentence that restates the topic of the theme.

Example:
Step 1: I dislike winter.
Step 2:
    I dislike cold weather.
    I dislike wearing the heavy clothing that winter requires.
    I dislike the colds that I always get in the winter.

Mather, N., & Jaffe, L. (2002). *Woodcock-Johnson III: Reports, Recommendations, and Strategies.* New York: John Wiley & Sons.

Steps 3 + 4:

I dislike cold weather. It makes me shiver. I hate to slide and slip on the ice on the streets and sidewalks. I hate to have cold feet, so I always wear two pairs of socks.

I dislike wearing the heavy clothing that winter requires. I have to wear earmuffs or a hat. I have to wear boots and a heavy coat. When it's really cold I have to wear long underwear. If I don't wear heavy clothing, I usually get sick.

I dislike the colds that I always get in the winter. I catch at least two colds a winter. My nose gets stuffed up and I cough all night. I have to take medicine that makes me sleepy. I miss school for several days.

Step 5: Clearly, winter is not my favorite season.

As skill improves, help the student focus on cohesion. In the first sentence of the second paragraph and every paragraph following, help the student learn how to insert a clear reference to the idea in the preceding paragraph. Demonstrate how to use explicit references, such as the same word in a sentence, an antonym or synonym of the word, a pronoun, or a connective (e.g., *for example, however, but*).

Adapted from: Kerrigan, W. J. (1979). *Writing to the point: Six basic steps* (2nd ed.). New York: Harcourt Brace Jovanovich.

KWLS STRATEGY

Know—Want to Know—Learned—Still Need to Learn

Purpose

KWLS is a strategy adapted from Ogle (1986) used to activate students' background knowledge about a topic and to help them set purposes for reading expository text.

Procedure

No special materials are needed for this strategy but a chart similar to the one below helps students organize information by category.

Know	Want to Know	Learned	Still Need to Learn

Steps

1. Students access what they KNOW.

   a) The teacher plans and leads a discussion designed to help the students think about what they already know about the topic of the reading material. To do this, students brainstorm what they know of the topic and also state how it is they came by that information.

   b) The teacher helps the students to categorize the information (e.g., types of people living in the new land; reasons why people left their own lands) so that students get an idea of the *types* of information they will encounter when they read.

2. Students determine what they WANT to learn.

   Using the categories of information developed in Step 1 and any other questions that the students and the teacher come up with, the class discusses what they want or need to learn from the reading. Specific questions should be written down.

3. Students write what they LEARNED.

   The class may first discuss what the students learned from the reading. Shared information will reinforce the students' comprehension and recall of the reading material, and the teacher may clarify any misconceptions. Students then write, individually or as a class, what they learned.

4. Students list what they STILL need to learn.

   If appropriate, the students and teacher discuss and list what they still need to learn about the topic.

Adaptation

Another adaptation of the KWL strategy adds mapping and summarization (Carr & Ogle, 1987). To add the mapping component, children categorize the information listed under L. The topic forms the center of the map. Lines are then added to show the relationships between the main topic and the facts that are gathered.

For the summarization component, children use the map. The center of the map becomes the title of the essay and each category is used as the topic for a new paragraph. Supporting details are then added to expand or explain the topic further. After practice with this procedure, some students are able to omit the mapping step and write their summaries directly from the KWL work sheet. The KWL strategy helps students: acquire, relate, and learn concepts; increase vocabulary; and, discuss important points and keywords.

Adapted from: Carr, E., & Ogle, D. (1987). K-W-L plus: A strategy for comprehension and summarization. *Journal of Reading, 30,* 626–631;

Mather, N., & Jaffe, L. (2002). *Woodcock-Johnson III: Reports, Recommendations, and Strategies.* New York: John Wiley & Sons.

and Ogle, D. M. (1986). K-W-L: A teaching model that develops active reading of expository text. *Reading Teacher, 39,* 564–570.

LANGUAGE EXPERIENCE APPROACH FOR SIGHT WORDS: MODIFIED

Purpose

This technique helps the beginning reader grasp the connection between spoken (or signed) language and written language while building an initial bank of sight words.

Procedure

Day 1

1. Explain to the student that he/she will practice reading by using his/her own stories.
   a. Have the student dictate an experience. Write the student's words exactly as spoken except for fixing pronunciation errors.
   b. Select a part of the story to work with, depending on the amount of words you think the student will be able to master. Read that section of the story to the student and ask for any corrections or changes.
   c. Reread the section of the story to the student and then have the student read with you until the student says that he/she can read it independently. Tell the student any words he/she has trouble reading.
   d. Type the section of the story you are working on and make a copy to use for monitoring accuracy. Also, make a list of the words and typed word cards for each word.

Day 2

1. Provide practice in reading the typed version of the story. Use choral reading and have the student read the story to others.
2. Have the student read the story silently, underlining the unknown words.
3. Have the student read the story aloud as you record pronunciation errors on your copy.

Day 3

1. Have the student practice reading the story, as in Step 1 of Day 2.
2. Have the student match word cards to the individual words in the typed story.

3. Order the word cards as in the story and have the student read the word cards. On your list, record the words the student reads correctly.

Day 4

1. Have the student repeat the procedures of practice reading and matching word cards to the story.
2. Lay out the cards in random order and have the student read them. Again, record the words the student reads correctly.

Day 5

1. Have the student read the cards in random order.
2. Have the student file the word cards for those words read correctly in a word box in alphabetical order.
3. Have the student illustrate the story and include it in an ongoing book of the student's stories. If you are working on a story in sections, the student can make it into a "chapter book."

The student continues to review the sight words using a variety of activities (see Word Bank Activities), while starting work on a new story.

Adapted from: Bos, C. S., & Vaughn, S. (2001). *Strategies for teaching students with learning and behavior problems* (5th ed.). Boston: Allyn and Bacon.

LOOK-SIGN-FINGERSPELL-WRITE

Purpose

The purpose of Look-Sign-Fingerspell-Write (LSFW) is to provide students who are deaf and hard-of-hearing with a multisensory technique for studying reading vocabulary and spelling independently. LSFW stands for the components of the technique, not the sequence of steps.

Materials

Index cards with one study word on each, typed or printed *neatly*. (Typing is preferable as that is how the student will see the word in text.)
Half-sheets of lined writing paper (cut vertically) for writing study words
Flow list for charting accuracy
Card box

Procedure: Primary Communication Mode: Sign

Introduce the Study Word

Introduce the word to be learned within the context of the reading selection or in written sentences that clearly communicate its meaning. Discuss the meaning of the word with the students or provide an activity to familiarize them with both the meaning and the visual representation of the word. Make sure the students know the meaning of and the sign for the study word, and can use it correctly in signed communication.

For multiple-meaning words or word combinations (e.g., *look up, buy into, run out on*), choose the two or three most common meanings, depending on the capability of the students, and introduce all of them. Provide activities in which the students can read the word in sentences at their reading level and decide the meaning of the study word in that context and which sign is conceptually accurate.

Teach the Steps

In teaching the procedure, go through all of the steps of instruction, modeling, guided practice, and checking independent practice before students use the method without supervision.

Students:

1. LOOK at the study word on the card *throughout* Steps 2–4.
2. SIGN the word.
3. FINGERSPELL the word.
4. SIGN the word again.
5. REPEAT Steps 1–4 until they can create a mental picture of the word and are *positive* that they can write it from memory five times without even one error.
6. WRITE the word from memory on the half-sheet of writing paper.
7. CHECK the spelling. Each time the students write the word, they compare their spelling with the card (not with their previous writing).

   • If correct, the students turn the card face down. They may either use the study card to cover the word they have just written or fold down the top of the paper to cover the writing.
   • If incorrect, the students must repeat Steps 1–4 until they are *positive* they can write the word correctly without looking at the model.

The students must write the word correctly five times in a row, checking each time, to complete the study process.

LSFW: STUDENT CUE CARD (Sign)

LOOK

STUDY: Sign–Fingerspell–Sign (Repeat many times)

WRITE & CHECK: *Turn* card over–*Write* word–*Check* the card.

RIGHT? Write & check until you have 5 correct spellings in a row.

WRONG? Do LOOK-STUDY until you can see the word in your mind.

Follow Up

Word Bank

The students file their study cards in word boxes, organized in alphabetical order or in groups such as *New Words, Review Words, Known Words* (and maybe *Hard Words*).

Flow List

To ensure and document retention, test or provide review activities frequently and track each student's accurate reading or writing (spelling) of the words studied on the Flow List. To be considered correctly spelled, students must write a word. They should, however, memorize its fingerspelling, as well, for use in signed communication.

Modification: LSFW with Tracing (LSFWT)

Purpose

Occasionally, a student with a severe learning disability in orthographic processing needs a more intense multisensory technique to enable him/her to retain and revisualize spelling patterns. In this case, a tracing step is added.

Materials

Add to the materials listed above: Large index cards (5" × 8") or a larger strip of rough paper (grocery bags work) with the word written in black felt tip pen (some students respond better to wide magic marker), in manuscript or cursive, depending on which the student is most comfortable using.

Steps

In this modification, the tracing step occurs between Step 3 and Step 4 as follows. The student signs the word, fingerspells it, traces it with the pads of his first two fingers, then signs it again. Make sure that the student is tracing the letters correctly, with the correct sequence and direction of strokes, and that he focuses on what he is doing while tracing. Then continue with Steps 5–7.

Mather, N., & Jaffe, L. (2002). *Woodcock-Johnson III: Reports, Recommendations, and Strategies.* New York: John Wiley & Sons.

```
┌─────────────────────────────────────────────┐
│  LSFWT: STUDENT CUE CARD (Sign, Trace)        │
│  LOOK                                         │
│  STUDY: Sign–Fingerspell–Trace–Sign (Repeat many │
│      times)                                   │
│  WRITE & CHECK: Turn card over–Write word–    │
│      Check the card.                          │
│  RIGHT? Write & check until you have 5 correct│
│      spellings in a row.                      │
│  WRONG? Do LOOK-STUDY until you can see the   │
│      word in your mind.                       │
└─────────────────────────────────────────────┘
```

Modification: LSFW for Students Using Sign-Supported English

For students who speak and sign simultaneously or who code-switch, add voicing to signing. Thus, Steps 2–4 are: sign & say, fingerspell & say letters, sign & say. The student may also verbalize the spelling of the word as he/she writes it.

For those students needing the addition of tracing, have the student say the word in parts (rather than saying the letter names) while tracing each part.

```
┌─────────────────────────────────────────────┐
│  LSFW: STUDENT CUE CARD (Sign and Speech)     │
│  LOOK                                         │
│  STUDY    Sign & say word                     │
│           Fingerspell & say letters           │
│           Sign & say word                     │
│           Repeat many times                   │
│  WRITE & CHECK: Turn card over–Write word     │
│      (voice spelling if it helps) Check the card. │
│  RIGHT? Write & check until you have 5 correct│
│      spellings in a row.                      │
│  WRONG? Do LOOK-STUDY until you can see the   │
│      word in your mind.                       │
└─────────────────────────────────────────────┘
```

Cautions

1. The effectiveness of LSFW depends on the students learning the procedure correctly and doing it correctly independently. The extra time spent in instruction, modeling, guided practice, and checking independent practice of the steps of LSFW is well worth it as, from then on, the students can be independent in learning new words for reading and spelling once they have been introduced.

2. Encourage students to do Steps 1–4 slowly, with concentration, and repeatedly. A student can repeat these steps 100 times or more if that's what it takes to create a mental imprint.

3. Active attention is a critical component. Without it, LSFW will not work and students will see it as a failure of the technique rather than a failure to follow the procedure correctly.

4. Make sure the students sign the word both *before* and *after* fingerspelling it. The rhythm should be: sign–fingerspell–sign–pause. (For LSFWT: sign–fingerspell–trace–sign–pause; for LSFW with Sign and Speech: sign & say–fingerspell & say letters–sign & say–pause.) Students have a tendency to shorten it to: sign–fingerspell–sign–fingerspell. This pattern is more likely to become automatic and thus is less effective.

5. If the student makes a mistake during the writing phase of this procedure, the student covers the error and returns to Steps 1–4.

6. Students will acquire words at different rates. Do not allow competition.

Reinforcement

Most students will learn the study words for reading and spelling and require reinforcement activities in both types of tasks. Some students, however, have such severe learning disabilities that even the addition of tracing does not enable them to revisualize the spelling patterns of some words, although they do learn to recognize them for reading. Eventually, you may decide that the amount of time required for a student to learn the spelling of a word, long after the student can recognize it in reading, causes an unacceptable reduction in the number of words the student is learning for reading recognition. In this case, you may decide to drop the reinforcement and tracking for spelling altogether, focusing only on reading recognition; emphasize fingerspelling as a bridge to written spelling; or choose only fingerspelled loan signs and frequently fingerspelled words used in American Sign Language and manually coded English for continued spelling study. (When deciding to de-emphasize spelling, however, consider that fingerspelling is an important component of signed communication, as many English words do not have corresponding signs, and writing is the major mode of communication with the hearing world for a person who is deaf.)

1. Sight words: The student may sign the word meaning(s) in response to the teacher or a peer-helper flashing the words on the study cards or commercial flash cards, or the student may scan text to find the word and sign it. If

Mather, N., & Jaffe, L. (2002). *Woodcock-Johnson III: Reports, Recommendations, and Strategies.* New York: John Wiley & Sons.

the word has multiple meanings, the task is to determine which sign is conceptually accurate in the context.

2. Spelling: The student writes the word in response to dictation from the teacher or a peer-helper or the student may use the word in his/her writing. Each time, however, the spelling must be reproduced from memory.

3. Use the Flow List (See Strategies: Flow List) to document students' retention of a word for reading or spelling.

4. Schedule: Reinforce new sight words and spelling words daily at first (more often for some students), then *slowly* fade reinforcement. The frequency of reinforcement will depend on the needs of the individual student.

Sample Schedule

Week 1: 3 to 6 words presented and studied (LFSW) Monday morning. Words reinforced and/or restudied daily.
Week 2: Words reinforced and/or restudied M, W, F.
Weeks 3 & 4: Words reinforced once a week.

Review all words once a month.

Additional Study Aids

1. To aid independent study, on the back of the study card, draw the sign for the word or a picture representing the word.

2. Write words on cards in "chunks" or common word parts with a slight separation between each (e.g., *s ing, con grat u late*). Color consonants in blue and vowels in red.

3. Write particularly difficult parts of the word (spelling demons) in a different color.

4. Point out parts of the words the students already know how to spell (e.g., vill*age*, cat*astrophe*). When possible, create a conceptual link between the two words (e.g., old village—*old* and *age* share a sign).

5. Teach common word parts as "chunks," on their own (e.g., *re, sub, tion, ed*) giving practice in visual recognition in a variety of words including the study words.

LOOK-SPELL-SEE-WRITE

Purpose

Look-Spell-See-Write is a study method that students may use independently to learn sight words and spelling words.

Procedure

Preparation
Print or type the word to be learned on an index card for the student. Ensure that the student already understands the meaning of the word and, when it is used for spelling, can read the word with ease.

Steps
1. Look at the word and say it aloud.
2. Say each letter.
3. Look carefully at the word, make a mental picture of it, then close your eyes, and try to see it.
4. Turn the card over and write the word from memory.
5. Check the spelling against the card.
6. If the spelling is correct, turn the card over and write the word again.
7. If the spelling is incorrect, start over from Step 1.
8. Continue writing and checking until you write the word correctly 5 times in a row without making a mistake.

LOOK-SPELL-SEE-WRITE: STUDENT CUE CARD

LOOK   Look at the word and say it aloud.
SPELL   Say each letter.
SEE   Look carefully at the word. Take a picture of it in your mind. Close your eyes and try to see the word.
WRITE   Turn the card over and write the word without looking at it.
CHECK   Check your spelling against the card.

• If your spelling is correct, turn the card over and write the word again.
• Continue writing and checking until you have written the word correctly 5 times in a row without a mistake.
• If you make a mistake at any time during the 5 writings, start over from LOOK (Step 1).

Mather, N., & Jaffe, L. (2002). *Woodcock-Johnson III: Reports, Recommendations, and Strategies.* New York: John Wiley & Sons.

MATH COMPUTATION FORMS

Name _____   Date _____

Teacher _____   Pages _____

Mather, N., & Jaffe, L. (2002). *Woodcock-Johnson III: Reports, Recommendations, and Strategies.* New York: John Wiley & Sons.

MATH COMPUTATION FORMS

Name _____   Date _____

Teacher _____   Pages _____

Mather, N., & Jaffe, L. (2002). *Woodcock-Johnson III: Reports, Recommendations, and Strategies.* New York: John Wiley & Sons.

MATH FACTS: INSTRUCTIONAL SEQUENCE

Purpose

When teaching addition and multiplication facts, using the following sequence helps students mentally organize this information, making it easier to retain and recall. Directly teach the commutative property (e.g., 3 + 4 = 4 + 3) and provide ample practice in its application.

Sequence

Addition Facts

+ 0 and + 1 principles
Doubles: 2 + 2, 3 + 3, 4 + 4, 5 + 5, 6 + 6, 7 + 7, 8 + 8, 9 + 9
Doubles + 1: 2 + 3, 3 + 4, 4 + 5, 5 + 6, 6 + 7, 7 + 8, 8 + 9
Doubles + 2: 2 + 4, 3 + 5, 4 + 6, 5 + 7, 6 + 8, 7 + 9
Plus Tens: 2 + 10, 3 + 10, 4 + 10, 5 + 10, 6 + 10, 7 + 10, 8 + 10, 9 + 10, 10 + 10
Plus Nines: [(any number – 1) + 10]: 2 + 9, 3 + 9, 4 + 9, 5 + 9, 6 + 9, 7 + 9, 8 + 9, 9 + 9

Remaining Facts

2 + 5	2 + 6	2 + 7	2 + 8
	3 + 6	3 + 7	3 + 8
	4 + 7	4 + 8	
	5 + 8		

Multiplication Facts

× 0 and × 1 principles
× 2 and 2 ×
× 5 and 5 ×
× 9 and 9 × (Magic Nines, Finger Nines)
Perfect squares: 1 × 1, 2 × 2, 3 × 3, 4 × 4, 5 × 5, 6 × 6, 7 × 7, 8 × 8, 9 × 9, 10 × 10

Remaining Facts

3 × 4	3 × 6	3 × 7	3 × 8
	4 × 6	4 × 7	4 × 8
		6 × 7	6 × 8
			7 × 8

MATH PROBLEM-SOLVING STRATEGY

Purpose

This strategy was designed to teach adolescents a procedure for solving math story problems. Adjust or modify the steps of the strategy depending upon the learner's characteristics.

Procedure

1. *Read the problem aloud.* Have a teacher help you identify any unknown words.
2. *Paraphrase the problem.* Reread the problem, identify the question that is asked, and summarize the information that will be important for solving the problem.
3. *Visualize.* Draw a picture of the problem or visualize the situation and tell what it is about.
4. *State the problem.* Underline the most important information in the problem and then complete the sentences: "What I know is . . . ," "What I want to find out is. . . ."
5. *Hypothesize.* Complete the sentence: "If . . . , then. . . ." For example, "If 7 people each want to buy 20 tickets, then I need to multiply to determine the number of tickets." For multiple-step problems, think through the series of steps and write the operation signs in the order they will be used.
6. *Estimate.* Estimate an answer that would make sense. Write it down.
7. *Calculate.* Calculate the answer and label it (e.g., 140 tickets, 5 rooms).
8. *Self-check.* Review the problem, check the computation, and ask if your answer makes sense.

Adapted from: Montague, M., & Bos, C. S. (1986). The effect of cognitive strategy training on verbal math problem solving performance of learning disabled adolescents. *Journal of Learning Disabilities, 19,* 26–33.

MEMORY: GENERAL PRINCIPLES FOR IMPROVEMENT

Increase Attention. Attention is necessary for all learning. Make sure that the student's memory problems are not really symptoms of attention problems. Use strategies for enhancing attention, such as intensifying instruction, using more visual aids and activities, and reinforcing attending behavior.

Promote External Memory. Encourage the student to write things down that need to be remembered, a practice known as "external memory." Encourage the student to keep an assignment notebook and maintain a calendar to help with memory. External memory is also useful for open-book exams.

Enhance Meaningfulness. Find ways to relate the content being discussed to the student's prior knowledge. Draw parallels to the student's own life. Bring in concrete, meaningful examples for the student to explore.

Use Pictures. Use pictures to help with memory. Use pictures on the chalkboard or on the overhead projector. Bring in photographs and show concrete images on videotape, when appropriate. If pictures are simply unavailable, ask the student to create images in his mind.

Minimize Interference. Avoid digressions and emphasize only the critical features of a new topic. Ensure that all examples relate directly to the content being covered.

Promote Active Manipulation. The student will remember content better if he experiences it for himself. For example, rather than lecturing the class on the effect of weak acid (such as vinegar) on calcite, have the student place calcite in a glass of vinegar and see what happens.

Promote Active Reasoning. Encourage the student to think through information rather than just repeating it. For example, rather than simply telling the student that penguins carry their eggs on the tops of their feet, ask the student why it makes sense that penguins would carry their eggs on the tops of their feet.

Increase the Amount of Practice. Provide opportunities for the student to practice and review information frequently.

From: Enhancing school success with mnemonic strategies by M. A. Mastropieri & T. E. Scruggs, March 1998, *Intervention in School and Clinic, 33,* 201–208. Copyright 1998 by PRO-ED, Inc. Adapted with permission.

MULTIPLICATION FACT CHART

Name _____

0	1	2	3	4	5	6	7	8	9	10	11	12
1	1	2	3	4	5	6	7	8	9	10	11	12
2	2	4	6	8	10	12	14	16	18	20	22	24
3	3	6	9	12	15	18	21	24	27	30	33	36
4	4	8	12	16	20	24	28	32	36	40	44	48
5	5	10	15	20	25	30	35	40	45	50	55	60
6	6	12	18	24	30	36	42	48	54	60	66	72
7	7	14	21	28	35	42	49	56	63	70	77	84
8	8	16	24	32	40	48	56	64	72	80	88	96
9	9	18	27	36	45	54	63	72	81	90	99	108
10	10	20	30	40	50	60	70	80	90	100	110	120
11	11	22	33	44	55	66	77	88	99	110	121	132
12	12	24	36	48	60	72	84	96	108	120	132	144

Mather, N., & Jaffe, L. (2002). *Woodcock-Johnson III: Reports, Recommendations, and Strategies.* New York: John Wiley & Sons.

MYSTERY MOTIVATOR

Purpose

The Mystery Motivator provides incentive for a student to demonstrate or refrain from demonstrating a target behavior for a specified time period. The following procedure is written for use with individual students although it can be adapted for use with a class.

Caution: This system may not be reinforcing for those students with very low frustration tolerance who might actually lose motivation if they demonstrate the target behavior and do not receive the expected reward.

Materials

Assortment of positive reinforcers

Reward cards: index cards, each bearing the name of one of the reinforcers

Envelope marked or colored in such a way as to distinguish it as special. Place one reward card in the envelope. Keep its content secret.

Chart with an X marked on a percentage of the squares. The higher the percentage, the more chance the student has to receive a reinforcer. Cover the center of *all* squares on the chart with tape so that the placement of the Xs cannot be seen.

Procedure

1. Set up a behavioral intervention with target behaviors, criteria for earning a reinforcer, and a recording system to track a student's performance of the behaviors. Explain the intervention and the Mystery Motivator reinforcement system to the student.

   Build up the anticipatory excitement of whether or not the student will meet the criteria and earn a chance at trying for the reward as well as the mystery of what the reward might be.

2. Each time the student meets the behavioral criterion, he or she may peel a piece of tape off of the chart. *If* an X is under the tape, the student takes the reward card out of the envelope and is given the reward on the card. If no X is under the tape, remind the student, with enthusiasm, that he or she can try again for an X the next time period

in which the intervention is used (e.g., next period, that afternoon, next day).

Adaptations

1. Use color-changing markers to make the Xs. One marker contains invisible ink that becomes visible when drawn over with a colored marker. Make Xs on the chart with the invisible ink. When the student meets the criteria, he or she colors in a square. If an X appears, the student gets the reward specified on the reward card in the envelope.

2. Wrap all rewards in decorative paper and put them in a grab-bag. If the student finds an X, he or she pulls one item out. Use film canisters or plastic medication containers (without labels) in which to place a strip of paper printed with rewards that cannot be placed in the bag such as larger tangible items, privileges, or coupons.

3. Mystery Motivators provide good incentives for a student to stay on task during evaluation sessions. For example, the student is allowed to peel tape off a square (or color it in) each time he or she finishes a subtest or a portion of a test with good effort and attention. So as not to break up the session, the reward cards are saved until a break and rewards given then.

Adapted from: Rhode, G., Jenson, W. R., & Reavis, H. K. (1995). *The tough kid book: Practical classroom management strategies.* Longmont, CO: Sopris West Educational Services.

NEUROLOGICAL IMPRESS METHOD

Purpose

The goal of this method is to build reading rate and fluency. Use the method 10 to 15 minutes daily for a period of from 8 to 12 instructional hours. Heckelman (1966) noted that the method is ineffective if the student has not made some progress after 4 hours of total instruction. The method works effectively with a student whose listening comprehension is higher than his/her present level of word recognition skill.

Procedure

1. Select high-interest reading materials that are slightly below the student's grade level.
2. Sit side-by-side, with the student slightly in front.

Mather, N., & Jaffe, L. (2002). *Woodcock-Johnson III: Reports, Recommendations, and Strategies.* New York: John Wiley & Sons.

3. Read material with the student in unison. In beginning sessions, read in a louder voice and at a slightly faster pace than the student. Reread initial lines or paragraphs until a normal, fluid reading pattern is established. Encourage the student to not worry about mistakes.
4. While reading, track the words with your finger. Later, as skill develops, have the student track the line of print with his/her finger.
5. By the end of eight 15-minute sessions, increase the difficulty level of the material. At this time, you may use materials at the student's reading frustration level.

Adapted from: Heckelman, R. G. (1966). Using the neurological impress reading technique. *Academic Therapy, 1,* 235–239; and Heckelman, R. G. (1986). N.I.M. revisited. *Academic Therapy, 21,* 411–420.

ORGANIZATION FOR EFFECTIVE INSTRUCTION

1. Organize the physical environment.
   a. Maintain the room with the appearance of orderliness & tidiness (e.g., wall posters colorful but organized so as to avoid the impression of a collage; orderly placement of furniture).
   b. Have materials categorized and placed according to function, frequency of need, and who needs to get them (e.g., texts used daily vs. the school policy manual; lined writing paper; reference materials such as a dictionary, computer disks, maps). Have them put away when not being used. Label cabinets and shelves.
2. Maintain a consistent schedule. Have daily activities planned in a consistent, and thus predictable, sequence. A consistent schedule facilitates:
   a. daily reinforcement of skills, concepts, and individual organization;
   b. students' independence in getting ready for and starting activities;
   c. students feeling in control and competent;
   d. students' ability to discuss their day and remember what they did.
3. Plan instruction and activities.
   a. Know your specific teaching objective. What is the student supposed to be able to do? For example, add 20 double-digit addition problems with regrouping with 85% accuracy; pronounce 10 real words and 10 nonsense words following the CVC pattern with 80% accuracy on each list.
   b. Plan how you are going to present the material or lesson (e.g., Place value: explain rules, model trading game with verbalization of the steps, pair students for guided practice, students practice while teacher checks dyads for comprehension and accuracy).
   c. Plan what the students will do for guided practice and independent practice.
4. Have the materials ready and immediately accessible.
5. State instructions clearly, briefly, and in the sequence you want them done. Don't modify midstream.
6. Teach transitions. Explain your expectations for behavior during transitions between activities. Teach transition behavior the same as you would any other skill. Provide practice.
   a. Explain meaning of term.
   b. List specific actions:
      1) Stop current activity.
      2) Put materials away.
      3) Take out materials for new activity.
      4) Move to appropriate area of the room.
      5) If you have a question, ask a classmate or raise your hand to ask teacher.
      6) Show readiness by sitting/standing quietly and looking at the teacher.
   c. Set a specific time limit for transitions (2 minutes is often sufficient).
   d. Establish specific start and end signals (e.g., 1 tap on a triangle to start, 3 to end). Consider a 30-second warning, if necessary.
   e. Give group credit for group success.
7. Establish a positive behavior management program.
   a. Rules express specific expectations for school behavior in demonstrable terms (e.g., Get your materials when you walk into the room; sit down and start work immediately; do not touch another student without his/her permission; follow the teacher's instructions immediately).
   b. Give frequent, specific recognition/reinforcement of positive behaviors.
   c. Have established consequences for rule infringements and be absolutely consistent in applying them when necessary.
   d. Whenever possible, use humor to request or redirect a specific behavior. Do not use anger or a judgmental manner when correcting behavior.

Remember: If you have—and stick to—a well organized teaching plan, you are less likely to have to depend on your behavior management program.

Mather, N., & Jaffe, L. (2002). *Woodcock-Johnson III: Reports, Recommendations, and Strategies.* New York: John Wiley & Sons.

	Subject	M	T	W	Th	F
(red)	Reading					
(blue)	Lang Arts					
(green)	Soc. St.					
(yellow)	Math					
(lt.blue)	Science					
	Notes					

Figure IV.7   Example of an Assignment Sheet to Help Students Remember Their Homework

ORGANIZATION OF MATERIALS AND ASSIGNMENTS

1. Set up the student's notebook in the following manner:
   a. Choose a 3-ring binder that has pockets and holders for pens, erasers, and other school supplies, as well as a transparent pocket in which to display a card with the student's name, address, and phone number in case it is lost.
   b. Insert a folder with pockets. Label the front cover HOMEWORK. On the inside, label the left pocket "Not finished" and the right, "Finished." Any papers given out in class—related to assignments—are to be placed in the Not Finished pocket and all completed assignments in the Finished pocket until they are handed in.
   c. Use a simplified week-by-week assignment sheet. Each week, tape a new one to the front of the homework folder so that it is easily accessible and less likely to be lost.
   d. Tape a month-long calendar to the back cover of the homework folder to fill in deadlines and schedule intermediate deadlines and work sessions for long-term projects. The student can color in the days of school breaks and special events on the calendar to display the schedule. Pictures representing major holidays may be added.
   e. Put tabbed dividers of different colors in the notebook, one for each subject. Plastic dividers are easier to handle and are more durable than paper dividers. On the assignment sheet, you may also color-code the row for each subject to match the color of the divider for that subject notebook. Let the student choose the colors. Figures IV.6 and IV.7 show dividers color-correlated to the academic subjects on the assignment sheet.
   f. In the back of the book, include a section for a stash of clean notebook paper.
2. To help the student write down assignments and bring home the proper materials, set up a system whereby the student writes down the homework in each class on an

assignment sheet. The teacher checks it for accuracy, legibility, and completeness, corrects it if necessary, and initials it. If inattention, handwriting, or other difficulties prevent the student from copying down assignments, the teacher should do so. The teachers may need to help the student remember to put the required materials in his or her backpack.
3. At home, the parents check the student's assignment sheet, make sure assignments are completed, initial the appropriate box on the assignment sheet, and watch the student put the assignment in the "Finished" pocket of the homework folder. The last row on the assignment sheet may be left open for the teacher and parent to communicate.
4. The teacher(s) reminds the student daily—and directly—to hand in his or her completed assignments and makes sure that the student does so.
5. For long-term assignments, the teacher or parent helps the student to break down the assignment into steps, schedule a deadline for each step, and schedule specific times on the monthly calendar (back cover of homework folder) for work on each step. Require the student to hand in each stage of the assignment for checking before going on.
6. The parents help the student set up a file system at home. Place files, each one labeled with the name of a class/subject, in a file drawer, file box, or accordion file. Periodically, a parent or tutor should go through the notebook with the student and pull out all of the papers that are no longer needed. File these, by subject, in the corresponding file. The student then has these papers to refer back to if necessary and the number of papers in the notebook are reduced.

Suggestion

To help the student begin to develop an understanding of time within the framework of months in a year, at the end of each month, put the monthly calendar up on the wall so as to create one row of twelve calendar pages by year's end. Refer back to different months and point out past events and how long ago they happened.

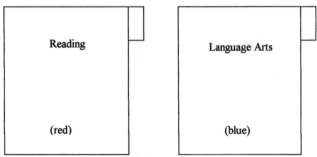

Figure IV.6   Examples of Notebook Dividers for Color-Correlation with Assignment Sheets

Mather, N., & Jaffe, L. (2002). *Woodcock-Johnson III: Reports, Recommendations, and Strategies.* New York: John Wiley & Sons.

PHONICS CHECK-OFF CHART

Consonants		Short Vowels		Initial Consonant Blends				Consonant Digraphs		Final Consonant Blends		Long Vowel Sounds	
				2		3							
b		ă		bl		scr		ch		ng		ai	
c		ĕ		br		spl		ch (k)		nk		ay	
d		ĭ		cl		spr		ph		tch		ea	
f		ŏ		cr		str		sh		mp		ey	
g		ŭ		dr		squ		th		nd		oa	
h		y		dw		thr		~~th~~		nt		oe	
j				fl		chr		wh		ct		ow	
k				fr		sch				ft		ue	
l				gl						pt		vcé	
m				gr						xt		a	
n				pl						nch		e	
p				pr						mpt		i	
r				st						lth		o	
s				sc						fth		ū	
t				sl						lfth		u(o͞o)	
v				sm								y	
w				sn									
x				sp									
y				sw									
z				tr									
qu				tw									
s (z)													
soft c													
soft g													

Mather, N., & Jaffe, L. (2002). *Woodcock-Johnson III: Reports, Recommendations, and Strategies.* New York: John Wiley & Sons.

Vowel Diphthongs and Digraphs	Initial Silent Letters	Silent Letters in Final Combinations	Word Patterns	Word Endings		
au	kn	ck	ar	le	al	cient
aw	gn	dge	er	ly	el	ture
ea (ĕ)	wr	stle	ir	ed (id)	able	tual
ea (ē)	gh	scle	or	ed (d)	ation	tuate
ei (ā)	h	mb	ur	ed (t)	er	ic
ei (ē)	pn	mn	igh	s	ery	ity
ey (ā)	ps	bt	eigh	s (z)	ar	ism
eu (ōō)	rh	gh	ear	(c) le	ary	ent
ew (ōō)	pt	pt	ind	less	or	ence
ie (ē)		lf	ild	ness	ory	ency
ie (ī)		lk	old	ful	tia	ant
oi			wa	ing	tial	ance
oy			qua	y	tian	ancy
ōō			quar	tion	tious	ia
ŏŏ			wor	sion (sh)	tient	ial
ou (ow)			al	sion (zh)	sia (sh)	ian
ou (ōō)			tu	ous	sia (zh)	ious
ou (ō)				ive	sial (sh)	fȳ
ou (ŭ)				ile	sial (zh)	
ow				ice	sian (sh)	
				ace	sian (zh)	
ui (ī)				ite	sient (zh)	
				ate	sient (zh)	
				ine (in)	cial	
				ine (een)	cian	
				ain (in)	cious	
					ceous	

Mather, N., & Jaffe, L. (2002). *Woodcock-Johnson III: Reports, Recommendations, and Strategies.* New York: John Wiley & Sons.

PHONOGRAM ACTIVITIES

Purpose

This approach to phonogram instruction and reinforcement is useful for deaf students who are deaf and who do not use audition in the reading process or for students who need practice seeing the common letter patterns in English words. It is intended to facilitate word recognition and spelling by helping students mentally convert common letter combinations into instantly recognized "chunks," and in doing so, reduce the burden on memory.

Instructional and Introductory Activity

Preparation

1. Choose phonograms to teach based on the sight/spelling words the students are learning in reading instruction and are encountering in their reading books. It is preferable, although not always possible, to choose high-frequency words.
2. If necesary, preteach the meaning of the words (including dual meanings) in the student's primary language (e.g., ASL, manually-coded English). Ensure that the students are completely familar with the meaning before introducing words for reading and spelling.
3. Introduce the words as you normally would, in context of the reading material, prior to phonogram study. Students should be familiar with the printed word as well as its meaning.
4. Explain that the same phonograms (agree on a sign, such as "letter-groups," or "letter friends" for younger students) occur in English words repeatedly and if the students can recognize these patterns, they will learn to read and spell words much more easily.
5. Provide each student with a set of word cards, each containing at least one of the phonograms intended for study (target phonograms). Use a print font and size that is easy for the student to read, or print the words neatly. Word cards that are typed or printed on a word processor are closest to what the student will see in text.
6. Make a large chart for each student. Students will use their charts to categorize their word cards. Write the target phonograms in the top row. The examples that follow are taken from Level 1 (red books) of Reading Milestones–Second Edition (PRO-ED, Austin, TX, www.proedinc.com).

7. To model the procedure, post a large chart on the board. To make the chart reusable, laminate it and write on it with dry

sw	ir	at	all

erase markers. Use tape to stick the word cards in place, or place a strip of Velcro down each column and on the back of each of your own set of word cards.

Note: In the descriptions of procedure below, words in uppercase letters are fingerspelled (e.g., G-I-R-L). Words in italics are signed (e.g., *girl*).

Procedure

1. *Instructions:* Explain to the students that they are to look at each word card and match it to one of the phonograms in the chart.
2. *Model the procedure* for two of the cards, thinking aloud as you do so. Example: "Let's see. Here's the word *girl*. G-I-R-L. [Point to sw and fingerspell it.] Does G-I-R-L have S-W? No." Do the same with the other phonograms until you come to the one that is in the word. Place the card in the column under that phonogram.
3. *Independent activity:* The students word independently, placing each of their word cards on their charts in the correct columns.
4. *Group activity (correction/reinforcement):* When students have finished, have them take turns coming up to the board to place your word cards in the column they chose. Have them explain the reason for that placement. Example: "This phonogram is I-R. Girl is G-I-R-L. It has I-R in it (student underlines ir with finger). Or, more simply, "I-R [pointing to phonogram on chart]—I-R [pointing to letters on word card] Same."

Guided Practice

1. Using the same word cards, have the students group their cards by phonogram. They should have at least 2 for each. Provide guidance as needed.
2. If a word can fit in 2 phonogram categories, and the student notices this, reinforce his careful analysis. Allow him to make a duplicate word card for the second match if he so desires.
3. Have students take turns telling you the words they put in each word group as you record them on the board. After recording each group, ask the sutdent to tell his or her

| ball | → | all
ball |
| fall | → | fall |

Mather, N., & Jaffe, L. (2002). *Woodcock-Johnson III: Reports, Recommendations, and Strategies.* New York: John Wiley & Sons.

reasoning for grouping those words. Write the phonogram over the words.

4. Pointing to the pattern, fingerspell the phonogram, then each word under it. Then have the students do it with you.

Independent Activity

Purpose

To begin to establish automaticity in recognizing the target phonogram in text and to strengthen its visual image in memory.

Preparation

Create a worksheet composed of rows of words containing the target phonogram and some words that do not contain it. You can use the same 6 to 10 words (containing the phonogram) repeatedly, in random order. Write the target phonogram at the top for reference.

ir
girl three flirt whirring bird and irk team third back quirk shirt first girl sir forth and swirl bird shirk dirty irk swirl whirl back dirt irk bird third three team girl birth whir frame firm

Activity

1. Specify the target phonogram. Have students scan the words, row by row, from left to right, circling or highlighting the phonogram (not the whole word) in each word containing it. Warn them that some words do not contain the phonogram.
2. Later, include words with an additional target phonogram (e.g., they will scan for ir and sw on the same worksheet).
3. As skill and familiarity with the task increases, include words that have letter combinations that might be confused with the target phonogram, such as grill and brim for the ir phonogram. This requires increased effort at visual discrimination.

Note: Inclusion of words that the student does not know how to read is acceptable in this exercise as it is solely for visual scanning and indentification of phonograms, not meaning.

Transfer

Preparation

1. Make copies of the reading material for words containing the phonogram(s) that you have specified and underline or highlight it (them).
2. As a group, have students write on the board the words they found and underline the target phonogram(s). Have them sign or explain the meaning of any they found in their reading text (if previously studied).

Reinforcement

1. Incorporate words that the students have studied in this way into writing/spelling actvities.
2. Assign Word Bank activities.

PIRATES TEST-TAKING STRATEGY

Purpose

The PIRATES test-taking strategy was developed to help students in middle and high school improve performance on multiple-choice tests. Use of the strategy has been documented to significantly improve students' test scores (Hughes & Schumaker, 1991).

Steps

Prepare to Succeed: Within the first 3 minutes, the student puts his name on the paper, writes the acronym PIRATES, states an affirmation regarding his ability to do well on the test, scans the test to ascertain the types of questions asked, and ranks the sections (if any) of the test from easiest to hardest.

Inspect the Instructions: Next, the student turns to the easiest section and reads the instructions, particularly focusing on information regarding *how* to answer the questions and *where* to write the answers.

Read, Remember, Reduce: Within this section, the student reads the first question, actively trying to understand its meaning, searches his memory for relevant information, and reduces the choices by eliminating the choices that he knows are incorrect.

Mather, N., & Jaffe, L. (2002). *Woodcock-Johnson III: Reports, Recommendations, and Strategies.* New York: John Wiley & Sons.

Answer or abandon: At this point, if the student can answer the question, he does so. If he still does not know the answer, he marks it with a symbol of his choosing. The symbols help to prevent penalties for skipped items. The student continues to attempt questions consecutively in this manner, repeating the I, R, and A steps, and moving from easier to harder sections of the test, until he has completed one pass through the entire test, with all test items either answered or abandoned.

Turn back: Having answered all of the questions he could, the student returns to the beginning of the test to tackle the rest. Often, just reading all of the questions and attempting to retrieve the needed information triggers recall of the information required to answer the remaining questions.

Estimate: If the student is still unable to come up with an answer to a question, he uses strategies to increase his chances of guessing correctly. For example, he would avoid absolute answers (e.g., all, always, never), eliminate choices with the same outcomes, or choose the longest or most detailed choice.

Survey: As a final step, the student quickly reviews the test to ensure that he has answered, or deliberately skipped (if there is a penalty for guessing), all of the questions.

A cue card, as shown in Figure IV.8 is often helpful to remind students of the steps in the PIRATES Test-Taking Strategy.

PIRATES Cue Card

Prepare to Succeed

Put your name & PIRATES on the test.

Allot time and order to sections.

State affirmation.

Start within 3 minutes.

Inspect the Instructions

Read instructions carefully.

Underline what to do, where to respond.

Notice special requirements.

Read, Remember, Reduce

Eliminate answers you know are wrong.

Answer or Abandon

Mark the questions you skip.

Turn back

Go to the beginning and try to answer the remaining questions.

Estimate

Avoid absolutes.

Choose longest or most detailed choice.

Eliminate similar choices.

Survey

Figure IV.8   Student Cue Card for PIRATES Test-Taking Strategy

Adapted from: Hughes, C. A., & Schumaker, J. (1991). Test-taking strategy instruction for adolescents with learning disabilities. *Exceptionality, 2,* 205–221; and Hughes, C. A., Schumaker, J., Deshler, D., & Mercer, C. (1988). *The test-taking strategy.* Lawrence, KS: Edge Enterprises.

Mather, N., & Jaffe, L. (2002). *Woodcock-Johnson III: Reports, Recommendations, and Strategies.* New York: John Wiley & Sons.

POSITIVE REINFORCERS

Many classroom management systems and individualized behavioral interventions incorporate the use of positive reinforcers. A positive reinforcer is something that increases the desired behavior. The effectiveness of a reinforcer will vary per student and activity. For some students, social praise from teachers may not be as effective a reinforcer as earned privileges or activities or tangible rewards. For the reinforcers to motivate behavioral change sufficiently, they must be uniquely interesting and attractive to the student. A positive reinforcer for one student could be negative to another. Thus, it is a good idea to request suggestions from the student as well as to note the activities that the student chooses. Regardless of the reinforcers selected, as their novelty wears off, their motivating power will diminish, and with it, the student's interest in the program. The following list provides examples of possible positive reinforcers from primary (edible) to secondary (social).

Edible

Coupons for fast food restaurants or ice cream parlors. (Many places will donate coupons for schools.)
Miniature candy bars
Earn a popcorn or pizza party for the class
Doughnut holes
Cookies
Assortment of individual-sized bags of chips
Long pretzel rods
Long licorice laces
Gummy worms or sour gummy worms

Material or Tangible

Novelty items, such as wax lips, vampire teeth
Fake tattoos
Tubes of plastic bubbles
Fast food restaurant toys that come with kids' meals
Wind-up figures
Stickers
Fuzzy or scratch and sniff stickers
Markers or any kind of art supplies
Origami papers with instructions
Preprinted and colored paper airplanes with fold-lines drawn on (can be purchased in pads)

Trading cards (sports, Magic, superheroes, cartoon characters)
Posters of sports stars or popular music artists
T-shirt saying "I survived Ms. or Mr. _____'s math class."
Fake rings
Money
Positive note, phone call, or e-mail home
Toys such as small vehicles or work machines
Jar of bubbles
Deck of cards
Comics
Anything depicting popular book or movie characters
Movie passes to the discount movie theater
Books
Old *National Geographic* magazines
Hair ornaments
Sticky objects (e.g., hands, frogs, bugs) that stick on walls when thrown
Rubber bugs

Privileges

Reduced or no homework for a day
Use of headphones and music while working in the classroom
Running errands
Acting as line leader
Use of art supplies
10 minutes on computer
Writing assignment on computer
Positive visit to the principal, counselor, or staff member of student's choice
Lunch with the teacher
Use of a Game Boy or similar device for short time
Time spent out of school with teacher
Use of candy or soda machine in teachers' lounge
Time to spend in library
Attending special school events that the student would not usually attend (e.g., performance for older classes)
Helping out in younger classes
Reading to younger students

Social

Statement specifying positive behavior demonstrated
Statement specifying accuracy, effort, care, or degree of completion evidenced in assignment

Mather, N., & Jaffe, L. (2002). *Woodcock-Johnson III: Reports, Recommendations, and Strategies.* New York: John Wiley & Sons.

Smile or wink
Pat on shoulder
Request for student to help teacher

PRECISION REQUESTS

Purpose

Precision requests reduce or eliminate the most common noncompliant behaviors—arguing, negotiating, refusing, procrastinating, and making excuses. Consistency among teachers in using precision requests greatly enhances the effectiveness of the technique.

Procedure

Before implementing precision requests, establish a hierarchy of negative consequences from mild to severe. Consequences must be carefully considered and chosen during the planning phase of this technique so that they are meaningful and appropriate to the level of noncompliance. In some instances, discuss possible consequences with school administration and/or make arrangements with other staff.

Explain the precision request and the hierarchy of consequences to the whole class. Make sure that all students, especially those most likely to need precision requests, understand exactly how the procedure works and what the consequences are.

Steps
When making a precision request of a student:

1. Stand close to the student, obtain eye contact, and make a quiet request in the form of a statement (not a question), using the word "please" ("Please take out your books and begin reading").
2. Wait 5 to 10 seconds after making the request but do not interact with the student during this time.
3. If the student starts to comply, verbally reinforce him or her for doing so, referring to the specific behavior (e.g., "I appreciate you following my instructions promptly").
4. If the student does not comply within 5 to 10 seconds, repeat the request using the signal word "need" (e.g., "I *need* you to take out your book and begin reading now").
5. If the student starts to comply, verbally reinforce him or her for doing so, referring to the specific behavior.

6. If the student still does not comply within 5 to 10 seconds after the second request, implement the first pre-established consequence.
7. Immediately after the consequence is completed, repeat the request using the signal word "need." If the student complies, verbally reinforce his behavior. If not, implement the next consequence in the hierarchy.

Important Components
- The use of the word "need" in the second request signals the student that lack of compliance will result in an immediate consequence.
- The same request must be made immediately after the consequence has been completed so that the student does not learn that he can get out of a request by receiving a consequence.
- Continue to use a quiet, unemotional, but firm manner in repeating the request and implementing the consequences. Do not allow yourself to become involved in a discussion about the request or the consequences.

Adapted with permission from: Sopris West Educational Services, *The Tough Kid Book: Practical Classroom Management Strategies* by Ginger Rhode, Ph.D., William Jenson, Ph.D., & Ken Reavis, Ed.D., Copyright 1992–1996 (6th printing).

PRECISION TEACHING

Purpose

Precision teaching is a measurement procedure that may be adapted for use with a variety of instructional materials. It is particularly appropriate for skills requiring accuracy, fluency, and maintenance, such as memorizing math facts or rapidly recognizing sight words.

Procedure

1. Select the behavior for change, such as memorizing multiplication facts. The behavior must be observable, repeatable, and able to occur at least 10 times during the timed period.
2. Decide how the skill will be presented (input) and how performance will be demonstrated (output). Examples include seeing, hearing, writing, and saying. A worksheet of multiplication facts would have a *visual* input with a *written* output.

Mather, N., & Jaffe, L. (2002). *Woodcock-Johnson III: Reports, Recommendations, and Strategies.* New York: John Wiley & Sons.

3. Define the goal necessary to demonstrate mastery. The goal may be determined by assessing three children who are performing the skill adequately and taking their average scores. For example, the goal on a multiplication worksheet may be to answer five one- by two-digit problems within a minute.

4. Design a diagnostic probe to sample a student's performance on the skill. Include more problems than can be completed in the time period. If the skill involves an oral output, a follow-along sheet is developed with spaces to score the items.

5. Determine how to score the probe. For example, on a multiplication worksheet, the number of correct digits written (with correct place value) could be counted, as an alternative to counting the number of correctly solved problems. The instructor may tally both the number of correct responses (c = correct) and the number of error responses (x = incorrect) on the same chart. Do not count incomplete problems as errors.

6. Administer the diagnostic probe to the student for a specified time period, usually 1 to 2 minutes, for 3 to 5 days, to establish a baseline. Chart the baseline results and draw a vertical line on the chart after the baseline data.

7. Analyze the student's performance. Determine if this is the appropriate skill level for instruction. If not, go back to an easier skill. If so, continue with the skill and begin instruction.

8. Identify the student's learning stage. If the student is in the acquisition phase, the count correct is gradually increasing; for the fluency stage, the number correct is two times greater than the number of errors; and in the maintenance stage, the predetermined goal has been met.

9. Record the student's daily performance and graph the results on an equal-interval chart or a semilogarithmic chart where the vertical axis is scaled with proportional distances between numbers.

10. Select an appropriate intervention based on the student's learning stage. Examples for the acquisition stage include instruction, prompting, cueing, modeling, and demonstrating; for the fluency stage, drill activities and reinforcers; for the maintenance stage, opportunities to apply the skill in practical situations.

11. Administer the probe daily or at least three times weekly and chart the results. Use the same probe until the goal is met.

12. Analyze and evaluate the charting of the student's learning patterns frequently to determine whether instructional changes should be made. Draw a vertical line on the chart any time a change in intervention is made.

Adapted from: Algozzine, R. (1990). *Problem behavior management*. Rockville, MD: Aspen.

PRECISION TEACHING GRAPH

Name _____   Number of Minutes _____

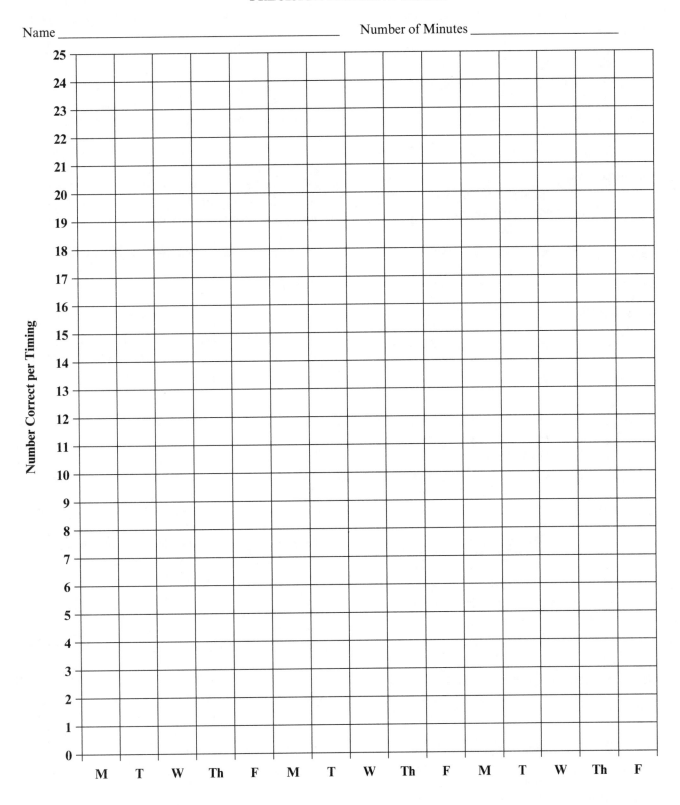

Mather, N., & Jaffe, L. (2002). *Woodcock-Johnson III: Reports, Recommendations, and Strategies.* New York: John Wiley & Sons.

PREREADING PLAN (PREP)

Purpose

PReP is a prelearning group activity for assessing students' background knowledge on a topic prior to starting a new unit or reading selection.

Preparation

Review the material to be taught and select a word, a phrase, or picture that represents the key concept to be presented. Present the stimulus to the students.

Procedure

1. Initial Association

Ask the students to tell anything they think of in association with the stimulus. Write all responses on the board. You may place a student's name or initials next to his or her comments to assist with later evaluation of each student's prior knowledge.

2. Reflections

Ask the students to explain what made them think of the responses they gave in Step 1. In this step, the students consciously connect their prior knowledge to the concept presented by the teacher and expand their knowledge through the responses of other students. Encourage participation from each student.

3. Reformation of Knowledge

After all students have shared their associations, ask them to think about the discussion and tell any new ideas about the topic. Students may elaborate ideas and modify ideas. This step helps students associate new knowledge with prior knowledge.

4. Evaluation

On a 3-point scale, evaluate the students' level of prior knowledge to determine whether or not further concept building is needed prior to reading or teaching the unit.

  a. *Much Knowledge*

  Responses reflecting knowledge of superordinate concepts for the topic (e.g., "type of geographical region" for *desert*) or related to the topic, definitions, and analogies indicate knowledge adequate for good comprehension.

  b. *Some Knowledge*

  Responses concerning examples and characteristics indicate that comprehension may be adequate but should be supported with activities to strengthen the association between new and prior knowledge.

  c. *Little Knowledge*

  Responses based on word associations rather than concept associations (e.g., affixes, rhymes) or on unrelated experiences indicate that instructional activities are required to enrich the students' knowledge of the superordinate concept before reading is assigned or the unit is taught.

Adapted from: Langer, J. A. (1981). From theory to practice: A prereading plan. *Journal of Reading, 25,* 152–156; and Langer, J. A. (1984). Examining background knowledge and text comprehension. *Reading Research Quarterly, 19,* 468–481.

PRESENTING TECHNIQUE

The Presenting Technique is a prereading method designed to provide a foundation for the reading process. This method may be effective for children with language impairments or for English Language Learners.

Procedure

To begin, a simple story is selected.

1. The student sits across from the teacher. The teacher reads aloud a short paragraph or two from a story, three times, as the student watches the teacher's face.
2. The teacher paraphrases the story using vocabulary that the student will understand.
3. The teacher rereads the original passage.
4. With cueing from the teacher, the student retells as much of the story as she or he can remember.
5. The teacher reads a short phrase or sentence and has the student repeat back the material. The length is determined by the ability of the student to repeat back the words.

After this procedure, the teacher may read short phrases or sentences with the student in unison. Once skill is gained with this technique, the teacher may use the Neurological Impress Method, reading the entire story with the student in unison.

Adapted from: Heckelman, R. G. (1986). N.I.M. revisited. *Academic Therapy, 21,* 411–420.

PRINCIPLES OF EFFECTIVE TEACHING FOR STUDENTS WITH LEARNING DIFFICULTIES

1. *Do not let the student fail.* Students who struggle often expect to fail. The most effective way to help the student overcome an expectation of failure is to provide consistent success experiences. Procedures include:
   a. Organizing materials and using methods that will lead the student to the right answer;
   b. Providing clues where necessary;
   c. Narrowing the choices for responding;
   d. Leading the student to the right answer by rewording the questions or simplifying the problem;
   e. Simplifying and guiding work so that the student does not make errors.
2. *Consider the best way for the student to receive information* but do not make assumptions. For example, a student who is hard of hearing may do best with a phonics approach to reading, whereas a student who has low vision may benefit from a sight approach.
3. *If the student is not learning the skill or concept, move back to a prerequisite skill.*
4. *Provide feedback for correct and incorrect responses.* Arrange lessons so that the student gets immediate feedback on the correctness of an answer. For example, if a student is learning to spell a word, have the student study the model, cover it, write the word, then compare the response to the model, thus getting immediate feedback. Not only does practice make perfect—practice makes *permanent.*
5. *Reinforce correct responses immediately.* Reinforcements can be tangible (e.g., stickers), in the form of privileges (e.g., computer time), or in the form of social approval (e.g., smile).
6. *Find the optimum instructional level for each task.* The level of materials will change according to the skill, concepts, and type of task. If the material is too easy, the student will not be challenged. If the material is too difficult, the student will face failure and frustration.
7. *Proceed in a systematic, step-by-step fashion.* Pay attention to the developmental sequence of the instructions. Go in order. Move slowly from simple to complex, lower to higher, less to more.
8. *Teach to mastery.* Ensure that the student has mastered a skill or subskill before introducing the next level. Provide consistent review to promote automaticity.
9. *Use minimal change from one step to the next to facilitate learning.*
10. *Provide for transfer of knowledge, skills, and use of strategies.* Create structured opportunities for the student to use them throughout the day in different situations (e.g., practicing a reading strategy in the math text during math class).
11. *Provide sufficient repetition to ensure learning.* Students with learning difficulties require more repetitions and practice than other students.
12. *Use massed, then distributed practice.* After ensuring that a skill, concept, or material is overlearned, space the practice and reinforcement over time, fairly frequently at first and then fading gradually.
13. *Consistently associate a given stimulus or cue with one and only one response in the early stages of learning.* Do not tell the student, "This letter sometimes says '*a*' and sometimes says '*ah.*'" Teach one sound until it is learned; teach the other sound later.
14. *Motivate the student* by reinforcing responses, varying the presentation of material, presenting materials enthusiastically, and adjusting the length of sessions according to the student's needs and attentional abilities.
15. *Limit the number of concepts presented in any one period.* Trying to learn too many new things at one time produces confusion. Introduce new material only after older material has been mastered.
16. *Arrange materials with proper cues for attention.* Set up the instructional setting and materials so as to direct the student's attention to the important information. Reduce distractions as much as possible.

Adapted from: Kirk, S. A. (1979). *Applying learning principles.* Unpublished manuscript, University of Arizona, Tucson.

A Simple Precept

Always make sure students know:

- what to do
- why they are doing it
- how to do it
- when they are done
- what to do next

From: Victoria Sperry (personal communication, November 12, 1977).

Mather, N., & Jaffe, L. (2002). *Woodcock-Johnson III: Reports, Recommendations, and Strategies.* New York: John Wiley & Sons.

RAVE-O

Retrieval Skills
Automaticity in Sublexical Processes
Vocabulary Elaboration
Engagement With Language
Orthographic Pattern Recognition

Purpose

The purpose of RAVE-O is to increase phonological and orthographic knowledge, semantic development, word-retrieval skills, and oral and reading fluency.

Summary

RAVE-O is a 70-session program that is taught in conjunction with a program of direct instruction in phonological processing. The RAVE-O program is based on the principle that a student only retrieves quickly what she or he knows well. The program is designed to increase children's knowledge and automatic use of decoding and word identification skills by teaching them to recognize common orthographic (letter) patterns instantaneously and fluently. "Magic Tricks" help children learn to segment words into smaller units, such as frequent rime patterns, initial consonant blends, and the most common prefixes and suffixes. Speed Wizard, a computer-based word identification program (Wolf & Goodman, 1998), reinforces children's daily practice of common orthographic patterns and increases the speed of their underlying visual and auditory recognition processes. RAVE-O further supports the development of reading decoding, word identification, and fluency by increasing speed and accuracy of word-retrieval skills, expanding understanding and use of new vocabulary, and improving spelling skills. RAVE-O is a new program that is currently under development and will be commercially available after the publication of this book.

Developed by: Wolf, M., Miller, L., & Donnelly, K. (2000). *RAVE-O.* Medford, MA: Tufts University.

RECIPROCAL TEACHING

Purpose

Reciprocal teaching was designed for middle school students with adequate reading decoding but low comprehension skills. The purpose is to help students develop critical thinking skills through the medium of reading. The student learns to set a purpose for reading, read for meaning, and self-monitor comprehension.

Rationale

The specific skills include: generating questions, summarizing, requesting clarification, and predicting upcoming information. Through the questioning and summarizing, the student demonstrates ability to extract key information from text. Through clarifying, the student demonstrates comprehension. Through predicting, the student uses prior knowledge as a link with incoming information.

Procedure

Explain the procedure to the student and model the steps. Subsequently, alternate in the leader role with the student.

1. The teacher and student read a segment of text.
2. The leader asks questions similar to those that would be on a test.
3. The leader summarizes the content of the segment of text.
4. The leader brings up and discusses any difficult parts of the text or material she or he did not understand. These are discussed with the partner.
5. The leader makes a prediction as to the content of the next segment of text.
6. The leader and partner read the next segment and repeat the process with the partner taking the lead.

Guidelines

1. Although you model the skills that the student needs to use within this procedure, you may need to prompt and instruct the student in asking questions about key ideas rather than details, reporting key ideas in the summary, and recognizing what was difficult about the passage.

Mather, N., & Jaffe, L. (2002). *Woodcock-Johnson III: Reports, Recommendations, and Strategies.* New York: John Wiley & Sons.

You also may need to modify parts of the task until the student can function effectively in the leader role.

2. Always provide instruction concerning questioning, summarizing, clarifying, and predicting within the context of the Reciprocal Teaching process.
3. Provide feedback consistently on the student's progress in performing the role of the leader.
4. Use Reciprocal Teaching in 30-minute sessions.

Modifications

1. Apply Reciprocal Teaching to content area materials.
2. Use Reciprocal Teaching as a listening-thinking activity where you read the material to the student. When presented orally, this technique may be used for younger students and students with reading decoding or language comprehension problems.

Adapted from: Palincsar, A. S., & Brown, A. L. (1984). Reciprocal teaching of comprehension-fostering and comprehension-monitoring activities. *Cognition and Instruction, 1,* 117–175; and Palincsar, A. S., & Brown, A. L. (1986). Interactive teaching to promote independent learning from text. *Reading Teacher, 39,* 771–777.

REPEATED READINGS

Purpose

Use the repeated readings technique to improve fluency in reading by increasing accuracy and rate. Use a graph or chart to provide visual reinforcement. This technique is appropriate for students who read slowly despite adequate word recognition, are unmotivated, or have listening comprehension ability higher than reading comprehension ability.

Procedure

1. Select a passage of from 50 to 150 words from a book that is at the student's instructional reading level.
2. Have the student read the selection orally while you time the reading and count the number of errors. Provide assistance with unknown words as needed.
3. Record the student's reading time and the number of words pronounced incorrectly on a chart. Use two different color pencils or two different symbols to differentiate the time and the number of errors (e.g., time: square, errors: circle).
4. Have the student look over the selection, reread it, and practice words that caused difficulty in the initial reading.
5. Have the student set goals for both reading speed and accuracy. Or, as an alternative, decide on a certain number of times the passage will be reread.
6. Have the student repeatedly practice reading the selection, charting progress after each trial. When the predetermined goal is reached, use a new selection and repeat the procedure.

Adapted from: Neill, K. (1979). Turn kids on with repeated reading. *Teaching Exceptional Children, 12,* 63–64; and Samuels, S. J. (1979). The method of repeated readings. *Reading Teacher, 32,* 403–408.

Repeated Readings

Number of words in passage:_____ Date: _____
Estimated Grade Level: ____
Student's Name: _____
Book: _____

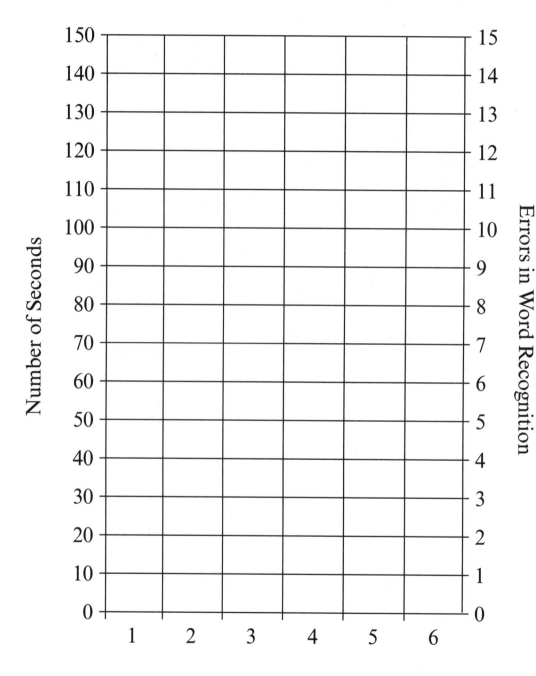

Mather, N., & Jaffe, L. (2002). *Woodcock-Johnson III: Reports, Recommendations, and Strategies.* New York: John Wiley & Sons.

REQUEST PROCEDURE

The purposes of this reciprocal questioning procedure are to help students set their own goals for reading and to teach students to raise questions independently. Before beginning, discuss with the student a purpose for reading the selection.

Procedure

Throughout the session, model questioning behavior and provide direct feedback to the student regarding the quality of his/her questions. Questions may require factual recall, recognition, evaluation, and critical thinking. As the procedure is continued, ask questions that will help the student integrate and evaluate what is being read.

Steps

1. Ask the student to read the first sentence of a passage silently.
2. Close the book and have the student ask questions about the sentence and what it means.
3. Ask further questions to enhance the student's understanding. Model good questioning behavior. In addition to asking detail questions about the passage, ask questions that require the student to relate personal experiences and prior knowledge to information in the passage.
4. Continue the process sentence by sentence until the student can make a reasonable prediction of what is going to happen in the rest of the selection. At this point, say: "Finish the selection to see if you were correct."
5. After the student has completed the passage, discuss whether the initial purpose raised was the best one for the selection.

Adapted from: Manzo, A. V. (1969). The ReQuest procedure. *Journal of Reading, 13,* 123–126; and Manzo, A. V. (1985). Expansion modules for the ReQuest, CAT, GRP, and REAP reading/study procedures. *Journal of Reading, 28,* 498–502.

REQUEST PROCEDURE—MODIFIED

Purpose

The purpose of this modified ReQuest procedure is to help students develop verbal reasoning abilities and build active reading skills. This approach is appropriate for older students with more advanced reading skills.

Preparation

Choose a literature selection at the student's independent reading level that is short enough that it can be finished by the end of the teaching session. Prepare comprehension questions pertaining to the selection or use questions provided in the teacher's manual or text. Include a mixture of literal, inferential, and evaluative questions.

Procedure

1. Read the first two paragraphs of the selection with the student, using the following procedure:
   a. the teacher and student read the first sentence silently;
   b. the student asks as many questions as he or she can think of about the first sentence and the teacher answers each question;
   c. the teacher asks as many questions as possible pertaining to the first sentence and the student answers or tells why a question cannot be answered. If the question can be answered, the teacher provides the answer. Proceed sentence by sentence through two paragraphs.
2. After two paragraphs have been read, write a question (teacher or student) pertaining to the outcome of the story or chapter and have the student attempt to answer it.
3. Have the student finish reading the selection silently and then answer the outcome question.
4. Have the student answer the comprehension questions orally (to the teacher or on tape) or in writing. Allow the student to choose the mode of response.
5. Determine the percent of accuracy on the questions and record the results on a chart.
6. Have the student reread parts of the selection to correct

Mather, N., & Jaffe, L. (2002). *Woodcock-Johnson III: Reports, Recommendations, and Strategies.* New York: John Wiley & Sons.

any incorrect responses and then answer any missed questions orally.

When the student consistently reaches 80% accuracy on the comprehension questions, increase the difficulty of the materials.

Adapted from: Alley, G. R., & Hori, K. O. (1981). *Effects of teaching a questioning strategy on reading comprehension of learning disabled adolescents* (Report No. 52). Lawrence, KS: Institute for Research in Learning Disabilities, University of Kansas; and Manzo, A. V. (1969). The ReQuest procedure. *Journal of Reading, 13,* 123–126.

RESPONSE-COST

(See also: Strategies: Classroom Behavioral Interventions and Strategies: Token Economy Systems)

Many students with ADHD tend to respond better and more consistently to behavioral intervention programs that emphasize positive reinforcement but also include mild negative consequences. Examples of negative consequences include: redirection to the task at hand; gentle but firm reprimands to stop a current behavior; loss of privileges; loss of interim reinforcers, such as points or tokens; or loss of a primary reinforcer, such as raisins or nickels. Before a program is initiated, the student must understand clearly the positive and negative consequences for targeted behaviors. Once the program begins, the teacher must adhere to it consistently. In this way, the rewards and consequences are not affected by the teacher's level of frustration or tolerance and the efficacy of the intervention is enhanced.

Response Cost

Response cost is a system in which the student starts out with the maximum number of reinforcers that it is possible to earn in a preset interval of time (e.g., a day, one class period). The student loses a reinforcer each time he/she demonstrates the negative target behavior (e.g., bothering another student, refusing to work). At the end of the set time, the student keeps what is left. If using interim reinforcers, the student may then exchange his or her tokens for a reward or save them for later to exchange for a "more valuable" reward.

Token Economy with Response-Cost

Using both a token economy and response cost increases on-task behaviors, independent work productivity, and academic accuracy of children with ADHD (DuPaul & Stoner, 1994). Tokens are awarded each time the student displays the positive target behavior and taken away when the student displays the negative target behavior (response-cost). For example, a student may earn four tokens each time the student raises his/her hand and waits to be recognized before speaking. The student loses one token each time he/she calls out before being recognized. Alternatively, the student can earn tokens for an interval of time during which he/she has stayed on task (e.g., 5 minutes of actively working on an assignment). Use a timer and monitor the student's time so that the interval is consistent and not too long. If the student displays an off-task behavior (e.g., getting up, talking, or looking around the room) before the time is up, he/she loses a token and the timer is reset to start the next interval. At the end of the preset time, the tokens can be exchanged for tangible items, privileges, or activities.

As with any behavioral intervention system, the student must be able to meet the criteria for earning sufficient tokens to trade for a reward. Earning rewards immediately stimulates the motivation to act in such a way as to continue to earn rewards. If at any time the student is losing more tokens than he/she is earning, analyze the program to see if it is necessary to reduce or change the behavioral criteria, shorten the intervals between rewards, or provide more attractive incentives.

SELF-MANAGEMENT STRATEGY FOR IMPROVING ADOLESCENT BEHAVIOR

Purpose

The Self-Management Behavioral Intervention is a systematic method for teaching students with behavioral difficulties to judge their behaviors as they are judged by others. Initially, teach this technique in a specific and limited time period such as one class. A limited time and setting allow the student to learn the procedure, assuring immediate success and providing the opportunity for the teacher to give corrective feedback as necessary. Only when the technique has been mastered in the training setting is the student guided to generalize it into other settings. Continue rewards throughout all phases of the technique.

Mather, N., & Jaffe, L. (2002). *Woodcock-Johnson III: Reports, Recommendations, and Strategies.* New York: John Wiley & Sons.

Procedure

1. Identify one to three specific behaviors requiring improvement. State these in positive terms. Examples: accepting classroom assignments courteously, starting assignments promptly, staying in seat, asking for help when stuck or confused on an assignment, handling irritating situations without anger. Many students need to be taught what specific behaviors comprise more general behavioral expectations. For example, "accepting classroom assignments courteously" includes looking at the person handing out materials, maintaining a pleasant facial expression, making sure the materials don't "fall" on the floor, and either listening to directions or starting work promptly.

2. Decide on times or class periods in which the situation lends itself to the requirements of the technique (e.g., the student evidences problems with one or more of the targeted behaviors, the teacher is able to meet individually with the student four times during the class).

3. Divide the class period into approximately four equal intervals (usually about 15 minutes), at the end of which the teacher uses a 6-point scale to rate the student's overall performance on the behaviors. Five indicates excellent behavior, three indicates mostly acceptable behavior with some minor problems, zero is unacceptable. (See Table 1.) Consistency in the criteria the teacher uses to rate the behaviors is critical as the student must be able to learn to match the teacher's ratings.

    Instead of one rating encompassing all target behaviors, the teacher may rate each behavior for the interval (0–6), total the points, then divide by the number of behaviors. For example, if the student is being rated on two behaviors, he/she receives an average of the points awarded for each.

4. To establish a baseline, rate the student's behaviors for 4 or 5 days without his/her knowledge.

5. Introduce the technique to the student, show the student the rating charts for the previous days, explain how you rated the behavior, and set up a menu of rewards (edible, tangible, or privileges) for which he/she can trade points earned. Rewards may be provided either in school or at home. (See Strategies: Token Economy Systems.)

6. Continue to rate the student as you have been but now, at the end of each rating interval, briefly show the student the points he/she has earned and provide verbal feedback. This enables the student to maintain awareness of the expected behaviors and gives him/her more immediate feedback on the degree to which his/her behaviors meet the criteria. Continue the behavioral technique until the target behaviors are consistently at an acceptable level over a period of about 10 days. If the student argues about the number of points awarded, he/she is given a warning and loses 1 point.

7. Give the student a rating chart and have him/her begin to monitor and evaluate his/her own behavior. For each interval, the student rates his/her performance on the target behaviors, then compares his/her points with the teacher's. If the student's rating is within 1 point of the teacher's (either overall or for each behavior), the student keeps the points he/she awarded him/herself. If the match is exact, the student keeps the points and earns a bonus point. If the student is off by more than one point, he/she loses all points for that interval. Thus, reinforcement is based on behavioral improvement as well as matching the teacher's rating. Continue the matching phase until the student consistently matches the teacher's ratings closely enough to keep his/her points for approximately 2 weeks. Gradually, lengthen the interval over which the student rates his/her behavior until the student is rating him/herself over the whole class period.

8. Begin to fade the comparison between the teacher and student ratings by comparing every other day, then twice a week, then once a week. Change to a random schedule of comparisons so that the student is never sure of when he/she will be required to match the teacher's ratings.

One method of randomizing comparisons is to have the student throw one die. If an odd number comes up, the student and teacher compare ratings. Ratings comparisons can be gradually faded by decreasing the probability that the student will roll a "comparison" number (e.g., fade from odd numbers to only 1 or 3, to only 3). Playing cards

Table 1. Criteria for Teacher and Student Ratings in a Student Self-Management Program	
Rating	Behavioral Expectation
5 = Excellent	Followed all rules for entire time period
4 = Very Good	One violation of a rule, but minor, within the time period
3 = Average	More than one violation of rules but no serious offenses
2 = Below average	Followed rules part of the time but behavior generally unacceptable due to one or more rule violations (e.g., aggressive, noisy talking)
1 = Poor	Broke one or more rules almost entire time period or engaged in more serious inappropriate behavior most of the time
0 = Unacceptable	Broke one or more rules entire time period

Mather, N., & Jaffe, L. (2002). *Woodcock-Johnson III: Reports, Recommendations, and Strategies.* New York: John Wiley & Sons.

may be used similarly. If at any point, the student's behaviors deteriorate or the teacher judges the student's self-ratings to be inflated, resume daily comparisons.

Although some students may eventually be able to maintain behavioral improvement without external reinforcers, students with ADHD are likely to require primary reinforcers indefinitely to sustain motivation.

Alternatively, criteria for work accuracy or completion can be added to each point level; however, in doing so, the teacher must take into account the level of work assigned relative to the student's capabilities (e.g., independent, instructional, or frustration level). Different behaviors targeted for modification will require adaptations in the wording of the performance criteria.

Adapted from: Rhode, G., Morgan, D. P., & Young, K. R. (1983). *Generalization and maintenance of treatment gains of behaviorally handicapped students from resource rooms to regular classrooms using self-evaluation procedures. Journal of Applied Behavioral Analysis, 16,* 171–188; and Shapiro, E. S., DuPaul, G. J., & Bradley-Klug, K. L. (1998). Self-management as a strategy to improve the classroom behavior of adolescents with ADHD. *Journal of Learning Disabilities, 31,* 545–555.

For more detailed information on implementing self-management techniques, see Shapiro, E. S., & Cole, C. L. (1994). *Behavior change in the classroom: Self-management interventions.* New York: Guilford; and Young, K. R., West, R. P., Smith, D. J., & Morgan, D. P. (2000). *Teaching self-management strategies to adolescents.* Longmont, CO: Sopris West.

SEMANTIC FEATURE ANALYSIS: CONCEPTS

Purpose

Semantic Feature Analysis is a prelearning activity designed to activate students' prior knowledge of a topic, introduce and organize the key concepts and vocabulary, and help the students relate new information to familiar information. This approach was designed for use with adolescents with learning disabilities in content area classes.

Procedure

Preparation: Developing the Relationship Chart
Having chosen a topic for study, the teacher reads the material to be introduced to the class and identifies the most important concepts. The teacher chooses vocabulary that

Consumer Credit

		Main Ideas					
+ positive relationship − negative relationship 0 unrelated ? unsure Key Vocabulary		Definition of credit	How to qualify for credit	Advantages of having credit	Problems related to credit	Consumer protection	Business protection
payment terms		+	0	+	+	+	+
Truth-in-Lending Law		0	?	0	?	+	0
balance (of a debt)		?	+	?	0	0	+
credit risk		0	+	?	+	0	+
credit reporting bureau		0	+	+	?	−	+
Fair Credit Reporting Act (1971)		?	?	?	?	?	0
Equal Credit Opportunity Act (1974)		0	+	?	0	?	0
credit record		0	+	?	+	0	+
starter account		+	+	0	0	+	+
credit rating		0	+	?	?	?	+
finance charges (interest)		+	+	−	+	?	+
consumer		+	0	+	0	+	0

Figure IV.9   Example Relationship Chart for Semantic Feature Analysis: Concepts

will be necessary for the students to know in order to understand the key concepts. The teacher then omits the vocabulary that the students are likely to know already. The teacher now develops a relationship chart—a grid with the key concepts written across the top, key vocabulary listed down the side (see Figure IV.9 for an example chart), and a code at the top of the page:

+ positive relationship
− negative relationship
0 no relationship
? unsure, need more information

Each student receives a copy of the relationship chart and the teacher uses an overhead projector for the model chart.

Introducing the Concepts and Vocabulary
The teacher introduces the main topic and encourages discussion concerning students' knowledge of and experience with the topic. For example, in a consumer education class, the teacher might introduce a unit on credit. Students then would discuss what they know about credit. The teacher introduces the key concepts across the top of the relationship chart, encouraging discussion and predictions on how each concept relates to the main topic. If students are unable to generate adequate definitions, the teacher explains the key concepts to them. The teacher introduces the key vocabu-

Mather, N., & Jaffe, L. (2002). *Woodcock-Johnson III: Reports, Recommendations, and Strategies.* New York: John Wiley & Sons.

lary, encouraging discussion and predictions as to how each word relates to the main concept. Again, discussion is guided so that the teacher helps the students generate the definitions of the words or tells them the definition.

Predicting Relationships

Starting with the first word in the vocabulary list, the teacher guides discussion and tries to gain consensus regarding the relationship between the vocabulary and each of the key concepts. The students may decide that the relationship between the two is positive or negative, or that no relationship exists between the two. If the class does not have sufficient knowledge of a vocabulary/concept pair to make a good prediction, a question mark is placed in the box. Students are always required to provide support for their decisions. When all of the vocabulary/concept relationships have been discussed, the students read the assignment with the intention of verifying their predictions, changing incorrect predictions, and finding information to help them fill in the boxes with question marks.

Correcting/Confirming Predictions

After reading, the teacher and students review the chart, confirming correct responses and changing responses where necessary.

Comments

Research with adolescents with learning disabilities demonstrated that Semantic Feature Analysis is more effective than traditional vocabulary study strategies for learning of new vocabulary and conceptual comprehension of text.

Adapted from: Anders, P. L., & Bos, C. S. (1986). Semantic feature analysis: An interactive strategy for vocabulary and text comprehension. *Journal of Reading, 29,* 610–616; and Bos, C. S., Anders, P. L., Filip, D., & Jaffe, L. E. (1989). The effects of an interactive strategy for enhancing reading comprehension and content area learning for students with learning disabilities. *Journal of Learning Disabilities, 22,* 384–390.

SEMANTIC FEATURE ANALYSIS: VOCABULARY

Purpose

The purpose of this activity is to guide students in analyzing the meanings of specific words while integrating the meanings of new words into their vocabularies. When introducing this activity, use concrete categories that are within the experience of the students. Later, progress to less familiar or more abstract categories.

Procedure

1. Select a category that relates to a topic to be studied or a reading selection. Select keywords related to the topic.
2. Make a chart with a topic heading at the top, keywords listed down the side, and columns across the page. Head some of the columns with terms that represent features shared by some of the words. Example:

Transportation in History				
	wheels	engine	speed	cost
horses	–	–	–	–
bicycle	+	–	–	–
car	+	+	+	+
train	+	+	+	+
airplane	+	+	+	+

3. Have the students place a plus or minus sign in each column across from each word, depending on whether or not the word has the feature heading the column. A question mark may be used if the student does not know.
4. Have the students discuss each word, tell why they chose a plus or minus, and explain how the word is similar to or different from the other words on the list.
5. Provide the planned lesson (e.g., lecture, reading, video).
6. Based on the information in the lesson, have the students change the signs in the matrix or fill in those that have question marks or were left blank.
7. Guide a discussion about the relationship between the words and features. During the discussion, use a class chart shown on an overhead projector or drawn on the board and fill in the signs that have attained group consensus.

Optional Steps

The following steps may be included after Steps 3 or 7:

1. Have the students add words to the list that fit the category.
2. Have the students add shared features in the empty columns.

3. Have the students complete the matrix with pluses and minuses.

Modification

When students become familiar with this activity, they may use a 10-point scale, rather than pluses or minuses, to indicate the degree of relationship between words and features (Johnson & Pearson, 1984).

Adapted from: Johnson, D. D., & Pearson, P. D. (1984). *Teaching reading vocabulary* (2nd ed.). New York: Holt, Rinehart, and Winston.

SEMANTIC MAPS: ADVANCE ORGANIZERS

Purpose

This technique is used to help students relate unknown information to known so that it is more easily understood and retained.

Procedure

1. Write the topic to be studied on the board in a complete sentence (e.g., Life abounds in the desert) and any words with which the students may be unfamiliar. Select new vocabulary that represents the most important concepts of the new unit.
2. Discuss the meanings of the new vocabulary and encourage students to share knowledge of and experience with any of the concepts. Encourage all students to participate.
3. Using the vocabulary, ask the students to identify which words go together in some way. Have them explain their rationale for the groupings they suggest. Group the words as suggested.
4. Ask students to provide a label for each group that describes the relationship among the words. These labels become the coordinate concepts associating the details (subordinate concepts) with the major topic (superordinate concept).
5. As the students suggest groupings and labels, generate a semantic map.

Follow-up Activity

Leave the map on the board or copy it onto a transparency or paper for later use. After the unit is presented, go back to the original map and: (a) add information and rearrange the map using the new information learned in the unit or (b) work in small groups to add information and rearrange the original map. Make transparencies for an overhead projector of the final map so that each group can present them to the class and explain the changes and why they made them.

SEMANTIC MAPS: EVALUATING/ACTIVATING PRIOR KNOWLEDGE

Purpose

This technique is used to activate and evaluate students' prior knowledge regarding the topic to be studied.

Steps

1. Write the major concept to be studied (superordinate concept) on the board.
2. Ask the students to brainstorm all words and phrases they associate with the topic, making sure that everyone participates. List all student responses on the board.
3. Ask the students to identify which words/phrases go together in some way. Have them explain their rationale for the groupings they suggest. Group together the words/phrases.
4. Ask students to label the groups. These labels become the coordinate concepts associating the details (subordinate concepts) with the superordinate concept.
5. As the students suggest groupings and labels, generate a semantic map.
6. Based on the students' responses to the mapping activity, decide whether or not preteaching of concepts and related vocabulary is necessary before presenting the unit or assigning the reading.

Modification for Evaluating Prior Knowledge

Based on the students' responses to the mapping activity, decide whether or not preteaching of concepts and related vocabulary is necessary before presenting the unit or assigning the reading.

Adapted from: Bos, C. S., & Vaughn, S. (2001). *Strategies for teaching students with learning and behavior problems* (5th ed.). Boston: Allyn and Bacon.

Mather, N., & Jaffe, L. (2002). *Woodcock-Johnson III: Reports, Recommendations, and Strategies.* New York: John Wiley & Sons.

SIGHT WORD ASSOCIATION PROCEDURE (SWAP)

Purpose

The SWAP procedure is a supplemental activity for teaching sight vocabulary.

Preparation

Make up flash cards with the student's words typed or neatly written, one to a card.

1. Prior to teaching, discuss the meaning of the words with the student.
2. Present each word for 5 seconds and say the word twice.
3. Shuffle the cards and ask the student to read each word as you show the flash card.
4. Supply the correct response if the student makes an error or doesn't respond within 5 seconds.
5. Repeat Step 2.

Continue until the student easily identifies all words. To aid retention, review the words for several days. As words are learned, file them in a word box.

Adapt this procedure by using flash cards with a word and picture on one side and only the word on the other side.

Adapted from: Bos, C. S., & Vaughn, S. (2001). *Strategies for teaching students with learning and behavior problems* (5th ed.). Boston: Allyn and Bacon.

SIX SYLLABLE STRUCTURES IN ENGLISH

SYLLABLE TYPE*	Examples	Explanation
Closed vc vc/cv	rabbit comment napkin	In a 1-syllable word, a single vowel is followed by a consonant. In a multisyllable word, single vowels are separated by at least 2 consonants. The vowel sound in a closed syllable is usually short.
Open v/cv	moment radar locate	An open syllable ends with a vowel. Only 1 consonant (or none) separates the vowel from the next syllable. The vowel sound is usually long.
R-controlled vR	bird port car	When followed by *r*, a vowel often loses its identity as long or short. It is coarticulated with the /*r*/ sound.
Vowel team vv	great boat cow out haul	Many vowel sounds are spelled with 2 adjacent vowel letters (e.g., *ai, ay, ee, ea, oi, oy, oa, au, aw, ew, ue, oo, ie, ei*). Vowel teams may represent the sounds of long or short vowels or vowel diphthongs. They may be followed by consonants or used at the end of a syllable.
Vowel-silent *e* vcE	like gate decide completely	These syllables spell the long vowel sound with a vowel–consonant–silent *e* pattern.
Consonant-*le*	table maple bubble little	If the syllabic /*l*/ comes at the end of a word and is preceded by a consonant, the consonant is usually part of that syllable. The nature of the preceding vowel determines if a doubled consonant is needed before the consonant-*le* (e.g., *little* requires a double consonant because the preceeding vowel sound is short, indicating a closed syllable; *bugle* requires a single consonant because the preceeding vowel sound is long, indicating an open syllable).

*v = vowel, c = consonant.

Mather, N., & Jaffe, L. (2002). *Woodcock-Johnson III: Reports, Recommendations, and Strategies.* New York: John Wiley & Sons.

SOFTWARE SELECTION TIPS

Tip 1–Choose software with limited distractions. Students with learning difficulties are prone to be distracted by too much stimuli on the screen at one time. Moreover, too many images, sounds, and animated activities can distract from the concept, skill, or procedure being studied. Choose programs that use simple screen displays and sounds that reinforce learning.

Tip 2–Choose procedures that match those being taught in school. Many students with learning difficulties get confused if the same task is presented in different ways, particularly in the early stages of learning. The method used by the software program for introducing or reinforcing concepts, skills, and procedures may be substantially different from the method of presentation used in the classroom. Weigh the other advantages of the software before introducing this type of conflict. If you decide to use software with differing procedures, take the time to point out the differences carefully and be ready to assist if confusion arises.

Tip 3–Choose modifiable software. Software that can be modified regarding speed, instructional levels, number of problems/questions requiring a response before moving to the next level, and content of activity (e.g., specific sight words, syllable structures, multiplication facts) will serve the needs of a wide range of students in a single classroom or an individual student over a long period of time. Sometimes requiring a speedy response is motivating but often it discourages careful thought and prevents a well-considered response. The difference depends on the student's personality and level of facility with the task.

Tip 4–Choose software with small increments between levels. Most software designed for typical students makes rather large jumps in difficulty from one level to the next. This is particularly true of retail software that purports to cover the entire K–8 curriculum within a subject area. Students with learning difficulties will often test out of Level 1 but then fail miserably on Level 2 because the tasks have gotten too difficult too fast. Special education publishers are more aware of this difficulty and incorporate smaller increments between levels. The other solution is to choose software that is specific to a student's current level of instruction.

Tip 5–Choose software with helpful feedback. Educational software should provide clues to the correct answer when a student makes an error; software that simply indicates a student is wrong is less helpful.

Tip 6–Choose software that limits the number of wrong answers for a single question or problem. A sure formula for creating student frustration is to require a student to guess repeatedly on a question or problem he or she doesn't know. It's also a sure formula for encouraging random guessing and other nonthinking behavior. The best software will limit the number of attempts, give clues as to the correct answer, provide the correct answer, and then reintroduce that same item at a later time. Test this feature on a software program by making deliberate errors.

Tip 7–Choose software with good record-keeping capabilities. We know that informative performance feedback can help students understand their errors and help them set realistic but challenging goals. Choose software that keeps records for each student. Young children might be told how many items out of the total number were correct. Older students can be given percentages correct. Ideally, information is made available on the types of tasks or questions that caused difficulties.

Tip 8–Choose software with built-in instructional aids. Guidance in figuring out the correct answer, or in understanding the process that would have led to the correct answer, can be extremely helpful. Some programs are constructed so that when a student gives a wrong response, he or she has the option of requesting guidance to the correct answer and earning partial credit. For example, the program moves step-by-step through the solution of the problem or task, asking a question at each step and giving the student feedback on his or her response.

Tip 9–Remember software is a learning tool—not the total solution! Instructional software is a tool in effective instruction and learning. With color, graphics, animation, sound and interactivity, it can capture and hold the attention of students so that they persist in tasks. When modifiable, it can support learning at the student's pace and on the student's level. It is important, however, for direct teacher instruction to lead technology-assisted instruction or reinforcement. Ensure that concept development and instruction in specific skills and procedures precede software use. Pencil-and-paper tasks still have a role to play in student learning. Although software can support student learning in a positive manner, software can rarely stand on its own. Instruction must precede software use and then extend beyond the software to help the student apply the concepts, skills, and procedures in many new settings.

Adapted from: Babbitt, B. C. (2000). 10 tips for software selection for math instruction (LD Online Reprint). *The LDA Gram, 34*(2), 11–12.

Mather, N., & Jaffe, L. (2002). *Woodcock-Johnson III: Reports, Recommendations, and Strategies.* New York: John Wiley & Sons.

SPEED DRILLS FOR READING FLUENCY AND BASIC SKILLS

Purpose

While most reading fluency techniques are intended to be used with text at the student's independent reading level, speed drills are developed at the instructional level. Speed drills provide practice in speeded recognition and pronunciation of word parts, word patterns, or whole words. Their purpose is to increase reading fluency by developing automaticity in recognizing the common spelling patterns in words and recalling the corresponding sounds. Speed drills are generally tailored to the needs of individual students but can be used for groups.

Materials

Stopwatch or timer
Pencil or pen
Progress chart

Preparation

1. Prepare speed drills (student and teacher copies). Target one specific skill the student has already learned but still makes frequent errors in, or hesitates before reading. Alternatively, you may have the student practice speed drills on all skills after the student has received instruction and understands the concept or rule but lacks automaticity with the patterns. These may include pronunciation of individual letters, common letter combinations, syllable types, spelling patterns, and/or sight words.
   Examples include:

   vowel teams: *oa, oi, oo, ou, oy*
   phonics rules: soft *g* vs. hard *g*
   consonant digraphs: *sh, ch, th, wh, ph*
   common endings: *ing, tion, able, ive*
   syllabication rules: vc/cv
   discriminating between syllable types: *pin/pine, glob/globe*
   sight words: *what, who, when, where, though, through*

2. Make a list of examples of the targeted skill. The number of examples depends on the skill. For example, if the ob-

ject is to pronounce short vowel sounds, only 6 items are possible. If the object is to recognize a specific syllable type, 10 to 15 examples might be used. If the student is to practice sight word recognition, the number will depend on the how many words a student can handle at one time.

   If you want the student to learn to discriminate between two patterns (e.g., hard c and soft c; closed syllable words and long vowel–consonant–*e* words), include examples of both.

3. Type them in 10 rows of 6 items each, in random order, repeating items as needed. Make a copy so that you and the student each have your own. Make sure that the student's copy is in a font and size that is easy to read.

Baseline Data

1. Before initiating speed drills, choose a book on the student's instructional level. Select two passages of approximately 300 words each and make a teacher copy for tracking errors.
2. Tape the student reading the passages aloud. For each passage, time the student's reading and mark any errors.
3. Calculate the number of words read correctly per minute and average the results of both passages. Errors include mispronunciations, substitutions, repetitions, partial repetitions, self-corrections, and omissions. Note, but do not count, omission of punctuation.
4. Keep the tape for later comparison.

Steps

1. Explain to the student that the drills are an activity that will help him or her recognize words faster and more easily.
2. Remind the student of the skill or rule on which the speed drill focuses (e.g., short vowel sounds; *c* followed by *i, e,* or *y* is soft).
3. Tell the student to read as fast as possible without making mistakes across the rows of items (left to right, moving down the page). The student has 1 minute to read as many items as possible.
4. The student starts out reading at a pace where he or she reads comfortably without errors. Gradually, the student will increase speed and continue without errors. If the student makes many errors because he or she is go-

Mather, N., & Jaffe, L. (2002). *Woodcock-Johnson III: Reports, Recommendations, and Strategies.* New York: John Wiley & Sons.

ing too fast, the exercise will not help the student improve.

5. Have the student start reading. On the teacher copy, mark each item on which the student makes an error, including stumbling on an item and/or self-corrections. Stop the drill after exactly 1 minute.

Documenting Progress

1. Chart the number of items that the student read correctly within the allotted time. The student should practice the speed drill independently three times daily but only the first reading of the day is charted.
2. The goal is for the student to read 60 items within 60 seconds with only one or two errors. When the student has achieved this, you may either proceed to another speed drill or use other speed drills for the same skill if you think that the student needs practice on a wider range of examples.

    For some students, 60 items in 60 seconds is not a sufficient level of fluency. For them, you may create speed drills with more items. For example, 90 items in 60 seconds increases the student's speed from 1 item/second to 1½ items/second.
3. At monthly intervals, repeat the fluency probe on the same book, using different passages. Try to use passages with approximately the same format, for example, limited or no dialogue. Document progress in the number of words read correctly per minute and share the information with the student. If the progress is noticeable on the new tape, listen to both tapes with the student, pointing out the differences.

Sample Speed Drill for Hard and Soft G

god	gallon	glad	gyp	grass	gas
giblet	gum	gypsy	sing	ground	gull
gym	gentle	gist	gem	gallon	gyp
gas	gum	sing	gull	gentle	gem
god	glad	grass	giblet	gypsy	ground
gym	gist	gem	gist	gentle	gym
gull	ground	sing	gypsy	gum	giblet
gas	grass	gyp	glad	gallon	god
gist	gym	ground	gypsy	giblet	grass
glad	god	gem	gentle	gull	sing

Adapted from: Fischer, P. (1999). Getting up to speed. *Perspectives: The International Dyslexia Association, 25*(2), 12–13.

SPELLING: GENERAL TEACHING PRINCIPLES

Word Choice

1. Choose words already in the student's oral vocabulary.
2. Make sure the student understands the meaning(s) of the word.
3. Emphasize a core of high-frequency words first.
4. Group words according to spelling patterns.
5. Pretest. Don't assign words the student already knows how to spell. Use study time for new words and reinforcement of previously learned words.

Method

1. Highlight any differences between what is seen and what is said.
2. Always have the student write from memory—never copy—then check for accuracy.
3. Work on immediate and delayed recall.
4. Consistently retest and reteach previous words.
5. Present two or three new words a day—or every other day—rather than a whole list at the beginning of the week. Determine with the student how many words he/she can learn in one session.

Materials

1. Study cards: The spelling word must be typed or written large and neatly.
2. Provide a computer/word processor if the student has visual–motor problems that interfere significantly with neat handwriting.
3. Use a flow word list.

Generalization

1. Integrate use of spelling words into daily class work.
2. Teach use of "bad spellers" dictionary, picture dictionary, or Franklin Spelling Ace if the student can approximate a phonetic spelling.
3. Teach the student how to proofread.

Mather, N., & Jaffe, L. (2002). *Woodcock-Johnson III: Reports, Recommendations, and Strategies.* New York: John Wiley & Sons.

SPELLING RULES: 43 CONSISTENT GENERALIZATIONS ABOUT THE ENGLISH LANGUAGE

I Introduced
M Mastered

I   M

____   ____ 1. Silent "*e*" on the end of a word usually makes the preceding vowel long (e.g., *name, Pete, time, home, mule, compose, imitate* [Silent e syllable]). See the Six Basic Syllable Patterns Overview.

____   ____ 2. Use "-*ck*" for /*k*/ at the end of one-syllable words after one short vowel (e.g., *back, deck, sick, clock, chuck*).

____   ____ 3. Use "-*tch*" for /*ch*/ at the end of a one-syllable word after one short vowel (e.g., *patch, etch, ditch, blotch, clutch*). Common exceptions: *such, much, which, rich.*

____   ____ 4. Use "-*dge*" on the end of a one-syllable word for /*j*/ after one short vowel (e.g., *badge, edge, bridge, fudge, dodge*).

____   ____ 5. In one-syllable words, double the final "*l, f, s, z*" after one short vowel (e.g., *tell, mill, fluff, bluff, pass, muss, fizz, fuzz*).

____   ____ 6. A single vowel in the middle of a syllable is usually short (e.g., *picnic, not, cabin* [Closed syllable]).

____   ____ 7. A vowel at the end of a syllable is usually long (e.g., *va/ca/tion, pre/tend, be/tween, pi/lot, lo/cate* [Open syllable]).

____   ____ 8. When a vowel comes before a double consonant, it is almost always short (e.g., *stripper, striper, supper, super*).

____   ____ 9. When two consonants stand between two vowels, the syllable division usually occurs between the two consonants (e.g., *nap/kin, ten/nis, but/ter*).

____   ____ 10. When one consonant stands between two vowels, the consonant may belong in the first syllable or it may belong in the second syllable (e.g., *trav/el, be/long, re/bel, reb/el*).

____   ____ 11. When three consonants stand between two vowels, the division occurs between a blend and the other consonants (e.g., *mon/ster, pump/kin*).

____   ____ 12. Separate prefixes and suffixes as syllables (e.g., *trans/port/a/tion*).

____   ____ 13. The letter "*c*" has the soft sound of /*s*/ when e, i, or y follows it (e.g., *city, center, cyclone*).

____   ____ 14. The letter "*g*" has the soft sound of /*j*/ when e, i, or y follows it (e.g., *gentle, ginger, gym*).

____   ____ 15. In a one-syllable word, with one short vowel, ending in one consonant, double the final consonant before adding a suffix beginning with a vowel (*-ing, -y,* or *-ed*) (e.g., *drop, dropping, dropped; sad, sadder, saddest; man, mannish; sin, sinner, sinning*). Keep the final consonant when adding a suffix beginning with a consonant (e.g., *sadly, manly, sinful* [1+1+1 generalization]).

____   ____ 16. Generalization 15 also applies to the final syllable in two- or three-syllable words, if the final syllable is accented (e.g., *confer, conferring; omit, omitted; begin, beginning* [2+1+1 generalization]).

____   ____ 17. Usually drop the final "-*e*" on words when you add a suffix beginning with a vowel (e.g., *late, later; shine, shiner; fame, famous*). Keep the final "-*e*" when adding suffixes beginning with a consonant (e.g., *homeless, movement* [Silent e generalization]).

____   ____ 18. If a word ends in a consonant followed by a "*y*," change the final "-*y*" to "-*i*" whenever adding suffixes unless the suffix begins with an "*i*" or the "*y*" has a vowel in front of it (e.g., *try, tried, trying; rely, relied, reliable, relying; play, playing, played, player* [y to i generalization]).

____   ____ 19. Use "*i*" before "*e*" except after "*c*," or when it says /*a*/ as in *neighbor* or *weigh* (e.g., *priest, chief, receive, ceiling, vein, freight*).

____   ____ 20. Use "*c*" for the final /*k*/ sound when the word has two or more syllables (e.g., *magic, terrific, Atlantic*).

____   ____ 21. Use double "*s*" after one short vowel in one-syllable words [see generalization 5] (e.g., *glass*). Use "-*se*" so words aren't confused as plurals (e.g., *grease, grouse, house*).

Mather, N., & Jaffe, L. (2002). *Woodcock-Johnson III: Reports, Recommendations, and Strategies.* New York: John Wiley & Sons.

___ ___ 22. Never end a word with a single "*z*." Double the final "*z*" when it follows one short vowel in a one-syllable word [see generalization 5]. Use "*ze*" after a long vowel sound or a double vowel (e.g., *buzz, freeze*).

___ ___ 23. "*Ai*" is most often followed by an "*n*" or "*l*" or "*d*" (e.g., *rain, sail, aid*).

___ ___ 24. "*Oa*" is almost always used in one-syllable words (e.g., *boar, roast, oat*).

___ ___ 25. "*Q*" is always followed by a "*u*" and at least one other vowel (e.g., *quit, quiet*). "*V*" and "*x*" are never doubled. "*X*" is never followed by an "*s*."

___ ___ 26. No words in English end in "*v*." They end with "*ve*," no matter whether the vowel is long or short (e.g., *have, gave, drove*). The "silent *e*" generalization is not consistent with "*v*" words.

___ ___ 27. To keep the hard sound for "*g*," follow the "*g*" with a "*u*" when used before an "*i*" or "*e*" (e.g., *guess, guide, guest*).

___ ___ 28. "*Igh*," "*ough*," and "*augh*" are usually followed by a "*t*" (e.g., *night, ought, caught*).

___ ___ 29. For most words, add "*s*" to make them plural (e.g., *oats, dogs, cars*).

___ ___ 30. When nouns end in "*s*," "*x*," "*z*," "*ch*," and "*sh*," add "*es*" to make them plural (e.g., *gases, taxes, buzzes, marches, brushes*). The /*ez*/ will be heard as an extra syllable.

___ ___ 31. Nouns ending in a vowel "-*y*" combination (*ay, oy, ey*) are made plural by adding "*s*" (e.g., *days, boys, keys*). Nouns ending in a consonant "-*y*" combination (*dy, ny*) are made plural by changing the "*y*" to "*i*" and adding "*es*" (e.g., *lady, ladies; pony, ponies*).

___ ___ 32. Most nouns ending in "*f*" or "*fle*" form their plurals by adding "*s*" (e.g., *roofs, rifles*).

___ ___ 33. Nouns ending in a vowel "-*o*" combination are made plural by adding "*s*" (e.g., *radios, studios*). Nouns ending in a consonant "-*o*" combination have no generalization, therefore, the dictionary must be used in each case.

___ ___ 34. Some common nouns have irregular plural forms (e.g., *man, men; mouse, mice; tooth, teeth; leaf, leaves*).

___ ___ 35. Use "-*est*" for the suffix when comparing three or more things (e.g., *tallest, youngest, nicest*). Use the "-*ist*" for people (nouns) who do things (e.g., *artist, projectionist, humanist*).

___ ___ 36. (1) For the suffix sound /*n*/ that indicates a person, a nationality, or a religion, use "-*an*" (e.g., *American, Lutheran*). (2) Use "-*ian*" when it sounds /*eyun*/ (e.g., *Indian, Cambodian*). (3) For the suffix saying the sound /*n*/, having a verbish quality, usually use "-*en*" (e.g., *ripen, redden, deaden*).

___ ___ 37. Use "-*ous*" as the suffix when the word is an adjective (e.g., *dangerous, marvelous*). Use "-*us*" when the word is a noun (e.g., *sinus, ruckus*).

___ ___ 38. Use "-*ize*" as the suffix to add to whole words or to roots (e.g., *modernize, authorize, criticize*).

___ ___ 39. "*Cise*" is a common Latin root and not really a suffix at all because the rest of the word cannot stand alone. The root "*cise*" means "to cut," but only makes sense when used with a prefix (e.g., *incise, excise*).

___ ___ 40. Usually use "-*er*" as a suffix for one-syllable words when you mean a person who "does" (e.g., *diner, jumper, hopper, runner*). Use "-*or*" for two or more syllable words when you mean a person or thing that "does" (e.g., *professor, editor, incinerator*). *Tractor, doctor,* and *actor* are common exceptions. Use "-*ar*" to form an adjective (e.g., *singular, regular, popular*). All others use "-*ure*" (e.g., *manure*).

___ ___ 41. Usually use the suffix "-*able*" when you are adding to a whole word and it means "able" (e.g., *serviceable, workable, manageable*) or when the root ends in a hard "*c*" or "*g*" (e.g., *despicable*). Use the suffix "-*ible*" when adding to a root (e.g., *visible, edible*) or when the root ends in a soft "*c*" or "*g*" (e.g., *forcible, legible*).

___ ___ 42. These suffixes mean people who do: -*ist*, -*ee*, -*cian*, -*eer*, -*ier*, -*er* (added to one syllable), -*or* (added to two or more syllables), and -*ess* (means female) (e.g., *pianist, employee, physician, engineer, brigadier, runner, editor, princess*).

___ ___ 43. Use "*wr*" as opposed to "*r*" for words that imply the meaning "twist" (e.g., *wrench, wrestle, wrist, write, wrought, wrap, wrong, wreck, wry*).

Developed by: C. Wilson Anderson, Jr., MAT, Educational Tutorial Consortium, 4400 South 44th Street, Lincoln, Nebraska 68516.

Mather, N., & Jaffe, L. (2002). *Woodcock-Johnson III: Reports, Recommendations, and Strategies.* New York: John Wiley & Sons.

SQ3R: SURVEY, QUESTION, READ, RECITE, REVIEW

Purpose

The purpose of the Survey, Question, Read, Recite, Review (SQ3R) study procedure is to provide a student with a systematic, efficient strategy that promotes independent study skills. The method is most appropriate for students in grade 4 and above who are studying content chapters in textbooks.

Procedure

1. Survey
Skim or preview the chapter to gain a general understanding of the chapter. Read introductory paragraphs, all headings, pictures, captions, graphs, summary paragraphs, and any comprehension questions. Attempt to determine what the chapter is about and the kind of information that the author is presenting. Depending upon reading proficiency and the length and complexity of the chapter, the student spends from 5 to 15 minutes on this step.

2. Question
Locate each boldface heading in the chapter and turn it into a question. This step provides more detailed study of the chapter and provides a purpose for reading the material.

3. Read
As soon as the questions are formulated, read to locate the answers. Begin with the first subtopic and find the answer. Move then to the next step of the procedure.

4. Recite
Pause and review the answer to the question. Paraphrase the answer to the question. Outline or underline the important material or write brief notes in a notebook for later review and study. Repeat Steps 2–4 with each question from the chapter.

5. Review
After completing the final subtopic of the chapter, rehearse the major points in the reading for about 5 minutes. Read each heading in the chapter and attempt to recall the major points. To aid in retention, review the material again at a later time.

Adapted from: Robinson, F. P. (1970). *Effective study* (5th ed.). New York: Harper & Row; and Tierney, R. J., & Readence, J. E. (1999). *Reading strategies and practices: A compendium* (5th ed.). Boston: Allyn and Bacon.

STORE THE STORY

Purpose

The purposes of this strategy are to improve comprehension, retrieval, and retelling of fiction or nonfiction stories by identifying consistent components, as well as to improve writing of stories by providing an outline or story frame.

Description

STORE is an acronym for:

    S = Setting (Who? What? Where? When?)
    T = Trouble (What is the trouble or problem?)
    O = Order of events (What happens?)
    R = Resolution (What is done to solve the problem?)
    E = End (How does the story end?)

Procedure

A. Introduce the Cue STORE
1. Discuss the meaning of the verb "to store" (save, hold, keep for a while, put away).
2. Discuss that the purpose of the strategy is to help understand and remember (store) any story the students read by recognizing and recalling each part. The strategy may also be used as a prewriting activity for developing a story.
3. Explain the story parts: Every story has a beginning, middle, and end. Every story also has a SETTING, TROUBLE, ORDER OF EVENTS, RESOLUTION, and ENDING.

B. Demonstration/Modeling
1. Read a short story aloud to the class. Fables provide good illustrations of story grammar.
2. Write the STORE frame on the board. Fill in the parts of the story.

C. Guided Practice
1. Have the students recall fairy tales (or other stories familiar to them) and identify the parts labeled by STORE.

Mather, N., & Jaffe, L. (2002). *Woodcock-Johnson III: Reports, Recommendations, and Strategies.* New York: John Wiley & Sons.

2. Tell the students that you will read a story to them and you want them to listen for the parts in the STORE frame.

3. Read a short story aloud and have the students follow along in their books.

4. Ask the students to help fill in the STORE cue sheet. On an overhead projector, write their answers on a transparency of the STORE form.

5. Have the students take turns retelling the story using the cue sheet as a guide.

D. Independent Practice

1. Have each student read a short story at his/her independent reading level and fill in the cue sheet. You may allow the students to work in pairs. Pair poor readers with good readers.

2. Ask each student to retell the story to the group using the cue sheet as a guide.

3. Provide further practice in reading, filling in the cue sheet, and retelling the stories on subsequent days.

USING STORE THE STORY FOR WRITING

Purpose

STORE the Story may be used as a framework to help students develop and organize their own stories, helping them to include the major story elements.

Procedure

A. Demonstration/Modeling

1. Model prewriting by thinking aloud the steps of topic selection and brainstorming ideas. Brainstorm ideas for the story, fill in the STORE cue sheet, crossing out ideas and adding others.

2. Read over the cue sheet to make sure that all parts of the story make sense and fit in relation to other parts.

3. Model drafting, revising, and rewriting. Explain how the use of STORE ensures continuity of the story line.

B. Guided Practice

The teacher guides the students to create a group story using the STORE format.

C. Independent Practice

The students create their own stories.

D. Adaptations for Extra Support

1. Provide picture cards to aid in generating story ideas.

2. Provide the Setting, Trouble, and some Events. Have the students add some Events and finish the story.

3. Provide the Setting or the Trouble and have the students generate the other parts.

Adapted from: Schlegel, M., & Bos, C. S. (1986). *STORE the story: Fiction/fantasy reading comprehension and writing strategy.* Unpublished manuscript, University of Arizona, Department of Special Education, Rehabilitation, and School Psychology, Tucson.

STORE the Story

Name _____   Date _____

Working Title: _____

SETTING

  Who _____

  Where _____

  When _____

TROUBLE

_____

_____

ORDER OF   1. _____

ACTION   2. _____

          3. _____

          4. _____

          5. _____

RESOLUTION

1. _____

2. _____

3. _____

ENDING

_____

_____

_____

_____

_____

Mather, N., & Jaffe, L. (2002). *Woodcock-Johnson III: Reports, Recommendations, and Strategies.* New York: John Wiley & Sons.

STUDY GUIDES

Purpose

Study guides may be adapted and used for a variety of purposes. A study guide may focus attention on key concepts in text, foster ability to process textual information at higher cognitive levels, heighten awareness of how content might be organized, and assist with evaluation of prior knowledge or information learned.

Preparation

When preparing a study guide, the teacher must read the material carefully, decide the purpose of the study guide, and identify the key concepts. The method of construction will depend on the type of study guide the teacher decides to use.

Types of Study Guides

Several types of study guides have been identified in the literature regarding reading in the content areas. Those described most often concern levels of comprehension, organizational patterns, and specific concepts.

Three Levels of Comprehension

A three-level study guide has questions that involve literal, interpretive, and applied comprehension. Depending on how information is presented in the text, any given question may require different levels of cognitive processing. Three levels of comprehension exist: (a) literal comprehension involves identifying factual material and knowing what the author said, (b) interpretive comprehension involves inferring relationships among the details and knowing what the author meant, and (c) applied comprehension involves developing generalizations that extend beyond the assigned material (Herber, 1978).

A single question cannot be considered as requiring a certain level of comprehension. To decide the comprehension level of a question, the teacher has to consider how the information is stated in the text and the level of cognitive processing necessary for the reader to come up with an acceptable answer (Pearson & Johnson, 1978). Even a question such as, "How might local endeavors toward recycling

eventually help global conservation?" would be a literal question if this information were directly stated in the text.

The items on a study guide may include open-ended questions, true-false statements, and fill in the blank. Matching items are not recommended as the separation on the page of two related concepts interferes with easy use of the guide for studying.

The three-level study guide is relatively easy to individualize according to students' abilities. For a fairly homogeneous class, the teacher may decide to prepare questions pertinent to the key concepts at only one level of comprehension. Alternatively, the teacher may decide to mix levels of questions. When adapting the study guide for learners at different cognitive levels or reading ability, the teacher may assign certain items to certain students, matching the level of comprehension required to the student's current ability level or scaffolding a student to the next level. An example of this type of chart is shown in Figure IV.10. For extra as-

---

**EXAMPLE STUDY GUIDE:
THREE LEVELS OF COMPREHENSION**

All students are to complete questions 1–5.
Mark each of these statements: T for True or F for False

___ 1. Count Camillo di Cavour became the first King of Italy.
___ 2. Garibaldi and his army won the battle in Sicily because the enemy ran out of bullets.
___ 3. The country called Italy did not exist in the year 1880.
___ 4. Garibaldi's victorious army was well-trained and well-equipped.
___ 5. After three weeks of fighting, Italy was free.

Of the questions below, answer only those you were assigned. Please answer in complete sentences on notebook paper so that you can use your answers later as a study guide.

**6. In 1834, Garibaldi escaped from Italy under sentence of death. Why do you think he had been sentenced to die?
**7. List three words or phrases that describe Garibaldi.
***8. This chapter is entitled, "The Fight for Italy." What would another good title be?
**9. For what reason was an army sent to capture Rome and central Italy even before Garibaldi reached there?
***10. Do you think that fighting a war is the best way for people to gain freedom? If so, explain your reason.
**11. Count di Cavour and Garibaldi were very different men who often clashed with each other. Describe one important way in which they were different and one important way in which they were alike.
***12. Today, Garibaldi is considered a great hero throughout the world; Count di Cavour's name is hardly known, although he was also very important in Italy's struggle for independence. What is one good reason for the difference in their fame?

Note: All of the true/false questions are literal; those with two stars are interpretive; and those with three stars are application questions.

Figure IV.10   Example Study Guide Utilizing Three Levels of Comprehension

---

Mather, N., & Jaffe, L. (2002). *Woodcock-Johnson III: Reports, Recommendations, and Strategies.* New York: John Wiley & Sons.

sistance, the teacher may write, next to the question, the page number where the answer may be found. For learners functioning at a lower reading level, the teacher may use the same study guide with adapted materials.

Organizational Patterns

To facilitate comprehension, study guides may be designed to heighten students' awareness of text organization. Some of the more common text patterns used include: main idea/details, cause/effect, comparison/contrast, and order of events. For example, a study guide emphasizing comparison/contrast might ask the students questions about similarities and differences between World War II and the Vietnam War. For a model of cause/effect, the teacher might list specific events down one side of the page with the heading "Cause" and leave blank the other side of the page with the heading "Effect." Figure IV.11 is an example of a study guide emphasizing temporal order.

Concept Development

A teacher may use the content of text to provide practice with a specific concept; the study guide is the medium. For example, a teacher who is trying to teach the class the concept of categorization could prepare a list of words or phrases, and a list of categories representing key concepts,

---

```
┌─────────────────────────────────────────┐
│        ORGANIZATIONAL PATTERN:           │
│            TEMPORAL ORDER                │
│                                          │
│ Number the sentences below according to │
│ the order in which they occurred in the  │
│ chapter.                                 │
│ ___ In 1854, Garibaldi left the United   │
│     States to go back to Italy.          │
│ ___ Although the Italians made several   │
│     attempts to revolt, they failed      │
│     each time.                           │
│ ___ The Sardinian King was made King of  │
│     Italy.                               │
│ ___ Garibaldi's army forced the austrians│
│     to retreat.                          │
│ ___ Much of Italy wa under the control   │
│     of foreign kings.                    │
│ ___ The Sicilians fought alongside of    │
│     Garibaldi and his men.               │
└─────────────────────────────────────────┘
```

Figure IV.11   Example Study Guide Representing Organizational Patterns

---

pertaining to the text chapter they are studying. The students are directed to place each item in the first list into the appropriate category. Categories from the Civil War might include: reasons for the war, immediate outcome of the war, long-term outcomes, results nobody had expected, and effect on the economy of the South. A concept guide designed to teach context clues might name and describe three types, with the requirement that, as the student reads, she fills in examples of each of the context clues.

Alternate Formats

Study guides may be constructed in alternate formats. For example, a teacher may copy a section of text and write questions and notations about key points, structure, or a specific concept in the margin next to the related information. Or, rather than copying the passage, he/she might write questions/notations on a piece of paper that is held next to the text while the student is reading.

Activities

Reading study guides may be completed by students independently, in pairs, or in cooperative groups. Class discussion should follow completion of the study guide to reinforce the purpose of the study guide and to ensure that everyone understands the correct responses.

Cautions
- Using a study guide or the same format of a study guide too frequently may become boring for students.
- Do not grade study guides. Use them diagnostically, for example, to see if a student can discern essential information from text. Ask the student why he/she answered as he/she did.
- Use the study guide as one activity within many in introducing or working with new information. Do not rely on it alone to introduce a new topic or section of text.

Adapted from: Herber, H. L. (1978). *Teaching reading in content areas* (2nd ed.). Englewood Cliffs, NJ: Prentice-Hall.

The study guide examples were written by Edith Jaffe and based on Johnson, W., Peck, I., Plotkin, F., & Richardson, W. (1976). *The modern world.* New York: Scholastic Book Services.

"SURE I WILL" PROGRAM: INCREASING COMPLIANCE

Purpose

The "Sure I Will" program enhances compliance in the classroom by developing a behavior that is incompatible with noncompliance. This program is an effective adjunct to Precision Requests.

Procedure for Individual Student

1. The student must respond to a teacher's "Please" request with "Sure I will" and *start the behavior* before the teacher issues the second request. The second request uses the word "need" ("Now I need you to . . ."). If the student waits, he or she is not rewarded.
2. The teacher should always socially reward the student's "Sure I will" response.
3. Intermittently, the teacher may give the student a tangible reward (e.g., toy, grab bag, coupon), a privilege, or opportunity to color in a square on the Mystery Motivator chart.

Group Adaptation

1. The class is divided into teams, and each team has its own compliance response (e.g., "Sure I will," "Right now," "No problem," "You got it"). Change students' groupings periodically.
2. The teams are named for their compliance response, which are listed on the blackboard. Each time a student responds with his or her team's compliance response *and* begins the behavior immediately, the team earns a point. Initially, the teacher should be liberal in recording marks. After several days, however, the teacher should only accept genuine efforts.
3. Each day, the teacher selects a number, secretly, and writes it down.
4. At the end of each day, the teacher announces the secret number. The teams that have marks equaling or exceeding the secret number get to participate in a group reward.
5. The teams that have marks lower than the secret number continue to do what is normally scheduled at that time of the day.

Adapted with permission from: Sopris West Educational Services, *The Tough Kid Book: Practical Classroom Management Strategies* by Ginger Rhode, Ph.D., William Jenson, Ph.D., & Ken Reavis, Ed.D., Copyright 1992–1996 (6th printing).

TALK-TO-YOURSELF CHART

Purpose

This activity encourages students to reflect on, and therefore process more thoroughly, the spelling of words and the specific relationship between the sounds and the letters in each word.

Procedure

1. Introduce a keyword such as *right* and ask the student to stretch out the sounds and raise a finger for each sound that she or he hears. (If the student has difficulty, provide instruction in phoneme segmentation.)
2. After the student responds with "three," write the word on a card. Ask the student to count the number of letters.
3. Ask the student to attempt to match the letters he/she hears with the letters that he/she sees. (The letters *r* and *t* each represent one sound; three letters, *igh,* represent the vowel sound.)
4. Place the chart shown in Figure IV.12 on the board to remind the student of the steps involved.

Example

Using the word *right,* the student would say.

1. The word is *right.*
2. When I stretch the word, I hear 3 sounds.

TALK-TO-YOURSELF CHART

1. The word is _____ .
2. When I stretch the word, I hear _____ sounds.
3. There are _____ letters because _____ .
4. The spelling pattern is _____ .
5. This is what I know about the vowel:_____ .
6. Another word I know with the same vowel sound is:_____ .
7. Other words that share this same spelling pattern are:_____ .

Figure IV.12   Model of Talk to Yourself Chart

Mather, N., & Jaffe, L. (2002). *Woodcock-Johnson III: Reports, Recommendations, and Strategies.* New York: John Wiley & Sons.

3. There are 5 letters because it takes *i-g-h* to represent the /i/ sound.
4. The spelling pattern is *ight*.
5. This is what I know about the vowel: the vowel is the only vowel in the word and it says its own name.
6. Another word that I know with the same vowel sound is: *pipe*.
7. Other words that share this same spelling pattern are: *night, might, sight,* and *fright*.

Adapted from: Gaskins, I. W. (1998). A beginning literacy program for at-risk and delayed readers. In J. L. Metsala & L. C. Ehri (Eds.), *Word recognition in beginning literacy* (pp. 209–232). Mahwah, NJ: Lawrence Erlbaum.

TAPED BOOKS

Purpose

The use of books on tape enables students to read materials that are at their frustration reading level. Books on tape may also be used to help a student build reading speed and fluency as he reads along with the tape.

Taped books are available from *Recordings for the Blind and Dyslexic* (RFB&D), a national, nonprofit organization that provides textbooks for individuals unable to read standard print because of a visual, physical, or learning disability. The master-tape library has educational books that range from kindergarten through postgraduate level. If a book is unavailable, an individual may request that it be recorded. If deemed to fit within the scope of the collection, the book will be recorded.

In late 2002, RFB&D made available a library of digital textbooks on CD-ROM which can be run on standard multimedia PCs or specialized players, allowing students to navigate the book/disk by page, chapter, or heading. RFB&D records educational and reference materials that are not available on tape or disk from other sources, in areas such as history, math, science, and economics. Members can search the catalog for specific recordings and order them online.

To register as a member (borrower) or volunteer as a reader, write or call RFB&D or contact them through their website (www.rfbd.org). A one-time registration fee and an annual membership fee for individuals provides access to the entire library. Applications can be downloaded from their website. Applications require the signature of a certified professional in the field of the applicant's disability attesting to the applicant's limits regarding the use of standard print.

Recordings for the Blind and Dyslexic, The Anne T. Macdonald Center, 20 Roszel Road, Princeton, NJ 08540, phone: (800) 221-4792, website: www.rfbd.org.

Public Libraries

Public libraries also provide a wide selection of recorded books for loan.

Commercial Availability

A wide selection of unabridged audio books is also available for rental or sale from either *Books on Tape* or *Recorded Books*. Selections include best-sellers, classics, history, biographies, and science fiction. Books on compact disk are also available. Tapes may also be ordered for purchase or rental online. Tapes may be rented for a month and then returned by mail. Prices vary.

Books on Tape, P.O. Box 7900, Newport Beach, CA 92658, phone: (800) 888-BOOKS, website: www.booksontape.com.

Recorded Books, LLC, 270 Skipjack Road, Prince Frederick, MD 20678, phone: (800) 638-1304, website: www.recordedbooks.com.

TELLING TIME STRATEGY

Purpose

This strategy, originally designed to teach students with low vision how to tell time on an analog clock face, is also useful for students who have difficulty processing the visual–spatial components of a clock face.

Prerequisite Skills

Rote count by 5's to 60
Identify the long and short hands on the clock
Comprehension of concepts: before, exactly, close to, top, start, stop

Procedure

1. Assess and activate prerequisite skills.
   a. Have student rote count by 5s to 60.
   b. Using an analog clock, have the student:
      (1) identify the long and short hands;
      (2) point to and name each number on the clock face;
      (3) name the number that comes before 12;
      (4) place the short hand exactly on the number 7;
      (5) place the short hand so it is close to the number 7;
      (6) place the long hand at the top of the clock;
      (7) move the long hand around the clock on the command, "Begin";
      (8) stop moving the long hand on the command, "Stop."
2. Give the student a clock with the numbers covered by circular markers. Point to each marker in sequence and have the student name the number under it. Once the student can name the numbers in sequence, point to markers out of sequential order for the student to name.
3. Beginning with "0" and starting at the top of the circle, have the student count by 5 as he touches the markers in sequential order.
4. Using the long hand of the clock rather than his finger, have the student repeat Step 3, counting by 5 each time the hand points to a marker.
5. Remove the markers from the clock. Repeat Steps 3 and 4.
6. Teach the student the following three-step procedure for telling time to 5-minute intervals.

   FIRST I look to see what number the short hand is on and say that number. If it's not exactly on the number, I always go to the number before.
   NEXT I start at the top of the clock and count by 5s until I find the long hand. I say the last number I counted aloud.
   LAST I say the time beginning with the first number I said (short hand), then the next number I said (long hand).
   Note: Until the procedure becomes sufficiently familiar that it does not tax memory, students may find it helpful to write the numbers.

7. When students are able to tell the time fairly easily using this strategy, begin teaching the other common phrases used to state the time of day (such as "a quarter after," "twenty to").

Created by Kathie Frankel, Arizona State Schools for the Deaf and the Blind, Tucson, Arizona.

TOKEN ECONOMY SYSTEMS

Purpose

Token economies are behavioral reinforcement systems used to increase the frequency with which a person demonstrates specific target behaviors.

Procedure

1. *Determine the behavior requiring intervention.* Using a variety of methods (e.g., teacher interviews, observations, situational rating scales), identify the student's behaviors that present the most serious impediment to learning, or require immediate intervention for safety reasons.

   Many educators choose a specific work habit or some aspect of academic performance as the target behavior. This type of intervention is generally easy to monitor, helps to improve academic skills and knowledge, and is incompatible with inattentive and disruptive behaviors. A positive and effective way to diminish a negative behavior is to promote the development of a behavior that is incompatible with it. For example, a student who frequently refuses work may earn 2 tokens each time he/she pleasantly accepts work, 2 tokens each time he/she starts to work within 0 seconds, and frequently as he/she continues to work. If necessary, combine an intervention of this type with a negative consequence such as losing 1 token each time the student refuses to take the materials in a cooperative manner, does not start to work within 10 seconds, or stops working for at least a minute.
2. *Identify the situation* in which the problematic behavior is most likely to occur (e.g., independent work in reading or writing, cooperative groups of two or more).
3. *Take baseline data.* Before initiating the intervention, take baseline data on the frequency, severity, and/or intensity of the behaviors targeted for intervention and establish a system for objectively monitoring progress. Some of the monitoring systems commonly used in schools include documenting the percent of work completed, counting the number of times the behavior occurs in a given time period, or counting the number of time periods (e.g., 5 minutes) during which the negative behavior does not occur.

Mather, N., & Jaffe, L. (2002). *Woodcock-Johnson III: Reports, Recommendations, and Strategies.* New York: John Wiley & Sons.

4. *Select the primary and secondary reinforcers.* Token economies include primary reinforcers (the privileges, activities, and tangible items that the student is trying to earn) and secondary reinforcers (tokens that measure progress toward earning the desired reward, such as poker chips checkmarks, or pennies). Decide on the secondary reinforcers you will use, taking into consideration the developmental age of the student. Younger or less mature students usually require tangible items, whereas older students and adolescents often prefer checkmarks on a card.

   Students under the age of 5 generally do not understand the complexity of a two-tiered program and, consequently, need an immediate "reward" each time they produce the target positive behavior. Intangible and tangible reinforcers to be given on a frequent basis may include: verbal praise specific to the behavior, a note to the parents, stickers on a card to bring home, or a grab bag of small, inexpensive things.

5. *Assign point values to the behaviors.* Determine a point value for each demonstration of the target positive behavior or for refraining from the negative behavior. If you are targeting more than one behavior, determine and list the point value for each, assigning more difficult tasks or behaviors higher point values. Break down complex tasks into their parts, assigning a point value to each, so that the student receives credit for those parts done well even if he/she does not complete the whole task.

6. *Develop a menu* of privileges, activities, or tangible items for which the student can trade his/her tokens. Assign a point value to each menu item according to its attraction for the student (e.g., toy from "treasure box," art supplies, helping to deliver the school newspaper). Make sure that some rewards are valued low enough that a student could earn them in half a day or less. Initially, many students will not be able to delay gratification for more than a few hours, even with the intervening reinforcement of tokens.

7. *Choose reinforcers.* Ensure that the rewards chosen are highly motivating to the student and are not easily available except within the behavior program. To this end, it is helpful to include the student in developing the menu. Do not make reinforcers time-dependent (e.g., participating in a scheduled field trip). The student *must* have the opportunity to earn the reward. The variable element is *when,* not *if,* he will earn it.

8. *Teach the student the relationship between the tokens and the primary reinforcers.* Depending on the developmental age of the student, this might include modeling the exchange of tokens for different objects. Activities and privileges on the menu can be represented by pictures.

9. *Immediate success.* Initially, set the behavioral criteria for earning tokens at a level the student is already capable of meeting (e.g., writing one complete sentence in an essay, completing 50% of a worksheet, raising his hand even if calling out at the same time). The student must earn enough tokens to cash them in for a reward at least daily and should be encouraged to do so. Immediately, the system becomes real and the student experiences success. Remember that the tokens are only interim reinforcers. If they are not converted into rewards on a frequent and regular basis, they will lose their effectiveness as motivators.

10. *Change rewards to maintain effectiveness and interest.* Monitor the effectiveness of the behavioral program on an ongoing basis. Typically, rewards have to be changed periodically so that they maintain their novelty and motivational power. Criteria for rewards may need to be lowered or altered. When the student is maintaining the target behaviors at an improved level, gradually increase the criteria for earning the same number of tokens. When the student is maintaining the behavior at a lesser level of support, incorporate another problematic behavior into the intervention. Continue to reinforce the previous target behavior intermittently but with sufficient frequency that the student remains aware of the behavioral expectation and his ability to meet it.

11. *Promote generalization.* A student with behavioral difficulties is unlikely to generalize the positive behaviors developed in one situation spontaneously to another situation. In all probability, the student will need guidance or direct training to do so, even in situations similar in structure and expectations. Typically, the student has more difficulty maintaining behavioral control in situations wherein rules, structure, and supervision are relaxed (e.g., assemblies, lunch). Although behavioral interventions in such situations are more difficult to establish, they are usually necessary.

Adapted from: DuPaul, G. J., & Stoner, G. (1994). *ADHD in the schools: Assessment and intervention strategies.* New York: Guilford.

Mather, N., & Jaffe, L. (2002). *Woodcock-Johnson III: Reports, Recommendations, and Strategies.* New York: John Wiley & Sons.

TOUCH MATH

Purpose

Touch Math is a systematic, multisensory program used to introduce and improve basic computational skills. This program is effective for students who have difficulty memorizing math facts and the steps of the four basic operations. This supplemental program is used in conjunction with the existing math program in kindergarten through third grade or with students at any level who need help with basic math skills.

Procedures

Students are taught to use a pencil to touch the Touchpoints, designated with dark circles, on the numbers 1–9, as illustrated in Figure IV.13. Use of the Touchpoints helps the student associate the number with its value while avoiding the errors that come with counting on fingers. When the student no longer needs them, the Touchpoints are gradually removed from the numbers (the student continues to "touch" them from memory), at which point the student can begin to use general classroom materials while continuing instruction in the Touch Math materials. The Touch Math program emphasizes the need to provide frequent practice in math facts with, and eventually without, use of the Touchpoints.

The steps within each operation are taught systematically, progressing from simple to more complex. At each stage, visual cues and simple rule statements reinforce the student's learning of the sequence of steps. For example, in Step 1 addition, the student begins by touching and counting all of the Touchpoints. In Step 2, the student names the larger number and touches points of the smaller number, point by point, while counting on. The student also verbalizes the procedure: "I touch the larger number, say its name and continue counting." When the student advances to two-digit addition, an arrow is drawn over the units column and

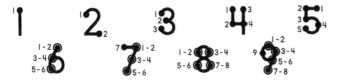

Figure IV.13   Touch Math: Illustration of the Touchpoints on Numbers 0–9

Figure IV.14   Touch Math: Example of Visual Cues for Addition with Regrouping

Reprinted with permission from: Innovative Learning Concepts, *Touchmath: The Touchpoint Approach for Teaching Basic Math* (5th ed.), Copyright 1999.

the student learns, "I start on the side with the arrow. The arrow is on the right side." A square over the tens column serves as a reminder to "carry over" a number. Figure IV.14 illustrates the visual cues for addition with regrouping. For subtraction, the student touches the top number, says its name, and counts backward. For multiplication and division, the student uses sequence counting. The student is taught strategies for both short and long division. The computation program is adaptable and a remedial kit is available for use with older students.

Additional Materials

The Touch Math Story Problems Kit provides for reinforcement of the concepts of each operation, instruction in the related language, and application to practical problems. The terms specific to each operation (e.g., add, all together, total) are introduced systematically with ample practice in using each new term with pictures, cut-outs, and coloring. A kit is available for each of the four basic operations. The Story Problems and computation programs can be easily integrated for simultaneous instruction. The materials of the Story Problems program are clearly intended to be at-

Mather, N., & Jaffe, L. (2002). *Woodcock-Johnson III: Reports, Recommendations, and Strategies.* New York: John Wiley & Sons.

tractive to young students and are not easily adaptable for older students.

A variety of reproducible masters, workbooks, posters, and games are available for teaching Touch Math. Innovative Learning Concepts also has a Fact Mastery Kit for each operation, a Place Value Kit, a Fractions Kit, a Money Kit, a Shapes & Sizes Kit, and a Time Kit.

Program materials, a videotape demonstrating how to teach the program, and sample program materials can be ordered from Innovative Learning Concepts, 6760 Corporate Drive, Colorado Springs, CO 80919-1999, phone: (888) 868-2462, website: www.touchmath.com.

TRANSITIONS BETWEEN ACTIVITIES

Purpose

Teaching students the behaviors expected during a transition from one activity to another increases instructional time and decreases the likelihood of problems occurring during this less structured time.

Procedure

1. Make and enforce a rule that as students complete each step of a transition, they are to be quiet and look at the teacher for the next set of instructions.
2. Before the end of any activity, give the class a 2-minute warning. Keep it brief (e.g., "You have 2 minutes to finish this activity"). Offer time later in the day for students who have not completed the assignment to do so (e.g., "If you cannot finish, I will give you time this afternoon to do so").
3. Choose a signal to end the activity and use it consistently. Announce that the activity is over, ring a bell, or set a timer to ring. At the signal, have the students stop working and look at the teacher. Wait until all students have done so.
4. Tell the students what to do with the assignment they were working on and the materials they were using. Depending on the class and the next activity, you may want to wait until they have completed this step before giving instructions for the next step.
5. Tell the class what materials to take out for the next activity, where to move to in the room, or to stay in their seats. If materials are to be given out, plan for this to be

done quickly and efficiently. Set a time limit for the transition.
6. Praise the class (if warranted) for an efficient transition and, if necessary, explain what can be improved during the next transition.
7. Give instructions for the next activity and tell the students how long the activity will last.
8. Encourage questions for clarification or requests for repetition. Students are not to start working until you give them the go-ahead and students have had time to ask questions. (Once all the instructions are given, allow students to begin work. Meet in a small group with any students who still need repetition or clarification.)
9. When students have begun to work, write the instructions on the board as back up for students who need reminders.

WILSON READING SYSTEM

The *Wilson Reading System* (WRS) is a 12-step, multisensory system for teaching decoding and encoding (spelling) beginning with phoneme segmentation. WRS directly teaches the structure of words in the English language in an organized, sequential system with extensive, controlled text to help teachers implement a multisensory structured language program.

The basic purpose of the Wilson Reading System is to teach students fluent decoding and encoding skills to the level of mastery. It includes sight word instruction, vocabulary, oral expressive language development, and comprehension. The ten-part lesson plans are highly interactive between teacher and student. The lessons progress from easier to more challenging tasks for decoding and then spelling. The program ends with fluency and comprehension work.

The Wilson program has twelve steps. Steps 1 and 2 emphasize phonemic segmentation skills (the ability to separate the sounds in a word) and blending the sounds together again. Initially, the student learns to segment sounds within one-syllable words using sound cards and a "sound tapping" procedure. For example, in teaching the word "map," three letter cards, representing the three sounds in a word, are placed on the table. The student is taught to say each sound while tapping a different finger to his or her thumb, as follows:

- As he says the /m/ sound, he taps his index finger to his thumb.

Mather, N., & Jaffe, L. (2002). *Woodcock-Johnson III: Reports, Recommendations, and Strategies.* New York: John Wiley & Sons.

- As he says the /a/ sound, he taps his middle finger to his thumb.
- As he says the /p/ sound, he taps his ring finger to his thumb.
- He then says the sounds as he drags his thumb across the three fingers, starting with his index finger and ending with his ring finger.

As the student succeeds at reading and spelling both real and nonsense words with three sounds, he then moves on to words with four sounds, then five, until by the end of Step 2 he is fluently blending and segmenting up to six sounds in a syllable.

Beginning in Step 3, the student is systematically taught to segment syllables in multisyllable words. Steps 4–6 teach vowel–consonant–*e* syllables, open syllables, suffix endings, and consonant-*le* syllables. The students have extensive practice with controlled vocabulary for decoding and spelling application. Comprehension is addressed through vocabulary work and literature read by the teacher to students.

Progression to a new step is dependent on mastery and fluent application of the previous step. Instruction after Step 6 combines continued work in decoding and spelling, comprehension, and application of skills in both controlled and noncontrolled text. In Steps 7–12, complex word structure is taught.

Information available from Wilson Language Training, 175 West Main Street, Millbury, MA, 01527-1441, phone: (800) 899-8454, website: www.WilsonLanguage.com.

WILSON READING SYSTEM FOR STUDENTS WITH VISUAL IMPAIRMENTS: ADAPTATION

As the Wilson Reading System (WRS) was originally designed for older students with reading disabilities, it does not depend on pictures for any of the activities or tasks, making it uniquely adaptable for students with visual impairments. The following adaptation was developed at a state school for the blind for use with middle school-age blind students and students with low vision, most with additional disabilities, who were reading at primer to early second-grade levels. Now in its second year, all of the students have made steady progress and are enthusiastic participants. Components of the system not noted below have not, as yet, been adapted.

Figure IV.15   Velcro Board for Wilson Reading System as Used with Students with Visual Impairments

1. Five is the maximum number of students that can be efficiently accommodated for organization, individualized planning, and fast-paced participation. Additionally, a group of this size requires an instructional aide during WRS instruction.
2. Rather than looking at writing on the board or at a class-sized letter/word card, each student has a flannel-covered board, approximately 2' × 1', bordered with strips of Velcro and with three horizontal strips of Velcro across the board. Figure IV.15 illustrates the flannel board with strips of Velcro.
3. Each letter, letter combination, and word card (element) is embossed with the corresponding Braille symbol(s) so that all cards have both print and Braille. Smaller print cards can be made to accommodate print readers with small visual fields. Braille readers learn to read and spell words in both Grades I and II Braille. The cards are backed with Velcro so that they stay immobile on the board until moved intentionally.
4. The students are seated in a horseshoe configuration and the teacher goes from student to student placing the card with the element each is supposed to read on his board. When she comes around again, the student reads his card, the teacher replaces it with another card and moves on to the next student. As students do not change levels until they have mastered the current one, they make few errors.
5. When students use the accompanying workbooks, enlargements are made for those who need them or they use their magnifiers or a CCTV. Braille copies are made for the Braille readers.
6. In preparation for each class, the teacher decides which elements and sentences each student will read so that there is minimal wait time as she moves between students. An instructional aide, using a record sheet that corresponds to the elements and sentences planned for each student, keeps data on each student's errors so that problem areas can be retaught and receive stronger emphasis the next day.

Mather, N., & Jaffe, L. (2002). *Woodcock-Johnson III: Reports, Recommendations, and Strategies.* New York: John Wiley & Sons.

7. Spelling and writing are done as a group, except for students who have already moved up to a higher level. Students use whatever materials and accommodations they need such as typing onto the computer, writing on raised-line paper with black felt-tip marker, or typing on a Braille Writer.

8. Strategies and mnemonics are used to help students differentiate between easily confusable letters, such as i/e in Braille and b/d in print.

9. Print readers code the letters in words to depict their pronunciation; braille readers do not. Extra emphasis is placed on the braille reader's ability to explain the relationship between the spelling pattern and the pronunciation of a word.

10. When students are asked to find the letters for certain types of sounds (e.g., welded sounds such as /nk/), the Braille readers erase the letters instead.

To ensure retention of the concepts and components that make WRS so successful, it is recommended that the teacher take the training offered by WRS and earn their certification. It is important for the teacher to understand the reading process and the reasoning underlying the organization and components of this system before adapting it to the individual needs of students with visual impairments.

Adaptation developed by Ruth Parsons, Arizona State Schools for the Deaf and the Blind, Tucson.

WORD BANK ACTIVITIES

Purpose

After studying a word, the student places it in a word bank to be used for a variety of reinforcement activities. Word bank activities help students establish and recall sight words. A plastic recipe box makes a convenient container.

Caution: Ensure that word cards are written neatly and accurately, and that they are sufficiently consistent in format (e.g., print style, color) that the student is not able to use incidental clues to identify words (e.g., I know this says "what" because it's green).

Activities

1. To facilitate independent study for reading or spelling, have the student draw a picture representing the word on the other side of the card. He can then try to read the words and look at the picture to check his accuracy. Similarly, he can go through the cards with the picture side up, write the spelling of the word on a piece of paper, and turn the card over to check his spelling.

2. Have the student classify words from his sight word box into a variety of categories, such as grouping all the words that relate to action, those used to describe, or semantic categories (e.g., animals, colors).

3. Have the student alphabetize the words.

4. Help the student think of other words in the same word family and write them on the back of the card. Then have the student choose a word, write a list of words that would fit in its family, and check them against the words on the back of the card.

5. Have the student make up individual cards for each member of a word family, mix up all the cards, and sort them by family.

6. Have students pair up to challenge each other to read or spell their word cards (either their own or the other student's).

7. Suggest ways for students to categorize the cards (e.g., long versus short words, antonyms and synonyms, words sharing the same beginning consonants, words with similar spelling patterns). Alternatively, brainstorm with the students a variety of ways to categorize the word cards, have small groups of students categorize their cards differently, then share their categorization principle and the word groups they came up with.

8. Have the student put together as many words as possible to form a sentence. Have the student write the sentence and add in any extra words that are necessary for it to make sense.

9. Group the students and give them a pile of word cards, face down. The first student picks up a word card and makes up the first sentence of a story, using the word. Each student in turn picks up the next card and continues the story, using the word in a sentence. The student who picks up the last card ends the story.

10. Use Activity #9 but have the students write a progressive story rather than tell it. Then choose a student to read it aloud.

11. Have the student practice using the words in both spoken and written sentences.

12. Teach the student how to use a flash method to teach another student to read the words.

13. Have the student practice the word cards by looking at the word, saying the word, tracing the word, and then turning over the word and writing it from memory.

14. Have two students team up, initial their own word cards, and then mix them together. Place all of the

Mather, N., & Jaffe, L. (2002). *Woodcock-Johnson III: Reports, Recommendations, and Strategies.* New York: John Wiley & Sons.

cards face down on the table. Each player selects a card, turns it over, and tries to pronounce it. If the player pronounces it correctly, he or she keeps it. If not, the other person tries to pronounce the word and if correct, takes the card. Any words missed by both students are placed in the middle to be restudied.

15. Use the word cards as part of a board game, such as Chutes and Ladders. Players place their cards, each in a separate pile, face down on the board. When it is the player's turn, he or she picks up the top card in his or her own pile and reads it. If correct, the player throws the dice (or spins the spinner) and progresses the appropriate number of spaces. If incorrect, play passes to the next person. Before picking up a card from his or her own pile, a player may choose to pick up a card from any other player's pile and try to read it instead. If the player is correct, he or she throws the dice and moves his or her marker, then has another opportunity to read the top card in his or her own card pile for another turn. If the student tries to read another player's card and is incorrect, he loses his turn and play passes to the next player.

16. Use cards in games incorporating finding or matching phonograms, syllable patterns (e.g., silent *e* syllables, double vowel syllables), or spelling demons (e.g., words with double consonants, words with silent letters). A spinner, dice, or game board can turn almost any reinforcement activity into a "game."

17. For additional practice with sight words, create modified cloze exercises. Have the student fill in the blanks in sentences using words from a word box.

WRITING AS A PROCESS

Purpose

Viewing writing as a process acknowledges that writing is composed of several interactive, overlapping, and recursive stages (Flower & Hayes, 1980; Graves, 1983). Although one focus of instruction is upon improving basic writing skills (editing), the central emphasis is upon communication. Writing requires time for planning (prewriting), composing (writing), revising (rewriting), and sharing.

Procedure

Prewriting

For the prewriting stage, provide the students assistance for generating writing topics (e.g., family, experiences, reading).

Have the students select their own topics from the lists they generate. Generating a topic list includes individual brainstorming and sharing ideas with others for additional topics. As students think of new topics, they add them to ongoing topic lists in their writing files. Students' selection of their own topics enhances both interest in writing and ownership of the piece. As students become familiar with the process, more teacher-directed writing assignments may be incorporated.

The planning step may simply involve thinking out what one wants to say before composing a first draft or may incorporate strategies for facilitating the planning process. In the planning process, students consider the purpose for the composition, as well as the intended audience. Examples of strategies often used in this stage include brainstorming and clustering ideas by using semantic mapping, a story frame, or self-questioning.

Writing

Once a topic has been selected, students create a first draft. Students are encouraged not to be overly concerned about handwriting, spelling, or other basic skills in this step and to place their full attention on developing their ideas.

Any time during writing, the students may drop back to an earlier stage. For example, in the writing stage, students may realize that they do not have enough information on the topic and drop back to researching it; or, students may realize during brainstorming or drafting that they are not interested in their topic and select a new one.

Revising and Editing

When revising, the students focus on the clarity of their message, such as organizing ideas and selecting more precise vocabulary. In editing, the students proofread for and correct errors in spelling, punctuation, capitalization, and usage. In both revising and editing, the teacher may introduce a variety of strategies for helping the students develop independence. Some of these are: peer editing, using a thesaurus or electronic spelling checker/thesaurus, learning to use and read proofreading symbols, learning an editing strategy or using a revision guide. During this time, the teacher also may note skills that require more instruction, allowing for grouping of students for specific skill lessons and incorporating practice activities into the daily writing plan.

During the process of writing, students have frequent, brief, individual conferences with the teacher. The teacher asks questions to highlight strengths or guide attention to weaknesses in specific areas. For example, the teacher may guide certain students to focus on elaborating ideas, modifying organizational structures, or editing basic skills. Dur-

Mather, N., & Jaffe, L. (2002). *Woodcock-Johnson III: Reports, Recommendations, and Strategies.* New York: John Wiley & Sons.

ing the writing stage, a student may confer and revise several times before feeling satisfied with the final product.

Sharing

When students feel they have completed their papers or stories, they read them to a peer or an assembled group for comments, questions, and suggestions. Students may then choose to revise the story again, publish the story, or begin work on another writing project.

When a piece is completed, students may wish to type it or have it typed, illustrate it, and create a cover for it. Subsequently, it may be placed in the classroom, school newspaper, or library for others to read. Through conferencing, sharing with peers, author's chair, and publication, students develop the sense that they are writing for an audience and that their writing can be read and understood by others.

Adapted from: Bos, C. S. (1988). Process-oriented writing: Instructional implications for mildly handicapped students. *Exceptional Children, 54,* 521–527; Bos, C. S., & Vaughn, S. (2001). *Strategies for teaching students with learning and behavior problems* (5th ed.). Boston: Allyn and Bacon; Flower, L., & Hayes, J. R. (1980). Writing as problem solving. *Visible Language, 14,* 388–399; Graves, D. H. (1983). *Writing: Teachers and children at work.* Exeter, NH: Heinemann Educational Books; Schlegel, M. (1986, October). *Remediation of written language: Group teaching techniques.* Workshop presented at Arizona Association for Children with Learning Disabilities, Phoenix, AZ; and Vallecorsa, A. L., Ledford, R. R., & Parness, G. G. (1991). Strategies for teaching composition skills to students with learning disabilities. *Teaching Exceptional Children, 23,* 52–55.

WRITING PROCESS WITH MAPPING FOR INDIVIDUAL TUTORING

Purpose

Guiding a student through the process approach to writing provides the student with a technique for deciding a topic, teaches him/her the components of a paper, gives him/her a method for organizing ideas, and reinforces the idea that writing involves numerous steps and stages.

Procedure

Begin by telling the student that you will be teaching him a new method of writing that has several steps. Explain that

good writers never complete a paper or story in just one draft.

Because several drafts of a paper are usually necessary, have the student use a word processor if one is available and the student has word-processing skills.

Prewriting

1. Select a topic.
   a. Provide the student with a broad topic on which to write. Within the broad topic assigned, have the student brainstorm and list as many ideas for subtopics as possible.
   b. Have the student cross out the subtopics that seem least interesting and then rank the remaining ones from most to least interesting.
   c. Have the student select the top choice as the topic and make up a working title (subject to change) that can evolve into the main idea statement for the paper.
2. Conduct research

   If necessary, have the student research the topic, taking notes on paper or note cards.
3. Generate idea statements
   a. Have the student dictate or write on paper everything about the topic he/she knows or can remember from reading. Have the student write only one idea to a line, skipping lines between statements.
   b. Have the student cut the paper between the statements so that he/she has a pile of separate ideas on the topic. Alternatively, the student can write each idea on a page from a sticky pad. These are easier to reorganize than slips of paper.
4. Organize the idea statements
   a. Ask the student, "How can you group these so that the ideas that are similar in some way are together?" Have the student then go through the ideas and group the pieces of paper. Help only as much as necessary.
   b. Have the student organize the ideas within each group according to the information present. Some ideas may be organized sequentially, others as statement and support, and others as comparison/contrast. Within each group, have him/her arrange the strips of paper one above the other on the table.
5. Generate main idea statements
   a. Ask the student why he/she put certain ideas together. Help him/her make a general statement that encompasses the ideas. Have the student write the general statement down and place it at the top of the stack.
   b. Have the student title all idea groups in the same

manner. If one statement in the stack serves as a main idea already, it may be placed at the top.

6. Add and reorganize information
   a. Encourage the student to write and add related ideas to any of the groups.
   b. Have the student review the ideas within each group. Encourage him/her to move ideas among the groups if any seem to fit better under some other heading.
7. Design the semantic map

Using the main idea statements as a guide, help the student to design a semantic map depicting the relationship among the main idea statements. The overall topic is the first level, the main idea statements are the second level, and the details are the third level. When drawing the map, however, it may become obvious that one or more of the main idea statements works better as a third-level statement placed as an offshoot of one of the second-level statements.

8. Explain the relationships and add to the map
   a. When the map is drawn, have the student explain why the main ideas were placed where they were and explain the relationships among them. Have the student make any changes in design or levels at this point.
   b. Have the student place the more detailed ideas in the semantic map associated with the main idea statements.
   c. Have the student explain how the information interrelates in the map.

Writing

1. Using the information in the semantic map, have the student write a first draft of the body of the paper. Each second level of the map becomes a paragraph. The idea statement at this level provides the main idea.
2. Have the student write an introduction and a conclusion.

Revising/Editing

1. Help the student read through the paper, making revisions in organization, sentence structure, and vocabulary.
2. Have the student write transitional sentences where needed to facilitate the connection between paragraphs.
3. Have the student rewrite the paper with revisions, read it again for further revision, and write another draft.
4. When the student and teacher are satisfied with the paper, help the student edit it for errors in mechanics, such as spelling, punctuation, and capitalization.

Final Copy

Have the student write and then hand in a final copy of the paper.

Adapted from: Buckley, M. H., & Boyle, O. (1981). *Mapping the writing journey.* Berkeley: University of California Berkeley/Bay Area Writing Project, Curriculum Publication No. 15; Graves, D. H. (1983). *Writing: Teachers and children at work.* Exeter, NH: Heinemann Educational Books; and Pearson, P. D., & Johnson, D. D. (1978). *Teaching reading comprehension.* New York: Holt, Rinehart, and Winston.

TESTS CITED WITHIN THE BOOK

Woodcock-Johnson III
Riverside Publishing Company
425 Spring Lake Drive
Itasca, IL 60143-2079
(800) 323-9540
http://www.riversidepublishing.com

Achenbach Child Behavior Checklist
ASEBA (Achenbach System of Empirically Based Assessment)
Room 6436
1 South Prospect Street
Burlington, VT 05401-3456
(802) 656-8313 or (802) 656-2608
Fax: (802) 656-2602
E-mail: mail@ASEBA.org
http://www.aseba.org

Analytic Reading Inventory, Sixth Edition
Prentice Hall Inc. / A Pearson Education
    Company / Simon & Schuster / A Viacom Company
Upper Saddle River, NJ 07458
(781) 455-1200
http://vig.prenhall.com

Beck Anxiety Inventory
The Psychological Corporation
555 Academic Court
San Antonio, TX 58204-2498
(800) 211-8378
TTY (800) 723-1318
Fax: (800) 232-1223
http://www.PsychCorp.com

Beck Depression Inventory—II
The Psychological Corporation
555 Academic Court
San Antonio, TX 58204-2498
(800) 211-8378
TTY (800) 723-1318
Fax: (800) 232-1223
http://www.PsychCorp.com

Beery-Buktenica Developmental Test of
    Visual-Motor Integration (4th Ed.)
Modern Curriculum Press
299 Jefferson Road
Parsippany, NJ 07054
(800) 321-3106
www.mcschool.com
http://www.ehhs.cmich.edu

Behavior Assessment System for Adolescents:
    Parent Rating Scale
AGS—American Guidance Service
4201 Woodland Road
Circle Pines, MN 55014-1796
(800) 328-2560
Fax: (800) 471-8457
http://www.agsnet.com

Boehm Tests of Basic Concepts—3
The Psychological Corporation
555 Academic Court
San Antonio, TX 58204-2498
(800) 211-8378
TTY (800) 723-1318
Fax: (800) 232-1223
http://www.PsychCorp.com

BRIGANCE Diagnostic Inventory of Basic Skills
Curriculum Associates
5 Esquire Road
Billerica, MA 01862-2589
(800) 225-0248
Fax: (800) 266-1158

Children's Auditory Verbal Learning Test—2
Psychological Assessment Resources, Inc.
16204 N. Florida Avenue
Lutz, FL 33549
(800) 331-8378

Children's Memory Scale
The Psychological Corporation
555 Academic Court
San Antonio, TX 58204-2498
(800) 211-8378
TTY (800) 723-1318
Fax: (800) 232-1223
http://www.PsychCorp.com

Clinical Evaluation of Language Fundamentals—3
The Psychological Corporation
555 Academic Court
San Antonio, TX 78204
(800) 872-1726
TTY (800) 723-1318
Fax: (800) 232-1223
http://www.PsychCorp.com

Colorado Perceptual Speed Trial III
DeFries, J. C., & Baker, L. A. (1983). Colorado family reading study: Longitudinal analyses. *Annals of Dyslexia, 33,* 153–162.

Comprehensive Test of Phonological Processes (CTOPP)
PRO-ED
8700 Shoal Creek Boulevard
Austin, TX 78757-6897
(800) 897-3202
www.proedinc.com

Conners' Rating Scales—Revised
Multi-Health Systems Incorporated
908 Niagara Falls Boulevard
North Tonawanda, NY 14120-2060
(800) 456-3003;
Fax: (888) 540-4484

Controlled Oral Word Association Test
    Benton, A. L., & Hamsher, K. (1976). Multilingual aphasia examination. Iowa City: University of Iowa Press.
    Spreen, O., & Strauss, E. (1998). A compendium of neuropsychological tests: Administration, norms and commentary (2nd ed.). Oxford University Press.

Expressive Vocabulary Test
AGS—American Guidance Service
4201 Woodland Road
Circle Pines, MN 55014-1796
(800) 328-2560
Fax: (800) 471-8457
http://www.agsnet.com

Goldman-Fristoe Test of Articulation
American Guidance Service
4201 Woodland Road
Circle Pines, MN 55014-1796
(612) 786-4343 or (800) 328-2560
Fax: (612) 786-9077
http://www.agsnet.com

Illinois Test of Psycholinguistic Abilities—3
PRO-ED
8700 Shoal Creek Boulevard
Austin, TX 78757-6897
(512) 451-3246 or (800) 897-3202
Fax: (800) FXPROED
http://www.proedinc.com

Key Math Diagnostic Arithmetic Tests—Revised (NU)
American Guidance Service
4201 Woodland Road
Circle Pines, MN 55014-1796
(612) 786-4343 or (800) 328-2560
Fax: (612) 786-9077
http://www.agsnet.com

The Listening Test
LinguiSystems, Inc.
3100 4th Avenue
East Moline, IL 61244-9700
(800) PRO-IDEA
(800) 776-4332
(309) 755-2300
http://www.linguisystems.com

Nelson-Denny Reading Test
Riverside Publishing Company
425 Spring Lake Drive
Itasca, IL 60143-2079
(800) 323-9540
http://www.riversidepublishing.com

Oral and Written Language Scales
AGS—American Guidance Service
4201 Woodland Road
Circle Pines, MN 55014-1796
(612) 786-4343 or (800) 328-2560
Fax: (612) 786-9077

Peabody Picture Vocabulary Test—III
American Guidance Service
4201 Woodland Road
Circle Pines, MN 55014-1796
(612) 786-4343 or (800) 328-2560
Fax: (612) 786-9077

Phonological Awareness Test
LinguiSystems, Inc.
3100 4th Avenue
East Moline, IL 61244-9700
(800) PRO-IDEA
(800) 776-4332
(309) 755-2300
http://www.linguisystems.com

Qualitative Reading Inventory—3
Longman
1185 Avenue of the Americas
New York, NY 10036
http://www.ablongman
(800) 666-9433

Rey Complex Figure Test and Recognition
    Trial (RCFT)
The Psychological Corporation
555 Academic Court
San Antonio, TX 58204-2498
(800) 211-8378
Fax: (800) 232-1223
TDD of Publisher (800) 723-1318
http://www.PsychCorp.com

Speech Sounds Perception Test
    Reitan, R. M., & Wolfson, D.
    (1985).
*Halstead-Reitan neuropsychological test
    battery: Theory and clinical interpreta-
    tions.* Tucson, AZ: Neuropsychology
    Press.

Stanford-Binet Intelligence Scale (4th Edi-
    tion)
Riverside Publishing Company
425 Spring Lake Drive
Itasca, IL 60143-2079
(800) 323-9540
http://www.riversidepublishing.com

Test of Language Competence-Expanded
    Edition, Level 1
LinguiSystems, Inc.
3100 4th Avenue
East Moline, IL 61244-9700
(800) PRO IDEA
(800) 776-4332
(309) 755-2300
http://www.linguisystems.com

Test of Mathematical Abilities—2
PRO-ED
8700 Shoal Creek Blvd.
Austin, TX 78758-6897
(512) 451-3246 or (800) 897-3202
Fax: (800) FXPROED
http://www.proedinc.com

Test of Word Finding—2
PRO-ED
8700 Shoal Creek Blvd.
Austin, TX 78757-6897
(512) 451-3246 or (800) 897-3202
Fax: (800) FXPROED
http://www.proedinc.com

Test of Written Language—3
PRO-ED
8700 Shoal Creek Blvd.
Austin, TX 78757-6897
(512) 451-3246 or (800) 897-3202
Fax: (800) FXPROED
http://www.proedinc.com

Vineland Adaptive Behavior Scales: Inter-
    view Edition
AGS—American Guidance Service
4201 Woodland Rd.
Circle Pines, MN 55014-1796
(612) 786-4343 or (800) 328-2560
Fax: (612) 786-9077
http://www.agsnet.com

Wechsler Adult Intelligence Scale—III
The Psychological Corporation
555 Academic Court
San Antonio, TX 58204-2498
(800) 211-8378
TTY (800) 723-1318
Fax: (800) 232-1223
http://www.PsychCorp.com

Wechsler Intelligence Scale for Children—
    III
The Psychological Corporation
555 Academic Court
San Antonio, TX 58204-2498
(800) 211-8378
TTY (800) 723-1318
Fax: (800) 232-1223
http://www.PsychCorp.com

Wechsler Memory Scale—III
The Psychological Corporation
555 Academic Court
San Antonio, TX 58204-2498
(800) 211-8378
TTY (800) 723-1318
Fax: (800) 232-1223
http://www.PsychCorp.com

Wide Range Achievement Test—3
Jastak Associates/Wide Range, Inc.
P.O. Box 3410
Wilmington, DE 19804-0250
(800) 221-9728
Fax: (302) 652-1644

Woodcock-Muñoz Language Survey. En-
    glish and Spanish Forms
Riverside Publishing Company
425 Spring Lake Drive
Itasca, IL 60143-2079
(800) 323-9540
http://www.riversidepublishing.com

The Word-R Test
LinguiSystems, Inc.
3100 4th Avenue
East Moline, IL 61244-9700
(800) PRO-IDEA
(800) 776-4332
(309) 755-2300
http://www.linguisystems.com

References

Adams, M. J., Foorman, B. R., Lundberg, I., & Beeler, T. (1998). *Phonemic awareness in young children*. Baltimore, MD: Brookes.

Algozzine, R. (1990). *Problem behavior management*. Rockville, MD: Aspen.

Alley, G. R., & Hori, K. O. (1981). *Effects of teaching a questioning strategy on reading comprehension of learning disabled adolescents* (Report No. 52). Lawrence, KS: Institute for Research in Learning Disabilities, University of Kansas.

Anders, P. L., & Bos, C. S. (1986). Semantic feature analysis: An interactive strategy for vocabulary and text comprehension. *Journal of Reading, 29,* 610–616.

Babbitt, B. C. (2000). 10 tips for software selection for math instruction (LD Online Reprint). *The LDA Gram, 34*(2), 11–12.

Barbe, W. B., Lucas, V. H., Wasylyk, T. M., Hackney, C. S., & Braun, L. A. (1987). *Zaner-Bloser handwriting, basic skills and application book I.* Columbus, OH: Zaner-Bloser.

Base, G. (1986). *Animalia.* New York: Harry N. Abrams.

Bassler, O. C., Beers, M. I., & Richardson, L. I. (1975). Comparison of two instructional strategies for teaching the solution of verbal problems. *Journal for Research in Mathematics Education, 6,* 171–177.

Bellanca, J., & Fogarty, R. (1986). *Catch them thinking: A handbook of classroom strategies.* Palatine, IL: IRI Group.

Blachman, B. A., Ball, E. W., Black, R., & Tangel, D. M. (2000). *Road to the code: A phonological awareness program for young children.* Baltimore, MD: Brookes.

Bos, C. S. (1988). Process-oriented writing: Instructional implications for mildly handicapped students. *Exceptional Children, 54,* 521–527.

Bos, C. S., Anders, P. L., Filip, D., & Jaffe, L. E. (1989). The effects of an interactive instructional strategy for enhancing reading comprehension and content area learning for students with learning disabilities. *Journal of Learning Disabilities, 22,* 384–390.

Bos, C. S., & Vaughn, S. (2001). *Strategies for teaching students with learning and behavior problems* (5th ed.). Boston: Allyn and Bacon.

Bowen, C. (1972). *Angling for words: A study book for language training.* Novato, CA: Academic Therapy.

Bradley, L. (1981). The organization of motor patterns for spelling: An effective remedial strategy for backward spellers. *Developmental Medicine and Child Neurology, 23,* 83–91.

Brinckerhoff, L. (1996). Making the transition to higher education: Opportunities for student empowerment. *Journal of Learning Disabilities, 29,* 118–136.

Brooks, R. B. (1991). *The self-esteem teacher.* Loveland, OH: Treehaus Communications.

Bryant, D. P., & Dix, J. (1998). Mathematics interventions for students with learning disabilities. In W. N. Bender (Ed.), *Professional issues in learning disabilities: Practical strategies and relevant research findings* (pp. 219–259). Austin, TX: PRO-ED.

Buckley, M. H., & Boyle, O. (1981). *Mapping the writing journey.* Berkeley: University of California Berkeley/Bay Area Writing Project, Curriculum Publication No. 15.

Bullock, J. K. (1991). *Touch math series* (4th ed.). Colorado Springs, CO: Innovative Learning Concepts.

Caldwell, J. H., & Goldin, G. A. (1987). Variables affecting word problem difficulty in secondary school mathematics. *Journal for Research in Mathematics Education, 18*(3), 187–196.

Campbell, K. U. (1996). *Great leaps reading program.* Micanopy, FL: Diarmuid.

Canfield, J., & Wells, H. C. (1994). *100 ways to enhance self-concept in the classroom* (2nd ed.). Boston: Allyn and Bacon.

Canter, L. (1993). *Homework without tears: A parent's guide for motivating children to do homework and succeed in school.* New York: HarperCollins.

Carbo, M. (1989). *How to record books for maximum reading gains.* New York: National Reading Styles Institute.

Carlisle, J. F. (2001). Using writing and study skills to improve the reading comprehension of at-risk adolescents. *Perspectives, 27*(2), 10–13.

Carnine, D., & Kinder, D. (1985). Teaching low-performing students to apply generative and schema strategies to narrative and expository material. *Remedial and Special Education, 6*(1), 20–29.

Carr, E., & Ogle, D. (1987). K-W-L plus: A strategy for comprehension and summarization. *Journal of Reading, 30,* 626–631.

Carreker, S. (1999). Teaching reading: Accurate decoding and fluency. In J. R. Birsh (Ed.), *Multisensory teaching of basic language skills* (pp. 141–182). Baltimore, MD: Brookes.

Carver, R. P. (1990). *Reading rate: A review of research and theory.* San Diego, CA: Academic Press.

Cotterell, G. C. (1973). The Fernald auditory-kinaesthetic technique. In A. W. Franklin & S. Naidoo (Eds.), *Assessment and teaching of dyslexic children* (pp. 97–100). London: Richard Madley.

Cunningham, P. M. (1979). Teaching vocabulary in the content areas. *NASSP Bulletin, 613*(424), 112–116.

Cunningham, P. M., & Cunningham, J. W. (1992). Making words: Enhancing the invented spelling-decoding connection. *Reading Teacher, 46,* 106–115.

Cunningham, P. M., & Hall, O. P. (1994). *Making words: Multilevel, hands-on, developmentally appropriate spelling and phonics activities.* Torrance, CA: Schaffer.

D'Ailly, H. (1995). Strategies in learning and teaching algebra. In E. Wood, V. Woloshyn, & T. Willoughby (Eds.), *Cognitive strategy instruction for middle and high schools* (pp. 137–170). Cambridge: Brookline.

Davidson, J. (1969). *Using the Cuisenaire rods.* New Rochelle, NY: Cuisenaire.

Deshler, D. D., Ellis, E. S., & Lenz, B. K. (1996). *Teaching adolescents with learning disabilities: Strategies and methods.* Denver: Love.

Devine, T. G. (1986). *Teaching reading comprehension: From theory to practice.* Boston: Allyn and Bacon.

DuPaul, G. J., & Stoner, G. (1994). *ADHD in the schools: Assessment and intervention strategies.* New York: Guilford.

Elkonin, D. B. (1973). *U.S.S.R.* In J. Downing (Ed.), *Comparative reading* (pp. 551–579.) New York: Macmillan.

Ellis, D. (2000). *Becoming a master student* (9th ed). Boston: Houghton Mifflin.

Engelmann, S., Bruner, E. C., Hanner, S., Osborn, J., Osborn, S., & Zoref, L. (1983–1984). *Reading mastery.* Chicago: Science Research Associates.

Engelmann, S., Johnson, G., Hanner, S., Carnine, D., Meyers, L., Osborn, S., Haddox, P., Becker, W., Osborn, J., & Becker, J. (1988). *Corrective reading.* Chicago: Science Research Associates.

Fernald, G. (1943). *Remedial techniques in basic school subjects.* New York: McGraw-Hill.

Fischer, P. (1999). Getting up to speed. *Perspectives: The International Dyslexia Association, 25*(2), 12–13.

Flower, L., & Hayes, J. R. (1980). Writing as problem solving. *Visible Language, 14,* 388–399.

Forte, I., & Pangle, M. A. (1985). *Selling spelling to kids: Motivating games and activities to reinforce spelling skills.* Nashville, TN: Incentive Publications.

Fry, E. (1994). *1000 instant words: The most common words for teaching reading, writing, and spelling.* Laguna Beach, CA: Laguna Beach Educational Books.

Fry, E. B. (1980). The new instant word list. *Reading Teacher, 34,* 284–289.

Fry, E. B., Kress, J. E., & Fountoukidis, D. L. (2000). *The reading teacher's book of lists* (4th ed). Paramus, NJ: Prentice-Hall.

Gaskins, I. W. (1998). A beginning literacy program for at-risk and delayed readers. In J. L. Metsala & L. C. Ehri (Eds.), *Word recognition in beginning literacy* (pp. 209–232). Mahwah, NJ: Erlbaum.

Geary, D. C. (2000). Mathematical disorders: An overview for educators. *Perspectives, 26*(3), 6–9. Baltimore: International Dyslexia Association.

Gillingham, A., & Stillman, B. W. (1973). *Remedial training for children with specific disability in reading, spelling, and penmanship.* Cambridge, MA: Educators Publishing Service.

Glass, G. G. (1973). *Teaching decoding as separate from reading.* New York: Adelphi University.

Glass, G. G. (1976). *Glass-analysis for decoding only teacher guide.* Garden City, NY: Easier to Learn.

Graham, S., & Harris, K. R. (1989). Components analysis of cognitive strategy instruction: Effects on learning disabled students' compositions and self-efficacy. *Journal of Educational Psychology, 81,* 353–361.

Graves, D. H. (1983). *Writing: Teachers and children at work.* Exeter, NH: Heinemann Educational Books.

Greene, V., & Enfield, M. L. (1994). *Project read.* Bloomington, MN: Language Circle Enterprises.

Gresham, F. M., & Elliott, S. N. (1990). *SSRS: Social skills rating system.* Circle Pines, MN: AGS.

Gurney, D., Gersten, R., Dimino, J., & Carnine, D. (1990). Story grammar: Effective literature instruction for high school students with learning disabilities. *Journal of Learning Disabilities, 23,* 335–342, 348.

Halpern, D. F., Hansen, C., & Riefer, D. (1990). Analogies as an aid to understanding and memory. *Journal of Educational Psychology, 82,* 298–305.

Hanau, L. (1974). *The study game: How to play and win with statement-pie.* New York: Barnes & Noble.

Hanover, S. (1983). Handwriting comes naturally? *Academic Therapy, 18,* 407–412.

Harris, K. R., & Graham, S. (1985). Improving learning disabled students' composition skills: A self-control strategy training approach. *Learning Disability Quarterly, 8,* 27–36.

Heckelman, R. G. (1966). Using the neurological impress reading technique. *Academic Therapy, 1,* 235–239.

Heckelman, R. G. (1986). N.I.M. revisited. *Academic Therapy, 21,* 411–420.

Heddens, J. W., & Speer, W. R. (2000a). *Today's mathematics: Part 1. Concepts and classroom methods* (10th ed.). New York: Wiley.

Heddens, J. W., & Speer, W. R. (2000b). *Today's mathematics: Part 2. Activities and instructional ideas* (10th ed.). New York: Wiley.

Henry, M. K. (1990). *WORDS: Integrated decoding and spelling instruction based on word origin & word structure.* Austin, TX: PRO-ED.

Henry, M. K., & Redding, N. C. (1996). *Patterns for success in reading and spelling: A multisensory approach to teaching phonics and word analysis.* Austin, TX: PRO-ED.

Herber, H. L. (1978). *Teaching reading in content areas* (2nd ed.). Englewood Cliffs, NJ: Prentice-Hall.

Herold, M. (1982). *You can have a near-perfect memory.* Chicago: Contemporary Books.

Horn, E. (1954). *Teaching spelling.* Washington, DC: American Educational Research Association.

Hughes, C. A., & Schumaker, J. (1991). Test-taking strategy instruction for adolescents with learning disabilities. *Exceptionality, 2,* 205–221.

Hughes, C. A., Schumaker, J., Deshler, D., & Mercer, C. (1988). *The test-taking strategy.* Lawrence, KS: Edge Enterprises.

Hutchinson, N. L. (1993). Effects of cognitive strategy instruction on algebra problem solving of adolescents with learning disabilities. *Learning Disability Quarterly, 16,* 34–50.

Johnson, D. D., & Pearson, P. D. (1984). *Teaching reading vocabulary* (2nd ed.). New York: Holt, Rinehart, and Winston.

Johnson, W., Peck, I., Plotkin, F., & Richardson, W. (1976). *The modern world.* New York: Scholastic Book Services.

Kerrigan, W. J. (1979). *Writing to the point: Six basic steps* (2nd ed.). New York: Harcourt Brace Jovanovich.

King, D. H. (1985). *Writing skills for the adolescent.* Cambridge, MA: Educators Publishing Service.

King, D. H. (1993). *Writing skills 2.* Cambridge, MA: Educators Publishing Services.

King-Sears, M. E., Mercer, C. D., & Sindelar, P. T. (1992). Toward independence with keyword mnemonics: A strategy for science vocabulary instruction. *Remedial and Special Education, 13,* 22–33.

Kirk, S. A. (1979). *Applying learning principles.* Unpublished manuscript. Tucson, AZ: University of Arizona.

Kirk, S. A., Kirk, W. D., & Minskoff, E. H. (1985). *Phonic remedial reading lessons.* Novato, CA: Academic Therapy.

Kratoville, B. L. (1989). *Word tracking: High frequency words.* Novato, CA: Academic Therapy.

Kroese, J. M., Hynd, G. W., Knight, D. F., Hiemenz, J. R., & Hall, J. (2000). Clinical appraisal of spelling ability and its relationship to phonemic awareness (blending, segmenting, elision, and reversal), phonological memory, and reading in reading disabled, ADHD, and normal children. *Reading and Writing: An Interdisciplinary Journal, 13,* 105–131.

Kucera, H., & Francis, W. N. (1967). *Comparative analysis of present day American English.* Providence, RI: Brown University Press.

Langer, J. A. (1981). From theory to practice: A prereading plan. *Journal of Reading, 25,* 152–156.

Langer, J. A. (1984). Examining background knowledge and text comprehension. *Reading Research Quarterly, 19,* 468–481.

Lenz, B. K., Schumaker, J. B., Deshler, D. D., & Beals, V. L. (1984). *The word identification strategy* (Learning Strategies Curriculum). Lawrence: University of Kansas.

Lindsley, O. R. (1991). From technical jargon to plain English for application. *Journal of Applied Behavior Analysis, 24,* 449–458.

Longo, A. M. (2001). Using writing and study skills to improve the reading comprehension of at-risk adolescents. *Perspectives, 27*(2), 29–31.

Lynch, J. (1998). *Easy lessons for teaching word families.* New York: Scholastic.

Maccini, P., McNaughton, D., & Ruhl, K. L. (1999). Algebra instruction for students with learning disabilities: Implications from a research review. *Learning Disability Quarterly, 22,* 113–119.

Malone, L. D., & Mastropieri, M. A. (1992). Reading comprehension instruction: Summarization and self-monitoring training for students with learning disabilities. *Exceptional Children, 58,* 270–279.

Manzo, A. V. (1969). The ReQuest procedure. *Journal of Reading, 13,* 123–126.

Manzo, A. V. (1985). Expansion modules for the ReQuest, CAT, GRP, and REAP reading/study procedures. *Journal of Reading, 28,* 498–502.

Mastropieri, M. A., & Scruggs, T. E. (1998). Enhancing school success with mnemonic strategies. *Intervention in School and Clinic, 33,* 201–208.

Mastropieri, M. A., & Scruggs, T. E. (1999a). *Teaching students ways to re-*

member: Strategies for learning mnemonically. Cambridge, MA: Brookline Books.

Mastropieri, M. A., & Scruggs, T. E. (1999b). *Teaching test taking skills: Helping students show what they know.* Cambridge, MA: Brookline Books.

Mather, N. (1985). *The Fernald kinesthetic method revisited.* Unpublished manuscript, University of Arizona, Department of Special Education and Rehabilitation, Tucson.

Mather, N. (1991). *An instructional guide to the Woodcock-Johnson—Revised.* New York: Wiley.

Mather, N., Wendling, B., & Woodcock, R. W. (2001). *Essentials of the WJ III Tests of Achievement Assessment.* New York: Wiley.

Mather, N., & Woodcock, R. W. (2001a). Examiner's Manual. *Woodcock-Johnson III Tests of Cognitive Abilities.* Itasca, IL: Riverside Publishing.

Mather, N., & Woodcock, R. W. (2001b). Examiner's Manual. *Woodcock-Johnson III Tests of Achievement.* Itasca, IL: Riverside Publishing.

McCoy, K. M., & Prehm, H. J. (1987). *Teaching mainstreamed students: Methods and techniques.* Denver: Love.

McGrew, K., & Woodcock, R. W. (2001). *Woodcock-Johnson III Technical Manual.* Itasca, IL: Riverside Publishing.

McGuinness, C., & McGuinness, G. (1998). *Reading reflex: The foolproof phonographix™ method for teaching your child to read.* New York: Free Press.

McIntosh, R., Vaughn, S., & Bennerson, D. (1995). FAST social skills with a SLAM and a RAP: Providing social skills training for students with learning disabilities. *Teaching Exceptional Children, 28*(1), 37–41.

Mercer, C., & Campbell, K. (1998). *Great leaps reading program.* Gainesville, FL: Diarmuid.

Mercer, C. D., Mercer, K. D., & Campbell, K. U. (2002). *Great leaps math program.* Gainesville, FL: Diarmuid.

Meyer, G. J., Finn, S. E., Eyde L. D., Kay, G. G., Moreland, K. L., Dies, R. R., Eisman, E. J., Kubiszyn, T. W., & Reed, G. M. (2001). Psychological testing and psychological assessment: A review of evidence and issues. *American Psychologist, 56*(2), 128–165.

Minskoff, E. H. (1982). Training LD students to cope with the everyday world. *Academic Therapy, 17,* 311–316.

Montague, M., & Bos, C. S. (1986). The effect of cognitive strategy training on verbal math problem solving performance of learning disabled adolescents. *Journal of Learning Disabilities, 19,* 26–33.

Montague, M., & Graves, A. (1993). Improving students' story writing. *Teaching Exceptional Children, 25*(4), 36–37.

National Reading Panel. (2000). *Teaching children to read: An evidence based assessment of the scientific research literature on reading and its implications for reading instruction.* Bethesda, MD: National Reading Panel, National Institute of Child Health and Human Development.

Neill, K. (1979). Turn kids on with repeated reading. *Teaching Exceptional Children, 12,* 63–64.

Norris, M. (1992). *Specialized text screen readers for students with learning disabilities* [On-line]. Available: http://www.htctu.fhda.edu/publicat/csun92.pdf.

O'Conner, R., Notari-Syverson, A., & Vadasy, P. (1998). *Ladders to literacy: A kindergarten activity book.* Baltimore, MD: Brookes.

Ogle, D. M. (1986). K-W-L: A teaching model that develops active reading of expository text. *Reading Teacher, 39,* 564–570.

Ormrod, J. E. (1986). A learning strategy for phonetic spellers. *Academic Therapy, 22,* 195–198.

Palincsar, A. S., & Brown, A. L. (1984). Reciprocal teaching of comprehension-fostering and comprehension-monitoring activities. *Cognition and Instruction, 1,* 117–175.

Palincsar, A. S., & Brown, A. L. (1986). Interactive teaching to promote independent learning from text. *Reading Teacher, 39,* 771–777.

Pavri, S., & Monda-Amaya, L. (2001). Social support in inclusive schools: Student and teacher perspectives. *Exceptional Children, 76,* 391–411.

Pearson, P. D., & Johnson, D. D. (1978). *Teaching reading comprehension.* New York: Holt, Rinehart, and Winston.

Poteet, J. A. (1987). Written expression. In J. S. Choate, T. Z. Bennett, B. E. Enright, L. J. Miller, J. A. Poteet, & T. A. Rakes (Eds.), *Assessing and programming basic curriculum skills* (pp. 147–176). Boston: Allyn and Bacon.

Press, J. (1998). *Alphabet art: A to Z animal art.* Charlotte, VT: Williamson Publishing Co.

Pressley, M., & Woloshyn, V. E. (1995). *Cognitive strategy instruction that really improves children's academic performance* (2nd ed.). Cambridge, MA: Brookline Books.

Putnam, L. (1992). The testing practices of mainstream secondary classroom teachers. *Remedial and Special Education, 13,* 11–21.

Rak, E. T. (1984). *The spell of words: Teacher's manual.* Cambridge, MA: Educators Publishing Service.

Rasch, G. (1960). Probabilistic models for some intelligence and attainment tests. Copenhagen, Denmark: Danish Institute for Educational Research.

Rhode, G., Jenson, W. R., & Reavis, H. K. (1995). *The tough kid book: Practical classroom management strategies.* Longmont, CO: Sopris West.

Rhode, G., Morgan, D. P., & Young, K. R. (1983). Generalization and maintenance of treatment gains of behaviorally handicapped students from resource rooms to regular classrooms using self-evaluation procedures. *Journal of Applied Behavioral Analysis, 16,* 171–188.

Robinson, F. P. (1970). *Effective study* (5th ed.). New York: Harper & Row.

Rojewski, J. W. (1992). Key components of model transition services for students with learning disabilities. *Learning Disability Quarterly, 15,* 135–150.

Rooney, K. J. (2001). Notetaking strategy: Two-column format for content area subjects [On-line]. Available: http://www.ldonline.org/ld_indepth/teaching_techniques/two.html

Rosner, J. (1979). *Helping children overcome learning disabilities* (2nd ed.). New York: Walker.

Samuels, S. J. (1979). The method of repeated readings. *Reading Teacher, 32,* 403–408.

Scheid, K. (1999). *Helping students become strategic learners: Guidelines for teaching.* Cambridge, MA: Brookline books.

Schiever, S. W. (1991). *A comprehensive approach to teaching thinking.* Boston: Allyn and Bacon.

Schlegel, M. (1986, October). *Remediation of written language: Group teaching techniques.* Workshop presented at Arizona Association for Children with Learning Disabilities, Phoenix, AZ.

Schlegel, M., & Bos, C. S. (1986). *STORE the story: Fiction/fantasy reading comprehension and writing strategy.* Unpublished manuscript, University of Arizona, Department of Special Education, Rehabilitation, and School Psychology, Tucson.

Schoenfeld, A. H. (1979). Explicit heuristic training as a variable in problem-solving performance. *Journal for Research in Mathematics Education, 10,* 173–187.

Schrank, F. A., Flanagan, D. P., Woodcock, R. W., & Mascolo, J. (2001). *Essentials of the WJ III Tests of Cognitive Abilities Assessment.* New York: Wiley.

Schrank, F. A., & Woodcock, R. W. (2001). WJ III Compuscore and Profiles Program [Computer software]. *Woodcock-Johnson III.* Itasca, IL: Riverside Publishing.

Schrank, F. A., & Woodcock, R. W. (2002). *Report writer for the WJ III* [Computer software]. Itasca, IL: Riverside Publishing.

Schumaker, J. B., Denton, P. H., & Deshler, D. D. (1984). *The paraphrasing strategy (Learning Strategies Curriculum).* Lawrence: University of Kansas.

Schumaker, J. B., & Deshler, D. D. (1992). Validation of learning strategy interventions for students with LD: Results of a programmatic research effort. In B. Y. L. Wong (Ed.), *Contemporary intervention research in learning disabilities: An international perspective* (pp. 22–46). New York: Springer-Verlag.

Schumaker, J. B., Deshler, D. D., Alley, G. R., Warner, M. M. Clark, F. L., & Nolan, S. (1982). Error monitoring: A learning strategy for improving adolescent performance. In W. M. Cruickshank & J. Lerner (Eds.), *Best of ACLD: Vol. 3* (pp. 170–182). Syracuse, NY: Syracuse University Press.

Schumaker, J. B., Deshler, D. D., Nolan, S., Clark, F. L., Alley, G. R., &

Warner, M. M. (1981). *Error monitoring: A learning strategy for improving academic performance of LD adolescents* (Research Report No. 32). Lawrence: University of Kansas Institute for Research in Learning Disabilities.

Schumaker, J. B., & Lyerla, K. D. (1991). *The paragraph writing strategy.* Lawrence: University of Kansas Center for Research on Learning.

Schumaker, J. B., Nolan, S. M., & Deshler, D. D. (1985). *The error monitoring strategy.* Lawrence: University of Kansas Center for Research on Learning.

Schumaker, J. B., & Sheldon, J. (1985). *The sentence writing strategy.* Lawrence: University of Kansas Center for Research on Learning.

Scruggs, T. E., & Mastropieri, M. (1992). Classroom applications of mnemonic instruction: Acquisition, maintenance, and generalization. *Exceptional Children, 58,* 219–229.

Shapiro, E. S., & Cole, C. L. (1994). *Behavioral change in the classroom: Self-management interventions.* New York: Guilford.

Shapiro, E. S., DuPaul, G. J., & Bradley-Klug, K. L. (1998). Self-management as a strategy to improve the classroom behavior of adolescents with ADHD. *Journal of Learning Disabilities, 31,* 545–555.

Sheridan, S. M. (1995). *The tough kid social skills book.* Longmont, CO: Sopris West.

Slater, W. H., Graves, M. F., & Piche, G. L. (1984, April). *The effects of structural organizers on ninth-grade students' comprehension and recall of four patterns of expository text.* Paper presented at the American Educational Research Association Convention, New Orleans.

Slingerland, B. H. (1971). *A multisensory approach to language arts for specific language disability children: A guide for primary teachers.* Cambridge, MA: Educators Publishing Service.

Smith, E. M., & Alley, G. R. (1981). The effect of teaching sixth graders with learning disabilities a strategy for solving verbal math problems (Research Report No. 39). Lawrence, KS: Institute for Research in Learning Disabilities.

Smith, J. K. (1999). *The effects of practice on the reading speed, accuracy, duration, and visual fatigue of students with low vision when accessing standard size print with optical devices.* University of Arizona: Unpublished doctoral dissertation.

Spalding, R. B., & Spalding, W. T. (1986). *The writing road to reading* (3rd ed.). New York: William Morrow.

Spargo, E. (Ed.). (1989). *Timed readings in literature.* Providence, RI: Jamestown.

Sparks, J. E. (1982). *Write for power.* Los Angeles: Communication Associates.

Stauffer, R. G. (1969). *Directing reading maturity as a cognitive process.* New York: Harper & Row.

Tangel, D. M., & Blachman, B. A. (1992). Effect of phoneme awareness instruction on kindergarten children's invented spelling. *Journal of Reading Behavior, 24,* 233–261.

Thomas, K. (1978). Instructional applications of the cloze technique. *Reading World, 18,* 1–12.

Thomas, C. C., Englert, C. S., & Morsink, C. (1984). Modifying the classroom program in language. In C. V. Morsink (Ed.), *Teaching special needs students in regular classrooms* (pp. 239–276). Boston: Little, Brown.

Thomas, E. L., & Robinson, H. A. (1972). *Improving reading in every class: A sourcebook for teachers.* Boston: Allyn and Bacon.

Thompson, S. (1997). *The source for nonverbal learning disorders.* East Moline, IL: LinguiSystems.

Thornton, C. A., & Bley, N. S. (Eds.). (1994). *Windows of opportunity: Mathematics for students with special needs.* Reston, VA: National Council of Teachers of Mathematics.

Thornton, C. A., & Bley, N. S. (2000). *Teaching mathematics to students with learning disabilities* (4th ed.). Austin, TX: PRO-ED.

Thurber, D. N. (1983). Write on! with continuous stroke point. *Academic Therapy, 18,* 389–395.

Thurber, D. N. (1984). *D'Nealian manuscript: A continuous stroke approach to handwriting.* Novato, CA: Academic Therapy.

Thurber, D. N. (1988). The D'Nealian pencil grip. *Communication Outlook, 9*(4), 11.

Tierney, R. J., & Readence, J. E. (1999). *Reading strategies and practices: A compendium: From theory to practice* (5th ed). Boston: Allyn and Bacon.

Topping, K. (1987a). Paired reading: A powerful technique for parent use. *Reading Teacher, 40,* 608–609.

Topping, K. (1987b). Peer tutored paired reading: Outcome data from ten projects. *Educational Psychology, 7,* 133–145.

Udall, A. J., & Daniels, J. E. (1991). *Creating the thoughtful classroom: Strategies to promote student thinking.* Tucson, AZ: Zephyr Press.

Vallecorsa, A. L., Ledford, R. R., & Parness, G. G. (1991). Strategies for teaching composition skills to students with learning disabilities. *Teaching Exceptional Children, 23,* 52–55.

Vaughn, S., & Klingner, J. K. (1999). Teaching reading comprehension through collaborative strategic reading. *Intervention in School and Clinic, 34,* 284–292.

Venezky, R. L. (1970). Linguistics and spelling. In A. H. Marckwardt (Ed.), *Linguistics in school programs: The sixty-ninth yearbook of the National Society for the Study of Education* (pp. 264–274). Chicago: University of Chicago Press.

Wallach, G. P., & Miller, L. (1988). *Language intervention and academic success.* Boston: Little, Brown.

Wolf, M., & Goodman, G. (1998). *Speed Wizards: Computerized games for the teaching of reading fluency.* Tufts University and Rochester Institute of Technology.

Wolf, M., Miller, L., & Donnelly, K. (2000). *RAVE-O.* Tufts University.

Wong, B. Y. L. (1985). Potential means of enhancing content skills acquisition in learning disabled adolescents. *Focus on Exceptional Children, 17*(5), 1–8.

Wong, B. Y. L., & Jones, W. (1982). Increasing metacomprehension in learning disabled and normally achieving students through self-questioning training. *Learning Disability Quarterly, 5,* 228–240.

Wood, E., Woloshyn, V. E., & Willoughby, T. (1999). *Cognitive strategy instruction for middle and high schools.* Cambridge, MA: Brookline Books.

Woodcock, R. W. (1999). What can Rasch-based scores convey about a person's test performance? In S. E. Embretson & S. L. Hershberger (Eds.), *The new rules of measurement: What every psychologist and educator should know* (pp. 105–127). Mahwah, NJ: Erlbaum.

Woodcock, R. W., & Johnson, M. B. (1977). *Woodcock-Johnson Psycho-Educational Battery.* Itasca, IL: Riverside Publishing.

Woodcock, R. W., McGrew, K. S., & Mather, N. (2001a). *Woodcock-Johnson III.* Itasca, IL: Riverside Publishing.

Woodcock, R. W., McGrew, K. S., & Mather, N. (2001b). *Woodcock-Johnson III Tests of Cognitive Abilities.* Itasca, IL: Riverside Publishing.

Woodcock, R. W., McGrew, K. S., & Mather, N. (2001c). *Woodcock-Johnson III Tests of Achievement.* Itasca, IL: Riverside Publishing.

Wright, B. D., & Stone, M. H. (1979). *Best test design: Rasch measurement.* Chicago: MESA Press.

Young, K. R., West, R. P., Smith, D. J., & Morgan, D. P. (2000). *Teaching self-management strategies to adolescents.* Longmont, CO: Sopris West.

Zentall, S. S., & Goldstein, S. (1999). *Seven steps to homework success.* Plantation, FL: Specialty Press.